Introduction to Early Childhood Education

EQUITY AND INCLUSION

• • •

JOHNNA C. DARRAGH

Heartland Community College

Boston   Columbus   Indianapolis   New York   San Francisco   Upper Saddle River
Amsterdam   Cape Town   Dubai   London   Madrid   Milan   Munich   Paris   Montreal   Toronto
Delhi   Mexico City   Sao Paulo   Sydney   Hong Kong   Seoul   Singapore   Taipei   Tokyo

Vice President and Editor in Chief: Jeffery W. Johnston
Senior Acquisitions Editor: Julie Peters
Development Editor: Bryce Bell
Editorial Assistant: Tiffany Bitzel
Vice President, Director of Marketing and Sales Strategies: Emily Williams Knight
Vice President, Director of Marketing: Quinn Perkson
Marketing Manager: Erica DeLuca
Senior Managing Editor: Pamela D. Bennett
Senior Project Manager: Linda Hillis Bayma
Senior Operations Supervisor: Matthew Ottenweller

Senior Art Director: Diane Lorenzo
Text Designer: Candace Rowley
Cover Designer: Ali Mohrman
Cover Art: Johnna Darragh
Media Producer: Autumn Benson
Media Project Manager: Rebecca Norsic
Full-Service Project Management: GGS Higher Education Resources, PMG
Composition: GGS Book Services
Printer/Binder: Edwards Brothers
Cover Printer: Lehigh Phoenix
Text Font: Berkeley

Credits and acknowledgments borrowed from other sources and reproduced, with permission, in this textbook appear on appropriate page within text.

Every effort has been made to provide accurate and current Internet information in this book. However, the Internet and information posted on it are constantly changing, so it is inevitable that some of the Internet addresses listed in this textbook will change.

Photo Credits: Anne Vega/Merrill, pp. 2, 110, 234; Johnna Darragh, pp. 5, 13, 15, 21, 62, 65, 77, 88, 103, 125, 137, 158, 192, 213, 264, 291, 326, 387, 432, 439; Wendy Bareither, pp. 6, 49, 283, 308, 350, 361, 415, 418, 445; Linda Fritz, pp. 9, 54, 322, 400; Marion Volz, pp. 14, 23, 34, 39, 89, 155, 166, 169, 181, 406, 434; EyeWire Collection/Getty Images, Inc.–Photodisc, p. 18; Jo Scott, pp. 27, 84, 121, 184, 191, 223, 252, 344; Carissa Carlson, pp. 35, 51, 59, 79, 153, 163, 209, 317, 335, 429; David Mager/Pearson Learning Photo Studio, p. 46; Krista Greco/Merrill, pp. 72, 148, 200; Mo Kelly, pp. 112, 299, 382, 413; Karissa Zimmerman, pp. 143, 257, 365; Anthony Magnacca/Merrill, pp. 176, 274; Margaret Varney, pp. 178, 205, 369; Frank McMahon, pp. 229 (all), 238; Joyce Hall, p. 248; Kristin Bach, p. 287; Kristen Palmer/Merrill, p. 314; Mac H. Brown/Merrill, p. 356; Pearson Scott Foresman, p. 396; Scott Cunningham/Merrill, p. 424.

Library of Congress Cataloging-in-Publication Data
Darragh, Johnna.
    Introduction to early childhood education: equity and inclusion/Johnna Darragh.
        p. cm.
    Includes bibliographical references and index.
    ISBN 978-0-205-56954-0
    1. Early childhood education.   I. Title.

LB1139.23.D37 2010
372.21—dc22

2009013757

www.pearsonhighered.com

10 9 8 7 6 5 4 3 2 1
ISBN-13: 978-0-205-56954-0
ISBN-10:   0-205-56954-4

(continued)

Standard	Key Elements of the Standard	Chapter and Topic
	6b. Knowing about and upholding ethical standards and other professional guidelines	1: Ethics as the Foundation for Professional Practice, p. 13 1: Teaching and Learning Connections: Using Ethics as a Guide for Practice, p. 14 3: Table 3.4: Overview of Special Education Populations, p. 66 5: Teaching and Learning Connections: Responsibilities as a Mandated Reporter, p. 142 7: Professional Preparation Requirements, p. 179 7: Table 7.1: Educational Requirements by Employment Area, p. 179 7: Teaching and Learning Connections: Learning About Professional Preparation Requirements, p. 185 9: Table 9.1: Overview of National and Federal Standards Affecting Early Childhood Education, p. 237 9: Table 9.8: National Professional Preparation Standards, p. 265 13: Figure 13.1: Standards Affecting Early Childhood Programming, p. 398 13: Teaching and Learning Connections: Learning About Your Program's Standards, p. 399 13: Table 13.2: DEC Indicators of Program Effectiveness and Their Application, p. 407 13: Figure 13.5: Standards for Program Planning and Evaluation, p. 410 13: Figure 13.6: Template for Program Planning and Evaluation, p. 412
	6c. Engaging in continuous, collaborative learning to inform practice	1: Your Commitment to Lifelong Learning, p. 13 3: Becoming a Professional: Using the Internet as a Resource, p. 66 4: Becoming a Professional: Supporting Your Stage of Teacher Development, p. 104 5: Teaching and Learning Connections: Examining Your Own Biases, p. 130 7: Supporting Professional Preparation, p. 187 12: Table 12.5: A Focus on Supporting Professional Comfort with Curriculum, p. 390
	6d. Integrating knowledgeable, reflective, and critical perspectives on early education	7: Self-Advocacy: The Role of Reflection and Philosophy, p. 189 7: Table 7.3: Descriptions of Areas of Reflection, p. 191 7: Teaching and Learning Connections: Supporting Reflection, p. 192 7: Teaching and Learning Connections: Example of a Reflective Teaching Philosophy, p. 193 10: Teaching and Learning Connections: Learning About Your Own Hot Buttons, p. 284 14: Building Teaching Skills and Dispositions: My Plan for Success, p. 448
	6e. Engaging in informed advocacy for children and the profession	14: The Role of Advocacy in Advancing the Field, p. 430 14: Teaching and Learning Connections: Steps Underlying Effective Advocacy, p. 433 14: Teaching and Learning Connections: National Advocacy Days, p. 434 14: Teaching and Learning Connections: Creating Advocacy Messages, p. 436 14: Access and Equity for All: Education as a Tool of Social Change, p. 448

The Standards and Key Elements are from the *NAEYC Standards for Early Childhood Professional Preparation: Initial Licensure Programs* by the National Association for the Education of Young Children, Washington, DC. At the time of publication, these draft standards were anticipated to be approved in July 2009.

Correlation Matrix of Early Childhood Special Education/Early Intervention (Birth to 8) Professional Standards Topics and Chapter Content

Standard	Description	Chapter and Topic
1: Foundations	Know philosophies, evidence-based principles, laws, and diverse and historical points of view.	1: Mission of the Division for Early Childhood of the Council for Exceptional Children, p. 9 1: The Emergence of Special Education, p. 30 2: Figure 2.4: A Brief History of Special Education Legislation, 1954–1997, p. 31 2: Accountability Within Special Education, p. 32 2: The Emergence of Inclusion, p. 35 2: Becoming a Professional: Understanding Laws That Shape the Early Childhood Field, p. 37 3: Issues of Access and Equity: Universal Design for Early Childhood Education, p. 54 3: Early Intervention, p. 58 3: Early Childhood Special Education, p. 59 4: Family Systems Theory, p. 100 4: Teaching and Learning Connections: How Does Understanding Family Systems Theory Support Effective Teaching?, p. 100 6: Theories of Family Involvement, p. 163 6: Theories of Social Support, p. 164 13: Standards Gaps: Children with Disabilities, p. 406
2: Development and Characteristics of Learners	Know and demonstrate respect for children first as human beings, know characteristics between and among individuals with and without exceptional	4: Principle One: Interrelationships Between Developmental Domains, p. 77 4: Table 4.1: Overview of Children's Developmental Domains, p. 78 4: Principle Two: Sequences of Learning and Development, p. 78 4: Teaching and Learning Connections: Brief Overview of Strategies Supporting Cognitive Development, p. 79 4: Teaching and Learning Connections: Brief Overview of Strategies Supporting Psychosocial Development, p. 80 4: Principle Three: Individual Patterns of Development and Learning, p. 81

(continued)

(continued)

Standard	Description	Chapter and Topic
8: Assessment	Use the results of assessment to identify early learning needs and develop and implement and adjust individualized instructional programs. Know appropriate use of assessment.	9: Standards Informing Curriculum and Assessment, p. 236 9: Teaching and Learning Connections: Uses of Assessment, p. 239 9: Figure 9.2: The Ethics of Assessment, p. 240 9: Teaching and Learning Connections: Selecting Culturally and Linguistically Sensitive Assessment Instruments, p. 243 9: Play-Based Assessment, p. 245 9: Strengths-Based Assessment, p. 245 9: Teaching and Learning Connections: Supporting Effective Assessment, p. 245 9: Common Assessment Strategies, p. 249 9: Table 9.3: Common Observation Strategies and Their Usage, p. 250 9: Informal Assessment Tools, p. 252 9: Table 9.4: Description of Documentation Strategies, p. 253 9: Teaching and Learning Connections: Organizing Portfolios, p. 254 9: Table 9.5: Components of the Work Sampling System, p. 256 9: Screening and Formal Evaluation, p. 258 9: Developmental Screening and Checklists, p. 258 9: Table 9.6: Common Screening and Checklist Instruments, p. 259 9: Postscreening: Diagnostic Assessment, p. 260 9: Table 9.7: Mandatory Data for the IFSP and IEP, p. 261 9: Teaching and Learning Connections: Professional Portfolio Uses, p. 266 9: The Professional Development Plan, p. 267 9: Building Teaching Skills and Dispositions: Learning to Use Authentic Assessment and Practicing Observing Skills, p. 268 13: Assessing Program Effectiveness, p. 414 13: Table 13.4: Methods of Data Collection Evaluating Stakeholder Satisfaction, p. 417 13: Teaching and Learning Connections: Learning About Your Program's Stakeholders, p. 417 13: Building Teaching Skills and Dispositions: RTI: Considerations for School Leaders, p. 419
9: Professional and Ethical Practice		1: Becoming a Professional: Learning About the Field, p. 11 1: Your Commitment to Lifelong Learning, p. 13 1: Ethics as the Foundation for Professional Practice, p. 13 1: Teaching and Learning Connections: Using Ethics as a Guide for Practice, p. 14 2: Teaching and Learning Connections: Examples of People-First Language, p. 36 3: Becoming a Professional: Using the Internet as a Resource, p. 66 4: Becoming a Professional: Supporting Your Stage of Teacher Development, p. 104 5: Teaching and Learning Connections: Examining Your Own Biases, p. 130 5: Abuse and Neglect, p. 139 5: Teaching and Learning Connections: Responsibilities as a Mandated Reporter, p. 142 6: Becoming a Professional: Keeping Current in Public Policy, p. 160 7: Teaching and Learning Connections: Learning About Professional Preparation Requirements, p. 185 7: Self-Advocacy: The Role of Reflection and Philosophy, p. 189 7: Table 7.3: Descriptions of Areas of Reflection, p. 191 7: Teaching and Learning Connections: Supporting Reflection, p. 192 7: Teaching and Learning Connections: Example of a Reflective Teaching Philosophy, p. 193 10: Teaching and Learning Connections: Learning About Your Own Hot Buttons, p. 284 12: Table 12.5: A Focus on Supporting Professional Comfort with Curriculum, p. 390 14: Figure 14.1: Strategies Supporting the Success of the Field, p. 429 14: Teaching and Learning Connections: Steps Underlying Effective Advocacy, p. 433 14: Teaching and Learning Connections: National Advocacy Days, p. 434 14: Teaching and Learning Connections: Creating Advocacy Messages, p. 436
10: Collaboration	Know and use models and strategies of collaboration and consultation.	2: The Advent of Systematic Parent Education, p. 29 2: Family Involvement and Special Education, p. 33 5: Becoming a Professional: Effective Collaboration, p. 128 6: Creating Partnerships with Families, p. 161 6: Teaching and Learning Connections: Providing Social Support, p. 163 6: Table 6.2: Types of Family Involvement and Teacher Practices, p. 165 6: Figure 6.4: Supporting Co-Constructed Relationships, p. 168 6: Supporting Family Empowerment, p. 169 9: Teaching and Learning Connections: Formal and Informal Strategies for Communicating with Families, p. 258 9: The Mentoring Relationship as a Tool for Assessment, p. 267 10: Including Families in Addressing Challenging Behavior, p. 308 14: Embracing Families as Their Child's First and Most Important Teacher, p. 441 14: Supporting Children and Families Who Are Culturally and Linguistically Diverse, p. 442

Topics adapted from *What Every Special Educator Must Know—Ethics, Standards, and Guidelines for Special Educators* by the Council for Exceptional Children, 2009, Arlington, VA.

About the Author

JOHNNA DARRAGH has taught early childhood education courses at the associate, bachelor's, and master's degree levels. She is currently a Professor of Early Childhood Education at Heartland Community College and serves as faculty liaison to their inclusive Child Development Lab. Johnna is a member of several Illinois committees focusing on workforce development and inclusion and is the Illinois Liaison to the National Professional Development Center on Inclusion. She is a member of the Illinois Professional Development Advisory Committee (PDAC) Steering Committee and serves on the National Center to Mobilize Early Childhood Knowledge (CONNECT) Steering Committee. In 2008, Johnna was a participant in the 2008 Project Forum on Universal Design. She has experience teaching infants, toddlers, and preschoolers, and she has been a home visitor/family support specialist. Her recent publications and presentations focus on inclusion and universal design for early childhood education. Johnna has a Ph.D. in Human and Community Development from the University of Illinois.

Preface

Early childhood education has emerged from a rich history of programs and practices to become a thriving field that today impacts the lives of millions of children, their families, and early childhood professionals. It plays a vital role in building healthy, dynamic communities and provides the opportunity for success and equity for all individuals. In other words, the effects of high quality early childhood education and respectful, nurturing, developmentally appropriate practice can last far into every child's future.

The pathway to becoming a social, economic and political force has not been without challenges—its history has varied greatly in terms of *who receives early childhood services*, *where these services are delivered*, and *who is responsible for ensuring that our youngest citizens receive the care and education they need and deserve*. Today, the field has great potential in its mission to provide services to children between birth and age 8. One of the greatest challenges, however, is to ensure quality, inclusive programming that supports the learning and development of each and every child.

Historically, the field of early childhood general education and the field of early childhood special education developed separately. The growth of early childhood general education was largely driven by social forces, namely, increases in women working outside of the home. Early childhood special education, on the other hand, was predominantly created through legislative mandates responding to the civil rights movement and reflecting society's responsibility to provide an appropriate education to all children in environments with typically developing peers.

Along with an increasing commitment to recognizing and meeting the needs of children with varying abilities, those in the field are also asking essential questions with regard to meeting the needs of culturally and linguistically diverse populations:

- What do we, as a field, need to do in order to support the development and learning for children and families from culturally and linguistically diverse backgrounds?
- How can we incorporate effective practices within early childhood environments that will meet the specific needs of children and families who are culturally and linguistically diverse?

In other words, we are currently faced with not only a legislative but also a moral mandate to develop inclusive and equitable practices that embrace the strengths and needs of each individual child, including those who are culturally, linguistically, and ability diverse.

WHY I WROTE THIS BOOK

This book was written from a deep personal and professional commitment to inclusion. I am the parent of two children with disabilities and have experienced—both directly and through my children's eyes—the incredible importance of quality, inclusive practices in supporting the development and learning of each and every child. I am also a college professor and have worked to support my students in developing the knowledge, skills, and dispositions needed to ensure quality programming for all children, including the ability to create thriving classroom communities where each child is welcomed, valued, and supported. Through inclusive practices that embrace equity at their core—reflecting basic fairness and acceptance of that which makes us each unique—children can be viewed as children, and not defined, categorized, and placed according to one of many characteristics they have.

THE EQUITY AND INCLUSION FOCUS OF THIS BOOK

This book is about the field of early childhood education's intricate past, its promising present, and its vibrant future. You will learn about the children, families, and professionals within the field and effective, evidence-based practices that reflect current research and theory. Throughout this book, you will also learn about diversity and the importance of recognizing, valuing, and embracing the unique qualities we each possess. This book draws from the fields of early childhood general and special education and child development, and includes policies and practices designed to ensure that each and every child and family is included. But, this book is about far more than inclusion, as it stresses the development of a professional philosophy and related practices that celebrate children, childhood, families, community, culture, relationships, and respect.

While inclusion and equity represent the organizing framework of the book, the core of this text is about you, and the powerful role you play as a current or future early childhood educator. The words on the page mean little without the knowledge, dedication, and expertise of the professionals who directly impact the lives of young children and their families.

AUDIENCE

This book is written for current and future early childhood professionals. There are many different roles within the field, including teaching young children, working with families, coordinating and directing programs, collaborating with other professionals, and providing social services. It includes fundamental knowledge, skills, and dispositions needed to support varied professional pathways. Knowledge, application, and reflection activities are designed to meet the needs of professionals at various stages of development, from novices to those who have extensive experience and are furthering their education.

THEMES OF THIS BOOK

The central themes of this book are equity and inclusion, which provide a lens through which diversity can be supported. Interwoven throughout the text is an ecological systems approach to understanding the complex, bidirectional relationships between the child and family, professional, early childhood field, community, and larger society. These themes are supported within the organizational structure of the text; therefore, issues of equity and inclusion are embedded throughout, as opposed to relegated to a separate chapter or chapter insert.

FEATURES OF THIS BOOK

 MyEducationLab: a powerful online resource offering authentic in-class video footage, simulations, case studies, and examples of children's work. Margin notes integrated into the text direct you to these resources, which are each accompanied online by a set of assignable questions to deepen understanding. Additional assignable applied exercises are available in "Building Teaching Skills and Dispositions."

Go to MyEducationLab and select the topic "Curriculum/Program Models." Under Activities and Applications, watch the video *Head Start* and think about the varied ways Head Start supports children and families.

To start using MyEducationLab, activate the access code packaged with your book. If your instructor did not make MyEducationLab a required part of your course or if you are purchasing a used book without an access code, go to www.myeducationlab.com to purchase access to this wonderful resource!

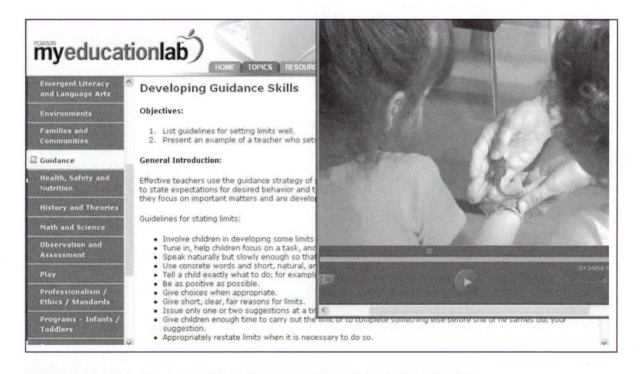

Opening Vignettes

Real-life situations designed to introduce the chapter topic

Teaching and Learning Connections

Features highlighting specific classroom practices that complement and extend course materials

---

TEACHING AND LEARNING CONNECTIONS

Supporting Cultural and Linguistic Diversity

- Learn about your own cultural and linguistic biases, and what this may communicate to families.
- Learn about each child and his or her family via a thoughtful questionnaire, a home visit, or daily conversations.
- Integrate knowledge of individual children and their families into the physical and social early childhood environment by including pictures, materials, and toys that reflect and respect the children's world.
- Be open to learning about new ways of interacting with the environment (including communication) and new ideas.

ISSUES OF ACCESS AND EQUITY FOR CHILDREN, FAMILIES, AND PROFESSIONALS
Early Childhood Education as a Tool of Social Justice

Childhood often evokes images of a carefree, happy time when children thrive within the care of stable, nurturing families. The reality for many children is that childhood is a time ripe with anxieties, fear, discrimination, and a lack of support for even their most basic needs.

Many families experience challenges in living conditions. These challenges can include a lack of safe shelter, the inability to put enough or nutritious food on the table, and violen... With... these families... children... develop... in... prese...

Issues of Access and Equity

A feature highlighting the impact of access and equity on children, families, and professionals within the field

Becoming a Professional

A feature highlighting ongoing professional development strategies as well as information on career pathways and opportunities within the field

• • • BECOMING A PROFESSIONAL • • •
Career Pathways

Home School Facilitator

"My job at the center is the home–school facilitator—I make sure there is a link between what is happening in the home and what is happening in school. One of the things that I work on a lot is making sure parents know how important it is for their children to be in school. Sometimes people just think this is babysitting. They don't really realize how important it is for children's later success."

Matt has a variety of responsibilities in the early childhood program where he works. One of his main challenges is coordinating child, family, and teacher needs. ...

CASE STUDY
Ensuring Access Through Inclusion

Myrna Children's Village (6 weeks to 6 years)

Sergio and April's bilingual preschool classroom at the Myrna Children's Village in New Mexico resembles many high-quality early childhood programs. Children are actively engaged in the curriculum. The teachers and staff spend their time observing, interacting with the children in meaningful ways, and supporting each child's individual development and

Case Studies

End-of-chapter features profiling an infant/toddler, preschool, kindergarten, or primary grade classroom. Case studies are tied to chapter content and conclude with constructed-response questions.

Reflecting on and Applying Effective Practices (NAEYC and CEC/DEC)

End-of-chapter questions and activities tied to the NAEYC and CEC/DEC standards

REFLECTING ON AND APPLYING EFFECTIVE PRACTICES (NAEYC AND CEC/DEC)

Ethics

• You have started a job teaching four-year-olds in a preschool classroom, and are greatly looking forward to applying all that you have learned in your college coursework. During your first week in the classroom, you carefully observe the children, working to get to know them and their interests. You also talk extensively with your new coworker. When you ask her what the children's interests are in the classroom so you can begin brainstorming possible ideas for a class project, she responds, "Oh, we just use themes in here. Our curriculum is planned for the whole year and we really don't have the time to add other material in." What would you do in this situation?

NAEYC Ideals
I-1.2. To base program practices upon current knowledge and research in the field of early childhood education, child development, and related disciplines, as well as on particular knowledge of each child.

I-3A.2. To share resources with co-workers, collaborating to ensure that the best possible early childhood care and education program is provided.

DEC: Professional and Interpersonal Behavior
3. We shall strive for the highest level of personal and professional competence by seeking and using new evidence based information to improve our practices while also responding openly to the suggestions of others.

Standards for Professional Practice

• Reflect on the various curricular models and approaches you learned about in Chapter 8. How do these models and approaches, in general, reflect theory and research in the field? What do professionals need to know about specific models to select one that 231is effective? How can a model be selected that is aligned with your own beliefs about children's development and learning?

NAEYC: Promoting Child Development and Learning
1c. Using developmental knowledge to create healthy, respectful, supportive, and challenging learning environments;

NAEYC: Teaching and Learning
Sub-Standard 4b. Using developmentally effective approaches;

Sub-Standard 4d. Building meaningful curriculum.

INSTRUCTOR AND STUDENT RESOURCES

The following resources are available for download by adopting instructors from www .pearsonhighered.com. Click on Educators, then register and download any of the following ancillaries:

- An *Online Instructor's Manual* includes focus questions, key terms, discussion questions, application activities, cooperative group activities, assessment activities, and related readings and resources for use with each chapter. The Instructor's Manual also includes fully prepared modules for use in **online courses**.
- An *Online Test Bank*, also available in *TestGen* and *BlackBoard* or *WebCT* course management formats, is available for each chapter.
- Instructor's slides for each chapter are available in *PowerPoint* format for enhanced classroom presentation.

The following resources are available in the text:

- A **Chapter Review** is based on guiding questions presented at the beginning of each chapter.
- **Key Terms** and their definitions are located within each chapter. A full **Glossary of Terms** is available on pages 463–471.

ACKNOWLEDGMENTS

I would like to thank many people for their extensive efforts, talents, and support contributing to the development of this text. Without these combined efforts and dedication, this text would not be a reality.

Thank you to Kelly Villella Canton for her commitment to the project, and for her extensive support and expertise in developing the first draft. Julie Peters deserves an abundance of credit and appreciation for making subsequent drafts into a publishable manuscript, and I am grateful for her diligence, vision, and creativity. I would also like to thank Bryce Bell for his thorough, thoughtful editing.

My wonderful colleagues and friends have played a huge role in this book's development, including the amazing staff at the Child Development Lab of Heartland Community College. I would like to specifically thank Darlene Wills, Kristin Bach, Wendy Bareither, Carissa Carlson, Linda Fritz, Joyce Hall, Barbara Parks, Joellen Scott, Marian Volz, Margaret Varney, and Karissa Zimmerman. My gratitude to Catherine Miller, for her personal and administrative support for the project. I would also like to thank Mo Miller, Brenda Nardi, Jennifer Graham, and Nancy Baptiste for sharing their professional knowledge and opening the doors of their programs. To the professionals who shared their professional passions in the Case Studies and Becoming a Professional feature and to my students, who I learn from every day, my many thanks. I am also appreciative of Frank McMahon's support and assistance with the photographs, and to the dedicated visionaries who provide leadership within Illinois early childhood system—they have provided me with wonderful colleagues, friends, and models of dedicated professionalism. And to Camille Catlett, for her inspirational leadership and vision in the area of inclusion, both nationally and within the state of Illinois.

Many thanks as well to contributing editor Teresa Walker and to Monica Fuller, both of whom demonstrated a great deal of patience in applying a fine-tooth comb to the manuscript, and my warm thanks to Jackie Bauer and Tom Neibur, for providing much of the

psychological propping up such a project entails. And, I would like to thank my friend and colleague Jane Schall, for her endless support, knowledge, passion, and triage skills.

I wish to thank the following reviewers for their helpful comments: Sara Jane Adler, Washtenaw Community College; Mary Cordell, Navarro College; Carol L. Devine, University of Kentucky; Dede Dunst, Mitchell Community College; Lori Fallon, Erie Community College; Deborah Greenlee, Mayland Community College; Caroline M. Hagen, Jamestown College; Tom Heffner, Asheville-Buncombe Technical Community College; Jeanne Helm, Richland Community College; Sydney Fisher Larson, College of the Redwoods; Michelle Burgess Morris, Wor-Wic Community College; Debra Pierce, Ivy Tech Community College; Frank A. Saraceno, Herkimer County Community College; and Priscilla Smith, Gwinnett Technical College.

Finally, I would like to thank my family—Alex, Megan, and John—for being a daily source of motivation and joy.

Brief Contents

Contents

Special Features

ISSUES OF ACCESS AND EQUITY

Introduction to Early Childhood Education

EQUITY AND INCLUSION

1 Introduction to Early Childhood Education

"Each time a person stands up for an ideal, or acts to improve the lot of others, or strikes out against injustice, he or she sends forth a tiny ripple of hope."

—ROBERT FRANCIS KENNEDY

Whether we are looking to the core of the field of early childhood education, the core of an individual early childhood program, or the core of this book, what we find is the same: you. As a present or future early childhood educator, you hold the promise of the field in your hands. You may touch the lives of individual children and families for only a brief period of time, but later in life they might remember your welcoming smile, warm embrace, gentle voice, or gift of time. Each of these can represent so much more than individual moments.

A teacher's memorable smile was a symbol of the safe and nurturing place a 5-year-old had found in his preschool classroom. This classroom was one of few such places in his life. The warm embrace between a 1-year-old child and her caregiver became the setting for important life lessons about trust, security, and relationships. And that gentle voice . . . For a 7-year-old, it was the voice of kindness. This voice that told him that he could solve problems, that he could make friends, that he could be successful, that he was valued for being himself. Although the face faded over time, the voice often came back to him with priceless messages. The gift of time, for a parent, came at a moment when life seemed to be crumbling at the edges. There was a feeling of being overwhelmed, isolated, and filled with growing anxiety. But the shared problem solving at the end of the day, the talk about his child's strengths and wonderful capabilities, and the phone call placed the next day proved to be the support he needed to deal with the pressures of the moment.

• • •

GUIDING QUESTIONS

• What is the field of early childhood education?

• What are issues of access and equity for children, and how can early childhood education support social equity?

• How does the sociocultural context affect families and professionals?

• What role do organizations such as the National Association for the Education of Young Children (NAEYC), and the Division for Early Childhood (DEC) of the Council for Exceptional Children (CEC) and frameworks such as developmentally appropriate practices (DAP) play in ensuring high-quality early childhood education services?

Welcome to the **field of early childhood education!** Our field provides an opportunity to have a positive impact on the lives of young children, their families, and society at large. You begin your journey by learning about this exciting field and your role—as a future or present professional—within it.

Professionals in the field of early childhood education have a dramatic ability to affect the present and the future. What children and their families learn within their relationship with you has a ripple effect. From safe and secure relationships we learn about our boundless capacity to love and be loved, to form rich relationships with others, and to connect with our world in meaningful ways.

First, *what exactly is early childhood education?* In broad terms, early childhood education refers to educational programs serving children from birth to age 8 and their families. Also, early childhood education is a field of study designed to prepare professionals for working directly or indirectly with children and their families in that age group.

Why is early childhood education so important? Early childhood is a period of tremendous cognitive, social/emotional, language, and physical growth. The quality of the care and education children receive during this time has an extensive, long-term impact on their development. Investment in high-quality early childhood education programs can yield both short- and long-term benefits for participating children (Cotton & Conklin, 2001; Galinsky, 2006).

Who should be eligible for quality early childhood education? All children infants through third grade have a right to quality care and education. All families have a right to programs that

field of early childhood education
Educational programs serving children between birth and the age of 8 and their families and the field of study that prepares professionals to work with children and families in this age group.

3

support their children's healthy development and learning. However, the early childhood education field has not been able to ensure that all children and families have access to quality programs. Access and quality represent two of the main challenges of the field today. Both of these are challenges that early childhood education professionals can positively affect. Recognizing these challenges and how to address them is an important part of your professional journey.

Who are early childhood professionals? Early childhood professionals hold many different positions in various settings. These include, for example, positions in child care centers, family child care homes, social services agencies, and public schools. Some professional roles in the field, such as teaching, involve working directly with children and their families. Other more indirect roles might include directing a program, working with families as a parent educator, or providing training to early childhood professionals. Professionals can be found working in the full range of age groups included in the field, from very young infants to third graders. Therefore, the answer to the question "Who are early childhood professionals?" is as broad and diverse as the field itself.

EARLY CHILDHOOD EDUCATION AS A TOOL SUPPORTING SOCIAL EQUITY

How does the field affect the children and families it serves? This text is developed around the idea that early childhood education is not only a vital service offered to children and families, but also committed to supporting and promoting **social equity**.

social equity

The just treatment of all members of society.

Social equity, in its broadest sense, refers to fair and just treatment of all members of society. Social equity within early childhood education means that all children and families have equal access and opportunity to benefit from all the field has to offer. Access to high-quality services, for example, is not dependent on monetary resources, a child's abilities, or program availability. Social equity through access and opportunity means high-quality early childhood education for all. Table 1.1 provides an overview of what equity is and is not.

What does the field have to offer young children and their families? The benefits of early childhood care and education are extensive (American Federation of Teachers, 2002). These benefits have the potential to close the large achievement gap that exists between students. In addition, supporting cognitive development and social skills can have a positive impact on children's success as students and productive citizens. High-quality early childhood education can reduce risk factors that can interfere with learning and succeeding in school (American Federation of Teachers, 2002).

TABLE 1.1   What Is Equity?

Equity Is . . .	Equity Is Not . . .
• Ensuring equitable opportunity and benefit within high-quality early childhood education environments, recognizing that some may need more or different supports. • Broad in scope to include diverse individual needs. • Curriculum, assessment, and teaching practices and materials that model and ensure equity. • Recognizing the value of different ways of learning and developing. • Ensuring that everyone can achieve within nurturing, supportive environments.	• Treating everyone the same. • Limited in scope or to a single target population. • A curriculum unit on equity or on a particular target group. • A single approach to learning or view of development. • Lowering standards.

Source: Adapted from Government of Saskatchewan (1997).

Social equity is achieved through policies, practices, and interactions that support diversity and inclusion. *Supporting diversity* requires accepting, respecting, and embracing the vast differences—in class, language, culture, ability, and age—that comprise American society. *Inclusion* is ensuring that the heart of programming for individual children, families, and communities respects this diversity in policy, practice, and interactions.

The impact of early childhood education as a tool of social equity is far reaching—beyond individual children to families, communities, and larger society. At first glance, however, one might not see the complexities of interrelationships, support, and opportunities provided by the field. Consider the following:

> Geraldo is a 4-year-old in Noel's preschool classroom. He is sitting at a sand and water table, pouring sand through a funnel. While he pours, he comments to another little boy at the table, "See, it goes through fast." As Noel walks by, she briefly rubs Geraldo's back, commenting, "I saw you pour the sand. It did go through fast!"

One way to look at this situation is at the fundamentals of the exchange. A boy is playing at the sand and water table, talking with another child, and a teacher walks by and makes a comment. Another interpretation may be invisible to the eye, but represents some of the most meaningful aspects of the field. The safety and security Geraldo feels within his preschool environment teaches Geraldo important lessons about relationships, respect, and community. Through engaging experiences that welcome his full exploration, Geraldo fulfills curiosities, flexes his experimental skills, and tackles each new task with a sense of wonder.

While Geraldo thrives within his preschool classroom, his mother is working for a nearby telemarketing agency. Between calls, she often thinks about what Geraldo is doing. She pictures him digging up to his elbows in the program's outdoor garden, insistent on finding just one more worm. Just last night, Geraldo's teacher had shared Geraldo's escapades in the garden and commented on how happy he seems within the program. She noted how much growth she had noticed throughout the year. Geraldo's mom had noticed the growth as well. She returned to her phone calls comforted by the thought that her son was thriving.

The local kindergarten program in Geraldo's community is also affected by his preschool participation. For every child that enters school ready to learn, the school district saves substantial dollars in costly interventions focused on "catching up." The high-quality preschool programming Geraldo is receiving supports his success now, in kindergarten, and in the future. The dollars saved can be given to other educational programs. In turn, additional members of the community are affected. This illustrates the ripple effect of one child's high-quality early childhood program.

Decisions made at the community and state level made Geraldo's participation in a quality early childhood program possible. His state's governor—with the knowledge, guidance, and support of numerous advocates—created a universal preschool program. This ensured that all 4-year-old children within the state had access to a preschool education. Members of Geraldo's community pooled resources, collaborated, and secured the grant funding for the universal preschool program. The director and

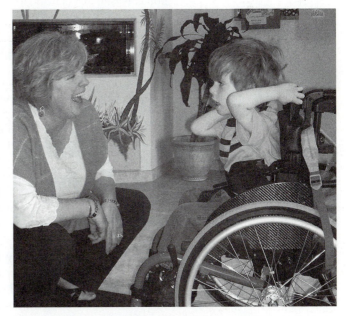

All children between infancy and age 8 have a right to access high-quality early childhood programming.

teaching staff (including Geraldo's teacher, Noel) made sure that the practices within the program were high quality and supportive of all children's development and learning.

Societal attitudes reflecting the important role of early childhood education also contributed to Geraldo's program participation. This **sociocultural context** includes values, attitudes, politics, and policies, and favors access to high-quality programming for *all children*. As you will learn in Chapter 2, this has not always been the case.

The central focus within early childhood education is children. Without children's needs for services and the benefits these services support, the field would not exist. Children, however, do not exist in isolation. Families and professionals also have social equity needs that are affected by the field of early childhood education.

sociocultural context

A combination of both social and cultural factors—such as politics and societal values—that affect the field.

Family Needs

Why do families need early childhood education? Families come to the field of early childhood education with a variety of needs. One parent needs care for her 6-week-old because she is returning to work. Another parent's preschool-aged child needs care and education. Yet another is looking for an opportunity for his 4-year-old to socialize with others for a few hours per week. The dramatic growth in the field is driven by the individual needs that parents have in caring for and educating their children. These individual needs are shaped by changes in family form, structure, and function.

The largest practical issue shaping this growing field has been the dramatic increase in women working outside the home. Sixty-five percent of mothers of children under the age of 6 and 79% of mothers with children under the age of 13 are in the workforce (Children's Defense Fund, 2005). Add to this the increase in single-parent families (doubled from 1970 to 1990), and the data indicates a compelling need for the care of children outside the home. Infant care, in particular, has been a rapidly increasing service. Statistics indicate that 50% of mothers with children under the age of 1 work outside the home (Children's Defense Fund, 2005).

Another reason that demand for early childhood education services has increased is that the field is particularly important for families from lower income backgrounds. "Affordable, quality and stable child care is the linchpin for working families, whether they are meeting TANF (**Temporary Assistance for Needy Families**) work requirements or are low income working families" (Ginsberg as cited in NAEYC, 2006a).

Temporary Assistance for Needy Families

A 1996 block grant program designed to move recipients into work and make welfare support temporary.

High-quality early childhood care and education can also provide other vital supports for families. This support was once thought of in the field as being an "expert–learner" relationship. Early childhood professionals were viewed as experts, and families were viewed as learners. But that's changing. Now, the family–teacher relationship is viewed as an essential *partnership*. Within this collaborative relationship, families act as their children's first and most important teacher(s). Professionals play the family's champion, connecting them with resources when needed, giving information as appropriate, and partnering with families to support children's development. Access to early childhood education *can help families sustain employment* and *strengthen the families' roles in supporting children's development*.

High-quality early childhood programming includes partnerships with families.

ISSUES OF ACCESS AND EQUITY FOR CHILDREN, FAMILIES, AND PROFESSIONALS

Early Childhood Education as a Tool of Social Justice

Childhood often evokes images of a carefree, happy time when children thrive within the care of stable, nurturing families. The reality for many children is that childhood is a time ripe with anxieties, fear, discrimination, and a lack of support for even their most basic needs.

Many families experience challenges in living conditions. These challenges can include a lack of safe shelter, the inability to put enough or nutritious food on the table, and violence. Within these families, children's development in the present, and their life opportunities in the future, can be seriously affected (Spodek & Saracho, 2005).

Lack of access to health care is an issue that affects more than 8.7 million children in the United States (National Coalition on Health Care, 2008). Children who lack health insurance, according to this report, are less likely to get preventive and primary care including immunizations, physicals, and care for common childhood illnesses. This affects their overall development.

Other children are victims of cultural and educational discrimination. In these cases, diversity issues such as language or familial differences may be ignored or scorned. In addition, many children lack access to quality education, which is often determined by the neighborhood a child lives in and/or families' economic status (Joint Economic Committee of the Congress, 1996). Some children may be discriminated against based on their diverse abilities and relegated to classroom environments that segregate them from more typically developing peers (Guralnick, 2001).

The term *social justice* refers to all members of society having the same basic rights, security, opportunities, obligations, and social benefits. Bill Clinton, in his 2007 book *Giving*, identifies the lack of social justice as a global concern. In his words:

The modern world, for all its blessings, is unequal, unstable, and unsustainable. And so the great mission of the early twenty-first century is to move our neighborhoods, our nation, and the world toward integrated communities of shared opportunities, shared responsibilities, and a shared sense of genuine belonging, based on the essence of every successful community: that our common humanity is more important than our interesting differences. (p. 4)

A socially just society embraces the rights of all society's members, regardless of age, gender, class, culture, or ability. Further, social justice ensures that individuals receive the supports they need to thrive. Social equity comprises practices that support members of society who are traditionally marginalized, meaning that they lack access to basic societal supports. Social equity, therefore, is a tool that supports social justice.

As a field, early childhood education can connect children and families with the resources they need. In turn, this can ensure healthy development and future ability to fully participate in society. Because of these benefits, early childhood education can serve as a tool supporting social justice.

TEACHING AND LEARNING CONNECTIONS

Teacher–Parent Partnerships

Old Teacher–Parent Paradigm	New Teacher–Family Paradigm
Teachers are experts.	Families are experts.
Parents are learners.	Teachers are facilitators and co-learners.
Parent's role is to follow the teacher's guidance in supporting their developing child.	Teachers and families partner to support the developing child.

Children and families represent an essential part of the field of early childhood education. Professionals are a vital component of the field as well. Therefore, the core of early childhood education consists of children, families, and professionals.

Professional Needs

Is early childhood education a profession? The answer is an absolute, resounding "YES!" Knowledge of children and how to support children's development is specialized; it emerges from concentrated, reflective education and application. The field benefits from the extensive work of the **National Association for the Education of Young Children** (NAEYC), which is the largest association of early childhood professionals. NAEYC is concerned with education, advocacy, and the provision of high-quality early childhood environments for young children. NAEYC has a **Code of Ethical Conduct** that governs professional conduct. NAEYC also provides a series of accreditation, or quality, guidelines for programs serving young children and for professionals preparing to work in the field.

One of the main challenges within early childhood education is the lack of recognition professionals receive (Whitebook & Sakai, 2004). This lack of recognition is shaped by the historical underpinnings of the field. In turn, this has led to confusion about the purposes of the field and the roles of professionals within it. This confusion is reflected in such terms as *babysitting* and *day care*, which lack recognition of the research-based practices the field of early childhood education is based upon.

One of the most exciting developments in the field is recent gains in professionalization. One example of these gains is the success of national efforts to increase early childhood teacher salaries (National Association of Child Care Resource and Referral Agencies [NACCRRA], 2008). However, significant work remains for the field to fully gain the recognition it deserves. One of your challenges, as a future or current professional, is participating in and supporting this ongoing development. An important tool supporting professionalism is making sure that the programming is of high quality.

HIGH-QUALITY EARLY CHILDHOOD EDUCATION FOR ALL

To support quality programming within the field, you need to understand the factors that determine quality. Quality, effective practices that support the development and learning of each and every child is a main focus of this text. The National Association for the

---

National Association for the Education of Young Children
The largest association of early childhood professionals, NAEYC is concerned with education, advocacy, and the provision of high-quality early childhood environments for young children.

Code of Ethical Conduct
NAEYC's guide to help professionals resolve ethical dilemmas.

Education of Young Children (NAEYC), the **Division for Early Childhood Education** (DEC) of the **Council for Exceptional Children**, the **National Association for Family Child Care** (NAFCC), federal and local governments, and advocacy groups have each developed policies, practices, and programs to guide early childhood professionals and positively affect the quality of care and education young children receive. Teacher education and preparedness has become a central focus in efforts to ensure quality. This focus is shaped by early childhood organizations, such as NAEYC and the DEC, and accepted frameworks for practice, such as developmentally appropriate practices (DAP).

Vision of NAEYC

NAEYC is the largest early childhood organization in the world. NAEYC's (2006b) vision statement reflects the organization's overall goals:

1. All children have access to a safe and accessible, high-quality early childhood education that includes a developmentally appropriate curriculum; knowledgeable and well-trained program staff and educators; and comprehensive services that support their health, nutrition, and social well-being, in an environment that respects and supports diversity.
2. All early childhood professionals are supported as professionals with a career ladder, ongoing professional development opportunities, and compensation that attracts and retains high quality educators.
3. All families have access to early childhood education programs that are affordable and of high quality and actively participate in their children's education as respected reciprocal partners.
4. All communities, states, and the nation work together to ensure accountable systems of high-quality early childhood education for all children.

NAEYC's goal of ensuring accountable systems of high-quality early childhood education for all children requires attention to the varied strengths and challenges children bring to classroom communities, including diversity in ability, language, and culture. For equity and inclusion to be supported—where each and every child benefits from high-quality services tailored to their unique development and learning needs—teachers must be prepared to respect and support children's diverse abilities and ways of processing and interacting with their world. Through an extensive ever-developing partnership supporting goals of equity and inclusion, the NAEYC and DEC have collaborated through companion papers, endorsements, and joint position statements.

Mission of the Division for Early Childhood of the Council for Exceptional Children

The mission of the DEC is to promote the optimal development of young children with special needs through promoting policies and advancing evidence-based practices (DEC, n.d.). Related goals include supporting the development of

Division for Early Childhood Education
Division of the Council for Exceptional Children for individuals who work with or on behalf of young children with disabilities and other special needs.

Council for Exceptional Children
The largest international professional organization dedicated to the improvement of educational outcomes for children with disabilities.

National Association for Family Child Care
An organization whose mission is to strengthen the profession of family child care.

Supportive, respectful interactions allow children to thrive.

children between the ages of birth and 8 with special needs and creating an integrated community of support for young children and their families. The DEC is one of 17 divisions of the Council for Exceptional Children, which is the largest professional organization in the world focused on improving educational outcomes for children with exceptionalities, **disabilities**, and/or children who are gifted.

disabilities

Disabilities refer to physical, cognitive, social and emotional, or genetic factors that have an impact on a child's ability to interact within the environment.

High-quality, inclusive practices represented through the extensive work of the NAEYC and the DEC are of particular relevance to early childhood professionals, as most preschool classrooms include at least one child with a disability (Winton, 2006, as cited by National Institute for Early Education Research). This, coupled with the increased cultural and linguistic diversity of children and families today (Beavers & D'Amico, 2005) create a strong demand for professionals who are prepared to provide high-quality, inclusive services.

Whether your career focus is going to be working with infants, toddlers, preschoolers, primary-age children, families, support agencies, or the college community, supporting equity and inclusion will be an important part of your work. Your role as a professional includes fostering children's healthy development and learning, partnering with families, and fostering the development of the field. Success in your professional role begins with knowledge of effective practices.

Impact of Developmentally Appropriate Practices

One of the most important publications for the field of early childhood education is NAEYC's *Developmentally Appropriate Practice in Early Childhood Programs Serving Children from Birth through Age 8* (Copple & Bredekamp, 2009). This book synthesizes what is known about children's development, organizes theory and effective practices in the field, and includes a series of **developmentally appropriate practices** (DAP) based on this information. DAP has significantly affected early childhood programs and practices. It has also influenced national and state policy and standards for teacher education preparation programs (Raines & Johnston, 2003). Copple and Bredekamp's book is so influential that the term *developmentally appropriate practices* has become one of the most recognized terms in the field.

developmentally appropriate practices

Series of practices that are age, individually, and culturally appropriate.

Overview of DAP. *What is developmentally appropriate practice?* DAP represents an ongoing, reflective process that strives to provide supportive early childhood services for each and every child. DAP is represented through three kinds of knowledge (Copple & Bredekamp, 2009):

1. What is known about child development and learning—referring to knowledge of age-related characteristics that permits general predictions about what experiences are likely to best promote children's development and learning.
2. What is known about each child as an individual—referring to what practitioners learn about each child that has implications for how to best adapt and be responsible to that individual variation.
3. What is known about the social and cultural contexts in which children live—referring to the values, expectations, and behavioral and linguistic conventions that shape children's lives at home and in their communities that practitioners must strive to understand in order to ensure that learning experiences in the program or school are meaningful, relevant, and respectful for each child and family. (pp. 9–10)

• • • BECOMING A PROFESSIONAL • • •

Learning About the Field

As a current or future professional taking an introduction to early childhood education course, you may be at varying points in your education and career. Some may be in the initial stages of considering a career within the field. Others may be pursuing education following several years of working with young children and their families. The pathway you have chosen to pursue your education may vary as well. Perhaps you are pursuing a **Child Development Associate** (CDA), taking courses toward your associate's degree, or pursuing a bachelor's degree. Career objectives are also likely to vary. Are you considering becoming a teacher in a child care center or Head Start program? A family child care professional? An early intervention specialist? A teacher in kindergarten or primary grade education?

Your success in the field is marked by your ability to provide quality educational services. Achieving this goal requires knowledge of the external factors shaping the field, present factors affecting children and families, and your own changing developmental needs. Thus, becoming a professional is not something that happens at one point in time, but rather is an ongoing commitment.

What strategies can you use to support your ongoing development? Many professional organizations provide current information on effective practices within the field. In addition, your colleagues can provide an important source of ongoing professional development. Joining a professional organization is an excellent way to learn about the field. In addition, professional organizations can provide opportunities to communicate with others who have similar passions and career pathways.

The following list provides a description of just a few early childhood organizations you can join:

Child Development Associate
Awarded through the Council of Professional Recognition, the credential recognizes competencies in all areas of child development.

American Federation of Teachers
http://www.aft.org/earlychildhood/index.htm
Represents the economic, social, and professional interests of classroom teachers.

Children's Defense Fund
http://www.ChildrensDefense.org
Works to ensure that every child has a healthy, safe, fair, and moral start.

Division for Early Childhood, Council for Exceptional Children
http://www.dec-sped.org/
Promotes policies and evidence-based practices that support families and enhance the optimal development of young children who are at risk for developmental delays and disabilities.

National AfterSchool Association
http://www.naaweb.org/
Advocates for after-school issues and professionals.

The National Association for Family Child Care
http://www.nafcc.org/
Advocates for the family child care professional.

National Association for the Education of Young Children
http://www.naeyc.org/
Is dedicated to improving the well-being of all young children, with a focus on the quality of educational and developmental services for all children ages birth through 8.

National Association of Child Care Professionals
http://www.naccp.org/
Serves owners, directors, and administrators of child care centers.

National Head Start Association
http://www.nhsa.org/
Represents children, staff, and Head Start programs across America.

World Association for Infant Mental Health
http://www.waimh.org/
Promotes education, research, and study on the effects of mental, emotional, and social development in infancy on later development.

(continued)

Your professional interests and goals will influence the organizations you choose to join. Many of these organizations have chapters you can join within your own community, supporting networking and field involvement. Exploring organizational websites will give you important information about opportunities available and how these might fit with your present career goals.

Developmentally appropriate practices are based on several interrelated themes (Copple & Bredekamp, 2009):

- Excellence and equity, which stresses that opportunities to learn must be provided for each and every child to eradicate achievement gaps and create an equal playing field.
- Intentionality and effectiveness, requiring early childhood teachers to be purposeful in their teaching practices as well as attend to the consequences of decisions made.
- Continuity and change, recognizing the changing and developing field that reflects such enduring values as commitment to the whole child; recognition of the value of play; respect and responsiveness to individual and cultural diversity; and partnerships with families.
- Joy and learning, reflecting the core value of creating childhoods that are filled with joy while cultivating children's delight in exploring and understanding their world.

What might DAP mean for a teacher in an early childhood classroom? For preschool teacher Wendy, DAP means getting to know each of her preschoolers as growing individuals. What do the children in her class like to do? What are their developmental levels? What are

FIGURE 1.1
How DAP contributes to Effective Practice

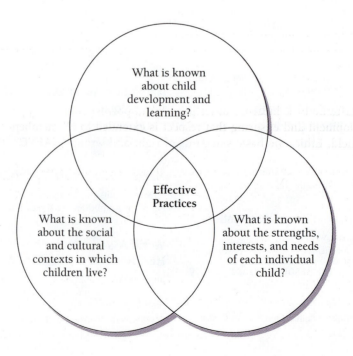

their strengths? What areas might strength-ening? It also means getting to know their fami-lies. Who are the important people in each child's life? How can these significant relationships be in-cluded and supported in the classroom environ-ment? The children in Wendy's classroom are also expected to attain developmental goals set forth by the state's early learning standards. DAP for Wendy means knowing what is expected of children developmentally and knowing how to support children in attaining developmental objectives. Figure 1.1 illustrates now DAP con-tributes to effective practice.

As is reflected in the theme of continuity and change that underlies developmentally appropri-ate practices, the needs of children, families, early childhood professionals, and society as a whole change over time. This continuous change leads to an important idea: early childhood profession-als must commit to being **lifelong learners**.

DAP requires supporting the individual development and learning needs of each child.

YOUR COMMITMENT TO LIFELONG LEARNING

lifelong learners
Those with a passionate commitment to acquiring new knowledge across the lifespan.

What does it mean to be committed to lifelong learning? Each one of you comes to this course with a variety of experiences. Some of you may have taught in the field for years and are looking for additional education. Others may be just beginning to explore the field as a possible profession. Regardless of your current level of experience, in this course you will acquire the knowledge, skills, and dispositions needed for success. The knowledge gained through this text and your course will mean different things at different points in time. Your ongoing experiences and development as a professional will support new inter-pretations, meanings, and applications. Throughout this development, reflection, where you carefully consider your relationship to the material, and ethical practice are essential.

Ethics as the Foundation for Professional Practice

The NAEYC Code of Ethical Conduct plays an important role in supporting profes-sional development and ensuring that respect is extended to all members of the early childhood field. Ethics are basic standards of right and wrong (NAEYC, 2005). From

---

TEACHING AND LEARNING CONNECTIONS

Committing to Lifelong Learning

Strategies supportive of lifelong learning include:

- A commitment to exploring emerging trends and new developments in the field.
- An investment in reflecting and improving on one's own professional practice.
- A shared dialogue with families and other professionals supporting continued growth through challenging values, beliefs, and practices.

Ethical practices guide professionals in their daily interactions with children, families, and other professionals.

these standards, decisions are made about supporting children and family development. The code outlines ethical expectations for all professionals, regardless of the type of work or population served.

The NAEYC Code of Ethical Conduct is a "living document" (Freeman & Feeney, 2004) developed from extensive interviews and applications with professionals in the field. The code is regularly revisited, with the goal of continuously working to encompass the variety of issues and challenges that face professionals. The code consists of seven core values (NAEYC, 2005):

- Appreciate childhood as a unique and valuable stage of the human life cycle
- Base our work with children on knowledge of how children develop and learn
- Appreciate and support the bond between child and family
- Recognize that children are best understood and supported in the context of family, culture, community, and society
- Respect the dignity, worth, and uniqueness of each individual (child, family member, and colleague)
- Respect diversity in children, families, and colleagues
- Recognize children and adults achieve their potential within relationships that are based on trust and respect

ideals

The aspirations of practitioners as represented through the NAEYC Code of Ethical Conduct.

principles

Guides for conduct and assistance in resolving ethical dilemmas.

From these core values, the code identifies **ideals**. Ideals represent the aspirations of practitioners. **Principles**, also identified by the code, guide conduct and assist practitioners in resolving ethical dilemmas. The goals of the ideals and principles are to "direct practitioners to those questions which, when responsibly answered, can provide the basis for contentious decision making" (Feeney & Freeman, 1999, p. 7). Please see Appendix A for the NAEYC Code of Ethical Conduct in its entirety.

Similarly, the Division for Early Childhood (DEC) of the Council for Exceptional Children (1996) has established its own Code of Ethics for working with children. See Appendix B for this code in its entirety.

TEACHING AND LEARNING CONNECTIONS

Using Ethics as a Guide for Practice

- Familiarize yourself with the NAEYC Code of Ethical Conduct.
- Use the code to work through challenges as they arise in the early childhood environment.
- Revisit the code regularly to ensure respectful, appropriate practices supportive of children and families.

The <u>NAEYC and DEC codes of ethics</u> provide a cornerstone for your professional development. Both <u>serve as important tools in ensuring that the development and learning needs of children and their families are met respectfully.</u>

Each chapter in this text concludes with a series of application activities entitled "Reflecting on and Applying Effective Practices." These are designed to support your development of the knowledge, skills, and dispositions needed for success in the field and are based on chapter materials presented. In this chapter, a description of ethical dilemmas and guiding questions to use in their resolution are presented. In all subsequent chapters, ethical dilemmas, related ideals from the NAEYC code, and related practice principles from the DEC code are presented.

Developing as a professional represents a lifelong journey.

MOVING FORWARD

The focus of this text is how the field of early childhood education can offer quality programs for *all* children and their families, and how you, as an early childhood professional, can make a difference in the lives of children, families, the profession, and society. You will learn about the basics of quality in the field. What are principles of developmentally appropriate practice? How do we assess and understand the strengths and needs of *each and every* child? Why should practices supporting inclusion be a central component of the field? What classroom practices engage and support young children's development and learning? What program philosophies and practices represent quality early childhood education? What strategies are used to collaborate with families and colleagues? How can respectful, supportive classroom communities be created? At the same time, you will learn about your role. How can you apply the knowledge, skills, and dispositions you acquire to support children, families, and the field as a whole? And ultimately, how can you play an important role in supporting social equity?

Understanding your role within the field of early childhood education requires knowledge of the field as a whole. You must also understand how the field's rich history has shaped the field today. Chapter 2, therefore, will focus on the history of early childhood education.

As you work through each chapter of this text, keep the following questions in mind. Reconsider them each time you've completed another stage of your learning:

- What do you see as early childhood education's role in supporting the development of each individual child?
- How would you explain the importance of the field to others?
- What contributions would you, as an early childhood professional, like to make to children, families, communities, and the field of early childhood education?

REFLECTING ON AND APPLYING EFFECTIVE PRACTICES (NAEYC AND CEC/DEC)

Ethics

Ethical dilemmas represent situations where individuals have to make decisions between two possible rights—in an ethical dilemma, there is more than one possible solution. Developed as moral compass for educators, dilemmas help you reflect on the question "What would a good early childhood educator do (Freeman & Feeney, 2004)?"

Each subsequent chapter ends with an ethical dilemma and related NAEYC Code of Ethical Conduct Ideals* and CEC/DEC Code of Ethics Practice Guidelines.** For each of these dilemmas, think about what you would do if faced with this situation, and consider the following:

- Who is involved in the dilemma, and what are your responsibilities to each individual or group?
- How can the NAEYC Ideals and CEC/DEC Practice Guidelines provided assist you in resolving the dilemma?
- What do you think a "good early childhood educator" would do in this situation?

CHAPTER REVIEW

- ### What is the field of early childhood education?

Early childhood education refers to practices and programs supporting the development and learning of children between the ages of birth and 8. In addition, it includes educational programming that supports the learning and development of professionals within the field. The parent organization within the field is the National Association for the Education of Young Children (NAEYC). NAEYC has worked extensively to develop education policy and what is considered best practices in supporting young children's development and learning. In addition to NAEYC and other organizations, the policies of federal, state, and local governments affect the education of young children.

- ### What are issues of access and equity for children, and how can early childhood education support social equity?

Access and equity for children is affected by the unique needs that children and their families bring to the early childhood environment. Early childhood education supports equity through responding to the needs of individual children, their families, and larger society. High-quality early childhood education is accessible to all—regardless of class, individual ability, or geographic location. It plays a key role in ensuring that all children have the ability to excel and succeed.

*NAEYC items in each chapter are from NAEYC (2005). Position Statement. Code of Ethical Conduct and Statement of Commitment. (Rev.). Washington, DC: Author. www.naeyc.org/about/positions/pdf/PSETH05.pdf.
**DEC items in each chapter are from Division of Early Childhood, Council for Exceptional Children (2009). Code of Ethics. http://www.dec-sped.org/uploads/docs/about_dec/position_concept_papers/Code%20of%20Ethics_Field%20Review%2011_08.pdf

- **How does the sociocultural context affect families and professionals?**

The social and cultural context creates several needs for early childhood education services. Changes in family form and function, such as the increased number of mothers in the workforce, have contributed to the need for the field of early childhood education. In addition, women play an important role in supporting families' economic well-being. Professionals within the field of early childhood education require specialized training. They also have clear expectations for conduct regarding the support of young children and their families. Further, persons within the field must meet various educational and training requirements. Despite these professional requirements, many view persons within the field as "babysitters." Although those negative stereotypes are changing, professionals in the field need to be aware of these challenges and work to eradicate them.

- **What role do organizations such as the National Association for the Education of Young Children (NAEYC), and the Division for Early Childhood (DEC) of the Council for Exceptional Children (CEC) and frameworks including developmentally appropriate practices (DAP) play in ensuring high-quality early childhood education services?**

NAEYC works to ensure high-quality programming. Their focus includes identifying, disseminating, and assessing indicators of quality within early childhood programs; focusing on the preparedness of early childhood professionals; addressing issues of access and affordability to quality programming for families; and strengthening support for the field as a whole. The focus of the DEC includes the creation of policies and the advancement of evidence-based practices supporting the development and learning of children with special needs between the ages of birth and 8. The DEC also works to create an integrated community of support for young children and their families. Developmentally appropriate practices provide guidance regarding effective practices, as they are based on current theory and application supporting children's development and learning. Also, they include a focus on supporting children's holistic development and are designed to support individual children and their needs. DAP leads to the creation of learning experiences supporting the success of children within the early childhood environment and the larger world.

2 History of Early Childhood Education

"You see things, and you say 'Why?' But I dream things that never were, and I say 'Why not?'"

—GEORGE BERNARD SHAW

Understanding the history of early childhood education requires looking through many lenses— historical, economic, political, cultural, sociological, and psychological. The different views these lenses provide combine into one core vision: society's role in supporting children. As a student in an introduction to early childhood education course, you may spend time in a variety of early childhood classrooms to learn about different programs, teaching styles, and approaches to caring for and educating young children. For example, you might observe an infant classroom serving children under the age of 15 months, a Head Start preschool classroom for 3- to 5-year-olds supporting bilingual learners, a classroom serving children with developmental delays and disabilities, a family child care program that includes children between the ages of 6 weeks and 6 years,

GUIDING QUESTIONS

- What are the origins of day nurseries, nursery schools, kindergarten, and parent education? Where do we see their influence in early childhood education today?

- How have historical social biases shaped early childhood education? Governmental policies? Educational philosophies?

- What are the goals of Head Start? Project Follow Through?

- How did the evolution of special education lead to today's focus on inclusion?

- What major contemporary challenges face early childhood education?

and/or a kindergarten classroom. The location and set up of these programs might vary. Some might be in church basements; others might be in people's homes, public schools, child care centers with multimillion-dollar architectural budgets, or other centers where the walls are dingy and gray.

The term diversity is certainly applicable when looking at program policies, practices, funding, ages of children served, and even the quality of services provided. This diversity means that defining early childhood education is a challenge felt by new and seasoned professionals alike. Where did this diversity come from? How does it affect the field today? Understanding the answers to these questions goes a long way toward ensuring that the development and learning of all children and their families are supported through high-quality early childhood education.

• • •

Early childhood education is a broad field with many programs and services addressing the needs of families and children between the ages of birth and 8. One family might need high-quality child care and kindergarten education for its infant and 5-year-old. Another might need early intervention services for a 1-year-old, Head Start services for its preschooler, and before- and after-school care for its third grader. Early childhood education encompasses many ages, settings, educational programs, and objectives, and therefore, has many different meanings for families, children, and teachers.

TEACHING AND LEARNING CONNECTIONS

Why Learn About the History of Early Childhood Education?

Understanding the history of early childhood education:

- Provides context for present-day practice so that you understand what has been tried out and worked or not worked by educators in previous centuries.

- Shapes your understanding of what is needed to meet present-day demands and support change in the future.

- Supports your ability to evaluate and explain the effectiveness of teaching practices today, such as to parents.

These many aspects of the field have been shaped by its rich, diverse history. This history includes children, families, and professionals. Knowledge of the history of the field will help you answer important questions. How did the field come to be? Why is there such a range of programs today? What is needed to meet present-day demands? What challenges does the field face in continuing to respond to the evolving needs of children, families, and professionals? As we examine the evolution of the field, we will consider the needs of three populations: children, families, and professionals.

OVERVIEW OF EARLY CHILDHOOD EDUCATION'S HISTORY

The care and education of young children are presently seen as inseparable, but this has not always been the case. For example, the kindergarten movement—originating from German traditions—focused on the education of young children. The goal of the kindergarten movement was to support children's academic success. Conversely the day nursery movement, which was derived from the French crèche model, focused on meeting a child's basic care needs such as feeding, sleeping, and toileting. Today, it is widely believed that one cannot care for children without educating them, and that educating children must involve caring for them as well.

Although we often talk about early childhood education as one field, varied historical underpinnings have led to at least five segmented areas of the field (Figure 2.1):

- *Day nurseries* refer to the care and education of children between the ages of birth and 5. These are now commonly referred to as *child care centers*.
- *Nursery schools* pertain to the education of children ages 3 to 5. Nursery schools are now commonly called *preschools*.
- *Kindergarten* meets the educational needs of children between the ages of 5 and 6.

FIGURE 2.1
The Five Segmented Areas of Early Childhood Education

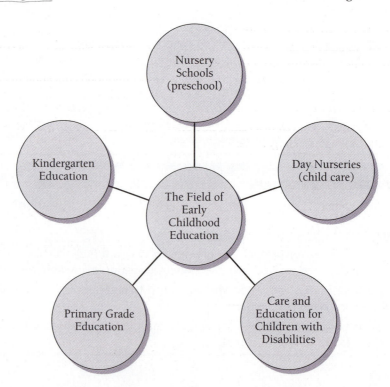

- *Primary grade education* meets the educational needs of children from first through third grade.
- The care and education of children with disabilities.

Primary grade education includes children between first and third grades.

With the inclusion of primary grade education, the field of early childhood education now encompasses children between the ages of birth and 8. However, not all children in this age range were originally included in the definition of whom the field served. Prior to the 1960s and President Lyndon Johnson's signing of the Elementary and Secondary Education Act and subsequent amendments, children with disabilities were largely educated within home or institutional environments. The signing of this act, and subsequent amendments that included attention to children with disabilities, placed an emphasis on the **inclusion** of children with disabilities into the **least restrictive environment** (LRE). LRE refers to the right of all children, regardless of their individual ability and to the greatest extent possible, to be educated in environments with typically developing peers.

Interestingly, the idea of inclusion is not new. Many individuals who have shaped our present-day ideas of children's learning and development considered environments inclusive of all children the most natural learning environment. The segregation of children with disabilities from schools that has emerged over time is predominantly a function of societal segregation. This segregation does not reflect the intent of major early childhood education philosophies.

As we explore the early history of early childhood education, an important question will emerge: Where are children with disabilities in this discussion? Despite compulsory education laws in place in the United States since 1918, children with special needs were relegated to home or institutional environments (Pardini, 2002). Discussion of the field of special education and its role in the evolution of early childhood education in general is found in "The Emergence of Inclusion" section of this chapter.

We will now turn to examining the origins of the field, which began with day nurseries (now commonly referred to as child care centers), nursery schools (now commonly called preschools), and kindergartens.

inclusion
Philosophical and practical approach emphasizing that children of varying needs and abilities should be educated in the same environment.

least restrictive environment (LRE)
Term referring to the right for all children, regardless of individual ability and to the greatest extent possible, to be educated within environments with typically developing peers.

EARLY HISTORY

Early childhood education in the United States evolved from a wide range of economic, social, and political contexts. Up to the 1960s, variation in program goals and funding led to the disjointed perception and implementation of services. This led to disparate early childhood education models, much evidence of which can still be seen today.

The Origins of Day Nurseries

Day nurseries originated in the United States in the late 1840s. The goal of day nurseries was to provide children of working parents with care in home-like settings that were considered preferable to their actual home environments (Rose, 1999). The first day nursery in the United States was the New York Day Nursery, which was established in 1854 through private charities. In day nurseries, the primary clientele were the children of parents who were poor. The persons caring for these children were largely untrained. Their primary role was to ensure that the children's custodial care needs were met.

At this time, there was a strong cultural bias against women working outside their homes. Employment outside the home had long been discouraged for women from middle- and upper-income backgrounds. The economic crisis of the Great Depression in the 1930s, however, made outside employment an economic necessity for many mothers. During this period, the federal government launched the first public child care program in U.S. history. Established through the **Works Progress Administration** (WPA), this program provided care for 75,000 children in 1,900 nursery schools while their parents pursued work outside the home (Rose, 1999). Only children who were qualified for "home relief" (which was an early version of public assistance) were eligible to participate (Illinois Facility Fund, 2000). Conventional ideology held that children were better off in these programs than at home, reinforcing the view that these nurseries were a form of "charity." The lower socioeconomic classes were day nurseries' main clientele, and the main focus of these programs remained providing custodial care for the children of mothers working outside of the home by necessity. Because of this custodial function, most nurseries were organized and run within social work, as opposed to education. Further, the use of day nurseries was exclusive to families experiencing economic hardship.

World War II represented a historical shift in government policies and support for the care of children outside the home. WPA centers were closing, and the war made it necessary for many women—not only those who were impoverished—to work outside the home, particularly in war industries. The **Lanham Act of 1940** authorized funding for governmental support of public and private agencies. The goal of this support was for the development and operation of public works. This act was later construed as including child care facilities in areas affected by the war (Cohen, 1996).

The Lanham Act had only a limited impact. Only children in war-impacted areas were served, and the intention was to provide funds only during this period of national crisis. Because of these funding constraints, only 13% of children who needed care were provided with public assistance (Cahan, 1989). Funding afforded through the Lanham Act was terminated in 1946 and most states, except for California, closed their programs.

Early federal involvement in child care services reflected the need for custodial services in the face of national crisis. Biases against care outside the home remained, based on the entrenched cultural view that families should raise their children without government interference (Cohen, 1996). These values—combined with a general distrust of nonmaternal care and the ambivalence about women working outside their homes—led to very limited government involvement in child care.

These prevailing views were tempered by an initially small but rapidly growing belief espousing equal opportunity for women and equality between the sexes: the **Women's Suffrage Movement**. In the early 1900s, women were asserting their rights and responsibilities, including the ability to work outside the home while their children were cared for by others. This growing movement garnished a small response from the federal government in 1954 when special dependent care deduction was added to the tax code. This deduction allowed child care services to become tax deductible up to $600 per year (Rose, 1999). These deductions were only afforded to persons who met particular criteria: widows or widowers, women whose husbands were incapable of working, and persons who were unmarried or separated from their spouses. It was not

Works Progress Administration
Federal relief program designed to ease the hardships of the Great Depression by offering jobs to the unemployed.

Lanham Act of 1940
Provided funds for the maintenance and operation of public works, including child care facilities in war-impacted areas.

Women's Suffrage Movement
Political campaign designed to support women's right to vote.

until the Equal Pay Act of 1963 and Titles VII and IX of the Civil Rights Act of 1964 that equal opportunity for women in education and employment became a national goal (Cahan, 1989).

These changing values coupled with the growing availability of day nurseries reflected an interesting development in the care and education of young children. As caring for children was traditionally assigned to women, the social and political issues involved in the care and education of young children have become women's issues. Consider, too, the substantive difference between the women who founded day nurseries and the persons who used them. The former were elite reformers and the latter composed of women from the lower class. These class and gender issues fostered a stigma toward day nurseries (Rose, 1999), which many argue still persists today.

stigma

The Origins of Nursery Schools

The children of middle-class families attended nursery school programs. These began as forums for the exchange of child-rearing advice and places where researchers and educators could study and foster children's social and emotional enrichment (Goffin & Wilson, 2001). The original model for preschools was the parent participation preschool, whose first nursery school was begun by a group of faculty wives at the University of Chicago in 1916 (Rose, 1999). These women were interested in a social experience for their children and parent education for themselves (California Council of Parent Participation Nursery Schools, Inc., 1996).

Nursery schools were most often in university settings. Child development researchers gathered and disseminated information based on their studies of children within the programs. The information shared applied most to practices supporting the care of children within the home and to efforts targeting professional preparation. The goal of professional preparation was to support children's development, with supporting social and emotional development considered a priority.

In 1922, Dr. Abigail Eliot founded the first public nursery school in the United States, and it enjoyed a rapid and significant popularity. In 1924 there were 28 nursery schools; by 1933, that number had grown to 1,700. In 1926, Abigail Eliot and Patty Smith Hill collaborated to found the National Association for Nursery Educators (Rose, 1999). This organization eventually became the National Association for the Education of Young Children (NAEYC).

The nursery school movement is credited with the birth of parent education. At this point, child development research and information designed to support child rearing was provided to the mothers of nursery school children (McLaughlin, 1990). Again, these parent education efforts were limited, as they, like nursery school child programming, predominantly affected the children of the middle class.

Education of Professionals. Nursery schools strongly influenced the preparation of early childhood education professionals. The National Association of Nursery School Educators (NANE)

Nursery schools were originally developed by parents.

was formed in response to the concerns of researchers and educators regarding the rapid expansion of nursery schools and related issues of program and teacher quality. In 1929 NANE's first book, *Minimal Essentials for Nursery School Education,* was published, which focused on quality within nursery school education. At the same time, **university laboratory schools** were developed in the United States through funding from the Laura Spelman Rockefeller Memorial Fund. These lab schools were typically housed within home economics departments, as the primary role of nursery schools included the gathering and dissemination of information related to children's development and learning.

Community-based schools and *normal schools* (so named for their focus on teaching children the norms of society) had also developed in various parts of the country. Training opportunities were viewed as important for all women and were designed to complement their roles as mothers and teachers. In 1927, the National Committee on Nursery Schools recommended a 4-year college degree for all nursery school teachers (National Association of Nursery School Educators, 1929).

During the Great Depression, the WPA and the Lanham Act spurred interest in nursery schools and teacher training, and both federal programs provided monies for teacher training. When the Lanham program closed following World War II, interest in professional training programs waned until the 1960s.

The Origins of Kindergarten Education

Coinage of the word *kindergarten* (German for "children's garden") is attributed to Friedrich Froebel, founder of the first kindergarten in Germany in 1840. Froebel (1826) believed that free self-activity, creativity, social expression, and motor expression were the foundations of successful educational experiences for children. These foundations were expressed through three main areas of activity: games and songs, construction, and **gifts and occupations**.

Elizabeth Peabody founded the first kindergarten in the United States in 1860. Peabody saw kindergarten as a viable option for all children, regardless of class background. She viewed the linkage of kindergartens to the established elementary education structure as essential (Rose, 1999).

The primary goal of **kindergarten** during this period was the support of children's social and emotional readiness for formal school. This was based on the assumption that intellectual development in children of that age did not benefit from environmental influence. Because of this assumption, academic achievement was not considered a goal.

In 1873, Susan Blow opened the first public kindergarten in St. Louis, realizing Peabody's goal by linking kindergarten education with the public school system. By 1883, every public school within St. Louis had a kindergarten classroom, and Blow's classroom was adopted as a model for kindergarten classrooms nationwide (Cahan, 1989).

As with day nurseries and nursery schools, issues of social class played a strong role in the evolution of kindergarten. Blow viewed kindergarten as a way to offer children who were poor an extra year of schooling before they were forced to work at the age of 11. A popular view emerged that kindergarten would perhaps provide a solution to urban poverty (Cahan, 1989). In addition, the large influx of immigrants to America created the need for kindergarten to integrate children of various language and social backgrounds into larger society.

Education of Professionals. The emergence of kindergarten education for young children included an emphasis on kindergarten teacher training. In 1874, Blow opened a kindergarten training school, which emphasized applying Froebel's ideas. By 1892,

---

University laboratory schools

Demonstration schools located in colleges and universities used for research, child education, and family–teacher training.

Gifts and occupations

Series of specific instructional materials designed by Frederick Froebel supporting children's experimentation within their environment.

Kindergarten education

Founded in the mid-1800s in the United States by Elizabeth Peabody, the original intent of kindergarten was to support social and emotional preparedness for education.

kindergarten education for both children and teachers had increased in popularity within the United States (Rose, 1999).

Figure 2.2 depicts a timeline of the early history of early childhood education.

FIGURE 2.2
A Brief Early History of the Day Nursery, Preschool, and Kindergarten, 1840–1964

Day Nurseries (now called child care centers)

1854–First day nursery in the United States, New York Day Nursery. Established through private charities.

Great Depression–First public child care program established through the Works Progress Administration. Served 75,000 children in 1,900 nursery schools. Only served children who qualified for "home relief." Last Works Progress Administration center closed in 1943.

Lanham Act of 1940–Funding provided for governmental support of public and private agencies including child care facilities affected by the war. Only served children in war-impacted areas. Program terminated in 1946.

Women's Suffrage Movement–During the early 20th century women asserted their right to work outside the home while others cared for their children.

1963–Equal Pay Act supported equal pay for similar work between men and women.

1964–Titles VII and IX of the Civil Rights Act afforded equal opportunity for women in education and employment.

Nursery Schools (now called preschools)

1916–First parent participation nursery school started by faculty wives at the University of Chicago. Goals included social experience for children and parent education.

1922–First public nursery school in the United States founded by Dr. Abigail Eliot.

1926–Abigail Eliot and Patty Smith Hill founded the National Association for Nursery Educators, which eventually became the National Association for the Education of Young Children.

Kindergarten Education

1840–Friedrich Froebel founded the first kindergarten in Germany.

1860–Elizabeth Peabody founded the first kindergarten in the United States. Goal was to support social and emotional readiness for formal school.

1873–Susan Blow opens first public kindergarten in St. Louis. First link between kindergarten education and the public school system.

1883–Every public school in St. Louis has a kindergarten classroom.

Kindergarten's Impact on Primary Grades

Before the onset of the kindergarten movement, primary grades were primarily teacher-directed forums where children were engaged in formal instruction (DuCharme, 1993). Increasingly, Froebelian ideas became accepted within kindergarten education. These ideals promoted children learning in home-like settings, completing tasks related to their daily lives, cooperating with peers during play and other activities, and developing an interest in the educational process. These ideals were considered appropriate not only for kindergartners, but also for children in the primary grades. As kindergarten and primary grade education became viewed as more similar than different, professional preparation and school organizations began to link the two. However, Froebelian views, which came to be called *child-centered education*, had a formidable philosophical foe: researchers had also documented the value of the teacher-directed, large-group, formal instruction approach (Bloch & Choi, 1990). This debate, still current among scholars, reflects differences in the philosophical roots of the field.

EARLY CHILDHOOD PROGRAMS: 1960s THROUGH THE 1980s

The 1960s were a time of great political and social upheaval. Attention had increasingly shifted to consideration of traditionally marginalized groups, including women, children, persons of color, and persons from impoverished backgrounds. A prevailing attitude emerged that centered on social equity. How could society meet individual needs and also create an egalitarian democracy that values each and every member of society? Activism during this period achieved results: the message of social equity was heard, and numerous legislative policies were developed in response. Head Start, Project Follow Through, and educational services for children with disabilities all emerged during the 1960s through the 1980s. Figure 2.3 summarizes the major developments occurring in Head Start during 1960s.

Head Start and the War on Poverty

Committed to supporting social equity, President Lyndon B. Johnson declared a **War on Poverty** in the United States. As part of this "war," Johnson signed the Economic Opportunity Act in 1964, thereby creating numerous programs designed to fight poverty, one of which was Head Start.

Head Start began in 1965 as an 8-week summer program to ensure later school success for preschool-aged children considered to be lacking in advantages. It attended to the emotional, social, health, nutritional, and psychological needs of children and families. Today, Head Start is part of the Administration on Children, Youth, and Families, which is itself part of the Department of Health and Human Services. In 2003, there were nearly 50,000 Head Start classrooms in the United States, and it has served over 21 million children since its inception (U.S. Executive Branch, 2006).

War on Poverty
Programs designed to eliminate poverty, including Job Corps, Head Start, Medicaid and Medicare, and the expansion of public housing and welfare programs.

Head Start
An intervention program that includes the provision of high-quality care and education to children from at-risk backgrounds, access to health care and social services, and parent education.

FIGURE 2.3
A Brief History of Head Start

1964–Economic Opportunity Act signed by President Lyndon B. Johnson.
1965–Head Start begins as an 8-week summer program for preschool-age children.
Mid-1960s–Head Start dedicates efforts toward emotional, social, health, nutritional, and psychological needs of children and families through high-quality educational programming.
1968–Project Follow Through begins, which focuses on evaluating the effectiveness of early childhood curriculum strategies.

Head Start supports children's development and prepares them for schooling. This mission is accomplished through a myriad of services including medical, dental, nutritional, and mental health services. Head Start also provides services supporting parent involvement through establishing family partnerships. Including children with disabilities and establishing community partnerships are also goals of Head Start.

Head Start's specific role in fighting poverty was based on the idea that early childhood education could shield children from families who are low income against turbulence in their homes and neighborhoods (Palmaffy, 2001). The argument was introduced and substantiated that dollars spent on early childhood education in the short term would save money down the road (Weikart, Bond, & McNeil, 1978).

Head Start was founded about the same time that academic research was making connections between IQ (**intelligence quotient**) development and environment. In simplest terms, IQ is a measure of present levels of cognitive functioning. IQ had been hotly debated among psychologists for years. Some researchers argued that intelligence was genetically determined, and therefore could not be modifiable by the environment. Others disagreed, arguing that environmental conditions can have a dramatic impact on intelligence.

In the early 1960s, three studies were published supporting the malleability of IQ (Hawes, 1999). In 1961, McVicker demonstrated the effect of experience on the developing brain. In 1964, Bloom published findings indicating that critical development of overall mental capacities occurred in the first four years of life. Finally, in 1966 Skeels published a follow-up to a study he had done in the 1930s. The original study, which had received extensive scorn from the academic community, was of children raised in an orphanage. The new study compared the children raised in the orphanage to a control group of children who had been moved from the orphanage to a nearby institution where they received extensive care and nurturing. Skeels found that, comparatively, the children who had remained in the orphanage suffered long-term negative effects. Skeels concluded that the early years matter, and that the quality of a child's environment plays a significant role in development. Each of these studies supported the development of Head Start.

In addition to being embraced as an academic intervention, Head Start was also seen as an environmental intervention—an opportunity to significantly improve the lives of children and families by providing nutritious meals, health care services, and parental support and education. Head Start also provided social support by educating communities on topics such as child-rearing practices, nutrition, and food preparation (Palmaffy, 2001).

Public attention to and investment in Head Start had many benefits. Early childhood education gained attention as a support for children's success in school. The program also renewed interest in identifying the best curricular models and strategies to support children's development and learning. Through Head Start, the benefits of preschool education were extended beyond the middle class to families who were lower income (Palmaffy, 2001).

intelligence quotient
Measure of intellectual functioning based on performance and verbal scales and evaluated through standardized tests.

The quality of a child's environment plays a significant role in his or her development.

Head Start and Beyond

The advent of Head Start brought numerous changes to early childhood education. First, the education of young children was seen as worthy of societal and government investment. Second, education was viewed as something that was important and necessary before the start of formal schooling, particularly for children from families who were living in poverty. Head Start, in many ways, followed the path of kindergarten education with similar results. Preschool was now seen as an important part of children's education.

Unlike kindergarten, however, Head Start was not linked to the public school system. Presidents Jimmy Carter and George W. Bush attempted to move Head Start to proposed Departments of Education; both met fierce resistance (Palmaffy, 2001). Head Start advocates feared a reduction in Head Start's ability to provide comprehensive services such as nutrition and health care. Proponents argued that linking Head Start to the public school system would assist in the professionalization of the field. This, in turn, would reduce the gap between the salaries earned by Head Start and public school staff. Both Carter's and Bush's proposals were defeated.

Head Start had a lasting effect on how Americans value teacher and staff preparation and training. Head Start adopted comprehensive educational strategies that included a focus on both children's development and practical strategies. Before Head Start, there had been few educational requirements for preschool teachers.

Head Start placed parent involvement at the center of appropriate educational practices for children. In recent years, Head Start has shifted from the language of "parent involvement and education" to that of "family involvement and education," representing inclusive language that acknowledges diversity in family form.

Finally, Head Start was also one of the first successfully concerted efforts to include children with disabilities. Responding to the Congressional mandate that 10% of the Head Start enrollment slots be reserved for children with disabilities, Head Start emerged in 1972 as a leader for supporting inclusive early childhood education services (Palmaffy, 2001).

THE EMERGENCE OF SPECIAL EDUCATION

The field of special education as a whole benefited extensively from legislation enacted during the same period as Head Start. Figure 2.4 summarizes the legal developments regarding special education that you need to be aware of in your teaching career.

Brown v. Board of Education

Landmark case within the U.S. Supreme Court that outlawed racial segregation in schools.

The 1954 *Brown v. Board of Education* decision extended equal educational opportunities to minority groups, created the climate for advocacy for children with disabilities, and led to the emergence of the field of special education. Following that landmark decision, the 1960s witnessed a virtual avalanche of federal legislation affecting the educational rights of children with disabilities (National Information Center for Children and Youth with Disabilities, 1996). Leading legislative attention to these issues was President John F. Kennedy, whose sister Rose suffered from a cognitive disability. Kennedy believed that Americans had a moral and constitutional obligation to provide for the needs of persons with cognitive disabilities. The 1961 President's Panel on Mental Retardation was the first significant federal activity aimed at improving the lives of persons with disabilities. The panel's first report, *A Proposed Program for National Action to Combat Mental Retardation* (1962), paved the way for the creation of new programs supporting persons with cognitive disabilities.

During the same general period, Title IV of the Civil Rights Act of 1964 was enacted. This act prohibited educational discrimination based on race, color, or national origin.

1954–*Brown v. Board of Education* decision extended equal educational opportunities to minority groups.

1961–President's Panel on Mental Retardation represented the first federal activity aimed at improving the lives of children with disabilities.

1964–Title IV of the Civil Rights Act passed, prohibiting educational discrimination based on race, color, or national origin, and leading to a national commitment to ending discrimination in education.

1965–Elementary and Secondary Education Act represented the first federal grant program targeting children with disabilities.

1968–Handicapped Children's Early Education Assistance Act represented the first government program targeted toward infants and toddlers with disabilities.

1973–Rehabilitation Act, through Section 504, prohibited discrimination of persons with disabilities by any agency, group, or entity receiving federal monies.

1975–The Education for All Handicapped Children Act, called P.L. 94-142, passed.

1986–Amendments to the Education of the Handicapped Act included provisions that entitle preschool-age children with disabilities to a free and appropriate education and special services to children between the ages of birth and 2.

1990–Education of the Handicapped Act renamed as the Individuals with Disabilities Education Act (IDEA). The term *handicap* was replaced with the term *disability*.

1990–American Disabilities Act (ADA) supported the removal of barriers for persons with disabilities by requiring public accommodations, employers, transportation programs, and communication systems to eliminate these barriers.

1997–IDEA amendments extended ADA requirements to public programs serving children ages birth to 3 and placed an emphasis on early intervention services for children who may be at risk for developmental delay.

FIGURE 2.4
A Brief History of Special Education, Legislation, 1954–1997

The act also marked a national commitment to ending discrimination in education (U.S. Department of Education, 1999).

During the presidency of Lyndon B. Johnson, the Elementary and Secondary Education Act of 1965, and its amendments of the same year, represented the first federal grant program that targeted children with disabilities. In two subsequent amendments (in 1966 and 1968), responsibility for the education of children with disabilities was moved from institutions to local schools (Pardini, 2002). Oversight programs through the newly developed Bureau for the Education of the Handicapped (now called the **National Council on Disability**) were established. In 1968, the Handicapped Children's Early Education Assistance Act represented the first government program targeted toward infants and toddlers with disabilities. This act provided funds to support model demonstration programs designed to educate infants and preschool-aged children with disabilities. Attention shifted to the importance of early intervention, which stressed that the earlier children receive special services targeted toward their individual developmental needs, the better the long-term outcomes (Pardini, 2002). This increasing awareness led to the development of the Office of Special Education and Rehabilitation Services within the U.S. Department of Education.

In the 1970s, several right-to-education cases were brought to court nationwide. The suits varied in whether they were filed by parents, children, or organizations. However, they shared important similarities, including the assertion that children

National Council on Disability

Independent council that makes recommendations to the president and Congress on issues affecting Americans with disabilities.

Education for All Handicapped Children Act of 1975

Also called P.L. 94-142, the act ensured a free and appropriate education (FAPE) to all children with disabilities between the ages of 3 and 21.

Go to MyEducationLab at www.myeducationlab .com and select the topic "Special Needs/ Inclusion." Under Activities and Applications, watch the video *PL 94-142* and consider the impact of PL 94-142 on education for students with diverse abilities.

free and appropriate education

Outcome of federal law ensuring that all children within the jurisdiction of the school district receive an education that meets their individual needs in an educational setting reflective of least restrictive environment law.

mainstreaming

Designed to integrate children with disabilities into the regular classroom environment, mainstreaming referred to strategies to support this goal.

should receive education within their public schools. Further, this education should be as similar as possible to the education of peers without disabilities. The severity of the disability should not exclude the publicly supported provision of services (Office for Civil Rights, 2005).

The Rehabilitation Act of 1973 brought increased rights to persons with disabilities, including children. Section 504 of this act, specifically, prohibited discrimination of persons with disabilities by any agency, group, or entity that received federal monies. This did not include private organizations, but did apply to the newly formed Head Start.

The Rehabilitation Act was followed closely by P.L. 94-142, the **Education for All Handicapped Children Act of 1975**. This law had four major purposes (DeStefano & Snauwaert, 1989):

- To guarantee that a **free, appropriate education** (FAPE), including special education and related service programming, is available to all children and youth with disabilities who require it.
- To ensure that the rights of children and youth with disabilities and their parents or guardians are protected.
- To assess and ensure the effectiveness of special education at all levels of government.
- To financially assist the efforts of state and local governments in providing full educational opportunities to all young children and youth with disabilities through the use of federal funds.

This legislation led to millions of children receiving educational services within their own community. It was during this time that the term *mainstreaming* was introduced. **Mainstreaming** refers to strategies that include children with disabilities within the existing mainstream of the American public school system (Mulligan, Morris, Green, & Harper-Whelan, 1999). A common form of mainstreaming is including children with disabilities with their typically developing peers during lunch or recess.

Until this point, the education of children with disabilities was a legislative movement. Public schools were charged with figuring out how to integrate children into existing school settings. The overall goal was to create one group of children—a diverse, cohesive whole. However, the mainstreaming movement failed to achieve this goal for several reasons (Gottlieb, 1981). One reason was the lack of attention to the infrastructure needed to support the routines and activities of all children. For example, children were included without attention to modifications or accommodations needed to support their inclusion. Another limitation was based on the original conceptions of children with and without disabilities. In the mainstreaming movement, children with and without disabilities were considered members of separate groups, with the goal of part-time integration. Another possible viewpoint is that all children are members of the same group. Viewing children as children regardless of individual abilities would support making adaptations and accommodations for individual children within the larger group.

Accountability within Special Education

Similar to the field of early childhood education, demands were placed on the field of special education to demonstrate that programs serving children were attaining anticipated results. The first model demonstration projects targeting children with disabilities were funded at the rate of one million dollars in 1968 through what is now the Early

Education Program for Children with Disabilities (Commission on Behavioral Social Sciences and Education, 1982). These programs provided locally designed ways to serve infants, young children, and their families. They also provided more specific information on effective programs and their techniques. Distribution of visible, replicable models throughout the country was encouraged (National Early Childhood Technical Assistance Center [NECTAC], 2007).

In 1968, 24 demonstration projects were begun, and by 1972, extensions including outreach projects were developed. The program has undergone significant expansion to this day, with funding levels currently reaching $20 million annually (NECTAC, 2007).

Family Involvement and Special Education

Family involvement in special education is seen as critical to the success of services. Based on this, family involvement is required at the very first stage of special education service implementation and throughout the process. The Education for All Handicapped Children Act mandated that schools include families in goal setting and service decision-making meetings. **Individualized Family Service Plans** (IFSPs), used to create family-centered goals to enhance the development of qualified infants and toddlers, and **Individualized Education Programs** (IEPs), a team-developed written program identifying goals and objectives supporting the development of children between the ages of 3 and 21 who have a disability, were implemented to carry out this mandate.

Although families were included in the structure of decision making, they were not given educational preparation to function well within this role. This barrier left many families feeling alienated (Furney & Salembrier, 2000). After having placed a great structural emphasis on the value of family involvement, professionals were faced with the difficult task of cultivating involvement.

Education of Professionals

The development of specific academic programs to support working with children with disabilities was bolstered in 1975 with the passage of the Education for All Handicapped Children Act. Special education teacher preparation programs existed before 1975, but the subsequent investment of the federal government in teacher preparation programs created substantive growth.

During the mid-1970s the focus was on working with children with special needs in general. The early childhood population was not specifically addressed. In addition, professional preparation programs were focused on specific areas of expertise: occupational therapists were trained separately in one program, whereas speech and language therapists were trained in another. Therefore, the segregation of special education as a field of professional study remained. This practice contradicts the overall goal of integrated and inclusive educational services (Bergen, 2003).

A MISSING PIECE: CHILD CARE AND LARGER HISTORICAL DEBATES

Thus far, you have explored how nursery school models influenced the development of Head Start, the emergence of special education, the origins of kindergarten education, and the relationship between each of these programs and the accountability movement.

myeducationlab

Go to MyEducationLab and select the topic "Special Needs/ Inclusion." Under Activities and Applications, view the simulation *What Do You See? Perceptions of a Disability* and consider the diverse abilities of the persons represented.

Individualized Family Service Plan

Written plan outlining family-centered individual supports and services to enhance development of a qualified child between birth and 3 years.

Individualized Education Program

A team-developed, written program identifying goals and objectives to support the development of a child between the ages of 3 and 21 who has a disability.

Attention to day nurseries (now commonly called child care centers) has remained left out in this larger debate. This neglected issue has affected not only children, but also professionals (Rose, 1999).

In the 1980s, our society still demonstrated vast ambivalence regarding women working outside the home. Some studies during that time raised the possibility of child care being harmful to children, with much of this concern centered on infant and toddler care, in particular (Belsky & Eggebeen, 1991; Belsky, 1994). These studies were used to support the idea that women should provide care to their own children in their own homes.

The focus of federal legislation targeting child care in the 1960s was to support entry into the workforce and financial independence for families living in poverty (Illinois Facility Fund, 2000). Guidelines for establishing quality preschool programs (including minimum requirements for preschool teacher preparation) were developing, but the educational needs of the infant-toddler population remained unaddressed.

A MERGING PERSPECTIVE: 1980s THROUGH THE 1990s

Just as national interest in early childhood education was renewed by Head Start in the 1960s, it was renewed in the 1980s by the findings of brain research. But there was an important difference. Head Start had drawn attention to issues affecting the preschool population. New findings of brain researchers were applicable to children at earlier stages of development, starting at birth and, in some cases, even before birth. These developments were followed in the 1990s by legislation aimed at the inclusion of children with special needs.

Attention to Child Care and the Birth-to-Age-3 Populations

As you will learn in Chapter 4, the first years of life are devoted to the development of future brain capacity, and relationship-based environments form a foundation from which brain development can occur (Shonkoff & Phillips, 2000). Early intervention (intervention during the first years of life) can be tremendously effective in addressing existing or potential adversities (Bailey, Scarborough, Hebbeler, Spiker, & Mallik, 2004). There is an unfortunate gap between what this research suggests might be the most effective practices and what current educational practices actually are. Here are a few startling facts:

- The earliest years of life receive the least attention from academic researchers.
- Many children spend their days in overcrowded programs with underprepared teachers.
- Investment in early intervention to prevent children from falling behind is comparatively limited.

The quality of child care that children receive during those first years of life is generally lacking. Half of the 15 million infants and toddlers of working families are in programs that do not support their development (Hancock & Wingert, 1997). In fact, the landmark Cost,

Inclusion celebrates the individual contributions of each person.

Quality, and Outcomes in Child Care Centers study (CQO Study Team, 1995), which provided a national picture of the quality of child care services, found that quality was poor to mediocre in half of the infant-toddler programs studied. In addition, families tended to overestimate the quality of care children receive. These findings led the Education Commission of the States to claim in 1995 that the quality of child care services should be upgraded and standards for the professional development of child care teachers should be created.

Attention has shifted away from whether or not children should be placed in child care to the effects of quality care on children's development. Further, research studies show that high-quality care has benefits beyond those traditionally thought to affect children from families who are low income. For example, the follow-up study to the 1995 Cost, Quality, and Outcomes study (Piesner-Feinberg et. al., 1999) found that children in high-quality care demonstrated greater mathematical ability, greater thinking and attention skills, and fewer behavioral problems. Although the negative effects from the lack of high-quality care apply to all children, they are demonstrably worse for children from families who have low income.

Quality care is essential to supporting the development and learning of all children.

The lack of attention paid to the birth to age 3 populations was also reflected in special education. Although debates over inclusion for the primary grade (and older) populations were long-standing, most researchers and practitioners agreed that inclusion within early childhood education was an increasingly feasible option (Bergen, 2003). Coupled with increased attention to the education and care needs of our nation's youngest children came additional legislative attention to children with disabilities. This included attention to the birth to 3 populations with disabilities and an overall societal goal on inclusion.

THE EMERGENCE OF INCLUSION

Integration became the goal of educational services in the 1980s. Rather than ask a child to adapt to the needs of the school, people began to think that perhaps the school needs to adapt itself to the needs of the child (Osgood, 2005). A child who was excluded from an activity because the room was not wheelchair accessible, for example, was an example of the child not meeting a need defined by the school. But when the school created an accessible environment by adding wheelchair ramps and space for wheelchairs in hallways, doorways, and classrooms, and the child was able to participate in the activity, the child was fully integrated. Other examples of physical adaptations supporting inclusion include rearranging classroom furniture or making sure tables are high enough to allow a child in a wheelchair to sit at the table. Including each and every child requires far more than making sure classrooms are accessible to those who use wheelchairs for mobility. Additional modifications to support a wide range of diverse needs will be discussed in Chapter 11.

Until 1986, legislation had only been enacted to accommodate the educational needs of children between the ages of 5 and 21. The Education for All Handicapped Children Act was amended that year to include preschool-aged children with disabilities, providing them with a free and appropriate education. Additional amendments ensured special services to children from birth through age 2 (referred to as early intervention), although

Individuals with Disabilities Education Act

Also called P.L. 94-142, IDEA is a federal program that provides funds to states and local education agencies to provide education services for children between the ages of 3 and 21. Passed in 1990, IDEA was the new name for the Education of the Handicapped Act.

Americans with Disabilities Act

Passed in 1990, the ADA required public barriers be eliminated for persons with disabilities.

natural environment

Under Part C of IDEA, the term *natural environment* stresses that early intervention services for infants and toddlers should be provided in settings in which children without disabilities participate.

people-first language

Use of language that places the child before the disability, as opposed to defining the child by the disability. Example: child with special needs versus special-needs child.

public funding for these services was not provided. The legislation also created the academic field of early childhood special education.

In 1990, the Education of the Handicapped Act was renamed as the **Individuals with Disabilities Education Act** (IDEA). The term *handicap*, which referred to an environmental limitation that was the result of a disability, was replaced with *disability*. To understand this rationale, imagine a child who does not have the ability to walk. It is literally true to say that the child is disabled. The child may use a wheelchair for mobility but cannot access a room at the top of a flight of stairs. He is handicapped in this context, but if an elevator were present, the handicap would be removed. The **Americans with Disabilities Act** (ADA) of the same year further supported the removal of barriers for persons with disabilities. This act required public accommodations, employers, transportation programs, and communication systems to eliminate barriers that might impede a person with a disability full interaction with the environment. The ADA considers child care programs public accommodations. Therefore, children must not be excluded from the program because they have a disability. The IDEA Amendments of 1997 extended these requirements to public programs that serve children ages birth to 3. An emphasis was placed on early intervention services for children who may be at risk for developmental delays.

Another linguistic change made by the IDEA Amendments of 1997 was the term **natural environment**. Under Part B of IDEA, the term *least restrictive environment* supported the education of young children with disabilities—appropriate to their needs—in environments with their typically developing peers. *Natural environment*, under Part C of IDEA, stresses that early intervention services for infants and toddlers should be provided within settings in which children without disabilities participate (Walsh, Rous, & Lutzer, 2000). In other words, early intervention services should be provided in the home and community, which includes child care settings (McWilliams, 2000). By emphasizing the term *natural environment*, the ideal that children should not be separated from their peers, homes, and communities to receive needed services is embraced as a core value and made a requirement.

Another change that came about in this period was the development of **people-first language**. Instead of referring to a 3-year-old as an autistic child, people-first language requires placing the child first. Therefore, the 3-year-old would be referred to as a child with autism. In other words, the disability no longer defines the child; it is just one of many characteristics that make the child who she is.

TEACHING AND LEARNING CONNECTIONS

Examples of People-First Language

Inaccurate Description	Appropriate Language
Disabled person	Person with a disability
Downs child	A child with Down syndrome
She is autistic	She has autism
He's learning disabled	He has a learning disability
She is a dwarf	She has short stature
She's crippled	She uses a wheelchair for mobility
Blind person	Person who is blind
He's in special ed	He receives special education services
Normal kid	Typically developing child
Handicapped parking	Accessible parking

• • • BECOMING A PROFESSIONAL • • •

Understanding Laws That Shape the Early Childhood Field

Becoming a professional within the field requires understanding the various laws that shape early childhood education policies and practices. At the federal level, there are several laws that influence program practices at the state and community level. The following provides a brief overview of some of the laws that have had an impact on the field:

- Americans with Disabilities Act
  - *Primary goal:* To remove barriers to equal access for persons with disabilities.
  - *Potential impact:* Design of early childhood environments, ensuring that access is supported for all individuals, regardless of individual ability.
- Section 504 of the Rehabilitation Act
  - *Primary goal:* To ensure that programs cannot discriminate against individuals based on their disability.
  - *Potential impact:* Program services and benefits for any program receiving financial services from any federal and state department or agency must extend equal opportunities to benefit from services to all individual, regardless of ability.
- Individuals with Disabilities Education Act
  - *Primary goal:* To ensure that children with disabilities have the same access to education as children without disabilities.
  - *Potential impact:* Ensures that all children between the ages of 3 and 21 are entitled to a free and appropriate education.
- No Child Left Behind Act
  - *Primary goal:* To close the gaps in achievement between different groups of students.
  - *Potential impact:* Influences the emphases within educational systems, such as emphasizing reading/language arts and mathematics, supporting English proficiency, supporting teachers receiving rank of highly qualified, and promoting learning environments that are safe and drug free.

Knowing and ensuring that these laws are met within your early childhood environment is an important part of your professional development. The following are strategies you can apply within your early childhood education setting (Downs, Blagojevich, Labas, Kendrick, & Maeverde, 2005):

- Review written materials to make sure they are nondiscriminatory.
- Evaluate the physical space to ensure that everyone has access to the building and areas within it, including each and every child with diverse developmental needs, such as a child who uses a wheelchair for mobility.
- Learn about community resources that will help meet the needs of individual children and families, such as parenting programs, resources for food and child care subsidies, and community programs providing children with supplemental services.
- Ensure that classroom practices and design are in line with federal and state laws and required parameters.

The focus of least restrictive and natural environments led to today's focus on inclusion. Inclusion reflects the basic attitude that children are children first. Further, it is the responsibility of society to create environments supporting the multitude of childhood developmental needs. This is in opposition to allowing children to be defined by the constraints (needs) of the environment.

A review of the disparate histories of day nurseries, nursery schools, kindergarten, primary grade education, and special education illuminates how they led to today's emphasis on inclusion and preparing professionals for inclusive practices during the early childhood years. The evolution of these five major strands of early childhood education also illuminates the way we treat family education today.

A Contemporary View of Family Education

No Child Left Behind Act

Signed into law by President George W. Bush in 2002, the NCLB Act promised sweeping reforms to the educational system focusing on standards of accountability, parent participation, and student performance.

Family education has benefited from extensive research and legislative attention. The **No Child Left Behind Act** (NCLB) of 2001 made parental involvement a legislative mandate. NCLB requires that all schools receiving Title I funding have a documented parent involvement plan and provisions for effective implementation. NCLB defines parent involvement and requires a regular, two-way, and meaningful dialogue on student academic learning and other school activities. It specified opportunities needed to exist for parents to:

- Assist in their child's learning.
- Be actively involved in their child's education at school.
- Serve as full partners in their child's education and being included, as appropriate, in decision-making and on advisory committees to assist in the education of their child.

myeducationlab

Go to MyEducationLab and select the topic "Families and Communities." Under Activities and Applications, read the case study *On the Frontlines: Connecting with Families* and consider how it relates to supporting family partnerships.

National Fatherhood Initiative

Sponsored through the federal government, the goal of the initiative is to strengthen the role of fathers in families.

Legislation mandating family involvement reflects the historical and philosophical belief that a family's role is critical. However, successful family education cannot be achieved by legislation alone. The challenge lies in the formation of strategies and policies that will support family involvement.

Interestingly, NCLB's use of the word *parent* is not reflective of the most current terminology in use in the field today. *Parent* (or *parents*) is not considered sufficiently inclusive of the various adult figures that may populate a child's immediate world such as a legal guardian, or the actual primary caregivers of a child such as an aunt, uncle, grandparent, and so forth. The term *family*, as is commonly used in Head Start, is generally preferred by professionals who seek to use and model inclusive language.

An important change during this period was an increased focus on the role that fathers play in their children's development. The U.S. Department of Health and Human Services **National Fatherhood Initiative** targets strengthening the role of fathers in families, addressing a historical lack of involvement in care and education. For example, the majority of Head Start program representatives surveyed said they included resident biological fathers, nonbiological fathers, and nonresident biological fathers (Fagan, 1999). However, only 16% of all fathers were highly involved in Head Start. This led Fagan to conclude that offering services to both moms and dads is not necessarily going to lead fathers to think that the services and activities are for them. The National Fatherhood Initiative seeks to distribute strategies supportive of father outreach and involvement.

Education of Professionals

Early intervention developed out of the related fields of early childhood education, **compensatory education**, and early childhood special education (Kunesh, 1990). Because early intervention developed from three different fields, great variation exists in the way professionals are prepared to work with children who have disabilities. Each professional discipline area has its own training sequence. Some require graduate degrees, whereas others require bachelor-level training. Knowledge bases also develop around particular disabilities. Professionals might focus on learning how to work with children who have cerebral palsy, for example, or children who have autism. This tends to relegate children to categories based on their disability. Based on this, a fundamental commonality—the fact that they are children first—can be overlooked. These variances in training are compounded by the fact that professionals from different disciplines may hold degrees in different areas. Some degrees focus on the entire span of life (birth to death), whereas others have degrees based on categorical separations of disabilities.

compensatory education

Movement to provide children from low-income backgrounds with educational experiences designed to compensate for potential challenges in learning and development.

PROGRAMMING AT THE END OF THE 1900s

Discrepancies remain between who was originally intended to benefit from various educational services when they emerged and who may actually benefit from those services today. Recall that child care, for example, was initially viewed as a social service for children from families who are low income. Education, however, was viewed as a service targeting the children and families of middle- and upper-middle-class communities within university lab school settings. It was not until the 1980s that the concept of care and education became inseparable. Figure 2.5 on page 40 provides an overview of the three principal movements influencing the field today.

EARLY CHILDHOOD EDUCATION IN THE 21st CENTURY

The 21st century has begun with reason for both great hope and serious concerns. The attention early childhood education has gotten for its important role in supporting the learning and development of young children is a reason for great hope. The conclusion is clearer than ever, and more people than ever understand it: the early years matter. Serious concerns remain at the professional level, however. Compensation is low, and there is not a clearly defined professional development system in place for all persons within the field. Families remain concerned about issues of quality and affordability. For society as a whole, debate remains as to how to best support quality child care at the national level. Most important, low-quality care is still prevalent, and many children are placed in care daily that damages their overall health and development.

The economic, political, and social climate of the United States is very different than it was in the 1800s.

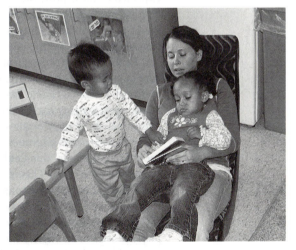

Professional preparation is essential to the provision of high-quality services.

that provide less cognitive stimulation (Guo & Harris, 2000). For example, families that are lower in income tend to provide less exposure to language, books, and informal learning opportunities, such as music lessons (Evans & Rosenbaum, 2008). They are also more likely to be raised by parents who have completed fewer years of education. In turn, this can affect children's cognitive and academic attainment (Haveman & Wolfe, 1995).

How pervasive is child poverty? Thirteen million American children under the age of 18 live below the poverty line. Children under the age of 3 are more impoverished than children in any other age group (National Center for Children in Poverty, 2006). The prevalence of child poverty is particularly alarming as poverty is linked to low achievement.

Children of poverty are more than twice as likely as their nonimpoverished peers to be held back in school. Further, they score significantly lower on measures of reading, math, and vocabulary tests (Children's Defense Fund, 2005b). The link between poverty and achievement was highlighted in a groundbreaking study conducted by Betty Hart and Tom Risley (2003) from the University of Kansas. They estimated that by the age of 3, a 30-million word gap exists between children in families on welfare and children in families with professional parents. The children of parents receiving welfare had vocabularies that mirrored those of their parents.

Hart and Risley (2003) also compared children's literacy skills at the age of 3 to achievement scores in third grade. The results indicated a strong association between skills at these differing points in time. They concluded that early language exposure and development is important to children's learning and performance in school. This research presents a compelling need for **early intervention** to reduce the achievement gap prior to school entry, with the overall goal of leveling the playing field.

What is the relationship between high-quality early childhood education programs and outcomes for children from low-income backgrounds? Success in school is predictive of success in life. Research has consistently found that children who have completed high-quality preschool programs are significantly more advanced in such important areas of development as language and literacy, creativity, music and movement, initiative, and social skills (Xiang & Schweinhart, 2002). High-quality early childhood preschool programs also contribute to children's eagerness to learn and their ability to get along with their classmates (Lee & Burkam, 2002). Preschool benefits all children, but the benefits are particularly great for children from families that are low income (NASBE Task Force on Early Childhood Education, 1988; Schweinhart, 1985; Schweinhart & Weikart, 1985; Schweinhart, Berrueta-Clement, Barrett, Epstein, & Weikart, 1985; Verzaro-Lawrence, 1981).

Neuroscience Research and Governmental Response

In 1990, President George H. W. Bush proclaimed the coming decade to be the "Decade of the Brain." This proclamation certainly bore true, as advances in magnetic resonance imaging (MRI) and positron emission tomography (PET) gave researchers an unprecedented window to the brain (Baum, 1999). This important research provided hard data on the importance of quality care and education during the first years of life and reinforced many current practices in the field. State policy makers and politicians responded to the findings by directing greater attention and resources toward the field of early childhood education.

Understanding the implications of recent brain research for the field is important. Studies in neurodevelopment, early intervention, and neurobiology show that the ages

early intervention
Practices designed to have an impact on both children's development and risk factors within children's environments.

from birth to 5 years are critically important for brain development (Perry, 2001; Shonkoff & Phillips, 2001). Further, the pace of brain growth between the ages of birth and 5 depends on whether the child's eagerness to learn is stimulated by the environment (Bowman, Donovan, & Burns, 2000). Finally, a child's ability to stay focused, follow directions, and pay attention is developed in the early years. Structured early learning fosters these abilities for later success in school and life (Bowman et al., 2000).

Advocates for children have utilized these findings to demonstrate the cost effectiveness of services. Research has consistently shown that investment in quality early childhood education services saves money in the long term. Specifically, for every dollar spent on early

Brain research findings indicate that the early years lay the foundation for future development and learning.

childhood education, it is estimated that there is a $13 return (Lynch, 2006). *Early Childhood Education for All: A Wise Investment* (Calman & Tarr-Whelan, 2005) summarized the economic benefits of early childhood education to taxpayers and the community. These benefits included preparation for success and school taxpayer savings for costly services down the road. Failing to sufficiently invest in quality care and education shortchanges taxpayers because the return on investment is great. In addition, access to available and affordable choices of early learning programs helps working parents fulfill their responsibilities.

Federal Government's Funding Involvement. The federal government's **Good Start Grow Smart** initiative recognized the importance of brain development during the first years of life. This initiative included continued funding for Head Start programs serving children ages 3 to 5 and **Early Head Start** programs serving children and families prenatally through age 3. Table 3.1 summarizes additional federal government initiatives designed to help the early childhood population.

As Table 3.1 reflects, federal spending on early childhood education is heavily targeted toward families with lower incomes and children with disabilities. This is a limitation of both present funding strategies and targeted populations (Ounce of Prevention Fund, 2005). Specifically, the focus of traditional services leaves out middle-income families who don't qualify for subsidized programs and who struggle to pay for quality programs. In addition, recent estimates indicate that (1) only one in seven children who are eligible for child care assistance actually receives it, (2) Head Start only serves about half of all eligible preschool-age children, and (3) Early Head Start serves less than 3% of eligible infants and toddlers (Children's Defense Fund, (2005b).

Continued funding of programs and increased political and economic advocacy demonstrate that state policy makers have responded to compelling data summarizing the importance of high-quality care and education. However, there is much more work to do to serve the populations who need it. As the data in Table 3.1 indicates, although many children benefit from government programs to support equity, large portions of the child population are left out. Low-quality care is a prevalent concern, as many children who are able to access services do not receive the care and education needed to support their development and learning.

Good Start Grow Smart

A federal early childhood initiative that focuses on strengthening Head Start; partnering with states to improve early learning; and providing information on early learning.

Early Head Start

Federal program designed to support economic and social well-being of pregnant women and children between the ages of birth and 3 and their families.

PEARSON
myeducationlab

Go to MyEducationLab and select the topic "Curriculum/Program Models." Under Activities and Applications, watch the video *Head Start* and think about the varied ways Head Start supports children and families.

TABLE 3.1   Federal Government Initiatives Designed to Influence Early Childhood Care and Education

Federal Government Initiative	Description of the Program	Link to Early Childhood Brain Development Findings
Child Care Development Block Fund	Uses majority of funding to provide access to child care for low-income populations; allocates 4% of funding toward increasing the quality of care children receive.	Provides access to quality child care for children from low-income populations.
Title I-supported preschool programs	Uses 2% to 3% of Title I funds to help children in high-poverty communities acquire skills needed to enter school ready to learn.	Addresses school readiness skills for children from low-income populations.
Early Reading First	Provides competitive grants to school districts and preschool programs designed to affect teacher support of literacy skills.	Supports school readiness skills for children from low-income populations.
Even Start	Provides educational services to families of low income through integration of early childhood education, adult education, parenting education, and family literacy programs.	Addresses school readiness skills and parent education/support for low-income families.
The Early Childhood Educator Professional Development Program	Provides competitive grants to early childhood educators working in high-poverty communities to participate in programs designed to increase their knowledge and skills.	Increases the quality of services through teacher education for children in high-poverty communities.
Special Education Preschool Grants and State Grants	Provides formula grants to states to make available special education and related services for children ages 3 to 5 with disabilities.	Addresses school readiness skills and reduced need for special education services in elementary school.
Special Education Grants for Infants and Families	Provides formula grants to states to make early intervention services available to children ages birth through 2 and their families.	Addresses school readiness skills and reduced need for special education services in preschool and elementary school.

Low-Quality Care Issues

We've learned that high-quality care and education experiences have a lasting impact on children, families, and society. Given this understanding, there is growing concern for the quality of care children receive. As you learned in Chapter 2, the 1995 Child Care Cost, Quality, and Outcomes (CQO) study examined the quality of care provided in four states—California, Colorado, Connecticut, and North Carolina. The results were startling. Most child care centers rated poor to mediocre (86%), with more than 40% of infants and toddlers in rooms of poor quality. Only one in seven centers was found to support healthy development. In one of eight centers, children's health and safety was threatened. Parents are unlikely to recognize low rates of quality, as they substantially overestimate the quality of the care their children receive.

The CQO study found that low-quality child care is related to high staff turnover, low staff-to-child ratios, low levels of teacher education, low teacher wages, and lack of specialized training. It also found that states with less-demanding **licensing requirements** have more low-quality programs. Further, centers that do not align with higher standards, such as NAEYC accreditation, have lower quality care overall.

The field of early childhood education today is shaped by many challenges and great promise and potential. Challenges center on ensuring that high-quality experiences

licensing requirements
Rules established through state licensing agencies that mandate minimum standards of health, safety, and practice for the field of early childhood care and education.

are accessible to all those who would benefit from it. Promise and potential is confirmed by data demonstrating what many in the field have known for years: The early years matter! Supporting children during these early years promotes their present and future success.

MEETING PRESENT CHALLENGES: INCLUSION AND FLEXIBILITY

The central mission of early childhood education supports the care and education of all children between the ages of birth and 8, regardless of their individual or family strengths or needs. Meeting this diversity requires creating a high-quality cohesive field that provides universal options. Universal options include access to high-quality care for each and every child and family; support for the unique development and learning needs of each child, family, and professional; and outcomes that support equity and success for all.

Inclusion and flexibility are essential to the field's ability to meet today's challenges and support the rich diversity of persons and communities affected by the field. Inclusion requires that the individual needs of each child, family, and professional are embraced. Flexibility requires policies, programming, and practices that respond to these individual needs.

Successfully attaining inclusion and flexibility means that the field must consider the diverse needs of the children, families, and professionals within it. In turn, each of these populations must have *access* to high-quality services, programming supportive of child and family needs, and support for ongoing professional development. Once access is attained, an intentional curriculum—reflecting the best research supporting individual children's development and learning within the context of their family and community—must be provided. Finally, the field—through accountability for equity and success—needs to create and maintain public support for the services it provides. This can be accomplished through creating a bridge between effective practices, societal requirements, and the assurance of positive outcomes for children, families, and professionals.

Understanding the field's need for inclusion and flexibility requires knowledge of present-day diversity. A series of statistics, however, does little to help understand the impact early childhood education has on individual lives. Understanding the interaction between individuals and their context serves to shape your knowledge of interactions and interrelationships. What is life like for this child, in this family, in this community, and

inclusion
The individual needs of each child, family, and professional are embraced and supported.

flexibility
Policies, programs, and practices are designed to respond to the unique needs of children, families, and professionals.

intentional curriculum
Content-driven, research-based curriculum reflecting active engagement with children, purposeful decision making, and attention to the consequences of decisions.

accountability for equity and success
Attention to the outcomes of early childhood policies, programs, and practices with the overall goal of supporting each child's success within his or her larger world.

TEACHING AND LEARNING CONNECTIONS

Supporting Inclusion and Flexibility

- Ensure access to high-quality services for children and families and quality educational experiences for professionals.
- Provide an intentional curriculum supportive of all children's development and learning and respectful of the context of family and community.
- Be accountable for equity and success through developing and maintaining public support.

All children are unique individuals with varied strengths.

what does this mean for your ability, as a professional, to support this child? The following are essential to understanding inclusion and flexibility:

1. *Children, families, and professionals have diverse needs and goals.* Each early childhood professional, child, and family brings to the early childhood environment a variety of needs, preferences, strengths, and ways of viewing and interacting with the world. Further, each individual, professional, family, and community has diverse needs and goals regarding the care and education of young children.

2. *Classroom communities have diverse needs and goals.* Each classroom community is unique, and therefore presents diverse needs, challenges, and strengths.

3. *The field of early childhood education has diverse needs and goals.* The uniqueness that children, families, and professionals bring to early childhood education creates the need for a field that is flexible and diverse in both its offerings and its professional opportunities.

4. *Community, society, and culture have diverse needs and goals.* The social and cultural context that early childhood education occurs within is shaped by changing community, societal, and cultural needs and goals. These needs include goals for the education of young children, and within this, expectations for children's learning and development.

ISSUES OF ACCESS AND EQUITY
Universal Design for Early Childhood Education

In 2006, Conn-Powers, Cross, Traub, and Hutter-Pishgahi described a framework for the "design of early education programs that meet the needs of all learners within a common setting and begin to move away from specialized programs" (p. 3). This goal, according to the authors, needs to be accomplished with a concurrent focus on standards and program accountability.

The main goals of their framework are to support learning for all children through equitable access and to create early education programs that engage and support all children. Building on and extending the work of Conn-Powers et al. (2006) is the framework for Universal Design for Early Childhood Education (UDECE) (Darragh, 2007). Although UDECE shares the learning goals of the Conn-Powers et al. model for children and families within the early childhood classroom, it extends this work through also focusing on access and equity for children, families, and professionals. UDECE looks specifically at what access to the field means for children, families, and professionals and how quality practices within the overall field can promote accountability for equity and success for each of these groups.

1. *Children, families, and professionals need multiple means of access to high-quality early childhood care and education.* Children, families, and professionals need to have varied opportunities to access high-quality care and education in

environments that (1) respect and welcome families, (2) meet the varied needs of individual children and families, and (3) support a variety of professional goals and opportunities. Access means that families can find care that is of high quality, is affordable, and supports their children's developmental needs.

2. *The field of early childhood education needs to provide multiple means of representation.* Multiple means of representation argues that learners require various methods of acquiring information and knowledge. In early childhood education, multiple means of representation refer to the numerous programs, philosophies, and educational approaches in the field. Programs support the breadth of the ages and provide families with a variety of choices. Some families, for example, might prefer a full-day Montessori program for their infant, whereas others are looking for a half-day bilingual program for their preschooler.

3. *Children need multiple means of engagement.* Multiple means of engagement focuses on creating appropriate environments and curricula that encourage children's overall development and support the developmental needs of the classroom community as a whole. For example, each classroom community is filled with children who have unique ways of viewing and processing the world. Curriculum needs to support these unique preferences through providing a variety of choices. At the same time, the choices provided need to support the development and learning of each individual child.

4. *Children and professionals need multiple means of expression.* Multiple means of expression provide assessment and documentation practices that reflect changes in child and professional knowledge and development over time. For example, teachers must develop documentation and assessment procedures built around the strengths of each child within the classroom community. Further, documentation and assessment procedures need to provide concrete information on how to utilize these strengths to support children's challenges. These same principles apply to professional assessment strategies.

5. *The field of early childhood education must be accountable for equity and success.* Equity and success can be thought of as a level playing field where children have equal access to and benefits from opportunities. Accountability requires policies, programs, and practices that ensure opportunities for equity and success are provided. Social equity in UDECE is provided through equitable access to programs and services and to experiences within the field that ensure each and every child's ability to participate in and benefit from all that larger society has to offer. Success means that early childhood education must meet the needs of children, families, and professionals. Additionally, the field must meet state and national standards for professional preparation, program quality, and goals for children's development and learning.

Accountability does not mean that only external standards are adhered to. In addition, equity does not mean that all children and professionals must reach a certain bar. At the most basic level, equity and accountability require human respect—respect for children, respect for parents, respect for professionals, respect for ourselves, and respect for each person's uniqueness. Modeling this respect, making sure we are accountable to ourselves, and striving to treat all persons in ways that support equity are core values of UDECE.

Present-day challenges in the areas of inclusion and flexibility lead to specific policies and practices important within your professional role. All professionals need to understand how to support access. Further, professionals must provide curricular practices that meet the needs of each individual child. Professionals also must provide services that reflect societal goals for children's development and learning *and* promote equity and success within the immediate context (the classroom community) and the larger context (the community and society the child is growing and developing within).

In Chapter 1 you were introduced to the term *social equity* and how early childhood education supports equity for children, families, and professionals. The concepts of inclusion and flexibility are central to attaining social equity. Inclusion and flexibility together support access to high-quality programming that supports individual strengths and challenges and success within the larger context. Without access, however, the quality of programming is rendered meaningless. Access within the field of early childhood education is supported through the wide variety of present-day program options, to which we will now turn.

DIVERSE SERVICES IN THE FIELD

Imagine a world where all children—from babies barely out of the protective embrace of the womb to 8-year-olds navigating from the shielding sphere of their parents into the larger world of their peers—have access to high-quality early childhood education. Children enter kindergarten ready to learn, and their learning and development flourish in accordance with the expectations of formal schooling. Educational environments are arranged by children's chronological ages, developmental needs, and diverse abilities. Programs meet the needs of all students—from the child who needs Head Start services to attain important literacy goals to the child who attends preschool to enhance burgeoning social skills. Primary grade environments support academic needs and embrace overarching needs for social and emotional literacy. The field, as a whole, is designed to support and enhance the development and learning of each child. No child is left out of this vital equation.

Journey back from this utopia to the present state of early childhood education. In reality, program participation in the United States is often shaped by **social class**, leaving the working poor and middle class unable, in many cases, to access quality education. Many families live in neighborhoods that do not have a high-quality child care center within walking distance or on the bus line. Even if a family qualifies for Head Start services, there may not be spots available (Children's Defense Fund, 2005b). Laws mandate inclusion, but children often remain segregated according to ability. Funding constraints translate into large class sizes, and therefore many children in kindergarten and primary grades are in environments that lack **individualized education**. Many elementary schools have teachers who are not trained in accommodating children's special education needs. Quality care and education services are difficult to find. In fact, a representative national study found that only 8% of infants and toddlers and 23% of preschoolers are in care environments that are of high quality (National Center for Early Development and Learning, 1997).

Despite extensive research demonstrating that early childhood education plays a key role in supporting children's development and, in turn, social equity, these realities remain. For children to benefit from all the field has to offer, they must have access to services.

social class

Hierarchal distinctions between social groups, often determined by income.

individualized education

Care and education based on children's individual needs.

Access through Inclusive, Flexible Approaches

Program options within the field include the full gamut of services available to children from birth to age 8. Within this larger category services are often presented as those impacting children between the ages of birth and 5, and those impacting children who are school-age, in kindergarten, and in the primary grades.

Services for Children Birth Through Age 5. Almost 72% of children under the age of 5 are in a regular child care arrangement (U.S. Census Bureau, 2008). Of this group, 73% are in nonrelative care. A description of center-based and family child care services and their prevalence are summarized in Table 3.2.

Focus on Kith and Kin Care. The majority of children not in center-based or family child care homes are cared for by relatives and friends, with 37% cared for by either their grandparent or father (U.S. Census Bureau, 2008). This kind of care is often referred to as **kith and kin care**. All 50 states exempt relatives and neighbors who provide care for a small number of children from licensing regulations.

There is great variance in who uses kith and kin care, but many of these persons share common characteristics. As a group, users tend to be African American or Latina women who are single and have lower levels of education and income (Porter & Kerns, 2006). Porter and Kerns identify the majority of children in kith and kin care as infants, followed by children who are school age.

The 1996 Welfare Reform Act drew attention to the quality of services children receive in kith and kin care. This attention emerged from the realization that many families on welfare used this kind of care, which does not require a license. Research has indicated that the providers of kith and kin care are generally similar to the persons who use this kind of care (Collins & Carlson, 1998). In addition, they tend to generally lack background knowledge in early childhood education (Brown-Lyons, Robertson, & Layzer, 2001).

kith and kin care
The care of children by relatives and neighbors who are considered exempt from licensing.

TABLE 3.2 Settings or Programs by Population Served and Percentage of Children Using Services			
Settings or Programs	**Population Served**	**Program Description**	**Percentage of Children Under 5 Using Services**
Child care center or other organized facility (such as a preschool or Head Start)	Children ages infant through school age	Early childhood services provided in a center program; children are typically in large groups that are segregated by age. In 2005, there were 105,440 regulated child care centers in the United States. (National Association for Regulatory Administration & the National Child Care Information and Technical Assistance Center, 2006).	23.1
Family Child Care	Children ages infant through school age	Early childhood services provided within a home environment, with children of varied ages being grouped within family child care homes or group homes. In 2005, there were 213,996 licensed regulated family child care homes in the United States.	22.3
In-Home Care	Children ages birth through school age	Services provided within the home by a nanny or au pair.	5.9

Similar to issues of quality within regulated care, the overall quality of care provided through kith and kin services is low (Brown-Lyons, Robertson, & Layzer, 2001). Based on the relationship between quality and children's present and future development, national initiatives have been targeted toward improving the quality of kith and kin services. This includes the work of the National Alliance for Family, Friend, and Neighbor Child Care. Its goals include influencing policies for family, friend, and neighbor care; enhancing access to services that support the quality of kith and kin care; and increasing awareness of the role that family, friend, and neighbor child care plays in the continuum of child care services.

Early Intervention. Early intervention (EI) services apply to children school age and younger who have developmental disabilities or delays. Early intervention services within IDEA include services to infants and toddlers between the ages of birth and 3. Each state determines criteria for qualifying for EI services. The goal of EI services is to lessen the impact of the disabling condition or to prevent negative developmental outcomes from occurring. Early intervention services include identification and intervention, and a focus on both the child and the context the child develops within. Early intervention has a positive impact on children's development and is cost effective (Bailey, Scarborough, Hebbeler, Spiker, & Mallik, 2004).

As you learned in Chapter 2, early intervention services require delivery within natural environments. This includes center- and home-based interventions. To have the greatest impact on children's development, early intervention services need to (1) start early, (2) include the family, and (3) have levels of intensity that respond to the child's overall needs (Bailey et al., 2004). Examples of early intervention services that children might benefit from in their first 3 years of life include:

- Assistive technology devices and services
- Physical therapy
- Audiological services
- Psychological services
- Family training, counseling, and home visits
- Service coordination
- Health services
- Social work services
- Medical services
- Special instruction
- Nursing services
- Speech-language pathology
- Nutrition services
- Transportation costs
- Occupational therapy
- Vision services

child find
Services that focus on early identification, screening, referral, and initial service coordination.

The ability to identify children in need of early intervention services is a defining feature of EI's success. Based on this, each state must attempt to identify, locate, and evaluate all children between birth and age 21 who need special education services. A well-known organization that provides these services is called **Child Find**. The identification and outreach services Child Find provides are diverse and could include ads summarizing developmental milestones with contact information should there be any concerns in the local newspaper, doctor's office waiting rooms, grocery stores, and community organizations and events where young children and their families can be found. Mass media campaigns are another tool Child Find utilizes, as are holding regular, accessible community screenings.

Early Childhood Special Education. Under IDEA, early childhood special education services include identification and intervention services for children between the ages of 3 and 5. Nearly half (48%) of all preschoolers receiving early childhood special education services have a speech or language impairment as their primary disability. Twenty-eight percent were identified as having a developmental delay as their primary disability (Pre-Elementary Educational Longitudinal Study, 2006). The average age at which children received special education services was nearly 3 years of age. Thirty-one percent of those who had an IFSP before the age of 3 experienced a 4.6 month gap between the end of services provided through

Early Head Start services are designed to reduce the effects of developmental delays and disabilities.

Part C of IDEA (applying to infants and toddlers) and the beginning of preschool services. Preschoolers with disabilities typically score lower in areas of emerging literacy, early math proficiency, social behavior, and motor performance (Pre-Elementary Educational Longitudinal Study, 2006).

Part C of IDEA
Federal regulations targeted toward infants and toddlers with disabilities.

Early Head Start and Head Start Services. Chapters 1 and 2 introduced you to the establishment and rationale behind Head Start services. Together, Early Head Start and Head Start have an impact on children between birth and kindergarten age. These programs are designed to erase the effects of genetic and environmental factors that place children at risk for developmental delays and disabilities. Identified risk factors include living in poverty (affecting 20% of children under the age of 6), having parents with low levels of education, being born with low birth weight, having limited preventative health care, living in high-risk neighborhoods, or living in linguistically isolated households (Karoly, Kilburn, & Cannon, 2005).

Forty-five percent of children receiving Early Head Start services are provided services through a home-based model. About half receive services in center-based care (Hamm & Ewen, 2006). Ninety-one percent of children who receive Head Start services do so in center-based care. The remaining 9% of Head Start services are delivered in home-based, family child care, or locally designed programs. Thirteen percent of children receiving Head Start services had been diagnosed with a disability, with the most common diagnosis (63%) being speech or language impairments (Hamm, 2006). Head Start is a federal program but is funded to local grantees through the Administration for Children and Families of the Department of Health and Human Services (HHS).

Child Care and Development Block Grant
Federal source of funding targeted toward supporting the financial independence of families who are low income.

Pre-Kindergarten At-Risk Programs. Through monies provided by the federal **Child Care and Development Block Grant**, many states are developing preschool programs for children who are considered at risk of educational failure. This is most commonly due to financial strains in the family. The main goal of pre-kindergarten at-risk programs is to reduce the **achievement gap** between children from economically impoverished backgrounds and their more affluent peers (Center for Public Education, 2006).

achievement gap
Disparity in academic performance between children from economically impoverished backgrounds and their more affluent peers.

As of 2005, 40 states offered pre-kindergarten at-risk programs, and many have moved toward offering universal programs to all children of preschool age (Center for Public Education, 2006). Access to these programs varies across the states. For example, many states offer services exclusively to 4-year-old children. Other states place caps on who can access programs based on family income levels. The rationale for **universal preschool**—the goal of which is to make high-quality preschool programming available to all children—is based on the compelling evidence of preschool education on children's present and future development.

There are numerous programs and services for children who are designated as having or are at risk for having developmental disabilities or delays. Interestingly, the different sources of program funding mean that children might concurrently participate in more than one program. For example, a child attending Head Start in the morning might also participate in an early childhood special education classroom in the afternoon. These arrangements can negatively affect continuity of care and require children to engage in numerous transitions throughout the day.

Focus on School-Age Child Care. Care for school-age children during nonschool hours is an important societal issue and an important part of early childhood education. Half of all children between kindergarten and eighth grade require nonparental care outside of school hours, requiring many programs and services to meet their needs (Children's Defense Fund, 2003). Many children use before- and after-school programs at schools, child care centers, and family child care homes. Many children, however, are left to care for themselves. How children spend their out-of-school time is a significant predictor of their school achievement and long-term success. Participation in structured, high-quality activities can have a positive impact on a young person's developing skills.

Access and Kindergarten Education. Although kindergarten education is not considered compulsory in each of the 50 states, nearly 98% of children attend kindergarten programs before entering first grade (National Center for Early Development and Learning, 1998). Because kindergarten has historically been viewed as a preparatory experience within a formal educational setting, the social and learning needs of children entering kindergarten vary greatly. Debate remains over the suitable age for entry into kindergarten, whether half-day or full-day programs are most effective, and what educational focus and curricula are most appropriate.

Age of Entry. The typical kindergartner is 5.5 years of age upon entering kindergarten (Education Commission of the States, 2007). As each state varies in requirements for age of entry, there is often a 12-month difference in age in children in the classroom. The range of developmental capabilities is even greater. Research on the best age for kindergarten entry is mixed. Some studies find no difference between children's ages and the impact on their mastery of basic reading skills (Magliacano, 1994). Others find that older children fare better on measures of academic achievement (Crosser, 1991).

The age-of-entry debate within kindergarten education has spurred two other issues: *redshirting* and *retention*. **Redshirting** refers to delaying kindergarten entry to allow children one more year in which to develop. Approximately 9% of kindergarten-age children are redshirted. Boys are more likely to be redshirted than girls. Further, children in affluent communities and those attending private schools are the most likely groups to be redshirted (National Center for Education Statistics [NCES], 2000). **Retention**, where children who have not met expectations for promotion to the first grade and therefore are kept (or retained) in kindergarten for another year, has a decidedly negative impact on

universal preschool
Programs offered within several states that are designed to support equitable access to high-quality early childhood education for all children, regardless of family income.

redshirting
Holding children out of kindergarten entry for an extra year, despite their meeting age requirements for entry.

retention
Practice of holding children back from promotion to the next grade because they have not met expected milestones.

TEACHING AND LEARNING CONNECTIONS

Retention Prevention

- Take the time to learn about each child's area of strength and challenge.
- Develop curriculum supportive of individual needs and reflective of individual strengths.
- Provide support for developing literacy skills.
- Partner with families to support child success.

children's growth and development. The idea behind retention is that a repeated year will give children the time they need to successfully enter and participate in the first grade.

There is no evidence that adoption of a retention policy has a positive impact on children's learning (Hong & Raudenbush, 2003). Further, kindergarten retention has a negative impact on the learning of all but children who were of the highest risk. Hong and Raudenbush (2003) concluded that retention has an overall negative impact on the learning and development of retained children. Their study focused on children's learning in mathematics and literacy. Other research identified the effects of kindergarten retention on social and emotional development as equally negative, with social stigma negatively affecting self-esteem and peer relationships (Shepard & Smith, 1985).

One of the issues that affects both redshirting and retention is the level of preparedness that children have for kindergarten. For example, teachers found that 48% of their kindergarten-age students were lacking in important preparatory skills, including following directions (46%), academic skills (38%), and the ability to work independently (34%) (National Center for Early Development and Learning, 1998). These findings illuminate a debate within the field: Are children not adequately prepared for kindergarten, or is kindergarten not adequately prepared for children?

Kindergarten Curriculum. One of the most important predictors of how children fare in kindergarten is the quality of the education they receive. Increasingly, there has been a **"push-down"** in the academic curriculum, with many of the skills considered a part of the first-grade curriculum now included in kindergarten. This shift, created by the standards movement, has caused a movement from a play-based curriculum to one that is more focused on academic skills (NAEYC, 1996). As a result, kindergarten education is pulled between the developmental, child-centered focus on early childhood education and the academic-achievement focus stressed in the K–12 system (Kauerz, 2005). To rectify this debate, the NAEYC has emphasized the need for kindergartens to provide child-centered practices that embrace children's social, emotional, and learning needs.

Historically, an important debate within the field centered on half-day versus full-day kindergarten curriculum. Many U.S. programs now deliver kindergarten curriculum in a full-day format. However, examination of the debate surrounding this trend provides an interesting lens into many of the economic, social, and educational debates that have shaped the field.

Half- vs. Full-Day Kindergarten. The prevalence of full-day kindergarten reflects social and economic pressures. Today's economy requires more parents to work outside the home, creating a demand for schools to provide full-day services. Relative to quality issues,

push-down
Used to describe increased expectations for knowledge of young children.

Go to MyEducationLab and select the topic "Environments." Under Activities and Applications, watch the video *Kindergarten Classroom* and reflect on the diverse populations kindergarten education supports.

research examining the effects of half-day versus full-day kindergarten has been fairly conclusive. For example, a longitudinal study of 8,000 kindergartners in 500 U.S. public schools found that full-day kindergarten education had significant positive effects on children's learning. These positive effects were recognized for all children, not only those who were from backgrounds considered low income and/or at-risk (Lee, Burkham, Honigman & Meisels, 2006). Researchers emphasized the impact of quality programming. Extra time in kindergarten should not focus solely on academics, but include attention to children's social and emotional needs. This emphasis complements the NAEYC position on high-quality kindergarten programming.

For most children, formal schooling begins with kindergarten, and their "early childhood education" continues through third grade. Primary grade education typically occurs in public schools, where it is regulated by additional standards. Therefore, although the standards of quality that embrace child-centered practices and support for social and emotional development remain, there is an increased focus on assessment and accountability.

Primary Grades, Assessment, and Accountability. Primary grade education requires careful attention to the broad, social context in which it occurs. As mentioned previously, societal goals include an increased focus on assessment and accountability. Unfortunately, this often encourages practices that contradict what is known about how to effectively support children's learning and development, including a focus on adult-centered goals for children's learning (Blaustein, 2005).

Despite the focus on performance, and the resulting academic-driven practices, many practices are considered appropriate for primary grade learning. Related to program structure, these include class size and mixed-age groupings.

Small class size in primary grade education has a positive impact on children's development and learning.

Class Size in Primary Education. School funding strategies often rely on state and local property taxes and have a direct effect on the number of children in classrooms. The research outlining the connection between increasing class sizes and children's outcomes is conclusive. Small class sizes (under 18) were found to have a larger advantage in supporting reading and math skills in the primary grades (Boyd-Zaharias, 1999).

Mixed-Age Groupings in Primary Grade Education. A mixed-age grouping model in the primary grades is thought to significantly support achievement (Katz, 1995). Mixed-age groupings represent the combination of multiple ages within one classroom. This is typically done with the grouping of first and second graders, and less commonly with second and third graders. It is often referred to as a *nongraded model.*

Mixed-age grouping forces a teacher to take a broad span of ages and developmental needs into consideration. In turn, this encourages a model that is both individually and developmentally appropriate.

Research on the effects of mixed-age grouping demonstrates a significant positive impact on attitudes toward school and self-concepts toward learning (Anderson & Pavan, 1993). Further, Pavan, (1992) found that the more time children spent in **nongraded classrooms**, the more positive their overall attitude toward school became.

Ensuring Access for All: Inclusive, Flexible Program Options

What does inclusive, flexible programming look like within early childhood education? High-quality inclusive programming, according to the 2008 Field Review Draft of the Joint Position Statement of Early Childhood Inclusion developed by the Division for Early Childhood (DEC) and the National Association for the Education of Young Children (NAEYC), consists of several defining features:

- Access: Children's active engagement in a wide range of learning opportunities, activities, settings, and environments is supported. For example, a center-based program for 3-year-olds might include children who qualify for Head Start services, early childhood special education services, and pre-kindergarten at-risk services along with those who do not qualify for any government-funded services all within the same classroom environment. In these environments, the learning opportunities and activities are accessible and support children's active engagement.
- Participation: Inclusive settings support belonging, participation, and engagement of children with disabilities and their typically developing peers through intentional strategies matched to the child's development and learning needs. Teachers, therefore, work to learn what each and every child needs within the classroom environment, and provide environments, experiences, and interactions tailored to those needs.
- Supports: Ongoing professional development and support is provided to families, practitioners, administrators, and specialists to ensure high-quality inclusive programming is developed and implemented. Complementing the knowledge, skills, and dispositions supported through this professional development and support are resources and program policies promoting communication and collaboration between each of these groups. Building from communication and collaboration is coordination and integration between specialized services and therapies and early childhood general education services.

Within the United States, there are programs that exemplify these inclusive, flexible practices. However, the goal of equity through access to inclusive, flexible programming is a goal for each and every child and family.

DIVERSE PROFESSIONAL ROLES

Your growth as a professional is influenced by opportunities that arise as well as your own internal development. Growing as a professional requires understanding the intricate context that influences your development, including employers, the field of early childhood education, and larger society (see Table 3.3). Before understanding the context, you must first understand who the early childhood professional is.

Who Are Early Childhood Professionals?

At any given time, there are 2.3 million professionals who work directly with children (Center for the Child Care Workforce, 2002). Twenty-four percent are working in center-based programs, which include public and private child care centers, Head Start

nongraded classrooms
Blend of first and second, or, less commonly, second and third grades.

Go to MyEducationLab and select the topic "Environments." Under Activities and Applications, watch the video *Primary Grade Classroom* and consider how children in the primary grades present varied developmental and learning needs.

TABLE 3.3 Early Childhood Education Programs, Populations Served, and Professional Roles

Settings or Programs	Population Served	Professional Roles
Child care center	Children ages infant through school age	Director, teacher, teacher assistant, teacher aide, education coordinator
Family child care	Children ages infant through school age	Teacher assistant, owner, group home provider
Child care resource and referral	Parents of children looking for child care and subsidies, professionals through development opportunities, the field through health services, training, and education programs	Parent counselor, subsidy specialist, training coordinator, child care nurse consultant, professional development advisor
Early childhood higher education	College students pursuing careers and/or information regarding early childhood education	Professor, adjunct professor, instructor
Early intervention	Children with developmental delays or disabilities between the ages of birth and 3, and their families	Developmental therapist, parent liaison, speech therapist, occupational therapist, infant mental health consultant
Early childhood special education	Children with developmental delays or disabilities between the ages of 3 and 6	Teacher, teacher assistant, parent educator, therapist, principal, superintendent, director
Head Start/Early Head Start	Children ages birth to 3 (Early Head Start) and 3 to 5 (Head Start) who meet federal guidelines for being at risk and their families	Director, teacher, head teacher, teacher assistant, home visitor, family support (or service) specialist, family resource coordinator, education coordinator, infant specialist
Family intervention programs	Families and children birth through school age	Director, home visitor, family support worker/specialist, program manager, supervisor, child development specialist, group services coordinator
Department of Children and Family Services	Children, families, and early childhood programs	Day Care licensing representative, program coordinator, early childhood consultant, policy specialist, program consultant, licensing administrator
Department of Human Services	Programs and policies designed to affect the field of early childhood education	Program coordinator, early childhood care and education consultant, policy specialist, program specialist
State Board of Education	Programs and policies designed to affect the field of early childhood education	Program coordinator, early childhood program consultant, policy specialist, program specialist
In-home care	Children birth through school age and their families	Nanny, au pair
Kindergarten through grade 3	Children ages 5 (although might vary with state entry requirements) to approximately age 8	Teacher, teacher assistant, parent educator, principal, superintendent, director
Pre-kindergarten at risk	Children ages 3 to 5 who have been identified as at risk and their families	Teacher, teacher assistant, parent educator, principal, superintendent, director
Prevention initiative/parent training	Families of children ages birth through school age	Family service worker, family resource coordinator, case manager, parent educator, program coordinator
School-age child care (also called the field of out-of-school time)	School-age children and their families	Director, recreation leader, youth leader, group worker, teacher, site coordinator

Source: Used with permission from the Illinois Network of Child Care Resource and Referral Agencies. http://spanish.ilgateways.com/careers/careersavailable.aspx

programs, and pre-kindergarten programs. Twenty-eight percent provide family child care as either providers or assistants. Thirty-five percent are paid relatives who are not family child care providers. Thirteen percent are paid nonrelatives who provide care for the child within the child's home (Center for the Child Care Workforce, 2002).

Of these providers, 49% are caring for toddlers (between the ages of 19 and 36 months), 29% are caring for infants (age 18 months and under), and 22% are caring for preschoolers between the ages of 3 and 5 (Center for the Child Care Workforce, 2002). The field of early childhood education also includes state-certified teachers who work with children who are in kindergarten through the primary grades (first through third) and those who work in out-of-school-time programs, such as before- and after-school programs.

In 2002, there were 168,000 kindergarten teachers in the United States (U.S. Department of Labor Bureau of Labor Statistics, 2003). Data on teachers working with first- through third-grade populations are not specifically broken out, but the number of elementary school teachers (serving children between first and sixth grade) numbered 1.5 million.

Out-of-school time programs present unique challenges in addressing the question of who are out-of-school-time professionals. Part of this difficulty lies in the fact that the out-of-school-time field lacks a national professional development system (National Institute of Out-of-School Time, 2003). Another challenge is that the field is so broadly defined. Professionals in the field can include persons who provide out-of-school-time programs to children and youth, work to prevent problematic behaviors such as drug use and teen pregnancy, work to support academic achievement, and work with children regarding specific hobbies and interests (Bodilly & Beckett, 2005).

out-of-school time
Time spent and services provided to children when not in school settings.

The breadth of services provided to children between the ages of birth and 8 who have developmental delays or disabilities presents challenges in defining the array of professional opportunities for working with them. One way to identify possible occupations is through examining the number of children receiving special education services under Part C of IDEA. In 2005, this number was 670,406 (National Center for Education Statistics, 2007).

Another potential source of professional occupation data is to look at the prevalence of children who are served in inclusive programs. The number of 3- to 5-year-olds with disabilities in regular classrooms has risen 32% between 1992 and 2001 (National Center for Education Statistics, 2007). Further, most preschool classrooms include at least one child who has a disability (Kirk, Gallagher, Anastasiow, & Coleman, 2006). Table 3.4 provides an overview of special education career options.

The job outlook for each of these occupations varies from very good to excellent depending on locale and the specific area of occupational interest. In particular, the need for early childhood special education teachers is expected to increase dramatically.

Another anticipated change in the field results from the increased national focus on inclusion. As you learned in Chapter 1, the

Professional opportunities in the field are extensive and diverse.

TABLE 3.4	Overview of Special Education Occupations
Occupation	**Description**
Developmental therapist	Provide assessment and intervention services to support a variety of developmental areas, including, but not limited to, cognitive processes, communication, vision, hearing motor, behavior, and social interaction.
Physical therapist	Provide services that help restore function, improve mobility, relieve pain, and prevent or limit permanent disabilities resulting from injuries or disease.
Occupational therapist	Work with individuals to improve their ability to perform daily living tasks.
Speech language pathologist	Assess, diagnose, treat, and help to prevent speech, language, cognitive-communication, voice, swallowing, fluency, and other related disorders
Audiologists	Identify and support hearing, balance, and related ear problems.

Source: Adapted from U.S. Department of Labor Bureau of Statistics (2009).

finding that most preschool classrooms include at least one child with a disability (Winton, 2006, as cited by National Institute for Early Education Research) means that there is great opportunity to develop and implement effective practices that are not only high quality, but inclusive as well.

Considerations of the changes in the field created through linguistic and cultural diversity of children and families today must also be noted. This need is reflected in the 2000 census data indicating that the number of children in immigrant families has increased by 63% during the past decade (Beavers & D'Amico, 2005). The Latino population (immigrant and nonimmigrant) grew by more than 50% during those years, and the African American population grew by a rate that exceeded that of the general population (U.S. Census Bureau, 2000). Unfortunately, research indicates that many teachers feel underprepared to teach children who are African American and children for whom English is not their first language (Pang & Sablan, 1998; Ray & Bowman, 2003; Valli & Rennert-Ariev, 2000).

There is no mistaking that each classroom community is filled with children of diverse needs. This creates a compelling need for professionals to be prepared to meet these diverse needs, and one that has been identified as lacking in professional development programs (Ray, Bowman, & Robbins, 2006). Your ability to recognize and respond to the diverse needs of each and every child within the classroom community is an essential component of your professional preparation.

• • • BECOMING A PROFESSIONAL • • •

Using the Internet as a Resource

Your ability to develop as a professional requires a commitment to supporting your continued education. There are many tools to assist you in acquiring the knowledge that you need, with the Internet serving as one of the most well-developed avenues for acquiring new knowledge. However, not everything on the Internet is substantive. You need to be able to sift through and determine what sources are reflective of quality, effective practices.

The Internet can be used as a storehouse of information, a virtual classroom, a diary or journal, and a network for consulting. This information can include online articles, web pages, electronic discussion groups, and blogs.

Guidelines to selecting Internet materials for early childhood education professionals include the following (Schanen, 2008):

- The curriculum must match your individual and program philosophy.
- The information must have developmentally appropriate content, including teaching practices, development and learning, and general expectations.
- The content should be thorough and current, free of stereotyping, and reflective of positive social values.

Where can you begin to look for quality Internet resources? Many major early childhood education professional organizations have content included in their site, and many provide online access to discussion groups, articles, and recommended websites. In addition to the websites presented in the Becoming a Professional feature in Chapter 1, some sites you might choose to explore include the following:

- Center on the Social and Emotional Foundations for Early Learning
  http://www.vanderbilt.edu/
- Child Care Exchange
  http://www.childcareexchange.com/
- Early Childhood Research & Practice
  http://ecrp.uiuc.edu/
- Edutopia
  http://www.edutopia.org/
- Early Head Start National Resource Center
  http://www.ehsnrc.org/
- National Association for the Education of Young Children
  http://naeyc.org
- National Institute on Early Childhood Development and Education
  http://www.ed.gov/offices/OERI/ECI/
- Scholastic
  http://www2.scholastic.com/browse/
- Zero to Three
  http://www.zerotothree.org/

An important consideration when conducting research and gaining knowledge from the Internet is that all information is not equal in its quality. Important factors to consider, adapted from NAEYC (2008), include the following:

- Ensure that the materials are well cited and reflect current practices within the field.
- Look for a sound basis in children's development and learning.
- Look for materials that are peer reviewed and placed on reputable sites that are well known in providing quality materials.

MOVING FORWARD

Meeting the diverse needs of children and families requires a variety of program options. Inclusion and flexibility within early childhood education supports the goal of success and equity for all and is responsive to the needs of the larger cultural and societal context. Your ability to apply these concepts within the field supports not only children and families, but also your own vibrant development as a professional. In this chapter, you have learned about diversity in terms of the depth of program options and professional roles available. The following chapters in your text will focus on diversity as it applies to children, families, and professionals.

CASE STUDY

Ensuring Access Through Inclusion

Myrna Children's Village (6 weeks to 6 years)

Sergio and April's bilingual preschool classroom at the Myrna Children's Village in New Mexico resembles many high-quality early childhood programs. Children are actively engaged in the curriculum. The teachers and staff spend their time observing, interacting with the children in meaningful ways, and supporting each child's individual development and learning. One of the main differences of this program, invisible to the eye, is that it represents extensive efforts reflective of a passionate commitment to inclusion. All the children are a part of one seamless classroom community. However, the classroom actually represents a unique collaboration between Head Start and early childhood special education, as the children in the classroom receive funding through these different programs.

At the core of the bilingual preschool classroom is access and equity. The children are all receiving services that respect their home language and support their emerging English proficiency skills. Access is also supported through inclusion. Regardless of individual abilities, the teachers in the classroom recognize that the best teachers for children are other children. The rich language and social experiences that occur in natural environments are well worth the bureaucracy the preschool director must manage: two funding streams, two sets of rules and regulations, and two populations of children who vary in the services they qualify for. However, they share the essential characteristic that they are all—foremost—children.

The success of Sergio and April's classroom is built on extensive collaboration—each teacher is familiar with the other's role. Sergio feels that his role as a special educator is to follow the parameters of the regular education curriculum. In addition, he provides children who are receiving special education services with the "salt and pepper" of instruction, representing enhancements (as opposed to modifications) that will promote their success in the classroom, such as slowing down the rhythm of the songs children sing and listen to in the classroom. For children with articulation and speech disorders, a slower pace might make the difference between successful participation and frustration. These enhancements are an important tool through which Sergio and April individualize the curriculum.

CONSTRUCTED-RESPONSE QUESTIONS

1. How does the composition of Sergio and April's classroom reflect inclusion within the program's design?
2. In what ways is flexibility built into program design?

REFLECTING ON AND APPLYING EFFECTIVE PRACTICES (NAEYC AND CEC/DEC)

- You are attending a meeting where a decision is being made regarding whether a kindergartner in your class should be retained for the coming school year. You feel that the child would be successful in first grade with some additional supports, and retention would be harmful to the child's self-concept and social relationships. The child's father, however, is advocating for retention. What might you do in this situation?

Ethics

NAEYC Ideals

I-2.4. To respect families' childrearing values and their right to make decisions for their children.

I-1.2. To base program practices upon current knowledge and research in the field of early childhood education, child development, and related disciplines, as well as on particular knowledge of each child.

DEC: Professional and Interpersonal Behavior

4. We shall serve as advocates for children with disabilities and their families and for the professionals who serve them by supporting both policy and programmatic decisions that enhance the quality of their lives.

DEC: Responsive Family-Centered Practices

1. We shall demonstrate our respect and appreciation for all families' beliefs, values, customs, languages, and culture relative to their nurturance and support of their children toward achieving meaningful and relevant priorities and outcomes families' desire for themselves and their children.

- Early childhood education is an important part of the lives of many young children and their families. What role does inclusion and flexibility play in ensuring that children's early childhood education services support learning and development? How can adopting inclusive and flexible practices help ensure that the needs of each individual child are considered?

Standards for Professional Practice

NAEYC: Promoting Child Development and Learning

1b. Knowing and understanding the multiple influences on development and learning.

DEC: Foundations

EC1K1: Historical, philosophical foundations, and legal basis of services for infants and young children both with and without exceptional needs.

DEC: Instructional Strategies

EC4K1: Concept of universal design for learning.

Chapter Review

- **What are some of the challenges to effective teaching today?**

  - *Readiness and the No Child Left Behind Act* (NCLB). The NCLB act focuses on school readiness for young children, particularly literacy. Readiness includes both social and academic skills, and stresses that the children enter school with the basic skills that they need for success. The challenges associated with readiness include what areas to target and what strategies effectively support this goal.
  - *The achievement of children from low-income backgrounds.* Research continuously identifies children from low-income backgrounds as being at risk for school failure. Further, research has shown that high-quality early childhood education experiences can support positive learning and development for all children. Part of the present-day challenge requires understanding the diverse needs of children from families who are low-income and designing appropriate educational experiences that support their learning and development.
  - *Neuroscience research.* Compelling neuroscience research has demonstrated that the first years of life lay the foundation for later life success. This data has been utilized as a resource supporting investment in high-quality care and education. Presently, the federal government invests monies in programs supporting healthy brain development through high-quality educational programs. These services are predominantly targeted toward children of families with low incomes and children with disabilities.
  - *Issues regarding low-quality care.* Recent research indicates that despite the enormous benefits of high-quality educational experiences for young children, a majority of children spend their time in early childhood environments that provide quality ranging from mediocre to poor. For the promise and potential of the field to be attained, all children must have access to high-quality services.

- **What are the components of inclusion and flexibility, and how do these support present-day challenges within the field?**

  The diverse history of the field has created present-day challenges in creating a high-quality, cohesive field providing universal options to all children between the ages of birth and 8. Foundational components of inclusion and flexibility consider the diverse needs of children, families, and professionals, and ensure responsiveness to the larger social and cultural context. From this foundation, access, quality experiences through the intentional curriculum, and accountability for equity and success could be supported.

- **What diverse services are offered within the field of early childhood education?**

  Services within the field of early childhood education cover a broad range. For children between the ages of birth and 5, the most common care arrangement occurs within child care centers. This is followed by family child care homes. The smallest percentage consists of children who are cared for in the home. The majority of children not in any of the above child care arrangements who still require regular child care services are in what is referred to as kith and kin care. Early intervention services apply to children between the ages of birth and 5 who have or are at risk for developmental delays or disabilities. Early childhood special education services are intervention services provided to qualifying children between the ages of 3 and 5. Early Head Start and Head Start services are offered to children between birth and school age. These services are designed to eradicate the potentially negative effects of genetic and environmental risk factors. Pre-kindergarten at-risk programs are preschool programs that exist within many states and are designed to reduce the achievement gap of children from low-income backgrounds. School-age child care consists of services offered to children of school age during nonschool hours. Kindergarten education supports the development and learning needs of children around the age of 5, whereas primary grade education encompasses first through third grades.

- **What issues are presently associated with kindergarten and primary grade education?**

Issues include uniform kindergarten age of entry requirements; redshirting, where children are held out for an additional year with the goal of "catching up"; retention, which is holding children back to repeat a year; and debates regarding the effectiveness of full- versus half-day programs. Within primary grade education, present-day challenges include class sizes, retention, and grouping practices.

- **What diverse career options presently exist for early childhood professionals?**

Within the field of early childhood education, there are many professional opportunities that occur within a variety of educational settings. These roles range from director to teacher to family home care providers and principals to family resource coordinators and parent educators. Within the field of early childhood special education, specialized roles include speech language pathologists and audiologists. The sheer breadth of opportunities requires attention to career goals and supportive educational pathways.

4 Understanding Development

"Keep me away from the wisdom which does not cry, the philosophy which does not laugh, and the greatness which does not bow before children."

—KAHLIL GIBRAN

On the first day of school, Margot greets each of her new preschool children at the door. For the past week, she has prepared for their arrival by arranging the room carefully, organizing and developing areas of related activities—or learning centers—based what she feels will interest the children, and placing materials strategically throughout the room. She has conducted home visits with all the children. This has allowed her to learn about their home life and habits, and about the expectations that they and their parents have for the first day and the year. Personal touches awaited the children in the classroom. She added their names on their cubbies, and placed photos of them and their families at the children's eye level throughout the room.

Figuring out who the children are and what they need is a great puzzle to Margot. Finding the right pieces to put in place to support each child is one of her favorite challenges. The information she has gathered to date is an initial glimpse into who they each are. Margot recognizes that the physical arrangement of the room, curriculum, and classroom practices will change dramatically as she gets to know the children, their developmental needs, and their diverse strengths and challenges. She is eager to apply what she has learned about growth and development and effective practices for supporting the range of individual strengths and needs that each child and family brings to the environment.

What are Margot's goals for each child in the classroom? These goals are as diverse as the children in her care. Each child presents individual histories and needs, and each family brings to the table its own motivations and expectations for what the preschool experience means. Sasha's parents, for example, hope that Sasha can improve her social skills and learn how to function well in both large and small groups. Toby's parents are focused on academic skills and are interested in Toby's successful identification of letters and numbers. Bon Filia's parents recently emigrated from Mexico, and their biggest hope is for their daughter to become fluent in English. Anna's parents worry about her placement in a fully inclusive classroom and hope that her autism will not separate her from meaningful interaction with her peers.

• • •

GUIDING QUESTIONS

- How do the following theories contribute to knowledge supporting high-quality early childhood education?

  - Ecological systems theory
  - Theory of cognitive development
  - Theory of psychosocial development
  - Hierarchy of needs theory
  - Attachment theory
  - Theory of multiple intelligences
  - Family systems theory

- How do the principles of children's development and learning relate to the framework of developmentally appropriate practices?

- How does knowledge of family systems theory affect the professional's ability to support children and families?

- How do stages of teacher development affect how one sees one's role as a professional and professionalism?

What are the fundamentals of child development and learning that guide effective practices in the field? What does each child need to grow and thrive? How does understanding this information contribute to your professional role? At this point in the text, you have learned about the field, its rich history, and the breadth of present-day opportunities. In this chapter, you will learn about the fundamentals of growth and development, which will serve as a framework for understanding effective practice.

DEVELOPMENT IN CONTEXT

context

External environments in which children grow and develop, such as the family, neighborhood, and community.

Understanding child growth and development begins with an understanding of the context in which children grow and develop. Each child has his or her own unique world—composed of such things as teachers, peers, family, and community. Within this world, children act and interact based on their own distinctive personalities, their ways of knowing and processing the world around them, and feedback they gather from this world. Two siblings, for example, might grow up in the same family, but their different ages and different personalities mean that they act, interact, and process their family in very different ways. Being a professional requires thinking about the child, his or her world, and the interactions between the two. Although it is only one of the many theories that you'll be learning, Urie Bronfenbrenner's **ecological systems theory** provides a useful template for understanding these complex, bidirectional interrelationships.

ecological systems theory

Theoretical model developed by Urie Bronfenbrenner that describes the interrelationship between children and the contexts of their development.

Ecological Systems Theory

Ecological systems theory (Bronfenbrenner, 1979) strives to provide an understanding of the interaction between a child and his or her world. This interaction is called bidirectional because the impact goes both ways: from the child to the world, and from the world to the child. Toward this goal, ecological systems theory identifies five systems that have an impact on the developing child:

microsystem

The immediate surroundings and relationships of a child's world.

mesosystem

The connections between different structures of the microsystem.

exosystem

The larger social system that affects the child, but that the child does not directly participate in.

- The **microsystem** includes the immediate surroundings and relationships of the child's world. The family, neighborhood, and early childhood program are all components of the microsystem. The microsystem has the greatest impact on the developing child, as these are systems the child has contact with on a day-to-day basis.
- The **mesosystem** represents the connections between different structures of the microsystem. For example, the relationship that families have with their child's teacher is a structure within the mesosystem, as are the relationships families have with other families in the community. The mesosystem can be thought of as a web of interconnections, where different members of the child's world interact together.
- The **exosystem** is the larger social system, which includes family work schedules or access to community resources. The child does not directly interact with structures within the exosystem; however, these systems have an indirect impact on the child's development. For example, 3-year-old Josh has never seen the inside of his father's workplace. However, the fact that his father often has to work long hours to make enough money to live on his minimum-wage salary means that the workplace has an indirect impact on Josh's life. Conversely, Annie's mother works for a local company that allows liberal family-leave policies. When Annie was born, her mother was able to take 6 months off work. When Annie is sick, her mother's workplace allows her to work at home. The policies of Annie's mother's workplace have an indirect impact on her development.

macrosystem

The outermost layer of the child's environment, which includes cultural values, customs, and laws.

- The **macrosystem** consists of the outermost layer of the child's world. This system includes cultural values, customs, and laws. Each of these is represented through a variety of factors. These include the policies that are in place to support children and families, the strength and support of the educational system, and the expectations for children and family learning and functioning. The macrosystem can also influence perceptions of the field of early childhood education. Are persons in the field viewed as babysitters who perform custodial tasks until family members can resume care? Or are persons in the field viewed as professionals performing work that can have a dramatic impact on society in the short and long term?

- The **chronosystem** refers to the dimension of time as it relates to children. One way time can be conceptualized is through the child's natural aging process, which creates changing developmental needs and ways of interacting with the environment. A toddler, for example, has very different needs than the same child as an infant, which will greatly differ from that same child's needs as a third grader. Time can also include the timing of a parent's death, a divorce, or other major life event.

Ecological systems theory stresses the importance of understanding the interrelationships between the children and their surrounding contexts (Figure 4.1). Within the field of early childhood education, the relevant context includes the family and the early childhood community (represented by the professional and the child's peers). The commonality in each context is the child, who creates overlap, or linkage between family and early childhood community.

How do child, family, early childhood community, and neighborhood community interact? Consider Lucy, a 3-year-old in a Head Start classroom. Her microsystem consists of her parents and brother, her Head Start classroom, and the neighborhood she lives in. Both her parents work full-time. Her early childhood programs only meet half a day, meaning that she spends an hour on the bus midday. After school she returns to her neighborhood. Her parents' concerns about the lack of safety in the neighborhood mean that she and her brother spend most of their time indoors. Her parents frequently communicate with Lucy's teacher, Isabel. They spend extensive amounts of time talking about Lucy's adjustments to the educational environment, as this is her first time in a formal educational setting. This communication is beneficial not only to Lucy, but also to her parents, as Isabel's efforts have ensured that they feel comfortable within the environment. Both of Lucy's parents are involved in the program in different ways: Lucy's father regularly volunteers, and her mother attends parent meetings. At these meetings, Lucy's mother has met other parents in the neighborhood and has arranged for play dates for both her children. These interconnections, represented in Bronfenbrenner's theory by the mesosystem, have provided Lucy's parents with important support in their parenting role.

Lucy's exosystem, represented through her parents' workplaces, presents the family with a variety of challenges. Her parents are able to adjust their schedules to take Lucy to school and to volunteer a bit in the program. However, their minimum-wage salary

chronosystem
The dimension of time.

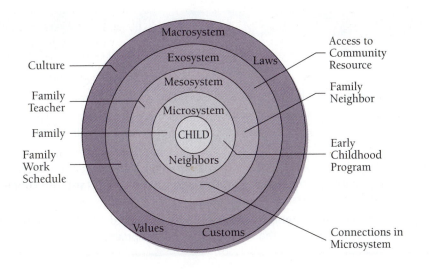

FIGURE 4.1
Ecological Systems

ISSUES OF ACCESS AND EQUITY FOR CHILDREN AND FAMILIES

Community Impact

Within the context of ecological systems theory, neighborhoods provide an important contextual influence on children's development and learning. The impact of neighborhoods is not hard to imagine. In some communities, children can play outside at night, whittling away the hours in neighborhood games of baseball, jumping on trampolines, or playing hide and seek. In other neighborhoods, safety requires that evenings be spent within the confines of their home, safely behind locked doors.

Neighborhoods can affect children's growth and development in a variety of ways. In Chapter 3, you learned that the impact of poverty is not a direct result of money per se, but rather challenges created by the lack of money. For example, financial strain can limit housing options. Many families who are impoverished live in communities with high crime rates and unemployment, low levels of resources, and a lack of relationships between neighbors (Brooks-Gunn & Duncan, 1997).

One of the challenges facing early childhood professionals in supporting children and families is responding to their contextual needs. When social isolation, crime, and the lack of resources combine to reduce opportunities within neighborhoods, part of the professional role includes working to build communities within the classroom environment. Strategies supporting this goal can include:

- Providing family members with opportunities to network and build relationships.
- Encouraging family get-togethers, including sponsoring safe places to play outside the early childhood environment.
- Familiarizing yourself with community resources and extending knowledge to families.
- Recognizing the potential impact of community stress on children's development and learning, and working to ensure that the classroom community is one in which children feel safe, accepted, and nurtured.

TEACHING AND LEARNING CONNECTIONS

Using Ecological Systems Theory to Support Children and Families

What does application of ecological systems theory provide professionals within their role of supporting children and families? Consider the following:

- By understanding the context in which children are growing and developing, professionals have an increased ability to support not only the individual child, but also the overall system.
- Supporting the overall system in which children grow and develop can serve to connect families with needed resources and support important interconnections between contexts.
- Strengthening the systems in which children grow and develop can in turn have a positive impact on their learning and development.

creates challenges in balancing budgets and a good amount of stress when things like gas prices rise. Neither parent has health insurance through their employer, and both parents are thankful for the health services offered through Head Start. These health services are supported by the macrosystem, as the current political climate provides continued financing to support Head Start services. The present chronosystem of Lucy's family is stable—at this moment in time both parents feel secure with their employment. Her brother has recently entered the public school system, creating challenges in maintaining involvement in both environments.

Knowledge of ecological systems theory can support professionals in their vital role of supporting child and family development. Professionals are most likely to affect the child's microsystem, which includes the child and his

Families and communities play a key role in supporting children's development and learning.

or her family. One important aspect of this impact is a basic understanding of child development, as understanding the unique needs of each child—as well as the general needs of children—supports connections between professionals, children, and families, and in turn informs effective practice.

To date, the most accepted framework for viewing, processing, and supporting young children's development is that of developmentally appropriate practices (DAP). Understanding DAP and the research and theory that has led to its development further supports your knowledge of the who, why, and how of quality early childhood practices.

THEORY AND RESEARCH SHAPING KNOWLEDGE OF CHILDREN'S DEVELOPMENT

Using DAP as its framework, NAEYC (2009) identified 12 principles of child development and learning that in turn affect decisions early childhood professionals make about DAP. These principles clarify theories of child development and learning, and organize developmental expectations based on children's ages, individual needs, and contextual needs.

Principle One: Interrelationships Between Developmental Domains

All the domains of development and learning—physical, social and emotional, and cognitive—are important, and they are closely interrelated. Children's development and learning in one domain influence and are influenced by what takes place in other domains. (NAEYC, 2009, p. 11)

Theory and research in child development includes the areas or **domains** of physical, social, emotional, and cognitive development. Physical development refers to such developmental tasks as cutting and writing (fine motor skills) and running and jumping (gross motor skills).

domains
General categories of development.

TABLE 4.1   Overview of Children's Developmental Domains

Developmental Domain	Description
Physical development	Physical growth and development of gross and fine motor skills; control of the body.
Social development	The ability to interact with others in a variety of contexts.
Emotional development	The ability to effectively control and communicate one's emotions.
Cognitive development	The ability to take in, process, and make sense of the environmental world.
Language development	The ability to comprehend and produce the spoken word.

Social development refers to the child's ability to interact in various contexts. One example would be how a child interacts in the context of adults. Another is how a child interacts in a group of his or her peers. How does a child approach a group? Participate in group play? How developed are the child's problem-solving skills? How strong is the child's emotional development?

Emotional development is the ability to effectively control and communicate one's emotions (**self-regulation**) and the belief that one can have a positive impact on his or her environment (**self-esteem**).

Finally, **cognitive development** refers to the ability to take in, process, and make sense of the environmental world. Language development is a major subcategory of cognitive development, and it encompasses the ability to understand and produce the spoken word. See Table 4.1 for an overview of children's developmental domains.

Although these distinct areas of development represent different skills and domains, they are closely interrelated, as each area of development influences the other. For example, babies who are not yet mobile are reliant on caregivers to bring the world to them. In turn, their cognitive development is influenced by the variety and quality of stimulation they experience.

Preschoolers, kindergartners, and primary-aged children, however, tend to have a greater ability to navigate the environment on their own. This ability to explore the environment is influenced by the physical skills used to negotiate the environment and the self-confidence needed to independently explore the environment. In turn, their exploration abilities support cognitive development through increased knowledge of the physical environment, covered in detail in Chapter 11.

Principle Two: Sequences of Learning and Development

> Many aspects of children's learning and development follow well documented sequences, with later abilities, skills, and knowledge building on those already acquired. (NAEYC, 2009, p. 11)

The work of stage theorists—who view development as proceeding through a series of unique stages—illuminates the relationship between the sequence of development and children's resulting skills, abilities, and knowledge. For example, the **theory of cognitive development** (Piaget, 1972) identified four distinct stages that describe children's cognitive development. Three of these stages are relevant to early childhood education:

---

self-regulation

Being able to effectively control and communicate one's emotions.

self-esteem

The belief that one can have a positive impact on his or her environment.

cognitive development

The ability to take in, process, and make sense of the environmental world.

theory of cognitive development

Piaget's theory that presented children's cognitive development in a series of four stages.

- **Sensorimotor stage (birth to 2 years).** Very young infants rely on their senses and reflexes as they explore the environment. For example, a 6-week-old flails her arm, which comes in contact with the mobile hung on the side of her crib. Her action, even though it was inadvertent, resulted in contact with the outer environment. Over time, children's actions become deliberate, and at 5 months that same baby will intentionally reach out and manipulate the mobile. Through this physical interaction with the environment, children develop schemes or ways of viewing and processing their world.
- **Preoperational stage (2 to 7 years).** Children's interaction with the environment begins to yield concrete strategies for comprehending and further interacting with the world. Consider the example of 2-year-old Casey, who has just completed a work of art and runs up to his teacher to show it to her. As Casey holds the picture up proudly for his teacher to view, he holds the picture toward himself, as opposed to showing that side to his teacher. He has learned to interact with people and objects in his environment. However, the **egocentrism** of the preoperational stage causes him to think that her view of the world is the same as his.

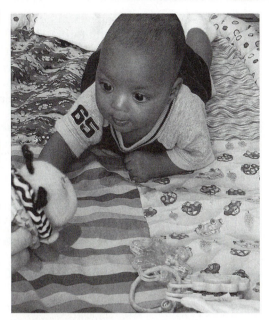

Physical interaction with the environment supports cognitive development during the sensorimotor stage.

- **Concrete operational stage (7 to 11 years).** Children have experienced and interacted with the physical world and are now able to apply their knowledge in a logical manner. They are not limited by what is right in front of them and can solve problems based on internal thought processes referred to as *abstract thinking*. For example, they are able to carry digits in their head when doing double-digit addition or think through the steps involved in remembering to bring homework back to school the next day.

Danish-American developmental psychologist Erik Erikson's work demonstrates how children pass through stages of psychosocial development marked by the successful attainment of developmental tasks. Through his **theory of psychosocial development** these tasks were viewed as a series of developmental crises. Successfully resolving each

egocentrism
Piagetian term referring to a young child's inability to understand a perspective other than his/her own.

theory of psychosocial development
Erikson's theory that development occurs based on internal psychological factors and external social factors.

TEACHING AND LEARNING CONNECTIONS

Brief Overview of Strategies Supporting Cognitive Development

- **Sensorimotor stage:** Provide children with opportunities to physically interact with the environment.
- **Preoperational stage:** Give the children opportunities to interact with people and objects in their environment, and provide feedback that reflects and extends their present level of cognitive understanding.
- **Concrete operational stage:** Provide children with opportunities to experiment and create new meanings based on environmental interaction.

developmental task during its appropriate stage provides the child with a psychosocial strength. Unsuccessful resolution results in potential challenges. Piaget claimed that the quality of experiences at each stage of cognitive development would have an impact on later learning. Erikson viewed the resolution at the psychosocial stage as having an impact on children's relationships for the rest of their lives.

Erikson (1950) identified four stages as relevant during early childhood:

- **Trust versus mistrust (ages birth to 2).** Children learn whether their caregivers will respond to their various attempts at communication. Erikson viewed the feeding relationship as critical and argued that caregivers needed to pay careful attention to quality interactions during that time. Quality interactions include eye contact, caressing, and the use of language.
- **Autonomy versus shame and doubt (ages 2 and 3).** Children need to learn that they have independence and that they can successfully exert this independence within their larger world. To support autonomy, or independence, caregivers allow children to complete tasks on their own, with the adult only providing assistance as necessary. Self-serve snacks, where children learn to serve themselves appropriate portions of food, is an application within early childhood education that supports autonomy.
- **Initiative versus guilt (preschool age).** During this stage children need to have purpose in exploring their environment and be allowed the space and opportunities to take risks and freely explore. In Margot's outdoor science lab, for example, children can freely choose from a variety of exploration materials, including tweezers and magnifying glasses.
- **Industry versus inferiority (primary grades).** Children need to develop a sense of competence and worth. The role of the adult includes knowledge of the child's capabilities. Further, the adult ensures that the child has opportunities for successful interaction with the environment. For example, second-grade teacher Monica places brushes with large handles in the art area to assist Jed, who has cerebral palsy and limited movement in his hands, in manipulating the art materials.

The work of both Erikson and Piaget challenges professionals to understand children's unique ways of viewing and interpreting the world. Each theorist asserts that one can derive general expectations from each stage. For example, children in Piaget's

---

TEACHING AND LEARNING CONNECTIONS

Brief Overview of Strategies Supporting Psychosocial Development

- **Trust versus mistrust:** Respond to children's cues for attention, and provide quality interactions including eye contact, caressing, and language experiences.
- **Autonomy versus shame and doubt:** Give children opportunities to complete tasks on their own, providing encouragement and assistance as necessary.
- **Initiative versus guilt:** Allow children opportunities to take risks and freely explore.
- **Industry versus inferiority:** Provide children with opportunities for successful interaction with the environment.

sensorimotor stage of development need physical interaction with the world to make sense of it and actually "think" with their eyes, hands, and mouths. To support exploration, professionals must ensure that the environment is safe and filled with interesting objects. Erikson's work stresses the significance of relationships in children's development. Specifically, each developmental stage presents unique challenges and requires different reactions from the professional. For example, one 6-month-old needs extensive physical cuddling. A 2-year-old might be glued to the teacher's lap one minute and refusing a hug the next. The ability of the teacher to discern these different needs and respond appropriately is essential.

Principle Three: Individual Patterns of Development and Learning

> Development and learning proceeds at varying rates from child to child, as well as at uneven rates across different areas of a child's individual functioning. (NAEYC 2009, p. 11)

In each classroom, a teacher might have children who are determined to explore all the environment has to offer with their physical bodies. Others take in the environment with skills of observation. One child might be very verbal and engage in extensive conversation with peers, whereas another may prefer solitary activities and needs coaching to interact with others. Another child might have extensive empathy for other children and strong skills of negotiation, but have a limited ability to process the environment through the written word.

The challenge for teachers is to appeal to the strengths of each child and use these to strengthen the other domains. A child with well-developed fine motor skills might be drawn to art and writing activities, but might shy away from exposure to mathematical concepts. To support this child's development in all areas, the teacher may incorporate experimentation with manipulatives into the art center, allowing the child to apply his growing artistic abilities to representations of Lego® designs and Duplo® structures.

Principle Four: Interactions between Biological Maturation and Experience

> Development and learning result from a dynamic and continuous interaction between biological maturation and experience. (NAEYC, 2009, p. 12)

Jordan and Elizabeth are both 8 months of age, and both negotiate and interact with the environment in distinctly different ways. Jordan uses her body to negotiate the environment; she crawls over, on, and through objects that are of interest to her. Elizabeth is more apt to explore the environment with her eyes and uses verbal and nonverbal cues as she looks around her world. Elizabeth will point to objects that she is interested in and protests when these objects are not immediately brought to her for examination. Despite their similarities in age, these children demonstrate their own preferences for navigating their environment. Each child's learning requires support for his or her unique ways of interacting with the world: Jordan needs ample opportunity to physically explore within a safe environment, and Elizabeth needs a clear line of sight and stimulating things to look at.

TEACHING AND LEARNING CONNECTIONS

Creating a "Good Fit" Between the Child and the Early Childhood Environment

- Get to know the learning and interaction preferences of each child in your classroom.
- Recognize that learning is supported through the creation of a match between the child's preferences and environment and teaching practices.
- Adjust environments and teaching practices based on each child's individual needs.
- Continuously monitor the effectiveness of your adaptations for each developing child.

---

nature

Genetic propensities and capabilities that represent internal qualities.

nurture

Personal experiences.

goodness of fit

Term coined by Thomas and Chess to describe the match between the environment and a child's temperament.

How to effectively measure catalysts of and factors that contribute to learning remains a question of research and theoretical debate. Arguments of nature versus nurture lie at the center of this debate. Nature refers to genetic propensities and capabilities, whereas nurture refers to the child's environment, or how personal experiences influence the developing child. The work of Scarr and McCartney (1983) demonstrates that nature and nurture are complexly intertwined, and serves to resolve this debate. These researchers view the child as an active participant in acquiring knowledge. This active participation changes over time, concurrent with the child's changing developmental needs. Based on this, children seek out environments that are compatible with their individual temperaments and talents. Learning occurs through a fluid interaction between the child's individual nature (as conceptualized through temperaments and talents) and the environment provided.

The concept of goodness of fit, originally coined to identify the relationship between environments and children's temperaments, illustrates the importance of creating a match between child and environment. Goodness of fit (Thomas & Chess, 1977) speaks to the need to match the environment and instruction to children's temperament styles, or unique ways of viewing and interacting with the world. A match between temperament and environment creates a safe, secure atmosphere in which children can grow and develop. A mismatch has an impact on children's self-esteem and overall self-concept. This model can be generalized to children's changing developmental needs. An environment that provides a good fit for children's learning needs continuously changes and adapts to fit the child's changing biology. An environment with a poor fit has a negative impact on the child's ability to process and learn.

Principle Five: Establishing Foundations and Supporting Optimal Development and Learning

> Early experiences have profound effects, both cumulative and delayed, on a child's development and learning; and optimal periods exist for certain types of development and learning to occur. (NAEYC, 2009, p.12)

A pervasive view within the field of early childhood education is that time and attention invested in children's present-day development is an investment in their future development.

TEACHING AND LEARNING CONNECTIONS

Brain Basics: Synaptic Development

- Synapses are the wiring of the brain and serve to allow children to both process and respond to their environment.
- Rapid synaptic development occurs during the first years of life.
- Children rely on interactions with people and exploration of the environment to support synaptic development.
- The brain operates on a "use it or lose it" principle, requiring active and continued exploration and interaction to maintain synaptic connections.

One way to explore the impact of present-day development on later development is by examining the recent research on overall brain development. Brain researchers have now quantified what theorists and practitioners in the field of early childhood education have known for years: The early years matter. In fact, one of the conclusions of the Carnegie Task Force on Meeting the Needs of Young Children (1994) was that "the influence of early environment on brain development is long lasting" (p. 7).

Overview of Brain Development. At birth, babies have 100 billion neurons, which represent foundational units involved in processing the world. Through interaction with the environment, synapses form to organize and connect neurons (Zero to Three, 2001). Synapses provide the basic wiring of the brain, allowing children to both process and respond to their environment. In other words, these synaptic connections between neurons allow thought to occur. Therefore, interaction with the environment is essential to healthy brain development.

During the first 6 to 12 months of life, synapses form at a faster rate than any other time in an individual's development. In fact, by the age of 8 months, a child might have one quadrillion synapses in his brain (Zero to Three, 2001). Synaptic development is based on the child's direct interaction with the environment. Appropriate stimulation that neither exceeds nor falls short of the child's needs provides the most effective foundation from which brain development can occur.

The recipe for appropriate stimulation is simple: Children rely on interactions with people, free exploration, and an engaging environment to support their developing mind. Children who lack appropriate levels of environmental stimulation (through both the physical and the human environment) form fewer synaptic connections between neurons when compared with children in stimulating environments.

The lack of stimulation at appropriate times can have a lifelong impact. The brain operates on a "use it or lose it" principle, and opportunities missed are difficult, if not impossible, to regain. The concept of windows of opportunity lends insight into prime opportunities for development and learning.

Supporting Windows of Opportunity. Windows of opportunity, also known as sensitive periods, refer to periods within a child's development when the brain is primed to learn foundational skills that subsequent development builds on. The information acquired during sensitive periods is affected not only by internal factors within the child, but also by factors within the environment. Children who miss opportunities for development during a critical period fight an uphill battle. Although brains can "rewire" themselves once a sensitive period has passed, it becomes more difficult.

windows of opportunity
Prime times for particular areas of brain development to occur.

Different windows of opportunity exist for basic motor development, music, vision, hearing, language, math and logic, and attachment.

Motor Development. Motor development can be divided into two categories: gross motor development, which refers to development in large muscle groups and skills related to reaching, crawling, walking, running, hopping, and skipping; and fine motor development, which includes the muscles related to grasping and writing. During the first 2 years of life, primary motor circuits connect to the brain's cerebellum and control posture and coordination. Physical experience of the environment through movement contributes not only to motor control, but also to early brain development in general. Vigorous exercise and activity provide the brain with glucose, which is the brain's chief source of energy. Increased glucose serves to increase blood flow, which in turn feeds the brain and enhances synaptic connections. Because of the important relationship between movement and brain development, children need free exploration of a safe and engaging environment. Children should have ample opportunity to practice skills that lead to both posture and movement, including crawling, creeping, rolling, and jumping (Berk, 2007).

In general, the window of opportunity for fine motor development follows gross motor development (Gabbard, 1998). The manual dexterity children gain from interaction with the environment supports later skills such as playing an instrument, sewing, or completing manual operations such as writing, building, and artistic design. To support these developing skills, children rely on opportunities that integrate visual–motor activities, commonly referred to as eye–hand or eye–body coordination. Such coordination activities include catching and kicking. In addition, opportunities within the classroom—including scribbling, drawing, coloring, and painting—support fine motor activities.

Music. Music also provides a vehicle for brain development. Exposure to music activities, such as singing and producing music, influences children's spatial skills (Rauscher, Shaw, Ky, & Wright, 1994). Spatial skills (the manipulation of shapes and figures in space), in turn, provide an essential building block for math and calculus skills.

Research shows that children's capacity to learn from music begins at birth (National Association for Music Education, 2000). Daily activities that include singing, listening, experimenting with musical instruments, and moving to music can support and develop this capacity.

Vision. Windows of opportunity for vision again points to the importance of early experiences. Children who are born with a visual impairment, such as cataracts, will become permanently blind in that eye if the clouded lens is not promptly removed (Agency for Health Care Research and Quality, 2006). The window of opportunity for visual development is thought to close around 18 months of age, creating a need for quality visual stimulation during infancy. By 1 month of age, infants can slowly track objects and are drawn to black-and-white objects. Their visual acuity is generally poor at this point, making black-and-white objects with checkerboards and angles particularly inviting.

Windows of opportunity create prime times for learning.

By 2 months of age, infants can attend to objects up to 6 feet away. In general, infants tend to track vertical movements more effectively than horizontal movements. Although they still prefer black-and-white objects, they have a growing awareness of colors, particularly the primary colors red and yellow (Berk, 2007).

By 3 months of age, infants begin to search for familiar objects in their environment (such as their primary caregiver). Cognitively, they are able to associate objects with events (such as a bottle and feeding time). Red, yellow, black, and white are still favorites, and the infant is noticeably interested in faces. At 4 months, the infant's interest in faces extends to his or her hands, and the child will spend extensive amounts of time gazing at his or her moving hand. Tracking abilities have significantly improved, and the infant can follow objects vertically, horizontally, and in a circle. At 5 months, infants are able to bring objects to their eyes for examination. Visual acuity enables them to look at objects placed close to them in the environment and ones placed far away. As children become increasingly adept at visually exploring their environment during their first 18 months of life, this ability expands (Berk, 2007).

Many practices common to early childhood education can actually interfere with healthy visual development. Bright, primary colors are often the decoration staple of early childhood classrooms. Although these might be appealing to the adult eye, bright colors can serve to overstimulate. Within early childhood classrooms, a neutral color scheme is considered most appropriate, with colors that stimulate visual development integrated through pictures, books, and materials (Glass, 2002).

Hearing. Infants' dependency on the environment for visual stimulation holds true for auditory stimulation as well. Access to a range of sounds can have a dramatic impact on the quality of infant hearing (Sireteanu, 1999). Early identification of hearing problems is vital. The fact that 27 states have adopted mandatory hearing tests at birth speaks to the importance of early hearing ability and the later production of language (National Conference of State Legislatures, 2006). Supporting hearing includes the provision of a sound-rich environment, but again, it is essential to avoid overstimulation. Background music, language, and singing are all auditory sources and need to be appropriately incorporated to complement activities. For example, soft background music can be appropriate during nap time. Tunes that are more energetic can accompany periods of the day where children are vigorous and active.

Language. Children have an enormous capacity to acquire language in the first years of life. Data on windows of opportunity indicate that the prime time for language learning is between birth and the age of 3. The first year of life is when the child's native language is "wired" into the brain (National Clearinghouse for English Language Acquisition, 2006). From this point to the age of 3, the brain creates synapses based on the vocabulary that children are exposed to.

Exposure to the spoken word supports language development. One of the most effective ingredients to healthy language development—not surprisingly—is talking to children. Talking helps to develop both language comprehension and production. The size of a child's vocabulary at 20 months is directly related to how much the child is spoken to. The children of chatty caregivers have on average 131 more words when compared with children whose caregivers do not speak to them often. By the age of 2, the gap between the word usage of children from chatty caregivers when compared with nonchatty ones had grown to 295 words (Huttenlocher, Haight, Bryk, Seltzer, & Lyons, 1991).

Math and Logic. The bases for math and logic skills are established between the ages of 1 and 4. During this period, children develop "number sense," which includes such skills as one-to-one correspondence and matching. Children exploring objects in the environment can stimulate logical processing. What does this object do? What happens if I manipulate the object in this way? These explorations can also provide opportunities to experiment with cause and effect. Introducing well-chosen materials is critical at this stage. Measuring cups in the sand and water table support experimentation with concepts of volume. Counting bears in the manipulative table can foster matching and grouping skills. Opportunities to design and build with Legos, blocks, or Duplos can also assist with these skills.

attachment relationship
Quality of interactions and resulting relationship between a child and the primary caregiver.

Attachment. The **attachment relationship** also represents a significant window of opportunity. During the first 18 months of life, children learn important information about how they are cared for and responded to within their environment. Interactive experiences, such as responding, talking, and cuddling, help a child to form expectations about how others will treat them. These expectations will, in turn, influence how children act with others. The concept of attachment is covered in more detail later in this chapter.

Piaget's writings on "readiness" complement the concept of windows of opportunity. According to Piaget, children construct knowledge of the environment in tandem with their brains' ability to process and make sense of their explorations. Therefore,

---

TEACHING AND LEARNING CONNECTIONS

Supporting Windows of Opportunity

- **Gross motor skills:** Provide children with physical experience of the environment through movement and free exploration of a safe and engaging environment. Children need many opportunities to practice posture and movement skills.

- **Fine motor skills:** Provide children with opportunities to develop manual dexterity, including visual–motor activities supportive of eye–hand and eye–body coordination.

- **Music:** Expose children to music activities such as thinking in producing music. Include daily activities related to sound, silence, listening, experimentation with musical instruments, and music-based movement.

- **Vision:** Provide visual stimulation based on developmental age, respecting needs for healthy visual development such as neutral color schemes in backgrounds.

- **Hearing:** Expose children to a wide range of sounds while avoiding overstimulation. Background music, language, and singing should be used to complement activities.

- **Language:** Expose children to the spoken word through talking, reading, and singing to children.

- **Math and logic:** Provide children with opportunities to explore, manipulate, and experiment with objects and well-chosen materials in the environment.

- **Attachment:** Foster quality relationships through low teacher–child ratios, primary caregiving experiences, and interactive experiences that include responding, talking, and cuddling.

what children focus on and process within their environment directly relates to their brains' capacities and drives for learning. A 2-year-old playing with measuring cups in the sand and water table has a very different experience of volume compared with a 5-year-old using the same measuring cups at the same sand and water table. Each will bring their present level of understanding to the situation, and each will interpret and derive different meanings from their interactions.

Principle Six: Progression of Development

Development proceeds in predictable directions toward greater complexity, self-regulation, and symbolic or representational capacities. (NAEYC, 2009, p. 12)

Imagine you are flipping through a photo album of a child's first 8 years of life. The pictures are of the same child, but the child is changing, growing, and developing over time. The picture of the child as a newborn is vastly different from the picture of the child as an 8-year-old.

At the same time that the child's outward appearance is changing over time, internal development is undergoing dramatic changes. The child as a newborn mainly communicated through crying and eye contact; the child as an 8-year-old reads, writes, speaks, listens, draws—he has a vast repertoire of ways to communicate with the world.

These communication skills do not develop in isolation. Rather, communication is only one dramatically changing developmental area, with physical abilities, self-regulation, social interaction, and problem solving—virtually each aspect of a child's development—changing and increasing in complexity over time (NAEYC, 2008).

What does this mean for the early childhood teacher? As you will learn in Chapter 5, knowledge of children's development is essential. In addition, recognizing development as predictable can provide important information about supporting development and learning overall, as where a child is presently at developmentally can provide important information about future developmental expectations. However, teachers must recognize that although development is predictable, children will develop based on their own unique timetables. Children's unique developmental strengths and challenges influence how they attain developmental milestones. For example, infants who are visually impaired can fall behind in language and communication if they do not have opportunities to extensively interact (e.g., poke, probe, pat, bang, mouth, throw, and compare to other objects) with objects in their environment (Texas School for the Blind and Visually Impaired, 2007). These interactions also need to be accompanied by rich verbal descriptors and labels that provide shared meaning to their explorations.

Consider as well a 5-year-old English language learner. When he joined his bilingual kindergarten classroom 3 months ago, he spoke no more than a handful of words in English. Within a few short months, his **social English**—represented by the language of everyday oral and written communications—began to flourish. He quickly learned to ask other children to play and was able to communicate his needs and preferences with growing skills to his widening circle of friends. His **academic English**—which is the language necessary for success in school—was far less developed. This gap between social and academic language acquisition is an expected developmental trajectory (Cummings & Wong Fillmore, 2000).

social English
Language of everyday oral and written communications.

academic English
Language necessary for success in school.

Academic English supports skills needed for school success.

Understanding that there is an expected variation in the acquisition of social and academic English for English language learners can provide teachers with important information about anticipated developmental pathways. It can also give teachers information about next steps. For example, one of the most effective strategies for supporting children's academic English is through building on their knowledge of social English (Eastern Stream Center on Resources and Training, 2003).

Knowledge of general developmental trajectories provides teachers with a fundamental understanding of present and anticipated future developmental pathways. However, understanding the unique developmental needs of each child provides teachers with the knowledge needed to create environments and interactions that respect and support each child's developmental path.

Principle Seven: The Importance of Relationships

Children develop best when they have secure, consistent relationships with responsive adults and opportunities for positive relationships with peers. (NAEYC, 2009, p. 13)

hierarchy of needs theory

Abraham Maslow's hierarchy of five levels of basic needs, culminating with attaining self-actualization.

The **hierarchy of needs theory** presents human needs in a pyramid fashion (Maslow, 1998). Physiological needs represent the base, where basic human needs for food, water, and shelter are met. Building from this foundation, safety and security support development. The early childhood classroom has clear expectations and routines and provides the child with an environment that incorporates needs for healthy and safe interactions. Next, Maslow's theory presents the needs of love and belonging, and speaks to the child's needs for secure relationships. Maslow's next level presents feelings of self-esteem and self-competence. From this, the child can eventually develop feelings of self-actualization, which is Maslow's highest stage. In this stage, children are able to attain and accept their ideal self. Figure 4.2 illustrates Maslow's hierarchy of needs pyramid.

Central to Maslow's model is support for children's social-emotional development, which in turn contributes to and is affected by relationships. Also referred to as social-emotional literacy, these skills represent one of the central tasks of early childhood development.

attachment theory

Ethological theory of development that posits that the quality of the caregiver–child relationship in the first 18 months of life will have a lifelong impact on the child's future relationships.

Social-emotional literacy depends on relationships: through relationships with others, children learn information about themselves and what they can expect from people in their world. One of the main theories supporting the vital role of relationships in children's development is **attachment theory**. According to attachment theory, the quality of relationships children form in their first years of life affects their lifelong quality of relationships (Bowlby, 1972). These include attachments with parents or other primary caregivers and other adults.

Bowlby's work was extended by Mary Ainsworth (1982), whose Strange Situation Experiment contributed to an examination of the quality of children's attachment. The

FIGURE 4.2
Maslow's Hierarchy
of Needs

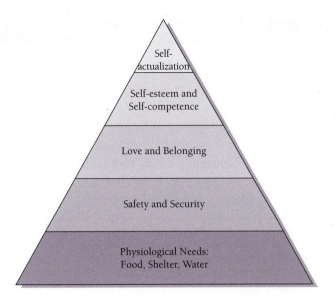

- Self-actualization
- Self-esteem and Self-competence
- Love and Belonging
- Safety and Security
- Physiological Needs: Food, Shelter, Water

Go to MyEducationLab and select the topic "Child Development." Under Activities and Applications, watch the video *Nurturing Relationships* and consider how warm, nurturing relationships are supported between children and the teacher.

strange situation consists of a series of separations and reunions designed to elicit anxiety in children. The idea behind eliciting anxiety is that the state would trigger attachment behaviors. Like the baby monkey in the jungle that clings to its mother's back in the face of danger, attachment theorists believe that the infant will seek out safety and security from a primary attachment figure in response to anxiety. Attachment theorists believe that how infants are treated in their first year of life has an impact on how they respond to their primary attachment figure when anxious. Securely attached infants will seek out comfort. Insecurely attached infants will respond in one of two ways. Either they will avoid seeking out comfort, as they have not learned they will be comforted, or they will react in a manner that demonstrates a desire for comfort coupled with anger or ambivalence.

The work of attachment theorists and Erik Erikson represents foundational theories that have contributed to the field's present-day focus on the development of social-emotional literacy, or competence. There are numerous examples of this focus. NAEYC (1998), for example, identifies the early years as critically important for the development of both future mental health and self-esteem. Its efforts include the "Supporting Teacher, Strengthening Families" initiative, designed to help early childhood professionals prevent child abuse and neglect and support healthy social-emotional development (Olson & Hyson, 2003). In addition to this national training effort, NAEYC has published extensive professional resources on this topic, and it is included in standards for both program and professional preparation accreditation.

Head Start has also identified the promotion of social-emotional development as a key responsibility of any early childhood program (Head Start Policy Book, 2006). Social-emotional school readiness is critical for children's successful transition to kindergarten, early school success, and later accomplishments in the workplace (Peth-Pierce, 1998). Finally, researcher Cybele

Secure attachments are based on trust and reciprocity.

> **TEACHING AND LEARNING CONNECTIONS**
>
> ### Supporting Attachment Within Infant-Toddler Settings
>
> - Focus on developing respectful, reciprocal relationships with each individual child.
> - Use a primary caregiving system, where one professional becomes a "expert" on the child's developmental needs and preferences.
> - Use daily routines as an opportunity for bonding and interaction.
> - Ensure that each child in the early childhood environment receives extensive physical contact and supportive verbal interactions.
> - Respect children's needs for space and comfort.

Raver (2002) identified children who are emotionally well-adjusted as having a significantly greater chance of school success. Children with emotional difficulties, by comparison, are at risk for early school failure.

The implications of this research points to high-quality early childhood environments that support social-emotional development. This goal relates to the seventh principle of DAP in that it ensures psychological security (NAEYC, 2008). Adopting Maslow's theory requires understanding that emotional security is supported by children feeling safe and valued and having their physical needs met. How to effectively support each of these goals will be covered in more detail in Chapters 11 and 12.

In addition to understanding children's development and learning, early childhood educators need to understand families. Having the largest impact on children's development, families are an essential part of effective early childhood education.

Principle Eight: The Influence of Social and Cultural Contexts on Development and Learning

> Development and learning occur in and are influenced by multiple social and cultural contexts. (NAEYC, 2009, p. 13)

Early childhood author and advocate Janet Gonzalez-Mena (2005) conceptualizes culture as invisible, and she argues that "one moves in culture the way a fish moves in water. The water is so much a part of the fish's experience, that the only time it becomes aware of the water is when it finally finds itself surrounded by air" (p. 239). Culture influences how we dress, eat, sleep, and celebrate. How we act when we are upset—whether it is acceptable to cry or stomp our feet, or whether emotional displays are frowned upon—is another facet of culture. Do teachers expect children to master math and science? The fine arts? Culture has an impact on societal expectations, and in turn, the expectations that families have for children's development are impacted by culture. Within an infant classroom, one child's parent might want you to allow babies to cry out their frustrations. Another expects you to respond to children when they are upset. Other parents might expect their child to be toilet trained at 1 year of age, and another considers the age of 3 a prime time for toilet training. The professional must respect the cultural expectations of each parent/significant family member within the community. However, professionals also have the responsibility to educate parents about effective techniques that support their child's development. Decisions about children's development and how to support it

---

TEACHING AND LEARNING CONNECTIONS

Becoming Culturally Literate

- Develop an understanding and appreciation of your own cultural perspective.
- Take time to get to know each family in your early childhood classroom.
- Work to develop collaborative partnerships with families through communication and establishing common ground (common ground includes the shared goals of supporting the child's development and learning).
- Actively listen to families with an open mind committed to learning from them.

---

become a partnership between professional and families. Both parties work to understand each other's viewpoints, and work in ways that most effectively respect the needs of each individual child. For professionals to effectively collaborate with family members, they must develop **cultural literacy**, reflecting the ability to understand and appreciate one's own cultural perspective as well as that of the family.

For professionals to be culturally literate, they must gather knowledge of the different contexts within which children develop, and act accordingly. The main goal is the establishment of common ground, and from this, mutual understanding and collaboration can blossom. Consider the parents who wish their child to be toilet trained at the age of 1. The teacher believes that children at that age lack physical and psychological preparedness for this task and is focused on toilet learning as opposed to training. The teacher must first work to understand the parent's perspective. From that point, the teacher can introduce information about readiness. In this case, the teacher can use norms about development and related expectations to inform and educate. However, the teacher must be open to the parents' perspective, and they all must reach a mutually agreed-upon solution.

cultural literacy
Ability to understand and appreciate one's own cultural perspective as well as that of the family.

Principle Nine: The Role of Effective Teaching

> Always mentally active in seeking to understand the world around them, children learn in a variety of ways; a wide range of teaching strategies and interactions are effective in supporting all these kinds of learning. (NAEYC, 2009. p. 14)

As you learned in the discussion of Principle Two, stages of cognitive development affect how children perceive the world around them and what factors of the environment are chosen for exploration. Two important theorists who have advanced our understanding of social, emotional, and cultural literacy and how children respond to the world around them include Jean Piaget and Lev Vygtosky. Both are thought of as constructivists, meaning that they believed that children gain knowledge (literacy) based on their interactions with the environment.

Constructivism and Piaget. Piaget described the mental structures that evolve in children as they interact with their environments and acquire knowledge as **schemes**. Schemes begin to form at birth, when interaction with the external environment helps shape ideas and conceptions. Piaget also described the process through which knowledge is constructed and applied as having two kinds of adaptation: **assimilation** and **accommodation**. When children assimilate, the knowledge they acquire fits within their

schemes
Logical mental structures that change based on the stage of cognitive development children are in.

assimilation
Incorporating new concepts into existing schemes.

accommodation
Altering existing schemes as a result of new information or experiences.

existing knowledge of the world. When they accommodate, the child's own schemes are adapted to make room for and use of their new knowledge.

Eighteen-month-old Will's fascination with the moon demonstrates the twin processes of assimilation and accommodation and his overall adaptation of knowledge based on the environment. According to his scheme (his existing knowledge) of the moon, it is a round, white object. It is no surprise that Will now happily labels all the objects in his environment that fit these criteria a "moon." To Will, the round, white tops of cottage cheese containers and the round, white plates used at the dinner table are all moons. Over time, Will encounters people labeling different objects in different ways. He continues to hear the round, white object that appears every night in the sky referred to as the "moon." Piaget argues that the differences between Will's current concept of moon and the information he is gaining about other round, white objects places him in a state of **disequilibrium**. In this case, the scheme he is applying to the existing concept of the moon as all round, white objects and the information he is receiving in the environment is mismatched. To return to a state of equilibrium, where there is a match between information presented in the environment and Will's existing scheme of the moon, he must *accommodate* his knowledge. This involves creating a new scheme for interpretation. Specifically, Will needs to refine his definition of the moon to include only the object in the sky, and to create new schemes (such as cottage cheese container tops or plates) for information that does not fit.

disequilibrium

Cognitive conflict resulting from a mismatch of interpretation and information presented in the environment.

Constructivism and Vygotsky. Lev Vygotsky, a Russian psychologist who emphasized the role of culture in cognitive development, also saw environment as central to development. He believed that constructing knowledge is a socially mediated process. In other words, it is the people in children's environments who influence how and what they learn. Let's linger on the example of Will and his definition of the moon. For Will to learn the correct concept of moon, this information must be within his **zone of proximal development** (ZPD). ZPD, according to Vygotsky (1978), is "the distance between the actual development level as determined by independent problem solving and the level of potential development as determined through problem solving under adult guidance or in collaboration with more capable peers" (p. 86). In other words, children can learn information through the assistance of adults and more experienced peers that they would not be able to learn on their own. The ZPD spans the distance from what children can learn independently to what children can learn with assistance. ZPD is often conceptualized as a ladder of cognitive development. The rungs of the ladder represent children's knowledge progression. The process of moving up the ladder is represented by the social guidance and informational assistance provided, for example, by teachers. Figure 4.3 provides a visual representation of ZPD.

zone of proximal development

Vygotskian concept that refers to the distance between what a child can accomplish on his or her own and what he or she can do with assistance.

Implications for Teachers. Both Piaget and Vygotsky viewed the teacher as vital in supporting children's development. Piaget believed that the teacher's responsibilities include designing an environment that supports children's knowledge of the world around them. Knowledge of children's developmental stage is critical in ensuring that teachers design appropriate environments (Kamii & DeVries, 1993). Vygotsky also viewed the teacher's role as critical to supporting children's development. He focused, however, on the process of teacher–child interactions as a means of children's learning about the world around them. Whereas Piaget focused on endpoints in development and learning, Vygotsky viewed learning as a process to be analyzed, as opposed to an end product to be attained (Riddle & Dabbagh, 1999). Another critical difference between the theorists' perspectives on children's learning was their focus. Piaget focused largely on the realm of

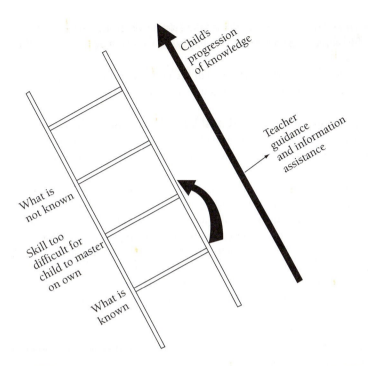

FIGURE 4.3
Visual Representation of ZPD

cognitive development, whereas Vygotsky broadened the focus of development to include social-emotional development as well. For children to learn, according to Vygotsky, their interests must be sparked, their imaginations must be engaged, and the climate that they are learning in must be emotionally safe and supportive of taking risks.

Principle Ten: The Importance of Play

> Play is an important vehicle for developing self-regulation as well as for promoting language, cognition, and social competence. (NAEYC, 2009, p. 14)

Play is another example of a familiar concept that is often misunderstood by many parents and professionals alike. Most people have heard adages such as "play is children's work" and "children learn through playing." The idea that professionals are merely guardians, referees, or police officers who intervene when everyday child's play gets out of hand is one that early childhood professionals have worked hard to eliminate.

To early childhood education professionals, play is not something that occurs haphazardly when a few children happen to share a bit of space and some random toys. Play is one of a multitude of methods by which children learn. Play fosters learning when children experiment with societal norms, roles, and values. Supporting play requires knowledge of children's developmental stages, curricular goals and strategies, observation, and assessment. It also requires the ability to design (and redesign) environments based on children's ever-changing needs.

There are five criteria that qualify play (Hughes, Noppe, & Noppe, 1988):

1. *Play must be* **intrinsically motivating**, *and therefore meaningful and motivational, to the child in absence of any external motivator.* A child, for example, who is putting together a block tower because he was told he would earn a sticker is not really playing.
2. *Participation in the activity must be freely chosen.* Children who are told by a timer when to move from one area of the classroom to another are not truly playing.

intrinsically motivating

Motivation or desire to do something based on internal drives and not external reinforcements.

TABLE 4.2 Supporting Meaningful, Engaged Play for Each and Every Child		
Area of Disability	Potential Challenges	Supportive Teaching Strategies
Physical	• Might be affected by access to toys and other materials within the environment • Might be affected by how toys and materials are played with once obtained	• Ensure that toys and materials are accessible to all through placement and organization • Modify toys and materials through such strategies as adding large handles, knobs, or Velcro to make sure they are easy to grasp and manipulate
Cognitive	• Might experience delayed development of play skills • Might experience challenges engaging in pretend play because of challenges in thinking abstractly • Might engage in more exploratory, as opposed to direct play, behaviors	• Support developing play skills through extensive modeling • Provide ample opportunities to imitate and learn specific play skills
Communication	• Might experience inability to initiate play with others; engage in a sustained play through conversation; or describe, control, or extend play with others	• Model strategies appropriate to the child's communication skills supportive of play entry and sustaining play • Provide extensive opportunities for communication through pictures, signs, and the written word
Vision	• Might experience challenges in orienting to play areas and materials • Might be limited in exploratory or imitative skills due to limited experience imitating models or manipulating objects	• Ensure that room lighting and object placement maximizes the visual capabilities of each child • Allow extensive opportunity for exploration of materials supportive of imitation
Hearing	• Might experience communication difficulties • Might experience challenges in responding to initiations of others	• Ensure background noise in classroom environment is minimized • Provide extensive opportunities for communication through pictures, signs, and the written word
Social, emotional, and behavioral	• Might withdraw from others or activities, limiting opportunities for engagement • Might experience challenges in maintaining concentration on play activities • Might be unwilling or fearful of risking exploration of materials with different textures, size, or functions	• Engage in social coaching, where children are encouraged and provided skills supportive of entering into and sustaining play • Provide ample opportunity and encouragement to explore various materials in the environment • Assist the child in maintaining focus on the play through commenting on the play experience

Source: Based on Owen (1998).

skills to put together a challenging puzzle, but also "talks himself" through the process. Marty uses private speech as she works at tying her shoe, and 8-year-old Mena uses private speech to guide her through a complicated subtraction problem. Children use private speech in a variety of situations, including pretend play.

Because pretend play is strongly related to cognitive, social, linguistic, and academic competencies, it is a common forum for private speech. Therefore, pretend play is an important experience for children in preschool through the primary grades (Bergen, 2002). Over time, children replace the private speech that they use during pretend and other kinds of play with something called self-regulatory internal thought.

TEACHING AND LEARNING CONNECTIONS

Piaget's and Vygotsky's Views of Development

Piaget	Vygotsky
The physical environment provides an essential conduit for learning.	The social environment provides an essential conduit for learning.
The teacher's role requires constructing an effective physical environment.	The teacher's role requires constructing effective interactions.
Cognitive development proceeds in stages.	Cognitive development is an ongoing, cumulative process.
Focus is predominantly on cognitive development.	Focus includes attention to cognitive, social, and emotional development.

Pretend play relates to the zone of proximal development as it supports practicing self-regulation. In turn, this supports their cognitive development. For example, in pretend play scenarios, children act out roles and rules, and they expand and restrain behaviors based on the complicated scenarios they have constructed. This type of play allows them to practice existing skills of negotiation and develop new ones that emerge as challenges surface during play. "In play it is as though he were a head taller than himself...as though the child were trying to jump above the head of his normal behavior" (Vygotsky, 1978, p. 74).

The role of the teacher in supporting children's pretend play experiences can be extended to general guidelines for supporting the practice of newly acquired skills and the acquisition of new ones. Bodrova and Leong (2003) recommend that teachers be aware of the developmental needs of each child in their care. Further, teachers should give roles to children who are reluctant to play. One way to support active engagement in sociodramatic play, according to these researchers, is by providing children with opportunities to act out stories. Teachers must also model ways that children can resolve disputes.

By directly encouraging and supporting children's pretend play, teachers utilize **scaffolding** to support the acquisition of new skills. Through scaffolding, the teacher responds to the child's interpretation of the events and supports the development of new interpretation and processing skills.

Principle Twelve: Supporting Positive Dispositions and Approaches to Learning

> Children's experiences shape their motivation and approaches to learning, such as persistence, initiative, and flexibility; these dispositions and behavior affect their learning and development. (NAEYC, 2009, p. 15)

Positive approaches to learning—including persistence, initiative, and flexibility—affect both social and academic outcomes (Hyson, 2008). Supporting children's enthusiasm and engagement is central to creating learning experiences and environments that support the development and learning of each and every child. An important strategy supportive of enthusiasm and engagement is designing learning experiences and environments that

scaffolding
Vygotskian concept that refers to the process of extending children's knowledge based on their present level of understanding.

> ### TEACHING AND LEARNING CONNECTIONS
>
> #### Benefits of Pretend Play
>
> - Provides opportunities for children to practice self-regulation.
> - Supports cognitive development through exploring and expanding on roles, relationships, and rules.
> - Allows children to expand or restrain behavior based on complicated, constructed scenarios.
> - Allows children to practice existing skills of negotiation and develop new ones.

reflect the processing preferences of each child within the classroom. One strategy supportive of individual children's processing is through respecting and incorporating multiple intelligences.

The theory of multiple intelligences was developed by Howard Gardner, a professor of education at Harvard University. Gardner (1983) believed that traditional conceptions of intelligence—which often focus on mathematical, verbal, and analytical reasoning—were far too limited. His theory proposes that there are eight types of intelligence that influence how children choose to process and interact with their larger environment. Responsibility falls on the teacher to ensure that the environment created responds to and supports the varied types of intelligence of children within the classroom. Table 4.3 provides an overview of each of Gardner's areas of intelligence and the implications for the early childhood classroom environment.

Gardner's work has numerous implications. First, Gardner advocates a strengths-based approach to designing environments and curriculum for young children. This approach views each child as having a vast capacity to uniquely contribute to his or her own development and learning. Teachers design educational experiences to complement and enhance children's strengths. Interestingly, Gardner argues that each area of intelligence is essential for successful functioning in society. Although cultures might value certain types of intelligence over others, each plays an important role in supporting effective functioning. Therefore, the early childhood professional should not only work to enhance children's strengths, but also use these strengths to build other areas of intelligence. For example, the curriculum and assessment practices in the United States demonstrate a bias toward verbal and mathematical intelligences (ERIC Development Team, 1996). Gardner's theory implies that this presents a limitation, and teachers should work to enhance a broader range of talents and skills, ensuring that all children have equal access to materials, their processing, and the demonstrated product of knowledge. The enhancement of various intelligences, therefore, should focus on both the processing and representation of knowledge.

One of the main advantages of Gardner's work is the challenge it extends to educators. This challenge encourages them to look beyond traditional conceptions of intelligence and the predominant cultural focus on skill development, curriculum, and testing (Kornhaber, 2001). Gardner's work reinforces the idea that each child is an individual. Based on this, one of the main challenges within the classroom context is to both enhance and embrace that individuality.

Understanding the 12 principles of developmentally appropriate practices can provide useful knowledge and skills benefiting the development and learning of young

TABLE 4.3 Intelligences and Implications for the Early Childhood Classroom Environment

Intelligence Proposed by Gardner	Description of Intelligence	Implications for Early Childhood Classroom Environment
Linguistic intelligence	Persons with linguistic intelligence display abilities in words and languages. Strengths of individuals with this type of intelligence include communication via the written and spoken word.	Environment should include many opportunities to interact with the written and spoken word. Within the linguistic environment, books, writing utensils, and opportunities for verbal expression abound.
Logical-mathematical intelligence	Logic, abstractions, reasoning, and numbers are strengths of persons with logical-mathematical intelligence. These individuals demonstrate abilities relative to reasoning, abstract pattern recognition, and scientific thinking and investigations.	Environment should include numerous opportunities for patterning, scientific exploration, and analytical processing. Manipulatives, such as tangrams, collections of objects, etc., experimentation, and opportunities for extensive exploration and analysis of materials within the environment are hallmarks that support this area of intelligence.
Spatial intelligence	Abilities relating to visualizing and mentally manipulating objects are strengths of persons with spatial intelligence. Persons with this type of intelligence are likely to have strong visual memories and good sense of direction.	Environments should include photos, puzzles, and challenging games, such as chess, that serve to exercise children's abilities to visually process and analyze their world.
Bodily-kinesthetic intelligence	Persons who demonstrate strengths in this area of intelligence tend to be adept at physical activities and rely on movement and direct interaction with the environment to support their knowledge.	Environment should include opportunities for physical exploration of the environment, often coined as *learning by doing*. Environment should also include extensive opportunities for active experimentation and manipulation, along with opportunities to physically express knowledge, such as sports, dance, or theatre.
Musical intelligence	Strengths in the area of musical intelligence translate into abilities related to music, rhythm, and hearing. Persons with musical intelligence are often able to sing, play instruments, or compose music.	Environment should include opportunities for listening to music, interaction with instruments, and for production and interaction with musical notes and sounds.
Naturalistic intelligence	Persons with naturalistic intelligence demonstrate a passion for and knowledge of nature and classification of objects within the natural world.	Environment should include opportunities to grow and learn from plants and animals and to share scientific knowledge and practices supporting the natural world.
Interpersonal intelligence	The ability to successfully interact with others is a propensity of persons with interpersonal intelligence. In general, these persons tend to be extroverts who are effective communicators and show strength in their abilities to empathize with others.	Environments should include opportunities to develop and explore relationships, as well as provide support for the communication efforts of individual children.
Intrapersonal intelligence	Persons with intrapersonal intelligence tend to be introverts who prefer to work alone. These individuals often have high levels of self-awareness and show strengths in knowing their own emotions and how relationships and interactions with others affect them.	Environment should include opportunities for children to be alone. Educators must respect the introverted qualities of these children.

children. As you have been learning, DAP goes far beyond addressing the individual needs of each child to include as a central component the need to support families in their vital role in the lives of their children. Understanding family development, therefore, is also critical.

FAMILY SYSTEMS THEORY

One of the challenges facing you as a professional is your ability to understand the diverse needs of families and to use that knowledge to support child and family development. **Family systems theory**, developed by Dr. Murray Bowen (1978) as a tool for understanding how the family as an emotional unit influences individual development, helps us understand and work with families within the early childhood profession (Christian, 2006). The following are the major components of family systems theory that apply to early childhood education (Chibucos, Randall, & Weis, 2005):

family systems theory
View of the family as a complex emotional unit that uses systems to describe the interaction among members.

- **Family systems have interrelated elements and structure.** The *elements* of the system refer to individual family members, and relationships develop between them. Each of these relationships is interdependent of one another, meaning that there is mutual dependence. Individual family members and their relationships provide an overarching structure, which, in turn, makes up the total system and its interactions with the outside environment.

  Emma is a 2-year-old who lives at home with her brother, mother, and grandmother. Emma has separate relationships with each of these people. She tends to play rough-and-tumble games with her brother, read books with her grandmother, and seek out her mother when she wants to be comforted. Her brother, mother, and grandmother have relationships not only with Emma, but with each other as well. Their family structure is the product of these relationships and represents their family unit. The teacher sees only Emma and her mother regularly. However, she needs to keep in mind that Emma has significant relationships with others that affect her on a daily basis. Emma's world is far more complex than the singular representations that home and school imply.

- **Family systems act in patterns, and these patterns provide members with information about how they should function.** At home, Emma is allowed to stay up playing at bedtime until she drifts off to sleep. Sometimes this happens in the middle of her pile of stuffed animals. During nap time at her child care program, Emma is resistant to lying down on the cot and often gets up and wanders over to the block area. Her teacher, Larissa, knows that Emma needs a nap and has tried many different strategies to encourage Emma to rest on her cot. Information important to Larissa includes Emma's behavior within the classroom and expectations for behavior at home. Knowledge of how Emma falls asleep at home might help both Emma and Larissa.

- **Family systems have boundaries that range on a continuum from open to closed.** Families with open boundaries are affected by external influences. They are responsive to information and ideas, and they tend to be independent and welcoming of

---

TEACHING AND LEARNING CONNECTIONS

How Does Understanding Family Systems Theory Support Effective Teaching?

- Supports understanding of the child within the family context.
- Enhances professional's ability to influence the child and family development.
- Provides opportunities to support the overlap between home and school through developing essential partnerships.

separateness and belonging (Christian, 2006). Closed families, however, have clearly defined boundaries that contain the family members. Members are isolated from the environment, and the family system is isolated from the environment.

Emma's family system is very open, and her mother welcomes Larissa's concerns about Emma not getting a nap during the day. The two women work together. Emma's mother shares information on how bedtime is handled at Emma's home, and welcomes Larissa's input on the benefits of limits and structure at bedtime. A closed family system would likely be resistant to questions about the child's home life and about information shared that differs from the family's own belief and/or child-rearing system.

- **The whole of the family is greater than the sum of its parts.** This tenet means that the totality of the family, composed of individual members, is greater than the individual elements. Based on this, a teacher cannot understand a family by observing one of the family members. To understand the child's development within the family, the teacher must recognize that children only represent one facet of this larger whole. Emma's behavior is shaped by her family and surrounding context.
- **Families shape behavior through messages and rules.** Messages and rules are guidelines families use to live by. These unwritten rules give family members information about what is important within the family system. Examples include such maxims as "respect your elders," "if provoked, fight," and "always do your best." The different rules and messages that families live by translate into different behaviors by family members. A child in a classroom, for example, might be following a family rule when he or she solves problems using physical aggression. Knowledge of this family rule and how it is influencing the child's behavior can assist teachers in effectively dealing with the aggression.

Knowledge of family systems can support your understanding of individual children in your care. Children come to school with rich histories that have an impact not only on their present development, but also on their future development. Working to understand children within the family system enhances your ability to have an impact on their overall development. Without careful attention to what might be going on at home, your role is limited to influencing the child exclusively within the classroom environment and you might be missing opportunities to support the overlap between home and school.

Children and families represent two essential facets of the early childhood education triad. The third component is represented by the teacher, and understanding your own professional development contributes greatly to your ability to effectively function within your important role.

STAGES OF TEACHER DEVELOPMENT

Professional development is not a fixed process, where one attends college or other training and is set for life for one's chosen occupation. Conversely, education alone does not breed expertise. It is the unique combination of education and appropriate experiences that shape professional success. Knowledge of your own professional development is central to your ongoing ability to support your own development, child development, and family development and learning. Lilian Katz (1972), a leading researcher and author in the field of early childhood education, argues that adopting a stage approach is a useful tool for understanding teacher development.

Stages of Teacher Development

The term *becoming a professional* implies an endpoint, where—as a professional—you will know how to interact with and process the environment around you. Interestingly, it might be more appropriate to think of your own professional development as a journey. Your professional needs, understandings, and ways of viewing and interacting with your world change and develop over time. Based on the concept that professionalism is a journey, and not a destination, Katz (1972) developed a framework based on four stages of teacher development.

stages of teacher development

Conceptual framework of four stages that Katz (1972) argues teachers move through in their professional development.

The Survival Stage. During the survival stage, teachers are novices in the classroom. The focus is on themselves and their own needs to function within the classroom atmosphere. Central questions teachers might ask themselves at this phase include: "Can I make it till the end of the week?" "Is there any way I can come back to work tomorrow?" "How will I ever make it to lunchtime?"

> Mark has just earned his associate's degree. In August, he began a position as a lead teacher in an early childhood classroom serving 4-year-olds. In his first weeks on the job, he was amazed by how exhausted he felt at the end of each day. Many of his questions centered on children's behavior. "How can I create a morning meeting where each child is engaged and actively participating?" "What should I do when Marci chooses to solve problems with her peers by physical means?"
>
> Mark had learned about many practices designed to support the development of all children. Still, he was surprised at how challenged he felt by his first weeks in the classroom. He often questioned his choice in occupation and wondered if he was well-suited for the daily challenges. Mark was thankful for the feedback and encouragement he received from his co-teacher and the center director. After about a month, he began to feel increasingly confident and began to develop and apply strategies consistently.

The Consolidation Stage. During this stage, the focus shifts from an internal "how will I make it in the classroom?" to an external "how can I support the development of children in my classroom?" As this implies, teachers in the consolidation stage feel more comfortable about their role and performance in the classroom. Subsequently, they are increasingly equipped to focus on meeting the needs of individual children.

> Xandra had been teaching in a classroom of 3-year-olds for 2 years and just recently felt that her confidence in guiding children's behavior was growing. Although each day presented numerous challenges, Xandra had well-developed strategies supporting the creation of classroom community and relationship building with each child and his or her family. Increasingly, her concerns were turning to curricular practices, and she found herself asking such questions as: "Is this the best activity I can design?" "Is the curriculum in the classroom supporting the learning and development of each child?" "Is there more that I should be doing to make sure that Jack's needs are being met?" Xandra appreciated the weekly planning time she had with her co-teacher and valued their brainstorming sessions targeted around these questions. Over the past 6 months, she felt as if she had more and more to contribute and really looked forward to this problem-solving time.

The Renewal Stage. During the renewal stage, teachers often find themselves increasingly comfortable with their classroom and the practices they have put into place. At the same time, teachers during the renewal stage often become bored with daily routines. Because of this, many teachers in the renewal stage are looking for new activities and ideas that they can implement in the classroom environment.

> During a recent conference highlighting the Project Approach, Wendy was thrilled to learn about a way of presenting and engaging children in curriculum that she felt really fit her overall philosophy. Following the conference, Wendy implemented the Project Approach within her own classroom. She was surprised and pleased not only by her reaction to this new challenge, but also by the reactions of the children. Internally, she felt invested in both her learning and teaching, and she looked forward to the new challenges that each day brought. From the children's perspective, there seemed to be a vigor that arose in the classroom, and Wendy marveled at the creativity and investment her students demonstrated.

The Maturity Stage. Teachers in the maturity stage look within themselves for additional ways they can have an impact on the field. "How is my work affecting the children and families I interact with on a day-to-day basis?" "How is my work affecting the field?" "In what ways can I make a larger contribution?"

> Riley had been a teacher within her school's first-grade classroom for over 20 years. She had benefited greatly from the expertise of others in the field over the years. This past year she decided that she would like to share some of her own ideas. After assessing her personal strengths, she decided to develop a presentation on building classroom community. At her first conference presentation on this topic, Riley was thrilled by the enthusiastic response she received from the participants. She was then motivated to write an article summarizing her presentation. The joy she felt from this accomplishment led to the desire to further share with colleagues. Within 2 years of her first presentation she had written four articles and given seven conference presentations.

Figure 4.4 shows the four stages of teacher development.

Understanding each of these stages has implications for you as a professional. Your overall development as a teacher will affect your views and practices within the classroom. Also, your developmental needs as a professional will change over time. For example, when seasoned teachers who have reached the maturity stage are faced with new situations, knowledge, and expectations, they might find themselves in the survival stage. Based on this, your comfort level might vary greatly depending on new challenges that you face. Understanding this, and the factors that help you move through the different stages, can be an important tool supporting your own professional development over time.

Similar to children, professionals pass through stages of development.

FIGURE 4.4
Stages of Teacher
Development

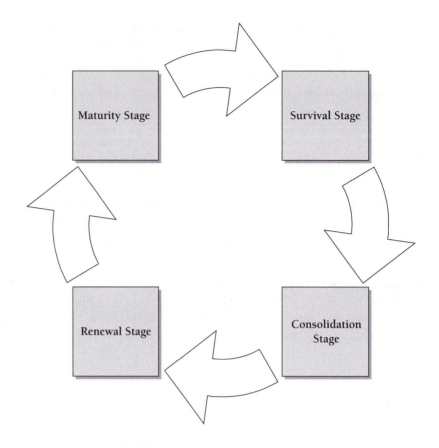

• • • BECOMING A PROFESSIONAL • • •

Supporting Your Stage of Teacher Development

Katz argues that early childhood professionals progress through different stages as they develop within their chosen career. The stages are not visited once and discarded; rather, new challenges can create situations where professionals revisit stages they have previously encountered. Your success as a professional requires recognition of the stage of development you are in. Further, you must develop appropriate strategies that meet your needs during this developmental stage. The following strategies can assist you in your journey:

- **Survival stage:** Seek out other professionals in the environment as resources for knowledge and feedback. Explore the possibility of finding a mentor.
- **Consolidation stage:** Use your strengths to support the individual needs of children in the classroom. Capitalize on reflection skills to ensure that practices are appropriate for each child.
- **Renewal stage:** Explore new activities and ideas to implement within your classroom. This exploration can include reading professional journals and joining professional organizations.
- **Maturity stage:** Explore different options within the field to influence children, families, and professionals in a variety of ways. This might include writing, conference presentations, and advocacy or mentoring.

Katz's stages of teacher development reflect general developmental issues influencing early childhood professionals. Again, similar to DAP for children, each individual professional has his or her own unique developmental needs that require consideration. The same general principles considered appropriate for supporting children's ongoing development can be applied to each professional's ongoing development.

MOVING FORWARD

Understanding development provides an essential precursor to effective practices within the field. Knowledge of development includes looking at the individual—child, family, or professional—and looking at the context in which they are growing and developing. Through understanding the bidirectional relationship between individual and context, you can begin to understand how to most effectively support, nurture, and enhance child development and learning.

The next chapters in this book explore child, family, and professional diversity. In this text, the term *diversity* is used to describe the wide, expansive range of personal experiences, interactions, and ways of being.

myeducationlab

Go to MyEducationLab and select the topic "Child Development." Under Building Teaching Skills and Dispositions, complete the exercises *Helping Children Develop Trust and Autonomy* and *"Get Moving": Creating a Newsletter Article on Physical Activity.*

CASE STUDY

Supporting Development

The Child Development Lab and Learning Center (6 weeks to 6 years)

Marian's interview for her position at the Child Development Lab and Learning Center, like many interviews, consisted of a variety of questions. For the most part, however, it was Marian asking the questions.

"How is mixed-age grouping going to work?" "What do you see as the advantages of adapting this primary caregiving system?" "How will no playpens or swings in the environment work?" "If each teacher has four infants and toddlers, I'm just not sure how that will be practical." "And what about inclusion? Who will we be including, and what are their needs?"

Marian had been a professional in the field for 30 years, and many of the things we were suggesting as practice within the program were new experiences not only for her, but also for us. The director and I had a clear vision of what we wanted to see happen within the program, but little practical experience in actually making it work. We were relying on seasoned professionals and visionaries, such as Marian, to bring our philosophies to life. This was a new journey for all of us, and it was not without challenges.

I regularly visited Marian's classroom in those first weeks to check on how things were going. By the third week, her skepticism had slowly started to change to a realization that this just might work. By the third month, she became an advocate for mixed-age grouping. By the sixth month, Marian and her co-teacher were giving workshops on using the Project Approach with infants and toddlers. In a short time, she had moved from a novice back to her previous stage of maturity.

Several weeks ago I asked Marian what helped her move from the novice to the maturity stage. Her response included commentary on her previous experiences and using what she knew about infants and toddlers to support this new situation. What she found most beneficial, however, was communicating with others adopting different strategies, and ultimately seeing how those worked.

CONSTRUCTED-RESPONSE QUESTIONS

1. Think about the strategies outlined for the new Child Development Lab and Learning Center program. In what ways did these strategies support children's development and learning?

2. As she adjusted to the program, Marian cycled through the stages of teacher development. What did Marian do to support her ongoing development? What additional strategies would you suggest?

REFLECTING ON AND APPLYING EFFECTIVE PRACTICES (NAEYC AND CEC/DEC)

Ethics

- You have just started working in a preschool classroom. On your first day, you develop a list of policies and strategies you would like to implement to involve families in the classroom community. When you show the list to your program director, she comments, "We have found it is easier to minimize family involvement. What would you do in this situation? I would prefer you just touch base with the families every once in awhile."

NAEYC Ideals

I-2.1. To develop relationships of mutual trust with families we serve.

I-3A.1. To establish and maintain relationships of respect, trust, and cooperation with co-workers.

DEC: Professional and Interpersonal Behavior

6. We shall build relationships with individual children and families while individualizing the curricula and learning environments to facilitate young children's development and learning.

DEC: Professional Collaboration

1. We shall honor and respect our responsibilities to colleagues while upholding the dignity and autonomy of colleagues and maintaining collegial interprofessional and intraprofessional relationships.

Standards for Professional Practice

- Imagine you are a student teacher in a first-grade classroom. One of your responsibilities is to develop an overview of policies supporting family communication within the classroom. Based on the material presented in Chapter 4, provide a brief rationale summarizing the importance of developing relationships with families. Be sure to consider in your response why knowledge of the contexts in which children grow and develop is so important.

NAEYC: Promoting Child Development and Learning

1b. Knowing and understanding the multiple influences on development and learning.

DEC: Development and Characteristics of Learners

EC2K2: Biological and environmental factors that affect pre-, peri-, and postnatal development and learning.

DEC: Individual Learning Differences

EC3K1: Impact of child's abilities, needs, and characteristics on development and learning.

CHAPTER REVIEW

- **How do the following theories contribute to knowledge supporting high-quality early childhood education?**

  - Ecological systems theory
  - Theory of cognitive development
  - Theory of psychosocial development
  - Hierarchy of needs theory
  - Attachment theory
  - Theory of multiple intelligences
  - Family systems theory

Each of these theories contribute to knowledge supporting to high-quality early childhood education in a variety of ways. Ecological systems theory supports understanding the complex, bidirectional interactions between a child and their environment, in turn impacting how educational services are designed to encompass and impact child, family, and community. The theory of cognitive development describes children's sequence of development based on their interactions with and processing of the environment. This knowledge provides teachers with information on how children view and process their world. Psychosocial theory describes children as passing through stages of psychosocial development based on the resolution of developmental crises, promoting teacher understanding of children's critical needs and appropriate caregiving behaviors. Goodness of fit is based on the premise that a match needs to be created between a child's temperament and their environment in order for an optimal environment for development and learning to be created.

Understanding children's needs within a hierarchy that begins with basic needs and culminates with self-actualization is the focus of hierarchy of needs theory. Through this theory, the critical importance of meeting children's foundational needs in order for higher-order needs to be developed is emphasized. Attachment theory stresses that the quality of relationships children develop during their first year of life has a lifelong impact, highlighting the importance of quality, stable relationships in early childhood environments. The theory of multiple intelligences presents eight types of intelligence and challenges educators to create educational environments and experiences that support each child's strengths. Finally, family systems theory supports understanding the individual components of families and their complex interactions, helping teachers understand and partner with families in early childhood settings.

5 Understanding Child Diversity

"Investing in [children] is not a national luxury or a national choice. It's a national necessity. If the foundation of your house is crumbling, you don't say you can't afford to fix it while you're building astronomically expensive fences to protect it from outside enemies. The issue is not are we going to pay—it's are we going to pay now, up front, or are we going to pay a whole lot more later on."

—MARIAN WRIGHT EDELMAN

When Grace was 3 years old, her mother learned that Grace qualified for early intervention services. Her programming would include speech, language, and occupational therapies. Her mother's overall attitude toward services was very positive. However, she was concerned that Grace would now be attending a segregated special education classroom on the other side of town. When she expressed her concerns to the team of specialists who were recommending Grace's placement in this environment, the specialists assured her that bus transportation would be provided. The team also informed her that children in this segregated classroom would be "included" with more typically developing children during gym time at the school. These children had qualified for special services under the "at risk for developmental delay" provisions of the school district.

GUIDING QUESTIONS

- How can early childhood education professionals use red flags to effectively support children's development and learning?
- What are the major areas and definitions of exceptionality?
- How can evidence-based practice support young children's development and learning?
- What strategies can early childhood education professionals use to support children from immigrant populations?
- How does stress affect the lives of children and families, and what role does the professional play in alleviating stress?

Grace's mom was not concerned about transportation; rather, she wanted her daughter at her neighborhood school with her peers. She approached the school team about a more inclusive option. The team's response was that she could pursue such arrangements on her own and access services through private organizations such as Easter Seals.

Grace's mother decided to pursue her own philosophy. She believed that finding an inclusive environment that would welcome, accept, and nurture Grace was the best option. After a long search, she found a preschool environment that was willing to include Grace. When she pointed out Grace's developmental differences to the program staff, they responded with "here, we work to individualize the curriculum, and we look forward to learning about and teaming with others to support her unique needs." When she expressed concerns about Grace's language to her teacher, the response she received was "I am learning about some different ways to support her language development. I can't wait to see her reaction, and I will be sure to let you know the impact." When Grace's mother picked her up after her first day of school, Grace's teacher said, "Wow! Does she love to draw. And she really seemed to enjoy interacting with two of the little girls in particular. It seems they are on their way to a fast friendship." After Grace's first week, her teacher let her mother know that Grace seemed to be responding to the language strategies she and her speech therapist were trying. Just that day, she observed that Grace had requested a refill on her milk with a clear pronunciation of the word more, followed by an emphatic gesture with her hands.

Within this environment, Grace was one child of 15 in the classroom community. Grace was more similar to the other children than different. To Grace's peers and her teachers, she was just another unique, amazing child.

● ● ●

In Chapter 4 you learned about general expectations for child, family, and professional development. In this chapter—the first in Part Two of your text—you will learn about diversity as it applies to children, including diversity in ability, culture, and linguistics, and the impact of familial stress on children's healthy learning and development. Chapters 6 and 7 will focus on family and professional diversity.

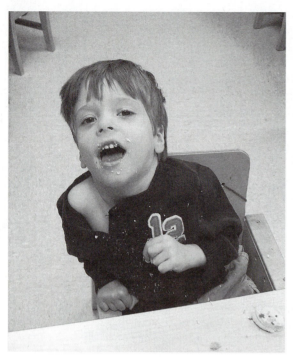

Labels cannot replace knowledge of each individual child.

When we hear the term *diversity*, we frequently think about *differences*. However, teachers must recognize what all children have in *common*: namely, that they are children. As indicated in the opening vignette, children are children first, and each child deserves appropriate, respectful, supportive services delivered within high-quality, inclusive early childhood environments. Some children might have labels that serve as descriptors for individual characteristics. However, these labels do not take away from the wonder, joy, and zest for living that should be a fundamental truth of each child's life, and the responsibility of the professional to treat each child with equity and equality.

This chapter discusses diversity through examination of ability, culture, and linguistics. This focus extends to a discussion of the impact of stress on children and families. Although each of these topics is presented under the category of diversity, it is essential to remember that diversity is cast as a wide net that includes each and every child and family. You can think of inclusion as the net, where—as you learned in Chapter 1—the heart of programming for individual children, families, and communities respects diversity through policy, practice, and interactions.

Diverse characteristics are not an add-on or addendum, but rather representative of the vast experiences and ways of interacting with and processing the world that encompasses those who participate in and benefit from the field of early childhood education. Diversity emphasizes that all children are different from one another, not that some children are different from others. Our exploration begins with understanding exceptionality through the lens of developmental red flags.

UNDERSTANDING EXCEPTIONALITY

Knowledge of children's development has long been informed through looking at ages and stages, where general expectations for such things as walking, talking, understanding concepts, and self-control shape knowledge of developmental patterns. The downside of presenting information in this manner is that ages and stages often lead to a checklist mentality of assessing children's development: either a skill is there and can be checked off, or it is lacking. Checklists of individual developmental skills ignore the complexity of children's development. As we know, children do not develop at the same rate or in the same ways. Further, checklists provide little concrete information about when there is a cause for concern. For these reasons, understanding red flags is becoming increasingly important for teachers.

Understanding Development through Red Flags

red flags

Developmental indicators that reflect atypical patterns of development.

Red flags can provide a useful tool in understanding children's development. Red flags consider general expectations for overall development and show when the absence of a developmental skill might be cause for concern or an indicator of atypical development. The focus on red flags is in alignment with the Centers for Disease Control and Prevention (CDC) of the Department of Health and Human Services. The CDC advocates shifting from a focus on typical behaviors to a focus on atypical growth. Knowing the

---

TEACHING AND LEARNING CONNECTIONS

Red Flag Resources

The following are red flag resources that can be used to help professionals determine if a child's development is progressing in a typical manner, or if there is reason for further investigation.

Autism Spectrum Disorders

http://firstsigns.org/concerns/flags.htm
First Signs

Autism and Other Developmental Disabilities

http://www.cdc.gov/ncbddd/autism/actearly/
National Center on Birth Defects and Developmental Disabilities: Learn the Signs: Act Early

Communication Delays

http://firstwords.fsu.edu/toddlerChecklist.html
First Words Project

General Child Development

http://www.york.ca/RedFlags.htm
York Region Early Identification Red Flags: A Quick Guide for Early Years Professionals

General Child Development with an Emphasis on Sensory Processing Disorders

http://www.sensory-processing-disorder.com/child-developmental-checklist.html
Sensory Processing Disorder Resource Center

---

signs of atypical patterns makes early intervention more likely, in turn supporting positive child outcomes (CDC, 2007).

Variations from typical development are not generally cause for concern. Red flags, however, are considered indicators of a potential developmental issue. As such, teachers should bring them to the attention of a parent and medical or developmental specialist.

TEACHING AND LEARNING CONNECTIONS

Benefits of Using Red Flags

Early childhood professionals can use red flags to:

• Demonstrate when the absence of a developmental skill might be cause for concern or an indicator of atypical development.

• Shift focus from general expectations for development to specific causes for potential concern.

• Support early identification of children who may benefit from early intervention.

An Overview of Exceptionality

Supporting access to and engagement in the early childhood environment for all children requires considering each child's strengths. In addition, professionals must work from a model that embraces diverse abilities. Knowledge of ages and stages provides a template for understanding development. Similarly, knowledge of exceptionalities—or differences in development—can provide a template by which early childhood professionals

exceptionalities
Differences in development including syndromes, impairments, disorders, and disabilities.

adaptations

Adjustments to the classroom environment, curriculum, and/or assessment.

accommodations

The provision of equipment, conditions, or an environment that supports the child's effective interactions with the environment.

modifications

A change in what is being taught or expected of a student.

can support strengths and abilities and attain access and engagement. Supporting access and engagement, in some cases, may require adaptations, accommodations, and/or modifications (National Dissemination Center for Children with Disabilities, 2008). **Adaptations** refer to adjustments to the classroom environment, curriculum, and or assessment. For example, an adaptation for a child with a visual impairment could be the use of low lighting. **Accommodations** refer to the provision of equipment, conditions, or an environment that support the child's effective interactions with the environment. Again, consider a child with a visual impairment. An accommodation supporting the child's interaction with the environment could include glasses or books provided in Braille. **Modifications** refer to a change in what is being taught or expected of a student. Again, using the example of a student with a visual impairment, a modification might include having written assessment read out loud and allowing the student to give verbal responses (National Dissemination Center for Children with Disabilities, 2008).

Inherently, exceptionalities are neither positive nor negative; rather, they are differences. Within this framework, exceptionalities include syndromes, impairments, disorders, and disabilities. See Table 5.1 for a glossary of terms. The following discussion provides a brief overview of exceptionalities as defined by the Council for Exceptional Children.

TABLE 5.1   Glossary of Exceptionality Terminology

Exceptionality	Brief Description	What Teachers Can Do to Support Learning
Autism	Challenges in the areas of communication, peer interaction, and leisure or play activities	Model and provide many opportunities for communication one on one and in small groups. Provide direct instruction and coaching during interactions with peers. Use alternative communication supports (such as pictures) for children who are developing functional verbal skills. Provide opportunities to develop independence.
Attention deficit disorder	Challenges in the areas of attention span, impulse control, and hyperactivity	Provide many opportunities throughout the day to move about. Provide children with choices. Limit distractions. Teach children to cue into and self-monitor their own behavior. Minimize transitions, changes in the schedule, and disruptions. Help children stay on task with daily written plan.
Behavioral disorders	Broad category applied when children's behavior deviates significantly from expectations; includes such disorders as ADD/ADHD, oppositional defiant disorder, and conduct disorder	Provide children with choices. Create buy-in for classroom rules and limits. Be consistent. Structure both environment and interactions for feedback—for example, in morning meeting child might sit next to teacher, who rubs child's back during activity.
Blindness/visual impairments	Challenges in sight that range in diagnoses from low vision to legal blindness	Use appropriate lighting suited to child's needs. Provide hearing, touch, taste, and smell sensory experiences. Use descriptive words such as *straight*, *forward*, or *left* based on the child's body orientation. Provide materials suited to child's visual needs, such as Braille or books in large print.

Exceptionality	Brief Description	What Teachers Can Do to Support Learning
Communication disorders	Variety of impairments that interfere with children's abilities to effectively communicate their thoughts and ideas to others; can include challenges in the areas of speech, language, or hearing	Model language, using enunciation to highlight sounds when appropriate. Provide many opportunities for nonverbal communication. Value communication opportunities, making sure children have adequate time and support to get their ideas across.
Developmental disabilities	Represents varied severe chronic conditions caused by physical and/or mental impairments	Create environment that reflects child's strengths. Provide many choices in activities and ways of interacting with environment.
Giftedness	Abilities reflective of significantly higher functioning in the areas of general academic ability, a specific academic aptitude or talent, overall creative and productive thinking skills, and leadership abilities	Provide challenging activities that complement the child's strengths. Use resources to expand curriculum in ways that reflect the child's needs.
Health impairment	Health issues that require the need for special health or educational services; issues include such things as a convulsive disorder, cystic fibrosis, heart disease, sickle cell disease, hemophilia, asthma, rheumatic fever, cancer, AIDS, or any other chronic or acute health problem impacting strength, vitality, or alertness	Create clear communication patterns with the family, documenting any special or emergency procedures. Should the child be frequently absent, make arrangements for the child to keep up with his/her work and engage in ongoing communication with peers.
Intellectual disability	Limitations of overall intelligence and adaptive behavior	Modify activities as needed to support child's full participation. Provide environmental activities that complement the child's strengths.
Learning disabilities	Represented by significant gap between potential achievement and actual performance	Use child's strengths to support areas of disability. Explore alternative forms for assignments that rely heavily on reading and writing skills.
Mental health disorders	Includes such things as depression, anxiety, conduct disorders, and eating disorders	Observe the child carefully to learn more about how he/she acts and interacts within the environment. Minimize triggers for anxiety.
Pervasive developmental delay	Significant delay or deviance in social, language, cognitive, and/or motor functioning	Create environment that capitalizes on child's strengths. Provide opportunities for modeling and peer coaching, particularly in the areas of communication and peer competence.
Physical disabilities	Broad range of impairments that include orthopedic, neuromuscular, cardiovascular, and pulmonary disorders; can include diagnoses such as cerebral palsy, spina bifida, amputations or limb absences, and muscular dystrophy	Design environment to maximize child access and interaction. Create opportunities for interactions that minimize differences in physical development and maximize opportunities for interaction.
Sensory processing disorders	Disorders of the brain that create difficulties in interpreting sensory information gathered from surroundings through touch, hearing, and moving about	Create environment that is sensitive to children's varied needs for sensory stimuli. Develop and follow appropriate sensory diet for the child. Provide opportunities for children to either receive more stimulation or regroup if overstimulated.

developmental disability

Assortment of severe, chronic, or ongoing conditions caused by physical and/or mental impairment.

pervasive developmental delay

Broad category that includes children who have a significant delay or deviance in social, cognitive, language, and/or motor functioning.

PDD-not otherwise specified

Diagnostic category for children who have significant impairments in social, cognitive, language, and/or motor functioning, but don't meet the criteria for an existing specified category.

autism

Specific diagnosis within pervasive developmental disorders that includes deficits in communication, social interaction, or creative and imaginative play.

Developmental Disabilities. The category of developmental disabilities represents an assortment of severe chronic, or ongoing, conditions caused by physical and/or mental impairments. Children with the diagnosis of **developmental disability** often have issues with language, mobility, learning, and participation in typical life tasks.

The American Psychiatric Association has created the term **pervasive developmental delay** (PDD) to describe children who have a significant delay or deviance in social, language, cognitive, and/or motor functioning. The broad category includes such diagnoses as autism, Asperger's syndrome, Rett syndrome, and **PDD-not otherwise specified** (PDD-NOS). PDD-NOS is a diagnostic category for children who have significant impairments in one of the designated areas, yet do not meet the criteria for an existing specified category. The breadth of the PDD category means that children who have this diagnosis display varied individual characteristics. For example, Assa is a 5-year-old who has been diagnosed with PDD-NOS. Assa experiences difficulties with transitions at school and often becomes frustrated when she has to complete a task. She has two good friends in the class, and when playing with these children, she prefers to play the same game of pretend play repeatedly, involving a scenario where she travels to Disney World. Her teachers know to give Assa warnings as transitions draw nearer, and they employ peer coaching to expand the depth and breadth of her play interactions.

Autism. Affecting as many as 1 in 500 children, **autism** is one of the fastest growing disability categories and exists within the larger category of PDD (Council for Exceptional Children, 2006). Autism exists on a spectrum, where severity depends on the overall characteristics. The impact of autism is mainly in the areas of communication and social skills.

Children with autism typically have difficulties in the areas of communication, peer interaction, and leisure or play activities.

Kyle is a 3-year-old who has been diagnosed with autism. He generally does not respond to his peers and engages in stereotypic play, where he continuously repeats the same behavior. Instead of moving cars around a track or pushing them across a floor, Kyle is fascinated by the car wheels and spends hours studying his rotations of the wheels.

Kyle is also very sensitive to touch and recoils when anyone unexpectedly places a hand on his shoulder. When someone communicates touch in a manner that is safe and respectful to him, such as when he expects it, he responds favorably. Busy, noisy environments are disconcerting to him, and he is likely to curl into a ball on the floor and slowly rock back and forth. Soft background music, on the other hand, is soothing to Kyle and he greatly enjoys the ritual of music before bedtime. Routines are very important, and any deviation from, for example, car seat, then buckle, then book placed in his hand can reduce Kyle to tears.

Although autism affects boys four times more than girls (Council for Exceptional Children, 2006), Emma also has been diagnosed as being on the autistic spectrum, with the specific label of Asperger's syndrome. Emma has some sensitivity to environmental stimuli but responds well to the removal of tags from her clothing and soft rather than glaring lights. Emma seeks out her peers, and these interactions are marked by alternating successes and frustrations when things do not go her way. She has responded well to social coaching and is learning how to respond to her peers in ways other than tears and anger. Emma likes experimenting with play dough and drawing, and she enjoys repetitive play where she continuously draws the same picture or creates the same dough structure.

The early childhood professionals in Emma's and Kyle's environments work hard to understand the unique ways that they process and interact with the world. Accommodations made within the environment include adjusting environmental stimuli based on a child's sensitivities and developing strategies to support particular

---

TEACHING AND LEARNING CONNECTIONS

Areas of Support Children with Autism Might Require

- Promoting receptive and expressive language development by providing an environment filled with books, language, questioning, songs, and finger plays.
- Supporting the development of social-emotional skills, including providing opportunities for coaching in one-on-one and small-group activities.
- Promoting independent living through targeting self-help skills, such as zipping coats, washing hands, and tying shoes.

---

behaviors. For example, Kyle's teacher is currently working with Kyle on expanding his play repertoire. Along with social coaching, Emma's teacher is working to enhance her ability to identify her own emotions and those of others.

Autism is diagnosed through evaluation by a team of experts, including neurodevelopmental pediatricians, speech and language pathologists, and physical and occupational therapists. How the child acts in different situations is essential information, so parent and teacher input is critical. The origins of autism are unknown. Prominent theories point to both genetic causes and environmental influences including pesticides, hormonal imbalances, and infections (Council for Exceptional Children, 2006). The treatment for autism is multifaceted and includes addressing and strengthening behaviors, regulating diet, and pursuing biomedical therapy. Because so little is known about the disorder, there is no definitive path for treatment.

Attention Deficit Disorder. Children with **attention deficit disorder** (ADD) and **attention-deficit/hyperactivity disorder** (ADHD) typically experience challenges in (1) attention span, (2) impulse control, and (3) hyperactivity (although this may not be present). Affecting between 3% and 5% of the school-age population, ADD was originally thought to be similar to autism in that it is more likely to affect boys. However, recent research indicates that ADD is just as likely to affect girls, although it looks qualitatively different and may require different treatment methods (Beauchaine, Hong, & Marsh, 2008).

David is a 5-year-old who has been diagnosed with ADD. He is eager to participate in class activities, but he often has difficulties in attending to tasks within his environment. Recently, David's teacher asked him to complete a painting at the art easel. David focused on his work for under a minute, and then wandered off to the book corner. At the teacher's request, David returned to the task at hand and proceeded to hum loudly as he worked. The teacher informed him that this was disrupting the work of the other children, and David's angry response was to throw his paintbrush down.

Lisa also has been diagnosed with ADD, but as her diagnosis includes hyperactivity, the appropriate label is ADHD. Lisa is in the third grade and has several friends in the classroom. Her overall disposition is positive and friendly. Lisa's challenges within the classroom environment occur when a task requires sustained attention. For example, Lisa's teacher practices "D.E.A.R." on a daily basis, which stands for Drop Everything and Read. During this time, Lisa has difficulty staying in her seat and often verbally and physically disrupts her classmates.

David's and Lisa's teachers work to create an environment that supports the children's preferred styles of interactions, and they provide clear boundaries, limits, and expectations for behavior. After David threw down his brush, his teacher employed a

attention deficit disorder

Disorder marked by challenges in maintaining attention and impulse control.

attention-deficit/ hyperactivity disorder

Disorder marked by challenges in maintaining attention, impulse control, and hyperactivity.

Go to MyEducationLab and select the topic "Special Needs/ Inclusion." Under Activities and Applications, watch the video *ADHD*. Consider how the development and learning needs of individual children can be supported.

logical consequence where he was required to pick up the brush and clean up the resulting mess. On a daily basis, she creates a list of what she expects David to accomplish in the classroom and goes over this list with him in the morning, as well as at various points in the day (should the need arise). When she reviews the list, she often prompts David to explore what kinds of behaviors might contribute to his completing the varied tasks and, through this, is supporting his further development of self-regulation skills.

Lisa's teacher recognizes that certain tasks are challenging for Lisa. Although she supports the students working with others and moving about the classroom to accomplish needed tasks, she also knows that helping Lisa acquire the skill of sitting and attending to material for a period of time is a necessary investment. She allows Lisa to pick where she wants to sit during D.E.A.R. and reminds her of the expectations for behavior (keeping hands to self, remaining quiet, staying in one place). The teacher has found that giving Lisa a large bean bag to sit on seems to help her settle in, and this, accompanied by her continuous verbal feedback, has supported Lisa's success at staying on task.

Like autism, the exact cause of ADD/ADHD is a mystery, but research has shown that it is a neurologically based impairment. There is no specified test for ADD/ADHD. Diagnosis is made by a team that includes teachers, family members, developmental and neurodevelopmental pediatricians, child psychiatrists, and/or a child psychologist. Treatment for ADD/ADHD might include behavioral, educational, and psychological therapy and, in some instances, pharmacological intervention.

Behavioral Disorders. According to the Council for Exceptional Children (2006b), a diagnosis of **behavioral disorders** (this is the favored terminology, although "emotional disturbances" is often employed) is made when a child's behavior deviates significantly from the expectations of others. Behavioral disorders are tricky to identify and diagnose, as it is often difficult to determine if problematic behavior is typical for the child's development stage. Identifying a behavioral disorder requires looking at the context in which a child is developing. Professionals also need to consider the possibility that one or more significant changes are affecting the frequency and intensity of the child's behavior and overall developmental profile.

The broad category of behavioral disorders includes, among many other disorders, ADD/ADHD, oppositional defiant disorder, and conduct disorder. Many of these behaviors can occur simultaneously, and conduct disorder often develops as a result of oppositional defiant disorder. Because conduct disorder typically affects children beyond the age of 8, our focus will be on oppositional defiant disorder (ODD).

A diagnosis of ODD includes frequent temper tantrums and excessive arguing with adults. In addition, children with ODD are actively defiant and refuse to follow adult requests and rules. Children tend to blame others for their mistakes or behaviors and are touchy or easily annoyed by others. There is frequent anger and resentment, and children's talking is described as "spiteful" when they are upset (American Academy of Child and Adolescent Psychiatry, 1999).

Tristan is a third grader who has been diagnosed with ODD. Throughout the day, Tristan is involved in numerous altercations. Lunch usually dissolves into Tristan throwing food or intentionally spilling, and outdoor playtime often involves physical disagreements with other children. Tristan's teachers have worked on a variety of strategies, such as instituting a positive behavioral support plan (which will be covered in more detail in Chapter 10) and giving Tristan continuous reinforcement for acting in what was considered an appropriate manner.

behavioral disorders
Diagnostic category reflecting that the child's behaviors deviate significantly from the expectations of others.

TEACHING AND LEARNING CONNECTIONS

Potential Teaching Strategies Supporting Children with ADD/ADHD and Behavioral Disorders

- Promote self-regulation skills by using written and picture schedules and verbal feedback.
- Reinforce positive behaviors through verbal feedback. For example, "I see that you have kept your feet on the floor."
- Provide clear, reasonable expectations and use charts, pictures, and the written word to post expectations throughout the room.
- Provide activities that capitalize on the child's strengths.
- Be consistent.

Blindness/Visual Impairments. **Visual impairments** affect about 1 in 1,000 school-aged children, and about 10% of this population is blind. Children with low vision can utilize what vision they have along with auditory (hearing) and tactile (touching) input to learn. Children who are blind rely exclusively on learning strategies that do not include sight (Council for Exceptional Children, 2007a). Educational considerations for these children require accommodations that build on the child's abilities to process the environment in ways that build on processing strengths, such as the capacity to learn through auditory stimulation (things they hear) or the ability to learn through hands-on experiences.

Two-year-old Jose has **low vision**, which for him means partial sight that cannot be corrected by conventional glasses or contact lenses. Each day, he joyfully barrels into the classroom and relies on the lighting adaptations (in his case, the use of bright lighting) to ensure that he does not come into contact with furniture in the classroom. He, like many of his peers, gravitates to the block center, where brightly colored, high-contrast blocks lay to support his varied architectural constructions. Jose also loves spending time in the book nook, where he pours over the brightly colored, high-contrasting pictures.

Misha is **legally blind** (meaning her visual acuity, or ability to see, is less than 20/200), and her kindergarten classroom also accommodates her learning needs in varied ways. Misha's teachers have constructed clear pathways in the classroom and have assisted her in developing an internal map of the classroom by guiding her through the location of furniture. They have provided tactile information in a variety of ways, from the rugs on the floor that designate various learning centers within the classroom to the use of Braille on labels throughout. With the assistance of the local university, her teachers obtained a wide variety of books and materials written in Braille, and Misha enjoys reading these materials and instructing her peers on the mechanics of Braille.

Communication Disorders. **Communication disorders** include varied impairments that interfere with children's abilities to effectively communicate their thoughts and ideas to others. These impairments may be in speech, language, or hearing. Speech disorders affect a child's ability to be understood. Language disorders affect spoken language, reading, and written communication. Hearing difficulties can range from hearing loss to deafness.

Go to MyEducationLab and select the topic "Environments." Under Activities and Applications, view the simulation *Accommodations to the Physical Environment* and think about adaptations and accommodations supporting diverse development and learning needs.

visual impairments
Impairments ranging in diagnosis from low vision to legally blind.

low vision
Partial sight that cannot be corrected through use of corrective lenses or contacts.

legally blind
Visual acuity less than 20/200.

communication disorders
Speech, language, or hearing disorders that impair a child's abilities to communicate thoughts and ideas to others.

TEACHING AND LEARNING CONNECTIONS

Potential Teaching Strategies Supporting Children with Visual Impairments

- Use descriptive words for learning activities. For example, "The goop is in a tub by your right hand. There are little animal shapes in the goop."
- Be conscious of glaring lights and their impact on vision.
- Describe and provide tactile information about the environment. For example, "The rug is in the back corner, and all the books and CDs are on the rug."
- Order appropriate materials based on the child's individual needs, such as materials in Braille, large print, or audio recordings.
- Verbally notify child of changes in room environment or class schedule. For example, "We had to add a chair in the morning meeting area because Mrs. Tile hurt her foot. Let's go examine where it is."
- Stress to other children that guide dogs are working and not to be treated as pets.

Amy is an energetic 3-year-old whose interests include the outdoors and playing in the dramatic play area. Her speech is often difficult to understand as, similar to 8% to 9% of the early childhood population, she often stutters (Council for Exceptional Children, 2006). Her teachers are invested in hearing what Amy has to say, and they support her speech by allowing ample time for her to communicate. In addition, they have coached Amy's peers to ensure that they allow Amy the time she needs to get her thoughts across. In the same classroom, Caroline has been diagnosed as deaf. Her parents have taught Caroline the fundamentals of American Sign Language, and Caroline's teachers and classmates are eager students as well. In addition to signing to communicate, her teachers have worked to label all aspects of the classroom environment to support Caroline's visual processing of this information. Caroline is quite adept at reading lips, so the teachers make sure to communicate with her at her level and when her eyes are on them.

TEACHING AND LEARNING CONNECTIONS

Potential Teaching Strategies Supporting Children with Communication Disorders

- Develop a classroom atmosphere respectful of various modes of communication, including opportunities for signing and communicating through pictures.
- Regularly consult with a speech and language pathologist to ensure that classroom practices support the child's needs.
- Provide students with speech impairments opportunities to speak in class and model active listening.
- Give children time to express themselves, without filling in gaps or rushing them.
- Provide an interpreter when appropriate, or support self and classroom acquisition of communication strategies such as American Sign Language.

Learning Disabilities. Children diagnosed with **learning disabilities** show significant gaps between potential achievement and actual performance. That is, although they are capable of higher levels of performance, neurological impairments impede their ability to accomplish it. Learning disabilities can fall into different categories, including challenges in reading, written language, math, memory, and metacognition (referring to the ability to monitor your progress as you learn and make changes and adaptations to learning strategies). The Council for Exceptional Children (2007b) estimates that somewhere between 5% and 10% of children between the ages of 6 and 17 have some kind of learning disability. Further, 50% of all school-age children receiving special education services have a learning disability.

learning disabilities

A significant gap in children's abilities and their performance.

Reagan has the learning disability of **dysgraphia** and experiences significant challenges in communicating through the written word. When Reagan verbally describes her ideas to her second-grade teacher, they are clear and well developed. In transcribing this world to paper, however, she experiences many challenges in letter and sentence formation. To support her development, Reagan is learning how to use a voice-activated computer program, which assists translating her thoughts to paper. She also has a special computer (called a NeoPad) that guides her through word creation by creating word prompts based on both the letters she is typing and the existing thoughts she has committed to paper.

dysgraphia

Challenges in expressing thoughts through the written word.

Stephen is a third grader who has been diagnosed as having a learning disability in reading. He has significant challenges in decoding and receives additional assistance from his teachers to help him break down and process individual words. On class trips to the library, his teachers help Stephen pick books that are targeted to his reading level, and within the classroom, they have adopted the practice of reading books aloud to the children during the class reading time. This accommodates Stephen's learning needs and his social and emotional needs by allowing him to share in the same stories as his classmates.

intellectual disability

Impairments in a child's overall intelligence and adaptive behavior.

Intellectual Disabilities. **Intellectual disabilities** (what used to be referred to as "mental retardation") are limitations of overall intelligence and adaptive behavior (which include personal and social skills). An accurate diagnosis of intellectual disabilities is based on (1) an IQ score of 70 or below, (2) a determination of difficulties in adaptive behavior, and (3) origins of the disability before the age of 18 (Hourcade, 2002).

The broad category of intellectual disability includes four levels of severity that are determined by IQ scores:

- Mild, where a child's IQ ranges from 70 to 50/55
- Moderate, where a child's IQ ranges from 55/50 to 40/35
- Severe, where the IQ score ranges from 40/35 to 20/25
- Profound, where the child's IQ score is below 20/25

High-quality care and education includes opportunities for communication and collaboration.

FIGURE 5.1
The Bell Curve

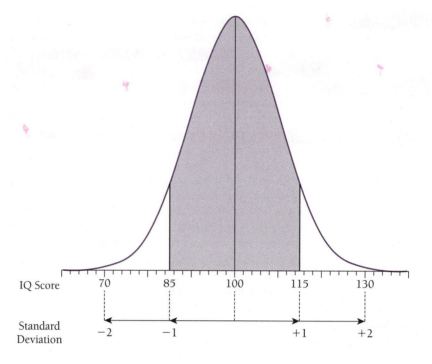

How does IQ translate into learning ability? As you learned in Chapter 2, the intelligence quotient (IQ) represents a measure of intellectual functioning with performance and verbal scales. IQ is evaluated with standardized tests. The statistical average for IQ is 100, and it is assumed that most of the population will score close to this mean. The bell curve looks at how far individual scores deviate from the mean and standard deviation. In this case, a child with an IQ of 70 falls two standard deviations below the mean, meaning that his or her score is higher than about 32% of the population, but lower than approximately 68% of the population (see Figure 5.1).

The label of intellectual disability provides information on a child's intellectual functioning as compared to the rest of the population. There are, however, many different types of intelligence. Howard Gardner's theory of multiple intelligence, presented in detail in Chapter 12, advocates using multiple ways to define, process, and enhance children's intellectual functioning. Although it is interesting to know that IQ is correlated with academic performance, it is also important to remember that children can contribute to society in many ways beyond performance in school.

Katie is a 3-year-old in an inclusive preschool classroom environment and has been diagnosed with a moderate intellectual disability. During songs at circle time, Katie's voice always rings out, and her daily play-dough creations are the source of great pleasure to her, her family, and her teachers. Many of Katie's peers are capable of identifying colors and are beginning to identify letters of the alphabet. Although Katie shows limited interest in these activities, she interacts with colors and letters mainly through her art and has not begun to formally identify different colors. The room has labels throughout to assist the children in self-regulation skills, and the teachers have ensured that pictures and words are on these labels to support the class's burgeoning literacy skills as well as Katie's need for concrete information. As her teachers embrace Gardner's theory of multiple intelligences, they work with Katie to develop some of her passions, including singing and dancing.

TEACHING AND LEARNING CONNECTIONS

Potential Teaching Strategies Supporting Children with Learning Disabilities, Intellectual Disabilities, or Giftedness

- Create an atmosphere supportive of multiple intelligences.
- Support varied contributions of each child, and create a classroom community that values varied contributions.
- Encourage participation in classroom activities based on individual strengths.
- Support positive peer relationships within the classroom environment, paying close attention to individual and classroom community social-emotional needs.

Gifts and Talents. Like intellectual disabilities, **giftedness** is measured according to how a child's abilities differ from those of the general population. Children who are gifted score one or more standard deviations above the mean. Children can demonstrate giftedness in a variety of different areas, including general academic ability, a specific academic aptitude or talent, overall creative and productive thinking skills, and leadership abilities (Clark, 2008). Although the national trend is toward cutting gifted services, children who are gifted do benefit, just like all children, from educational services that are tailored to meet their individual needs.

Will is a gifted third grader, whose IQ scores place him in the 99th percentile in terms of intellectual ability. Will has an amazing capacity for processing numbers and words, and he has responded well to the inclusion of various foreign languages in his educational environment. Although many of his peers are working on the fundamentals of multiplication, Will is working toward mastery of basic calculus. Will's teachers work to support his interests and aptitudes and include activities in their individualized curriculum that are tailored to his needs.

Physical Disabilities. **Physical disabilities** are a broad range of impairments that include orthopedic, neuromuscular, cardiovascular, and pulmonary disorders. Physical disabilities can also include such diagnoses as cerebral palsy, spina bifida, amputations or limb absences, and muscular dystrophy. Physical disabilities have many different causes and present varied challenges in terms of access. For example, children with physical disabilities may encounter challenges to gaining access to activities in the classroom or engaging in play with peers, toys, and materials.

Taylor is a 1-year-old whose cerebral palsy has limited the use of her arms. One of the goals her parents and teachers have for her is to work the arm muscles to support increased movement. Toward this goal, Taylor's teachers have placed several objects that are of great interest to Taylor in the environment, including water with various funnels, cups, and spoons in the sand and water table, and small colored balls in the block area. Taylor loves to explore in both of these areas, and the work out her fingers and wrists get in playing with the balls and by scooping and pouring at the sand and water table greatly enhance her overall dexterity. One accommodation the teachers made to support her developing skills involves the materials in the environment. They have added large-handled pitchers and spoons with handles that are easy for Taylor to grasp.

giftedness
Significant difference in ability in academics, aptitudes or talents, creative and productive thinking skills, and leadership abilities.

physical disabilities
Impairments that include orthopedic, neuromuscular, cardiovascular, and pulmonary disorders.

TEACHING AND LEARNING CONNECTIONS

Potential Teaching Strategies Supporting Children with Physical Disabilities

- Ensure access to the early childhood environment.
- Value the contributions of each child.
- Provide activities that support social inclusion, where children are able to participate in ways that highlight their abilities.

---

sensory processing disorders

Difficulties processing information in the environment, including touch, sound, and movement.

Sensory Processing Disorders. **Sensory processing disorders** are complex disorders of the brain, causing children difficulties in interpreting sensory information gathered from their surroundings through touch, hearing, and moving about (Sensory Processing Disorder Network, 2006).

Sensory processing disorders manifest themselves in many ways, including sensory modulation, sensory discrimination, and sensory-based motor disorder. The term *sensory modulation disorders* describes characteristics of children who are either overly sensitive to environmental stimuli or fail to notice sensory information that is perceptible to most others. *Sensory discrimination disorders* refer to impairments in the ability to process and make sense of common sensations in the environment. Children with this disorder are able to take in information accurately with their five senses, but they respond to this information atypically. Finally, *sensory-based motor disorder* translates into difficulties sequencing motor tasks, and as a result, the child appears clumsy.

Kadin is a 6-year-old who has been diagnosed with a sensory modulation disorder. Every time he gets new clothes, his mother cuts out all the tags, as the feel of the tags on the back of his neck is very annoying to him. In his kindergarten classroom, the teachers are responsive to his sensitivities regarding textures, and they encourage him to experiment with various textures and respect his choices not to participate. To assist him in processing the various inputs from the environment, the teachers use low lighting and keep background noise (such as loud or complex music) to a minimum.

TEACHING AND LEARNING CONNECTIONS

Potential Teaching Strategies Supporting Children with Sensory Processing Disorders

- Pay close attention to the child's interactions with the environment, noting sensory stimuli that overwhelm the child.
- Make appropriate adjustments and accommodations based on observations of the child's reactions to sensory stimuli.
- Respect individual needs regarding environmental interactions and preferences.
- Develop sensory diet and stimulation appropriate to the child's needs.

Health Impairments. **Health impairments** include a variety of health issues that require the need for special health or educational services (Venn, 1989). These affect about 1.2% of children receiving special education services. A health impairment may be a convulsive disorder, cystic fibrosis, heart disease, sickle cell disease, hemophilia, asthma, rheumatic fever, cancer, AIDS, or any other chronic or acute health problem that limits strength, vitality, or alertness (Venn, 1989). Health impairments can adversely affect the student's educational development.

Children have varied sensory preferences.

> Casey has cystic fibrosis and needs to receive medication daily at lunch. Her teachers ensure that her medication is delivered in an appropriate and timely manner. She often misses school, and her preschool teachers will send materials home with cards from the other children to ensure that Casey is aware that her role as a vibrant part of the classroom community. When Casey misses school for an extended time, her teachers work to coordinate her educational needs with her home environment.

Children's Mental Health Needs. How children view themselves and how they feel others view them is an expression of their mental health. Positive mental health is important to having positive relationships with others, coping with stress, and experiencing a full range of emotions associated with life's challenges.

One in five children, or as many as 6 million, are affected by **mental health disorders**, which are significant psychological syndromes that have an impact on daily living (U.S. Department of Health and Human Services, 1999). The causes of mental health issues are varied and complex, and are thought to develop based on both heredity and factors within the environment. Biological causes can include genetics, chemical imbalances in the body, or damage to the central nervous system. Environmental factors can include exposure to environmental toxins, including high levels of lead. Furthermore, exposure to violence contributes to poor mental health. Exposure can include either witnessing or

health impairments
Health issues that require special health or educational services.

mental health disorders
Broad range of issues that affect children's conception of themselves and their interactions with others. Can include depression, anxiety, conduct disorders, and eating disorders.

TEACHING AND LEARNING CONNECTIONS

Potential Teaching Strategies Supporting Children with Health Impairments

- Familiarize yourself with the child's health needs and make appropriate accommodations.

- Ensure that communication supports child's active involvement in classroom activities, even when a health impairment precludes the child from attendance.

- Build supportive classroom communities that respect the child's individual needs. For example, if children need to take medicine, have feeding tubes, or receive nebulizer treatments, model attitudes and provide appropriate information (while respecting privacy) that cultivates acceptance.

being a victim of abuse, or living in an area where violence is a regular part of the child's world. Chronic exposure to stress caused by living in poverty, experiencing serious hardship, and/or losing significant persons in the child's life through death, divorce, or broken relationships are also considered risk factors (U.S. Department of Health and Human Services, 1999).

Mental health issues include such things as depression, anxiety, conduct disorders, and eating disorders. Treatment of mental health issues is contingent on appropriate identification. The National Mental Health Information Center (2003) recommends that families and professionals watch vigilantly for signs that a child is troubled by his or her feelings, including persistent feelings of sadness and hopelessness; excessive, recurrent anger; expressions of worthlessness, guilt, or anxiety; extreme fear; expressions of feeling that his or her mind is out of control; and concerns about physical appearance or physical problems. In addition, families and professionals must look for *major differences in the child's interactions with others* through such things as poor concentration, an inability to focus attention, worries about being harmed or harming others, and/or the need to repeat actions to relieve anxiety.

Sean is a 6-year-old boy who started the year in his first-grade class filled with great anticipation and exuberance for all that the school year would offer. After the third week of school, his teacher noticed that Sean would frequently leave an activity he was engaged in and go into the bathroom to wash his hands. At the end of the day, when it was time to pack up his backpack, Sean would continuously check to make sure that what he had placed in the pack was still there. At recess, Sean would often ask to go inside the classroom to see that his pencils were where he had left them in his desk.

After consulting with Sean's mother and finding that similar behaviors were occurring within the home environment, Sean's teacher referred him to a mental health professional, where consultation led to treatment for obsessive-compulsive disorder. Sean's teacher developed a variety of strategies designed to assuage his anxieties with both patience and reassurance. She allowed him to perform and check and recheck, and encouraged him to write down his findings. For example, when he came in at

---

TEACHING AND LEARNING CONNECTIONS

Potential Teaching Strategies Supporting Children with Mental Health Challenges

- Learn about and respect the child's individual needs. For example, find out from a family member what comforts the child.

- Create a supportive classroom atmosphere, paying attention to potential "triggers" for challenges and working to alleviate these.

- Support the varied contributions of each child. For example, observe the children and make sure to acknowledge their efforts and accomplishments.

- Encourage participation in classroom activities based on individual strengths. For example, if a child prefers to communicate through pictures, make sure there are plenty of writing materials available.

- Create many opportunities for success, and work to support positive internal models of esteem and competence. For example, create a classroom community that values and respects each child's individual contributions.

recess to locate his pencils, he would write a note to himself indicating that the pencils were in the correct spot and then take the note outside with him. In this way, his teacher provided support for his anxieties, and tried to help him develop coping mechanisms to both relieve them and allow him to engage in meaningful play with his peers.

Knowledge of exceptionalities, in isolation, means very little. Rather, it is the merger between knowledge and practice that supports the development and learning of individual children.

Applying Your Knowledge of Exceptionalities to Practice

Knowledge of exceptionalities can be thought of broadly, in terms of general categories, or specifically, when this knowledge is applied to the individual child. General categories relating to developmental differences are often communicated through labels. Labels are diagnostic names used to describe certain characteristics, such as a child with autism, obsessive-compulsive disorder, or a mild intellectual disability, but labeling is both a complex and a controversial practice. Those in the field of special education have long debated the practice. Labels can be used to support access to services—such as a child with an intellectual disability qualifying for speech, physical, and occupational therapies; reimbursements for treatments through Medicaid; or participation in the Special Olympics. They may also provide important information about what families can expect or need to watch for. However, labels can have a negative impact if they are used to determine a child's ability and potential: children may be likely to live up (or down) to the expectations perceived.

Labels also can cause professionals to focus on broad categories, ignoring the fact that children they lump into one group are actually very different from one another (Greenspan, 2007). Greenspan cautions that using labels creates the danger of losing the uniqueness of each child and fails to account for variance in development and behavior.

How can labels be beneficial? Labels are not inherently problematic; rather, it is inappropriate usage that raises issues. Labels can provide general information about the challenges a child may have. For example, a child with low tone might need trunk support to assist in sitting at the table, or a child with a weak gag reflex might require extra vigilance when eating foods of a certain texture. It is knowledge of the individual child that will guide your practice. This knowledge, coupled with evidence-based practice, can ensure the provision of high-quality, inclusive programming.

Labels
Term applied to describe a particular set of characteristics.

Medicaid
Federal-state health care program for persons who are low income, including children who have disabilities.

TEACHING AND LEARNING CONNECTIONS

Potential Use of Labels

- Can be used to research and gain knowledge of specific challenges children are having in the classroom environment.
- Can support brainstorming about an individual child's potential needs.
- Can provide common, shared terminology with other professionals.

CAUTION: Labels can never replace knowledge of each individual child.

Evidence-based practice is an important component of the knowledge needed to support the development and learning of *all* children. Evidence-based practice is defined as "a decision-making process that integrates the best available research evidence with family and professional wisdom and values" (Buysse & Wesley, 2006, p.66).

Evidence-based practice originated in medicine and consists of a five-step evidence-based, decision-making process (Buysse & Wesley, 2006):

evidence-based practice

Process through which research and effective practices are evaluated and applied to support children's development and learning.

1. Pose the question. For example, "What are this child's specific needs?"
2. Find the best available evidence. "What research and practice recommendations can inform how I meet this child's specific needs?"
3. Appraise the evidence quality and relevance. "Are the research and practice recommendations I have gathered reflective of current knowledge in the field?" "Are these recommendations likely to benefit this child?"
4. Integrate research with values and wisdom. "How can I apply what I have learned in a way that respects my own and the child's family's ways of supporting the child's development and learning?"
5. Evaluate. "How effective were steps 1–4?"

• • • BECOMING A PROFESSIONAL • • •

Effective Collaboration

An important skill within the early childhood professional role is effectively collaborating with other professionals. Collaboration can take many forms, such as the following (Weasmer & Woods, 1998):

- Sharing teaching and learning strategies
- Exploring additional avenues for support and information exchange
- Exchanging ideas with the goal of developing a shared sense of purpose
- Obtaining feedback that leads to increased professionalism

The following are components of effective collaboration at the individual level (Kruse, Louis, & Bryk, 1994):

- Openness to improvement
- Trust and respect of colleagues
- Investment in exploring alternative knowledge and skills
- Development of personal practices based on individual situations
- Opportunities and investment in meeting and discussing new ideas
- Shared norms and values

Collaboration between professionals begins with providing collegial support. This support can be both interpersonal and professional. Professionals develop relationships with the people they work with and guide one another through challenging situations that might arise within the workplace (Horn & Jones, 2004). Designing effective collaborations targeted toward improving your own teaching and learning begins with trying to identify colleagues with similar goals and values with whom you would feel comfortable sharing vulnerabilities and challenges. From that point, you can commit to an open exploration of your own teaching, with the ultimate goal of your own continued professional development.

Evidence-based practice requires specific knowledge of each child's strengths and challenges and general knowledge of development and exceptionalities. From that point, teachers can look to research evidence to evaluate the effectiveness of various practices. It is important to note that evidence-based practices do not negate professional and family wisdom and values, but rather work to integrate wisdom, values, and research with the goal of making good decisions that benefit young children (Buysse & Wesley, 2006).

Understanding children's unique needs, therefore, is an essential component of evidence-based practices. In addition to diversity in ability, it is also important to have knowledge of cultural and linguistic diversity.

SUPPORTING CULTURAL AND LINGUISTIC DIVERSITY

One of the most dramatic changes in the demographics of the field is the cultural and linguistic diversity that teachers are likely to encounter in classroom communities. This change is based on the rich diversity reflected in the United States. Diversity might be visible or invisible to the eye and can include (but is not limited to) such things as language, child-rearing beliefs of family members, family composition and roles within the family, and beliefs and values regarding actions and interactions with the larger world. Young children come to early childhood education environments with unique ways of knowing, processing, and interacting with their world. Language and culture represent just two areas of uniqueness.

Imagine that you are beginning a new job. This job has a new set of responsibilities, people to meet and develop relationships with, and roles to enact. Your successful transition might rely on many things. This can include your ability to communicate, to create and respond to shared meanings, and to use others as guides in this process. On your first day in this new job, you realize that many of these skills are not likely to assist you in your transition. Your coworkers have patterns of communication that you cannot quite decipher. In addition, they meet your bids for assistance with barely decipherable comments that you need to "figure it out." You become an observer within the environment, trying to break the codes of communication and interaction. At the same time, you try to function successfully.

Now imagine you are a child in a similar situation, where you are transitioning into an early childhood classroom. Historically, **immersion strategies** have been common. Through immersion strategies, teachers expect children to learn language and appropriate interactions by merely being in the environment where the language being learned is commonly spoken. However, professionals no longer consider immersion strategies effective practice within the field (NAEYC, 1995).

Supporting each child within early childhood education requires knowledge and skills related to understanding the diverse needs of children and families and dispositions supportive of creating welcoming, nurturing, and respectful classroom communities in which all children can thrive.

immersion strategies
Expectation that children will acquire a second language through exposure alone.

Children of Immigrant Populations

The United States has a long history of immigration. Despite the numbers of immigrants to the United States, the educational system has historically ignored the needs of immigrant children (Future of Children, 1995). This is despite the fact that children of immigrants make up one-fifth of the children in the United States (Suarez-Orozco &

Suarez-Orozco, 2002) and that the number of children in immigrant families grew by 63% between 1990 and 2000 (National Conference of State Legislatures, 2002). Coupled with this lack of attention is a bias toward immigrant populations and non-English speakers. Within this bias, children's differences (language differences, in particular) are viewed as handicaps as opposed to resources (NAEYC, 1996a).

culturally and linguistically diverse
Term used by the Department of Education to describe children who are non-English proficient or have limited English proficiency.

Increased rates of immigration result in large numbers of **culturally and linguistically diverse** children entering the school system (Bhavnagri, Krolikowski, & Vaswani, 2000). The U.S. Department of Education describes the enrollment of children with limited English proficiency as a state of cultural and linguistic diversity. Therefore, teachers need to have knowledge of cultural and linguistic diversity and corresponding practices. It is not just immigrant populations, but native populations, too, that have diverse cultural and linguistic needs. For example, children within the same early childhood classroom might differ in their exposure to the written and spoken word, which in turn affects their readiness for literacy learning. Families of children in that same classroom might view the role of early childhood education very differently, with some seeing the field as providing babysitting services and others recognizing the importance of high-quality programming.

Supporting Culture in Early Childhood Classrooms. We often take culture for granted, as it is so implicit in our daily worlds. The fact that we are often unaware of culture can translate into perceptions that certain behaviors are "right" or "wrong." In turn, this can have an impact on our reactions to individual situations. For example, a parent and infant–toddler professional differ in their belief regarding how one should put down a young child for a nap. The caregiver feels that rocking is appropriate, whereas the parent feels that the child should be allowed to cry until he falls asleep. These differing beliefs, should respectful communication not occur, could be a source of anxiety and conflict. Supporting access to the field and engagement within early childhood programs requires recognizing your own values and beliefs regarding children's development and learning and understanding the role of family in supporting their child's development and learning.

English language learners
Term used to describe children who are acquiring English proficiency.

dual language learners
Children who are learning a second language while developing a basic competency in their first language.

Without abandoning the emphasis on learning as much as possible about children as individuals, or the idea that labeling children broadly can be problematic, let's look at the general knowledge available to us about children who are English language learners.

Supporting English Language Learners. Children who are **English language learners** can bring a rich diversity to the classroom environment. Increasingly referred to as **dual language learners**, these children are learning a second language while still developing a basic competency in their first language (Espinsoa, 2010), and can bring a

---

TEACHING AND LEARNING CONNECTIONS

Examining Your Own Biases

- Commit to learning about your own values and beliefs through reflection and paying careful attention to your reactions to individual situations.
- Examine classroom practices and procedures for bias, including messages conveyed in the environment through books, materials, and decorations.
- Discuss biases with other professionals and commit to supportive exploration.

rich collection of languages and ways of communicating to the early childhood classroom environment. To attain a classroom of many voices within a shared community, professionals need to encourage the use of the child's home language (the primary language that is spoken within the child's home) while they foster the acquisition of English (NAEYC, 1996a). This approach is respectful of the child's skills and learning needs. Respecting the home language supports the child's developing language proficiency so that she has a firm foundation on which to build English proficiency. It is also respectful of the family, as it communicates that how they live their lives is valued. Further, respecting the home language fosters success in the larger society through supporting the development of **bilingualism**, and thereby creating a bridge between home, school, and community.

bilingualism
Ability to fluently speak two languages.

Supporting English language learning requires support for the child's development and learning needs, as well as those of the family. To fully support children's English language learning, professionals can use the following strategies for working with both children and their families:

Strategies for Working with Children
- Explicitly link concepts to students' backgrounds and experiences. For example, before and after reading, have children respond to prompts that help them relate to the main characters or main theme (Saunders & Goldenberg, 1999). With the story "The Three Little Pigs," this might include asking children about the kinds of houses they have lived in.
- Emphasize key vocabulary through intentionally selecting words children are likely to use in conversation, providing direct instruction in word meaning, and making sure there are extensive opportunities to hear and apply the new words (Beck, McKeown, & Kucan, 2002).
- Use speech appropriate for children's level of language proficiency, being sure to avoid jargon, slang terms, and run-on sentences (Richards & Lockhart, 1996).

Strategies for Working with Families (NAEYC, 1996a)
- Actively involve parents and families in the early learning program and setting.
- Encourage and assist all parents in becoming knowledgeable about the cognitive value for children of knowing more than one language, and provide them with strategies to support, maintain, and preserve home-language learning.
- Honor and support children in the cultural values and norms of the home.

Supporting English language learners requires many of the skills that are fundamental for effective teaching. Namely, professionals must work to understand and accept the breadth of diversity of each child and family in their class, and support their ongoing development.

Supporting diverse child and family populations requires critical reflection by the professional. This reflection includes examining one's own values and beliefs coupled with critically looking at how those values and beliefs translate into practice (Thorp & Sánchez, 2008). Essential sources of knowledge for professionals include recognizing that *language and culture are interdependent*. Specifically, language is the primary way that families *translate their cultural lens* and socialize children to be members of their particular cultural and linguistic community. Language is the medium through which culture is communicated. Further, professionals must recognize that *maintaining home language is often a struggle for families and communities*, as schools are not always supportive of bilingualism. Further, there is a *developmental sequence to English language acquisition*.

TEACHING AND LEARNING CONNECTIONS

Supporting Cultural and Linguistic Diversity

- Learn about your own cultural and linguistic biases, and what this may communicate to families.
- Learn about each child and his or her family via a thoughtful questionnaire, a home visit, or daily conversations.
- Integrate knowledge of individual children and their families into the physical and social early childhood environment by including pictures, materials, and toys that reflect and respect the children's world.
- Be open to learning about new ways of interacting with the environment (including communication) and new ideas.

Therefore, professionals must be aware of and use this developmental sequence to support development and create effective learning activities for individual children.

Children who are English language learners are at risk for being labeled as having a developmental delay or disability (Ladner & Hammons, 2001). This can happen when professionals lack an understanding that learning English is a long developmental process, and they mistake the process as indicative of developmental challenges. When considering these misconceptions, keep in mind that children who lose fluency in the home language lose their ability to communicate across generations.

Cultural and linguistic diversity are types of developmental diversity. Additionally, diversity is apparent in family form and function. Family diversity will be covered in depth in Chapter 6.

Diversity implies a broad range of realities. It can take many forms, including diversity in development, language, and ways of viewing, processing, and interacting with the world. In addition, the amount and kinds of stress children are exposed to on a daily basis is another kind of diversity requiring professional knowledge, skills to support, and dispositions reflecting respect.

types of stress
Stress includes positive, tolerable, and toxic levels of intensity.

positive stress
Daily stressors resulting from not being able to engage in a desired activity.

tolerable stress
Stress responses that can be overcome by warm and consistent caregiving.

toxic stress
Ongoing stress that is not buffered by adult support for extended periods.

CHILDREN, FAMILIES, AND STRESS

Although there are many historical and present-day representations of childhood as a carefree and happy time, professionals must recognize that children are exposed to stress daily. The kind of stress children experience, and how effectively they deal with stress, presents different outcomes for children.

Children experience three **types of stress** (National Scientific Council on the Developing Child, 2007). **Positive stress** is the daily stressors that result from not being able to engage in a desired activity—a child being told she can't have a second cookie, for instance, or learning how to share. The second category is **tolerable stress**, which is damaging, but through assistance and support, children can deal with it effectively. Examples of tolerable stress include the death of a loved one, a natural disaster, or a terrorist attack. The third category is **toxic stress**, which is chronic, excessive, and unmanageable. With toxic stress, child buffers, or emotional resources in the environment, are not there to help children deal with the stress. Examples of toxic stress include growing up in extreme poverty, being exposed to domestic violence or abuse, or being the victim of abuse or neglect.

ISSUES OF ACCESS AND EQUITY
Stress and Children's Brain Development

Stress might not be a term commonly associated with childhood; however, it is important to recognize that children are exposed to stress on an ongoing basis. Daily stressors can include transitioning from home to school, dealing with a brief separation from a parent, or having to end a favored activity. Some children might experience chronic stressors, such as extreme poverty or neglect, extended maternal depression, or family violence. Children's brains are equipped to cope with stress, but excess amounts of stress can have an overall negative impact on brain functioning. Early childhood educators must have an understanding of the relationship between stress and brain functioning. They can then provide support to help reduce stress.

The body reacts to periods of stress by releasing the stress hormone *cortisol*, along with adrenaline. In turn, this influences reactions to stress. Reactions might include an elevated heart rate, decreased memory and problem-solving skills, and an overall fight-or-flight response to the stressor. Learning to deal with low levels of stress is an important developmental task. However, chronic stress can disrupt the brain's architecture and create stress management systems that respond at lower thresholds. Lower stress thresholds are problematic in that they are related to physical and mental illness (Gunnar, 2000).

Social relationships play an important role in helping children regulate their levels of cortisol, and thereby control their stress reactions to different situations. In settings where children receive extensive attention, support, and guidance from their teacher, children's levels of cortisol are low; when these behaviors are lacking, cortisol levels are higher (Gunnar, 2000).

Professionals need to provide a stable, consistent, appropriate environment that minimizes children's exposure to stress. In addition, families and professionals need to remember the vital role they play as a buffer to stress: Stress is mediated through social relationships, and therefore these relationships should be valued as the core of children's ability to learn and develop.

TEACHING AND LEARNING CONNECTIONS
Understanding Types of Stress

- *Positive stress:* Stress that children experience daily. Within the context of positive stress, teachers need to support self-regulation skills.
- *Tolerable stress:* Potentially damaging stress that requires coping and assistance support. Teachers need to support self-regulation and provide ongoing social support and coping mechanisms for both the child and family.
- *Toxic stress:* Pervasive stress marked by the absence of social support factors. Requires supporting both the child and family. It is important to connect families with community resources and social support systems.

Why focus on the impact of stress on young children? Chronic exposure to stress can affect the overall functioning of the brain and place children in a perpetual state of high alert. Because cortisol affects the brain's ability to respond to and process information in the environment (see Issues of Access and Equity Feature), it has a great impact on children's development and learning. The professional who understands these things can act as a helpful buffer to both tolerable and toxic stress for the children in their care.

The Impact of Tolerable Stress

Tolerable stress includes stress responses that could have an impact on overall brain development, but in the face of warm and consistent caregiving, can be overcome (Shonkoff & Richmond, 2007). Tolerable stress generally appears for a limited time, which serves to provide the brain with the opportunity to recover. Examples of tolerable stress include divorce, the death of a parent, disaster, and growing up in a time of war.

Divorce. The impact of divorce on children is varied and complex. Much of the psychological literature has focused on the child's age and gender as predictive of child adjustment to divorce. Teachers, however, need to look at factors in the child's immediate world to understand the impact of divorce on children (Hughes, 2005). This approach complements the definition of tolerable stress, pointing to factors within the environment that affect children's ease of adjustment both during and after the divorce.

Hughes (2005) cautions that, when looking at divorce, researchers and practitioners must look at the diversity in outcomes for children. Specifically, although children with divorced parents are about twice as likely to experience problems when compared with children in nondivorced families, most children (75% to 80%) do not experience difficulties (Hughes, 2005). The ill effects children are more likely to demonstrate include:

- Academic difficulties
- Problems with aggressiveness
- Low self-esteem
- Depression
- Relationship difficulties
- Engagement in delinquent activities
- Early sexual activity
- Experimentation with illegal drugs in adolescence

Practitioners should consider risk factors that may contribute to a child's adjustment (Hughes, 2005). *Parental loss* is a risk factor created by children lacking continued contact with one of their parents. *Economic loss* is another risk factor, as children in single-parent families are more likely to experience the stress of a change in economic resources. *Changes in the child's living situation* can create more life stress, which is magnified by *poor parental adjustment*. Other risk factors include a *lack of parental competence* and *exposure to conflict between parents*.

The impact of divorce on children is as diverse and individualized as their family situation, resources, and presence of support in their lives. Similarly, the impact of parental death on children is also diverse.

Parental Death. Parental death can represent tolerable stress, depending on the effectiveness of the child's support system in serving as a buffer. Popular psychological literature proposes that persons go through three main stages in dealing with death. These stages apply to children in the following ways (Rice, 1996):

- **Shock:** During this stage, children experience shock and grief, and they have a difficult time dealing with the fact that their parent has died.

- **Great disturbance**: In this stage, children might show signs of loss of sleep, anxiety, upset stomach, depression, and loss of appetite.
- **Gradual reawakening:** During this stage, children are able to readjust their lives and continue without the parent they lost.

The ability to understand and cope with death varies by age (Fitzgerald, 1992). Infants and toddlers sense a loss, and many demonstrate changes in their overall eating and sleeping habits. Between the ages of 2 and 6, children generally lack a concept of time and the permanence of death. Often children in this age group use magical thinking. The child might think, for example, that the dead person continues to engage in daily activities and that this person might come back to life. Children between the ages of 6 and 9 have a general understanding of death. However, they often fear that death is contagious and, therefore, is likely to affect them or other people in their lives. In addition, children during this stage are likely to become preoccupied with death, its causes, and what happens following death.

Disaster. Another example of tolerable stress is a childhood experience with disaster. Disaster comes in many forms, from weather issues to automobile deaths, drowning, or the loss of family members to violence. Because they are both unexpected and often large in magnitude, disasters precipitate a wide variation of reactions in both children and adults. Common reactions often include a *loss of control due to the magnitude of events*. In addition, a loss of stability can serve to *destroy trust and internal equilibrium*. Children might also have *self-centered reactions* where they fear what will happen to them and for their own safety (Waddell & Thomas, 1992).

Responding to children after a disaster includes many of the principles in helping children deal with the loss of a parent through death or divorce. Teachers can assist children in coping with disasters by giving them reassuring personal contact. In addition, teachers can provide children with factual information and current plans for safety, including a disaster plan. They can also encourage children to talk about their feelings and focus on reestablishing routines. It is important to understand that children will have a wide range of ongoing reactions (Federal Emergency Management Agency, 2006).

TEACHING AND LEARNING CONNECTIONS

Helping Children Cope with Death

- Use precise words, such as *dead* and *death,* as opposed to using clichés, such as *gone to sleep*.
- Reassure children when talking to them about death, particularly regarding that fact that they will still be cared for.
- Respond to children's questions and requests for information factually and simply, responding to their need to acquire more information over time.
- Allow children to participate in the grieving process.
- Allow children to explore their emotions physically through clay or artistic expressions.
- Respond to the child's continuing and changing need for knowledge and information (Edinberg, 2000).

One of the most salient characteristics of disasters is their unpredictability. By acknowledging the potential for disaster and educating themselves accordingly, teachers can avoid or reduce some of the negative effects of disasters on children.

Growing Up in a Time of War. The 21st century has brought a time of insecurity and international conflict to the United States. For the first time since Pearl Harbor, America was attacked on its own soil on September 11, 2001. The resulting political and international fallout affects children in both direct and indirect ways.

The death of a parent or prolonged separation is an outcome for many children post-September 11, due either to loss of life during the terrorist attacks or to loss of life or prolonged separation from the wars in Afghanistan and Iraq. Young children are unlikely to grasp politics. However, news, information, and some visual imagery of the war can provide an honest and useful context to their developing understanding.

Much of the information presented on dealing with tolerable stress can be applied to children's coping with the impact of September 11 and the aftermath. Note, however, that for children in war-torn Afghanistan and Iraq, or refugees from other countries experiencing violence or hunger, the level of stress is much more marked. The daily reality of the war permeates every aspect of their lives. For these children, therefore, stress would most likely be toxic.

Helping children cope with stress from war requires addressing children's questions as they arise, making sure to follow routines, using accurate and concrete words, and providing children with reassurance and comfort. War and terrorism have unique aspects that merit professional attention (Myers-Walls, 2003):

- War is a new topic for many adults. Most parents do not discuss war with their children. In fact, almost 25% of parents reported they had not spoken with their children about war. Over 40% of children reported not having such a conversation with their parents.
- Naturally, perceptions of the wars in Iraq and Afghanistan and their handling contribute to a hot cultural topic. Adults often present political views and opinions with vehemence. Parents may demonstrate support for or against the war, or offer strong opinions of the current administration. But professionals must present a temperate view, addressing children's questions with respect and leaving politics aside. Professionals should also provide a temperate view for other issues raised by war between countries, such as religious and ethnic differences. Using the basic idea of respect for all persons is a good place for a professional to start.

Professionals can take many actions supporting children in times of war (NAEYC, 2003), such as limiting exposure to media coverage of the war. In addition, professionals can offer children reassurance through physical closeness. Many children might be interested in talking about the war, and professionals should respond to these interests in a calm, reassuring manner. Professionals can model peaceful resolutions to conflict by problem solving through discussion and through negotiation and compromise. Children need opportunities to release tension, which teachers can provide through allowing for dramatic play, exploration of artistic mediums, and physical activity (Myers-Walls, 2003). Professionals must also watch for changes in children's behavior, including a loss of appetite, trouble concentrating, and the appearance of regressive behaviors. In addition, professionals must make sure they are taking care of themselves—including coping effectively, getting enough rest, and eating and exercising well.

The Impact of Toxic Stress

Maslow's hierarchy of needs provides a useful template for understanding the impact of toxic stress on young children's development. Within the hierarchy, needs are represented as developing in a pyramid structure. Physiological needs such as food, water, and shelter represent the base, and psychological needs such as self-actualization represent the pinnacle. Factors that create toxic stress, where ongoing stress is coupled with a lack of adult buffering for extended periods, are likely to affect needs at the base of the shelter. Put simply, unsupportive environments tend to create toxic stress.

A basic assertion of Maslow's framework is that if foundational needs are not met, children do not proceed to its higher levels, establishing love and belonging, self-esteem and self-competence, and self-actualization. The toxic stress created by homelessness and chronic poverty might affect base-level physiological needs. The toxic stress caused by abuse and neglect might affect safety and security. Figure 5.2 illustrates where these toxic stresses fall on Maslow's hierarchy of needs pyramid.

Stress is a daily part of children's lives.

Homelessness. Each year over 1.5 million or one out of 50, children are homeless, and half of these children are under the age of 6 (National Center on Family Homelessness, 2009) The impact of homelessness on children begins before their birth. Parents who are homeless experience many obstacles to healthy pregnancy, including a lack of prenatal care and chronic health problems (Hart-Shegos, 1999). Infants who are born homeless have a higher rate of premature birth and are at a greater risk of death (Hart-Shegos, 1999). Families who are homeless in general have less access to health care, so these children are more likely to lack essential immunizations.

By 18 months of age, children who are homeless often display significant developmental delays. These, in turn, affect both their learning and behavior. As preschoolers, children who are homeless are more likely to be separated from their parents, causing

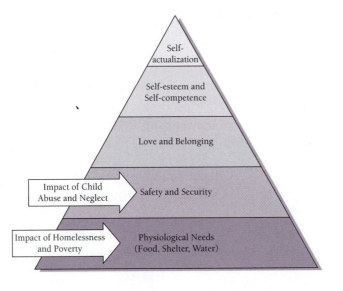

FIGURE 5.2
Impact of Toxic stress on the Developing child

attachment and behavioral issues. Due to a lack of access to preventative health care and immunizations, children who are homeless have very high rates of acute illness, including twice as many ear infections, five times more diarrhea and stomach problems, and four times the rate of asthma as children who are not homeless. The impact on children's mental health is also daunting, with 74% of children who are homeless worrying that they will have no place to live, 58% worried they will have no place to sleep, and 87% worried that something bad will happen to their family (National Center on Family Homelessness, 2009). Not surprisingly, children who are homeless between the ages of 6 and 17 struggle with significantly higher rates of mental health problems when compared to their peers who are not homeless. Despite this, less than one-third are receiving mental health treatment (National Center on Family Homelessness, 2009).

McKinney-Vento Homeless Assistance Act

Passed in 1987, the act provides federal funds for shelter programs and related services to populations who are homeless.

Women, Infants, and Children

The mission of this government program is to provide support to women with low income and children under 5 who are at nutritional risk.

extreme poverty

Families who earn less than one-half the federal poverty level.

Early intervention and education services are a right provided to children who are homeless through IDEA's 2004 requirement that states comply with the 1987 **McKinney-Vento Homeless Assistance Act**. Amendments to this Act in 2001 mandated that schools and school districts provide equal access to educational services and do their best to remove any barriers to the educational success of students who are homeless (Myers & Popp, 2003). Successful education of children who are homeless requires an ecological systems approach that focuses on providing consistent, high-quality care that addresses children's social, emotional, and learning needs. Services need to focus on providing family education and family support. Families and children also must have access to needed community resources. These can include connections to housing programs, **Women, Infants, and Children** (WIC), job placement services, and screening and early intervention programs (Myers & Popp, 2003; National Center on Family Homelessness, 2009).

Poverty. Since 2000, poverty rates in the United States have escalated dramatically (12.4%). Nearly 13 million children in the United States are considered poor (Children's Defense Fund, 2004). Of those, one in three are considered *extremely poor*. The term **extreme poverty** applies to those families who get by on less than one-half the poverty level; or less than $7,412 per year for a family of four (Children's Defense Fund, 2004).

TEACHING AND LEARNING CONNECTIONS

Examining Classroom Practices and Potential Biases

Many of the practices commonly used in early childhood education may actually serve to alienate some populations based on access to monetary resources or disregard for present living situations. The following practices may merit examination within your classroom environment:

Potentially Biased Practices

- Show and tell, which often focuses on possessions and turns into competition
- Discussions of living arrangements, which can serve to highlight differences
- Practices such as dressing in costume on Halloween, which can potentially highlight differences in access to resources

Alternatives

- Showing and telling about a favorite toy in the classroom
- Focusing on the wide variety of living arrangements available within the community
- Using dress-up materials within the classroom

Note: Halloween can also be a culturally exclusionary practice; it is important to consider alternative events.

The impact of poverty on development is pervasive and severe. Children who are impoverished are less likely to be healthy, and poor health affects learning and development. The resulting achievement gap begins early. Children who have grown up in poverty are likely to be 18 months behind developmentally (Knitzer, 2007). This gap in development is still present at the age of 10.

Early childhood education can make a difference in the lives of children from families who are impoverished. High-quality educational experiences predict positive outcomes. Research demonstrates, for example, that the odds of completing high school rose from 39% to 53% for children who were exposed to high-quality preschool experiences (Knitzer, 2007).

Children who are impoverished tend to enter school significantly behind their peers who are nonimpoverished (Klein & Knitzer, 2007). Effective strategies supporting these children's readiness skills require knowledge of early literacy and math skills. Teachers can cultivate these skills by giving children regular exposure to storytelling, book reading, pretend play, work with manipulatives, and opportunities to explore and experiment with objects in the environment. Teachers must be knowledgeable regarding how children grow and develop and how to support growth and development over time. Providing healthy snacks and meals and participating in the USDA's **School Breakfast Program** can ensure that children's nutritional needs are met. Teachers must also learn about the *cultural traditions and practices* of children who are from immigrant families or who have limited English proficiency (Klein & Knitzer, 2007). Cultural traditions and practices might include the important holidays, daily customs, and how they celebrate important family events.

The impact of poverty on young children's development represents a toxic stress that affects the first two levels of Maslow's hierarchy. Children who are impoverished, for example, are more likely to suffer from homelessness and its consequences. Even among children who are not homeless, poverty can be an obstacle to their physiological needs and their safety and security. Children who are impoverished are more likely to grow up in unstable neighborhoods and suffer a greater exposure to crime.

Supporting positive outcomes for children who are homeless and impoverished includes m*aking sure that all young children from families with low income enter school with the skills that they need to learn*, regardless of the setting they are in or the work status of their parents. Further, *investing in infants, toddlers, and their families through expansion of Early Head Start services is essential. Policies must be developed that strengthen parenting and include attention to low education, poor work histories, substance abuse, and domestic violence* (Knitzer, 2007).

Homelessness and poverty are each examples of toxic stress that can have an impact on a family system and, consequently, child development. Families under stress are more likely to adopt poor coping mechanisms, which can include abuse and neglect (Nunez, 1996).

Abuse and Neglect. Abuse and neglect take many forms. Even children who do not suffer direct abuse may suffer its effects indirectly when there is violence among significant people in their lives. As abuse and neglect are most likely to occur in the home, and parents are highly unlikely to report abusive and neglectful behaviors themselves, social service agencies must rely on indirect means of identification, such as referrals made by pediatricians, emergency room doctors, and teachers (Perry, Conrad, Dobson, Schick, & Runyan, 2000).

Costs associated with failing to support children affected by abuse and neglect are dramatic. These include economic costs associated with identifying, educating, protecting, healing, and sustaining these children (Perry, Pollard, Blakely, Baker, & Vigilante,

School Breakfast Program
Government program providing cash assistance to states to operate nonprofit breakfast programs.

1995). Professionals play a key role in ensuring that children and families receive the support they need, and the importance of this role must be recognized and embraced. In 2004, 1% to 2% of children were victims of child abuse or neglect (Child Welfare Information Gateway, 2006). Of these victims, 60% experienced neglect, 18% were physically abused, 10% were sexually abused, and 7% were emotionally maltreated. The remaining 5% of cases fit into other state-defined categories (Child Welfare Information Gateway, 2006). Each state government determines what constitutes child abuse and neglect. Despite this, the federal government does provide guidelines. According to the **Federal Child Abuse Prevention and Treatment Act**, child abuse and neglect is defined, at a minimum, as:

- A recent act or failure to act by a parent or caregiver that results in death, serious physical or emotional harm, sexual abuse or exploitation; or
- An act or failure to act which presents an imminent risk of harm.

The broad category of child abuse and neglect includes several subcategories. Early childhood professionals spend so much time with young children that familiarity with these categories of abuse and neglect (and their signs) is vitally important. In fact, all 50 States, the District of Columbia, the Commonwealth of Puerto Rico, and the U.S. territories of American Samoa, Guam, the Northern Mariana Islands, and the Virgin Islands have statutes requiring child care providers to be **mandated reporters** (Child Welfare Information Gateway, 2006). Persons must issue a report if they suspect or have reason to believe that a child has been abused or neglected. Teachers, principals, center directors, aides, and so on are responsible for reporting informed suspicion and turning the investigation over to the responsible parties. Table 5.2 provides a summary of the types of abuse and neglect and their related signs.

Federal Child Abuse Prevention and Treatment Act

Public Law 93-247, which provides federal monies to the states to support prevention, assessment, investigation, prosecution, and treatment activities.

mandated reporters

Professionals who must issue a report should child abuse or neglect be suspected.

TABLE 5.2   Categories of Child Abuse/Neglect and Their Related Signs and Symptoms

Category of Child Abuse/ Neglect	Description	Related Child Signs and Symptoms	Related Parent Signs and Symptoms
Neglect	The failure to provide for a child's basic needs	Begs or steals food or money. States that no one is at home to provide care.	Appears to be indifferent to the child. Seems apathetic or depressed. Behaves irrationally or in a bizarre manner. Is abusing alcohol or other drugs.
• Physical	Failure to meet child's needs for food, shelter, or supervision	Is consistently dirty and has severe body odor. Lacks sufficient clothing for the weather.	
• Medical	Failure to provide necessary health treatments	Lacks needed medical or dental care, immunizations, or glasses.	
• Educational	Failure to educate a child or attend to his/her needs for specialized services or education	Is frequently absent from school.	
• Emotional	Failure to attend to a child's emotional needs or the failure to provide physical care	Uses self-deprecating comments or reports that others use derogatory comments.	

Category of Child Abuse/ Neglect	Description	Related Child Signs and Symptoms	Related Parent Signs and Symptoms
Physical abuse	Intended or unintended harm to a child in the form of punching, hitting, throwing, kicking, or otherwise causing the child direct bodily harm	Has unexplained burns, bites, bruises, broken bones, or black eyes. Has fading bruises or other marks noticeable after an absence from school. Seems frightened of the parents and protests or cries when it is time to go home. Shrinks at the approach of adults. Reports injury by a parent or another adult caregiver.	Shows little concern for the child. Denies the existence of—or blames the child for—the child's problems in school or at home. Asks teachers or other caretakers to use harsh physical discipline if the child misbehaves. Sees the child as entirely bad, worthless, or burdensome. Demands a level of physical or academic performance the child cannot achieve.
Sexual abuse	Exposure to or coercion to perform various sex acts	Has difficulty walking or sitting. Suddenly refuses to change for gym or to participate in physical activities. Reports nightmares or bed-wetting. Experiences a sudden change in appetite. Demonstrates bizarre, sophisticated, or unusual sexual knowledge or behavior. Becomes pregnant or contracts a venereal disease, particularly if under age 14. Runs away. Reports sexual abuse by a parent or another adult caregiver.	Is unduly protective of the child or severely limits the child's contact with other children, especially of the opposite sex. Is secretive and isolated. Is jealous or controlling with family members.
Emotional abuse	Adopting patterns of behavior that impair a child's overall sense of self-worth or emotional development	Shows extremes in behavior, such as overly compliant or demanding behavior, extreme passivity, or aggression. Is either inappropriately adult (parenting other children, for example) or inappropriately infantile (frequently rocking or head-banging, for example). Is delayed in physical or emotional development. Has attempted suicide. Reports a lack of attachment to the parent.	Constantly blames, belittles, or berates the child. Is unconcerned about the child and refuses to consider offers of help for the child's problems. Overtly rejects the child.

myeducationlab

Go to
MyEducationLab and
select the topic
"Diverse Learners."
Under Building
Teaching Skills and
Dispositions, complete
the exercise
*Addressing the Needs
of Culturally and
Linguistically Diverse
Learners.*

Conversely, children in low-quality care situations experience elevated levels of cortisol during the day (National Scientific Council on the Developing Child, 2005).

This information provides concrete evidence of the relationship between brain development and stress. It also reemphasizes the role professionals play in supporting children's present and future development.

MOVING FORWARD

Learning about diversity is little more than learning about children and the unique qualities and characteristics that make them who they are. Diversity in the field must not be viewed as an exception, but rather as the rule that applies to each of us, whether our diverse characteristics are tangible or intangible, visible or invisible. The terms *inclusion* and *flexibility* mean that a great, expansive net is cast in defining the parameters of whom the field serves and what kinds of services it provides. This net encompasses the needs of each child and family. Succeeding within your chosen role depends on your commitment and acceptance of diversity and your willingness to embrace that which makes us each unique.

CASE STUDY

Comprehensive Approach to Supporting Diversity

The Child Development Lab and Learning Center (6 weeks to 6 years)

On any given day, the walls at the Child Development Lab and Learning Center (CDLLC) in Normal, IL are bustling with professionals and busy children between the ages of 6 weeks and 6 years. Many of these professionals work at the center regularly, and others visit to provide numerous different support services.

One of the most vital aspects of the CDLLC program is the support services provided by early intervention staff. The program is committed to inclusion and embraces this aspect of its mission by identifying disabilities, delays, and other needs, and intervening with individualized services.

Local developmental therapists support identification through regular visits. The therapists use screening instruments to identify children whose development might be atypical. Should a child demonstrate red flags during these assessments, CDLLC notifies the appropriate family members and refers families to the local early intervention program.

If a child qualifies for services, therapies are conducted within the home and/or the CDLLC. CDLLC professionals believe that they are well suited to incorporate developmental interventions within their program. For example, infant-toddler teacher Marian has learned a series of exercises to develop the low muscle tone of a 9-month-old in the class. Jo incorporates a series of speech exercises into her daily work, benefiting both the child who is targeted for services and the entire class. Many of the familieswhose children receive services through the CDLLC allow therapists to alternate between visits to their home and the CDLLC. This practice ensures that each team member (family members, CDLLC staff, and early intervention staff) is equipped to support the development of individual children. The CDLLC is a natural environment for these children and therefore embraces the role it has in supporting children's development.

CONSTRUCTED-RESPONSE QUESTIONS

1. How can early childhood programs ensure access for diverse populations? In what ways does the CDLLC support these populations?

2. Describe the importance of identification and intervention strategies for young children and the specific strategies utilized within the CDLLC.

3. Identify the goals of intervention within natural environments, and explain the strategies CDLLC used toward meeting these goals.

CASE STUDY

Ensuring Access for Diverse Populations

Myrna's Children's Village (6 weeks to 6 years)

Similar to the CDLLC, the Myrna's Children's Village is committed to supporting access to education through high-quality early childhood education services to children of students who are pursuing a college education. The Village is located within student housing on the New Mexico State University–Las Cruces campus, providing students with easy access to the facilities. Programs serve children ranging from 6 weeks through 5 years. Each program is designed to meet varied family needs, including Early Head Start services, Head Start programming, Early Childhood Special Education services, and university sponsored-early childhood programs. Strategies for meeting family needs include social support, access to college and community resources, and—in many cases—access to health and social services.

Myrna's Children's Village has also formed programs and partnerships supporting child and family needs. For example, the Women, Infants, and Children (WIC) office is located within the Village and is staffed two days a week. Here, qualifying families can receive information about services available to them and can access needed resources. A Family Resource Center is also located within the Village. The center is open to all NMSU families, and partners extensively with the families of the Village. Here, family members can attend parenting classes and learn about community resources.

The Village contains many different early childhood programs. The Village has focused recent efforts on developing a coordinated community calendar for families and staff. Such coordination would relieve duplicate efforts and streamline program offerings.

In addition to serving the needs of families, the Village gives special consideration to supporting cultural and linguistic diversity. Sergio and April's preschool classroom is located near the border of Mexico. Many of the children and their families speak different Spanish dialects. Some have dialects reflecting their origins deep within Mexico, others reflect the dialects of border towns, and still others use a combination of Spanish and English. To ensure that proper dialect and meaning is supported, materials are reviewed by a small number of family members to check for appropriate language before they are distributed widely.

CONSTRUCTED-RESPONSE QUESTIONS

1. How can early childhood programs ensure access for diverse populations? In what ways does Myrna's Children's Village support these populations?

2. In what ways can the community serve as a buffer to stress? How is this demonstrated within the Children's Village?

REFLECTING ON AND APPLYING EFFECTIVE PRACTICES
(NAEYC AND CEC/DEC)

Ethics

- Hector's family has recently emigrated from Mexico, and he has enrolled in your 3-year-old preschool class. On his first day of class, his mother and father requested that he be spoken to exclusively in English. You explained that you were bilingual and felt Hector's development and learning would best be supported if you spoke to him in both English and Spanish. The parents insisted Hector would learn English faster if that was all he heard, and remained adamant in their request. Presently, there are no other English Language Learners in the classroom. **What would you do in this situation?**

NAEYC Ideals

1-1.11. To provide all children with experiences in a language that they know, as well as support children in maintaining the use of their home language and in learning English.

I-2.5. To respect the dignity and preferences of each family and to make an effort to learn about its structure, culture, language, customs, and beliefs.

I-1.2. DEC: Evidence Based Practices
1. We shall rely upon evidence based research and interventions to inform our practice with children and families in our care.

DEC: Responsive Family Centered Practices

1. We shall demonstrate our respect and appreciation for all families' beliefs, values, customs, languages, and culture relative to their nurturance and support of their children toward achieving meaningful and relevant priorities and outcomes families' desire for themselves and their children.

Standards for Professional Practice

- Develop a summary sheet of the ways in which using red flags can be beneficial to supporting young children's development and learning. How might you use knowledge gained through red flags to support children's healthy development and learning within your classroom?

NAEYC: Promoting Child Development and Learning

1a. Knowing and understanding young children's characteristics and needs.
1c. Using developmental knowledge to create healthy, respectful, supportive, and challenging learning environments.

DEC: Development and Characteristics of Learners

EC2K3: Specific disabilities, including the etiology, characteristics, and classification of common disabilities in infants and young children, and specific implications for development and learning in the first years of life.

- What strategies do you feel are most important to support children who are under stress? Do you feel there any situations that might make supporting families under stress more challenging? What strategies might you use to ensure that your interactions with all children and families are professional?

NAEYC: Building Family and Community Relationships
2b. Supporting and empowering families and communities through respectful, reciprocal relationships.

CHAPTER REVIEW

- **How can early childhood education professionals use red flags to effectively support children's development and learning?**

Professionals can use red flags to help them determine when children are displaying concerning behaviors or a pattern of development. Red flags are indicators of a potential developmental issue, and professionals should bring them to the attention of families and medical specialists.

- **What are the major areas and definitions of exceptionality?**

Table 5.1 provides a summary of areas of exceptionality presented in this chapter.

- **How can evidence-based practice support young children's development and learning?**

Evidence-based practice provides a process for exploring the individual development and learning needs of each child, understanding research and effective practices that exist relative to those needs, and applying that information in a way that is reflective of professional and family values and wisdom. Through careful attention to the individual child, the validity of research and practice information, and the impact on the child, the professional can use this process to move from knowledge to effective practice.

- **What strategies can early childhood education professionals use to support children from immigrant populations?**

Children from immigrant populations can be culturally and linguistically diverse. If professionals do not support this diversity effectively, children can experience incredible personal challenges, delays, and academic failure. Teachers must familiarize themselves with strategies supporting linguistic development, including supporting the child in communicating in their home language. Further, teachers must work to create supportive environments that reflect and respect cultural diversity. This requires examining your own biases, including a variety of materials, and implementing teaching strategies that complement the child's cultural world.

- **How does stress affect the lives of children and families, and what role does the professional play in alleviating stress?**

The three kinds of stress children typically experience include positive stress, tolerable stress, and toxic stress. Chronic exposure to stress can affect the overall functioning of the brain and children's development and learning. Understanding the kinds of stress they are experiencing is critical to developing strategies supportive of their overall development and learning. The development of nurturing relationships to promote child and family resilience is foundational to successfully supporting children.

6 Understanding Family Diversity

"The parent is, and remains, the first and most important teacher that the child will have."

—RABBI KASSEL ABELSON

Myra rouses her three children from a sound sleep each day at 6:00 A.M. There is a nice cadence to their routine: breakfast, brush teeth, and then the great tumble into the car. Myra makes two stops before she gets to work. The first is the local elementary school, where her second-grade son, Toby, will spend time with his friends in the before-school program. The second stop is the family child care home where 3-year-old Kasey and 7-week-old Caleb spend their days. Myra is due at work by 7:15, and she is particularly hurried today because she was late twice last week. Transitioning back to work 6 weeks after Caleb's birth hasn't been smooth. She wanted more time at home with baby Caleb, but the pressure to make ends meet just didn't allow them that luxury.

Carla's day also begins at 6 A.M., when she powers on her computer to respond to a few emails before her baby wakes up. After tending to a few morning details, she hears the baby begin to cry and picks her up from her crib. Carla is due at work around 8 A.M. She has already decided that today she will go in a bit later than normal to try to sneak in a few extra cuddles with her 14-week-old before dropping her off at a local child care center. Back at work now for only 2 weeks, Carla feels a bit resentful at missing time with her daughter. But there are bills to pay, and she does, overall, enjoy her job. Her management position allows her some flexibility, and her company has tried to support her transition. One of the tasks that she is looking forward to today is offering one of her employees, Myra, a promotion. Surely the extra money and more flexible hours will help her balance her work–family responsibilities.

Three hours later, Carla sits in her private office, pumping breast milk into a plastic bottle and reflecting on her conversation with Myra. Carla was sure Myra would eagerly jump at the promotion and was surprised when she asked for time to think about it. One of the issues with the proposed raise, Myra informed Carla, was that she would lose the financial support she was getting for her children's early childhood education services. This would lead to a net monetary loss. Carla was struck by the inequity of their positions and the varied challenges they faced balancing work and family. Even the fact that she was pumping breast milk in her private office highlighted this disparity, as Carla knew Myra's only option for pumping was a chair in the corner of the public restroom.

● ● ●

GUIDING QUESTIONS

- What is the structure and composition of America's families, and why is this knowledge relevant to your role as a teacher?

- What is the child care trilemma, and how does it affect access to education and services?

- What issues affect access for the infant-toddler, preschool, and K–3 populations?

- How do employer-based solutions affect access?

- What role does co-construction play in supporting relationships with families?

- How is social support effectively provided to families?

- How does family empowerment affect family functioning?

The difference between Carla's and Myra's situations represents some of the diverse issues of class and family structure that you may encounter as a professional. Furthermore, this vignette demonstrates social inequities and the often-tenuous balance between work and family that many families face. Partnering with families requires understanding this diversity and developing skills that create overlap between home and school.

The layers of knowledge, skills, and dispositions needed to partner with families are similar to those required to implement developmentally appropriate practices. This includes general knowledge of families and particular knowledge of the families of children

149

in your classroom. This particular knowledge is shaped through recognition that families are part of a dynamic and changing system of relationships; their interactions with other family members, their places of employment, and their neighborhoods, for example, have an impact on them and their children. In addition, these factors affect the needs they bring to the classroom. Meeting, or not meeting, these needs can have a dramatic impact on family functioning, which in turn can positively or negatively affect the developing child.

Who are America's families? What are their needs relative to the field? What role does the teacher play in meeting those needs? Knowledge in each of these areas—and the ability to apply that knowledge in a way that is supportive of family and child development—is critical to your success as a teacher.

WHO ARE AMERICA'S FAMILIES?

family structure

Descriptive characteristics of a family.

single-parent families

Families in which one parent cares for one or more children without the assistance of another adult in the household.

dual-earner families

Families where both parents are working outside the home.

Who is in a family, and how does this affect their interactions with their children, the early childhood classroom, and the larger community? Family structure, which is a description of the characteristics of a family, can provide important information about who is considered a member of a family (see Figure 6.1). Knowledge of family structure, however, is meaningless without knowledge of individual family functioning. For example, single-parent families are statistically more likely to live in poverty (Federal Interagency Forum on Child and Family Statistics, 2008). However, certainly not all single-parent families have low incomes. Dual-earner families, where both parents are working outside the home, may experience challenges in balancing work and child-rearing responsibilities. This, too, is not always the case. As we explore family structure, therefore, it is essential to keep in mind that this information represents a general description and cannot replace knowledge of each individual family.

How can professionals use information on family structure? Chapter 5 introduced the five-step decision-making process referred to as evidence-based practice. The five steps include (1) posing a question; (2) finding the best available evidence; (3) appraising the evidence quality and relevance; (4) integrating research with values and wisdom; and (5) evaluating the effectiveness of steps 1–4 (Buysse & Wesley, 2006). As families represent an important part of each step in the process, knowledge of family structure can guide teachers in developing partnerships with key family members. In some families, for example, teachers may form partnerships with a mother and father, in others with a grandmother, and in others with a foster parent. These partnerships can be critical to successfully evaluating evidence-based practice for each individual child.

FIGURE 6.1
General Family Structure Statistics

Family Structure	Families with Children Under the Age of 18
Dual-parent (married) families	67%
Single-parent families, female headed	23%
Single-parent families, male headed	3%
Dual-parent (unmarried) families	3%
Foster families	4%

Note: From "America's Children in Brief: Key National Indicators of Well-being," by Federal Interagency Forum on Child and Family Statistics, 2008. Retrieved December 1, 2008, from http://www.childstats.gov/index.asp

Figure 6.1 provides a general schema of family structure based on who lives with the child and whether they are married or unmarried. Within this general depiction, there is great variance. For example, dual-earner families outnumber two-parent families with one breadwinner by 2 to 1. Unmarried births accounted for 38% of births in 2006, and the rate of births to adolescents grew in 2006 for the first time since 1991. The majority of children who live with neither parent are living with grandparents or other relatives, and 42% lived in foster families (Federal Interagency Forum on Child and Family Statistics, 2008).

How might these variations affect children? Consider children who are born to adolescents, or **teen parents**. The United States has the highest rate of teen pregnancy in the industrialized world, with 35% of all girls getting pregnant at least once prior to the age of 20 (National Campaign to Prevent Teen Pregnancy, 2005). Some teen parents fare well, despite numerous adversities (FSU Center for Prevention and Early Intervention Policy, 2005). However, as a group, the children of teen parents share the following characteristics:

- They are more likely to be born prematurely and at a low birth weight.
- They are 50% more likely than the children of nonteens to repeat a grade, are less likely to complete high school when compared with the children of older mothers, and have lower performance overall on standardized tests.
- They suffer higher rates of abuse and neglect than the children of mothers who delayed childbearing.
- They are more likely to live in poverty.

These poor outcomes occur because teen parents as a group are less skilled in their communications with children (Culp, Appelbaum, Osofsky, & Levy, 1988), are more likely to be depressed, and are less knowledgeable overall about children's development (Osofsky, Hann, & Peebles, 1993).

Certainly teen parenting is not an absolute guarantee that children will demonstrate the above characteristics. However, children of teen parents are considered *at risk,* or more likely, to experience challenging outcomes. Having knowledge of the risk factors associated with teen parenting, therefore, can lead to acquiring additional information about potential supports and resources.

In addition to family structure, **family composition**, or who is included in the family, can also vary. Step, blended, gay and lesbian, foster, and cohabitating families represent a few family relationship patterns. See Table 6.1 for an overview of family type by composition.

foster families
Certified "parents" or family who care for minor children who have been removed from birth or custodial parents by state authority.

teen parents
Persons age 19 and under who become parents.

family composition
Persons included in a family.

TABLE 6.1 Family Type by Composition

Type of Family	Description
Binuclear	Postdivorce family with children, consisting of the original nuclear family divided into two families, one headed by the mother, the other by the father
Blended	Couple containing two or more children, at least one of whom is the biological child of both members of the couple and at least one of whom is the stepchild of one member of the couple
Extended	Three generations or more living in the same household
Foster	Family where the parent is not biologically related to the child but is committed to being a short-term or primary and permanent caregiver
Lesbian or gay	Family headed by either a lesbian or a gay couple
Nuclear	Family consisting of two married parents and their biological children
Step	Family containing one or more children where at least one of the children is the stepchild of one member of the couple and none of whom is the biological or foster child of both members of the couple

As you can see in Table 6.1, families take many different forms. Among the children found in one early childhood classroom, for example, one might live with his grandmother, another with two men as his parents, another in foster care, and so on. In addition to variation in living arrangements, how families live (culture) and communicate (linguistics) can vary greatly as well. For example, 20% of families in the United States speak a language other than English within their home (Federal Interagency Forum on Child and Family Statistics, 2008). General knowledge of this information can lead professionals to research specific ways to incorporate linguistically sensitive practices. With knowledge of how to support linguistically diverse families, teachers can apply respectful, supportive strategies to specific families.

Sensitivity to family diversity requires that professionals employ a broad and inclusive view in their definition of family. From this broad knowledge, teachers can look at how the field of early childhood education, specifically, presents unique challenges and support for families in terms of accessing quality services.

Equity Issues Affecting Families

In general, the American cultural view of child rearing as a private concern requires parents to secure and, for many, finance their own child care arrangements. Parents' ability to both access and finance child care depends on a variety of factors, such as the availability of care and financial resources. When considering social equity, the field of early childhood education frees parents to work outside the home, which in turn affects individual livelihood. The field also supports transitioning from welfare to work. Further, social equity is supported through equal access for all children to high-quality early childhood services. This access supports school readiness and success.

Equity issues facing families are similar to those for children. Families require program options that meet their diverse and individual needs. This means that families have access to services for the full age range of early childhood, in a variety of quality settings. Families need to be included in a way that respects their role as the child's first and most important teacher. In this chapter, you will learn the challenges families face in securing care that is high quality, affordable, and accessible. In addition, you will explore strategies to help you welcome families and respect and nurture the vital role they play in the lives of their children.

THE CHILD CARE TRILEMMA

Effectively supporting equity for families requires attention to issues of access. Access is accomplished when families can participate in services that are of high quality, affordable, and accessible (see Figure 6.2). Solving this **child care trilemma**, as it is referred to in the field, requires expanding the focus to potential business, community, and governmental solutions.

child care trilemma

Interrelated issues of quality, accessibility, and affordability that affect a parent's ability to find care.

Issues of Quality

As you learned in Chapter 3, much of the care and education provided to young children is mediocre at best (CQO Study Team, 1995). Discussing issues of quality without discussing issues of affordability and access is difficult, as they are so deeply interdependent. Issues of affordability are shaped by the relationship between quality early childhood education and the cost of services—high-quality child care is more expensive (Culkin, Helburn, & Morris, 1990). This leaves many parents unable to access services based on

FIGURE 6.2
The Child Care
Trilemma

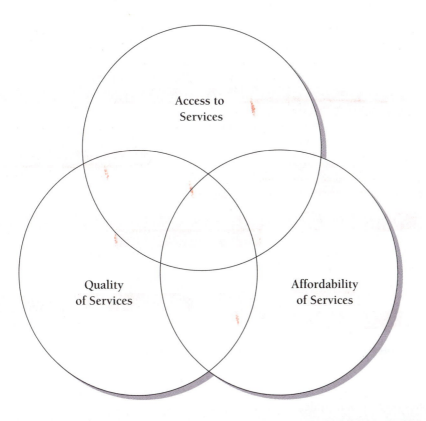

their income. Access to child care is affected by the fact that demand exceeds supply, which is an issue that is particularly noticeable for infant care. Professional knowledge of the field requires an understanding of the issues parents face in securing high-quality education for their children.

Issues of Affordability

Full-time child care expenses can range from $4,000 to $10,000 a year per child (Friedman, 2006). Consider this data in the light of the following: One-third of families with young children earn less than $25,000 per year (Friedman, 2006). For a point of reference, a family with two adults working full-time at minimum wage earns a combined income of $21,000 per year. Those families who fall below the federal poverty line ($21,200 for a family of four) pay as much as 25% of their income on child care (U.S. Census Bureau, 2002). Although government assistance for child care services is available, only 22% of families who received Temporary Assistance for Needy Families (TANF) received this kind of assistance, compared with 6% of families not receiving TANF (U.S. Census Bureau, 2002). This fact represents an interesting

Quality care is the cornerstone of effective practice.

dilemma facing many families who earn enough money to no longer qualify for TANF. Although their overall income has increased, they actually experience a drop in take-home income when covering child care costs independently. It is easy to see how child care costs can be prohibitive for families of middle and lower incomes.

As child care services affect a greater percentage of overall family budgets for children from families with low incomes, affordability is greatly affected. Child care expenses can erode the financial benefits of employment, influencing whether families with low income (such as Myra from the opening vignette) can subsist on low earnings without public assistance (Giannarelli & Barsimantov, 2000). The main source of subsidies for child care expenses is the Child Care and Development Fund. This fund serves 10% to 15% of families who are eligible for these monies (U.S. Department of Health and Human Services, 2006).

The high cost of child care services can affect families in financial and nonfinancial ways (Giannarelli & Barsimantov, 2000), regardless of family income. The costs of child care can influence the number of hours a parent works and whether two-parent families choose to work split shifts. Child care costs, in other words, affect families in a variety of ways.

The lack of affordable child care affects, in turn, the productivity of the workforce. For example, mothers are more than twice as likely to quit their jobs when employers offer inadequate child care or none at all (Hofferth & Collins, 2000). There are numerous strategies that would support public investment in care, including welfare reform and universal preschool programs. These strategies have had limited success.

Government Support. Government efforts supporting access to quality early childhood services include:

- Temporary Assistance for Need Families (TANF)
- Child Care and Development Block Grant

TEACHING AND LEARNING CONNECTIONS

Connecting Families with Community Resources Supporting Affordability

One of your roles as a professional is ensuring that you connect families with community resources. Regarding affordability, the following strategies can be beneficial:

- Familiarize yourself with the local, state, and national resources, including grants, scholarships, and subsidies that can help families pay for early education services. For this information, contact your local Child Care Resource and Referral Agency.

- Ensure that your program is taking advantage of government programs that benefit families, including subsidies for such things as food. Check with your local health department, licensing representative, and Child Care Resource and Referral Agency for more information about available subsidies.

- Take an active role in educating members of your community about the importance of quality care and issues of affordability that many families face. Consider writing a letter to the editor, talking to board of education members, sponsoring an awareness and information activity, or talking to local business leaders and politicians.

- **At-Risk Child Care Program** (targeted toward the working poor)
- Head Start programs
- State-funded universal or voluntary pre-kindergarten programs

Each of these programs serves children who are considered at risk because of developmental issues or poverty status, as research has consistently demonstrated that high-quality early childhood services have the greatest positive effect on children with these characteristics (Stegelin, 2004). However, high-quality early education services can benefit many more children than those served by these programs. In addition, these programs are not able to serve the number of children who qualify: Recent estimates by the Children's Defense Fund (2005) indicate that (1) only one in seven children who are eligible for child care assistance actually receives it, (2) Head Start serves only about half of all eligible preschool-age children, and (3) Early Head Start serves less than 3% of eligible infants and toddlers.

In addition to these programs, taxpayers can offset some of the costs of care through the income tax credits. The ability to claim this benefit depends on family income, with middle and upper classes qualifying.

Employer-Based Solutions. Employers can offer a range of programs that help make child care services affordable. Employer funding of child care is one of the most direct ways to have an impact on families. However, less than 2% of employers provide this form of assistance (Bureau of Labor Statistics, 1998). The kinds and prevalence of programs employers offer is also regionally based. In rural America, most employers are small, family-run businesses, making the extension of employer-based solutions difficult. A more common benefit offered to employees is reimbursement accounts, where employers set up accounts funded through employee pre-tax contributions to cover expenses for dependent care (U.S. Department of the Treasury, 2008).

The challenges families face regarding child care affordability are very real and serve, for many, as a barrier to employment. Along with affordability, access to quality early childhood education services also represents an important facet of the child care trilemma.

Issues of Access

Early childhood education plays many significant roles in the lives of children, families, and overall society. Whether early childhood education services are used by working parents or through welfare programs, they are critical foundations for an equitable start in life for all children. Additionally, these services can serve as vehicles for social change. NAEYC's Call for Excellence in Early Childhood Programs (2000) identifies the removal of barriers for all children to attend high-quality programs as a vital goal. Note that issues of access affect infants and toddlers, preschoolers, and the school-age population differently.

At-Risk Child Care Program

Enacted in 1990, the ARCCP is designed to fund child care services for children of families with low income who do not receive Aid to Families with Dependent Children monies.

Go to MyEducationLab and select the topic "Families and Communities." Under Activities and Applications, watch the video *Head Start*, which you may recognize from Chapter 3. Consider the various strategies Head Start uses to involve families and communities.

Children and families must have access to the field to benefit from quality services.

Issues of access in the field are strongly shaped by issues of affordability. Despite the documented benefits of preschool services, only 45% of children from low-income backgrounds were enrolled in preschool services, whereas almost 75% of children from high-income backgrounds were enrolled (National Education Goals Panel, 1997).

Early Childhood Education Compared with the K–12 System. Why are issues of access so different regarding birth through preschool services as compared with K–12 education? Some of the reasons are that the programs are differently managed, differently administered, and different in the *way* families qualify for them. Most birth through preschool services operate in a price-sensitive environment that is supported mainly by fees from families and supplemented from private and public contributions (NAEYC, 2000). In the K–12 system, educational services are publicly funded and have a relatively stable funding base. This stability translates into options that are shaped by the diversity of child and family needs. In contrast, families and children needing early childhood education services must struggle to receive them.

Infant-Toddler Populations. The lack of care and education services for the infant and toddler population is an issue of great concern within the field. According to a study that represented a 12-country comparison of quality and access to services, the demand for infant and toddler services in the United States far exceeds the present supply (Organisation for Economic Cooperation and Development, 2006). Most other countries included in the study, such as Sweden and Belgium, had addressed this issue through liberal parental leave and job assurance policies, enabling parents to stay home and care for infants. The field of early childhood care in the United States has struggled to respond with similar strategies.

It is hard to overstate the impact that cost has on access. Infant care costs can range from $3,803 to $13,480 a year. In 42 states, the fees associated with infant care are higher than tuition at a 4-year public university (NACCRRA, 2006). Where care is more affordable (Arkansas and Georgia, for example), the state-regulated ratio of caregivers to infants is higher (1:6 compared with NAEYC's recommended 1:3). In turn, program quality is affected (NACCRRA, 2006). The strong reliance on parent fees produces a certain irony. More children in the classroom means more parent fees and more revenue to work with, which would seem to provide for higher quality care. More children in the classroom, however, also mean lower quality care.

Preschool Populations. Although increasing numbers of preschool-aged children have access to education services, the United States remains dramatically behind when compared with other countries. In France, for example, nearly all preschool-aged children attend publicly funded programs, as do most 4-year-olds in England, Luxembourg, and the Netherlands (Stipek, 2005). In the United States, 2004 statistics indicate that 42% of 3-year-olds and 67% of preschoolers attend preschool services regularly (Stipek, 2005).

Attendance in preschool populations is largely shaped by race/ethnicity, poverty status, and maternal education. Hispanic children are the least likely to be enrolled (40%), and black children are the most likely to be enrolled (64%) (Karoly, Kilburn, & Cannon, 2005). Forty-seven percent of children of families living in poverty are enrolled in services, compared with 59% of children in families at or above the poverty level. Regarding levels of maternal education, 38% of the children of mothers with less than a high school education enroll in preschool services, compared with 70% of mothers with at least a college degree. Interestingly, the Karoly, Kilburn, and Cannon (2005) study found little

ISSUES OF ACCESS AND EQUITY FOR FAMILIES
Understanding the Working Family with Low Income

Many American families struggle to pay the bills, even though their incomes are above the poverty line. Historically, persons in this group have been referred to as the "working poor." Because many of these families make twice the poverty line and still face hardship (such as challenges in paying the bills and keeping food on the table), the preferred term is the *low-income working family* (Acs & Nichols, 2007). Reflecting the goal of using people-first language, the term working families with low income will be used.

Working families with low income face challenges similar to families who are impoverished, and they are particularly vulnerable to crises and unexpected expenses. Five hundred dollars for a car repair, for example, becomes a budgetary crisis. One-third of these families lack health insurance, despite the definition of working family with low income including at least one family member who is working full time.

Access to quality child care is an issue for these families. Their income is too high to qualify for government-subsidized services such as Head Start and too low to pay for the estimated 10% additional cost of high-quality care. In states that have adopted universal preschool programs, this is the group that is predominantly targeted. However, at present only 10% of states have embraced universal preschool (Acs & Nichols, 2007).

Although the context might shape our thinking of economic groups as either impoverished or nonimpoverished, some levels of income present unique challenges. As a professional in the field, you can use this knowledge to shape your understanding of family systems and stress and to effectively advocate for family issues of access and equity.

difference in the enrollment patterns of children in single- and two-parent families. They did, however, find maternal employment to be predictive of program participation. At a societal level, attendance in preschool programs has become an increasingly political issue. A result of this focus is preschool that is funded by the states.

Universal Preschool. Head Start was the federal government's first major investment in preschool education, targeting funds specifically for children who were considered at risk for developmental issues. However, the benefits of high-quality preschool educational services are not limited to populations considered at risk:

> The evidence is in: quality early education benefits children of all social and economic groups. There are both short- and long-term economic benefits to taxpayers and the community if early education that meets high standards is available to all children, starting with those who are most disadvantaged. Indeed, universally available quality early education would benefit everyone and be the most cost-effective economic investment. (Calman & Tarr-Whelan, 2005, p. 2)

Universal preschool programs (UPKs) are state-funded programs to ensure that preschool is accessible to all children. UPKs come in many different forms. In the states

Universal preschool programs

Also referred to as Preschool for All, these programs work to ensure that preschool is accessible for all children.

that have programs, some are accessible only to 4-year-olds, whereas others, such as Illinois, extend UPKs to include children who are 3. Currently, eight states (Florida, Georgia, Illinois, Iowa, Louisiana, New York, Oklahoma, and West Virginia) and the District of Columbia are phasing in or offering voluntary pre-K services for all age-eligible children (Pre-K Now, 2008). UPKs might also be called by different names, such as Preschool for All. Additionally, there is great variance in the percentage of the population served by public pre-K programs. For example, in Georgia and Oklahoma, 50% or more of all 4-year-olds are in public pre-K (Pre-K Now, 2008).

The view that high-quality preschool should be accessible to every child has received extensive support. For example, Steve Barnett of the National Institute for Early Education Research (NIEER) claims that high-quality early education services play a large role in supporting school readiness. These high-quality services reflect needs that continue up the income ladder. Universal preschool is critical to the success of children and society and is a matter of social equity (Barnett, Brown, Finn-Stevenson, & Henrich, in press).

School-Age Populations. Twenty percent of children in kindergarten through eighth grade access nonparental child care. Fifty percent have nonparental child care arrangements after school (National Center for Education Statistics, 2004). The most common arrangements for children after school include center-based or school-based programs (19%), relative care (17%), and self-care (13%).

Accessibility issues in school-age populations have less to do with whether arrangements are available and more to do with what children are doing in their before- and after-school hours. Children who spend 20 to 35 hours per week engaging in constructive learning activities are more likely to succeed in school. Furthermore, out-of-school hours play a key role in overall development (Children's Defense Fund, 2003). These positive outcomes include an increase in academic achievement, school attendance, time spent on homework and extracurricular activities, efforts in school, and student behavior (American Youth Policy Forum, 2006).

Center-based or school-age programs are the most common kinds of care before and after school.

Unfortunately, many children are in self-care situations before and after school. Nearly 9% of children ages 5 to 11 supervise themselves during some part of the week, and 42% of children between the ages of 11 and 14 spend time unsupervised (Children's Defense Fund, 2003). The time children spend unsupervised increases dramatically during the summer months.

Research indicates that children in unsupervised situations are more likely to engage in delinquent behavior and are missing out on the positive contributions that structured out-of-school time can have on children's development. One of the issues affecting children's participation in out-of-school programs is access, both in terms of the cost and availability of programs. For example, metropolitan areas have far fewer out-of-school programs than are needed (National Association of Elementary School Principals, 2001). Further, most programs rely heavily on parent fees, which in turn presents access challenges similar to the affordability of child care.

Addressing issues of access within the field of early childhood education requires looking at family and community needs; thinking about resources that are available to address those needs; and developing, implementing, and evaluating solutions. Employers are one potential resource for addressing access issues.

Employer-Based Solutions. Employers might find that supporting family access to child care is beneficial for many reasons. These include the improvement of employee morale and reduction in turnover and absenteeism. Further, access to child care can increase productivity. All of these efforts serve to benefit the overall community (U.S. Department of the Treasury, 1998).

Partnerships with Child Care Resource and Referral Agencies (CCRRAs). Partnerships with local CCRRAs can provide families with a low-cost way to access information about child care opportunities in their community. Information provided by CCRRAs includes elements of quality care, providers located in the community, and information on selecting an appropriate provider.

Flexible Workplace Policies. Employers can adopt numerous strategies to make the workplace more family friendly (Galinsky, Bond, & Friedman, 1993). These include *family leave*, in which maternity and paternity leaves are granted (Breidenbach, 2003). Following leave, a return to the same or similar position is ensured. Telecommuting is another strategy reflected in **family-friendly** workplaces, as is job sharing. Many workplaces allow a compressed work schedule, which enables parents to work longer days in order to work fewer overall days. Finally, flextime allows workers to set their own arrival and departure times, therefore allowing flexibility to meet family responsibilities.

On-Site Child Care. Nearly one-fifth of all employers offer on-site or near-site child care (Hewitt Associates, 2003). Benefits of on-site care include convenience, the opportunity for parents to visit their children on breaks, the demonstration of a company's commitment to their employees, and the potential for the company to play a role in the quality of care that children receive.

Off-Site Child Care. Off-site child care takes a variety of forms. Some companies sponsor near-site care, which provides many of the advantages of on-site care without the presence on company grounds. Other employers arrange for a certain number of slots at community centers, enabling their employees to have first pick of availability. Off-site care can support parent choice and address space needs that might prevent companies from providing on-site care.

Businesses represent one potential source of support for families. Other sources of support include local, state, and national programs, which can serve to offset some of the high costs of quality care (Kinch & Schweinhart, 2004). One national program that serves as a model for both supporting families and providing high-quality care is military child care.

family friendly
Policies and practices that support families.

Solutions to the Child Care Trilemma

Military child care represents an exemplary model of employer-sponsored care. With 400 facilities and 2,800 family child care homes worldwide (U.S. Army, 2005), a cost-sharing system between military families and the government, and outside accreditation through NAEYC, military child care provides a solution to the child care trilemma. The military

• • • BECOMING A PROFESSIONAL • • •

Keeping Current in Public Policy

As the importance of high-quality education and its impact on young children's development and learning gains more recognition, the field must continue to advocate for appropriate public policy that supports critical functions.

Fortunately, the field has many well-developed organizations that engage in advocacy. The following provides a brief overview of professional organizations and their related public-policy efforts:

Organization	Focus of Public Policy	Opportunities for Involvement
Children's Defense Fund (http://childrensdefense.org) Organization's major goals include ensuring that each child receives a: • Healthy Start • Head Start • Fair Start • Safe Start • Moral Start	• Child welfare and mental health • Early childhood development • Child health • Youth development • Family income • Budget analysis	• Internships • Leadership Network • Ongoing development initiatives • Internet email list • Facts, reports, and resources • Advocacy action plans
National Association for the Education of Young Children/Public Policy (http://www.naeyc.org/policy/) Organization's major goals include the promotion of national, state, and local public policies supporting high-quality early childhood programming	• Current public policy issues and legislation affecting early childhood education at national, state, and local levels	• NAEYC email list • Children's Champion Action Center • Early Childhood Workforce Systems Initiative • Advocacy Toolbox • Facts, reports, and resources
Division for Early Childhood of the Council for Exceptional Children Policy/Advocacy (http://www.dec-sped.org/index.aspx/PolicyAdvocacy) One of organization's major goals includes supporting high-quality programming and services for children with disabilities	• Current public policy issues and legislation affecting early childhood education at national, state, and local levels with an emphasis on influencing laws and regulations	• Children's Action Network • DEC email list • Pubic Policy/Legislative Updates • Public Policy Resources • DEC Advocacy News Updates
Kids Count (http://www.aecf.org/MajorInitiatives/KIDSCOUNT.aspx) This organization is in charge of a national and state-by-state project sponsored by the Annie E. Casey Foundation to track the status of children in the United States (such as immunization rates or the number of children living in poverty or without health insurance)	• Data reflecting the status of young children at the national, state, and community level	• Data, publications, and resources • State advocacy networks • News alerts

supports this solution by creating varied child care options, requiring accreditation for programs, and ensuring equitable salaries for staff (Zellman, Johansen, Meredith, & Selvin, 1994).

Access Within Military Child Care. Military child care is the largest example of employer-sponsored care in the country. Issues of military access present many unique challenges, including early morning and irregular duty hours, field exercises, and extended periods away from home (Lucas, 2001). A variety of services have been developed to meet these unique needs, including home- and center-based care and programs for out-of-school hours. Entry into the range of services is coordinated through one central point that is similar to nonmilitary Child Care Resource and Referral Agencies. Parents can choose full, part, or hourly care, and options exist for long-term care when parents will be on extended leave. Centers take children at 6 weeks of age, child care homes can begin care as early as 4 weeks of age, and some newborn homes accept babies from birth.

Quality Within Military Child Care. Military child care programs are licensed through the Department of Defense (DoD). The DoD provides both standards and oversight through four unannounced visits per calendar year (NAEYC, 2001). In addition to meeting DoD standards, the Military Child Care Act was amended in 1996 to mandate that all programs become NAEYC accredited. In 2001, 98% of military child care programs had attained accreditation, as compared with only 10% of nonmilitary programs (NAEYC, 2001).

Cost Within Military Child Care. The fees associated with military child care are shared between the government and families. Parents pay fees on a sliding scale, and the average cost to parents is about 50% of the overall cost. These costs are shared regardless of the age of the child in child care. Although the total cost of child care is similar to high-quality, nonmilitary centers, military parents pay significantly less than civilians (Lucas, 2001).

Having access to programs and services, although important, is not enough to ensure the successful development and learning of children. Quality practices require that families are welcomed and that the relationship between families, professionals, and children is cultivated in the early childhood environment. Without family input, a teacher's ability to support each individual child is severely limited. Conversely, families who are not connected to their child's education are missing important opportunities to support their children. Children, in addition, benefit from strong connections between home and school. Theory and effective practices underlying the creation of partnerships with families, therefore, is important knowledge that will contribute to each professional's role.

CREATING PARTNERSHIPS WITH FAMILIES

The intersection between family and early childhood education has been referred to as overlapping spheres of influence (Epstein, 1994), with home and school representing the separate spheres. At the center is the child. What is also represented in this overlap is opportunity and potential. The early childhood professional has both the opportunity and the potential to strengthen both spheres and ultimately benefit the developing child.

Professional opportunities to strengthen these overlapping spheres of influence are marked by two pathways. One pathway consists of professionals working to draw members of the family system into the classroom community through family involvement.

family involvement
Strategies designed to support the familial goal of involvement in the early childhood community.

FIGURE 6.3
Overlapping Spheres
of Influences

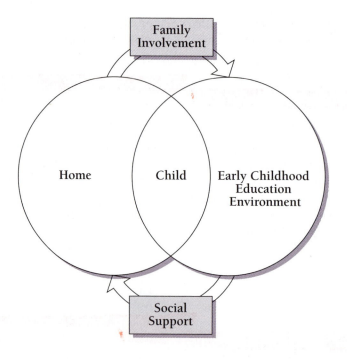

social support
Strategies designed to
support the child's
family system.

The other pathway focuses on classroom communities strengthening family systems through the provision of **social support**. Figure 6.3 provides an illustration of these pathways. Efforts toward family involvement and social support share the common goal of working to have a positive impact on the developing child. The goal of family involvement requires getting parents to participate in the classroom. The goal of social support, on the other hand, requires teachers getting involved with families outside the classroom.

Family involvement in 1-year-old Caleb's Early Head Start program is supported through his dad's regular visits to the classroom. Through these visits, his dad learns more about Caleb's development in the classroom, and the teacher learns more about Caleb's family. Social support is developed through the visits Caleb's teacher makes to their home and the relationships that are encouraged with other families in the classroom. On home visits, Caleb's teacher has given his father a variety of literacy resources. Further, she has shared strategies for reading aloud in ways that will maintain Caleb's interest. At one of the family activities, Caleb's dad met another classroom parent who lives in the same apartment complex, and these families have begun to exchange babysitting favors.

Family needs often dictate the kinds of services offered and the role of the professional in providing these services. Family goals also differ. One parent might be interested in seeing a mastery of the alphabet. Another parent may be more interested in seeing her child learn how to enter groups and sustain play. Vygotsky (1978) argues for the importance of family voice in determining expectations for their child's development. For professionals to effectively support children's development, they must have knowledge of the general field of early childhood and their professional role along with knowledge of family systems and how these influence children and the early childhood environment.

TEACHING AND LEARNING CONNECTIONS

Providing Social Support

- Create a welcoming educational environment with comfortable space for families to gather and open-door policies. Include chairs in the lobby area, a bulletin board, and relevant, informative reading materials and pamphlets.
- Communicate positive attitudes toward families by actively listening and expressing interest.
- Demonstrate openness and enthusiasm regarding children's development.
- Respect family diversity by learning about individual families.

Theories of Family Involvement

There is no question that a strong family–school connection has a positive affect on children's attitudes and academic outcomes (Hickman, Greenwood, & Miller, 1995). One of the goals of the National Education Goals Panel, the precursor to NCLB, was that "by the year 2000, every school will promote partnerships that will increase parental involvement and participation in promoting the social, emotional, and academic growth of children" (North Central Regional Laboratory, 1995, p. 1). The only debate that remains is about *how* to most effectively support family involvement. This is particularly relevant when a family member's ability and desire to become involved depends on such factors as social class and comfort in the school environment.

Relationships between home and school environments are strongly correlated with social class (Rothstein, 2004). A strong predictor of social class is education. In turn, levels of education can affect family expectations for education and beliefs regarding the impact families can have on the educational process. Family involvement is further exacerbated by family comfort in the school environment and the ability to participate in classroom-based activities with their children. Many strategies supporting involvement in the early childhood education environment (such as family–teacher conferences, classroom volunteering opportunities, and participation in family meetings) assume that all families feel equally welcome and comfortable in the school. The challenge to teachers is to provide a variety of opportunities that meet the different access needs and cultural needs of families.

All families, of course, do not feel equally welcome and comfortable in the early childhood environment. Supporting family comfort and involvement in early childhood education can be thought of in the same way that the field thinks of readiness and supporting the individual

social class
Social groups that arise from economic relationships between members of society.

Family involvement can be cultivated through program-sponsored activities.

Go to MyEducationLab and select the topic "Diverse Learners." Under Activities and Applications, watch the video *Incorporating Home Experiences of Culturally Diverse Students–Part 1* and consider the role of home experiences in the early childhood environment.

development of each child. Therefore, highly individualized culturally appropriate strategies supporting home–school partnerships need to be adopted. One of the inhibiting factors to adopting individual strategies for family involvement is that schools tend to dictate the who and how of involvement (Lopez, Kreider, & Caspe, 2004). This one-size-fits-all approach is often at the expense of unique family concerns and expertise regarding their children's development.

In Andrew's third-grade class, families are given a list of potential involvement opportunities and when these occur during the school year. These opportunities include helping at lunch, during library and computer time, and as a playground supervisor. Andrew's parents both work full time, making participation in these activities next to impossible. When Andrew's father asks if he can occasionally participate during computer time, he is told that an ongoing commitment is required. In this case, the school is in the leadership role of determining the when and how of involvement. Andrew's parents must either change their schedules or choose not to participate.

co-constructed

Shared power between families and the educational system that supports a mutual vision of children's education.

As opposed to relying on parent involvement strategies where schools hold all the power and dictate involvement, Lopez, Kreider, and Caspe (2004) advocate that relationships between home and school are **co-constructed**. In co-constructed relationships, power and input into the form and function of relationships is shared. In Andrew's third-grade class, this translates into his teacher finding out when the parents are available and designing opportunities to support their availability.

What kinds of family involvement can be cultivated within the early childhood classroom? School–family partnerships can take many forms, which are summarized in Table 6.2 on the next page.

Theories of Social Support

social support theory

Theory stating that the support provided by other humans is predictive of mental and physical health.

Social support theory has a long history in psychological research. The main idea behind **social support theory** is that the support provided by other humans is predictive of mental and physical health. The positive impact afforded through supportive networks is particularly beneficial during times of stress (Lincoln, Chatters, & Taylor, 2005). Social support occurs within social networks, which are composed of persons with whom individuals have regular contact. However, not all members of a social network are supportive. Research has shown that the quality of overall support received is significantly predictive of overall development (Hughes, 1994).

Abraham Maslow's hierarchy of needs theory, covered in Chapter 4, provides the theoretical foundation for theories of social support. Social support meets a person's needs for belonging and love. Through positive interaction, affirmations, and support, an overall feeling of self-esteem and competence emerges (Lincoln, Chatters, & Taylor, 2005). In the face of stress, social support is thought to have a buffering effect. This effect helps alleviate the stress by allowing individuals outlets for their anxieties and the opportunity to problem solve. Social support is also an important precursor to family involvement. Families are more likely to become involved in their child's education when they feel supported by the child's teacher (Cotton & Wikelund, 2001).

Social support strategies seek to provide a positive climate in the educational environment. Strategies include positive attitudes toward families, openness and enthusiasm toward children's development, and respect for family diversity.

TABLE 6.2   Types of Family Involvement and Teacher Practices

Type of Family Involvement	Description	Teacher Practices
Parenting	Helping families establish home environments supportive of children as students	• Ongoing, regular communication • Home visits to promote communication • Parenting education through workshops and courses • Connecting families with community resources such as WIC and local Child Care Resource and Referral Agencies
Communicating	Developing effective school-to-home and home-to-school communications	• Ongoing, regular, communication via phone, email, and/or face-to-face contact • Language interpreters to assist families as needed • Newsletters and written notes informing families of classroom events and activities • Regular (at least twice per year) conferences
Volunteering	Recruiting and organizing family involvement and support	• Initial survey of families to determine kinds of potential involvement • Varied opportunities provided for involvement, including classroom and home-based activities • Structure for communicating with families about opportunities, including phone trees, parent room coordinators, or notes home
Learning at home	Providing families with information and ideas to support children at home with targeted learning activities	• Information on how to support children in mastering targeted knowledge and skills • Opportunities for at-home activities, including book bags, links to learning activities, and hands-on explorations
Decision making	Including families in school decisions and developing family leaders	• Developing parent advisory committees • Including opportunities for meaningful family involvement on board of directors • Developing family advocacy and action networks organized around school goals
Collaborating with community	Identifying and integrating resources from the community with the goal of strengthening the quality of school programs and services	• Information for families on community health, education, social support, and recreational resources • Developing partnerships with community service organizations • Coordinating family, child, and school personnel service to the community

Note: From "Theory to Practice: School and Family Partnerships Lead to School Improvement and Student Success," by J. L. Epstein, 1994, in C. L. Fagnano & B. Z. Werber (Eds.), *School, Family and Community Interaction: A View From the Firing Line*, Boulder, CO: Westview Press. Copyright 1994. Adapted with permission.

Co-Constructed Relationships

Relationships between home and school are co-constructed, requiring professional attention to family needs and opportunities in the early childhood environment. There are five dimensions that support co-construction in the overall goal of supporting family involvement (Lopez, Kreider, & Caspe, 2004):

- **Dimension One: Responding to Family Interests and Needs.** Co-construction responds to the needs of both families and educational environments. First grader Ani's mother, Lena, is interested in improving Ani's reading skills. Lena indicated this interest in a family survey sent home at the beginning of the school year. The desire to support their child's reading skills at home was also noted by several other families with first graders. To respond to family interests and needs, the first-grade teacher, Mr. Grimes, held a family literacy night early in the school year. The focus of this night was on at-home strategies to support literacy development. To ensure that each of the families who indicated an interest in literacy felt welcome, he surveyed their availability before setting the literacy night date. Mr. Grimes also made sure that food and activities for the whole family created event accessibility.
- **Dimension Two: Engaging in Dialogue with Families.** Home–school relationships are born out of trust and mutual respect; ongoing dialogue based on families' own experiences and areas of expertise are essential ingredients in support, trust, and mutual respect. Teachers can provide information about what to expect within the early childhood community, how children spend their day in the classroom, how to effectively support learning at home, and how to implement strategies that complement what is occurring within the classroom walls. Families can provide similar information based on the home environment and a long-term perspective on their child's development that the professional might be lacking. Based on this, the goal of dialogue is bidirectional: Both teachers and families provide information that shapes the nature of home–school involvement.

Co-constructed relationships begin with attention to family strengths.

- **Dimension Three: Building on Family Funds of Knowledge.** Embracing the co-constructed nature of family involvement means recognizing that families have an important role in the lives of their children and that strengthening the families' ability to support their child's development promotes positive developmental outcomes (Moll, 1992). As experts on their child's development and learning, families are treated as important sources of information. For example, Ella's mother can provide important information about Ella's overall development. As a poet, she can provide the teacher and class with knowledge and skills in her area of expertise in the fine arts.
- **Dimension Four: Training Families for Leadership.** Participation in early childhood programs is a learned skill, and early childhood professionals should work to cultivate family leadership skills. "In a system where schools hold the power, parents must acquire the skills to be effective advocates for change" (Lopez, Kreider, & Caspe, 2004, p. 2). Families might advocate for the use of new or different classroom strategies, different curricula, or alternative methods for

their own involvement. The skills families acquire through early childhood programs can continue to benefit them as their children navigate successive school environments, empowering them to become long-term advocates for their children. At the Mulberry parent co-op, parents are expected to take a leadership role in the administration and functions of the school. To support families in adopting this role, workshops are held at the beginning of each year that serve not only to inform families about overall goals of the school, but also to provide specific information about the various forms that involvement might take and about how families can have a positive impact on their child's educational outcomes.

- **Dimension Five: Facilitating Connections Across Children's Learning Contexts.** Families are managers of their children's time within home, school, and community contexts. For families to successfully negotiate the overlapping spheres, they must feel empowered and have specific skills to support and advocate for children. In Jorge's infant–toddler classroom, families not only are equal participants in the quality education their children receive, but also receive ongoing education and training about the importance of quality care in the lives of their children and how to evaluate care and advocate for quality. This education and training is of particular importance because much of the population served in Jorge's class are children of college students. Therefore, they will be seeking alternative care arrangements for their children as their time at the college comes to a close.

Figure 6.4 illustrates the five dimensions of co-constructed relationships.

Supporting co-constructed relationships between home and school requires careful attention by the educator. Specific goals include supporting the leadership skills and advocacy efforts of families and drawing attention to the long-term benefits of such actions. Early childhood educators become agents of social support who work to create a level playing field in terms of family competencies in supporting their child's overall development. The field has moved from being characterized as an expert-learner relationship, in which early childhood professionals were viewed as experts on children's development and families their targeted audience, to one of partnership and

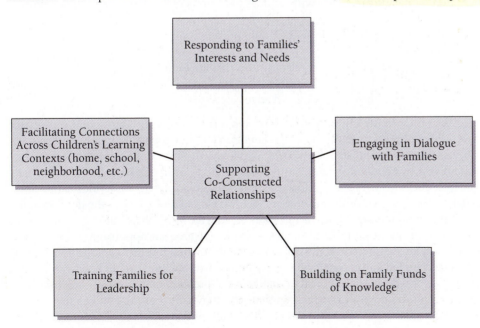

FIGURE 6.4
Five Dimensions
supporting
Co-Constructed
Relationships

> ## TEACHING AND LEARNING CONNECTIONS
>
> ### Supporting Co-Constructed Relationships
>
> - Get to know the individual interests and needs of each family.
> - Communicate with families regularly.
> - Recognize families as experts on their child's development and treat families as both resources and sources of important information.
> - Support families in developing leadership roles in their child's educational experiences by creating opportunities, providing needed information for success, and providing appropriate encouragement.
> - Work to support family empowerment by embracing and supporting their role as their child's first and most important teacher.

shared power. This partnership includes acquiring important knowledge of children and their daily lives and family systems. Effective ways to collaborate as well as being a supportive member of the family's social network are essential to a successful partnership. Along with providing support for family involvement, professionals must also adopt strategies that provide families with social support.

Social Support Strategies. Providing social support is an important goal, as such support can serve as a buffer against stressors. Specific strategies designed to promote social support include (Epstein, 1994):

- Reaching out to families through home visits designed to break down barriers and establish trust.
- Learning about the diverse backgrounds of children in the class and creating comfort zones based on respect for this diversity.
- Communicating regularly with families to keep them informed about their children's development.
- Using written and other forms of communication presented in ways that families can understand.
- Building close, professional relationships that are built from mutual respect.
- Working with families to increase their knowledge of children's development and assist them in their parenting and advocacy skills.

According to these guidelines, social support begins with interest and acceptance. From this, it builds over time through communication supporting long-term goals that can have a positive impact on children's development. For example, Margot begins each school year by conducting home visits to the families of her classroom. On these visits, she introduces herself to the child and family and provides them with information about what can be expected in the classroom. She interviews families about the developmental goals they hold for their children and about the degree of involvement they would like to have in their education. Then, Margot works to ensure that opportunities for involvement meet family interests and work with their schedules. But the relationship with families does not end at the conclusion of the home visit. Margot touches base with families on a daily or weekly basis. Verbal exchange is the predominant mode of communication for families who drop off and pick up their children daily. For the families she does not see on a regular basis, she relies on telephone calls and email. Margot's communications focus not only on children's development, but also on ongoing family concerns and interests. Throughout the year, Margot holds a variety of evening family events, where food and child care are provided. Although Margot often chooses educational topics and activities for these events based on family interest, she also ensures that there is ample time for families or other primary caregivers to network and form socially supportive relationships. Margot's attitude toward her classroom is that it includes not only the children, but also the significant relationships they have with family members. By facilitating both family involvement and social support, Margot is attaining a fundamental professional goal of family **empowerment**.

Supporting Family Empowerment. Empowered families feel as though their efforts make a difference and they are effective advocates for their children. Disempowered families, however, often feel alienated and that their involvement will make little difference. Family empowerment has long been a goal in the field of special education, where family input is an expected and valued part of setting goals for children's development. Through Individualized Family Service Plans (IFSPs) for infants and toddlers and Individualized Education Programs (IEPs) for children preschool-aged and beyond, family input into goals for children's development is not only welcomed, but considered a mandate.

Goals for educators regarding family involvement in both the IFSP and the IEP should include (1) meeting the legal rights of families to be informed and help make decisions, (2) obtaining information about the life of the child at home, (3) using families' ideas to set goals and objectives, (4) enlisting the families' help in carrying out certain learning projects at home, and (5) reinforcing the parent–child relationship and the parent's sense of competence in his or her role (Disability Rights Center, 2006). These goals speak to the importance of providing both family involvement strategies and social support. The overarching goal of support is empowerment, supporting families' beliefs that they can make a difference in their child's education.

Empowering families requires fostering their ability to effect change at the community, organizational, and individual level (Perkins & Zimmerman, 1995). Family roles in early childhood education include "information seeker, problem solver, committee member, public educator, political activist, and most importantly, spokesperson for the needs of their children" (Minnes, Nachen, & Woodford, 2003, p. 665). Empowerment encompasses each of these roles. At its core, empowerment speaks to a family's ability to participate in and have an impact on their child's education. Goals for family empowerment recognize the fluidity of the early childhood professional's role. In many cases, children and their families are only members of the professional's community for a brief time. To empower families is to promote a long-term impact, and through this impact, support the developmental trajectory of the child.

Education is one of the most critical facets of empowerment. The areas of education families can benefit from are determined by their

Family empowerment promotes child advocacy.

empowerment
The expansion of individuals capacities to negotiate with, influence, and control facets of their world.

TEACHING AND LEARNING CONNECTIONS

Empowering Families

- Learn to recognize the strength of each individual family.
- Utilize these strengths to partner with families in addressing areas of challenge.
- Offer families opportunities to share their knowledge with you and other families through daily communication, family group meetings, and so on.
- Create a safe atmosphere for the exchange of ideas by demonstrating openness and acceptance.
- Respect families' perspectives, even if they differ from your own.
- Use families as resources, both for yourself and for other families.

own individual needs. For example, one parent in the classroom might require education regarding his child's development and how to effectively support it. Another parent in the same classroom might benefit from education on advocacy and how to effectively advocate for her child's inclusion in natural settings.

Obstacles to family empowerment include a lack of information about the meaning of taking an active role in their children's education, school staff using alienating jargon, and educators not valuing or cultivating the family role. Understanding families, the role they play in children's lives, and the interrelationship between families and the early childhood community provides an essential foundation from which support strategies can build (Disability Rights Center, 2006).

MOVING FORWARD

Central to the success of early childhood education is the field's ability to meet the diverse needs of the children and families it serves. As you have learned, meeting these needs requires supporting quality, affordable, and accessible programs and practices that recognize the vital role families play in their children's development and learning. Families will not benefit from services they cannot access, nor will they benefit from services that do not respect and value the important role they play in their children's lives.

myeducationlab

Go to MyEducationLab and select the topic "Families and Communities." Under Building Teaching Skills and Dispositions, complete the exercise *Helping Parents Build Children's Social Skills*.

CASE STUDY

A Comprehensive Approach to Access

The Child Development Lab and Learning Center (6 weeks to 6 years)

Heartland Community College's Child Development Lab and Learning Center (CDLLC) includes in its mission a commitment to serving students (70%) and faculty/staff (30%). The program is structured to support the development of both children and families.

One of the most distinctive factors at the lab school is the diversity of the program's families. The staff at the CDLLC employs various strategies to cast a wide net that encompasses this vast diversity and brings it together in a unified community. A central goal in this community is co-construction, where the program embraces family involvement, works to provide social support, and promotes family empowerment. The following are examples of how each of these goals is attained:

1. **The promotion of family involvement.** The CDLLC provides employer-sponsored care for some families. The open-door policy of the center means that families are welcome to drop by anytime. Many parents come on their breaks and lunches to gather a few cuddles and check on how their child is doing. Many of the students whose children are in the program drop in between classes, stealing time away from computers in the library to catch a smile. Each of the CDLLC's classrooms has a one-way observational window, allowing parents to check on their children without the child knowing.

    Each semester the program offers numerous opportunities for families to get involved in the classroom. In Wendy's and Jo's preschool classroom, for example, families are asked to attend the children's plays and puppet shows. These events are scheduled right before pick-up time, so most family members can attend. Marian and Korissa sponsor many involvement activities in their infant and toddler classroom as well. These tend to be less formal in nature and include invitations on walks or opportunities to ride with the children on the city bus (a favorite trip of the children). What each teacher tries to do is create varied experiences that ensure that each family member can become involved. Coupled with this is extensive communication and relationship building, which goes a long way toward ensuring that each family member feels empowered to become involved.

2. **The promotion of social support.** At the CDLLC, teachers work to incorporate daily communication strategies into their routine. Parents are greeted each morning, and pick-up time becomes a prime time for information exchange about the child's day. In the infant and toddler classrooms, family members receive a sheet of paper that provides eating, toileting, and napping habits for the day. These strategies are a precursor to social support. The foundations of established relationships can develop into opportunities for mutual learning about supporting children's development as well as opportunities to support parents in their role. This support could include the connection with community resources, the provision of information, and a patient ear and mutual problem-solving attitude.

    The staff members at the CDLLC recognize that they are one potential avenue for social support and that the relationships developed between family members can provide expansive support. To facilitate these relationships, the CDLLC has a central foyer that leads to each of the classrooms. The couches and chairs say "Welcome, come sit a while," and many family members will gather and chat throughout the day. Family nights sponsored by the CDLLC also serve to support these developing relationships. The teachers recognize that the relationships cultivated within the program's walls can be a source of enduring support.

3. **The promotion of family empowerment.** Family empowerment can only be cultivated from within. Environmental factors, however, can contribute to the personal belief that one's thoughts, feelings, and ways of viewing and interacting with the world are both valid and worthwhile. Strategies that empower family members include taking the time to listen, engaging in reflection, and validating families'

thoughts, feelings, and actions. At the CDLLC, the staff members recognize that the gift of time and focus is one of the most precious things they can give their families. Therefore, they work to ensure that meaningful connections occur on a regular basis. At times, this means stepping back, taking a deep breath, and taking the time to focus, recognizing that the time given to a family can be much more precious in the long run than the act of checking off items as done.

CONSTRUCTED-RESPONSE QUESTIONS

1. Identify strategies for creating effective partnerships with families, and explain how the CDLLC works to build these essential partnerships.

2. Identify how the strategies used in the CDLLC have a potentially long-term impact on family functioning. How might this, in turn, influence children's development?

CASE STUDY

A Comprehensive Approach to Access

Mulberry School (preschool through 3rd grade)

As a parent cooperative, the Mulberry School has built parent involvement into the infrastructure of the program. Families not only are required to engage in 50 hours of program involvement per year, but are charged $30 per hour should they not meet this obligation. Families must find strategies for involvement, and the school provides a wide variety of opportunities. These include opportunities to join the parent board and to participate in the classroom on a daily, weekly, or monthly basis. These opportunities include serving lunch, supervising a short time, accompanying children on field trips, or showcasing family talents or abilities. Families also are encouraged to join fundraising and committee work.

By making family involvement a requirement and providing options for involvement, the staff creates both the expectation and the opportunity for participation and social support. The teachers see most of the parents on a regular basis and develop relationships with them. In addition, the teachers see relationships develop and flourish between family members. All of this works to support the co-construction of relationships between home and school.

CONSTRUCTED-RESPONSE QUESTIONS

1. Identify opportunities for creating effective partnerships with families, and explain how the Mulberry School works to develop these essential partnerships.

2. Identify how the strategies used in the Mulberry School have a potentially long-term impact on family functioning. How might this, in turn, influence children's development?

REFLECTING ON AND APPLYING EFFECTIVE PRACTICES
(NAEYC AND CEC/DEC)

Ethics

- Naomi is a 2-year-old in your early childhood class. Every day, her grandmother drops her off in the morning and picks her up in the afternoon. As you do not see Naomi's mother regularly, you have sent notes home, and placed several phone calls with the goal of developing a partnership supporting Naomi's development. Naomi's mother has not returned your calls, nor has she attended any of the family activities you have invited her to. You have recently become concerned about Naomi's language development, and have intensified your efforts to contact her mother, to no avail. What should you do in this situation?

NAEYC Ideals

I-2.2. To develop relationships of mutual trust and create partnerships with the families we serve.

I-2.5. To respect the dignity and preferences of each family and to make an effort to learn about its structure, culture, language, customs, and beliefs.

DEC: Enhancement of Children's and Families' Quality of Lives

1. We shall demonstrate our respect and concern for children, families, colleagues, and others with whom we work, honoring their beliefs, values, customs, languages, and culture.

4. We shall advocate for equal access to high quality services and supports for all children and families to enhance their quality of lives.

- Co-constructing relationships with families is the cornerstone to developing effective partnerships with families. Explain the term *co-construction* and describe two or three strategies you would use to support co-construction.

Standards for Professional Practice

NAEYC: Building Family and Community Relationships

2a. Knowing about and understanding family and community characteristics

2b. Supporting and empowering families and communities through respectful, reciprocal relationships.

2c. Involving families and communities in their children's development and learning.

DEC: Professional and Ethical Practice

EC9S3: Respect family choices and goals.

CHAPTER REVIEW

- **What is the structure and composition of America's families, and why is this knowledge relevant to your role as a teacher?**

American families reflect extensive diversity. Who a child lives with—be it a two-parent or single-parent family; a foster, blended, or gay family; or a single-parent family where the mother is a teen parent—is an important consideration for teachers when working to create effective family partnerships. Within the framework of evidence-based practice, information on structure and composition can be used to gather, process, apply, and evaluate data. However, this data is only meaningful if it is relevant to specific families.

- **What is the child care trilemma, and how does it affect access to education and services?**

The three facets of the child care trilemma include issues of quality, accessibility, and affordability. Each of these issues can negatively affect family access to the field. For example, high-quality programs are typically more expensive than low-quality ones, restricting access based on affordability.

- **What issues affect access for the infant–toddler, preschool, and K–3 populations?**

Issues of access are shaped by affordability and the unique characteristics of varied populations. For example, the number of infants and toddlers needing care in the United States far exceeds the available supply of child care centers. Preschool access is largely shaped by income. Families of low income may not qualify for government funding and make too little to afford high-quality care. One solution for the preschool population is universal preschool, which is designed to provide high-quality care and education services to all preschool-aged children. Although this program is gaining popularity and political attention in the United States, less than 10% of the states offer universal preschool programs. School-age child care also presents issues of access. Children who are engaged in learning activities before and after school are more likely to succeed. However, parent fees associated with these programs make access difficult for many.

- **How do employer-based solutions affect access?**

Employer involvement in supporting access for families has numerous positive benefits for the workforce. These include increased morale, reduction in turnover or absenteeism, and increased productivity. Employers can provide on-site and off-site care and partnerships with community agencies to assist employees in finding quality care. Family-friendly workplace policies, such as allowing for parental leave and flexible work hours, are other strategies that support parents in balancing work and family.

- **What role does co-construction play in supporting relationships with families?**

The co-construction of relationships embraces families as equal partners in the education process. Further, co-construction works to involve families in schools, supporting families in their role as the child's first and most important teacher.

• **How is social support effectively provided to families?**

Social support requires that professionals begin with interest and acceptance toward families and builds through communication over time to support families' long-term goals. Social support involves the professional provision of support and the creation of ties that enable families to gain support from other members of their social network.

• **How does family empowerment affect family functioning?**

Family empowerment involves supporting parents' ability to effect change at the community, organizational, and individual level. Strategies that support empowerment include attending to family needs and providing the skills that enable families to become advocates for their children's development and education.

7 Understanding Professional Pathways

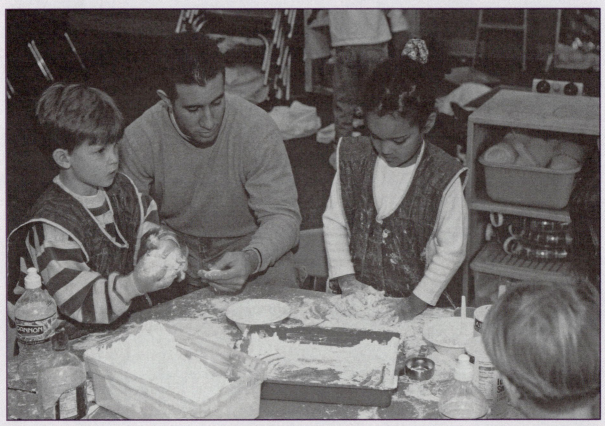

"No social advance rolls in on the wheels of inevitability. It comes through the tireless efforts and persistent work of dedicated individuals."

—MARTIN LUTHER KING, JR.

Meta knew early in her college career that she wanted to work with young children. Her first experience in a supervised setting was in her Introduction to Early Childhood Education class. In this class, she was required to conduct 10 hours of observation in the college's lab school during the semester. Her first hour was spent in a state of nervous trepidation: "Will the children accept me?" "What if I do something 'wrong'?" "How am I to interact with them?" Within that first hour, she was taken by the fact that the children were so welcoming, so accepting. These attitudes were demonstrated in a variety of ways. A few of the children were happily glued to her lap during her entire observation. One child would continuously catch her eye, and then shyly look away. Meta was thrilled when, toward the end of the hour, the child gave her a shy smile. By the end of her visit, Meta knew that this is where she needed to be.

GUIDING QUESTIONS

• What is meant by the term *early childhood education profession*? What factors present challenges in the profession?

• In what ways can your level of education, skills, and dispositions help you to become an early childhood professional?

• What issues contribute to challenges in compensation and turnover in the field, and how can these be addressed?

• What are the roles of reflection and the development of an educational philosophy in professionalism?

Her interest was quickly translated into a plan when she met with her college counselor. There were prescribed classes to be taken and an education plan for her to follow. She was assured that her hard work, determination, and persistence would pay off. In 4 to 5 years she would earn her degree and be able to embark on a career working with young children.

Amber's career pathway was very different. Her background was in the field of economics, and after the birth of her first child, she elected to stay home. The need for an income drove her to open a family child care home. At first, this was a temporary arrangement, just until her child was old enough to enter kindergarten. Over time, however, her family child care home became her passion. Although her initial goal was to meet basic licensing requirements, within 3 years, she was pursing accreditation from the National Association for Family Child Care for her family child care home. This transformation was shaped by the recognition of the incredible role she played in the lives of young children in her care. Further, she believed that she could advocate for quality care in her own unique way. Amber's advocacy focus included ensuring that she provided high-quality care herself and assisting other home child care programs in their pursuit of quality. To accomplish this, she shared her knowledge with members of the local family child care association and benefited from the knowledge of others in the group. Another important part of her journey was ongoing education. Through courses at the local community college, Amber learned how to provide quality care, the importance of family–professional partnerships, and the importance of her work for both children and larger society. What began as an economic necessity became a professional journey.

Sam's role in the field of early childhood education represented yet another unique, evolving path. His involvement began when his son attended Head Start. Sam's flexible schedule allowed him to volunteer in the classroom and see first-hand the benefits the program had for his son and the other children. Within a year of his son's entry to the program, he was hired as a teacher's assistant. Eventually, he wanted to have his own classroom. One challenge in meeting this goal was further schooling. Sam's work and family responsibilities precluded him from attending school full time, and the nearest early childhood education program was over an hour away. At a staff meeting, he learned of an online program run by a local college, and he quickly found out what he needed to do to participate. For him, the online environment was a boon. In 3 years he was able to complete degree requirements and earn an Associate of Applied Science (A.A.S.) degree in Early Childhood Education.

• • •

Each individual in these scenarios had very different career pathways, and each pathway was shaped by the opportunities open to them. Although they all used different routes to access the field of early childhood education, their ultimate goal was working with young children. Their experiences in the field are likely to be different as well, as their individual ability to continue education and secure needed compensation will vary with the career paths they select.

In the two previous chapters, you learned that early childhood education plays an important role in supporting equity for children and families. Equity is also an incredibly important issue for professionals. Each professional has diverse individual needs, including **compensation**, the need to feel valued, and the need to advance in their chosen career. Further, as you learned in Chapter 3, the incredible variance in program settings, missions, and ages of children served in early childhood education requires that professionals prepare themselves for the possibility of many different career roles. Career paths may not form a straight line, but instead might be a winding path with varied options and opportunities. These available choices affect your ongoing development. How effectively professionals are prepared for their career roles can affect the quality of care children receive and the support extended to their families. Issues of access and equity for children, families, and professionals, therefore, are complexly intertwined.

compensation
The amount of money earned for professional activity.

profession
The body of people in an occupation that is learned.

equitable compensation
Fair wages based on the professional requirements of employment.

THE EARLY CHILDHOOD EDUCATION PROFESSION

What does the term *early childhood professional* mean? There is a difference between the concepts of the early childhood *field* and the early childhood **profession**. The *field* of early childhood comprises anyone who provides early childhood services (NAEYC, 1993). The *profession* is represented by persons who have acquired some professional knowledge and are on a professional path. NAEYC's definition of a professional path includes those who have either completed or are enrolled in a credit-bearing early childhood professional preparation program. This program, typically provided by community colleges, technical schools, and 4-year colleges and universities, must meet recognized guidelines. Furthermore, persons who are participating in ongoing, competency-based training are considered to be on a professional pathway.

What do professionals need to grow and develop within the field? Professional access to the field requires attention to each individual's unique developmental characteristics. Professional development opportunities that support access must complement these developmental characteristics and prepare individuals for varied career paths. Career options need to be respected as part of the profession and **equitable compensation**, or fairly paid. All of these factors play a role in social equity, as they have an impact on the field's ability to attract and retain well-prepared

Professionals in the field have diverse needs.

professionals who provide high-quality services. In turn, these high-quality services support the growth and development of both children and their families. This vital role cannot be realized, however, unless professionals are adequately prepared.

PROFESSIONAL PREPARATION REQUIREMENTS

How do you prepare yourself to be an early childhood professional? This simple question has a complex response that is shaped by the position sought after, region of the country one lives in, and resources available. Were you to examine professional preparation requirements across the United States, you would find little agreement about the knowledge needed for successful performance. These vast discrepancies directly affect the quality of care and education that children and families receive.

For example, some states require only a high school diploma to work with young children in center-based care. Others require a college degree for the same occupation (U.S. Department of Labor, Bureau of Labor Statistics, 2007). Public school teachers in most states, however, must have at least a bachelor's degree (B.A. or B.S.), complete an approved teacher education program, and be licensed. Special education teachers in all states must be licensed. These licensing requirements include the completion of a teacher training program and at least a bachelor's degree. Many states require a master's degree (U.S. Department of Labor Bureau of Labor Statistics, 2007). Table 7.1 provides a summary of educational requirements in the field.

The lack of consistent professional preparation requirements emerged from the disparate origins of the field presented in Chapter 2. The fact that caring for and educating children originated as two separate fields with separate goals, coupled with the legislative emergence of the field of early childhood special education, has lead to numerous disparate threads within the larger field of early childhood education. This disparity can affect the quality of services that children and families receive, the compensation earned by professionals, and the ongoing professional development that is available.

Variance in professional development requirements, opportunities, and compensation affects equity in a variety of ways. Adequate preparation translates into quality educational services, supporting equity for *all* children and families. Professional development systems, as well as compensation that values working with children between birth and age 8, support equity for professionals. Supporting the goals of equity and inclusion requires attention to the preparation that *all* early childhood professionals need, regardless of their chosen occupation.

What information do professionals need to provide high-quality care and education? Professional preparation programs must support the development of needed knowledge, thereby supporting an understanding of the knowledge, or the "why," of the field (Katz,

TABLE 7.1 Educational Requirements by Employment Area	
Area of the Field/Occupation	**Educational Requirement (requirements will vary by state)**
Direct work with young children in center, family child care, or Head Start program	Varies from high school diploma to a bachelor's degree
Teaching in a program affiliated with a public school	Bachelor's degree and licensing
Teaching in special education	At least a bachelor's degree, with many states requiring a master's degree

FIGURE 7.1
Components of
Effective Teaching

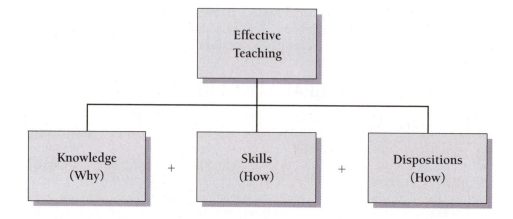

1999). Knowledge translates into practice, or skills, which provide the "how" components of the field as applied in work with young children and their families. Another skill, also focused on the "how," is the development of appropriate dispositions. *Dispositions* reflect teacher attitudes that create environments and interactions that support, respect, and nurture (Katz, 1993). Knowledge and skills have historically been represented by education and experience, whereas support for and measurement of dispositions represent an emerging area of the field. Figure 7.1 illustrates these components of effective practice.

Level of Education

**accreditation
standards**

Series of standards developed by NAEYC to ensure quality in early childhood programs and teacher preparation institutions.

Professional education is tied to classroom quality (Burchinal, Cryer, Clifford, & Howes, 2002; Early et al., 2006). In view of this, the NAEYC requires adequate levels of professional preparation for child care administrators and teachers as a part of its **accreditation standards**. The link between education and quality has been so well established that Head Start has mandated that 50% of all its early childhood teachers must have a bachelor's degree by 2013. Further, all teachers must have an associate's degree in early childhood education or a related field by 2013 (Administration for Children and Families, 2008).

Despite this link between level of education and quality of care, many professionals do not have the required levels of education. For example, many of those working with young children lack either a Child Development Associate credential or a college degree. Although many of these persons provide care that is consistent, caring, and beneficial to children's overall development (NAEYC, 1993), the general relationship between education and program quality reflects that higher levels of education are associated with stronger early childhood programs.

How does education influence practice? Education provides knowledge of children's development, and this knowledge forms a basis for practice. Consider a 2-year-old who responds to boundaries and limits in the classroom with an avid "No!" and who insists that classroom materials are "Mine!" Understanding developmental issues facing 2-year-olds in general helps teachers to know that these behaviors are important milestones in social-emotional development. Children at this age experiment with asserting themselves, trying to become more independent, and creating schemas where their actions and interactions with others and the environment can have an impact. Knowing this relationship between development and behavior results in teacher practices that guide and shape the child's behavior based on developmental needs. This is contrary to often-used practices that punish the child for behaviors that are considered "problematic." Knowledge of children's development contributes to the finding that early childhood educators with increased levels of professional preparation provide more developmentally appropriate, nurturing, and responsive care and education experiences (NAEYC, 2005). In addition to knowledge of general development, teachers should also be knowledgeable of atypical development. For example, as you learned in Chapter 5, knowing how to identify developmental delays and disabilities through red flags is critical to supporting children's development and learning.

Challenges in Pursuing Education. Similar to programs serving children, professional preparation programs vary greatly in their ability to meet the needs of persons in the field. Part of this variance emerges because not all professionals have equal access to ongoing education. An ideal of education is that it is open to all. The reality is

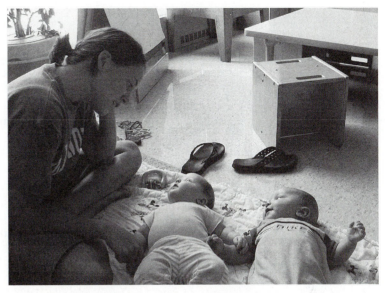

A teacher's level of education is positively associated with the quality of care children receive.

that education requires access to resources, which include both monetary resources and time. Although many in the field might have access to the money needed to support education, time might be a factor. For others, there might be time to pursue education, but a lack of financial resources makes pursuit impossible. NAEYC (2007) identifies this relationship as particularly problematic for women of color with low incomes who have limited access to education, particularly at the bachelor's level. For many, a combination of time and monetary obstacles might be present.

Education is one important professional preparation requirement. In addition, professionals need skills that support children's overall growth and development and establish effective partnerships with families.

TEACHING AND LEARNING CONNECTIONS

Continuing Your Education

- Explore federal financial aid and available funds through college financial aid offices.
- Contact your local Child Care Resource and Referral Agency to find out about opportunities supportive of continuing education in your community.
- Talk to your program director or principal about accommodations that can support your education, including tuition reimbursement, flexible hours to complete a practicum, field experiences or student teaching, and increased compensation based on increased levels of education.
- Explore varied course delivery methods, including online, weekend, and intensive course offerings.
- Explore options for financing your continuing education, including scholarships and programs such as T.E.A.C.H.

Skills

Skills can be thought of as applications of knowledge within a particular situation. Whereas knowledge provides the "why" of teacher behaviors, skills provide the "how." For example, the child might know why a paper needs cutting, but without the ability to cut the paper, little is likely to happen. A teacher, for example, might know that providing children with quality literacy experiences is essential, but without the ability or skill to create an engaging, literacy-rich environment, this knowledge does very little. Teachers could also have extensive knowledge regarding activity development, but without the skills to adapt instruction and/or make accommodations to support the engagement of each child, the lesson will lack equity for all children.

The application of skills is both an art and a science. The art is represented through knowing *when* to apply particular skills, and the science is based on knowledge of *how* to apply this information. Knowledge and skills, however, represent only two facets of professional need, with dispositions representing the third.

Dispositions

dispositions

Habits of mind or ways of responding to situations that focus on the *how* of applying the skills and knowledge that individuals have.

Dispositions are "habits of mind or tendencies to respond to certain situations in certain ways" (Katz, 1995, p. 3). Dispositions differ from skills and knowledge in that dispositions focus on *how* we apply knowledge and skills. For example, two teachers in a kindergarten classroom might have similar knowledge and skills. Differences in their passion for learning, friendliness, and creativity, however, will result in two very different classroom environments.

Consider these rationales for focusing on dispositions (Egertson, 2004): First, *having a particular knowledge or skill does not mean that it will be applied.* For example, Andi attended college for 4 years. She graduated with honors with a bachelor's degree in Early Childhood Education and certification to work with children between birth and age 8. After Andi's first year of teaching in a kindergarten classroom, the principal at Andi's school, Marin, was concerned about her performance. Andi was very knowledgeable and could apply a variety of appropriate skills in the classroom, but Marin felt there was something missing in Andi's classroom interactions. On one occasion Marin observed Andi as she developed a topic web with the children in her classroom. Although her prompts for children's ideas for the topic web were sound in terms of practice, the way that Andi approached the task seemed to lack passion or interest in the activity. As a result, the children seemed bored. They responded to Andi's prompts with what Marin felt was apathy about the subject they were discussing and the resulting topic web. Marin decided that what was missing in the curricular environment were dispositions that supported each child's learning and engagement.

Marin recognized that dispositions are an important facet of the educational environment and decided to provide Andi with experiences that would develop her dispositions. This decision reflected the second core rationale for the development of dispositions, centering on the fact that dispositions *work along with knowledge and skills to support learning* (Egertson, 2004). Further, Marin believed that all individuals have *natural tendencies toward appropriate dispositions* and that these *inclinations could be supported through learning.*

Marin set out to develop a plan for enhancing Andi's dispositions toward children's learning. Before developing this plan, Marin explored what dispositions were appropriate for an early childhood professional. In general, she believed that appropriate dispositions included cultivating children's love of learning, respect for the world around them, and desire to explore and experiment. Marin considered what specific dispositions might lead to these general outcomes for children and how these dispositions could be cultivated.

• • • BECOMING A PROFESSIONAL • • •

Career Pathways

Child Care Resource and Referral Network Training Coordinator

Jill has been with the Child Care Resource and Referral Network (CCRRN) for 12 years. She started as an intern in the AmeriCorps program as she pursued her bachelor's degree in early childhood education. When a full-time job opened up, Jill was ready—she nearly had her degree, and she had gained valuable experience. Jill knew that the Provider Services Manager position was right for her. She had previously worked as a center director, and although she enjoyed working with children, she felt her talents lay more in the training and coordination aspects of the field.

Jill's position has enjoyed dramatic growth during the past decade. Right now, she supervises three people and is responsible for making sure that the training and coordination needs of a large community in Illinois are met. Most of the providers who attend training are family child care professionals, and the state's new Quality Rating System (QRS) is one of the catalysts that is bringing them in. In Illinois, the QRS is specifically designed to reach out to kith and kin care providers, encouraging them to receive additional training. This training, in turn, qualifies them for increased subsidies from the state government and ultimately increases the quality of care children receive.

Along with this growth, the nature of Jill's job has changed. Originally, the CCRRN would sponsor a few training sessions a year, based on what the staff felt people would like to learn about. Now, it offers training that is shaped by various programs and agencies, including the Illinois Department of Human Services. In addition, the agency conducts yearly assessment surveys, determining what professionals in the field most want to learn about.

On any given day, Jill is involved in a variety of different tasks. She conducts training, supervises staff, talks with professionals about what they're interested in, and talks with state agencies to coordinate opportunities. She loves this incredible diversity and feels lucky to have a job that is so stimulating and challenging. At the same time, her job has offered her a great deal of flexibility. For example, Jill was able to bring her young children to work with her and work at home part-time during their early years of life.

The greatest reward Jill identifies is her ability to have an impact on quality care. "I see so many people on a regular basis, and see their growth and development over time, and I know how much that is benefiting the children in their care. It is great to be a part of such a dynamic organization that creates so many positive changes."

Jill's position fits in the general category of educational administration. This area has a good occupational outlook, with growth anticipated to be as fast as the average for all occupations through 2014 (U.S. Department of Labor Bureau of Labor Statistics, 2007).

Positive professional dispositions cultivate a love of learning in young children.

Effective teachers are effective people who are warm and caring, enjoy life, and are enthusiastic about helping others grow and develop (Taylor & Wasicsko, 2000). Essential dispositions for effective teachers include *empathy*, or the ability to understand and accept the perspectives of others. Teachers must also have a *positive view of both self and others*, where dignity and self-worth are both internally and externally validated. Being honest and genuine, reflected through *authenticity*, communicates to others a desire to connect. And finally, effective teachers need both *purpose and vision*, where beliefs and values permeate their actions and provide a framework for interactions and goals for both themselves and others (Usher, 2004). These dispositions—coupled with knowledge of cultural, linguistic, socioeconomic, and ability diversity—can create equitable, welcoming, and engaging environments for *all* children, their families, and other professionals.

Go to MyEducationLab and select the topic "Diverse Learners." Under Activities and Applications, watch the video *Explode Stereotypes* and reflect on how stereotypes can impede the development of positive dispositions supporting children's learning.

Once Marin selected dispositions that she wanted to cultivate, she turned her attention how to support Andi's development of these dispositions. Marin decided to observe Andi in the classroom and give her *positive feedback* to support dispositions; this would also give her an opportunity to *model appropriate dispositions.* Further, she encouraged Andi to learn about and implement the Project Approach (covered in detail in Chapter 8) with the children in her class. She anticipated that the co-construction of curriculum with the children would create feelings of empowerment and connection. In turn, both Andi and the children developed dispositions of curiosity by taking risks and experimenting, showing a willingness to explore options, allowing flexibility, and expressing a sense of wonder (Ros-Voseles & Moss, 2007). Finally, the principal made dispositions a part of *evaluation and assessment* for all the teachers and other professionals within their early childhood program.

Supporting the ongoing development of professionals requires attention to these factors. In turn, this attention can support the knowledge, skills, and dispositions required for success in the field. The workplace, the field of early childhood, and society as a whole are important contextual factors to examine.

ISSUES IN THE PROFESSION

Understanding the professional development of practicing teachers and other early childhood professionals requires being aware of the challenges facing the field. One of these challenges is the low level of compensation, making continuing education (after obtaining a certificate or a degree) and higher education difficult to afford. Because education is sometimes not directly tied to increased compensation, many are deterred from pursuing higher education and other professional training opportunities (National Center for Early Development and Learning, 2001). Other potential obstacles include a lack of

---

TEACHING AND LEARNING CONNECTIONS

Learning About Professional Preparation Requirements

- Learn about the professional preparation requirements for different career opportunities in your state by discussing opportunities with a college advisor or career counselor or by exploring the Internet. (To look for professional preparation requirements in your state, for example, you can type into a search engine the words *professional preparation, early childhood*, and the name of your state.)

- If you are taking courses at an associate degree level, speak with an academic advisor about courses that articulate or transfer easily to baccalaureate programs.

- Keep in mind that even if you are not contemplating pursuing further education right now, you may change your mind in the future.

---

benefits and the lack of a coordinated system of career paths (National Center for Early Development and Learning, 2001).

Challenges in Professional Preparation

Challenges in professional preparation can be understood by revisiting the separate histories of the field. As was presented in Chapter 2, one distinct strand of early childhood education emerged from the provision of child care services. This strand focused on the service of caring for children while their mothers were away at work. Until the advent of Head Start, this strand was predominantly a vehicle used by the middle and upper middle class to ensure appropriate educational experiences for their children. Another strand is represented by early childhood special education and originated through legislative mandate. Two additional strands include kindergarten education and primary grade education.

Similar to programming for children, teacher preparation programs in the United States remain segregated in their educational focus. Course offerings and educational options are offered separately in the areas of child care, early childhood education, and special education. Further, a clear path, or transfer of credits, between educational programs is often lacking. This means that education obtained at one level (such as at an associate degree level) will not always transfer to another (such as a baccalaureate program).

In addition to the challenges in professional preparation are challenges related to the issues of compensation and turnover.

Challenges of Compensation and Turnover

Challenges in compensation and turnover can best be understood by examining challenges faced in professionalizing the field as a whole. As was once believed of the field of nursing, the care and education of young children has been perceived by society as women's work. Historically, women have cared for children without pay. As this work was not viewed as specialized, the field has not been acknowledged as having the professional status it deserves. In addition, there has been a pervasive societal attitude that learning begins when children enter formal schooling, at about age 5. This negative viewpoint of professionalism, coupled with the failure to recognize the great importance of the first years of life, impedes accepting the viewpoint that caring for and educating children are inseparable activities that begin at birth. Consequently, many parents viewed persons working with very young children as little more than babysitters, whose basic responsibilities include keeping children out of danger until parents can resume their care.

Over the past decade, a variety of studies have contradicted this negative stereotype of early childhood educators. For example, the National Child Care Staffing Study (Whitebook, Howes, & Phillips, 1990) found that a skilled and educated early childhood education workforce was linked to high-quality early childhood programs with positive outcomes for children. The importance of the early childhood education workforce has also been bolstered by the findings of brain research. Related research highlights the huge amount of development in the early years of life and that the development that occurs in these first years has a dramatic impact on children for the rest of their lives. Research indicates that the quality of care influences not only brain development, but also school readiness (Bailey, Scarborough, Hebbeler, Spiker, & Mallik, 2004; Piesner-Feinberg, et. al., 1999). This positive relationship is particularly important for children and families with low incomes (Whitebook & Eichberg, 2002).

Despite the growing awareness of the importance of the early years, compensation levels of some areas of early childhood services are dramatically low. The average salary for child care workers is $7.90 per hour, and the average wage of preschool teachers is $9.53 per hour (Center for the Child Care Workforce, 2004). Child care center staff compensation, including wages and benefits, is exceptionally low, with child care workers comprising one of the lowest paid of all classes of workers in the United States (National Center for Early Development and Learning, 2000).

Interestingly, the varied origins and histories of child care, early childhood education, and special education have lead to different levels of compensation for professionals. In general, program directors and early childhood professionals working with kindergarteners through third graders earn more than professionals working in a child care center. Center-based staff earn more than family child care providers (North Carolina Institute for Early Childhood, 2001), and staff working with preschool populations earn more than those working with the birth to 3 population (NAEYC, 1993). Finally, professionals working in early childhood special education make the most when compared with each of these other occupations (McCormick Tribune Center for Early Childhood Leadership, 2005).

turnover rate
Statistical measure of number of professionals who leave the field.

This discrepancy in pay creates differences in turnover rates, with those being paid less for their work—not surprisingly—being more likely to leave the field. The low compensation of early childhood professionals contributes directly to the dramatic **turnover rate**. The staff turnover rate of child care center personnel is between 25% and 50% per year (National Center for Early Development and Learning, 2001). The American Federation of Labor-Congress of Industrial Organizations (AFL-CIO) (2007) reported the turnover rate of child care professionals to be more than 33% annually. This striking turnover rate is occurring despite the significant job prospects in the field. Projections indicate that job opportunities will increase as much as 10% to 20% between 2002 and 2012 (AFL-CIO, 2007).

One of the top reasons for concern about the turnover rate in the field is the relationship between the quality of care children receive and workforce stability. Specifically, continuity of care is a predictor of quality and child outcomes. Excessive turnover rates undermine quality and directly affect children's abilities to benefit from early childhood education services (Belsky et al., 2007). Resolving the challenges related to professional preparation, compensation, and turnover requires solutions that take into account the complex relationship of a system with disparate origins that lacks a clear, substantive funding stream.

EXPLORING SOLUTIONS

Recall from Chapter 4 the discussion of ecological systems theory, where children are influenced by the contexts (such as family, early childhood program, neighborhood) in which they grow and develop. Similarly, professionals are influenced by their developing contexts, with their workplace, as an environment in which they directly interact, representing an important part of their microsystem. This microsystem includes working conditions and practices that support ongoing development in the profession.

Supporting Professional Preparation

You learned about workplace policies that are considered "family friendly" in Chapter 6. These policies include flexible work hours, partnerships with local Child Care Resource and Referral Agencies (who can provide information about child care opportunities), on-site child care, and access to child care programs off-site. Military child care was presented as a solution to many of the challenges that military families face in accessing quality child care. Specifically, as military child care provides a variety of child care options—oversight to ensure safety, training, and improved wages for staff; accreditation to support and ensure program quality; and cost sharing to improve program affordability—it is an excellent model of supporting access. The family-friendly template can be applied to professional needs as well. Table 7.2 provides information on how families' access to high-quality care and education for their children relates to issues of access faced by professionals.

How do these factors work together to support professional access? Consider Libby, who is a teaching assistant in a Head Start classroom. After her first year on the job, Libby decided that she would like to pursue additional education. Her goal was to become a lead teacher in her Head Start program. She presented this goal to her program director,

TABLE 7.2 Ensuring Access for Professionals

Family Access Factor	Application to Professional Access
Flexible work hours	Flexible work hours to pursue education
Partnerships with local Child Care Resource and Referral Agencies	Partnership with local training and education agencies, including Child Care Resource and Referral Agencies, community training programs including programs that provide food service and CPR training, and partnerships with community colleges and universities to support continued education
On-site child care	Educational programming at the early childhood program site
Off-site child care	Ensuring that community programs provide the educational opportunities staff need
Varied child care options	Varied educational programs, including online, evening, and weekend training opportunities
Oversight to ensure safety, training, and improved wages for staff	High-quality educational services that provide professionals with an ongoing professional development system, including the development of articulation systems that allow professionals to transfer from one program to the other without having to repeat previous education
Accreditation to ensure program quality	Accreditation of community colleges and universities to ensure program quality, articulation, and professional preparedness
Cost sharing to improve program affordability	Monies available for professional development, through both programs of employment and community-based programs (such as Child Care Resource and Referral Agencies)

T.E.A.C.H. scholarship

Scholarship opportunity that links education to compensation. As of early 2009, T.E.A.C.H. scholarships were offered in 23 states.

who informed her that staff development funds were available to support her education. In addition, her director informed her that community and state programs were also available that provided monetary support. These included small scholarships from the local Child Care Resource and Referral Agency to cover the costs of books and Teacher Education and Compensation Helps (**T.E.A.C.H. scholarships**) in her state of Michigan. These scholarships would cover most costs associated with tuition and books, reimbursement for substitute teachers to cover Libby's college attendance at classes she took during the day, monies to help pay for her travel to and from the college, a bonus when Libby completed her credit goals, and academic counseling to help her meet her overall goals. In exchange for receipt of the scholarship, Libby agreed to stay with her Head Start program for a year following her contract completion.

Libby began her studies at the community college in her area. She took such courses as Child Growth and Development, Introduction to Early Childhood Education, and Curriculum for Young Children. After her first semester, she decided to transfer to the local university.

In addition to her college training, Libby took advantage of the food services and CPR training that were offered on-site at her Head Start program. Staff development days also provided on-site learning opportunities, and her employer partnered with a variety of local agencies and individuals to ensure that the training provided met staff development needs. In one case, a presenter was brought in to address how to support positive guidance with young children. Libby found this session particularly helpful, as she and the other teacher in her classroom had been struggling with how to effectively support the challenging behavior of one of the children in the classroom.

Rebecca, as an in-home family child care provider, faced unique challenges in her pursuit of ongoing education. She too qualified for a T.E.A.C.H. scholarship. However, her position as the only person in her home providing care for several young children made it extremely difficult for her to attend college courses during the day. Fortunately, Rebecca was able to take evening and weekend courses at the local community college and several courses online. Although Rebecca was most interested in courses on infant–toddler development and curriculum, only one course in this topic area was offered. When it came time for Rebecca to complete her first practicum in her course of study, she was particularly frustrated by the challenge presented. How would she take the time off that she needed to complete her practicum hours?

Professional preparation reflects one aspect of challenge in the field. In addition, compensation and turnover are two other pervasive issues that have an impact on the quality of care and education provided.

Addressing Compensation and Turnover

Issues of compensation and turnover are so important in the field that NAEYC's Conceptual Framework for Early Childhood Professional Development (1993) includes the following recommendations:

- Compensation should not be differentiated on the basis of the ages of children served.
- Early childhood professionals should be encouraged to seek additional professional preparation and should be rewarded accordingly.
- Early childhood professionals with comparable qualifications, experience, and job responsibilities should receive comparable compensation regardless of the setting of their employment. This means that a teacher working in a community child care

---

TEACHING AND LEARNING CONNECTIONS

Addressing Issues of Compensation

- Represent yourself as a professional at all times by dressing in a professional manner, using appropriate language, and maintaining professional topics in conversation in the work environment.
- Advocate for the importance of the field by joining your local NAEYC affiliate and by educating others about early childhood education through conversation, letters to the editor of your community paper, and class presentations.
- Commit to pursuing ongoing education.
- Provide care and education that is consistently of high quality and in alignment with the best of what is known about supporting young children's development and learning.

---

center, a family child care provider, and a primary grade teacher who each hold comparable professional qualifications and carry out comparable functions or responsibilities should also receive comparable compensation for their work.
- Compensation for early childhood professionals should be equivalent to that of other professionals with comparable preparation requirements, experience, and job responsibilities.
- The provision of an adequate benefits package is a crucial component of compensation for early childhood staff.
- Career ladders should be established, providing additional increments in salary based on performance and participation in professional development opportunities.

Determining where the money will come from is an inherent challenge in addressing issues of compensation and turnover. As you have learned, the field of early childhood education relies heavily on parent fees to support programs. Many parents are spending a substantial amount of their income on services. Because of the existing challenges families face in paying for early childhood services, charging families additional monies to support increased teacher salaries is not seen as a viable option. If additional monies are not to come from families, they must come from other sources, which may include the program, corporations, communities, or the government.

The impact of professional preparation, compensation, and turnover can be measured at the workplace, field, and societal levels. Policies developed at each of these levels can and do have significant positive changes. In addition, your self-advocacy regarding your role as a professional can also have a positive impact.

Self-Advocacy: The Role of Reflection and Philosophy

Learning how to advocate for yourself is an important part of your professional development. Representing yourself as a professional and acquiring the needed knowledge, skills, and dispositions—as well as communicating those to others—is referred to as **self-advocacy**.

Self-advocacy requires personal reflection. Reflection, in turn, plays an important role in representing abilities. Based on this, self-advocacy requires developing reflection skills and personal philosophy.

self-advocacy
The ability of professionals to articulate and advance the public perceptions of their work.

Constructivists

Constructivism synthesizes the debate between behaviorists and maturationists. Constructivists see an inextricable link between development and environment, reflecting a belief in the complex interaction between nature and nurture. Children are driven to act on their environment, and in turn, the environment—and the child—changes based on these interactions.

Although Jean Piaget is often referred to as the father of constructivism, the idea that child development is influenced by interaction with the environment preceded the work of Piaget by nearly a century. For example, Jean-Marc Gaspard Itard (1775–1838), a self-taught physician during the French Revolution, is considered one of the first true constructivist theorists. After the revolution, he received formal training, becoming an expert in working with persons who were deaf and lacked speech (referred to as mute at that time). He developed strategies for the education and treatment of persons who were deaf, efforts that have led to him being commonly referred to as the "patriarch of special education."

One of Itard's most notable accomplishments was his work with a boy called Victor, or "The Wild Boy of Aveyron" (Itard, 1962). Victor was a 12-year-old boy when he was found in the woods by a group of hunters. It was apparent to Itard that the boy had lived on his own for some time, perhaps as long as 7 years. The boy lacked human speech and, according to Itard, had a profound aversion to society. Itard embarked on an intensive, 5-year training plan with Victor, targeting social-emotional goals as well as speech and communication. After 5 years, Victor had made many gains. Itard's contributions represented the first systematic attempts at specialized education based on the individual needs of a child. These efforts spoke to Itard's belief that development can be enhanced based on environmental stimuli.

Edouard Sequin (1812–1880) was a student of Itard and shared Itard's belief that appropriate educational methods could have a dramatic impact on children's development. In France, Sequin opened the first school dedicated to the education of persons with intellectual disabilities (then referred to as the mentally handicapped) in 1839. A decade later, he opened similar schools in the United States. Sequin's approach centered on observation and supported tasks fostering both physical and intellectual development, which in turn promoted self-reliance and independence. Sequin wrote extensively on the education of persons with intellectual disabilities. He was the first president of the **American Association on Intellectual and Developmental Disabilities** (formerly the American Association on Mental Retardation) (Spodek, Saracho, & Davis, 1987).

Despite its initial popularity, the work of both Itard and Sequin lost favor. The preferred treatment for persons with disabilities in both the United States and Europe became institutionalization and segregation from society. Sadly, this did not change significantly until the work of Maria Montessori became popular and the social and political reforms of the 1960s took place.

As you learned in Chapter 4, the work of Jean Piaget (1896–1937) formalized and advanced the concept of constructivism in many ways. His theory of cognitive development offered a stage-based theory of children's learning and development. The theory reflected his belief that a child's development and learning are affected by the interaction between the child's own internal drives and the surrounding environment. Through this theory, Piaget offered specific information regarding what children needed at each respective stage.

Constructivism remains one of the most widely accepted theories in the field and has shaped High/Scope Curriculum and the Kamii-DeVries Approach, which will each be covered in detail later in the chapter.

pro
phi
Stat
beli
rega
of e
edu
role

American Association on Intellectual and Developmental Disabilities

Called the American Association on Mental Retardation until 2007, the AAIDD is the oldest organization in the United States focusing on the intellectual disabilities of children and adults.

Com

Lev Vygotsky: Sociocultural Theory. Lev Vygotsky believed that supporting children's development and learning is a **socially mediated process**. Through this process, children learn societal expectations and gather knowledge through interactions with adults and other more experienced peers. Vygotsky's impact on the field of early childhood education in general and teaching practices specifically was extensive, and his work will be discussed in more detail in Chapter 12.

Vygotsky thought that the most effective way to support learning was by attending to a child's need for developing significant social relationships (Vygtosky, 1986). Mixed-age groupings and looping are two applications of Vygotskian theory that focus on the support, development, and maintenance of essential relationships.

Applications. **Mixed-age grouping** places children in groups with others of different ages. There are typically two ranges of ages for children between the ages of birth and five by which children are grouped: birth

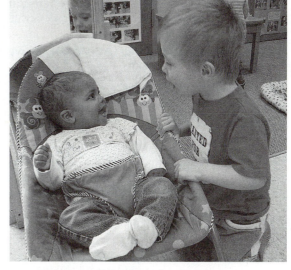

Mixed-age groupings have many advantages.

to 3 and 3 to 5. In this model, a child entering care at 6 weeks of age will be in the same classroom until he or she reaches the age of 3, only experiencing one classroom transition before kindergarten. This model supports relationship development and complements the work of Vygotsky by allowing children to learn from more experienced peers. Mixed-age groupings in the primary grades have other advantages, too. Specifically, children and teachers have more time to develop relationships, an essential foundation on which learning and development can be built. Mixed-age groupings are also reflective of natural family groupings.

Many administrators argue that mixed-age groupings are not financially feasible because staff–child ratios are mandated according to the age of the youngest child in the classroom. For example, state licensing requirements might call for one caregiver for every four infants, five toddlers, and six 2-year-olds. In a mixed-age grouping, even if there is only one infant in the environment, a one-to-four ratio must be maintained. One cost-effective solution to this concern is **looping**. In a looping arrangement, the teacher transitions into a new classroom along with a group of children of similar ages, thereby eliminating the need to modify staff–child ratio based on the youngest child in the group. Looping maintains relationships between teachers and children, despite the structural changes imposed by programs.

socially mediated process
Children's learning is based on their interactions with other members of society.

mixed-age grouping
The placement of children of varying ages (usually a 2- to 3-year span) in one classroom environment.

looping
Arrangement designed to support continuity of care through professionals transitioning to a new classroom with the children.

TEACHING AND LEARNING CONNECTIONS

Benefits of Mixed-Age Grouping

- Requires fewer classroom transitions as children stay in same room for longer period of time.
- Promotes development of meaningful relationships with caregivers.
- By creating groups that include older and younger children, structures the environment so children can learn from more experienced peers.

John Dewey: A Focus on Pragmatism. John Dewey (1859–1952) was part of the progressive education movement. He believed that the most effective education occurs in an interactive social context, advocating a bustling, supportive community (Dewey, 1916/2004). He saw the world's everyday problem-solving tasks as valuable learning opportunities, a view that led him to be known as the father of pragmatism because of the value he placed on everyday, unremarkable experiences. To Dewey, true education lay in teaching children to learn, as opposed to delivering them subject matter. He saw experience and growth as being complexly intertwined and considered children's free exploration of the environment an essential component of their education. In 1896, he founded the University of Chicago Laboratory Schools, the primary goal of which was the rigorous testing and evaluation of his theories in a practical setting.

Applications. Dewey's ideas about supporting children's innate curiosity and respecting their ability to "learn by doing" are still widely respected today. His ideas are reflected in such things as support for home–school continuity, teaching children practical living strategies, a focus on the acquisition and application of basic skills, learning that focuses on problem solving and collaboration, and the development of learning experiences that support and reward children's inherent curiosity (University of Chicago Lab Schools, 2006).

Maria Montessori

Italian educator who founded the first children's school and developed materials and a training program based on her philosophy for educating children.

Maria Montessori. Maria Montessori (1870–1952) was considered a counterpart to John Dewey and others in the progressive education movement. Her views were similar to Dewey's in that she saw education as a catalyst in individual and social development (Smith, 2005). The two also agreed that childhood is a time in which support for curiosity and inquiry is critical. They differed, however, regarding how education should be provided and the method by which development and learning should be supported.

Montessori was the first woman in Italy to receive a medical degree. She accomplished this at a time when there was a strong bias against professional women. This created an unwelcome climate for her medical practice, and she was sent to supervise a school for "deficient and insane" children in Rome. Before Montessori arrived at the school, treatment of children was marked by a lack of respect and attention. She was interested in creating a different approach and based her work on the work of Itard and Sequin. She was systematic and scientific and provided warm, loving care in a stimulating environment. Further, Montessori tailored her care and teaching to the individual needs of each child. Montessori's caring, conscientious approach showed impressive results. Children who were once deemed uneducable thrived. They passed exams and earned grades comparable to the grades of other children in the public school system (Edwards, 2002).

Montessori felt that teaching methods supporting child achievement for this population would be successful in the public school system as well. She devoted her life to developing an effective method for the education of all children (Edwards, 2002). These methods were based on the premise that the child is a dynamic, curious person with an inner need and drive to master his or her world. Montessori believed that children come to know the world through their senses. Supporting this requires experiences that allow for exploration, learning, and development through and of the senses. She also believed that children **auto-educate**, meaning that they actively construct knowledge based on their interactions with the environment. This means that children's personal interests provide the cornerstone of curriculum and that children should be allowed opportunities to repeat activities until they are mastered.

auto-educate

Montessori concept stressing that children actively construct knowledge based on their interactions with the environment.

Montessori wrote both philosophical works related to children and specific guidelines for teachers. The guidelines include an emphasis on teacher observation of the individual child's interests and conscientious preparation of the environment based on these

TABLE 8.3	The Beliefs of Constructivists
Constructivists	**Beliefs**
Jean-Marc Gaspard Itard (1775–1838)	• Developed strategies for educating and treating persons who are deaf. • Known as the patriarch of special education. • Made the first systematic attempts at specialized education based on individual needs of the child. • Believed that development can be enhanced based on environmental stimuli.
Edouard Sequin (1812–1880)	• Student of Itard who shared belief the that appropriate educational methods can markedly affect children's development. • Opened first school dedicated to the education of persons with intellectual disabilities. • First president of the American Association on Intellectual and Developmental Disabilities.
Jean Piaget (1896–1937)	• Developed stage-based theory of children's learning and development. • Believed that children developed based on interactions between child's own internal drives and the surrounding environment. • Theories of cognitive development shaped High/Scope Curriculum and the Kamii-DeVries Approach.
Lev Vygotsky (1896–1934)	• Believed that children's development and learning is a socially mediated process. • Children learn societal expectations and gather knowledge through interactions with adults and other more experienced peers. • Placed relationships at the center of children's development and learning.
John Dewey (1859–1952)	• Believed that the most effective education occurs within an interactive social context. • Advocated for problem solving as a valuable learning opportunities. • Known as the father of pragmatism.
Maria Montessori (1870–1952)	• Saw education as a catalyst in individual and social development. • Devoted life to developing an effective method for the education of all children. • Saw children as the center of learning, and child-centered curriculum as essential. • Viewed the environment as a third teacher.

observations. She saw the environment as so pivotal that she often referred to it as the "third teacher," with children and the teacher consisting of the other two.

Applications. Applications of Montessori extend beyond its specific methodology and teacher training. The philosophical applications of inclusion, the relationship between movement and cognition, the importance of active learning, and the importance of order in the lives of children should be staples in all high-quality early childhood programs (Lillard, 2005). Further discussion of the structure and effectiveness of the Montessori approach will be covered in Chapter 11.

Table 8.3 summarizes the beliefs of the constructivists discussed here.

From these philosophical underpinnings, several curricular models and approaches have emerged, many of which influence the field today. Understanding each of these perspectives helps you process and analyze the effectiveness of each model and approach based on your own value system and beliefs about how children develop and learn.

UNDERSTANDING CURRICULAR MODELS AND APPROACHES

Curricular models and approaches are tools that can support theory, planning, implementation, and evaluation. They are derived from child development research and theory (Goffin & Wilson, 2001) and base their varied approaches on underlying philosophies.

TEACHING AND LEARNING CONNECTIONS

Caution: Prepared Curriculum!

Prepared curriculum, in this context, refers to curriculum—often commercially distributed—that presents a series of activities based on general age categories. For example, a curriculum for 3-year-olds might include a week-by-week guide to different classroom activities and themes that can be implemented.

Although prepared curricula might provide some useful ideas for activities, teachers must remember the following:

- Prepared curricula do not take into account individual variation in children's development and learning styles.
- Themes based on the time of year or a set schedule (for example, Dinosaurs in April) fail to take into account children's interests.
- Themes often ignore context—children learning about snow in Hawaii or the ocean in Iowa lack important experiential knowledge in which to couch their learning.

Because of the link between curriculum and theory, many in the field argue that a purist approach to curriculum must be adopted. In the purist approach, particular models are followed in totality to the exclusion of others. Still others recommend an eclectic approach, where curriculum is designed representing the best of effective practices and tailored to the individual needs of each child. Prepared curricula are another option, which can include a series of activities and environment-design strategies presented in specific units or areas of investigation and knowledge. For example, a prepared curriculum on the topic of dinosaurs might include books, art activities, manipulatives, songs and finger plays, and pretend play props centered on dinosaur exploration. Typically, these activities occur over a specified time, such as one week.

An important caveat to remember if you are considering adopting a prepared curriculum is that the curricular design might not adapt well to individual children. Further, many curricula are designed around individual content areas (such as a curriculum focused specifically on math, science, or literacy skills). This "piecemeal" approach can result in disconnected activities and teaching practices that lack integration and cohesiveness (NAEYC & NAECS/SDE, 2002).

Evaluating the effectiveness of curricular models, therefore, becomes an important consideration. Curriculum in general should support the *active engagement* of all children; it should not be something that is haphazardly put together but rather reflective of *clear goals that are shared by all*. Curriculum needs to be *evidence-based* where what is happening in the classroom reflects effective practice as evidenced by research. In addition, curriculum needs to be *intentional*, where teaching and learning occurs through investigation and concentrated focus. Teachers must have a clear understanding of where they are going and how they intend to get there. Effective curriculum *builds on prior learning and experiences* and is *comprehensive* in scope. Goals of curriculum are *derived from professional standards*, and the curriculum, overall, is *likely to benefit children* (NAEYC & NAECS/SDE, 2002).

These guidelines speak to the importance of providing curricular experiences that are engaging, meaningful, and rigorous. Through *engaging experiences*, children are likely to be drawn in and benefit from all that the curriculum has to offer. *Meaning reflects connections between the curriculum and the children's daily lives. *Rigor* reflects intentional, concentrated focus. Although curriculum can and should be fun, it also must reflect goals for children's development and learning.

Whether you follow a particular model or take an eclectic approach often depends on your place of employment and the flexibility offered to you. Many states are currently adopting specific curricular models in the face of increasing accountability standards. The logic behind this move is that if a particular model is adopted, there is greater continuity within and across programs.

Regardless of the approach that you take, effective curriculum shares fundamental components. These components are reflected through attention to inclusion and flexibility.

Effective curriculum supports the development and learning needs of all children.

Foundations of Effective Curriculum

Curriculum models and approaches must reflect and support the inclusion of diverse developmental needs and learning capabilities (Division for Early Childhood of the Council for Exceptional Children [DEC], 2007). To accomplish this, the DEC recommends:

> To benefit all children, including those with disabilities and developmental delays, it is important to implement an integrated, developmentally appropriate, universally designed curriculum framework that is flexible, comprehensive, and linked to assessment and program evaluation activities.

In addition to ensuring curriculum meets the needs of children with varying abilities, it is also essential that curriculum models and approaches support cultural and linguistic diversity. Therefore, regardless of the curriculum model you may choose to adopt, there are several fundamental components that must be included (DEC, 2007). First, the curriculum must support *access and full participation by all children*. Curriculum should be *aligned with the program's mission and standards* and *reflect accountability to agency and state standards and mandates*. Finally, curriculum needs to *ensure that the needs of individual children and families are met*.

Universal Design for Learning (UDL) represents a curricular framework that ensures that the development and learning needs of each and every child in the classroom are met. Founded in 1984, the Center for Applied Special Technology (CAST) has advanced the use of UDL in the field of education. UDL has three primary principles (CAST, 2008):

- **Multiple means of representation.** This principle provides diverse learners with options for acquiring information and knowledge, including activities and materials that stimulate children's curiosity, their senses, and their desire to experiment and explore.
- **Multiple means of action and expression.** This principle provides learners with options for demonstrating what they know, such as through songs, artwork, plays, language, and varied forms of assessment.
- **Multiple means of engagement.** This principle focuses on tapping into learner interests, offering appropriate challenges, and increasing motivation through teaching strategies and environments that welcome each child, are respectful of diverse needs, and provide feedback that stimulates their interest and investment.

Universal Design for Learning

Framework for applying universal design principles to instructional materials, curricula, and educational activities so that they are engaging and accessible to each and every learner.

How can universally designed frameworks be created? Cohesive, universally designed frameworks are based on assessment and progress monitoring designed to support individual children's access and participation in appropriate learning opportunities, scope and sequence strategies that focus on children's present levels of development or content knowledge and next steps supporting development and learning, and access and intervention strategies designed to provide rich learning opportunities (DEC, 2007). Collaboration with team members is essential. These team members may include, but are not limited to, families and other teaching professionals. Table 8.4 summarizes each of the components of a universally designed curriculum framework.

Curriculum used in early childhood education programs also must meet the parameters of developmentally appropriate practices. This means that the curriculum must

TABLE 8.4   Components of Universally Designed Curriculum Frameworks

Component	Description
Assessment and progress monitoring	Curriculum includes attention to each child's developmental and learning needs to ensure access and participation and that appropriate learning opportunities are developed based on these needs. Modifications to assessment and progress monitoring strategies might be required to accommodate all children's needs, including: • Using alternative measures when necessary. • Changing how a child performs a particular skill or task. • Assessing underlying or prerequisite skills. • Reducing the number of items assessed/monitored.

Scope and sequence	Curriculum scope refers to broad interrelated areas of development or content knowledge that are targeted within the curriculum, whereas sequence pertains to the order in which materials will be introduced. Sequence is often based on age levels or developmental hierarchies (easier to more difficult). To support the diversity of learning needs, curriculum scope and sequence needs to:
	• Include all areas of learning, not only those presented in the targeted areas for a particular age group or developmental level.
	• Provide accommodations, when needed, to ensure that children are progressing through the scope and sequence outlined. These accommodations might include:
	  • Adapting the learning environment.
	  • Providing additional supports.
	  • Allowing children alternative forms of communication to demonstrate knowledge or a particular skill.

Activities and intervention strategies	Activities and intervention strategies need to provide rich learning opportunities that are not relegated to contrived experiences designed by adults. The three principles of Universal Design for Learning provide the template for the creation of meaningful learning, and accommodations are created when necessary. These accommodations might include, but are not limited to: • Providing children with needed social supports including peer-mediated intervention strategies and cooperative learning opportunities. • Using visual, auditory, and kinesthetic methods to communicate information. • Providing encouragement and ongoing feedback for children's efforts. • Adapting toys and materials as needed to support child access. • Altering the physical, social, or temporal environment to support child needs. • Altering the scheduling of routines and activities to accommodate and support child engagement. • Adjusting the amount and type of support needed based on children's needs. • Dividing activities into smaller steps to support acquisition of knowledge and skills.

Source: From "Universal Design for Learning Guidelines 1.0," by CAST, 2008, Wakefield, MA: CAST. Retrieved July 1, 2008, from http://www.cast.org/publications/UDLguidelines/version1.html

meet the individual needs of each and every child in the classroom. In addition, it must support expectations for children's learning and development and consider and respond to the child, family, and program context.

Types of Early Childhood Curriculum Models and Approaches

Curriculum models provide a conceptual framework and organizational structure for decision making and prioritizing, administrative policies, instructional methods, and evaluation criteria (Goffin & Wilson, 2001). Models tend to be formalized and provide specific materials and training-centered relevant topics. **Curricular approaches**, on the other hand, tend to be less formal. Approaches provide professionals with guidelines for effective practice, believing that the fluidity of children's development and needs necessitates a more generalized approach. To demonstrate the difference between the two terms, think of images they each evoke. *Models* are structured, defined, and representative (a model of an airplane, for example). An *approach* implies individuality in how it is carried out (movement is implied, with no specific directives on how to carry out that movement).

Over time, distinct curricular models and approaches have emerged:

Models
- The Direct-Instruction Approach (DISTAR)
- High/Scope Curriculum
- The Montessori method
- Bank Street Model
- Creative Curriculum

Approaches
- Kamii-DeVries Approach
- Developmentally appropriate practices
- Reggio Emilia education
- Project Approach

Each of the models and approaches listed above is based on theories of how to effectively support children's growth and development. It is helpful to understand their underlying philosophies.

Behaviorist Theory and Philosophy: DISTAR. **DISTAR** was originally developed in the late 1960s to support children from at-risk backgrounds through direct instruction in reading and mathematics. Today, what was then known as DISTAR is commonly referred to as **direct instruction**. DISTAR embraces two Skinnerian concepts, including shaping and behavior modification. As you have learned, shaping consists of reinforcing behaviors in successive approximations to the desired behavior. Children are provided positive feedback or rewards for behavior that comes increasingly closer to the desired outcome. A child who is expected to sit and take turns at circle time, for example, is given tokens for each short time that he is able to maintain his focus on this goal.

Another example of shaping commonly occurs during toilet learning. Kris has taken a behaviorist approach to toilet learning in her class of 2-year-olds. She relies heavily on stickers and candy to reward children's efforts toward the desired goal of eliminating on the toilet. Each child in the class has a sticker chart in the bathroom. Kris has listed each of the targeted behaviors that she feels are important (beginning with lifting the toilet seat, should it be down, and ending with flushing) down a column she has made on the

---

curriculum models
Conceptual frameworks and organizational structures for program planning, implementation, and evaluation.

curricular approaches
Generalized approaches that provide guidelines for effective practice.

DISTAR
Commonly known as direct instruction, DISTAR is based on behaviorist principles that support teacher-directed learning.

direct instruction
Behaviorist curricular model utilizing shaping and behavior modification.

side. Children get a sticker for each behavior they complete, and for every five stickers, they receive a piece of candy.

Behavior modification focuses on extinguishing behaviors considered problematic. This is accomplished through removing a reinforcer (something that is thought to contribute to present behaviors) and replacing it through reinforcement with a desired behavior. In the DISTAR curriculum, teacher-directed activities focus on acquiring specific skills. To teach reading, for example, teachers provide direct instruction and reward children based on their mastery of units of knowledge. Children are frequently assessed to determine their knowledge acquisition and are grouped based on their abilities. Subsequent knowledge and reinforcement is presented, toward the overall goal of mastering reading and arithmetic.

Although DISTAR enjoyed early research-documented success, long-term studies showed that the gains children demonstrated in academic areas were short lived (Marcon, 1992). Much of the academic advantages were lost by the third grade. Many in the field still subscribe to the teacher-directed approach advocated by DISTAR, where activities are teacher-driven and focused on transmission of specific, targeted information.

Constructivist Theory and Philosophy: High/Scope Curriculum and Kamii-DeVries Approach. One of the central figures in the constructivist movement was Jean Piaget. Piaget believed that children learn from interaction with their environment, where the child affects the environment and the environment is affected by the child. The changing nature of interactions requires a dynamic perspective of children's development that embraces the fact that children's needs change over time.

Today, the **High/Scope Curriculum** and the **Kamii-DeVries Approach** represent the most structured applications of Piaget's theory. Both models rely on the same theory to justify their practices. Interestingly, the underlying rationale for effective practice in each case is based on differing interpretations of theory (Goffin & Wilson, 2001).

The High/Scope Curriculum. The High/Scope Curriculum was a component of President Johnson's efforts to reduce the impact of poverty on developing children. The prevailing belief was that early childhood education was a tool that might alleviate the negative impact of poverty. Based on this, the political and social climate of that time supported the development of preschool programs and accompanying curricula. As part of this effort, the High/Scope Curriculum was launched in 1962 to serve children considered at risk in impoverished neighborhoods in Ypsilanti, Michigan (Hohmann & Weikart, 1995). High/Scope emerged under the leadership of David Weikart, who was the director of special services for the public schools in Ypsilanti. Weikart and his colleagues embraced preschool as an effective early intervention with great potential for positive long-term results. The resulting school, **Perry Preschool Project**, broke new ground in preschool education as a form of intervention. It also served as a catalyst for the High/Scope model, as there was no existing curriculum that Weikart and his colleagues felt adequately supported children.

Practices in the High/Scope Perry Preschool Project embraced all children as active learners. These researchers saw the responsibility of the professional as supporting children as they develop, carry out, and reflect on activities. Environment is a critical component of this approach. High/Scope learning centers are well designed, are clearly labeled, and contain assorted materials supporting children's own abilities to create meaning from their interactions (High/Scope, 2009). Let's consider Tamika's High/Scope classroom.

Tamika has many different goals for her children's development and learning. First, she wants children to learn through active involvement with people, materials, events, and ideas. To accomplish this, she plans activities for discovery learning, in which the

Go to MyEducationLab and select the topic "Curriculum/Program Models." Under Activities and Applications, watch the video *High/Scope* and reflect on how the curriculum model supports young children's development and learning.

High/Scope Curriculum

Curriculum model derived from Piaget's theory that served as the underlying model for the Perry Preschool Project.

Kamii-DeVries Approach

Curricular approach based on Piaget's theory.

Perry Preschool Project

The project provided high-quality preschool education services to African American children who were living in poverty. Follow-up studies have been conducted when the original children were 27 and 40.

materials around them help children "discover" things about topics she introduces. A second goal of the curriculum is to bolster confidence. Tamika recognizes that the ability to participate in activities and direct one's own learning is a valuable and life-long skill. Therefore, she allows children ample time and opportunity to complete tasks on their own. A third goal Tamika embraces, based on the High/Scope Curriculum, is the support of individual initiative and learning, which she accomplishes through careful observation of and interaction with each child. Tamika also values parental involvement in the program. She invites parents into the classroom and conducts numerous home visits during the year. Daily routine is also valued. The schedule focuses on predictability and routine. Tamika and her students conduct a Plan-Do-Review cycle every day, where first the children brainstorm and agree on their learning experiences (Plan). Then they execute the activities while interacting and experimenting (Do). Afterward they explore and reflect on the activities as a classroom community (Review). Figure 8.2 illustrates the Plan-Do-Review cycle.

The High/Scope Curriculum enjoys a unique place in the expansive body of research examining program effectiveness. As a research project designed to determine the effectiveness of High/Scope, the Perry Preschool Project followed a group of children who participated in the High/Scope Curriculum and followed up with them when they were 27 and 40. The results are compelling. Researchers concluded that, compared with a matched control group, the children had unique characteristics, including that 63% fewer were habitual criminals, 68% fewer had been arrested for drug dealing, and 26% fewer received adult welfare or other social services. Furthermore, 31% more of the Perry Preschool participants graduated from high school or completed a GED, and nearly twice as many were home owners (Parks, 2000).

The research made a compelling argument favoring high-quality early childhood care and education, underscoring the premise that success in one's early years can have a positive and profound impact throughout one's life.

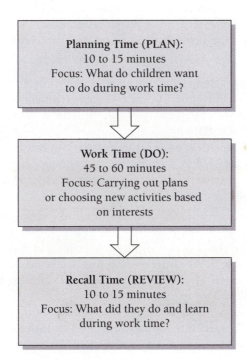

FIGURE 8.2
High/Scope Plan-Do-Review Cycle

TEACHING AND LEARNING CONNECTIONS

Implementing the Plan-Do-Review Cycle

- **Plan time:** Provides children with the opportunity to express their ideas to adults. Supports viewing themselves as individuals who can make and act on decisions.

- **Do:** Allows children to gather information and to interact with their peers and solve problems.

- **Review:** Provides opportunity for children to represent work experiences in a variety of ways.

The Kamii-DeVries Approach. Like High/Scope, the Kamii-DeVries Approach was established in the 1960s. It got its start when David Wiekart and Constance Kamii developed a curriculum supporting youth who were disadvantaged in the Ypsilanti (Michigan) public school system where they taught. Both practitioners adopted Piaget's theory. Weikart focused on Piaget's conceptual structure, which had provided the foundation for High/Scope, and Kamii focused on Piaget's constructive processes directed at advancing cognitive development. Later, in the 1970s, Kamii collaborated with Rheta DeVries at the University of Illinois-Chicago campus, and the new model flourished (Goffin & Wilson, 2001).

The Kamii-DeVries Approach is based on the idea that children interact in a logical-mathematical framework. Within this framework, children develop knowledge, intelligence, morality, and personality (Kamii, 1985).

> Jessie's classroom is based on the Kamii-DeVries Approach. The children explore their environment freely, and physical activity is encouraged as essential; the children are rarely idle. Group game playing is considered an activity that promotes social and moral development. Relationships are considered important, and Jessie works to create a cooperative atmosphere based on mutual respect. She creates an environment supportive of active exploration, child observation, and responsiveness based on children's current conceptions of the world.

Montessori Education. Montessori education supports learning and development from birth through adulthood with curricula, materials, environments, and teacher preparation programs (Edwards, 2002). Montessori education reflects the fundamental belief that children learn best in a social environment supportive and respectful of each child's unique development. Montessori—similar to Vygotsky—advocated mixed-age groupings and thought a 3-year age span in a group was appropriate. Specific components of the Montessori philosophy include the prepared environment, specific materials, and a clearly articulated teacher's role.

myeducationlab

Go to MyEducationLab and select the topic "Curriculum/Program Models." Under Activities and Applications, watch the video *Montessori* and consider the unique aspects of the Montessori model.

- **The prepared environment.** Montessori's "third teacher," represented through the environment, reflects the environment's role in maximizing learning and independence. Children work on activities of their own choice at their own pace. One child may be setting a table in the housekeeping area, while another uses beads to solve a multiplication problem. Environments are prepared with the physical and the psychological in mind and are designed to be simple, beautiful, and orderly, cultivating culture with language, plants, art, music, and books.

- **Materials.** Materials specific to Montessori education include solid geometric forms, knobbed puzzle maps, colored beads, and specialized rods and blocks. Each material demonstrates a single quality. For example, rods may differ in size alone, and colored beads may differ only in shape. Because children choose their own activities, the materials are stored accessibly on low, open shelves.

Montessori materials are designed to be self-correcting. A child constructing a block tower of Montessori materials demonstrating size will note an error if the pieces don't fit together correctly. Such feedback encourages children to try new approaches to solve problems. Montessori materials are also designed to meet the needs of children at different stages of development. A child may learn to group rods based on color one year and then use the same rods the following year to explore numerical concepts.

- **The role of the teacher.** A Montessori teacher serves four principal roles: (1) *awakening the child's spirit and imagination*; (2) *encouraging independence and high self-esteem*; (3) *helping the child develop the kindness, curiosity, and self-discipline* needed for participation as a full member of society; and (4) *helping the child observe, question, and explore ideas independently*. Observation is an important tool supporting attainment of these goals. The teacher uses observation to gain knowledge of individual children's needs and designs the environment accordingly.

Montessori education enjoys great popularity in the United States. According to 2000–2001 statistics, there were about 1,400 Montessori schools in the United States serving approximately 85,000 students. Compared with 1993–1994 statistics, this represents an 88% growth in the number of schools and a 98% increase in the number of students served (National Center for Education Statistics, 2003). Teacher credentials are offered through the American Montessori Society and courses and train-the-trainer programs through the Association of Montessori Internationale. In 2006, there were over 60 teacher education programs that offered the credential in the United States, Canada, Mexico, and Korea.

The Bank Street Approach. Like Montessori education, Bank Street provides educational programs for both children and teachers. The **Bank Street Approach** was founded by Harriet Johnson, Caroline Pratt, Elizabeth Irwin, and Lucy Sprague Mitchell, who studied under John Dewey, an avid supporter of progressive education. The Bank Street Approach represented an interesting mix of social and political factors. The time was 1916, just 4 years before women were granted the right to vote in federal elections. The Women's Suffrage Movement was at its peak. With financial help from Elizabeth Coolidge, these women developed what became known as the Bureau of Education Experiments. The goal of the bureau was to identify practices that supported the development and learning of young children and to provide training to teachers based on these practices. From this organization, the Bank Street Approach emerged (Bank Street, 2006).

The Bank Street Approach attends to children's overall developmental and learning needs and emphasizes the relevance of information to children's daily lives. The approach involves children and families and includes a focus on strengthening community.

Bank Street children interact with their environment; construct knowledge based on interaction with people, places, and things; and interpret their experiences (Bank Street, 2006). The Bank Street philosophy identifies several key components of education, including attention to experiential education, stressing that children learn by doing. The focus is based on constructivism, and support for children's ownership of learning is a key component of this approach.

Classrooms using the Bank Street philosophy provide a variety of hands-on learning experiences that are supported and enhanced by the teacher. Teachers create experiences

Bank Street Approach

Curricular approach that Inspired both a child- and teacher-training program.

that support child discovery and design curriculum to support children's interpretations of these experiences. Collaboration is a key aspect of the learning environment, and teachers support children in both developing a sense of community and cultivating social responsibility.

The Creative Curriculum. The Creative Curriculum is the most widely used curriculum in Head Start, with about 40% of programs indicating that they used it in an ongoing federal evaluation of Head Start services (Family and Child Experiences Study, 2006). The Creative Curriculum draws on the constructivist principles of Piaget and Vygotsky and stresses the importance of the physical and social environment in supporting play.

The Creative Curriculum is designed for infants and toddlers, preschool-aged children, and children in the primary grades. The core of the infant-toddler program is developing respectful, nurturing relationships between teachers, children, and families. At the preschool level, the curriculum emphasizes social-emotional and cognitive development via active interaction with the environment. Rooms are arranged in 10 interest areas, focusing on such content areas as literacy, mathematics, social studies, science, the arts, and technology. These same content area themes carry over into the primary curriculum.

Classrooms using the Creative Curriculum contain a variety of interest areas: blocks, dramatic play, toys and games, art, sand and water, library, music and movement, discovery, cooking, computers, and outdoor environments. The Creative Curriculum relies on observation and assessment by teachers to inform the curriculum. The curriculum respects the interaction between heredity, environment, and learning and views a stress-free environment as the foundation for healthy development. Developing supportive and respectful relationships with primary caregivers is considered essential in the curriculum. The curriculum was also created with consideration for Maslow's hierarchy of needs, with a priority of building safe and healthy environments that support belonging and self-esteem.

Challenges of Curricular Models and Approaches

One of the main goals of each of the curricular models and approaches outlined above is to provide teachers with guidance in structuring learning experiences. The heightened recognition that the early years matter, coupled with increased demands for accountability, has resulted in many individual programs utilizing a specific curricular model. Further, many state and federal agencies, such as Head Start, increasingly require that a particular model be used. Although Head Start does not endorse a particular curriculum, the largest percentages of children are in Head Start programs that use the High/Scope Curriculum or the Creative Curriculum (Family and Child Experiences Study, 2006).

The advent of curricular models has also created a competitive environment, which has created both innovation and discord (Goffin & Wilson, 2001). This discord has emerged from the belief that there is one best way to support children's learning. Some models and approaches are designed to advance children's social-emotional development, whereas others focus predominantly on cognitive development.

Much of the debate between models is represented through the disparity between behaviorists and maturationists. In behaviorism, the child is viewed as dependent on adults' instruction in academic knowledge and skills (Banks, 2003), and, therefore, it places a great value on cognitive development. The maturationist's child-initiated approach, on the other hand, views young children as having primary responsibility for determining their interactions with the environment. A high value is placed on social-emotional

• • • BECOMING A PROFESSIONAL • • •

Career Pathways

Head Start Teacher

April's present career as a Head Start teacher followed a winding path that began in 1994. Originally, she was a substitute in a child care setting and then moved to an Early Head Start program. During this time, she earned her first of two Child Development Associate (CDA) certificates.

As April gained more experience, she continued to take additional classes at the local university. Her education was primarily funded through Head Start, and in 2005 she achieved her goal as a teacher in a Head Start classroom. Attaining this goal was not without challenges—April found that balancing her education with work and family was a complicated juggle. As a nontraditional student, navigating the system was a particular challenge.

In her present role as a Head Start teacher, one of the things April most appreciates is her ability to see positive changes in the children and families that she works with. "We start the school year focusing on routine and really working to make sure that children understand the classroom community and its related expectations. By the end of the year, I really see this great blossoming in both their play and imagination."

One of the main challenges April presently faces is meeting the extensive standards required by Head Start. Her program uses the Creative Curriculum, which she finds very beneficial, particularly in the areas of observation and documentation and meeting these varied standards. "There is a data collection component to that Creative Curriculum. I have to collect and enter data on each child in different developmental areas. The program then compiles the data and gives me information on where each child in the classroom is developmentally. It also tells me what additional observation and assessment data I need to collect. It also aggregates the whole community, allowing me to see classroom strengths and global challenges. This really helps me plan and ensure that I am meeting each child's individual needs."

April graduated in May 2008 with a bachelor's degree and is unsure what the future will bring. For right now, she is happy in her Head Start classroom and the impact that she is able to have on the children and families in her care.

The 2008 Reauthorization of the Head Start bill requires that by September 30, 2013, at least 50% of teachers in center-based Head Start programs have a baccalaureate degree in early childhood education or a baccalaureate or advanced degree in a field related to early childhood education with experience teaching preschool-age children. All Head Start teaching assistants, by 2013, will be required to have at least a CDA and be enrolled in a program leading to an associate or baccalaureate degree (U.S. Department of Health and Human Services, 2008). As of 2006, the current average salary for a Head Start teacher is $26,500 per year (National Head Start Association, 2007).

development. This debate has been historically represented in the field by instructivist and constructivist camps.

The debate between instructivist and constructivist approaches limits examination of curricular options that lie outside this traditional dichotomy (Katz, 1999). To resolve this debate, early childhood theorist Lilian Katz imagined a curriculum that relies in part on both instructivist and constructivist principles, but does not favor one over the other. She suggested an early childhood curriculum that was "trichotimized" to focus on social-emotional, intellectual, and academic skills.

Constructivists had long embraced support for social-emotional development. Support for intellectual goals, on the other hand, is generally thought of as a feature of curricula developed in response to more recent research. **Intellectual goals** specifically relate to the dispositions and habits of mind a child uses to interpret experience. Curiosity is an example of a disposition that supports exploration and problem solving. Children also need to master academic skills, although these are usually not encountered spontaneously or through exploration (Katz, 1999). One approach that reflects Katz's curricular strategy was found in Reggio Emilia, Italy.

Reggio Emilia

In the late 1980s, the early childhood education systems of the northern Italian community of **Reggio Emilia** gained the attention of educators in the United States. The teaching practices in Reggio Emilia transcended the instructionist–constructionist dichotomy in the form of a child-originated and teacher-framed curriculum.

The groundwork for the Reggio Emilia approach was established shortly after World War II, when parents built new schools for their young children (New, 2000). Government sponsorship of early care and education in Reggio Emilia, however, began with the 1968 founding of preprimary schools for children ages 3 to 6. In 1971, care was expanded to include children 4 months to 3 years of age. The schools were initially organized and run by families, and a strong spirit of collaboration between teachers and families remains to this day. Loris Malaguzzi oversaw the school until his death in 1994.

Curricula based on the Reggio Emilia approach enhances and promotes a child's construction of "his or her own powers of thinking through the synthesis of all the expressive, communicative and cognitive languages" (Edwards, Gandini, & Forman, 1993, p. 457). In this approach, teachers use reflective practices to create their own theories about how to effectively support children's development. This process differed from the most popular thinking in the United States, which at that time advocated prescriptive practices to shape teacher's actions in the classroom community.

Reggio Emilia schools are amiable communities designed to support the well-being of children, families, and teachers. Children are seen as competent, capable learners, and families are viewed as essential partners in their child's education. Teachers are valued members of the community who act as learners, researchers, and advocates for children.

The Reggio Emilia approach embraces several other pedagogical approaches, including the idea that curriculum should be emergent and build on the interests of children. And emergent, in-depth study of concepts, ideas, and interests of the children in groups are represented through project work. The graphic arts are used as tools to represent cognitive, linguistic, and social intelligences, which is referred to as representational development. There is a strong focus on collaboration, and children are often gathered in small and large groups designed to support group membership and individual uniqueness. Teachers within Reggio environments are viewed as *researchers* who serve as a resource and guide who lends expertise to children. The Reggio approach embraces documentation, including comprehensive portfolios. Included in these portfolios are pictures of children as they work, written dictation summarizing their processes, and visual media that graphically represent learning. Finally, similar to Montessori, the environment in Reggio classrooms is viewed as an essential "third teacher." In the environment, there is space for small and large group gatherings,

trichotimized

Curricular strategy advocated by Katz that focuses on social-emotional and intellectual learning and support for meaningful and useful academic skills.

intellectual goals

Dispositions or habits of mind that children use to interpret experiences.

Reggio Emilia

Town in Italy whose pedagogical approach to caring for and educating young children has been widely studied in the United States.

myeducationlab

Go to MyEducationLab and select the topic "Curriculum/Program Models." Under Activities and Applications, watch the video *Reggio Emilia* and consider how this is an effective approach in Italy, and why aspects of the approach have been adopted within the United States.

representations of children's work adorning the walls, and common spaces where children can work together.

Reggio Emilia teachers have many responsibilities.

A teacher named Chiara explores the learning experience with children in a preschool environment. She gains an understanding of the learning process herself while she also observes and processes the children's interactions with the environment. Ideas are very important in her classroom, and she asks the children a lot of questions supporting their developing knowledge. Chiara spends a lot of time ensuring that the environment is well organized, pleasing, and structured to reflect both children's work and their interests. Documentation is also impor-

The emergent curriculum is based on children's interests.

tant. She uses notes, videotapes, tape recorders, pictures, and portfolios to document the children's development. Her role extends far beyond the classroom as she partners with the children's families. She follows the children for 3 years and therefore has extensive time to build relationships with both the children and their families. Chiara is also an important resource herself in weekly debates on teaching practices and learning processes.

The variety of historical, economic, and political factors that coincided in Reggio Emilia to create and sustain its remarkable success has been the subject of much scholarly debate in the United States. Although Reggio schools exist only in Reggio Emilia, Italy, many U.S. educators have explored how to implement a Reggio-inspired approach. The educational climate in the United States makes the adoption of some of the Reggio approaches difficult. Among students, families, and schools in the United States, it is schools that hold the most power. The idea of a full partnership with families, although practiced in small enclaves around the country, would require such a broad, cultural shift that few see it as immediately feasible. However, the most prevalent form of Reggio Emilia curriculum in the United States is the **emergent curriculum**, which includes the **Project Approach**.

THE EMERGENT CURRICULUM

The emergent curriculum is based on curricular practices and applications that follow the interests of the child. These interests are often contextually based, emerging from their daily interactions with their own world. In the context of supporting the emergent curriculum, professionals have many responsibilities. These include noting and documenting the interests of children and developing effective, vibrant curricular activities and strategies that embrace and extend those interests. At the same time, the teacher must introduce and support learning defined by society, or expectations for learning. The focus becomes the child's creation of meaning regarding the world around them. This meaning is represented through the introduction of knowledge and

emergent curriculum
Curriculum based on the interests of the child.

Project Approach
Developed by Sylvia Chard and Lilian Katz, the Project Approach represents an investigation of a real-world topic worthy of children's attention and effort.

Go to MyEducationLab and select the topic "Curriculum/Program Models." Under Activities and Applications, watch the video *Emergent Curriculum on Children's Interests: Hospital Project* and consider the role of the emergent curriculum in creating engaging classroom environments.

skills guided by children's unique interests and ways of viewing and interacting with their world.

What does the emergent curriculum look like? The answer to this question will vary greatly, based on both the ages of the children in question and how they process and experience their world. For infants and toddlers, the focus of the emergent curriculum is on the development of relationships. For preschool-age and older children, the focus is on in-depth investigations, which is represented by the Project Approach.

Emergent Curriculum for Infants and Toddlers

Infants and toddlers are learning about the world around them and their role in it. Curriculum begins with the establishment of secure relationships and builds from there to include focused attention on sensory, motor, and language experiences. Professionals working with infants and toddlers must provide care that is both responsive and supportive to each child's unique needs.

One of the main developmental tasks of infancy and toddlerhood is that of building relationships. Relationships allow children to securely interact with and experience all their environment has to offer in terms of explorations and interactions. When thinking about implementing an emergent curriculum for infants and toddlers, therefore, the central focus should be on relationships.

Chapter 4 introduced you to the critical importance of young children's formation of a secure attachment relationship. You also learned about the interrelationship between different areas of development. It is widely believed that if children do not form successful relationships with others during their first years of life, all areas of development will be negatively affected. Further, the lack of secure relationships during the first years has a lifelong impact on relationship development (Bowlby, 1988).

Infants and toddlers are searching for trusting and secure relationships and a safe base for learning and development (Lally, 2000). This safe and secure platform allows infants to incorporate behaviors perceived as appropriate and imitate actions, communication patterns, and the emotional and social behaviors of others. This base provides experiences that allow infants to explore and process their world. How do things move and fit in space? How are objects, people, and ideas used as tools? How can I cause things to happen? Each of these questions, fundamental to learning about their immediate world, begins from safe and supportive relationships.

TEACHING AND LEARNING CONNECTIONS

Developing Respectful and Supportive Relationships with Infants and Toddlers

- Provide extensive opportunities for physical contact, including cuddling, rocking, and allowing children to sit in your lap.
- Note children's explorations of the environment and provide appropriate behavioral reflections.
- Take joy in children's development, conveying to them that you notice them and their interactions with the world.
- Minimize or eliminate the time children spend in constrictive objects, such as playpens and swings.

Supporting the Infant-Toddler Emergent Curriculum

The term **"educarer"** was coined by educator and infant specialist Magda Gerber, who developed a philosophy of meeting infant-toddler needs based on respect and support for relationships. Of central importance to appropriate educaring is the time the educarer spends with the infant and the infant's free exploration of the environment. These two factors are considered interrelated and dependent on each other. "Only a child who receives undivided attention from his educarer during all routine care-giving activities will be free and interested to explore his environment without needing too much intervention of the *educarer*" (Gerber, 2002. p. 3).

Components of the educaring philosophy include the following:

- *Basic trust* in the child to be an initiator, an explorer, and a self-learner.
- An *environment* for the child that is physically safe, cognitively challenging, and emotionally nurturing.
- Time for *uninterrupted play*.
- *Freedom to explore* and interact with other infants.
- An environment that involves the child as an *active participant*.
- *Sensitive observation* of the child in order to understand his or her needs.

Caregiving routines based on this philosophy are the foundation of effective infant-toddler emergent curriculum. What practices lead to an educaring philosophy? *Primary care arrangements*, where a teacher works to develop a bond with the child and become an expert on his or her development are important. *Small groups* that allow each child *individualized attention* are critical. Continuity of care, reflecting minimal transitions between caregivers supportive of ongoing bonds is another essential practice, as is cultural continuity, where a bridge between home and early childhood environment practices is developed and cultivated. Finally, practices in an educaring philosophy respect, embrace, and *include children with diverse abilities* (Gerber, 2002).

Successful development of infant–toddler curriculum requires that these foundational practices be in place. From this foundation, professionals can turn their attention to activities that support infant-toddler learning.

Developing the Infant-Toddler Emergent Curriculum

Infant-toddler curriculum, similar to curriculum for older children, takes into account children's developmental and learning needs and the needs of the family and larger context (such as age-related expectations for knowledge, skills, dispositions, and feelings).

educarer

Gerber's term for infant-toddler caregivers who implement a philosophy based on respect and support for relationships.

continuity of care

Minimal transitions between caregivers, supporting development of ongoing relationships.

cultural continuity

Creation of a bridge between home and early childhood environments and child-rearing practices.

TEACHING AND LEARNING CONNECTIONS

Developing Primary Caregiving Groups

- Look at age range of children in the classroom and their developmental needs.
- Stagger grouping based on individual needs of each child, with maximizing caregiver's ability to give attention as primary goal.
- Get to know the developmental needs and preferences of each child in group.
- Develop system of communication with other professionals regarding children in primary caregiving group.

The natural curiosity of infants and toddlers provides a springboard for learning: Children are primed to learn and well equipped to explore. Creating an appropriate curriculum for infants and toddlers is based on careful observation and planning (Lally, 2000).

Observation. Knowledge of individual children comes from careful observation of how they interact with their environment. Teachers can ask the following questions as they observe children:

- What strategies do the children use in their play? What does this tell us about their learning and development?
- What are their overall developmental needs?
- How might we support or extend play?
- How might experiences we design support the child's needs?

To effectively support development, teachers must document these observations and reflections. Documentation provides important information on where the child is and where the child is going. Further, this documentation can provide a road map for future experiences and serve as a critical tool in planning.

Planning. Planning curriculum for infants and toddlers provides connected experiences that support a framework of understanding (Maguire-Fong, 1999). Connections are forged in many ways. These include connections between the child's present learning and development needs and overall goals, connections between a child's interests and experiences provided in the environment, and connections between people, objects, and events. Following observation, questioning and reflection, and documentation, teachers can select and develop a topic of investigation for children.

Topics of Investigation. Investigations provide a natural fit for the child's learning style (Maguire-Fong, 1999). Investigations begin with knowledge of individual children and are developed through knowledge of what appears to interest children. Indicators of interest include what children choose to play, what they seem focused on in conversations and interactions, and activities and objects they are drawn to.

After selecting an investigation topic, teachers develop a list of possible learning encounters that support child interest and complement development and learning goals. Topic webs are a useful tool for this process.

Developing a Topic Web. A topic web for investigations with infants and toddlers begins with observation of their development and learning and builds on this by incorporating children's interests and curiosities. Steps to completing a topic web begin with selecting a topic of investigation. For example, Carissa has noticed that the children in her toddler class are very interested in the construction that is going on around their center—they can often be found with their faces pressed against the window, observing the trucks as they go by. Their favorite destination on walks is the construction site, where the children never seem to tire of viewing the activity. Carissa decides that trucks would be a great topic of investigation for her class.

Carissa then begins developing the web and places the topic of "trucks" in a center circle. From this point, two sets of "connections" are created. One set of connections reflects activities related to the topic of trucks that she feels the children will enjoy. The other set of connections, which radiate from the activities, are the developmental areas the activities support. Once this initial brainstorming is complete, Carissa is ready to move on to developing a timescape.

TEACHING AND LEARNING CONNECTIONS

Developing a Topic Web

- Begin by placing the topic in the center of web. For example, a project based on bugs would include the word *bugs* in the center of the topic web.
- Let the children know that you are going to brainstorm topics related to the proposed bug project.
- As children produce ideas ("What do bugs eat?" "Do bugs sleep a night?" "What kind of bug bites really hurt?"), record these ideas around the main topic.
- Further develop listed areas, asking children questions to determine knowledge and interest ("Do you think bugs only sleep at night?" "Have you even seen a sleeping bug?" "How can we find out the answers to our questions on bugs?").
- Based on agreed-upon classroom procedure (such as voting or drawing a topic from a hat), select topic from web and proceed.

Creating a Timescape. A **timescape** represents a plan of action, or a potential sequence for the investigation (Maquire-Fong, 1999). Teachers need to remain flexible, as children's interests are one of the main factors driving the investigation. Carissa's timescape includes a list of the activities she selected and the corresponding areas of development and learning supported through the activities.

timescape
Planned sequence of activities for a topic of investigation.

Each activity Carissa plans is accompanied by a general template of what she hopes to accomplish. This includes an overview of what will happen in the activity and how the activity will support children's development and learning. One of Carissa's planned activities, for example, is to create a mudscape in the sand and water table complete with trucks, wooden blocks, and plastic people. She will set up the activity before the children arrive in the classroom and has decided that the activity will remain a part of the environment until her observation leads her to conclude the children are no longer interested. Carissa plans for the activity to support development and learning in a variety of ways—children will be interacting in small groups supporting social-emotional skills, she will sit with the children at the table and provide behavioral reflections supporting language development, and the variety of engaging materials will support cognitive development through experimentation. Carissa also sends home a note to the children's families letting them know about the truck investigation, and inviting them to contribute photos, story books, or any related items (including their time) that they are willing to share. Carissa's activity is designed to capitalize on children's interests, and she has made sure that her plan specifies the materials needed, who is involved in the investigation, and how families would be involved in the process (Maquire-Fong, 1999).

Emergent curriculum for infants and toddlers begins with establishing relationships and extends from that point to include experiences reflective of young children's interests. For children preschool-age and older, the Project Approach is a common and well-accepted approach supportive of the emergent curriculum.

The Project Approach

The Project Approach embraces Katz's (1999) assertion that the early childhood curricular debate needs to embrace practices that support knowledge, skills, dispositions, and feelings, and it supports the principles of the emergent curriculum outlined through Reggio Emilia philosophy. The Project Approach was originally developed by Sylvia Chard and Lilian Katz. According to Katz (1999), the approach supports intellectual dispositions, offers good processes that support rich content, and leads to high-quality products. The approach relies, as its name implies, on projects. But they are projects that have a few important distinctions. The projects must emerge from children's own ideas and interests. Teachers provoke the interests of children with appropriate questions to decide what the projects will be, and they then establish appropriate academic goals that are embedded within the projects. The teachers must continue to provoke the children with questions as the projects progress and the children's learning and development continues over time. The projects must also be large enough to support a diversity of ideas and allow for various types of expression. The context of knowledge is very important in the Project Approach, as is the role that learning plays in this larger context (Katz & Chard, 1989).

Teachers must carefully plan the project before the topic is introduced to the children and make a topic web to explore the viability of the topic (Katz & Chard, 1989). Viability is determined through addressing such questions as "Is this topic likely to sustain children's interests?" "Is the topic rich with opportunity to support children's development and learning goals?" "Are there opportunities to introduce targeted knowledge, skills, and dispositions in the topic?"

Should the topic be established as viable, the teacher creates an outline of key events and plans for possible experiences such as fieldtrips or investigations. Each of these steps informs the collection of necessary resources.

The Project Approach website (http://www.projectapproach.org) describes its three main phases:

myeducationlab

Go to MyEducationLab and select the topic "Math and Science." Under Activities and Applications, watch the video *Exploring Eggs in a Study of Birds* and reflect on the role of fieldwork in developing an engaging curriculum.

- **Phase One:** This phase represents the opening of the project and can include three key events. The first of these is *the initial starting point*, at which time the project is introduced. The second key event is the *topic web plan*, where the class collects and maps out ideas according to what children know about the topic. The third key event is *listing questions*. Here, emergent questions are collected and responded to over the course of the project.

- **Phase Two:** This phase of the project focuses on the collection of information. The first key event is *preparation for fieldwork*. During this event, children prepare to investigate an aspect of the project more closely. This may include trips outside the classroom environment. These investigations should be shaped by the children's hypotheses about anticipated findings, questions for exploration, and tools needed to process information. This event is followed by *fieldwork*. During fieldwork, children actively investigate the selected topic, writing field notes and sketches to transcribe their knowledge and record additional questions they might have. The next key event is *fieldwork follow-up*. Here, children discuss and process information gained during their fieldwork, develop new questions, and consult resources based on additional emerging questions. *Visiting experts* are an important part of Phase Two. These experts are people who come to the class to share knowledge with children on a particular topic. Children can prepare for the visiting expert by developing questions. During the visit, children can transcribe information and generate new questions.

- **Phase Three:** Phase Three of the project is the culmination and distribution of knowledge. Key events include the *culminating event*. During this event children present the results of the project to others, including such people as other children and/or family members. Children could, for example, elect to put on a play, share a song, or create pictures that summarize the project. These efforts are shaped by children's reflection on the project itself and result in children *personalizing new knowledge*. Then, through a variety of mediums (such as art and the written and spoken word) children make the information presented during the project meaningful to them.

Examples of Project Approach panels.

Scott created a Project Approach curriculum for his pre-K class. Children encountered the topic of ants in the book *Busy Ants* by Kristin Nelson (2004). At morning meeting time, Scott and the children brainstormed on topics related to ants. The developing topic web included "where ants live," "what ants eat," and "the purpose of anthills." To begin project exploration, Scott encouraged the children to observe ants in their natural environment. The children then transcribed their notes (represented by drawings and some letter formations) onto provided clipboards. They transformed the classroom's block area into an intricate web of ant tunnels, and Scott provided large, plastic ants for the children to weave through their creations. They put dirt in the sand and water table and experimented with developing and destroying representations of anthills. Children made written and pictorial representations of the knowledge they acquired, adding new information and new questions to the project record. Scott brought in new picture books each week to facilitate research, and they learned about the role of ants in the ecosystem from a local entomologist who spoke to the class. In the culminating phase of the project, the children demonstrated their knowledge by creating a picture book about ants, constructing a clay model of an anthill, and performing a short play they wrote about a day in the life of an ant.

The Project Approach targets four distinct types of learning: knowledge, skills, dispositions, and feelings. Table 8.5, demonstrates how each is addressed.

TABLE 8.5   Learning Goals Within the Project Approach

Type of Learning Goal	Application with the Project Approach
Knowledge	• Information: facts, cultural perspectives, stories, works of art • Concepts: schemas, event scripts, attributes and categories • Relations: cause and effect, how objects and processes relate, part–whole • Meaning: personal experience of knowledge, individual understanding
Skills	• Basic academic skills: talking, reading, writing, counting, measuring • Scientific and technical skills: observation, data management, use of computers and scientific equipment • Social skills: cooperation, discussion, debate, negotiation, teamwork • Personal relationships: give and take, appreciation, assertiveness
Dispositions	• Habits of mind: wondering, figuring out, predicting, explaining, etc. • Approaches to work: challenge seeking, persistence, reflection, openness • Preferences: cooperating/alone, longer/shorter time, active/passive • Strengthening and weakening: promoting useful dispositions and discouraging dysfunctional ones
Feelings	• Setting realistic expectations for achievement • Dealing with success and failure, learning from errors of judgment • Coping with frustration, disappointment; appreciating success • Appropriately expressing feelings and seeking support when needed • Recognizing moods, crises, and blocks, as potential obstacles to learning • Helping children find ways to deal with personal problems

Source: Information from "Four Types of Learning Goals," from the Project Approach Website, 2007, Alberta, Canada: Project Approach Retrieved May 6, 2009, from http://www.projectapproach.org/index

Each of the contemporary approaches presented—Reggio Emilia curriculum and the emergent curriculum—share foundational characteristics. Namely, they are each built on the premise that supporting children's development and learning requires child-centered curriculum.

Child-Centered Curriculum

child-centered curriculum

Curricular approach focused on developing children's thinking skills and supporting them in making connections between internal and external worlds.

In addition to the term *emergent curriculum*, another term you are likely to encounter in your studies and work in the field is **child-centered curriculum**. The focus of the child-centered curriculum is on developing children's own original thinking and supporting them in making their own unique connections to their internal and external worlds. One of the main goals of the child-centered curriculum is developing children's problem-solving skills, stimulating their interest and imagination, and supporting their ability to process and interact with their environment (Barton & Booth, 1990).

The child-centered curriculum can be directly contrasted to the teacher-directed curriculum. Goals of teacher-directed curriculum are to transmit facts, support skill development, and develop prescribed values based on mastering knowledge presented. In the teacher-directed curriculum, the children are a receptacle for knowledge, as opposed to active participants and processors of the world around them. Today, it is largely believed that the child-centered curriculum is the most effective way to structure curriculum in early childhood education (Almy, 2000).

MOVING FORWARD

The field of early childhood education has a rich history composed of innovative ideas and practices. Today, the curricular models and approaches available to the field—and effective teaching practices derived from those—provide a template for creating nurturing, stimulating classroom environments. From this sound base of theory, you will now explore the planning of curriculum through a focus on assessment, which is the topic of Chapter 9.

myeducationlab

Go to MyEducationLab and select the topic "Curriculum/Program Models." Under Building Teaching Skills and Dispositions, complete the exercise *Considering Montessori and High/Scope Models*.

CASE STUDY
Applying Early Childhood Theory

The Child Development Lab and Learning Center
(6 weeks to 6 years)

Marian and Korissa's infant-toddler classroom is a busy environment currently filled with children between the ages of 8 weeks and 3 years. The teachers have worked extensively to involve each child in the daily activities. Children are sitting at the table and the chairs are of varying heights supporting each child's developing strength and ability to sit up. The two infants who are awake in the classroom are being held by their primary caregivers and included in the family atmosphere the teachers have created. Following snack, the children have various choices about activities to pursue. Most of them are engaged in an art activity. The young infants are held and supported as they participate by placing their hands in paints and making handprints on the available paper. Careful planning went into this activity, with the teachers ensuring that each child will be able to participate. Planning included the reality that many of the younger children would be exploring the paint with their mouths. The paint placed on the table, therefore, was conducive to such explorations.

The teachers identify themselves as constructivists and believe that supporting children's active interaction with the environment is key to their development and learning. As such, the environment is designed for safe exploration and includes a variety of mediums for the children to explore. The sand and water table are always filled with interesting textures, including dirt, snow, Styrofoam packing materials, and leaves.

Their primary caregiving system allows teachers to be versed in each individual child's needs and communicate extensively with other teachers and support staff to ensure that those needs are met. The system creates success for the children. The teachers report that this makes their job much easier, as they develop an expertise that they can then employ with each individual child. Primary care arrangements are developed based on the children's ages—each teacher has a range of ages in the classroom environment, making it easier to meet individual children's developmental needs.

CONSTRUCTED-RESPONSE QUESTION

1. Describe constructivist theory and how this is reflected in Marian and Korissa's infant-toddler classroom.

REFLECTING ON AND APPLYING EFFECTIVE PRACTICES (NAEYC AND CEC/DEC)

Ethics

- You have started a job teaching four-year-olds in a preschool classroom, and are greatly looking forward to applying all that you have learned in your college coursework. During your first week in the classroom, you carefully observe the children, working to get to know them and their interests. You also talk extensively with your new coworker. When you ask her what the children's interests are in the classroom so you can begin brainstorming possible ideas for a class project, she responds, "Oh, we just use themes in here. Our curriculum is planned for the whole year and we really don't have the time to add other material in." What would you do in this situation?

NAEYC Ideals
I-1.2. To base program practices upon current knowledge and research in the field of early childhood education, child development, and related disciplines, as well as on particular knowledge of each child.

I-3A.2. To share resources with co-workers, collaborating to ensure that the best possible early childhood care and education program is provided.

DEC: Professional and Interpersonal Behavior
3. We shall strive for the highest level of personal and professional competence by seeking and using new evidence based information to improve our practices while also responding openly to the suggestions of others.

Standards for Professional Practice

- Reflect on the various curricular models and approaches you learned about in Chapter 8. How do these models and approaches, in general, reflect theory and research in the field? What do professionals need to know about specific models to select one that 231is effective? How can a model be selected that is aligned with your own beliefs about children's development and learning?

NAEYC: Promoting Child Development and Learning
1c. Using developmental knowledge to create healthy, respectful, supportive, and challenging learning environments;

NAEYC: Teaching and Learning
Sub-Standard 4b. Using developmentally effective approaches;

Sub-Standard 4d. Building meaningful curriculum.

DEC: Development and Charecteristics of Individual Learners
EC1K2: Trends and issues in early childhood education, early childhood special education, and early intervention.

DEC: Instructional Planning
EC7K1: Theories and research that form the basis of developmental and academic curricula and instructional strategies for infants and young children.

DEVELOPING YOUR PHILOSOPHY

Describe the role of curriculum in supporting children's overall development. What factors do you see as most important in determining the curriculum, the teacher, the child, the family, or external factors (such as NCLB)?

CHAPTER REVIEW

- **What theoretical and philosophical perspectives have shaped the field of early childhood today?**

  The major philosophical perspectives that affect the field today are those of behaviorism, maturationalism, and constructivism. Behaviorists believe that the environment and behavior are shaped largely by external factors such as rewards and punishments. Maturationists, on the other hand, believe that the child's naturally unfolding development provides the catalyst for his or her interactions with the environment. As such, a child's drive to learn plays a central role in his or her interactions with the environment. Constructivists view nature and nurture as complexly intertwined, and constructivism is considered the prevailing viewpoint in the field today.

- **What are the major curricular models and approaches in the field, and how do these reflect the field's philosophical underpinnings?**

  a. High/Scope Curriculum and Kamii-DeVries Approach are based on the work of Piaget.
  b. The DISTAR curriculum is based on behaviorism.
  c. Montessori education and the Bank Street Model are based on constructivism.
  d. Reggio Emilia, the Project Approach, and the Creative Curriculum are based on contemporary conceptions of children's development and learning.

- **What is emergent and child-centered curriculum, and how do these support effective curricular practices?**

  The emergent curriculum is based on the interests of the individual child. A main goal of emergent curriculum is supporting children's knowledge and meaning regarding the world around them. Creating curricular experiences that inspire and support continued growth and learning are an important component. For infants and toddlers, the focus of the emergent curriculum is on the development of relationships. For preschool-age and older children, project work is a tool supporting the emergent curriculum.

  Child-centered curriculum is grounded in supporting children's unique connections between their internal and external worlds. In the child-centered curriculum, the child's interest and abilities provide the catalyst for curricular experiences. This is in direct contrast to the teacher-directed curriculum, in which the major components of curricular experiences include mastering facts, specific skills, and predetermined areas of required knowledge.

9 Assessment

"Assessment is a means, but by no means an end."

—SAMUEL MEISELS

Elias enters his pre-K classroom on his first day of formal schooling, and both his parents are there to drop him off. Elias met his teacher, Lucia, the week before at a home visit. He is glad to see her familiar face when she greets him at the door.

Lucia, too, is filled with excitement about the new class of 4-year-olds. She and her co-teacher have met each of the children and are excited that four of the children in their class are English language learners. Elias is one of these children, and his parents, recent immigrants from Mexico, are both nervous and enthusiastic about all they hope Elias will learn in the coming year. Lucia is bilingual and well versed in practices that support children becoming bi- and multilingual. One of her main challenges is ensuring that Elias and his fellow students are supported in their home language as they work to attain concurrent English proficiency. She recognizes that this support will emerge from a team effort, with the team composed of her and her co-teacher, Elias, his parents, and the other children in the classroom.

Down the hall, Noma is welcoming Elias's sister, 6-month-old Beatriz, to her infant-toddler classroom. One of Noma's challenges is designing experiences that meet Beatriz's ongoing developmental needs. Noma also recognizes the importance of teamwork in ensuring that Beatriz's development is supported at home and in the early childhood classroom. She views herself, Beatriz, and her family as essential members of the team.

● ● ●

GUIDING QUESTIONS

- How do standards inform curriculum and assessment?
- How do effective assessment practices support equity, accountability, and success?
- What are challenges to effective assessment, and how are these addressed?
- In what ways do observation and other common assessment strategies contribute to knowledge of children's development and learning?
- What roles do screening and formal evaluation play in answering questions about a child's development?
- How do self-advocacy and reflection support professional assessment?

Lucia and Noma share important goals in their early childhood classrooms, with their foundational goal of getting to know each child in the classroom and his or her development and learning needs. Both teachers understand that families, schools, and states hold expectations for children's development and learning. Teachers are responsible for knowing *what* children should be learning and *how* they should be developing, which are informed by *standards*, and how well they are learning, developing, and making progress, which is informed by *assessment*.

This chapter focuses on effective assessment and includes applicable strategies for early childhood environments. In Bredekamp and Rosegrant's (1995) four stages of the curriculum process, effective assessment shapes knowledge of children's development and learning, as it provides information about the strengths and areas of challenge for each child. In turn, knowledge of children informs planning, which provides the foundations for developmentally appropriate curriculum implementation. The effectiveness of the curriculum in supporting children's development and learning is again determined through assessment, and the cycle repeats itself. Figure 9.1 illustrates the role of assessment in the curriculum process.

FIGURE 9.1
Role of Assessment
in the Curriculum
Process

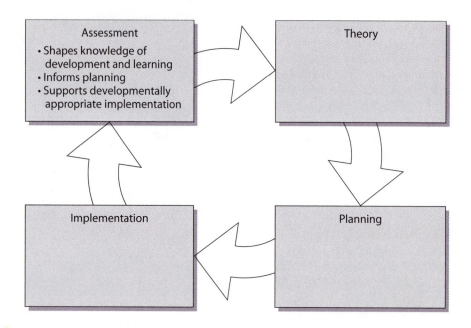

STANDARDS INFORMING CURRICULUM AND ASSESSMENT

The question of what young children should be learning is strongly influenced by the goals of larger society. Cultural knowledge—representing information, skills, attitudes, conceptions, beliefs, values, and other understandings of expectations for interactions with the immediate world—varies from society to society, as does the means of determining what knowledge is expected. For example, children in a Mayan community might gain cultural knowledge through stories passed down from generation to generation. A child in the United States, conversely, might gain this knowledge through formal schooling. In the Mayan society, members might look to elders for information on what children are expected to learn. In the United States, state and national standards are one important source of this information.

Standards at the Forefront

standards

Generalized goals for children who are learning at varying ages of development.

What are standards for early childhood education? **Standards** represent expectations for learning. For children, standards are typically presented for an age and grade level, often indicating knowledge, skills, and dispositions that children need to master to proceed to the next stage of learning. Standards affect what is taught in early childhood education and how the success of the field is measured. This success is often referred to as *accountability*, representing how effectively the teacher, program, and/or school is meeting its defined goals.

content standards

Broad expectations of knowledge, skills, and dispositions that individual children should have at a particular age in a specified subject.

As of 2006, 49 states have standards describing expected learning for children prior to kindergarten age, and Head Start has developed a Child Outcomes Framework (NAEYC & NAECS/SDE, 2002). In addition, numerous national organizations have developed **content standards** to guide learning and development in specific content areas, such as mathematics, literacy, science, social studies, music, dance, technology, and the arts.

Standards vary in both their content and the ages of children included. For example, most states (49 including the District of Columbia) provide standards for preschool populations, but significantly fewer (14) provide standards for infant-toddler populations (Scott-Little, Lesko, Martella, & Milburn, 2007). The development of infant-toddler standards is lagging because infant-toddler education represents an emerging field and research guiding standard development is much newer (Scott-Little et al., 2007). As discussed in Chapter 2, this lack of attention emerges from the historical underpinnings of the field, where care and education for infants and toddlers was seen as more custodial in nature.

Yet another example of the pervasive viewpoint of early childhood programs as custodial and not educational is the fact that of the 49 states that have **early learning standards** in place, most are used in state pre-K programs, which are predominantly associated with the public school systems (Scott-Little et al., 2007). In most center-based and family child care programs, use of standards is viewed as voluntary.

The application of standards to young children varies not only within states, but also between states. This variance results from each state being responsible for developing its own standards for children in K–12 education. Therefore, different states have different requirements for kindergarten and primary grade children, which can result in different learning standards for children preschool age and younger. These sets of standards do not act independently—expectations for younger children feed into expectations for older children. For standards to be developmentally appropriate, they must not be "watered-down" versions of standards for older children (Kostelnik, 1992). Rather, standards should represent age-related expectations, individual needs, and the unique larger contexts in which children learn and develop. Ensuring that standards are developmentally appropriate and complementary is referred to as **alignment**.

The source of standards for children between birth and the age of 8 is shaped by national organizations. Table 9.1 provides a list of curriculum standards that exist at the national level.

Many of the standards in Table 9.1 were based on existing elementary standards and, therefore, may not always be developmentally appropriate. Part of the teacher's role,

early learning standards

Expectations of knowledge, skills, and dispositions that children should have at a particular age.

alignment

Process through which standards at various age levels and in varied content areas are matched, ensuring that children can make a seamless transition between sets of standards.

TABLE 9.1 Overview of National and Federal Standards Affecting Early Childhood Education	
Name of Organization	**Content Area**
American Association for Health Education (AAHE)	Health
Center for Applied Linguistics	English as a Second Language Standards
Consortium of National Arts Education Associations	Fine Arts
International Reading Association (IRA)/National Association for the Education of Young Children (NAEYC) Joint Position Statement	Reading and Writing
International Reading Association and National Council of Teachers of English	Standards for the English Language Arts
International Society for Technology in Education National Educational Technology Standards for Students	Technology
National Association of Music Education (MENC)	Music
National Council of Teachers of Mathematics (NCTM)	Math
National Council for the Social Studies (NCSS)	Social Studies
National Research Council	Science

FIGURE 9.2
The Ethics of
Assessment

*Source: From the Code of
Ethical Conduct, by the
National Association for the
Education of Young
Children, 2005. Retrieved
January 15, 2007, from
http://www.naeyc.org/about
/positions/PSETH98.asp*

Responsibilities to Children

Ideals

I–1.6—To use assessment instruments and strategies that are appropriate for children to be assessed, that are used only for the purposes for which they were designed, and that have the potential to benefit children.

I–1.7—To use assessment information to understand and support children's development and learning, to support instruction, and to identify children who may need additional services.

Principles

P–1.5—We shall use appropriate assessment systems, which include multiple sources of information, to provide information on children's learning and development.

P–1.6—We shall strive to ensure that decisions such as those related to enrollment, retention, or assignment to special education services, will be based on multiple sources of information and will never be based on a single assessment, such as a test score or a single observation.

Responsibilities to Families

Ideals

I–2.2—To develop relationships of mutual trust and create partnerships with the families we serve.

Principles

P–2.2—We shall inform families of program philosophy, policies, curriculum, assessment system, and personnel qualifications, and explain why we teach as we do, which should be in accordance with our ethical responsibilities to children (see Section I).

P–2.6—As families share information with us about their children and families, we shall consider this information to plan and implement the program.

P–2.7—We shall inform families about the nature and purpose of the program's child assessments and how data about their child will be used.

P–2.8—We shall treat child assessment information confidentially and share this information only when there is a legitimate need for it.

Responsibilities to Community and Society

Ideals

I–4.5—To work to ensure that appropriate assessment systems, which include multiple sources of information, are used for purposes that benefit children.

Principles

P–4.5—We shall be knowledgeable about the appropriate use of assessment strategies and instruments and interpret results accurately to families.

TABLE 9.2 Common Assessment Terms and Their Meanings

Common Assessment Terms	Meanings
Authentic assessment	Any assessment strategy designed to estimate children's knowledge, understanding, ability, skill, and/or attitudes in a consistent fashion. Authentic assessment occurs across individuals and emphasizes methods other than standardized achievement tests, particularly those using multiple-choice formats. Authentic assessment or Performance-based assessments typically include exhibitions, investigations, demonstrations, written or oral responses, journals, and portfolios.
Content standards	Statements that provide a clear description of what a child should know and be able to do in a specified content area (such as literacy, mathematics, the arts, and science) at a particular level.
Developmental assessment	An ongoing process of observing a child's current competencies (including knowledge, skills, dispositions, and attitudes) and documenting growth and change over time. Information is used to help children develop further in the context of family, caregiving, and learning environments.
Developmental checklist	A brief guide to the development of children in a particular age range, checklists require the assessor to place a check to indicate if a developmental milestone has been met. Checklists are most effective when used along with other measures.
Developmental screening	Identifying children likely to be members of groups who may be at risk for developmental or health issues.
Diagnostic assessment (also called Evaluation)	Tool used to indicate child's present level of functioning in comparison to expected developmental levels. These are typically used to identify a disability or developmental problem.
Documentation	Documentation keeps track of and preserves children's work as evidence of ongoing developmental progress or of a program's development. Documentation can also focus on children's behavior or examples of how developmental milestones are met or illustrate projects or class activities. Projects may be displayed on walls or in portfolios.
Early learning standards	Statements that describe expectations for the learning and development of young children across the domains of health and physical well being, social and emotional well being, approaches to learning, language development and symbol systems, and general knowledge about the world around them.
Evaluation	The measurement, comparison, and judgment of the value, quality, or worth of children's work and/or of their schools, teachers, or a specific educational program based on valid evidence gathered through assessment.
Formal assessment strategies	Procedure for obtaining information that can be used to make judgments about characteristics of children or programs using standardized instruments.
Informal assessment strategies	Procedure for obtaining information that can be used to make judgments about characteristics of children or programs using means other than standardized instruments (examples include observations, self-reflections, portfolios, and narratives).
Observational assessment	A process in which the teacher systematically observes and records information about the child's level of development and/or knowledge, skills, and dispositions to determine what has been learned, improve teaching, and support children's developmental progress.

(*continued*)

TABLE 9.2 Common Assessment Terms and Their Meanings *(continued)*

Common Assessment Terms	Meanings
Outcomes	Changes in behavior, knowledge, understanding, ability, skills, and/or dispositions that occur as a result of participation in a program or course of study, receiving services, or using a product.
Portfolio assessment	A collection of work, usually drawn from children's classroom work, which, when subjected to objective analysis, become an assessment tool. This occurs when (1) the assessment purpose is defined; (2) criteria or methods are made clear for determining what is put into the portfolio, by whom, and when; and (3) criteria for assessing either the collection or individual pieces of work. These are identified and used to make judgments about children's learning.
Program standards	Expectations for the characteristics or quality of early childhood settings in homes, centers, and schools. Such characteristics typically include the ratio of adults to children, the qualifications and stability of the staff, characteristics of adult–child relationships, the program philosophy and curriculum model, the nature of relationships with families, the quality and quantity of equipment and materials, the quality and quantity of space per child, and safety and health provisions. Program standards are often developed at the program, state, and/or national level.
Readiness tests	Testing instruments designed to measure skills believed to be related to school learning tasks and are considered predictive of school success.
Rubrics	Descriptive scales for organizing and interpreting data gathered from observations of children's performance on a learning task and/or of children's developmental status. Rubrics describe levels of performance of children's work or a particular area of knowledge by defining varying levels of quality or mastery and providing indicators of each level.
Standardized test	A testing instrument that is administered, scored, and interpreted in a standard manner. It may be either norm referenced or criterion referenced.
Standards	Widely accepted statements of expectations for children's learning or the quality of schools and other programs.
Standards-based assessment	A process through which the criteria for assessment are derived directly from content and/or performance standards.
Test	One or more questions, problems, and/or tasks designed to estimate a child's knowledge, understanding, ability, skill, and/or attitudes in a consistent fashion across individuals. Information from a test or tests contributes to judgments made as a part of an assessment process.

Source: From The Words We Use: A Glossary of Terms for Early Childhood Education Standards and Assessment, by Council of Chief State School Officers, 2004. Retrieved June 15, 2007, from http://www.ccsso.org/Projects/scass/early_childhood_education_assessment_consortium/publications_and_products/2838.cfm

Well-designed assessment practices reflect what children need to know, expectations for children's development and learning in general, and knowledge of individual children in particular. Daily assessment supports the development and learning of each individual child and can serve as a tool that supports equity, accountability, and success.

ASSESSMENT PRACTICES

Historically, much debate in the field of early childhood education has centered on how to effectively assess children's development and learning. Challenges have included: *How should assessment data be gathered? How well do assessments measure what they are intended to measure? In what way should assessment results be used?*

Challenges of Effective Assessment

One of the main challenges of assessment centers on how results are used. For example, because of the standards and accountability movement, some professionals use **standardized tests** and other assessment measures to determine whether a child will be admitted to a particular program, promoted to the next grade, or retained. In addition, professionals often use these tests to determine a program's effectiveness.

Further, some professionals are concerned that many of the assessment practices used are not effective at measuring what they are intended to measure. One of the most significant areas of concern centers on the reality that many assessments are not **culturally and linguistically sensitive**. Consider Elias, the English language learner from the opening vignette. If given an assessment instrument that did not consider his developing English proficiency, his test scores in reading and language would be much lower. In this case, the assessment used would not provide an accurate picture of his literacy development.

Another criticism of assessment instruments is that they are **biased** in their development. This bias emerges from the fact that most instruments are developed based on children from middle-class, European American backgrounds. This is related to the historical underpinnings of the field, where lab schools—in which most assessment tools were developed—served families who were predominantly from middle- and upper-middle-class backgrounds. Therefore, tests were **normed**, or averaged, based on these children's learning and development and therefore not representative of a valid sample of all children.

Challenges in assessment are further complicated by how development and learning are assessed and the inherent challenges associated with assessing young children's development. Effective assessment provides a holistic picture of the child's development over time. This picture often develops through sampling representing snapshots of children's development. Professionals must take care to ensure that the

standardized tests
A testing instrument that is administered, scored, and interpreted in a standard manner.

culturally and linguistically sensitive
Assessment practices based on the individual cultural and linguistic backgrounds of each child.

biased
Assessment instruments that have prejudice, toward either a particular learning style or a content area, inherent in their design.

normed
Assessment tests used as a basis of comparison, where the norm is considered a representation of typical expectations.

TEACHING AND LEARNING CONNECTIONS

Selecting Culturally and Linguistically Sensitive Assessment Instruments

- Ensure that the assessment instruments are delivered in the child's primary language.
- Consider children's experiences with testing and make appropriate accommodations.
- Communicate with children and families about the assessment process, general expectations, and use of results.
- Avoid use of high-stakes testing practices.

whole of children's development—including physical, cognitive-language, and social-emotional areas—are represented. Further, as mentioned earlier, the field of early childhood education has adopted many strategies typically used with older children, due to assessment pressures created by the No Child Left Behind Act. These include **high-stakes testing**, where assessment results have important consequences for children, families, professionals, or programs and are reflective of many commonly used assessment practices being ill-suited to providing a holistic picture of children's overall development. Finally, children are greatly affected by internal moods (such as hunger and amount of rest) and influences from the external environment (such as noise and activity level). Because of this, assessment that is not a composite of children's development over time might not present a realistic picture of the child's strengths and areas of challenge.

Developmentally appropriate assessment takes into account each of these challenges. Assessment must meet several criteria for it to be considered reliable, valid, and appropriate (National Institute for Early Education Research, 2004). **Reliability** in assessment data means that you and your coworker are likely, under similar circumstances, to attain similar results. **Validity** in assessment data means that the instrument measures what it is designed to measure. Assessing a child's fine motor skills, for example, leads to a snapshot of the child's fine motor development.

Although the following assessment criteria were developed for the preschool population, they have been adapted to include application to infants and toddlers.

- **Assessment should not make children feel anxious or scared.** To accomplish this, assessment should be performed in natural environments, when possible, and administered by persons with whom the child feels comfortable. Further, assessment should be viewed as an opportunity for children to demonstrate what they know. This is in direct contrast to assessment practices that focus on a perceived lack of knowledge or skills.
- **Information should be obtained over time.** Children are very sensitive to internal and external factors, such as whether they are tired, hungry, or distracted. Because of this, a one-shot approach to assessment only provides information on the child's internal state and not the data being sought after in the evaluation.
- **Assessment data around individual areas of development should be obtained in a variety of ways.** The application of knowledge and skills is integrated across a variety of settings. For example, a 3-year-old child might demonstrate one-to-one correspondence when placing napkins next to plates at a family-style lunch or when matching Unifix cubes and counting bears in the manipulatives area. For assessment data to be useful, it needs to account for the wide variety of ways that children demonstrate knowledge within their learning context.
- **The collection of assessment data must be sensitive to young children's interests and attention spans.** Targeted assessment includes the need to gather data in a way that represents children's developmental needs. Within this broad goal, therefore, assessment should be embedded in natural environments and daily activities. When more formal means of assessment are required, such as through testing, assessment periods should be short—no longer than 35 to 45 minutes for a 4- or 5-year-old child and significantly shorter for an infant, toddler, or 3-year-old.

Meeting each of these criteria, in turn, supports reliable, valid assessment.

high-stakes testing
Assessment practices that have important consequences for children, families, professionals, or programs.

reliability
Measurement of how likely assessment data are repeatable with similar results.

validity
Measure of how effectively assessment data are measuring the concepts they were designed to measure.

TEACHING AND LEARNING CONNECTIONS

Supporting Effective Assessment

- Conduct assessments in natural environments.
- Gather information over time.
- Use a variety of strategies to gather information on different developmental domains.
- Base data collection on children's interests.
- Be respectful of children's attention spans.

The challenges associated with assessment can be further illuminated through examination of your own experiences with assessment. You most likely have been assessed many times throughout your scholastic career. These assessments might include taking paper-and-pencil tests, giving speeches, or writing papers. In many of these cases, the assessment practices focus on your ability to provide responses to questions in an unnatural environment. For example, it is highly unlikely that later in life someone will pop up in front of you on the street, hand you a paper and pencil, and command that you write out the six substages of Piaget's sensorimotor stage of development.

Similarly, assessing children in ways that contradict how they are likely to use information in life can provide skewed representations of what children know and how they apply this information. To address concerns with inappropriate data collection, the field has turned to play-based assessments.

Addressing the Challenges of Assessment

Play-Based Assessment. **Play-based assessment** focuses on how children demonstrate development and learning in their natural interactions with the environment. As a natural behavior, play provides windows into not only children's social-emotional, cognitive, and motor development, but also their strengths and coping strategies. Furthermore, play provides important information about the qualities of children's relationships. Play can also serve to establish a common language supporting communication with families and the development of a family–professional partnership (Segal & Webber, 1996).

Play-based assessment has gained popularity in recent years as a sound tool to assess how children navigate and interact with their environments. This form of assessment is seen as particularly beneficial for infant-toddler populations, as this group is least likely—due to their developmental nature—to respond to more formal assessment practices.

In addition to assessing children's development through play, strength-based assessment practices are considered a remedy for challenges associated with assessment.

Strength-Based Assessment. Historically, assessment practices have been criticized for their focus on what a child can and cannot do. For example, Moira, a preschool teacher, used a **checklist** in her early childhood program. The checklist consisted of such items as "Can hop three times on one foot" and "Can color within lines." This checklist gave Moira information about what children in the classroom could accomplish relative to age-related expectations. However, it gave her very little information about how children accomplished tasks and navigated their environments. For example, if a child

play-based assessment
Tool focusing on how children demonstrate development in their natural interactions with the environment.

checklist
Assessment based on whether a child can complete particular age-related skills.

was not able to walk up steps in a manner that alternated legs, how were they navigating the environment? Were there other effective strategies they were using? If so, how did these help them accomplish needed tasks?

Strength-based assessment

Assessment practices that focus on what a child *can* do and that provide a holistic picture based on the child's capabilities.

Strength-based assessment focuses on what a child *can* do and how the child uses his or her knowledge and skills to meaningfully interact with the environment. This represents a significant shift from traditional assessment practices that sought to identify risk factors or tasks children could not complete. Supporting each child's development, embracing what a child can do, and seeing the child through the lens of his or her amazing capabilities reflects dispositions that can dramatically affect your view of a child's growth.

Strength-based assessment focuses on a child's capabilities. Changes in attitudes toward English language learners represent one of the most notable shifts toward strength-based dispositions in the field and larger culture. Originally, children whose primary language was not English were seen as deficient in their prior learning, and great efforts were made to teach English while extinguishing their primary language. Recently, cultural changes have created the viewpoint that children who are bi- and multilingual have great strengths. Certainly, the prevalence of programs teaching preschool-aged and younger children a second language speaks to the cultural shift. As a field, the view of bi- and multilingualism as strengths is demonstrated through advocacy for and development of culturally and linguistically sensitive instruments.

Culturally and Linguistically Sensitive Assessment. Good assessment is both culturally and linguistically sensitive, respecting and responding to the individual learning needs of each child. Appropriate assessment of English language learners has historically been a challenge in the field, as there are very few assessment instruments designed toward this specific population, despite the present and anticipated growth in the English language learner population (NAEYC, 2005b). Further, those assessments that exist are often used inappropriately. These limitations can affect the teacher's ability to make sound decisions about how and what to teach. Further, inaccurate assessments can lead to an under- or overidentification of developmental delays or specific disabilities.

What criteria exist for selecting linguistically and culturally appropriate assessment instruments? All screenings and assessments used with English language learners must be culturally appropriate, considering children's cultural knowledge and preferred ways for viewing and interacting with their world. Assessment tools must also be linguistically appropriate, considering the child's language when selecting instruments. In addition, translations of English-language instruments must be free of linguistic and cultural bias before being used with young English language learners. Translations need to focus on more than a word-for-word translation by including attention to the contexts within which children learn (NAEYC, 2005b). Consider a first-grade reading comprehension assessment. Children are required to read a paragraph and respond to a series of prompts testing their knowledge of the sequence of events in the paragraph. The topic of the paragraph is a game of baseball, and in the paragraph are a series of questions about what is happening in the game. Although knowledge of baseball is not specifically being tested, the game of baseball is the main topic of the paragraph. In this case, the topic of baseball may introduce bias if the game does not reflect the local and cultural experiences of the children taking the test (Hagie, Gallipo, & Svien, 2003).

culture-bound

Assessment practices that assume a child has particular areas of knowledge related to overall culture. Assessment should be culture-free, where children's abilities can be highlighted without test bias.

Assessment instruments that incorporate these characteristics are not **culture-bound**, where performance is dictated by having knowledge of a particular culture. For assessment to be culture-free, meaning that it is free from cultural bias, it must take into account children's different levels of cultural knowledge, including language.

Acquiring knowledge of each individual child is supported through play-based, strength-based, and culturally and linguistically sensitive assessments. A common tool

ISSUES OF ACCESS AND EQUITY FOR CHILDREN

Assessment Practices Within Head Start

The 2007 reauthorization of the Head Start Act mandated that all Head Start programs must assess children's progress toward specific learning outcomes in the areas of cognitive and language development. This reauthorization reflects the importance of assessment in ensuring that children in Head Start programs are benefiting from *teaching and learning practices* that support individual education needs. In addition, the screening and assessment practices selected by each Head Start program are utilized to determine whether individual children would benefit from *focused intervention* to address *significant developmental concerns*.

Assessment, data analysis, program assessment, and continuous improvement are each guided by Head Start's Child Outcomes Framework. This framework is composed of 8 general domains (language development, literacy, mathematics, science, creative arts, social and emotional development, approaches to learning, and physical health and development), 27 domain elements, and 100 examples of children's skills, abilities, knowledge, and behavior (Chicago Public Schools, 2005). The 2007 Reauthorization of Head Start requires more specific education performance standards in the areas of reading, math, science, and other aspects of cognitive development (National School Boards Association, 2008).

Head Start's focus on the development of individual children extended to ensuring appropriate practices at the program level. Toward this goal, local programs are required to analyze the data gathered on all children. In turn, programs use this information to determine the *educational and developmental interventions on which that program can improve*.

Together, the assessment practices of Head Start provide useful examples of integrating assessment across the early childhood program to meet varied goals. As for access and equity for children, these practices can ensure that children and society are benefiting from the services offered.

for assessment in early childhood environments is observation. Observation focuses on getting to know the children and how they interact with their environment by watching and listening to them. In turn, this knowledge supports your ability to make sound decisions about teaching and learning.

OBSERVATION

A 3-month-old pushes himself up on his arms, lifting his head and arching his back as he looks into the mirror placed in front of him on the floor . . . a 2-year-old takes a ball of play dough and rolls it out into a snake shape, saying "ake!" as she finishes her creation . . . a 5-year-old climbs up the slide ladder, proceeding with his left leg continuously leading . . . an 8-year-old writes her name on the bottom of a piece of paper, reversing each of the letters (such as LEAHCIM) and placing each letter so they overlap one another.

What do each of these individual snapshots of children's development mean? In isolation, very little. For assessment to be effective, it must be *collected over time* and *include*

myeducationlab

Go to MyEducationLab and select the topic "Observation and Assessment." Under Activities and Applications, watch the video *Observing Children in Authentic Contexts* and reflect on how you can use these skills in your daily practice.

information that represents the whole of children's development. Further, assessment practices must be authentic, where children are assessed in natural environments engaging in everyday tasks. Ongoing observation, where children's development is observed and recorded in a strategic manner, is an effective informal assessment tool. For observation to be effective, it must be objective.

Objectivity

objectivity
Representation of observed facts, without the insertion of opinion.

What does **objectivity** mean? Objectivity refers to a basic representation of facts, without the introduction of opinion. Consider each of the previous examples above, which are provided as an objective presentation of events. In each case, the child's actions are presented without professional commentary on the interpretation, or subjective analysis, of their actions. The following examples are subjective interpretations, of the same actions:

A 3-month-old happily pushed himself up on his arms and with great strength lifted his head and arched his back as he looked curiously into the mirror placed in front of him on the floor.

A 2-year-old takes a ball of play dough and clumsily rolls it out into a snake shape, saying "ake!" as she finishes her creation.

A 5-year-old lumbers up the slide ladder, proceeding with his left leg continuously leading as if he can't use his right one.

An 8-year-old anxiously writes her name on the bottom of a piece of paper, reversing each of the letters and making the writing impossible to read.

subjectivity
Reporting of assessment data that includes professional opinion.

In each of these cases, the interpretations represent the thoughts of a professional. Including subjective language makes recorded data difficult to interpret through any lens other than the one the professional has added. **Subjectivity** can serve as a block to effective assessment, as bias from the recording professional can affect his or her interpretations and those of others who may review the data.

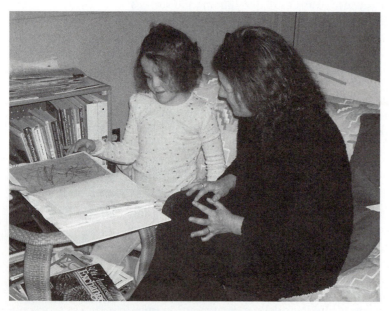

Families are an important part of meaningful assessment.

Who might also be involved in the interpretation of assessment data? Families are one population that benefit from shared assessment, as this information can help support a foundational understanding of children's development. You have learned that one of the core practices of appropriate assessment is the maintenance of confidentiality. Assessment data, however, can be shared on an as-needed basis within the realm of confidentiality with family consent. Persons in this category might include your co-teacher, when assessment data is used to support effective classroom practices, or other professionals, when assessment data might be utilized to determine whether a child is in need of further evaluation and/or intervention services.

The objective recording of assessment data provides information that can be used for interpretation in a variety of ways. First, objectivity allows professionals to reflect on children's development over time, without the interference of changing opinions and perceptions. For example, a child's behavior might initially be viewed as defiant but, over time, is viewed as a strong need for support and positive attention. Second, *objective assessment allows other professionals to be able to process the data collected without being influenced by another's opinion.* As teamwork is an essential component of the field, objective data allow each member of the team to interpret the data through his or her own professional lens. Finally, *subjective perceptions are largely shaped by individual values and attitudes*, which may or may not coincide with the child's reality.

How can information gathered be presented in an objective manner? Information presented should focus exclusively on a description of events occurring. Also, all information gathered in a particular period of time should be presented.

There are many commonly used strategies supporting effective observation. Use of these strategies requires more than knowledge and skills: Effective observation is also shaped by appropriate dispositions (Jablon, Dombro, & Dichtelmiller, 1999). An important disposition supporting developmentally appropriate observation is an *attitude of openness*, where observing creates an *attitude of wonder* about the children you work with daily (Jablon et al., 1999). Further, your interest in individual children and their development can serve as a cornerstone to developing trusting relationships with their families. The resulting relationships with children and families in turn can promote effective, supportive practices.

Viewing observation as a tool that creates openness and a sense of wonder about each child in the classroom helps move the task of observing from something that you have to find time to do to an important part of your everyday work with children in the classroom. Therefore, the development of appropriate dispositions regarding assessment can support your regular use of assessment practices.

Common Assessment Strategies

Positive dispositions toward observation require familiarity with common strategies and the skills to employ these strategies. Observation is far more than looking at a child; rather, effective observation consists of numerous strategies that have varied uses and applications in the environment. Table 9.3 summarizes common observation strategies, their potential use, and suggestions for how to incorporate these into the early childhood environment.

Time is one of the most critical factors associated with effective assessment. In a busy early childhood environment, finding time to observe the development of all children is challenging, so you must *develop a recording system that is effective for you.* Your own ways of processing and interacting with the environment mean that some forms of assessment will be more conducive to your temperament and learning needs. You also need to *make a plan for who and what you will observe.* In cases where the child is an English language learner, *arrange for a staff person who speaks the child's language to observe that child and write up the observation.* Finally, if you have coworkers, *figure out a system that allows you to cover for one another while someone steps out of the action to observe for a few minutes* (Mitchell & David, 1992).

Knowledge gained through observation provides a cornerstone for effective practices that meet the individual needs of each child. Observation needs to be a daily part of effective teaching. However, observation alone does not fully address all practices needing to be in place to support effective teaching and learning. Rather, observation is one form of

TABLE 9.3 Common Observation Strategies and Their Usage

Observation Strategy	Description	Potential Use	Suggestions for Incorporation
Running records	Detailed narrative accounts of events as they occur. Running records record everything observed in a factual manner. Sasha bent over the puzzle, reaching for each new piece with her left hand, and using both hands to place it in its correct spot. She placed 10 pieces in their places before taking a brief break to look around the room.	Running records can serve as a tool for documenting children's behavior for later reflection, where the information provided is processed and analyzed in the larger context.	Running records require time to observe and attention to the times in which you are most interested in observing. Comfortable chairs, notepads, and writing instruments are effective tools.
Anecdotal notes	Detailed narrative accounts that describe a particular event. Ben came into the room today, put his bag in his cubby, and asked the teacher for help finding his folder. When she asked him if he had taken it out of his bag, he replied "no."	Anecdotal notes can present information in a story format, which are recorded after an event has concluded. Anecdotal notes, over time, can provide stories of a child's development and interactions with the environment.	Anecdotal notes require material considerations similar to running records. However, the transcription of events can be done at a convenient time and does not require real-time notations.
Brief notes	Quick written records that provide a reminder of events observed. Marina shared two stories during morning meeting. Jessica sat by herself during snack.	Brief notes can be compiled on a daily or weekly basis to present a cumulative picture of children's development.	Placement of sticky notes throughout the room with easy-to-access writing instruments. Notes are collected daily and placed in a child's folder.
Checklist	Form used to indicate whether a particular behavior or developmental	Checklists can provide a quick assessment of children's development and	Strategic observation organized around particular content items. Checklists can

	milestone is present or absent. |	Present	Absent
Hops on one foot.	✓	
Walks up stairs with alternating feet.	✓	
Uses two hands to catch ball.		✓		serve as an indication of where further observation or more formal assessment measures should be targeted.	be completed in real time by asking a child to complete certain tasks, or—more appropriately—by deriving information to address checklist items from collected observations.
Event sampling	Observing the occurrence of a specific event and what happens before and after the event. A: Jake looks and points at Adam's truck and says "Mine." Adam does not respond. _____ B: Jake takes Adam's truck. _____ C: Adam begins to cry and walks away. Jake takes the truck over to the sandbox. _____	Also called ABC sampling, this can be used to look at factors that might reinforce or contribute to particular behaviors. (A) represents what happens right before the event, (B) the event itself, and (C) what happens right after the event.	Event sampling requires time and materials that are conveniently placed. In addition, skilled observers will focus on the child's interactions with the environment on a continuous basis to "catch" what precedes the actual event.
Tallies	Recording of the number of times a specific event occurs in a specified time. Behavior / Time period / Frequency Hair pulling / Snack ‖ / Transition outside ‖ / Transition to nap ‖‖	Tallies can be used to target the prevalence of specific behaviors and can serve as an indication of where further observation or more formal assessment measures should be targeted.	Tallies require a set observation target, such as the number of times a child physically interacts with a peer during snack.
Time sampling	Observing the occurrence of a specific event during a designated time or a specified event at a	Time sampling occurs at selected intervals and requires recording targeted behaviors during these intervals.	Time sampling requires targeting a particular behavior and developing and adhering to a schedule

(continued)

TABLE 9.3	Common Observation Strategies and Their Usage *(continued)*		
Time Sampling *(continued)*	particular interval of time (for example, is a child doing *x* behavior when observed at 5-minute intervals).		for sampling. In addition, the observer must recognize that the designated behavior might occur outside of the designated sampling times.

Behavior	Time period: 5-minute intervals	Presence (*x*) or absence of behavior (0)
Hair pulling	00	0
	05	X
	10	0
	15	0
	20	X
	25	X
	30	X

documentation

A strategy used to record children's development and learning over time.

documentation that can be utilized to create a bridge between developmental needs and classroom practices that support teaching and learning.

Informal Assessment Tools

Knowledge of each individual child is critical to supporting his or her development. Table 9.4, adapted from Helm and Gronlund (2000), provides a description of informal assessment tools that can be used to provide knowledge of individual children.

What strategies ensure that the documentation is used appropriately? Documentation and assessment practices should be based on routine classroom activities. These practices also require attention to each child's individual learning styles. A child's progress over time must be a focus of documentation and should include natural products of learning experiences. Figure 9.3 provides a sample document strategy for two children's handwriting.

Systematic means of collecting materials and documenting children's progress over time has gained increasing attention in early childhood education. Two popular approaches of systematic collection that represent the whole of children's development include portfolios and the Work Sampling System.

Learning to document is an important part of becoming a professional.

TABLE 9.4 Description of Documentation Strategies

Type of Documentation	Description
Individual portfolios	Content items collected at specific intervals designed to show children's learning styles, interests, and unique ways of viewing and interacting with the world. Portfolios can be used as a tool for documenting growth and development over time, communicating with families, or demonstrating how content standards are met.
Individual or group products	Products can include concrete items that children have developed, samples of written and spoken language, pictures of constructions (such as in the block area and/or with Legos or clay), or examples of a child's creativity (such as samples of their writing or drawings).
Child self-reflections	Children's statements of their own preferences, responses to activities, or individual ways of processing information in the early childhood classroom.
Narratives of learning experiences	Anecdotal stories of individuals, small groups, or the whole class. These can be recorded in: • Teacher journals • Displays on projects and units • Books or explanations for families • Books or stories for children

Source: Adapted from "Linking Standards and Engaged Learning in the Early Years," by J. Helm and G. Gronlund, 2000, *Early Childhood Research and Practice,* 2(1). Retrieved June 4, 2007, from http://ecrp.uiuc.edu/v2n1/helm.html

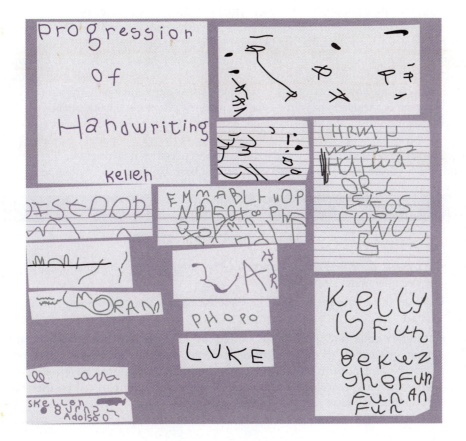

FIGURE 9.3
Sample Documentation Strategy
Collection of two children's handwriting samples over 9-month period.

TEACHING AND LEARNING CONNECTIONS

Observation and Documentation Tools

The following can be useful tools in recording observations:

- Sticky notes and notepads placed in easily accessible positions throughout the classroom
- Audiotapes
- Videotapes
- Cameras
- Clipboards and paper

---

authentic assessment

Assessment practices that reflect expectations for development as demonstrated in the natural environment and that include a focus on how the child would use assessed knowledge, skills, and dispositions.

Each of these represents strategies that support **authentic assessment**, where children are involved in the documentation and evaluation of their own achievements. In addition, each approach summarizes children's *performance*, is *realistic*, and is *appropriate for the overall goals of instruction* (Pett, 1990).

Using Portfolios. Portfolios represent collections of children's work and are a record of the child's process of learning over time. Toward this end, portfolios include what the child has learned and the processes that have supported this learning; how the child thinks, questions, analyzes, synthesizes, produces, and creates; and how the child interacts (socially, emotionally, and intellectually) with others (Grace, 1992).

The contents of portfolios can be divided into three major categories. *Showcase models* consist of work samples that are chosen by the child. *Descriptive models* contain representative work of the child and are characterized by a lack of evaluation. *Evaluative models* also include representative products but are evaluated by particular criteria, which can include how effectively the work meets external standards (Grosvenor, 1993).

screening

Assessment practice used to determine if children require additional assessment or services designed to support development and learning.

What can be included in a young child's portfolio? Collections of work can be guided by each of the previously outlined documentation strategies and the results of **screening** or other more formal assessments. Purposeful collection is one of the most important aspects of portfolio development. Without an overall framework for collection, it is merely a collection of a child's work (Grace, 1992). Individual goals of the classroom determine the purpose of the

---

TEACHING AND LEARNING CONNECTIONS

Organizing Portfolios

- In general, portfolios should be arranged by categories of development, content, or documentation strategies.
- Within these categories, portfolios should be arranged chronologically and dated.
- Materials collected in portfolios should include a variety of materials documenting a variety of different developmental domains. For example, writing samples and photos of artwork can document fine motor development, whereas voice recordings, transcriptions, and writing samples can be used to document language and literacy development.

portfolio. These goals can include *documenting growth and development over time*. For example, teachers can compile a series of paintings that show progression of color mixing or documentation of children's friendships. Portfolios can also be used to *demonstrate how the child is meeting external standards*. These standards can include scores on developmental inventories or samples of work showing mastery of content standards. Portfolios can also be used to *showcase a child's strengths*. This kind of portfolio might include work samples of the child's favored activities or video of a child interacting with others. Portfolio goals can include *supporting self-reflection* in children. Self-reflection portfolios could include video or written commentary on a child's work. Another effective use of portfolios is as a *tool for communicating with families about children's overall development* (Mitchell & David, 1992).

Materials for a child's portfolio should be collected and reviewed regularly. These items should be dated as they are obtained. Specific portfolio items might be determined by overall curriculum needs, and other items might emerge based on ongoing reflection and assessment of the child's evolving development.

The Work Sampling System. Another popular approach to assessing and documenting children's development over time is the **Work Sampling System** (Meisels, Jablon, Marsden, Dichtelmiller, Dorfman, & Steele, 1995). Widely used within Head Start, the Work Sampling System consists of three main tools for documenting children's development: (1) developmental guidelines and checklists, (2) portfolios, and (3) summary reports.

The *developmental guidelines* provide a framework for observation, providing teachers with specific criteria to observe for that are derived from national standards and current knowledge of children's development. Information about the developmental guidelines gathered through observation is then used to complete the *checklists*.

Portfolios are collections of work that document children's efforts, progress, and achievements (Meisels et al., 1995). Two types of work samples (core and individualized) are included as portfolio items. Core items reflect data on the same area of development collected at three different points in time over the course of a school year. For example, a cutting sample collected three times a year would document fine motor growth and appropriate use of scissors, and a photo and transcribed dictation of a block structure would document using words and representations to describe mathematical ideas. Individualized items are collected with the goal of reflecting the larger curriculum as well as the unique aspects of each child's work (Meisels et al., 1995).

Documented information is used to develop *summary reports* three times a year. To complete the summary reports, teachers compile the information collected through the developmental guidelines and portfolios and—combined with their knowledge of children's development and learning—assess and summarize the student's progress and performance. Each of these strategies, in turn, is used to individualize instruction, communicate with families, and meet federal reporting mandates. Table 9.5 provides a summary of each of the components of the Work Sampling System.

Go to MyEducationLab and select the topic "Families and Communities." Under Activities and Applications, watch the video *Portfolio Exhibitions* and consider the role of portfolios in showcasing young children's development and learning.

Work Sampling System

Assessment process consisting of developmental guidelines and checklists, portfolios, and summary reports.

TABLE 9.5	Components of the Work Sampling System

Component	Description
Developmental guidelines and checklists	Focusing on personal and social development, language and literacy, mathematical thinking, scientific thinking, social studies, the arts, and physical development, developmental guidelines and checklists are designed to assist teachers in observing the developmental growth of each child (Meisels, 1995). Guidelines and checklist items are informed by local, state, and national standards for children's development.
Portfolios	Used as a tool to provide documentation of children's experiences throughout the year, portfolios allow children to participate in the selection of relevant materials (Meisels, 1995). Items included in portfolio development include core items, which reflect learning in a particular learning domain, and individualized items, which are based on the child's unique interactions with the environment. Core items are typically collected three times per year.
Summary reports	Included three times per year in the Work Sampling System, summary reports are based on teacher observations of the child's learning and materials collected. The intention of the summary report is to replace traditional report cards. This is accomplished through providing a picture of the child's development based on the varied data collected and the child's own perceptions of that data.

Source: Meisels, S. (1995). Performance Assessment in Early Childhood Education: The Work Sampling System. Urbana, IL: CEEP Clearinghouse on Early Education and Parenting (CEEP Document Reproduction Service No. ED EDO-PS-95-6).

• • • BECOMING A PROFESSIONAL • • •

Career Pathways

Infant-Toddler Teacher

Kathryn's career pathway as an infant-toddler teacher has been well supported through the military child care system. The greatest benefits came from the combination of extensive education and experience in their high-quality system. "They have a well-developed series of trainings here and really excellent programming—in combination, I feel like I have really benefited from both in terms of tackling the day-to-day challenges of my work, as well as making sure I am prepared for the future."

These day-to-day challenges are numerous and center on the extensive documentation and assessment required. Kathryn finds the numerous guidelines she has to follow challenging. These include military, NAEYC, and state regulations. Tending to these can present some obstacles in doing what she loves the most: working with the children. "Our days and weeks have many different things required of us. We have to observe every day, work on the children's portfolios, and develop lesson plans. Sometimes I feel overwhelmed in getting this all done, but I think it really helps me make sure that the kids are getting what they need. This makes it all worth it."

In addition to the training received through the military program, Kathryn has obtained her associate's degree and is working toward her bachelor's degree. "I think I might want to teach kindergarten eventually. But really, the pay and benefits are so great here—I just might stay."

Military child care is not dependent on parent fees exclusively for teacher wages. The subsidies received from the federal government have a direct impact on the quality of salaries and benefits offered to teaching staff and personnel. The rate of growth in the program is directly related to the needs of military families for child care and the latest services. In 2009, for example, the demand for qualified employees is great, reflective of the wars in Afghanistan and Iraq.

The Work Sampling System represents a strategy for **performance assessment**. In this form of assessment, children's experiences and demonstrated learning are used to document how effectively external standards are met.

Both portfolios and the Work Sampling System embrace children as active participants in their own learning and can be effectively used as tools for communicating with families about their child's development. As families play a critical role supporting children's development and learning, this communication is vital.

You have learned about formal and informal strategies for supporting partnerships with families. Assessment is a tool that can complement these strategies. Lucia uses a variety of informal strategies supporting communication with parents in her early childhood classroom. Her use of ongoing assessment complements these strategies. For example, she regularly assesses Elias's communication progress in the classroom, observing and taking careful note of how he uses language to interact with both his peers and teachers. Through daily communication at drop-off and pick-up,

performance assessment
Form of assessment that requires children to perform tasks in order to demonstrate knowledge, skills, and dispositions.

Lucia reports on Elias's progress to his family. She also shares notes suggesting strategies that they might incorporate in their home to support his continued development. Lucia also encourages Elias's parents to conduct their own observations and report back to her about his development.

Lucia collects portfolio items regularly throughout the school year supporting more formal organization that will provide a way to communicate progress. The items she collects are informed by her state Early Learning Standards, which provide a guide for general expectations for children's development. In addition, Lucia works to incorporate objects in the portfolio that embrace Elias's strengths and unique ways of processing and interacting with his world. As Elias is very verbal and creative, this documentation includes many samples of his art, digital photos of his sculpture creations, and transcribed samples of his language interactions. Elias also selects items to include in his portfolio and participates in the conference Lucia has with his family by explaining the varied contents.

Using authentic assessment as a means of communication provides both families and professionals with a holistic summary of children's development. Both parties have the opportunity to provide input into the process and comment on the child's development over time. Family participation in assessment can begin before the child's entry into the program, where data is collected from the family on the child's perceived strengths and areas of challenge. These, in turn, can serve to inform and guide assessment, allowing the professional to provide ongoing feedback and interpretations based on the family's input.

Observation and documentation strategies, as a group, represent informal assessment practices. There are a

Assessing children's development often happens during naturally occurring activities.

TEACHING AND LEARNING CONNECTIONS

Formal and Informal Strategies for Communicating with Families

- Daily conversations
- Classroom visits
- Opportunities for family volunteering
- Daily notes and phone calls
- Written questionnaires
- Program orientations
- Newsletters
- Family–teacher conferences

---

variety of more formal assessment practices that can provide specific information about children's individual development, as well as their development in the context of their peers. In developmentally appropriate assessment, this data can serve to *identify significant concerns that may require focused intervention for individual children.*

SCREENING AND FORMAL EVALUATION

"Is my child's development typical?" "How does she compare with her peers?" "She isn't walking, should I be worried?"

These questions are ones you might encounter when working with families. Further, you might have your own concerns about an individual child's development and wonder if these concerns are warranted. Informal assessment strategies, such as the observation and documentation strategies outlined previously, can give you information about each individual child's development. They are typically used on a regular, ongoing basis. More formal strategies can be used to assess young children's development relative to that of their peers. Formal assessment practices include developmental screening, checklists, and diagnostic assessment. They tend to be applied less often and serve to address specific questions about young children's development.

Developmental Screening and Checklists

Developmental screening is used to identify children who are at risk for health or developmental problems. Developmental checklists and screening tools can provide information on perceived developmental progress. These can be filled out by family members and early childhood professionals. Further, screening and checklists are tools often used at the community level as a means of identifying children whose development may not be proceeding in a typical manner.

An example of checklists and screening measures at the community level are Child Find projects. Child Find is a part of the Individuals with Disabilities Education Act (IDEA). It requires states to locate, identify, and evaluate all children with disabilities between birth and age 21 who are in need of special education services.

Although Child Find projects vary from state to state, screening tools play a key role in locating and identifying children who may be in need of further evaluation. In addition, developmental checklists—which focus on whether a child can meet general expectations for development in expected age ranges—are a tool that can provide information about whether further assessment is needed.

One way that developmental checklists are used in Child Find is through mass dissemination and placement in public places. The public places might include the local paper, doctor's offices, or places where children and families are likely to be found. Checklists used in this manner might be organized by the age of the child and include such questions as "Can your child _____?" In this context, the overall purpose is to encourage families and professionals to ask questions about a child's health or development that can lead to further screening and/or evaluation.

An example of screening that is widely used in the United States is newborn hearing screening. Screening newborns for hearing is considered an essential part of determining whether children need early intervention services. The benefits of early intervention on children with hearing impairments are dramatic. The clear rationale for these services has resulted in the universal newborn hearing screening movement. In 2007, 27 states and the District of Columbia have mandated early hearing screening programs (National Conference of State Legislators, 2008).

Many considerations need to be taken for screening instruments and developmental checklists to be conducted in a developmentally appropriate manner. For example, screening needs to occur regularly and should happen in a setting where the child is comfortable. Many checklists are filled out based on a family member's or professional's existing knowledge of the child and therefore do not require direct assessment. Table 9.6 provides an overview of common developmental screening and checklists used with young children.

Screening and developmental checklists can play a key role in determining whether children and families need to participate in more formalized assessment procedures.

TABLE 9.6   Common Screening and Checklist Instruments

Name of Instrument	Age Included in Assessment	Intended Usage/Area of Measurement
Brigance® Screens	Infants–preschool age	Overall development
DIAL-3	Preschool aged	Overall development
Early Screening Inventory-Revised	Preschool aged	Overall development
Early Screening Profiles	Toddlers–preschool age	Overall development
FirstSTEP Preschool Screening Tool	Preschool aged	Overall development
Parent's Evaluation of Developmental Status (parent administered)	Infant–preschool age	Overall development
Infant Development Inventory (parent administered)	Infants–toddlers	Overall development
Child Development Review Parent Questionnaire (parent administered)	Toddlers–preschool age	Overall development
Brief Infant-Toddler Social and Emotional Assessment (parent administered)	Infants–toddlers	Social and emotional development
Ages & Stages Questionnaires (parent administered)	Infants–preschool age	Overall development
Ages & Stages Questionnaires: Social and Emotional (parent administered)	Infants–preschool age	Social and emotional development
Pediatric Symptom Checklist (parent administered)	4–16 years of age	Social and emotional development
Newborn Hearing Screening	Newborns	Hearing

Therefore, these procedures serve as gateway instruments, where results—along with other informal assessment strategies—indicate whether further evaluation is needed. Similar to diagnostic assessments, many formalized assessment instruments require specific training and certification for administration and interpretation.

After a screening is conducted, there are several possible outcomes. One outcome is that the screening indicates no need for further evaluation. Another indicates that further evaluation is warranted. A child might score below the cut-off on a screening instrument, or the family and professionals have significant concerns that—despite screening results that fall within the typical range—might warrant further evaluation. The third outcome indicates the need for rescreening, where instrument, assessment, or developmental considerations create the need to reexplore the original screening results. Regardless of the outcome, developmental screening provides information about children's development. This information can be utilized to communicate with families about a child's present level of functioning and what families can anticipate in terms their child's development. In addition, developmental screening can provide a launch pad for discussions of professional or familial concerns.

Postscreening: Diagnostic Assessment

Diagnostic assessments are formal tools used to determine whether a child meets criteria for a developmental delay or disability. Conducting diagnostic assessments requires special training and certifications or degrees, and similar to screening, diagnostic assessments have individual measures of validity and reliability. At this stage in your career, it is not likely that you will implement diagnostic assessments, as they require specialized training. However, you should be familiar with their composition and usage, as they may affect many children and families in your early childhood environment.

Diagnostic assessments are (1) norm referenced, where scores are compared with others taking the test; (2) criterion referenced, where specific knowledge or skills are measured; and (3) performance based, where the child's actions during the assessment affect overall results. Most diagnostic assessment is task based, where children are assessed in terms of their abilities to complete particular tasks. Limitations of **task-based assessment** include that the child might not be willing or able to perform a particular task at a given time, as removing a behavior from the context it occurs in might make the requested tasks meaningless to the child.

task-based assessment
Assessment practices that require a child to perform a particular task at a given point in time.

From Assessment to Intervention

You have learned that one of the primary outcomes of assessment is determining whether children are in need of early intervention services. The benefits of early intervention services are extensive, and research has demonstrated that the earlier intervention occurs, the better the overall results (Pardini, 2002). This information provides a strong and clear rationale for intervening as soon as possible, placing a great importance on assessment and intervention occurring during the first years of life.

For children who require early intervention services, assessment plays a key role in the development of Individual Education Programs (IEPs) and Individualized Family Service Plans (IFSPs). Although there are many similarities between the IFSP and IEP, one of the main differences is the age of children served. The IFSP covers children from birth through age 2, and the IEP covers children and youth between the ages of 3 and 21.

TABLE 9.7 Mandatory Data for the IFSP and IEP	
IFSP	**IEP**
• The infant's or toddler's present levels of physical development, cognitive development, communication development, social or emotional development, and adaptive development, based on objective criteria • The family's resources, priorities, and concerns relating to enhancing the development of the family's infant or toddler • The major outcomes expected for the infant or toddler and the family, and the criteria, procedures, and time lines to be used to measure progress toward achieving the outcomes and whether modifications or revisions of the outcomes or services are necessary • Specific early intervention services necessary to meet the unique needs of the infant or toddler and the family, including the frequency, intensity, and method of delivering services • The environments in which early intervention services shall appropriately be provided, including a justification of the extent, if any, to which the services will not be provided in a natural environment • The projected dates for initiation of services and the anticipated duration of the services • An identification of the service coordinator from the profession most immediately relevant to the needs of the infant or toddler or family (or who is otherwise qualified to perform all applicable functions) who will be responsible for the implementation of the plan and coordination with other agencies and persons • Steps to be taken to support the transition of the toddler with a disability to preschool or other appropriate services	• Present level of educational performance • Goals • Special education and related services • The extent to which child will participate with children with and without disabilities in the school environment • Whether the child will take state and district-wide tests, with or without accommodations, or have an alternative assessment • When services will begin, where and how often they'll be provided, and how long they'll last

The IFSP and IEP use assessment data in a variety of ways. For the IFSP, assessment provides information on the child's present level of functioning in each developmental domain as well as family concerns, strengths, and resources. In the IEP, the focus on the child's present level of functioning is maintained; however, there is minimal focus on the families' strengths and needs. Table 9.7 provides an overview of information required by the federal government for inclusion in the IFSP and IEP.

Data provided through assessment provides the foundation for services: Assessment specifically shapes the kind, frequency, and anticipated goals of intervention strategies. A sample showing a portion of an IEP/IFSP form is included in Figure 9.4.

Assessment practices occur at an individual level, affecting the development of each child and the ability of the professional to support this development. In addition, they occur at the family level, affecting family–professional partnerships and the family's ability to support their child's development. Assessment also occurs at the societal level, such as within and among school districts, affected by the standards that influence expectations for development and learning. Finally, for effective assessment to occur, there must be support at the program level, such as evaluating quality in child care centers, preschools, elementary schools, and other such settings.

FIGURE 9.4 Sample Portion of IEP/IFSP Form

Child's Name:	Date of Birth:	Date:

Chronological Age:	If Premature, Adjusted Age:

Child's Current Developmental Status

Informed clinical opinion to determine eligibility must be based on the integration of all 4 of the following sources of information. (Check all that have been used.)

❏ **Developmental History**   ❏ **Health Status**   ❏ **Observation of Parent & Child**   ❏ **Developmental Evaluation**

❏ Date of *Early On* Multidisciplinary Evaluation_____ Date of MET (if different):_____

❏ See Attached Report incorporating the above 4 sources

Eligibility: Established Condition:	**Developmental Delay:**
Special Education Category:	**Rule #**

Area	Present Level of Development		Method/Tool/Date	Family
	Parent Input	Result of Dev. Evaluation	Person Completing: Name/Title	Priority

Health
❏ See Attached
   Report
		❏ Does health effect participation
		   in Early Intervention Activities		

Hearing ❏ See Attached Report		❏ Language needs considered		
Vision ❏ See Attached Report		❏ Braille needs considered		

Fine Motor
❏ See Attached
   Report
		❏ Assistive Technology
		   considered		

Gross Motor
❏ See Attached
   Report
		❏ Assistive Technology
		   considered		

Cognitive/ Thinking ❏ See Attached Report				

Communication
❏ See Attached
   Report
		❏ English proficiency
		   considered
		❏ Communication needs
		   considered		

**Social/
Emotional**
❏ See Attached
   Report
		❏ Positive behavioral supports
		   considered		

Adaptive ❏ See Attached		❏ Assistive Technology Report considered		

Where will this evaluation take place?
Who should be present?

Child's Name:		Date of Birth:	Date:

IEP Goal

GOAL/OUTCOME STATEMENT – What the parent would like to see happen for this child/family, including:
A – Audience (Person targeted); **B** – Behavior (Procedures to be used); **C** – Criteria; **D** – Duration (Timeline)
Priority: *(Please circle)* 1   2   3   4   5   6   7   8

Progress made on this goal will be reviewed at the "six month review" unless stated otherwise.

Concern of Parent:

Present Status – What is happening now?

Steps/Objectives – To reach this outcome	Method & Criteria of Evaluation	Review Code	Expected Time Frame
Evaluation Schedule: Progress will be evaluated at least every 6 months	1 – New/Revised 2 – Still a need 3 – Partially Accomplished 4 – Accomplished		

Strategies/Methods - for working on this outcome during this child & family's daily routines and activities.	Persons Responsible

If this outcome cannot be met in the natural environment with supplementary supports explain why it cannot not be met there and the timeline for its inclusion into the child's natural environment. See page 8.

Service Code	Parents Initials	Frequency (how often?) Intensity (How long?)	Individual Or Group	Starting Date	Ending Date	Location Code	Payor

Other Services

To the extent appropriate, the IFSP must document services that are not required or covered under Part C. Listing the non-required services does not mean that those services must be provided, however, their identification can be helpful to both the family and the service coordinator to assist in securing those services, including those through public or private sources. These services must correspond to family identified outcomes.

Service	Outcome #	Start Date Mo/Day/Yr	Duration (months)	Provider Information	Funding

Source: From Early On, Michigan Individualized Family Service Plan (IFSP) Individualized Education Plan (IEP). Retrieved April 1, 2009, from http://www.michigan.gov. Adapted with permission.

PROFESSIONAL ASSESSMENT

Assessment is a familiar component in the life of any college student. As a professional, you are likely to experience a variety of different forms of assessment, from those that provide you with access to the profession (such as **teacher licensure and certification exams**) to those that are reflective of a certain level of mastery being attained (such as **credentialing**). These assessments typically are given at one point in time and reflect the attainment of particular knowledge, skills, and dispositions. Ongoing assessment that supports professional growth, however, is an important part of the professional's role.

Chapter 7 introduced you to self-advocacy as a tool for advancing individual professionalism and the field as a whole. Components of self-advocacy include reflection and the development of a professional philosophy. Together, these provide a systematic way to process and reflect on professional growth.

What assessment strategies support professional growth over time? Reflection is seen as central to professional growth (Jones, 1993). Tools such as portfolio writing support a teacher's telling and reflecting on his or her stories of development.

Developing a Portfolio

Child portfolios provide documentation of growth and development over time, usually within a finite period that is determined by the environment's calendar year. For professionals, the time span of a portfolio is much greater, as it includes their individual development over the course of a career. To begin portfolio writing, Jones (1993) recommends addressing broad questions: What do you do? Why do you do it in that particular way? What lessons have you learned from your experience that will be helpful to you in your classroom and potentially to other teachers as well?

Portfolio writing is informed by standards for professional development. In addition to NAEYC and DEC/CEC standards presented in Chapter 7, standards can include expectations in particular programs of study. For example, one teacher who is working toward a CDA would include standards relevant to that credential. Another teacher who is working toward certification for teaching in the public school system would look to professional teaching or content standards as a guide.

At the national level, there are several standard sets that can guide portfolio development. Additionally, international guidelines have been developed by the **Association for Childhood Education International** (ACEI). This organization is focused on the education and development of children from birth to adolescence at the global level. The overall goal includes supporting children's developmental needs in a changing society. Table 9.8 provides a list of national standards and what professional populations are likely to document using these strategies.

How can these standards be effectively used in portfolio development?

teacher licensure and certification exams
Educational tests used to determine if candidate has academic and general knowledge and teaching skills needed to earn a state-issued license or certification.

credentialing
Process that verifies a practitioner's professional qualifications.

Association for Childhood Education International
Organization focused on the education and development of children between birth and adolescence at the international level.

Developmental screening and assessment take into account the input of families and professionals.

TABLE 9.8 National Professional Preparation Standards

Standard Set	Population Set	Use in Portfolio Development
		Documentation of how the professional has met standards focusing on:
Council for Professional Recognition, Child Development Associate (CDA)	Persons pursuing the CDA credential	• Creating a safe learning environment • Creating a healthy learning environment • Creating a quality learning environment • Supporting children's physical, cognitive, social, creative, communication, and self development • Using positive guidance strategies • Supporting productive and positive relationships with families • Developing programs that meet participants' needs • Maintaining a commitment to professionalism
NAEYC Standards for Professional Preparation	Professionals pursuing Associate, Initial Licensure, and Advanced degrees	• Promoting child development and learning • Building family and community relationships • Observing and documenting • Making assessments to support children and families • Teaching and learning • Growing as a professional
Division for Early Childhood, Council for Exceptional Children Early Childhood Special Education/Early Intervention (birth to age 8) Professional Standards	Professionals preparing for initial careers in early childhood special education endorsements and early intervention at the bachelor's and master's degree level	• Foundations • Development and characteristics of learners • Individual learning differences • Instructional strategies • Learning environments/social interaction • Language • Instructional planning • Assessment • Professional and ethical practice • Collaboration
National Professional Teaching Standards (Early Childhood/Generalist subgroup)	Professionals preparing to work with children between the ages of 3 and 8	• Understanding young children • Equity, families, and diversity • Assessment promoting child development and learning • Knowledge of integrated curriculum • Multiple teaching strategies for meaningful learning • Family and community partnerships • Professional partnerships • Reflective practice
Association for Childhood Education International	Professionals preparing to work with children between birth and the age of 8	• General education • Foundations of early childhood education • Child development • Learning and teaching processes • Professional laboratory experiences
Head Start Performance Standards	Professionals working with children in Early Head Start and Head Start settings	• Early childhood development and health • Family and community partnerships • Program design and management

Standards can be used to tell the professional world how you have met guidelines deemed important for effective work with young children. In turn, your accountability as a professional is supported through demonstrating how these guidelines have been met. Accountability can only be attained, however, if portfolios are used effectively.

Developing a professional portfolio is similar to the processes for developing portfolios for children, where documentation and assessment guidelines and expectations inform the contents of the portfolio. The professional portfolio also requires active participation and evaluation of portfolio materials by each individual.

Professional portfolios should also provide experiences in a content-arranged, chronological context. The guiding factor for organization is the purpose of the portfolio. Ones used for a job interview might vary from ones used to demonstrate learning in a college course on early childhood development. However, each will share fundamental components that include the professional's own interpretations of development. Portfolios represent a tool for communicating learning and development over time and supporting self-reflection and professional growth. Another form of assessment you are likely to experience, particularly while you are a student preparing for your professional career, is testing. Testing might include course-based assessments, designed to master knowledge of topic matter, and state and national tests to determine if you have foundational knowledge needed to pursue a career in the field.

State and national requirements for assessment will vary with the program you are studying in and the intended purpose of your course of study (for example, certification). Assessment instruments that are common to early childhood professionals at the Associate, Initial Licensure (bachelor's degree), and Advanced (master's degree) levels include the basic skills test. This test consists of multiple-choice items in reading comprehension, language arts (grammar and writing), and mathematics. Many professionals take the Assessment of Professional Teaching Test for Early Childhood, which consists of assessment of professional and pedagogical knowledge of the field of early childhood education. Others are required to take content-area tests, designed to assess knowledge in particular subject areas.

In addition to increased assessment protocols, many states require ongoing professional development for all professional educators. These guidelines vary based on the area of the field, programs professionals are operating within, and content standards in each area. For example, most states require family child care professionals to participate in ongoing education on a yearly basis to maintain licensure of their program, and Head Start and center-based programs require professionals to participate in a particular number of hours of additional training on a yearly basis. The topics of training can be determined by the program or are based on the professional's assessed needs.

Your own professional development, therefore, can be determined by numerous factors, including the educational pathway you are pursuing, program needs, and your own assessed needs. An important factor for professionals to keep in mind is that they must

---

TEACHING AND LEARNING CONNECTIONS

Professional Portfolio Uses

- As a tool for communicating learning and development over time
- As a tool for self-reflection and professional growth
- As a tool to be used in pursuing employment or continuing your education

take an active role in their ongoing development. In this active role, professionals must determine what their own areas of strength and needs are. They must also establish how to effectively pursue the knowledge, skills, and dispositions necessary to support ongoing development. A professional development plan is an effective tool to guide ongoing development.

The Professional Development Plan

Adopting the framework of the Individual Family Service Plan and the Individualized Education Plan, a **professional development plan** includes information on strengths and needs, contextual factors that can support ongoing development, and timelines and/or strategies for meeting individual plan needs. A well-designed professional development plan includes (Vermont Early Childhood Work Group, 2001):

- Assessment of current interests, knowledge, and skills.
- Identification of specific areas for growth.
- Development of strategies and identification of resources to address areas for growth.
- Documentation of professional growth.

> **professional development plan**
> Systematic plan designed to support ongoing professional development based on individual needs and goals.

The portfolio can be an effective tool that supports documentation of your plan and growth over time. The framework you select can be based on the area of the field you are in, standards for professional development within that framework, and your future professional goals.

Support for ongoing professional development can also be provided through establishing a mentor–mentee relationship.

The Mentoring Relationship as a Tool for Assessment

A mentoring relationship can be conceptualized as a learning relationship, where both the mentor and the mentee gain knowledge over time. Drawing from Vygotsky's sociocultural theory of development, the knowledge gained by the mentee emerges from interactions with a more experienced member of the profession. Benefits for the mentor include supporting another teacher's development and revisiting one's own knowledge, skills, and dispositions.

Assessment for professionals requires the active participation of the mentee in their ongoing development. A successful mentoring relationship is based on mutual respect, trust, and caring. In mentoring relationships, each party shares of themselves, takes risks, and reflects on ongoing learning in the context of the professional relationship (Zachary, 2000). Both parties need to be committed to collaboration and exploration of strengths and weaknesses, and both grow and develop through the evolving relationship.

In this context, mentoring is shifted from an expert–learner relationship—where knowledge is transmitted from one person to another—to one of mutual exploration, goal setting, and ongoing reflection and assessment. In this respect, effective mentoring relationships can reflect the co-construction of relationships advocated for professional relationships with families.

The mentee's responsibilities in this relationship include developing and demonstrating dispositions of openness. This openness can be manifested by welcoming feedback, taking risks, and investing in the process. It is important to have the courage to share one's strengths and areas needing strengthening. Ongoing attention should be devoted to open assessment of the nature of the mentor–mentee relationship and how effectively it is meeting your individual needs. Self-advocacy, therefore, becomes critical, and reflection as a tool of self-advocacy, as presented in Chapter 7, becomes an important skill.

myeducationlab

Go to MyEducationLab and select the topic "Observation and Assessment." Under Building Teaching Skills and Dispositions, complete the exercises *Learning to Use Authentic Assessment* and *Practicing Observing Skills.*

MOVING FORWARD

In this chapter, you have learned about assessment in supporting the continuing developmental needs of children and professionals. Assessment is an ongoing process, and as such, requires attention to changes in needs, growth over time, and contextual factors that affect expectations for learning.

In Chapter 8 you learned about the theory and planning aspects of effective curriculum. Assessment supports access, and before effective teaching and learning can occur, knowledge of the individual child—and the professional—must be developed. Based on developmentally appropriate practices, your interactions with children are informed by knowledge of children's needs in general, each individual child, and the impact of the larger context on children's development and learning. Concurrently, your ability to implement effective practices in the field is affected by your own knowledge, skills, and dispositions, manifested through your individual strengths. Therefore, learning about how to best support children's development and learning is mirrored through your own ongoing assessment of professional effectiveness. To support development of assessment and reflection, each of the remaining chapters of this text will conclude with a Developing Your Portfolio activity.

CASE STUDY

Effective Assessment for Children

The Child Development Lab and Learning Center: Infant-Toddler Classroom (6 weeks to 3 years)

August marks the beginning of the school year, and the teachers look forward to the new children who will be in their classrooms. Home visits are conducted each fall. The goal of these visits is to get to know each child and their family and to begin to establish open lines of communication. The teachers come to these visits with basic information about their classroom and inform families of ongoing assessment practices in the classroom. At the CDLLC this includes daily observation and the administration of the Ages & Stages Questionnaires (ASQ) and the Ages & Stages Questionnaires: Social-Emotional (ASQ:SE) three times a year. During these home visits, families sign consent forms for screening and ongoing evaluations.

During the first 2 weeks of the school year, the teachers conduct the ASQ developmental screening on each of the children in their care. They also asked families to complete the family screening instrument based on their perceptions of their child's development. The data gathered through these screenings provide the professionals with baseline data about children's development. They also indicate whether the child might be experiencing any developmental challenges. Each of the teachers in the two infant-toddler classrooms are invested in early intervention. Should screening instruments indicate a need, they communicate with families about more formal assessment practices. With family consent, children, when needed, are referred to the local Easter Seals program for formal assessments.

In addition to more formal screening practices, the teachers engage in informal assessment in a variety of ways. Children's development is observed daily, and the environment has been developed to support this observation. Hooks are placed throughout the room for clipboards, and sticky notes are placed strategically throughout the room. At the end of the day, the teachers gather their varied notes and place them in the child's folder. Weekly, the teachers use part of planning time to transcribe their notes into the child's record, discussing the implications of what they have observed for classroom practices. Just last week, Marian noticed that Abe is pulling himself up on furniture and beginning to cruise throughout the room. She and her co-teacher make sure he has room to develop this emerging skill, and they develop a plan to place themselves strategically throughout the room to try and cushion his frequent falls.

Each teacher communicates assessment with families in a variety of ways. Daily communication includes brief "Today I did…" sheets that include the child's eating, sleeping, and toileting habits throughout the day and major accomplishments. Eva's daily communication sheet on last Tuesday, for example, included that she had eaten part of her meal with a spoon and asked for more milk by stating "ore!"

Last year the teacher referred three children for more formal assessment. In each case, the children did eventually qualify for early intervention services. The teachers wanted to be a part of the initial IFSP meeting. Their reasoning for attendance included ensuring that the developmental goals and practices adopted in their environment complemented the child's needs. The observations the teacher completed were then shaped by these goals. The objective was providing ongoing information about how effectively the child was meeting developmental goals. Observational data was used to determine what adjustments needed to be made to classroom interactions to ensure that goals were most effectively met.

CONSTRUCTED-RESPONSE QUESTIONS

1. Identify the components of effective assessment, and describe how these are supported in the CDLLC.

2. Explain the process of identifying children who may be in need of early intervention services. In what ways do practices at the CDLLC reflect this process?

3. In what ways does effective assessment reflect family–teacher partnerships? What strategies does the CDLLC utilize to cultivate and support these partnerships?

CASE STUDY

Professional Portfolios and Mentoring

Mulberry School

As the director of the Mulberry School and a teacher in the multiage classroom, Brenda's responsibilities in the program are numerous. As the director, she is responsible for new hires. One of the tools that Brenda relies on to inform her judgment on hiring are the portfolios that job candidates bring to interviews.

Brenda feels that the professional portfolio provides so many advantages over the traditional résumé that candidates used to offer. First, the portfolio showcases the work of the candidate and gives information about how he or she constructs activities and experiences to support children's overall development. Second, the portfolio indicates the candidate's level of professionalism. Time and attention to portfolio development reflects pride in one's work and acknowledgement of the need for professional representation. Finally, Brenda appreciates the opportunities to talk with the candidates about their portfolios. Through these conversations, she is able to get a sense of what the potential employee feels is important and how these knowledge, dispositions, and skills translate into practice.

Brenda is interested in learning about each potential employee's perceived strengths. What do they feel they are good at, and how do they feel these strengths support children's development and learning? Through a focus on strengths, Brenda believes that areas needing strengthening will be more easily addressed.

Once a person is hired, Brenda works to establish a mentoring relationship. She not only observes the novice teacher, but also provides time for them to come and observe her. Along with these observations is discussion—Brenda provides supportive and constructive feedback and encourages the mentees to ask questions of her and her practices. Brenda is both open and honest in her responses. At times this honesty means acknowledging that there might be more effective practices that she could have adopted. Through this openness, Brenda sees this relationship as an opportunity not only for the teacher to grow and develop, but for her to grow and develop as well.

CONSTRUCTED-RESPONSE QUESTIONS

1. Identify the components of effective assessment for professionals. What strategies are used at the Mulberry School to support these goals?

2. What is the role of mentoring in supporting professional development? How does the Mulberry School use mentoring as a tool?

REFLECTING ON AND APPLYING EFFECTIVE PRACTICES (NAEYC AND CEC/DEC)

Ethics

- At the beginning of each school year, you and your co-teacher are responsible for completing assessments on the children in your preschool class. Of the 20 children in your class, 3 are English language learners. As the two of you are going over the assessment results, you notice that the 3 children who are English language learners have scored significantly lower, when compared to the rest of the class, in the areas of language, literacy, and logic. You point out to your co-worker that you are not sure the results are valid, and question whether there were more appropriate assessment tools and practices you could have used with this group. She responds, "Well, this is the assessment tool we are supposed to use, so I don't think there is much we can do except report the results and go from there. I don't really see what we could do differently anyway." What would you do in this situation?

NAEYC Ideals: Ethical Responsibilities to Children
I-1.6. To use assessment instruments and strategies that are appropriate for the children to be assessed, that are used only for the purposes for which they were designed, and that have the potential to benefit children.

I-1.10. To ensure that each child's culture, language, ethnicity, and family structure are recognized and valued in the program.

DEC: Professional and Interpersonal Behavior
5. We shall use individually appropriate assessment strategies including multiple sources of information such as observations, interviews with significant caregivers, formal and informal assessments to determine children's learning styles, strengths, and challenges.

DEC: Evidence-Based Practice
2. We shall use every resource, including referral when appropriate, to ensure high quality services are accessible and are provided to children and families.

• •

- Family involvement in authentic assessment is paramount for children's development and learning to be supported. In what ways can families contribute to the assessment process? How does this involvement support goals for familial involvement in children's education?

Standards for Professional Practice

NAEYC: Observing, Documenting, and Assessing to Support Young Children and Families
3a. Understanding the goals, benefits, and uses of assessment.
3b. Knowing about and using observation, documentation, and other appropriate assessment tools and approaches.
3c. Understanding and practicing responsible assessment.

DEC: Foundations
EC1K2: Trends and issues in early childhood education, early childhood special education, and early intervention.

3. Based on your readings in this chapter, develop an assessment plan for an early childhood program. Include in your plan:
   - Safeguards you will use to ensure appropriate assessment.
   - Strategies for involving families.
   - An overview of assessment tools and strategies you will use.
   - How your assessment plan will assess each area of children's development.
   - Your reporting plans for assessment data.

NAEYC: Observing, Documenting, and Assessing to Support Young Children and Families
3a. Understanding the goals, benefits, and uses of assessment.
3b. Knowing about and using observation, documentation, and other appropriate assessment tools and approaches.
3c. Understanding and practicing responsible assessment.

DEC: Assessment
EK8S4: Select and administer assessment instruments in compliance with established criteria.

EK8S5: Use informal and formal assessment to make decisions about infants and young children's development and learning.

EK8S9: Emphasize child's strengths and needs in assessment reports.

DEVELOPING YOUR PHILOSOPHY

In what ways do you feel observation and assessment informs practices in early childhood education? How can you work to ensure that observation and assessment does in fact inform your classroom practices?

DEVELOPING YOUR PORTFOLIO

Develop a list of strengths and weaknesses of each of the observational strategies presented on pages 250–252 in your text. Based on this list, create a summary table of situations in which each strategy can be employed and advantages and disadvantages of each method. Next, review the screening instruments profiled on page 259 in your text. Select three of these instruments, and identify why you feel these would support knowledge of children's development.

CHAPTER REVIEW

- **How do standards inform curriculum and assessment?**

  Standards represent expectations for learning, and if appropriately designed, answer the question "What should children be learning?" Standards can provide a guide for selecting and developing appropriate curriculum. In turn, standards can inform assessment by providing guidelines about what young children should be learning. Standards, curriculum, and assessment, therefore, do not exist in isolation, but should be complementary processes in early childhood classrooms.

- **How do effective assessment practices support equity, accountability, and success?**

  Effective assessment practices support equity, accountability, and success in a variety of ways. First, assessment practices that are based on expectations for children's learning and development ensure that children are acquiring the knowledge, skills, and dispositions needed for success. Through this process, accountability to the larger context can be supported. Specific accountability factors that affect equity and success include identifying children who may require additional intervention and helping programs improve their educational and developmental interventions.

- **What are challenges to effective assessment, and how are these addressed?**

  Challenges of effective assessment included the use of standardized and high-stakes testing that fail to account for children's developmental needs. Further, there are many concerns in the field that assessment practices are not always culturally and linguistically sensitive. Another common criticism of tests is that they are biased and fail to reflect the needs of the populations being assessed. Play-based assessment, strength-based assessment, and culturally and linguistically sensitive assessment practices take these challenges into account and work to develop assessment strategies reflective of children's strengths and capabilities.

• **In what ways do observation and other common assessment strategies contribute to knowledge of children's development and learning?**

Observation and other common assessment strategies can be effective tools in supporting children's development and learning if they meet certain criteria. First, they must be objective, focusing on a factual representation of what is observed. Second, data need to be collected over time, providing a holistic view of development and learning that captures the progression of development. When these criteria are met, teachers have knowledge of children over time, and if collected in a variety of situations, across different environments. The breadth of data collected, in turn, can serve as an important planning tool. Observation, as a tool of documentation, is one of the most common assessment strategies. Other common assessment strategies include portfolios and the Work Sampling System.

• **What roles do screening and formal evaluation play in answering questions about a child's development?**

Screening and formal evaluation are designed to address specific questions about young children's development. Developmental screening can be used to measure developmental progress, and is used to identify children who are at-risk for health or developmental problems. If a screening indicates the need for further evaluation, a diagnostic assessment is used to determine if a child meets the criteria for a developmental delay or disability.

• **How do self-advocacy and reflection support professional assessment?**

Professional assessment provides opportunities for self-advocacy and reflection. Regarding self-advocacy, professionals are able to document their growth and development over time and clearly communicate their professional goals. This serves as an advocacy tool, clearly communicating to the larger context efforts toward a documentation of professionalism. Further, professionals who utilize ongoing assessment can use this as a tool for reflection, looking back over their changing developmental needs and strengths over time.

10

Supporting Social-Emotional Development Through Guidance

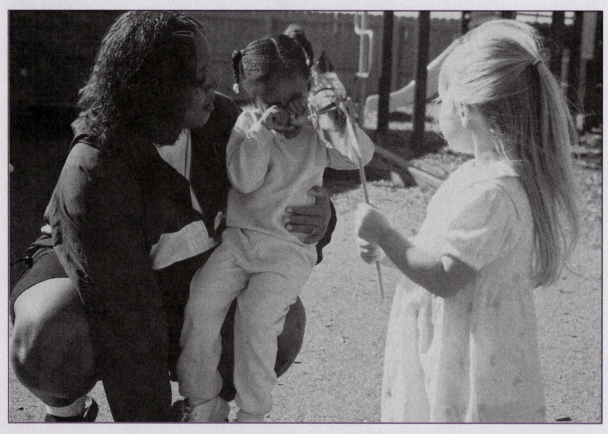

"If we wish to create a lasting peace we must begin with the children."

—MAHATMA GANDHI

Georgia feels a flash of anxiety as she enters her classroom of 4- and 5-year-olds. It is her third week in the classroom, and she feels that many issues have become particularly challenging. When she settles the class in for morning meeting, she has to remind the children three times to keep their hands to themselves, and two of the children wander off to the sand and water table. When the children are preparing to go outside, three of the children need to be separated, and one of them has a hard time settling down after crying for an extended time. Lunch involves a mini-food fight, and two children are sent to the director's office. At rest time, none of the children are able to settle in and stay on their cots for long. By the end of the day, Georgia is wondering if she has picked the wrong profession.

GUIDING QUESTIONS

- What is social and emotional development, and how do these areas of development interrelate?
- How do the theories of Maslow, attachment theorists, and Erikson provide a rationale for supporting social-emotional development?
- What role does guidance play in supporting children's development and learning?
- What is the relationship between developmentally appropriate practice and positive guidance?
- How do practices at the primary, secondary, and tertiary level support children's social-emotional development?
- What role do families play in the guidance process, and how can effective partnerships with families be developed?

Abril is one of the children in Georgia's classroom, and the days are as taxing for her as they are for Georgia. Abril moves from one challenging encounter to another—first, she and one of her classmates have a disagreement about who gets to use the funnel at the sand and water table. Then, another child takes her favorite seat at snack time, reducing Abril to tears. At outdoor playtime, several of her attempts at playing with other children are rebuffed, and Abril sits in the corner of the play garden, kicking at gravel with her foot.

Down the hall, Dameeka's experience with her class of 4- and 5-year-olds is very different. The children know the routine so well they rarely need reminders and seem to enjoy their relationships with Dameeka and with one another. Transitions between activities run smoothly, and the arguments that do emerge are often settled without Dameeka needing to intercede. Dameeka looks forward to lunch, as it always provides her with an opportunity to talk to the children about what is happening in their lives. During nap, she transfers her observation notes to each child's portfolio. Although not all the children nap, those who don't seem to appreciate the opportunity to curl up with a book or listen to the soft music playing. When Dameeka leaves her classroom at the end of the day, she is confident that she has chosen the right profession.

Stacie, a child in Dameeka's classroom, experiences challenges similar to Abril's. She often begins her day with a disagreement with other children and is often told "no" when she asks children if she can play. To cope with these challenges, Stacie often yells and occasionally chooses to solve problems with her hands firmly grasping a shock of another child's hair. Dameeka and her co-teacher work extensively with Stacie on her developing social skills, often coaching and intervening as necessary.

● ● ●

The teaching experiences of Georgia and Dameeka are not unique to them. Many in the field experience great challenges when dealing with children's behavior on a day-to-day basis, and many have great success. Both children in the vignette, Abril and Stacie, require individual attention, and each professional must work to make sure that the children experience success with their peers. Dameeka has spent extensive time ensuring that children in her classroom feel a sense of community, leaving her with more time to manage the challenges that individual children present. Georgia is often putting out fires in her classroom, making her less likely to be able to tend to children's individual needs.

The challenges Georgia and Dameeka experience in their classrooms affect their conceptions of their daily work and their ability to work effectively in the classroom. These classroom challenges can affect the children's self-concept, learning, and interactions with other children. Though it might be easier to focus on the challenges occurring in Georgia's class, it is important to pay attention to the extensive work and effort that has gone into Dameeka's smoothly run classroom.

INTRODUCTION TO SOCIAL-EMOTIONAL DEVELOPMENT

The successes and challenges in each environment largely relate to the teacher's ability to support each child's social-emotional development, which represent two separate, though complexly intertwined, areas of development and learning. **Emotional development** refers to the ability to identify and understand emotions within oneself and to respond appropriately to the emotions of others. **Social development** influences one's interactions with others and how effectively one navigates interactions and relationships. How one feels about oneself emotionally affects social interactions; conversely, the success of social interactions can affect how one feels about oneself.

Developing social-emotional skills is one of the central tasks of early childhood and has been identified as a central focus of early childhood programs (NAEYC, 1998; Olson & Hyson, 2003; Head Start Policy Book, 2003). An overarching goal is for children to be able to successfully navigate their own internal feelings in the context of relationships.

Failing to tend to children's social-emotional needs has serious consequences. Behavior problems appearing early in a child's preschool career are the single best predictor of delinquency in adolescence, gang membership, and adult incarceration (Dishion, French, & Patterson, 1995). Supporting children's positive social-emotional development benefits children and larger society in terms of dollars saved toward costly interventions and incarcerations down the road (Lipsey & Derzon, 1998).

Tending to children's social-emotional development supports positive outcomes for children. However, the increasing focus on academic curriculum, espoused by such government policies as the No Child Left Behind Act, has targeted the scholastic achievement of American children, placing less emphasis on the importance of social-emotional development. Interestingly, the reforms supported through NCLB—most notably, high-stakes testing—have had little long-term impact on children's achievement (Darling-Hammond, 2005). The reason such reforms have had limited impact centers on the failure to recognize that social-emotional skills are as important to children's success as cognitive ones (Comer, 2005; Ray, Bowman, & Brownell, 2006). **Social-emotional adjustment**, or the child's ability to socially and emotionally adapt to new situations, predicts children's early school success (Raver, 2000). Therefore, social-emotional development is an important tool of social equity.

How can children's social-emotional development be cultivated in early childhood programs? In this chapter, you will learn about guidance and how to use effective guidance strategies that support and nurture each child in vibrant classroom communities. Before discussing guidance specifically, you need to understand factors that shape and influence children's behavior. These include both developmental factors and environmental factors, or contextual factors.

---

emotional development

The ability to identify and understand emotions within oneself and to respond appropriately to the emotions of others.

social development

How effectively the child navigates interactions and relationships.

social-emotional adjustment

The child's ability to socially and emotionally adapt to new situations.

Overview of Social-Emotional Development

In Chapter 4 you were introduced to theories that have shaped present-day understanding of social-emotional development. The most relevant of these theories include Maslow's hierarchy of needs theory (Maslow, 1998), attachment theory (Bowlby, 1972), and Erikson's theory of psychosocial development (Erikson, 1950). Table 10.1 summarizes the contributions of each of these theories to understanding social-emotional development.

This theoretical foundation shapes several skills, or behaviors, that reflect underlying capabilities. According to the National Scientific Council on the Developing Child (2005), these key skills include the ability to:

- Understand and recognize one's own feelings (**self-awareness**).
- Accurately read and comprehend emotional states in others.
- Manage strong emotions and how they are expressed in a constructive manner (**self-regulation**).
- Develop **empathy**, or shared understanding of emotions, for others.
- Establish and maintain relationships (**social skills**).

These skills do not develop in isolation. Rather, because of the complex interaction between emotional and social development, these skills are influenced and affected by external relationships. The context of social-emotional development, therefore, is important to understanding children's behavior.

self-awareness
Understanding and recognizing one's own feelings.

self-regulation
The ability to manage strong emotions and express them in a constructive manner.

empathy
The capacity to share and understand the emotions of others.

social skills
Skills needed to establish and maintain relationships.

TABLE 10.1   Theories Supporting Knowledge of Social-Emotional Development

Theory	Brief Overview	Aspects Relevant to Social-Emotional Development
Maslow's hierarchy of needs theory	Pyramid model that presents a hierarchy of human needs; physiological needs represent the base, whereas self-actualization represents the pinnacle.	Children need environments in which they feel safe and secure. Children need secure relationships, supporting love and belonging. Children need to feel valued and competent, supporting self-esteem and self-competence.
Attachment theory	The quality of relationships children have in their first years of life affects their lifelong quality of relationships (Bowlby, 1972).	Children need to develop trusting, nurturing relationships with primary caregivers.
Erikson's psychosocial theory	How children pass through stages of psychosocial development is affected by the successful attainment of development tasks.	Children learn trust through quality interactions and consistent responses to their attempts at communication. Children learn autonomy (independence) through completing tasks on their own. Children learn initiative through free exploration and taking risks. Children develop a sense of competence and worth (industriousness) through successfully interacting with the environment.

The Context of Social-Emotional Development

Children's behaviors are best understood in the context of their families and the larger social world in which the children live (Bowman & Brownell, 2007). To demonstrate the interaction between child behavior and context, consider the following quote by Barbara Bowman (Bowman & Brownell, 2007), professor and co-founder of Erikson Institute, a leading graduate school in child development:

> Some families, under economic or personal stress, may be too disorganized to provide stability and consistency in the home, and, as a result, their children may not learn to regulate their emotional reactions in various situations. Some children from minority cultures, more attentive to physical cues than verbal ones, may exhibit challenging behaviors in mainstream situations that are highly dependent on language. Any factor—biological, family, or linguistic—when viewed against another set of circumstances—for example, different social contexts—can evoke different responses from children. It is the interaction of individual and societal factors that determine the ability of children to meet societal standards for behavior. (p. 3)

Successful social-emotional development is shaped by the child's developmental context and biological factors that may place an individual child at risk for developing social-emotional challenges. The following list provides a summary of environmental and biological risk factors that can affect children's behavior (Michigan Public Policy Initiative, 2002).

Environmental and Social Risk Factors
- Family and Community
  - Parental physical illness
  - Homelessness
  - Poverty
  - Family separation or divorce
  - Domestic violence
  - Parent mental illness
  - Community violence
  - TV violence

- Parenting
  - Diet and nutrition in the home
  - Quality of parent–child relationship
  - Demanding parental schedules and increased stress
  - Teen parenting
  - Kinship or foster care
  - Child abuse and neglect

- Child Care
  - Group size
  - Training for caregivers
  - Caregiver–child relationships
  - Consistency in caregiving
  - Lack of appropriate guidance strategies
  - Peer victimization

Biological and Congenital Risk Factors
- Physical
  - Fetal alcohol syndrome
  - Drug exposure
  - Low birth weight
  - Allergies
  - Chronic illness or hospitalization
  - Sleep disorders
  - Lead poisoning

- Child Mental Health
  - Sensory integration difficulties
  - Emotional regulation
  - Attention deficit hyperactivity disorder
- Oppositional defiant disorder
- Autism

- Developmental
  - Developmental delays
  - Language or hearing impairments
  - Traumatic brain injury

Professionals must understand children's behavior in the larger context of their families and community. They will serve children and families better not only by understanding the stress factors in their lives that can affect children's behaviors, but also by developing strategies that respond to their unique needs. In addition, attention to both child and family can support the development of effective partnerships with families. These partnerships play a key role in prevention, identification, and intervention (Division for Exceptional Children, 2006).

Understanding both developmental and environmental influences on children's behavior provides the foundational knowledge needed to provide nurturing environments that communicate a sense of safety, security, and belonging to the young child. This knowledge is also central to developing classroom communities where every child feels welcomed and respected for who they are and for their individual contributions, where their feelings of personal self-worth are viewed as a central classroom goal, and where children's internal feelings of competence and worth translate into rewarding interactions with others filled with compromise, negotiation, and mutual appreciation. This knowledge alone, however, is not enough to create an emotionally vibrant, socially nurturing classroom community. Early childhood professionals must also have a variety of skills, represented through supportive teaching practices that can be tailored to the needs of individual children. These supportive teaching strategies are referred to as guidance.

GUIDANCE

Children learn from everyday interactions. Infants learn trust from your responses to their cries of distress and your exclamations at their interactions with the environment. Toddlers learn acceptance from how you deal with their pursuit of bodily explorations, which might include biting, hitting, or pulling hair. Preschoolers might learn these same lessons of acceptance from how you respond to their angry kicking down of another child's block structure: Do you address the behavior without belittling the child, or do you treat the child as a problem and cast him or her away from the rest of the group? Similarly, a second grader labeled as a bully learns about acceptance from your reactions to "bullying" behavior. Is the child deemed a "bully" and treated with contempt by you and other members of the class? Or do you model acceptance and nurturance by trying to figure out the child's social needs and working to integrate her into the group?

The term **guidance** is used in the field to refer to specific strategies teachers can use to support children's positive conceptions of self and successful interactions with others. Guidance is distinctly different from punishment. For example, **punishment** is

guidance
Series of practices that support children's social-emotional development.

punishment
Intervention strategy focused on extinguishing behaviors perceived as challenging.

TABLE 10.2 Guidance Versus Punishment	
Guidance	**Punishment**
Strategies supportive of children's positive sense of self and positive interactions with others	Extinguishing of behaviors
Focus on developmental needs of individual children	Focus on external rules
Supports long-term self-regulation	Focuses on a quick fix for challenging behaviors
Focus on prevention	Focus on intervention

often focused on extinguishing behaviors, with little attention to their root cause. Guidance, however, respects children's individual developmental needs and embraces and responds to these needs while supporting positive ways of interacting with the others. Punishment is often a quick fix, but because little attention is paid to the child's needs that are causing behaviors, it does little in supporting long-term social-emotional developmental goals (New & Cochran, 2007). See Table 10.2 for a comparison of guidance and punishment.

Guidance is most often used as a preventive strategy that works to bypass challenging behaviors. Conversely, punishment is an intervention strategy. To exemplify the difference between the two, consider two kindergarten teachers. In Nathan's classroom, the children are busily pursuing varied tasks. Some are listening to a story in the book corner, and others are examining rocks that had just been collected from outside. Another small group is building with blocks, and two children are sharing one side of an art easel.

Nathan is walking slowly around the room with a clipboard in his hand. On this clipboard, he is jotting down a variety of notes to be added to the children's portfolio. In addition, he is commenting on the various tasks the children are engaged in, adding a bit of information here, a suggestion or exclamation there.

In Casey's classroom, the first thing that is noticeable is the noise. Children are speaking in loud voices, and the occasional argument breaks out over the din. Although children are also gathered in different areas of the classroom, the groups that are formed seem to be in constant rotation between working cooperatively and arguing about some perceived injustice. Casey is spending her time moving from group to group to put out various fires as they emerge. These fires are extinguished with a variety of tactics, including coercion (either you do this or . . .), threats of punishment (losing outside time), and the placement of children in time-out. Nathan spends his time focusing on observing and supporting children's development, whereas Casey is spending her time trying to overcome challenges in the classroom.

Implementing effective guidance practices requires recognition that children's interactions with the environment represent behaviors and that some behaviors children exhibit can be challenging. For example, children might be *experimenting* with behavior in pursuit of a specific outcome. Consider Lenny, a 4-year-old who has been waiting patiently for his turn on a trike during an outdoor playtime. After several minutes of waiting, he decides to take things into his own hands by pushing a nearby child off of her trike. In this case, the behavior of focus is Lenny pushing a child off the trike. However, what leads up to this event and what happens after provides the professional with important information. The behaviors leading up to the event might indicate the need for more trikes in the outdoor environment, a way to manage shorter wait times, or the need for additional engaging activities for children to participate in. What happens after the event provides important knowledge as well: Does Lenny successfully obtain the trike, with no intervention? If so, he may learn that pushing the child off the trike is an effective behavior and repeat it in the future. If Lenny, the teacher, and the child who was pushed off the trike engage in discussion that supports increased empathy for the child who was pushed and problem-solving skills during times of frustration, Lenny may be less likely to repeat that behavior in the future.

How do young children learn behavior? One prevalent viewpoint is that behavior is learned through *modeling* (Gartrell, 2006). Modeling occurs when children see others engage in behaviors that provide an outcome they see as positive, and in turn, engage in the same behaviors in the hopes of obtaining similar outcomes. For some children, attention—either positive or negative—can be a desired outcome. A 3-year-old who lets out a string of profanities during self-serve snack time might be modeling language she hears at home. The resulting exclamations of the teacher can serve to satisfy the child's need for attention. The context of behavior, therefore, is important in understanding modeling. This importance is twofold: First, knowledge of the context in which behavior occurs can contribute to understanding. Second, professionals must be careful not to send negative messages about behaviors children are choosing to model. For example, it might be perfectly acceptable in the child's home environment to use profanity. Therefore, professionals must teach children appropriate behaviors in their classroom environment.

Young children's challenging behavior might emerge from *strong needs* (Gartrell, 2006). For example, a child whose basic needs for safety, security, social needs, and self-esteem are not met may interact with the environment in a way that is reflective of those strong needs (Maslow, 1998). This might include such things as a 5-year-old who solves problems with his fists, a 6-year-old who throws herself on the ground in protest of requests, or a third grader who spends lunchtime demanding food and money from other children.

In each of these cases the professional must recognize that common interventions focusing on punishment are ineffective, particularly in the larger goal of supporting social-emotional development. Placing Lenny in time-out is a reaction to his behavior of pushing a child off the trike, but does little to teach him how to deal with his frustrations or to address wait time. Telling a child who uses profanity in the classroom that those words are "bad" or "inappropriate" might give negative messages about the persons

myeducationlab

Go to MyEducationLab and select the topic "Guidance." Under Activities and Applications, watch the video *Peaceful Conflict Resolution* and reflect on the role of the teacher in supporting children's conflict resolution skills.

TEACHING AND LEARNING CONNECTIONS

Sources of Mistaken Behavior

- **Experimenting:** "How will this behavior support my achieving a desired outcome?"
- **Modeling:** "I saw her do it and get what she wanted."
- **Strong Needs:** "I have nothing and no one."

he learned those behaviors from. It also does little to provide examples of what is considered appropriate language. Punishing children by removing them from the group, taking away privileges or toys, or placing checkmarks on a board next to their name does not teach a child appropriate ways to deal with their problems and may serve to humiliate them as well.

Motivation and Self-Regulation

**extrinsic
motivation**

Factors outside the child that serve to motivate behavior.

**intrinsic
motivation**

Internal motivation to act in a particular way.

As these are common punishment practices in the field, it is important to address the effects of behavioral charts and time-out separately. As you have learned, behavioral charts emerged from behaviorism, with a focus on controlling children's behavior through external means. This focus on **extrinsic (external) motivation** creates a situation where behavior is based on feedback from the environment, as opposed to supporting children's **intrinsic motivation**, or their desire to act in a particular way that comes from within. A child who is intrinsically motivated uses his or her own internal compass of right and wrong as a guide for behavior. As one of the goals of guidance is to support children's regulation of their own behavior, developing this internal compass is of primary importance. Therefore, practices such as behavioral charts (also called sticker charts or reward systems) are largely considered inappropriate.

Motivation, however, is a complex issue: Most of us are motivated by both internal and external factors. For example, an individual's salary (an external motivator) may influence choice in occupation, as may passion for the occupation (an internal motivator). In the case where one earns a low salary for something one enjoys and feels passionately about, the internal motivator may outweigh the external motivator. The opposite is true as well: One could elect to stay in a job one loathes because of the high salary. For children, external motivators have been found to increase motivation and interest in tasks that are initially of low interest (Cameron, Pierce, Banko, & Gear, 2005). The external motivator, in this case, can serve to create a feedback loop, where the external motivator serves to facilitate initial interest, which, over time, can serve as a channel for internal motivation (Jalongo, 2007). Consider, for example, a child who is engaged in toilet learning. Taking time away from an activity to sit on a toilet may not, initially, seem particularly motivating. When coupled with an external motivator, such as the promise of "big girl" pants, however, initial interest might be engaged. This kind of private,

---

TEACHING AND LEARNING CONNECTIONS

Supporting Intrinsic Motivation

- Support persistence through providing challenging tasks with appropriate levels of support.
- Encourage children to complete tasks on their own.
- Provide activities that capitalize on children's interests.
- Allow children extensive choices in the environment.
- Give children opportunities to evaluate their efforts.
- Avoid praise and rewards.

individual use of an external motivator is much different from the public, potentially shaming use of a behavioral chart.

Time-out represents another common application of punishment in the field. In a time-out, children are removed from the situation for a period of time. Often, this time period is determined by the child's age, with a 2-year-old being placed in time-out for 2 minutes, a 3-year-old for 3 minutes, and so on. Several assumptions are often made in the implementation of time-out, including that children will reflect on their behaviors and be less likely to engage in these behaviors in the future. This assumption ignores that children learn from direct interaction with the environment. If the goal is to guide children's behavior in a way that is both respectful and responsive, a more appropriate practice is called **time-in**. During time-in, the teacher spends focused time with a child. For a child who is engaging in inappropriate behavior, such as pulling another child's hair to get a book from her, this might mean teaching appropriate problem-solving strategies. For a child who is emotionally very upset or angry, this might include rubbing his back and helping him calm down, with the goal of emotional self-regulation. Note, however, the child's preferences for physical contact must be respected.

The two instances in which time-out is advocated as a positive guidance practice are when a child is a danger to him- or herself or to others. In these cases, removing the child from the situation can reduce the potential for harm. This form of time-out should be accompanied by time-in, where the teacher spends time with the child to calm him or her down and support self-regulation skills.

Promoting intrinsic motivation supports children feeling pride in their own accomplishments.

time-in
Guidance strategy used as a replacement for, or in conjunction with, time-out. The focus of time-in is to help children regulate their own emotions.

Understanding Your Reaction to Guidance Challenges

One of the challenges associated with appropriate guidance practices is recognizing that you might have a negative reaction to children's behavior. For example, it is challenging not to view in a negative light the behavior of a child who dumps out her milk while looking at you or of one who spits at you while you are talking to him. You must, however, keep in mind the context of behavior and recognize that the behaviors children engage in are an opportunity to teach. Challenging behavior, therefore, can be seen through the lens of "Okay, I see what we need to work on next."

In addition, much of children's challenging behavior can be viewed as developmentally appropriate. It could be difficult to view a 2-year-old who is thrashing on the floor, flailing his hands and feet on the ground, and screaming at the top of his lungs as a child who is pursuing an important developmental task (such as autonomy). However, viewing the behavior in this light can support your respectful and responsive interpretation and reaction to this event.

Your own values play a key role in guidance, as these can dictate what behaviors you expect from children. Your culture, for example, might lead you to expect that children look you in the eye when you are talking to them. For some children, their cultural context might indicate that looking an adult in the eye is a sign of defiance. In this case, your values and expectations might directly conflict with a child's and become a source

FIGURE 10.1
Impact of Culture on
Expectations for
Children's Behavior

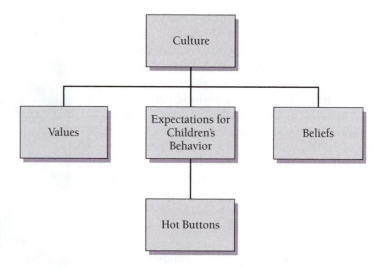

FIGURE 10.1
Impact of Culture on
Expectations for
Children's Behavior

of a cultural clash. It is also important to keep in mind that the field of early childhood has its own culture. Many practices common in the field are not shaped by evidence-based practice, but rather laden with values and beliefs regarding how to effectively support children's development and learning. Many of these values and beliefs were shaped by theorists and researchers who made significant contributions to the field, which were processed through their own cultural lens. The field's increasing focus on evidence-based practice serves to address cultural biases that may exist regarding effective practices supporting children's development and learning. Figure 10.1 shows how culture affects the expectations for children's behavior.

How can you get in touch with your values regarding children's behavior? An effective strategy is to look for "hot buttons," or behaviors that cause you to feel an emotional reaction. For example, you might feel a flash of anger when a child throws a toy at another child but not feel this same anger when a child verbally admonishes another. Your hot buttons are key to understanding your own values. Careful reflection on these values can lend insight into understanding your own expectations for behavior and how these might positively or negatively affect the learning environment.

As a professional, you must also realize that some children may match your preferences and expectations for behavior more closely than others. Certainly, as adults there are some adults whom we "click" with and others whom we don't. This behavioral match can translate into your feeling more in tune or positive toward certain members of your class. Although these responses are normal, children in the classroom must never pick up on differences reflective of personality preferences.

TEACHING AND LEARNING CONNECTIONS

Learning About Your Own Hot Buttons

- Pay careful attention to behaviors that are frustrating to you.
- Explore why the child might be displaying particular behavior.
- Reflect on how these behaviors might challenge your own beliefs and values.
- Explore how these beliefs and values might affect the learning environment.

Developmentally Appropriate Practice and Effective Guidance

The foundations of effective guidance mirror the foundations of developmentally appropriate practice. First, *you must learn about each child in the classroom*. This includes observation that illuminates each child's strengths and areas of challenge and how each child interacts with his or her environment. Second, *you must have knowledge of the child's family* and their expectations for their child's behavior and how they support these behaviors. Informal assessment through daily interactions with families is a useful way to achieve this goal. Finally, *you must have knowledge of the context of learning*. This includes knowledge of your own expectations for children's social-emotional learning and expectations reflected through the larger environment. This can include standards for children's learning and/or precursors to school readiness.

Beyond knowledge of DAP and its role in effective guidance, a three-tiered approach to supporting positive behavior in the classroom is recommended (DEC, 2006). The first tier focuses on *universal practices*, which are applied to each child in the classroom. These practices play a key role in prevention. The second tier of intervention focuses on the *targeted instruction of social-emotional skills and effective communication skills*. Teachers use strategies at this level with children who are at risk for developing challenging behaviors. The third tier of intervention provides an effective approach for teachers to *address concerns about children who are persistent in their use of challenging behaviors*. At this level, individualized interventions are provided, which are based on the child's unique behaviors, family situations, and desired outcomes. All children benefit from universal practices, 5% to 15% of children require secondary interventions, and 1% to 10% need tertiary intervention (Catlett, Winton, & Hemmeter, 2004). Figure 10.2 illustrates this three-tiered approach to behavior in the classroom.

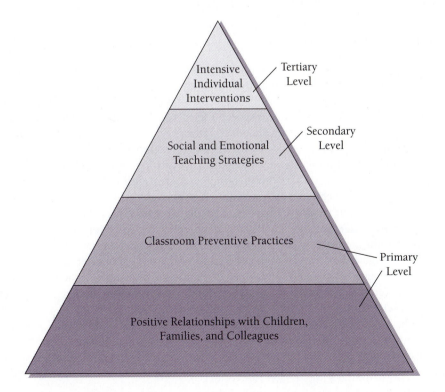

FIGURE 10.2
The Teaching Pyramid

Source: From "The Teaching Pyramid: A Model for Supporting Social Emotional Competence and Preventing Challenging Behavior in Young Children," by L. Fox, G. Dunlap, M. L. Hemmeter, G. Joseph, and P. Strain, 2003, *Young Exceptional Children, 58,* pp. 48–52. Reprinted with permission.

UNIVERSAL PRACTICES SUPPORTING SOCIAL-EMOTIONAL DEVELOPMENT

How can guidance practices be supported in the early childhood environment? A focus on prevention requires universal practices. These practices begin with the following (Honig, 2000):

1. *Be clear about what behaviors are acceptable and unacceptable.* In the context of this expectation, you must focus on *what you expect a child to do*, as opposed to what you don't want them to do. Clear statements of expectations, such as "use your words," "keep your feet on the floor," and "walk, please," provide children with specific information about what type of behavior is expected. Further, *rules should be stated simply*, and professionals need to be *consistent* in enforcing rules on a day-to-day basis. Clear guidelines for acceptable behavior are most effective when used in conjunction with modeling and appropriate support for the desired behavior .
2. *Express pride, interest, and pleasure.* Be sure that children know you are interested in them and take note not only of their challenges, but also of their day-to-day accomplishments and general ways of interacting with their world. Remember that this focus should support intrinsic motivation and avoid competition. A good rule of thumb is to avoid focusing on what *they have* or *what they are wearing*.
3. *Be positive. Focus on the wonder and unique journey of each child* and provide support that is nurturing and positive as they navigate their world.

In addition to these foundational practices, there are specific guidance techniques that support effective prevention of challenging behaviors. These include behavioral and affective reflections, mirroring, choices, encouragement, effective classroom rules, and sensory-responsive environments.

Behavioral Reflections

Nina is a preschooler in your classroom who has displayed a variety of challenging behaviors in recent weeks. During your brief morning meetings, she often refuses to participate, hanging at the edge of the group and distracting other children with frequent bids for their attention. During center time, you have observed her wandering aimlessly through the room. When she does choose to interact with her peers, it is often through physical means. She often takes away other children's materials in order to enter a group or deals with a lack of duplicate toys by taking the toy of another child. Your anecdotal observations have revealed that Nina is receiving a great deal of negative attention for these behaviors. Other children are protesting her interactions, and you have found that both yourself and your co-teacher have been giving Nina negative feedback.

behavioral reflections

Simple statements identifying a child's behavior.

Behavioral reflections are simple statements reflecting what you see a child doing. These reflections are made without judgment and are objective in that they only report facts. When Nina enters the classroom and chooses the sand and water table, for example, an appropriate behavioral reflection is "I see you are playing with the sand." When Nina moves on to the book corner and is reading a book on ants, another example of a behavioral reflection is "You are reading a book on ants."

The beauty of behavioral reflections is that they are completely nonjudgmental in their nature and therefore do not provide a source of extrinsic motivation. Rather, these are objective statements that tell a child that you notice them, regardless of the activity they are engaged in. This nonjudgmental feedback, in turn, can give children a sense of

Mirroring

A key to the development of emotional self-regulation is the ability to identify emotions. Recognizing feelings creates a bridge between feeling and thought. Consider Isabel, a 4-year-old who has been diagnosed as having an autistic spectrum disorder. Isabel often has strong emotional responses to factors in her environment: She becomes very upset during disagreements with her peers and will often scream, yell, and cry in response to arguments. She often turns to the teacher for support, stating, "She won't let me play" or "They don't like me."

Often, these reactions are not related to classroom occurrences. For example, once a child selected a toy that Isabel intended to play with. Isabel's response in this situation was a loud cry of "She won't play with me." Isabel's feelings are guiding her interpretation of the situation—should her teacher try to rub her back to calm her down, she might be missing a cue of what Isabel needs. In this case, emotions and her thoughts about emotions lack continuity—a first step, therefore, would be to help her experience and label these emotions and then apply thought to processing this situation.

In Isabel's case, employing **mirroring** strategies is more appropriate than using an affective reflection. With affective reflections, labels are provided to emotions. With mirroring, the teacher matches the emotional level and language of the child. Therefore, as opposed to saying "You seem angry," mirroring would include "She won't play with you?" proclaimed with the same level of intensity. This could be followed with "She won't play with you?" and varied repetitions until Isabel herself can bring her emotions under control.

The advantages of mirroring include that children are allowed to work through their emotions, feeling all the moment has to offer and then applying their own developing emotional regulation skills to the situation. As opposed to helping children manage their emotions by diffusing them, mirroring allows children to fully experience their emotions and then be supported in linking cognition to that emotion ("She took the toy so you felt she did not want to play with you."). For children who are developing a bridge between thought and emotion, mirroring can be particularly effective.

Choices

In addition to behavioral and affective reflections and mirroring, **choices** can provide children with a means of navigating their environment as they develop essential self-regulation skills. Consider Sophie, a 3-year-old who has difficulty wrapping up her play at the end of the day and transitioning home with her father. Often, when he comes to pick her up, there are numerous protests that include "Just one more activity!", "I'm not ready!", and "I'm not done playing."

The teachers have noticed that pick-up time for both Sophie and her father has not only become longer over time, but also resulted in a good amount of stress for both parties. Her father makes frequent bids for Sophie to leave, and she protests in a variety of ways. To intervene, the teachers decide that offering Sophie choices is an effective teaching practice.

First, they begin to inform Sophie when her father will be coming, giving her 10- and then 5-minute warnings. When her father arrives, Sophie has agreed that she can show him one activity in the classroom. Following this, it is time to go, and Sophie's choice is that she can either walk to the car or be carried.

On the first day, Sophie complies with all aspects of the plan until her father tells her it is time to go and informs her "You can either walk to the car or I will carry you." At this point, Sophie throws herself on the floor, crying in protest. Her father, in a calm voice, importance in their environment, where they are noticed for their day-to-day interactions and not for behaviors that you deem extraordinary or problematic. A good rule of thumb to follow with behavioral reflections is that each child should receive at least five per day.

Affective Reflections

Affective reflections are simple statements that identify how you perceive a child to be feeling. These statements lack judgment and present children with labels for the emotions they seem to be experiencing. Saying "you look angry!" to a child who is stomping through the room or "you seem sad" to a child sitting alone on a swing with tears in her eyes are examples of affective reflections.

Upon separation from his mother each morning, 2-year-old Patrick enters the classroom and proceeds immediately to the corner of the room that is furthest from the door. Here, he begins to yell and scream, repeatedly calling out "mommy!" and throwing whatever objects are in his immediate reach.

One of the co-teachers in the classroom is always by his side when these episodes begin, and she spends extensive amounts of time asking Patrick questions about his life. "What do you think Joe (his brother) is doing now?" "How was your doggy this morning?" "What did you have for breakfast?" The goal of this teacher's interactions is to distract Patrick from his concerns in the hopes of getting him to calm down and join the rest of the group.

One day, the other co-teacher in the room approached this duo, looked down at Patrick, and said, "You seem very sad." Patrick stopped screaming for a minute, looked at her, and said "Yeah." The teacher then proceeded to sit down next to Patrick, rub his back, and ask him questions about what was so upsetting to him. Within minutes, Patrick had calmed down a bit and was talking about "missing ma."

The different approaches are both commonly found in the field. As opposed to confronting the source of serious emotions, many focus on distracting the child in the hopes of diffusing the situation. This practice ignores one of the fundamental concepts of emotional self-regulation; specifically, before children are able to effectively control their emotions, they need to be able to identify them. The process of learning how to emotionally self-regulate begins at birth; however, around 18 months to 2 years of age, children begin to be able to label their own emotions, which is considered a foundational emotional self-regulation skill (Bretherton, Fritz, Zahn-Waxler, & Ridgeway, 1986).

Each of these approaches focus on helping the child: The first approach focuses on creating short-term changes in the child's behavior, whereas the second approach focuses on helping the child learn emotional self-regulation skills. Through supporting emotional self-regulation skills, teachers can help children assess their own internal states. Identifying internal states helps children cope with challenging, frustrating, and stressful situations. Similar to behavioral reflections, a good rule of thumb with affective reflections is to provide these five times per day to each child in the classroom.

The development of empathy is a ke

tells her, "I see you are lying on the floor, so I assume that you want me to carry you." He picks her up and begins to carry her to the car.

What might happen if Sophie then protests and asks to be put down so that she can walk? The overall goal of choices is to allow children some control over their environment and to support them as they meet the varied expectations placed on them. A protest to walk, therefore, might be greeted with agreement, and her father allows her to walk the rest of the way. Should she fall onto the floor again, Sophie's father picks her up and reminds her that she made this choice as he carries her the rest of the way to the car.

Encouragement

You have learned about the importance of supporting children's intrinsic motivation. When children are intrinsically motivated, they base their actions on internal models of expectations rather than on external rewards to shape behaviors. Intrinsic motivation supports social-emotional development by allowing children to act out of their own expectations and models of behavior as opposed to relying on adults to constantly shape their behavior.

Encouragement is an effective tool to support intrinsic motivation. Through encouragement, professionals can focus on the efforts that children put forth, as opposed to outcomes for behavior. Encouragement reflects the belief that all children have strengths and an internal desire to learn. Further, through encouragement children benefit from respectful interactions with adults that help them develop skills supportive of healthy self-esteem. These skills build on emerging self-control (Mulligan, Morris, Green, & Harper-Whelan, 2003).

When compared to **praise**, encouragement has many advantages. Praise is often used as an *external motivator to shape children's behavior* (Hitz & Driscoll, 1989). Therefore, the motivation to behave in a particular manner is provided through the environment. In addition, praise is often used as a *classroom management tool*, where external rewards are given to children who are behaving in an expected manner. This includes such comments as "I like how Jose is sitting" or "Look at how Nomi is following the rules by lining up for outside time." In each of these scenarios, some children are marked as being "good," and a clear message is sent to others to behave in this expected manner. This practice negates clear directives, where children are told what behavior is expected of them, and rather, forces children to look at others, determine what behavior they are engaging in, and act appropriately. For many children, the observation and processing steps involved in shaping their own behaviors in this manner can be particularly challenging. Further, this kind of feedback can create winners and losers, where some children are the recipients of praise and others forced to figure acceptable behaviors out based on these responses that other children receive. Table 10.3 provides a comparison of encouragement and praise.

encouragement
Statements that reflect a child's efforts or progress and that are supportive of intrinsic motivation.

praise
Statements that focus on a child's product and are supportive of extrinsic motivation.

TABLE 10.3 Encouragement Versus Praise	
Encouragement	**Praise**
"You worked really hard on that!"	"I love it."
"I see you used the whole page for your picture."	"That is so pretty."
"What an accomplishment."	"Good job!"
"Let's all work to sit down so we can start our morning meeting."	"I like the way Jose is sitting."
"It is nice to see you enjoying that so much."	"I have never seen someone do such a good job."

Use of encouragement offers several distinct advantages. These advantages emerge from specific strategies (Hitz & Driscoll, 1989):

- **Offering children specific rather than general comments.** For example, as opposed to saying "great job," encouragement focuses on specific behaviors the children are engaging in. Behavioral reflections can be an effective tool providing encouragement. Reflections might include "I see you are sitting and waiting for the story to begin" or "I noticed that you washed your hands and sat right down for snack."
- **Focusing on improvement and efforts rather than the evaluation of a specific product.** As opposed to saying "I like your painting," a teacher instead says "I see you used four different colors in your work" or "You really spent time on that. I can see your effort in covering the whole page."
- **Avoiding competition or comparison with others.** Therefore, instead of saying "I like how Brian is lined up to go outside," say "You are working hard to put your coat on."
- **Setting children up for success.** Children can become reliant on your praise of "great job," "terrific," or "fantastic." In the absence of these comments, children might experience a sense of failure and/or a lack of satisfaction with their work. Encouragement, therefore, gives children the space to focus on their own efforts and contributions.
- **Helping children develop an appreciation of their behaviors and achievements.** Specifically, instead of "great work," giving a child feedback that includes "you worked hard on that till it was completed" provides feedback on the results of their efforts, as opposed to the end product.

Encouragement is most effective when it is used in *teacher-initiated and private situations*, where an honest exchange of ideas is supported and children are allowed to talk about their work. Further, encouragement should comprise *sincere, direct comments that are delivered in a natural tone* (Hitz & Driscoll, 1989). Table 10.4 provides an overview of guidance strategies.

Behavioral and affective reflections, mirroring, choices, and encouragement are foundational guidance practices, meaning that they should be applied to all children during daily interactions. By using these foundational guidance tools effectively, professionals can communicate to children the importance of *belonging and significance*. For example, behavioral reflections tell a child that you notice him or her and support the child's feelings of belonging, whereas choices allow children control over their environment and support their feelings of significance within it.

Each of these foundational strategies provides children with *personal power*, where they can have an impact on their environment. Finally, foundational guidance practices provide information about expected behaviors and expectations and therefore are a form of *guidance that teaches*.

TABLE 10.4 Overview of Guidance Strategies	
Technique	**Brief Description**
Behavioral reflections	Simple statements identifying what you see a child doing
Affective reflections	Simple statements identifying your perception of a child's emotions
Mirroring	Supporting and imitating the intensity of children's emotional reactions to events
Choices	Simple statements that outline options between A and B
Encouragement	Statements that reflect a child's effort or progress

In addition to these foundational guidance strategies, another important source of information for children in the classroom is rules for children's behavior. Rules provide children with general expectations for behavior in the classroom community and are equally applied to each child in the classroom. Rules are shaped by classroom community needs and should address the question of "What behaviors can support our existing in this classroom community together?"

Effective Classroom Rules

Condi is a second-grade teacher who is responsible for 26 students in her class. Each year before the school year starts, Condi writes out a list of classroom rules and posts them at the door and near the white board at the front of the room. These rules are the product of extensive efforts on Condi's part, and every year the list of rules gets longer and longer. Her list of 28 rules includes such things as:

- No other toys with the play dough.
- Each center's materials stay in the same place.
- All materials must be put away before moving to next area during center time.
- No Legos or blocks left on the floor.
- Sit criss-cross applesauce during morning meeting.

At the beginning of the school year, children are informed of the rules, and the list is reviewed on a weekly basis. Further, children are given information on the consequences of not following the rules: Each time a rule is not adhered to, a check is placed next to their name. Whenever a child receives five checks, they will not be able to participate in outdoor recess the next day. Condi is always amazed by the time it takes her to make sure the children are following the classroom rules. Often, she feels like a police officer.

Now consider Devarsi's second-grade classroom, which provides a more positive example of community building. On the first day of school, Devarsi sits down with the children and discusses what it means to be a member of a community and how each person's behavior in a community affects others. The children are asked to give an example of someone in their community who helps them and explain why their behavior is helpful. He then reads the book *I Got Community* by Melanie Cooper (1995) and asks the children to think about how the community members supported the main character.

Next, Devarsi explains that they are each members of their own community in the classroom, and he uses this as a prompt to brainstorm possible behaviors that might be beneficial to the development of community. He creates a list based on these behaviors and places it on the wall next to the white board. Once the list is posted, the children and Devarsi talk about what it means to follow the rules. For example, one of the rules was "treat other's belongings with respect." To explore the application of this rule, the children and Devarsi talked about specific examples of being respectful and examples that might demonstrate a lack of respect. On a weekly basis, Devarsi asks the children if they would suggest any additions to the list, and, based on the input of each community member, the list is updated. By the end of the school year, the children have a total of 10 rules listed.

There are many differences between Condi's and Devarsi's approach to rules. First, Condi

Classroom rules provide clear expectations for behavior.

> ## TEACHING AND LEARNING CONNECTIONS
>
> ### Establishing Classroom Rules
>
> - Establish rules in the classroom with children.
> - Allow children opportunities to generate examples of what the rules mean—for example, "keep feet on the floor" means "no climbing on the table."
> - Regularly revisit the established rules and use as a tool in problem-solving discussions.

based her list of her own ideas of rules in the classroom, as opposed to creating buy-in to the list based on *children's input*. Second, Devarsi spent time to *teach the importance of following the rules*, based on the fact that their classroom was a community and that communities can support members in a variety of ways. Finally, Devarsi spent time *teaching the children the rules* by allowing them to brainstorm, with his input, what specific behaviors are associated with each rule.

Mutually developing and revisiting rules in the classroom community allows Devarsi and his class to create a list of value-based rules shaped by their unique community. The rules constructed were responsive to children's ongoing needs, giving them a sense of empowerment and allowing them opportunities to share their voice in the community.

Sensory-Responsive Environments

Many of the challenges that occur in the early childhood environment can be bypassed through careful attention to children's sensory needs. Some children are hypersensitive to environmental stimuli and require calming input to help them organize and respond. Other children might need stimuli in the environment to increase their level of responsiveness. All children benefit from sensory environments that are respectful to their unique sensory needs.

sensory diet
Personalized activity schedule that matches the unique nervous system needs of each child.

The term **sensory diet** was developed by occupational therapist Patricia Willbarger (Biel & Peske, 2005) and refers to a personalized activity schedule that matches the nervous system needs of each child.

Determining the workings of a child's nervous system needs begins with careful observation. Questions that observational data can address include: When does the child seem to need stimulation? Relaxation? What activities in the environment seem to calm the child? Are there activities that seem to stimulate the child?

Sensory profiles can be developed for each child in the classroom and appropriate diets planned. Andre, for example, has difficulty sitting and attending during morning meeting. He often gets up, walks around the room, and pokes other children. To help guide his behavior through attention to his sensory needs, he is encouraged to jump around before sitting down and is given a heavy sit pillow to hold onto during meeting time. The goal of this object is to provide weight to give him sensory feedback and assist in organization. As movement before sitting seems to help each child focus more during meeting time, Andre's teacher always begins their meeting with an active activity.

For some children, movement alone can serve to wind them up further. For these children, combining a movement activity (such as swinging on the swings) with activities stimulating bodily awareness through input to the joints, muscles, and connective tissues (such as pushing, lifting, or pulling heavy objects) can serve to help them organize their nervous system. Again, recognizing universal benefit, these activities can be structured throughout the day.

Each classroom might include a variety of children with different—and potentially competing—sensory needs. How can one child's needs for movement, another child's need for bodily awareness activities, and another child's need for relaxation be accommodated in the daily classroom routine? The key to meeting each of these needs is to make tending to children's sensory needs a part of the routine. Just as curricular activities need to be adapted to support each child, sensory activities also need to become a daily part of the classroom.

Each of the aforementioned practices can be used to develop a strong, preventive foundation for guidance in the early childhood classroom. As these are preventive, their appropriate usage will serve to bypass many challenging behaviors. Many children, however, will require more than these preventive measures. These behaviors are often referred to as "challenging," and difficulties dealing with these behaviors have been identified as one of the main reasons novice teachers leave the field (Darling-Hammond, 2000).

ADDRESSING CHALLENGING BEHAVIORS

How many children in the classroom might exhibit difficulties in social-emotional development? Approximately 10% to 13% of preschoolers between the ages of 1 and 6 have been diagnosed with emotional and behavioral disorders (Institute of Medicine, 2001). Additionally, 28% of a large sample of preschool students meet the criteria for the diagnosis of a psychiatric disorder (Lavigne et al., 1996). Therefore, professionals in the field are working to support a large range of social-emotional needs. Some children might require little support. Others—who potentially exhibit challenging behaviors in the environment—require more of your attention.

Addressing challenging behaviors begins with attention to the root causes of children's behavior (DEC, 2006). Questions to ask yourself include: Why is the child acting in a particular way? What are they hoping to achieve? How is their behavior achieving desired outcomes?

Answering these questions begins with careful observation and sometimes requires more formal screening and assessment. Based on this, effective interventions are developed through knowledge of behavior, its antecedents, and consequences. Let's begin with exploring what challenging behaviors are.

Defining and Understanding Challenging Behaviors

Challenging behavior is "any repeated pattern of behavior, or perception of behavior, that interferes with or is at risk of interfering with optimal learning or engagement in prosocial interactions with peers and adults" (U.S. Department of Education Center for Evidence-Based Practice, 2002, p. 2).

The source of children's challenging behaviors is varied and complex. For example, children might engage in challenging behavior because they lack the language skills to problem solve verbally. Other children might have challenges with impulse control, which in turn affects their interactions with the environment. Still others might lack social skills for entering a group and because of this "ask" other children if they can play by knocking down their block structure. Some children might have learned that using physical aggression is an appropriate and expected means of dealing with anger and solving problems in the environment.

challenging behavior
Repeated pattern or perception of behaviors that interferes with children's interactions with others and/or the learning environment.

TEACHING AND LEARNING CONNECTIONS

Tools for Understanding Challenging Behavior

- Know the child.
- Carefully observe to target the source of challenging behavior.
- Think about triggers in the environment.
- Use families as a resource and problem-solving partner.

Understanding the source of children's challenging behavior leads to effective intervention. Observation, therefore, is a critical tool in developing appropriate guidance strategies. Observational strategies that identify the source of challenging behavior include *event sampling* and *time sampling*. Event sampling focuses on what happened before and after the behavior occurred. Time sampling examines the frequency and environmental context of the challenging behavior. Techniques such as running and anecdotal records can help you identify the challenging behaviors. Following identification, the DEC (2006) recommends using logical and natural consequences and social and communication skills training to address challenging behaviors at the secondary level of intervention.

Logical and Natural Consequences

logical consequences

Reasonable, related, and respectful teacher-initiated consequences that respond to challenging behaviors.

Logical consequences are teacher-initiated consequences that address individual behaviors in the classroom. For consequences to be considered logical, they must be reasonable, related, and respectful. A consequence for a child who kicks down the block structure of another child, for example, would be experiencing a *reasonable* consequence if they rebuilt the block structure. This consequence would also be *related*, in that it pertains to the action of the child. Finally, this consequence would also be *respectful*, as it allows a child to take responsibility for his or her behavior.

natural consequences

Consequences that occur naturally in the environment and do not require teacher intervention.

Natural consequences, on the other hand, occur naturally in the environment without teacher intervention. For example, a natural consequence for a child who is repeatedly told "put your mittens on to go outside" might be allowed to go out without his or her mittens and experience cold hands. Then this consequence is followed up with a behavioral reflection "you did not put your mittens on and now your hands are cold."

The problem with natural consequences is that, professionally, we are unlikely to let a child be hurt or uncomfortable in order to demonstrate the consequences of behavior. The example of a child experiencing cold when outdoors on a mild winter day could be acceptable, but were the temperatures at or below freezing, such a consequence might harm the child.

If used appropriately, logical and natural consequences can help children forge a link between their behavior and its outcomes. Logical and natural consequences can be used with children as young as toddlers, although the anticipated effects on their behavior might be different from that of a preschooler or school-age child. For example, when I was in graduate school we experimented with consequences for toddler and 2-year-old biting behavior. We knew that biting was a developmentally typical behavior for this age group but also felt that employing consequences was an important facet of children's social-emotional development. When children bit others in the classroom, we instilled the consequence of the biter having to care for the child who had been bitten. The "biters" were taken with us as we gathered wet paper towels and ice cubes. They sat as we applied the cold, wet paper to the other child's bites (this was often done with their help). While applying the compress, we used both behavioral ("You have been bitten on the arm") and affective ("I see you are crying; biting hurts") reflections.

This strategy was compared with a former strategy that had been employed, which included removing the child who had bitten from the situation. We were surprised by the results: Children did not bite any less frequently. Upon reflection, however, we decided that—as biting is a developmentally appropriate behavior—we would not expect it to extinguish. Rather, as our goals were supporting children's respect for others in the environment and appropriate problem solving, we were teaching children about the consequences of their actions. Whether toddlers and 2-year-olds could synthesize and apply that information in the present sense was not a goal. Rather, the focus was on the development of behaviors supporting children in the long term.

As a side note, there are many effective ways to prevent biting from occurring. As with all guidance strategies, determining the root of the child's behavior is an important first step. Is the child teething? Teething rings and cool washcloths can provide relief. Is the child expressing him- or herself? Providing children with appropriate words to express their feelings can decrease biting behaviors.

The Social Skills and Communication Curricula

Supporting children who are at risk for challenging behaviors requires teaching children social skills and supporting and responding to children's social-emotional development needs. The challenges a child demonstrates influences the strategies selected. Strategies that include the child, the classroom community, and the family are most likely to be effective.

What behaviors should be supported through the **social skills curricula**? This question can be addressed by determining the challenging behaviors the child demonstrates, their age, and their developmental needs. The social skills curriculum includes three stages (Fox & Lentini, 2006).

During the first stage, called *skill acquisition*, the desired skill is introduced to the child. For example, Marcus is interested in teaching Lupe how to ask a group of children to play. The skill, walking up to a group and asking "Can I play with you?" is introduced to Lupe, first through role playing with Marcus. Then, the skill is used on a small group of children who are playing in the block area. Marcus gives Lupe plenty of opportunity to practice the skill in the classroom, providing guidance and feedback, until Lupe has reached the second stage, which is called *fluency*. In this stage, children have learned the skill and can apply it easily. When Lupe is able to apply the skill in his neighborhood, he has reached the third stage, called *skill maintenance and generalization*. Through using the skill outside the classroom environment, Lupe is demonstrating that he has mastered the skill and is able to apply it across varied situations. Within these stages, children benefit from training in four basic areas of interaction. These include participation, where children are actively engaged in the process of skill development; communication, represented through two-way dialogue regarding the skill; cooperation, reflecting classroom support for the skill development; and validation-support, provided through ongoing feedback (Williams & Asher, 1993). Figure 10.3 illustrates the stages of the social skills curricula.

How can each of these stages be taught? For younger children, teachers can use modeling and behavior and affective reflections. For example, focusing on the skill of turn-taking with a 3-year-old might include modeling, taking turns in a conversation

social skills curricula
Series of practices designed to support children's social skills.

FIGURE 10.3
Stages of the Social
Skills Curricula

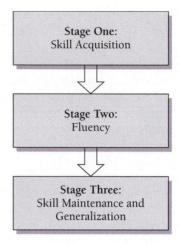

with the child, then using behavioral reflections to comment ("I see you waited until I was done speaking to say something."). "You look happy! We took turns" is an appropriate affective reflection that could be added to this.

An important teaching strategy is coaching. With older children, coaching begins with discussing different concepts with them and determining how these might be demonstrated. For example, a teacher might ask a 5-year-old, "What does it mean to co-operate?" Based on the child's response, and teacher-provided guidance if necessary, behaviors can be identified.

Next, children are allowed to practice the new skill with feedback. Similar to coaching, this strategy allows the child to focus on particular skills and be provided with specific feedback. The last step focuses on review, where feedback is given and new strategies developed.

Addressing the Challenging Behavior of Infants and Toddlers. There are several important factors to remember when considering the challenging behaviors of infants and toddlers (Fox, 2006):

- It is never too early to address concerns about a child's problem behavior. One of the major challenges associated with addressing problem behavior, however, is determining whether the behavior is developmentally expected or of a level of development and intensity that exceeds normal development.
- Before exploring possible interventions, it is essential to understand children's physical–medical status, developmental status, and intervention history.
- Intervention strategies for infants and toddlers must focus on children in the context of their family and the early childhood environment.
- Effective intervention supports the development of new caregiver and family skills in interacting with the child.
- The natural environment, where behaviors are demonstrated, is the most effective location for intervention.
- Interventions demonstrated must be culturally and linguistically respectful and responsive.

Social skills and communication training can help alleviate children's challenging behaviors. The first step in providing support is to identify—through observation, screening, and assessment—the challenging behaviors and whether they fall outside the

---

TEACHING AND LEARNING CONNECTIONS

Implementing Effective Interventions

- Understand children's developmental needs contributing to challenging behavior.
- Carefully select an intervention strategy that is related to children's needs and respectful of their development and learning.
- Strive for consistency, and to achieve this goal, communicate extensively with families.
- Recognize that effective interventions need to be implemented over time.
- Regularly revisit and reassess the child's needs and the effectiveness of the intervention strategy.

---

range of what is considered typical. By identifying what infant–toddler skills might require additional support, knowledge is supported. For example, observation of a toddler who uses his body to solve problems might suggest that specific guidance is needed in using words. Observation of another toddler who also uses her body to solve problems might lead you to the conclusion that, in this child's case, support for emotional self-regulation might be required.

Applying effective interventions does not mean that behaviors are going to immediately be extinguished. Any developmental intervention undertaken needs to be applied consistently and over time. As the goal is to teach children appropriate behavior, the same general principles of developmentally appropriate practices apply. These include that each child's ability to take in, process, and apply information varies with the developmental needs of the child.

Language represents one of the most important skills in self-regulation, as communication provides a means of expression. Children with language delays are at risk for using challenging behaviors to communicate their point to others, and in this light, the challenging behavior actually serves as a form of communication. Part of the challenge for professionals is determining what communicative function a child's behavior serves.

Addressing the Challenging Behaviors of Preschool and School-Age Children.
Effectively addressing the challenging behaviors of preschool and school-age children is based on the same factors that apply to infants and toddlers. First, the challenging behaviors must be addressed as early as possible. In addition, knowledge of the child's physical, medical and developmental status, and intervention history is essential. Families must be involved in the intervention process for it to be most effective, and the natural environment is the most effective locale for intervention. Finally, the intervention practices employed must be culturally and linguistically sensitive to the child and his or her family.

For older children, the same strategies used with infant-toddler populations can be applied. For example, observing children can indicate whether helping them express themselves verbally is a useful strategy or whether they need additional support to develop self-regulation skills. As children grow and develop, increased demands and challenges in the world of peer interactions might create the need for social skills intervention.

FIGURE 10.4
Teachable Moments

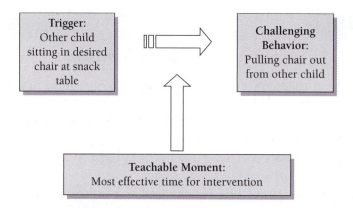

Supporting children's social skills requires knowledge of when guidance strategies are most effectively used. Professionals are most likely to intervene when they see a problem behavior occurring or right after the behavior has occurred (Center on the Social and Emotional Foundations for Early Learning [CSEFEL], 2006). The most effective time for intervention, however, is before the actual time of occurrence. The period before the occurrence of a behavior is described as a **teachable moment**, where the triggers for a potential behavior have emerged, but the behavior has not occurred. It is during this time that children can most effectively learn the application of language or self-regulation strategies. Figure 10.4 illustrates a teachable moment.

Once you have determined the child's needs, you need to develop a general idea of the behaviors you want to support. Research has indicated that there are several specific behaviors that children engage in during play that are related to forming friendships (CSEFEL, 2006). These include *organizing play*, where children make statements that suggest activities and how to proceed with the activity. *Sharing* is also related to forming friendships, as is *assisting others*, where children use a variety of different methods to help their peers. Finally, *giving compliments*—where children compliment the efforts and products of their peers—has been identified as important in friendship formation.

In addition to these factors, *reciprocity* plays an important role in friendship formation. For reciprocity to occur, children must not only initiate play with others, but also respond to the play bids of other children.

Messages given through the environment and learning activities, including literature, play a large role in assisting children in successfully developing relationships. Some children, however, require more direct forms of intervention in order to develop and apply appropriate skills. These interventions are commonly referred to as social skills guidance.

Social Skills Guidance

Social skills include communication, problem solving, decision making, self-management, and peer interaction abilities that allow children to develop and maintain positive interactions with others. Children's success in these areas is related to their overall **peer competence**, which refers to their basic abilities to form relationships with others.

Supporting social skills requires attention to different areas of children's development and how these developmental areas affect their interactions with others. The five-step process for supporting children's social skills includes (Bellini, 2003):

1. Identify social skill challenges.
2. Distinguish between skill acquisition and performance challenges.

---

teachable moment

Point in time when children are most likely to respond to instructional strategies.

peer competence

Ability to interact successfully and independently with peers.

3. Select intervention strategies.
4. Implement intervention.
5. Assess and modify intervention as necessary.

Successful interactions are informed by appropriate social skills.

What is the child's present level of functioning? Determining the answer to this question can lend insight into the appropriate social skills curricula. The first step in addressing children's challenges in social skills is determining the child's present level of functioning. Through careful observation, family interviews, and formal assessment procedures such as screening and checklists, professionals can gain important knowledge about what social skills areas are particularly challenging for the child. One child in a classroom, for example, might demonstrate challenges in one-on-one interactions, such as not making eye contact or responding to the bids of peers. Another child in that same classroom might have these skills in place, but become agitated and distracted in group interactions. Each of these children will require different types of intervention, with guidance targeted toward their specific needs.

Following assessment of a child's area of challenge, professionals must determine whether the child's challenges reflect challenges in skill acquisition or performance. Specifically, is the child demonstrating the absence of a particular skill or behavior (challenge in skill acquisition) or does the child not seem to be able to apply the skill (performance)? In the former case, the child will need to be taught the specific skill; in the latter, the focus of intervention would be to teach the child how to effectively apply the skill. If a child lacks a skill, encouraging him or her to apply it in specific situations is likely to be fruitless. For example, Andre is a 4-year-old who demonstrates challenges in entering and exiting group play. Your observations of Andre indicate that he lacks the language skills to successfully enter play. Your intervention, therefore, must begin with the provision of appropriate language ("Hi, can I play?") before teaching him when and how to apply this language.

Once a child's present functioning is determined and skill and/or performance challenges identified, professionals can move to the third stage of the process, where a social skill intervention is selected, and the fourth stage, where it is implemented. Effective social skill strategies and their applications are summarized in Table 10.5.

The fifth step of implementation is assessing and modifying the intervention. This stage is often planned before the start of the intervention, as data can then be collected on the impact of the intervention throughout the process. Using this assessment data as a foundation, professionals can make decisions regarding effectiveness and, if necessary, implement modifications.

Many other strategies can be helpful to children who require social skills training. For example, professionals can use **social prompts**, where children are coached with specific verbal or physical cues to assist them in interactions with other children. For example, Matthew provides 6-year-old Jordan with a light touch on his shoulder to indicate when he should respond to another child's questions. One of the challenges in using social prompts is to learn when to withdraw them to ensure that children can use suggested behaviors in the absence of the prompts. Observation can be a useful guide, with continuing use of a strategy despite the absence of prompts indicating that prompts might not be as needed.

social prompts
The provision of verbal or physical cues to guide children in social situations.

TABLE 10.5   Descriptions of Social Skills Intervention and Their Applications

Social Skills Intervention	Description	Application
Peer mentors	Peers who are trained in supporting social interactions interact with the targeted child throughout the day. Peer mentors should be children who have age-appropriate play and social skills and have a record of regular attendance.	Peer mentors are provided with specific strategies to support the targeted child's development of social skills. Focusing on a peer allows the teacher to be in the role of facilitator and allows the targeted child to utilize newly acquired skills in social interactions.
Thoughts and feelings activities	Thoughts and feelings activities can be used to support social interaction skills such as empathy and perspective taking.	Through the use of picture cards, stories, and children's books, targeted children can be coached with prompts that include "What do you think she is thinking?" "Why might she be acting this way?"
Facilitating reciprocal interactions	Reciprocal interactions can be supported through direct skill and on conversational give and take. Included in this might be coaching on turn taking, the use of appropriate questions, and responding to the conversational cues of others.	Picture cards, stories, and children's books can again be an effective tool in supporting reciprocal interactions, where children are coached to identify turn-taking behaviors that are occurring. Further, daily conversations that occur between peers and adults can be turned into coaching opportunities, where the child is provided specific information about the interchange taking place.
Social stories	Social stories are tools that present a brief social concept to children in the form of a story. Stories selected should be based on the interest and needs of the child and should be presented in a way that is respectful of the child's developmental needs.	Social stories are best utilized when they are paired with an opportunity for the child to practice the learned skill. For example, after reading a social story on turn taking, the child would then be allowed to practice that skill in a group setting. Although there are many social stories available for purchase, these can be made to fit the child's individual developmental needs.
Role playing/behavioral reversal	Role playing is used to address basic interaction skills, where children are provided opportunities to practice developing skills. Behavioral reversals allow the child the opportunity to practice skills from the perspective of another.	Role playing and behavioral reversals should focus on social situations the child is likely to encounter. In addition to creating scenarios between the child and adult, other props, such a puppets or small toys, can be utilized.

Source: Data from Bellini, S. (2003). Making (and keeping) friends: A model for social skills interaction. *The Reporter*, 8(3), 1–10.

prime

The process of preparing children for upcoming social interactions.

reinforcement

Encouragement coupled with behavioral reflections that are provided following a play episode.

In addition to the use of prompts, teachers can **prime** children for social situations. For example, before going out on the playground to play ball, Marrisa primes Ally for the outdoor situation by saying, "Whom would you like to play ball with?" "How will you ask her to play?" "What might you do with the balls?" Priming not only gets the child ready for the upcoming situation, but also can use specific prompts to facilitate peer interaction.

Another effective social skills strategy is the use of **reinforcement**. Reinforcement typically occurs after a play episode, as giving reinforcement during play can actually have a negative impact on the duration of the play (Joseph & Strain, 2006). Using reinforcements can be thought of as a type of encouragement coupled with behavioral reflections. For example, after two children engage in sustained play in the block area, a reinforcement might be "You and Gretchen played together in the block area. I noticed you were taking turns with the animals." In this example, the child is provided with specific information about her behavior and given direct feedback. This is in direct contrast to comments such as "You did such a great job playing," where the child does not gain concrete information about the play episode.

Supporting Emotional Self-Regulation

In addition to social skills training, early childhood professionals can assist children in developing emotional self-regulation skills. For many children, universal practices that support social-emotional development result in well-developed regulation skills. For some children, particularly in dealing with anger and controlling impulses, additional training is required.

Supporting children's self-regulation skills requires modeling the behavior that you want the child to develop (Joseph & Strain, 2006). When children are angry or having a difficult time controlling impulses, professionals must *model remaining calm*. This includes when responding to children and when responding to situations that are frustrating to you. In addition to serving as a good model for calm behavior, professionals can teach children *how to control their anger and impulses*. Although many adults tell children to "calm down," this does little in the way of providing children with specific strategies that assist them in the process of calming.

The **turtle technique** is an effective tool for teaching children to regulate their own emotions. This technique begins with children learning to recognize when they are experiencing overwhelming feelings. Following that recognition, children are taught to say "STOP!" and then to envision themselves going into their "shell." Children are then encouraged to take three deep breaths and think thoughts that can help calm them down. These thoughts might include a focus on what they are feeling ("I am so angry I can't think, I need to think.") or possible interpretations of the situation ("It was a mistake. I can build the tower again. It is okay.") After calming, children come out of their shell and work on solutions to solving their problem. Figure 10.5 illustrates the steps involved in the turtle technique.

Go to MyEducationLab and select the topic "Guidance." Under Activities and Applications, watch the video *Managing Challenging Behaviors: Discussing Choices* and reflect on how supporting children in discussing choices can help manage challenging behaviors.

turtle technique
Series of strategies designed to help children deal with overwhelming feelings.

FIGURE 10.5
Turtle Technique

TEACHING AND LEARNING CONNECTIONS

Strategies Supporting Self-Regulation

- Provide children the opportunity to identify their own emotions, using affective reflections when appropriate.
- Prepare children to handle disappointment through providing specific strategies to help them cope.
- Recognize and comment on when children remain calm, helping them identify strategies that they used in doing this.

Another effective strategy to teach children self-regulation is *preparing children to handle disappointment.* Using priming, professionals can coach children on what might happen in a particular situation should things not go as anticipated. Priming examples can include "We might not win the game, but it is great that we get to play" or "Remember that everyone will get a chance to be the line leader."

Finally, behavioral and affective reflections and encouragement can be used to *recognize and comment when children remain calm.* In these cases, children are provided with specific feedback ("I saw you get really angry in the block corner and pick up a block. Then, it looked like you took three breaths and calmed down."). The child, in this case, is given feedback about your observations of his feelings and the strategies he undertook to help get these feelings under control.

Conflicts between children are an inevitable part of classroom communities. Although many conflicts can be warded off by a strong foundation supporting social-emotional development, the nature of existing with others in a group environment means that many conflicts are unavoidable.

Conflict Resolution

Joshua and Daniel are playing in the block corner, seemingly absorbed in constructing a tower for their race cars to drive down. Suddenly, Joshua yells "That's mine" at Daniel and takes a car out of Daniel's hand. Daniel responds by yelling "MINE!" and reaching over to grab the car out of Joshua's hands. Neither is willing to give up their claim on the car, and both are screaming and yelling as they try to gain control of the object.

The argument between Joshua and Daniel reflects a common occurrence among young children. The professional's responsibilities in dealing with conflict resolution include (1) preventing conflicts from becoming too serious to resolve easily and (2) ensuring that conflicts are resolved peaceably, no matter how serious they become (Gartrell, 2006). Together, these strategies are referred to as **conflict management**.

Teaching children to resolve their own conflicts requires direct instruction in negotiation skills. Gartrell (2006) suggests using the five fingers on the hand to remember the following steps:

1. *Thumb: Cool everyone down.* The first step in conflict management is to cool everyone down. For Joshua and Daniel, this requires their teacher, Janette, to approach them and help them regulate their emotions. Janette speaks to the boys in a calm voice and places her hands on each of their shoulders, telling them "Okay, let's take a few breaths and see what is going on here."

2. *Pointer finger: Agree about what the problem is.* During this phase, Janette and the two boys determine what the problem is. To Janette's question of "Why are you two

conflict management

Series of strategies designed to help children respond to and resolve interpersonal conflicts.

yelling at each other?" both Joshua and Daniel protest in varied "He took my car! That was my car! I had that car!" After listening to the boys, Janette responds "Oh, so you both want that car and feel you had it first," to which the boys respond, "Yes!"

3. *Tall finger: Brainstorm possible solutions.* After identifying the problem, Janette and the children brainstorm possible solutions. These include that they take turns using the car or that perhaps they can use the car in some way together. Janette also points out to the boys that there is another car in the bin that is exactly like the one they are using, except that it is a different color.

4. *Ring finger: Agree on a solution.* After listing out the possibilities, Janette asks the boys what they want to do. She is not surprised when neither is willing to give up the car. She tells the boys, "It seems as though none of the solutions we have come up with will work for you; what else might we do? Remember, we only have about 20 minutes left before lunch." After a few more prompts, the boys agree to each play with one of the two cars and that they would switch after 10 minutes so they had equal time to play with the desired car. Janette agrees that she will tell the boys when 10 minutes is up.

5. *Pinky: Facilitate the solution.* Facilitating the solution requires carrying out the agreed-upon plans and recapping the conflict resolution strategies that were used. After 10 minutes had elapsed, Janette told the boys it was time to exchange cars. They agreed to, and when it was time to clean up, Janette sat down with the boys and recounted—using behavioral and affective reflections—what she had seen occur. These included: "You were pulling the car back and forth and yelling at each other. You both looked so angry." She then repeated to the boys what steps they had taken to resolve their conflict, and at the end stated, "You really worked hard at building this tower. It seemed you had so much fun together."

Figure 10.6 illustrates the steps involved in teaching conflict negotiation skills.

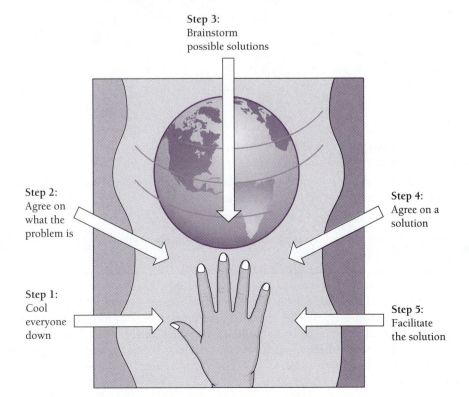

FIGURE 10.6
Steps in Teaching Conflict Negotiation Skills

Step 3: Brainstorm possible solutions
Step 2: Agree on what the problem is
Step 1: Cool everyone down
Step 4: Agree on a solution
Step 5: Facilitate the solution

ISSUES OF ACCESS AND EQUITY FOR CHILDREN

The Many Faces of Bullying

Bullying is a behavior that can represent particular challenges in the early childhood environment. Bullying not only is a hot button for many, which may tax personal resources in dealing with challenging behaviors, but also can have a dramatic impact on the learning environment.

The label of "bully" has many negative connotations that can impede successfully dealing with the child's challenging behavior. As a professional, your first responsibility is to identify the child's challenging behaviors and their potential causes. Aggression is often a behavior associated with bullying. Referring to a child's aggressive behaviors—as opposed to using the label of bully—can support successful intervention and reflect respect for the challenges that child is experiencing.

Aggressive behaviors, in many cases, represent a cyclical interaction. The children who engage in aggressive behaviors are often the victims of relational aggression. Children who are bullied are often less skilled in assertive skills and, as a group, tend to be socially isolated. Effectively dealing with aggressive behavior in the classroom, therefore, requires efforts targeted toward the children who are displaying aggressive behaviors and those who are the recipients of these behaviors.

Tertiary level interventions can be employed to support positive behaviors that replace aggression. Professionals also must teach other children assertiveness skills that respond to aggression (NAEYC, 1995). NAEYC identifies the following strategies professionals can use to support assertiveness skills:

- Use role playing and demonstrations to model assertive behaviors.
- Intervene before the occurrence of conflict and model how to solve problems in a positive way.
- Teach children when to seek the help of adults when confronted with challenging situations.
- Remind children that some behaviors (such as teasing and verbal provocations) are sometimes best ignored.
- Teach children how to use appropriate language with one another.
- Following a conflict, give children the opportunity to replay the scene. During the replay, model and offer suggestions for how the situation might have been resolved.
- Teach children how to stand up for themselves and not to give away objects or territory in response to aggressive behaviors.
- Identify acts of aggression and teach children not to accept them.
- Show children the importance of standing up for themselves using their self-concept and personal power.

During each of the five steps of conflict management, Janette used primary and secondary guidance strategies. This included designing an environment that had many options for play and assisting the boys in developing emotional self-regulation. Further, Janette used affective and behavioral reflections, choices, coaching, and social prompts to support conflict resolution.

Teaching children conflict resolution skills is an important part of supporting social-emotional development. The increasing prevalence of violence in children's lives and the accompanying decrease in models for appropriate conflict resolution makes supporting children in negotiating conflict an important part of the curriculum.

Despite your best efforts, some children may not respond to specific social skills and self-regulation interventions. These children may continue to frequently engage in challenging behaviors. These children require more intensive individualized intervention, representing the third phase of the DEC model.

INTENSIVE, INDIVIDUALIZED PLANS

Intensive, individualized interventions include identifying and addressing specific behaviors in a systematic way. Within the three levels of challenging behavior, children who require intensive, individualized plans often fall in the category of strong needs (Gartrell, 2006). The first step in developing interventions is to assess the child's behavioral challenges.

Kristin is a first-grade teacher who is concerned about Jack's behavior. On a daily basis, Jack seems to lose control of his emotions. When this occurs, he will often yell, scream, and strike out at persons and objects in his immediate reach. Kristin recognizes that to support Jack's positive behaviors, she needs to first gather additional information. Questions she needs to address include:

"Are there environmental factors that seem to trigger his behavior?"

"Does Jack lack necessary skills in interpreting and responding to situations?"

"What happens after his behavior has occurred, and what impact might this have on the behavior?"

Kristin's initial plan represents important components of **functional assessment**. Functional assessment is composed of five basic steps (Kern, 2007):

functional assessment
Five-step process designed to identify, intervene, and evaluate children's persistent challenging behaviors.

1. *Prioritize and define the challenging behavior.* For Kristin, this means that she must determine what the challenging behavior is, how harmful the behavior is to the child or others, how it might interfere with learning and activities, and if the behavior will impede positive social relationships and acceptance.

   Prioritizing and defining the behavior begins with Kristin's reflection on what it is that Jack does that is so challenging. Careful observation leads her to conclude that his tendency to yell when upset, throw objects, and hit other children are behaviors of particular concern. She concludes that this behavior is harmful not only to Jack, but also to other children in the classroom, and that his learning and participation in class activities is greatly affected by his behavior. Further, observation has led her to conclude that other children in the class are beginning to avoid Jack and refusing his attempts at playing with them.

2. *Conduct a functional assessment.* During this phase, information is gathered by professionals who know the child well. Techniques used during functional assessment include interviewing family members and other professionals who work with Jack and conducting careful observation.

   Kristin's functional assessment focuses on "what function (or purpose) does Jack's behavior serve?" To address this question, Kristin develops an observational plan that includes running records, time sampling, and event sampling. Running records are selected to get detailed information about Jack's behavior during a particular time period. Time sampling allows Kristin to zero in on points in the day that she feels might be problematic. Event sampling is used to give Kristin information about what happens before and after a specific behavioral event.

In addition, Kristin spends time talking with Jack's mother and grandmother, who drop him off and pick him up from school every day. Although they exchange general information during these times, Kristin views drop-off and pick-up times as important for basic communication. For more extensive conversations, she tries to create concentrated times around the family schedule, such as phone calls or private meetings. Questions she asks them during these periods include "Are you seeing this behavior at home?" "What happens when Jack engages in these behaviors?" "Is there anything that seems to trigger these behaviors?" "What happens after these behaviors occur?"

3. *Develop a hypothesis statement.* The third step in functional assessment is to develop a hypothesis, or theory, as to why specific behaviors might be occurring. Hypothesis statements include information on (1) what happens before a behavior occurs (its antecedents), (2) a description of the behavior itself, and (3) the presumed function the behavior serves.

The results of Kristin's observation and interview indicate that Jack seems to engage in challenging behaviors during times when there is less structure in the classroom. For example, center time and outdoor playtime seem to be challenging for Jack. The less teacher attention and feedback he receives during these times, the more likely his behavior is to occur. In his home environment, Jack displays the identified challenging behaviors during times when neither his mother nor his grandmother is readily accessible. This includes when they are preparing dinner or putting his younger sibling to bed.

Identifying the function Jack's behavior serves is a challenge to Kristin. On the one hand, it seems that his behavior gains him attention. On the other hand, Jack seems filled with regret when his behavior becomes out of his control. Kristin wonders if somehow his behavior helps him to internally regulate. In absence of external guides for behavior, it seems that Jack becomes distressed and is unable to deal with this distress in a constructive way. In turn, his inability to regulate these emotions causes increasing anxiety, resulting in the observed challenging behaviors. Interviews with his family indicate that this might be the case in the home environment as well. Therefore, Kristin formulates the hypothesis statement: "When Jack is in situations that lack external input and feedback for his behaviors, he becomes distressed and engages in challenging behaviors." This hypothesis statement not only reflects the assessment data Kristin has gathered, but also provides information about triggering environmental events and the resulting behavior.

4. *Develop a support plan.* Based on hypothesis statements developed in step 3, support plans include strategies for making changes to antecedent events in order to prevent problems and providing skills instruction to build appropriate behaviors and decrease the likelihood of the child engaging in inappropriate behaviors.

Kristin's support plan for Jack includes providing him with additional structure throughout the day. A picture schedule is developed for Jack, providing him with detailed, pictorial information about the day's activities and expectations during these activities. Further, Kristin provides Jack with a timer so he can monitor the time he will be spending in varied activities. She also develops a system where she will provide Jack with additional behavioral reflections during times that are challenging to him.

In addition to these strategies, Kristin provides Jack with specific social skills training to assist him in regulating his emotions. For example, she provides Jack with direct instruction on how to use the turtle technique when he is feeling anxious and alternative strategies when he does become upset. These alternatives include direct instruction on how to effectively deal with emotions when angry and suggestions for areas of the room he can go to when angry in order to regroup. To support co-construction between the home and school environment, Kristin works with Jack's family to develop these strategies and assists them in determining how to implement these strategies in their home environment.

5. *Implement, evaluate, and modify the plan.* Before implementing the support plan, the frequency of both the challenging behavior and the occurrence of social skills behavior are collected. Decisions are made regarding what would represent progress in the plan, and following initial implementation, data is collected on a regular basis to determine if the plan is having an impact.

Kristin uses the previously collected assessment data as a launch pad for identifying specific problems she will observe for and the list of social skills that she is targeting in the classroom. Observation provides her with the frequency of data before the intervention and a means of collecting data regarding Jack's progress.

After a 2-week period, Kristin notes that there has been a slight increase in Jack's use of targeted social skills strategies, accompanied by a slight decrease in challenging behaviors. Consultation with his family reveals that they too have noticed a slight change in Jack's behavior at home. Kristin recognizes that effective intervention takes

• • • BECOMING A PROFESSIONAL • • •

Career Pathways

Home School Facilitator

"My job at the center is the home–school facilitator—I make sure there is a link between what is happening in the home and what is happening in school. One of the things that I work on a lot is making sure parents know how important it is for their children to be in school. Sometimes people just think this is babysitting. They don't really realize how important it is for children's later success."

Matt has a variety of responsibilities in the early childhood program where he works. One of his main challenges is coordinating child, family, and teacher needs. Helping families is the heart of his job, and he works to make sure that the vital role families play in their children's lives is less stressful. "When parents are overwhelmed, kids can feel that. I can be there to talk to parents and help them discover the right track. In turn, this can reduce their stress and the stress on the child."

Matt's original field was broadcast journalism, and it was his passion for helping children and families that led him to the field of early childhood education. His place of employment provides support for tuition and books, helping him realize his dream of earning a bachelor's degree in early childhood education. "The number-one challenge I face in getting my degree is time and willpower. This is particularly an issue as I'm already working in the field. But I know where I want to go, and I know what I need to do to get there."

Matt's role as the home–school coordinator falls in the U.S. Department of Labor's Bureau of Labor Statistics (2007) area of social assistance. Employment in this area is expected to grow rapidly, particularly in the area of individual and family services. However, growth in this area depends on the amount of funding available, as many job opportunities are contingent on federal budgets that embrace social services and strengthening families.

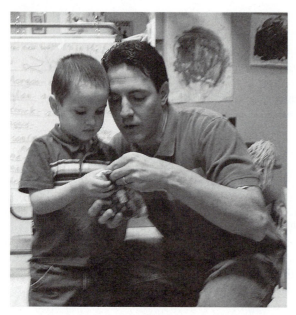

Relationships are the foundation on which effective guidance strategies are built.

time and that learning new skills, and extinguishing existing behaviors, is a significant process. Based on the improvements that she and Jack's family see, they decide to continue with the existing plan for one more month. At that point, they will determine if modifications are needed. Note that outside consultation from a behavioral specialist can be beneficial in understanding the source of behavioral challenges and developing a behavioral intervention plan.

Including Families in Addressing Challenging Behavior

The importance of including families as partners in supporting children's behaviors has been stressed. Families should be active participants in all areas of the process, beginning with identifying challenging behaviors and ending with implementing and evaluating interventions. When talking with families about a child's challenging behaviors, several practices need to be kept in mind (CSEFEL, 2006). To begin discussions with families, professionals need to express a concern about the child. In this conversation, they should focus on the behavior of concern and not on their reactions to the behavior or how they see this behavior affecting other children. In this light, professionals must be nonjudgmental and concrete in their description. They must communicate to families that their goal is to help the child and to let the family know that they are not solely responsible for addressing or "fixing" the child's behavior. At this point, the importance of partnership and working together to solve challenges a child is experiencing can be stressed.

Professionals should ask families if they have noted similar behaviors or situations and if they are also concerned about these behaviors. The goal of the conversation is for professionals to let the family know that they would like to work with them to help the child develop appropriate skills. The focus is on supporting positive behaviors, not addressing behaviors that may be viewed as negative.

Families need concrete information about what is happening in the classroom. When talking about behaviors, professionals should use language that includes "the child is having a difficult time" or "she seems to have challenges when. . . ." This language is preferred to "the child loses control" or "he always lashes out when. . . ." Professionals should conclude by offering to work with the family to develop a plan that supports the child's behavior at home and in school. The overall focus is creating continuity in partnership between the home and school environment.

MOVING FORWARD

In this chapter, you have learned about the importance of supporting children's social-emotional development. As social-emotional development is a predictor of school readiness and success, supporting literacy in these areas is of the utmost importance.

Successful strategies designed to support children's social-emotional development begin with understanding that children's behavior is influenced by a variety of factors. These factors include biology and the surrounding context (such as the early childhood environment and the family). From this foundation, supporting positive behaviors includes attention to universal practices, targeted toward all children in the classroom;

myeducationlab

Go to MyEducationLab and select the topic "Guidance." Under Building Teaching Skills and Dispositions, complete the exercises *Developing Guidance Skills* and *Helping Children Learn Social Skills*.

secondary interventions, supporting children who are at risk for developing challenging behaviors; and tertiary practices, addressing the challenging behaviors of children who have not responded to practices in place.

Supporting social-emotional development requires attention to relationships in the classroom and positive development between children and adults. Families are an essential part of the guidance process, with the knowledge that continuity between home and school is most likely to affect children's overall development.

CASE STUDY
Developing Relationships

The Child Development Lab and Learning Center: Infant and Toddler Classroom (6 weeks to 3 years)

Marian and Korissa believe that their most important role as early childhood professionals is supporting the relationship development of infants and toddlers in their classroom. From the moment a child enrolls in their classroom, one of the teachers becomes the child's primary caregiver. This role means that they will become the "expert" on that particular child and be responsible for making sure that his or her individual needs are met. Colin, for example, likes to be rocked and have his back patted when falling asleep. Marian makes sure that these needs are met by not only her, but also the other caregivers in the room should she be absent. Kendra needs cuddle time after waking up, and Korissa makes sure that ample time is provided to meet this need.

The children in their class are placed in their primary caregiving arrangements based on the age of the child, the hours the child is in the classroom, and the fit that exists between the child and a particular caregiver. Many of the children have picked their own primary caregiver, making it clear in their first days in the classroom which teacher seems to most effectively meet their needs. The teachers have tried to balance the children's ages in the mixed-age grouping format, recognizing four young infants for one and four older toddlers for the other might not create an effective match.

In addition to relationships with the teachers, the children are encouraged to develop relationships with one another. For infants, this includes supporting awareness of other children in the classroom through behavioral reflections: "I see you are looking at Grace," or "Jose just touched your leg." For toddlers, this awareness is further developed through behavioral reflections that comment on their interactions with other children: "You and Michael are pushing the truck together."

Affective reflections play an important role in supporting relationships in the classroom as well. A toddler in the throes of screaming at the top of his lungs while hitting the floor with his fist is told, "You look angry!" Another child who is hanging her head over her lunch is told, "You seem sad."

Getting along with others is another goal in the classroom, with the recognition that children's developmental needs shape behaviors. For example, the cries of "Mine!" in the classroom reflect toddlers' focus on autonomy. Because of the young children's focus on autonomy, Marian and Korissa recognize that sharing is not a feasible goal, but rather, prior to being able to share, the children need to learn true ownership of objects. This focus on true ownership reflects the idea that sharing comes from a place where children feel an object is theirs to give up.

Although the teachers have goals for children's interactions, there are no formal rules in the classroom. This is based on the recognition that a list of rules, for toddlers and infants, is an abstract concept that would not be grasped. Rather, the teachers use modeling and coaching to support such skills as using one's words to solve problems. Modeling includes showing children options for solving problems, whereas coaching provides children with the specific words they need to participate in their own problem solving. Coaching directions match the children's language capabilities, including "I want that" and "My turn please."

CONSTRUCTED-RESPONSE QUESTIONS

1. Identify the components of effective guidance and describe guidance strategies the CDLLC utilizes to support children's development and learning.

2. Explain the three levels of guidance practices and describe the strategies the CDLLC uses that apply to each of these levels.

CASE STUDY

Developing a Positive Behavioral Support Plan

Mulberry School: Multiage Classroom (1st through 3rd grade)

Tomaz is an 8-year-old in Brenda's and Pat's multiage classroom. By the end of the third week, other children in the classroom were calling Tomaz a bully and excluding him from many peer interactions. Tomaz's behaviors that have led to this label include calling other children names, taking toys away, and often becoming involved in physical altercations on the playground.

Brenda and Pat decide to develop a functional assessment to determine what behaviors are contributing to his challenges. This includes a brainstorming session where the teachers develop a list of challenging behaviors. Next, the teachers conduct a functional assessment, where they determine what happens before these behaviors and its consequences. Based on this, Brenda and Pat formulate a hypothesis statement that includes "When Tomaz is teased by other children, he often reacts in a physical manner. In addition, he seems to have difficulties entering groups to play and often chooses strategies that involve taking toys and physically interfering with children's activities. When these events occur, he appears to become agitated and uses physical strategies to problem solve."

Based on this assessment, the support plan Brenda and Pat develop includes helping Tomaz learn how to enter groups. Coaching is used to provide him with specific strategies, and the teachers will often shadow Tomaz to support strategy application. In addition, the teachers target children in the classroom who are often involved in the teasing, working with them on appropriate language and communication skills and coaching on how to be an effective community member.

Observational strategies to determine the effectiveness of their plan include documentation of Tomaz's defined challenging behaviors and the behaviors of children in the classroom that seem to trigger these behaviors. Observations are conducted biweekly, and the teachers meet and discuss on a weekly basis what progress has been made and what adaptations to their plan might be necessary.

CONSTRUCTED-RESPONSE QUESTIONS

1. Identify strategies that contribute to effective guidance and how the Mulberry School utilizes these strategies.

2. Explain the purpose of functional assessment and identify how the Mulberry School uses this kind of assessment.

REFLECTING ON AND APPLYING EFFECTIVE PRACTICES (NAEYC AND CEC/DEC)

Ethics

- Camilla is a 3-year-old in your preschool class. You have been increasingly concerned about her behaviors in the classroom, which include biting, kicking, and yelling at the other children. For the past several days, you have been observing and documenting these behaviors, and have noticed that the behaviors seem to be increasing. Throughout this process, you have been discussing your concerns with her family and working to determine if these behaviors are occurring in the home environment as well. This morning, her mother comes in and informs you, "We've decided that Camilla will be grounded if she misbehaves at school. Any trouble and its straight to bed without supper." When you respond that you were hoping to work together develop a plan to support Camilla's positive behaviors at home and school, she responds, "Well, we talked about this for a while and think it's best. So just give us a daily report on how she is doing." What would you do in this situation?

NAEYC Ideals: Ethical Responsibilities to Children
I-1.2. To base program practices upon current knowledge and research in the field of early childhood education, child development, and related disciplines, as well as on particular knowledge of each child.

NAEYC Ideals: Ethical Responsibilities to Families
I-2.6. To acknowledge families' childrearing values and their right to make decisions for their children.

DEC: Responsive Family Centered Practices
1. We shall demonstrate our respect and appreciation for all families' beliefs, values, customs, languages, and culture relative to their nurturance and support of their children toward achieving meaningful and relevant priorities and outcomes families' desire for themselves and their children.

Standards for Professional Practice

- The chapter states that social and emotional development is the core of the early childhood curriculum. Provide a brief (two to three paragraph) summary of the importance of children's social and emotional development as a foundation for development and learning.

NAEYC: Promoting Child Development and Learning
1a. Knowing and understanding young children's characteristics and needs.

DEC: Foundations
EC1K2: Trends and issues in early childhood education, early childhood special education, and early intervention.

- Several members of a community funding organization drop by your center for an observation. After they leave, one of the members calls you and comments on how the children seem to have too many choices and that there needed to be more direct consequences for children's behavior. He asked you if you were familiar with time-out and how he saw that as an effective punishment for young children. Briefly (two to three paragraphs) respond to the concerns this observer raised.

NAEYC: Building Family and Community Relationships
2a. Knowing about and understanding family and community characteristics.
2c. Involving families and communities in their children's development and learning.

- Supporting a child's social and emotional development requires knowledge of appropriate strategies, assessment, and reflection. This support not only occurs in direct interactions with children, but also in how you develop such things as classroom community and children's interactions with one another. What strategies do you feel are most effective in community building? How would you determine the effectiveness of these strategies?

NAEYC: Teaching and Learning
4a. Knowing, understanding, and using positive relationships and supportive interactions.

DEC: Learning Environments and Social Interactions
EC5S2: Organize space, time, materials, peers, and adults to maximize progress in natural and structured environments.
EC5S4: Structure social environments, using peer models and proximity, and responsive adults, to promote interactions among peers, parents, and caregivers.

DEVELOPING YOUR PHILOSOPHY

Develop a statement reflecting your beliefs regarding the importance of the social and emotional curriculum. Include in your statement what you see as your professional role in designing and supporting a curriculum that stresses social and emotional development.

DEVELOPING YOUR PORTFOLIO

Include in your portfolio each of the following:

- A description of five practices in the classroom structure that can support positive social and emotional development.
- A description of five practices between teacher and child that can support positive social and emotional development.
- A description of five practices in the early childhood environment that can support community building.

CHAPTER REVIEW

- ### What is social and emotional development, and how do these areas of development interrelate?

  Social development influences a child's interactions with others and their success in relationships, whereas emotional development refers to the ability to identify and understand internal emotions as well as respond appropriately to the emotions of others. The two influence one another—how one feels about oneself emotionally affects social interactions, and vice versa.

- **How do the theories of Maslow, attachment theorists, and Erikson provide a rationale for supporting social-emotional development?**

Each of these theories provides a rationale for supporting social-emotional development. From Maslow, we learn about the importance of foundational needs and how effectively meeting these needs allows children to develop more refined abilities. Attachment theory supports children's relationships, and Erikson's psychosocial theory emphasizes the child's need to master developmental tasks for social-emotional success. Together, each of these comprises an important model for supporting and understanding young children's successful interactions with others.

- **What role does guidance play in supporting children's development and learning?**

Guidance promotes children's positive concepts of self and successful interactions with others. Social-emotional development is linked to all other areas of development and learning, as how children feel about themselves and their relationships to others affects exploration, processing, and interaction with the environment. Therefore, effective guidance supporting social-emotional development also supports children's development and learning in all developmental domains.

- **What is the relationship between developmentally appropriate practice and positive guidance?**

Positive guidance strategies focus first on each individual child in the context of appropriate behaviors. In addition, positive guidance stresses that the behavior must be understood in the context it occurs within. Therefore, support for positive guidance mirrors DAP through understanding the individual child, developmentally appropriate behaviors, and the larger context.

- **How do practices at the primary, secondary, and tertiary level support children's social-emotional development?**

Guidance practices at the primary level focus on universal practices, which are applied to each child in the classroom community. At the secondary level, children who are at risk for social-emotional delays or the development of challenging behaviors are targeted. At the tertiary level, guidance strategies are targeted toward children who are persistent in their use of challenging behaviors. Strategies used at each of these levels ensure that children are receiving appropriate prevention and intervention strategies designed to support their individual needs.

- **What role do families play in the guidance process, and how can effective partnerships with families be developed?**

Families play a key role in the guidance process as continuity between home and school facilitates the success of strategies employed. Effective partnerships with families can be developed in a variety of ways, with ongoing communication providing an essential foundation.

11 The Learning Environment

"The greatest sign of success for a teacher is to be able to say,
'The children are now working as if I did not exist.'"

—MARIA MONTESSORI

The moment the door opens, Grace begins to take in the sights and sounds of her family child care home. Today the first thing Grace sees is the smiling face of her caregiver, Brenda, and Grace holds out her arms in greeting. After a few moments of snuggling with Brenda, Grace is down on the floor and crawls into the living room. There she is greeted by choices. Low shelving units are placed against the wall. Included on the shelves are large knobbed puzzle pieces to support her developing grasp, soft building blocks, and a basket filled with colorful scarves. She pulls the cloth blocks off the shelf and begins to arrange them in a teetering stack. Inevitably they fall, and Grace squeals at Brenda's response of "Uh-oh" each time the blocks scatter on the floor.

Dillon's preschool classroom is located in an old church basement, and is filled with choices as well. When the door to the room opens, he can see several play areas (referred to as learning centers) his teacher Ms. Hall has arranged in the classroom. Dillon's choices include playing with a variety of dress-up clothes and props in the dramatic play center, building and designing with the wooden blocks and plastic zoo animals in the block center, cozying up with a good book in the book corner, or spending a bit of time at the sand and water table. After considering his choices for a few moments, he chooses to join two other children in the dramatic play area. The wide pathways make it easy for him to negotiate the room in his wheelchair. As he approaches the other children, he is looking forward to this activity and the day ahead.

Anna has mastered her morning routine. Upon entering her kindergarten classroom, she picks up her writing journal and joins her group at their table. Journal time is a time of talking, sharing, and writing, and Anna writes and draws pictures of Olivia—her current favorite book character—in her journal. As she finished, she glances around the room, noting the different available activities. The class was doing project work on bugs, and Anna noticed that there were new bug books in the book corner. The science table also had something new—from Anna's vantage point, it looked like there might be an ant farm to explore. Just as Anna was about to move over to the science table, Mr. Gregory announced they were going outside. In his arms he carried a large box, filled with plastic magnifying glasses and specimen cups. Once outside, Mr. Gregory gave each child some exploring tools and suggested they go on a bug study. Anna chose to dig for bugs in the garden that she and her classmates had planted. It was under a row of tomatoes that she hit the jackpot: Three worms were gently pushing their way deeper into the sand. Anna watched their antics for several minutes and then used a clipboard and pencil located on the picnic table to document what she had seen.

● ● ●

Each of these children is interacting with the early childhood environment. For each of them, the environment supports different development and learning needs. For Grace, the activities in the physical environment are secondary to what she gets from interactions with her caregiver, Brenda. Trust and security are important to infants, and the time that Grace spends cuddling with Brenda, being sung to, and sitting in her lap provide her with information about quality relationships.

GUIDING QUESTIONS

• In what ways is the early childhood learning environment considered the third teacher?

• How has universal design contributed to understanding how learning environments affect children, families, and professionals?

• What general environmental design principles need to be considered in the goal of supporting children's development and learning?

• What specific environmental design principles need to be considered to support children's development and learning in the indoor environment? The outdoor environment?

• How does Maslow's hierarchy of needs contribute to conceptions of the social-emotional environment for young children, families, and professionals?

In Dillon's preschool learning environment, relationships he is forming with peers fulfill new developmental needs. Preschoolers need and thrive on friendships, and opportunities to interact in small groups allow children space to support burgeoning relationships. Dillon's relationship with his teacher is also important. She plays an important role in making sure Dillon's individual needs are met and that he participates equally in all indoor and outdoor activities.

Kindergartner Anna is developing new skills that support her independent interaction with the physical environment and negotiation in relationships with peers. Her increasing self-regulation skills mean that she can take responsibility for her own work and independently negotiate and interact with the environment and the people in it. Mr. Gregory, Anna's teacher, views himself as a guide. In this role he creates a learning environment that supports the development of self-regulation skills and peer relationships. Before the children arrive each morning, Mr. Gregory thinks about how the spaces and places in the room will meet the needs of the individual children and the classroom community as a whole. Not a morning goes by that he is not making some minor change. Today he added more Legos to the block corner to allow children to create an even larger structure. Yesterday he placed an extra pillow in the book corner to accommodate three children who seem to be increasingly enjoying one another's company as they poured over books.

Environments provide the context in which development and learning occur. In the field of early childhood education, the word *environment* refers to two very different factors—the physical and the social-emotional aspects of the *learning environment*. In part, the environment refers to the *physical aspects of a space*: Where are objects in the classroom placed? What kinds of toys and materials are in the classroom? What kinds of activities can children choose from? Are expectations for safety met? These same questions can be applied to the outdoor environment, where careful attention to activities, objects and materials, and safety is a must. The term *environment* also refers to *social-emotional aspects of the classroom*: How does the environment support children's needs for developing relationships? Security? Does the environment convey information about choices and limits, thereby supporting self-regulation skills? Are individual needs met, supported, and nurtured? Does the environment convey that all children belong and are important members of a larger classroom community?

Learning environments affect children through the spaces, attitudes, and atmospheres created for children's work and play. The environment affects families and professionals as well, with room arrangements, objects and materials, and décor contributing to messages that welcome or exclude, value or disregard, respect or ignore. Consider what the physical space offers to each of the professionals . . . for Brenda, her environment is her home. She needs to provide an environment that supports the developmental needs of each of the children in her care and her professional needs for comfort and interaction with children and families. Her rocking chair is one of the most used parts of her environment—the placement of a basket of books next to this chair supports interactions with individual children and the group. The old church basement in which Ms. Hall spends her days is a more institutionalized environment. Careful placement of nonpoisonous plants throughout the room, the use of warm soothing colors on the walls, and the creation of comfortable spots to gather with the children have contributed to the warmth and nurturance conveyed by her classroom. Mr. Gregory's environment is a traditional classroom in a public school. He strives to create a comfortable environment for everyone. In addition, observation and assessment are a daily part of his world, and he has designed his environment to facilitate access to needed materials supporting this goal.

The parents of Grace, Dillon, and Anna have unique needs in the learning environment as well. Grace's mom is still nursing and often takes breaks from work to meet Grace's feeding needs. The rocking chair is important to her, too: Here she and Grace spend comfortable bonding time. Dillon's mom is anxious about his inclusion in the preschool classroom. Ms. Hall's open-door policy means she can stop by anytime as a welcomed addition to the environment. Each visit she makes increases her comfort level, as her vantage point from the chair inside the classroom door assures her that Dillon is not only included, but also thriving. Anna's dad drops her off and picks her up every day. The space designed for family communication just beyond the classroom door allows him to learn about classroom happenings and touch base with Mr. Gregory on an ongoing basis about Anna's kindergarten world.

Well-designed learning environments play a critical role in achieving the goals of early childhood education, thereby providing high-quality services that meet the individual needs of each child. The role of the environment is viewed as so important that many researchers and theorists refer to learning environments as the "third teacher."

THE LEARNING ENVIRONMENT

The **learning environment's role as the third teacher**, with parents and teachers representing the first and second teachers, has been advocated throughout the history of early childhood education (Malaguzzi, 1994). One of the greatest proponents of the importance of the early childhood environment was Maria Montessori, who viewed careful attention to environment design as a critical component of building an effective classroom. Montessori's recommendations influenced a variety of design components: From the arrangement and placement of objects to the inclusion of child-sized furniture—Montessori left no area of the classroom unexamined. In a Montessori classroom, children are free to make their own choices, including working alone or in groups. Careful attention is paid to creating security and a sense of belonging. The teacher's role in the Montessori classroom is to carefully design the physical environment. Children are provided with a variety of sensory materials, such as blocks, Peg-Board, and yarn, and there is a strong focus on daily living activities. This focus is met through child-sized kitchen utensils, pots, pans, and plates to expose children to cooking activities and different-sized pieces of fabric to support cleaning and folding. Learning centers support children's interests, and each center is filled with objects and materials that facilitate active, hands-on exploration. By allowing children the opportunity to freely explore the carefully designed environment, teachers—who serve as guides in the environment—support children's drive for independence and responsibility.

learning environment's role as the third teacher
As part of a triad based on the child and the professional, the learning environment's role is thought to be equally important in supporting children's development and learning.

Well-designed learning environments engage young children.

Creating Effective Learning Environments

How can you as a teacher cultivate the learning environment's role as the third teacher? The foundational component of effective environments is access—without access to the environment, children and families will not benefit from all the environment has to offer.

Consider the needs of Dillon, the preschooler from our opening case. Dillon uses a wheelchair for mobility, and Ms. Hall needs to take that into account when designing the physical aspects of the environment. Can Dillon access different areas of the room in his wheelchair? Can he fully participate in activities in all areas of the environment? Are outdoor and indoor activities equally accessible? In addition to these physical aspects of the environment, Ms. Hall devotes attention to Dillon's social-emotional needs. Can he equally participate in room activities? Do space considerations take into account his wheelchair and accommodate his need to participate with small groups of children? Attention to the physical and social-emotional environment and Dillon's individual needs ensures equal access, and equal access ensures equity.

Access to the learning environment is also important to Dillon's mother. She plays an essential role in Dillon's development, and her participation and comfort in his education is of primary importance. Ms. Hall recognizes that families are the first and most important teachers for the children in her class, and her welcome extends to the families of all children in her classroom.

Designing effective physical and social-emotional environments is not a random process; rather, it is shaped by extensive research and theory. One of the most relevant bodies of knowledge supporting the development of early childhood environments is that of universal design.

universal design

Developed in the field of architecture, it ensures that all buildings are designed to meet the diverse needs of the populations using them.

Universal design was developed in the field of architecture. The goal was to ensure that all buildings were developed to meet the diverse needs of the populations who would be using them. For example, wide pathways and ramps allow for access for persons using wheelchairs for mobility and Braille panels in elevators allow use by persons who are visually impaired.

Seven principles support access and equity to buildings and products (Center for Universal Design at North Carolina State University, 1997). Each of these principles can be applied to environmental design in early childhood education and include that physical environments need to support:

- Equitable use
- Flexibility in use
- Simple and intuitive use
- Perceptible use
- Tolerance for error
- Low physical effort
- Size and space for approach and use

As each of these design factors has been well accepted and practiced in the field of architecture, they will serve as the organizing framework for our explorations of the physical environment.

The importance of the physical environment is matched in importance by the social-emotional environment. It is not hard to imagine a well-designed environment that leaves its occupants feeling uncomfortable, uneasy, out of place, or alienated. Again, consider Dillon. An environment might accommodate his physical needs for space, but if this is not complemented by a warm, enthusiastic, inclusive tone, the potential positive impact of the environment can be lost. For Dillon's mother, space might be provided for her to come and observe. However, without Ms. Hall's welcoming and accepting attitude, she might be less likely to feel comfortable in stopping by. The comfort—and appeal—of the environment Ms. Hall has created allows her to fully engage with the children and families during her 8-hour days.

We will now turn to the seven design principles, each of which plays a key role in ensuring equitable access to the environment.

Ensuring Equity

Children will not benefit from the environment if they cannot access all it has to offer. Access can also be thought of in terms of supporting both inclusion and flexibility. Careful attention to children's needs for access can ensure that all are included and that the environment's design is flexible. Further, providing access to each child ensures equity through supporting full participation and engagement in the environment.

One way that access is conceptualized and equity is supported, both in the field of early childhood and in larger society, is through the removal of barriers. The Americans with Disabilities Act (ADA) provides civil rights protections to individuals with disabilities in public places. As its main focus, the ADA supports the removal of physical barriers that keep people from equal participation in the public aspects of society.

How can physical access in the indoor environment be ensured? Consider the following:

- Can children physically access all areas of the classroom? Is there room to negotiate areas with a wheelchair? A walker?
- Can children who are new to walking—and a bit wobbly on their feet—safely access all areas? What about children who are crawling?
- Are materials in the room accessible to children? Are there a variety of choices in activities and materials resting on low shelves, making it easier for children to make their own selections and direct their own learning?
- For infants and toddlers, are materials arranged so they can be selected without worrying about pulling objects down on their heads?
- Are materials accessible in terms of logical placement and organization? For example, are all materials that might logically be found in the housekeeping area placed there? Are these materials organized and easy to access? Are the blocks neatly stacked in marked spots so children can easily make choices when designing structures and follow this organization system when they are putting objects away?

Accessibility focuses on the removal of physical barriers. Inclusion—another important tool of equity—focuses on the removal of social barriers (Christensen, 2003). Both need to be tended to in early childhood environments. Presently, laws such as the ADA ensure that physical access is supported; attention to social access requires careful consideration and appropriate action. A common effect of a child's disability is peer isolation, so attention to appropriate inclusion practices can serve to address this potential negative outcome (Christensen, 2003).

Indoor and outdoor environments produce unique challenges for children regarding access, inclusion, and flexibility. The attention given to maintaining access in outdoor environments has been more limited (Christensen, 2003). The most common methods for meeting outdoor ADA guidelines are transfer systems, where children are moved from one object to another (Christensen, 2003). Children similar to Dillon who use a wheelchair for mobility, for example, are likely to use an outdoor transfer system to move from one place to another. This transfer system typically involves being carried from area to area. This transfer system might accentuate Dillon's disability and place him in situations where his ability to participate in a way similar to his peers is significantly more noticeable.

Consider an outdoor environment where most activities provided focus on gross motor skills. In this environment are swings, a climber, and a slide. A riding path circles around the playground equipment, and there is blacktop area for basketball. Dillon's options in this environment are limited. His cerebral palsy means he has little controlled

---

TEACHING AND LEARNING CONNECTIONS

Supporting Social Access Outdoors

- Ensure a variety of outdoor play experiences supportive of each developmental and learning area.
- Provide choices based on children's interests, needs, and capabilities.
- Ensure that the indoor and outdoor environment mirror one another in terms of opportunities for learning.

---

movement in his legs, making climbing impossible. His teachers will often place him in the swing or assist him in sliding down the slide. However, the fact that he is carried to these activities and is unable to participate without their assistance serves to highlight his limited gross motor abilities.

How can social access be maintained in the outdoor environment? The following provisions are important:

- Varied play experiences that stimulate diverse play activities
- Activity choices outdoors mirroring those indoors, including art activities, block play, opportunities for dramatic play, games and puzzles
- Materials needed to support exploration of the outdoor environment, including tools for digging, collecting, and examining
- Materials and opportunities to plant and harvest

Without access, the attention paid to the physical and social environment is time primarily wasted. Once access is supported, professionals can turn their attention to the additional universal design factors.

Ensuring Flexibility in Use

Flexibility in use requires careful attention to the individual needs of children and the cultural context in which children are growing and developing. Based on children's developmental needs, the following are components of environments supporting flexibility in use:

1. Children are allowed to explore, experiment, and interact.
2. Children have opportunities for both work and play.
3. Many different areas of intelligence are reinforced through appropriate materials and activities, giving children opportunities to pursue and develop their own areas of strength.
4. Children's needs for independence and the development of secure relationships are supported through opportunities to independently explore and spend one-on-one time with primary caregivers and peers.

In addition to these broad goals, effective environments need to support the individual and cultural needs of each child in the classroom. In accordance with DAP, environmental design demands the consideration of children's ages, stages, individual needs, and cultural context. What information can the framework of DAP provide regarding environmental design?

DAP Revisited: The Needs of Children. Information regarding ages and stages is one important piece of designing effective environments. Ages and stages provide some information relative to young children, but additional knowledge of the child's individual development and cultural context provide the big picture. Because many of children's developmental needs relative to the environment remain constant, the fundamentals mentioned previously should be foundations for your practice.

Developmental Considerations for Infants. Infancy is a time of rapid growth and development. When thinking about an infant's environmental needs, you must consider each developmental domain.

Physical Development. For nonmobile infants who cannot access all an environment has to offer on their own, the role of the teacher is to bring the environment to the child. The teacher-caregiver must provide movement for infants to develop each of their senses and develop physical skills. For example, Brenda has two infants in her care. One is 10-month-old Grace, the other 3-month-old Ethan. When Grace sees something in the environment that interests her, she crawls over to the object of interest and looks at, touches, and often tastes it. Ethan is working on the developmental tasks of pushing up and rolling over. Brenda makes sure Ethan has extensive time on the floor to develop these skills. Brenda can tell from Ethan's enthusiastic gurgles and attempts at reaching when an object in the environment has caught his eye. Moving these objects to within his reach enables his reaching and grasping skills and allows him to more fully experience objects in the environment.

Many factors in the environment can impede these developing skills. Programs that have large numbers of infants relegated to few caregivers will often use swings, play pens, high chairs, and bouncy seats. Although these objects can be used to give children an important vantage point in the classroom, they should not be overused. These also interfere with healthy development by placing infants in positions they would not naturally find themselves in (Abbott & Bartlett, 2001). They can also prevent relationship building, as they remove opportunities for adults to be on the floor interacting with young children. As a rule of thumb, do not place children within these confining objects for more than 20 minutes total a day (American Academy of Pediatrics, 2004).

As infants age, the environment needs to further challenge their developing skills. Opportunities to crawl freely, pull up, and practice sitting in fall-safe areas are important. In addition, the mouth provides infants with sensory information about their world; as such, children need to have access to safe objects for this essential kind of exploration.

Social-Emotional Development. Relationships are as important to infants as food and water; therefore, designing an environment that effectively utilizes relationships is critical. This design should include couches, rocking chairs, and other comfortable places where professionals and children can spend quality one-on-one time.

Cognitive Development. An environment that supports the cognitive development of infants is one that provides opportunities for children to develop their senses in ways that are respectful of their overall need for stimulation. One of the most important factors to consider when designing environments that meet infants' cognitive needs is balance. Each of the senses needs to be challenged through stimulation but tempered by the need to protect the infant from overstimulation. Teachers need to pay careful attention to the signals infants give in response to the environment. Cries can indicate overstimulation, and looking away from objects can indicate an infant's need to regroup.

Developmental Considerations for Toddlers. Many of the environmental needs of toddlers build on those of infants. Despite continuity in development, where new skills build on existing ones, the period of toddlerhood represents a distinct developmental stage with its own unique needs.

Physical Development. The toddler's drive to explore the environment is often tempered by unsteady feet. To meet the physical needs of toddlers, environments must provide opportunities for toddlers to move around and exercise their developing walking (and running) skills. These areas must be free of objects likely to trip toddlers. In addition, the environment needs to provide the toddler with challenges for their developing skills.

Many of the skills that toddlers and older infants are developing can be augmented through environmental modifications. For example, crayons that are thin are likely to snap in the toddler's eager fingers, but the inclusion of thick crayons in the room can help the toddler develop the skill of drawing. A teacher might encourage toddlers to pour their own milk during snack time. The use of weighted pitchers designed to assist pouring skills can help to get more milk in the cup and less on the table.

Social-Emotional Development. Toddlers become focused on independence, and in any toddler classroom you can often hear the cry of "MINE" being chanted repeatedly. The environment should provide opportunities for autonomy to develop and, therefore, should have adequate toys and materials for toddlers to use individually. Often, teachers spend time telling toddlers to share; however, learning to share at this age is not an appropriate developmental goal. For toddlers to develop the ability to share, they first need to learn true ownership. In addition to

Stimulating environments for infants and toddlers allow action and interaction.

having duplicates of toys, games, and materials, the environment should be designed so that toddlers may interact with these materials on their own.

In addition to fostering independence, teachers must encourage toddlers to fulfill their need to play. Because toddlers engage in solitary and parallel play, large group interactions should be minimized or eliminated from the environment completely. When teaching in a toddler environment, supervise interactions with other toddlers.

Cognitive Development. Like infants, toddlers need environments rich in language and stimulating materials to effectively develop their senses and knowledge of the world around them. During toddlerhood, cultivating exploration requires that the environment provide stimuli for all areas of their developing bodies and minds. With exploration being the driving objective, teachers should fill the environment with opportunities for toddlers to exercise their increased ability and desire to create impact. Materials that toddlers can manipulate such as puzzles, play dough, and goop (made with cornstarch and water) can be welcome additions. With increased independence comes toddlers' increased interest in trying out new roles: A well-stocked dress-up area can support developing imaginations. Toddlers are becoming increasingly verbal, and their communication should be both encouraged and responded to. Verbal labels remain an important part of the toddler environment and aid their ever-expanding vocabularies. Literacy skills—composed of reading, writing, speaking, and listening—should also be a focus of teaching practices and environmental design. An environment that includes appropriate labels that contain the written and pictorial representations is one way to develop literacy. For example, children's cubbies should be labeled with both their name and a selected picture. Children will first focus on the picture and, over time, come to associate their name with the picture. Eventually, toddlers gain the understanding that their name is composed of symbols and that these symbols represent one designation of who they are.

Developmental Considerations for Preschoolers. As children grow and develop, many of their environmental needs remain stable. Consequently, preschool environments will share many characteristics with environments developed for infants and toddlers.

Physical Development. Preschoolers may have many of their basic developmental skills in place. For example, they typically can walk from place to place in the environment, have the reaching and grasping abilities to select items to interact with, and can engage in

myeducationlab

Go to MyEducationLab and select the topic "Emergent Literacy and Language Arts." Under Activities and Applications, watch the video *Creating a Print Rich Environment* and consider how you can apply this information in your own early childhood environment.

TEACHING AND LEARNING CONNECTIONS

Creating Effective Physical Environments for Toddlers

- Provide extensive opportunities and materials for children to practice their developing motor skills, including tools and materials for drawing and cutting, space for running and skipping, and equipment for climbing.

- Provide extensive choices and duplicate materials. For example, make sure that children have two to three choices at any given time and that there are duplicates of the most popular toys and materials.

- Focus on small group interactions.

- Provide materials that toddlers can successfully manipulate, such as large knobbed puzzles, thick crayons, and wide, weighted pitchers.

- Utilize language, songs, finger plays, and books to support literacy.

TEACHING AND LEARNING CONNECTIONS

Creating Effective Physical Environments for Preschoolers

- Provide tools and opportunities for preschoolers to develop burgeoning skills, including drawing, writing, and cutting materials; balls, jump ropes, and objects to balance on; and plenty of space to run, jump, and skip.
- Create opportunities for targeted social skills development in pairs and small groups.
- Provide opportunities and materials for experimentation, including large tweezers and magnifying glasses, binoculars, cylinders of different shapes, funnels, and malleable materials such as water, sand, and dirt.
- Use questioning and discussion as language-building opportunities.

---

selected activities in proficient ways. In preschool, children refine and expand their skills. In addition to walking, children often add hopping and skipping to the mix. Preschoolers need heavy materials that allow them to lift, push, and pull, supporting vestibular development (balance) and sensory integration. The scribbles that dominate the toddler stage become increasingly defined, so teachers must provide increased opportunities to write, draw, and cut. A well-stocked art area with a variety of tools at children's disposal can support these skills.

Social-Emotional Development. During the preschool stage, many children move from parallel to more cooperative play. This developmental stage includes an increased interest in peers. Because children do not innately know how to form complex relationships, they need to be taught a skill set that supports peer interactions. What are important skills to consider? Preschoolers must learn how to enter and exit a group, how to sustain play, how to introduce a topic of play, and how to negotiate disagreements as they arise. Children must have opportunities to interact in small groups that, at times, are teacher facilitated.

Cognitive Development. Preschoolers have an endless need to experiment. The environment encourages children's explorations and allows them to develop thinking skills. Open-ended materials, objects to build and manipulate, and materials to combine and dissect each provide children with needed feedback. Preschoolers' language skills continue to develop, and children have words to express wants, feelings, and perspectives. The teacher needs to extend language interactions through questioning and discussion. An environment filled with the written and spoken word supports literacy. Children should have ample opportunities not only to explore books, flannel boards, dramatic play props, stickers, or stamps to create books, but also to practice writing skills.

Developmental Considerations for Kindergartners. Kindergarten children often face distinct challenges. Many are functioning for the first time in a formal school setting. This setting might bring with it challenges regarding functioning in a large group and independently meeting curriculum expectations.

Physical Development. New friendships and group activities challenge kindergartner's physical skills. Organized sports may begin in kindergarten (or even sooner!) with many playground activities requiring complex physical ability. Throwing, catching, kicking, jumping rope, and playing hopscotch are a few playground favorites; the

• • • BECOMING A PROFESSIONAL • • •

Career Pathways

Preschool Teacher, International Schools

Tracey's role as a teacher of 4- and 5-year-olds is similar to many teaching roles in the United States. Her program follows the Illinois Early Learning Standards, and she and her assistant teachers work to support the developing English skills of many of the children in her care. One thing that makes Tracey's work unique is its location. She teaches at the American School of Kuwait, and her job, in addition to the rewards of working with the children and their families, has presented many unique opportunities. "Working in the International School System has been an incredible opportunity. I've been able to travel the world and have learned so much about different cultures and the people in them."

The children in Tracey's classroom are from different countries, including Lebanon, Pakistan, Sweden, and Indonesia. Many of these children are English language learners, and many of their parents have identified that they want them to learn English with an American accent. Tracey is not bilingual, but two of her assistants are—one speaks Urdu and understands Arabic, and the other speaks Taiwanese, Chinese, and English.

Many of the children in her classroom come in with developing English proficiency skills. Tracey finds that songs and games and the creation of a print-rich environment have supported the developing language skills of each child. Tracey reports that interactions with other children are often the children's best teacher. It is the conversations that occur in the block area or science center, for example, that seemed to create opportunities for their English proficiency skills to blossom.

Tracey has been in the field of early childhood education for the past 15 years. She started in Head Start and then worked in private preschools. Her CDA was begun during her Head Start years, and she completed her associate's degree while working in private preschools. At this point in her career, she is pursuing her bachelor's degree in the United States through an online educational program.

Tracey feels fortunate to have been able to tap into the International School System and feels that this is an incredible opportunity that many early childhood professionals are not aware of. She found out about these opportunities through a recruiting fair.

Tracey's professional journey was supported by two main factors. The first of these was that she carefully considered each of her places of employment, looking for a match between her own and their philosophies of early childhood education. Tracey also greatly benefited from mentors along the way: "I have worked with wonderful people who have been amazing mentors and have found this to be of tremendous help."

teacher's challenge is to provide children with noncompetitive opportunities to develop these skills.

Social-Emotional Development. Kindergarten children are often expected to function independently in a large group setting. The teacher needs to provide children cues, including well-organized routines and choices that help develop these expectations of autonomy. Children need concrete opportunities to complete work at their own pace and

Environments for kindergartners need to be organized and support autonomy and creativity.

organization strategies that help them work toward their individual goals.

In addition, kindergartners engage in cooperative play, and friendships often define the social climate. Environments that provide for small group activities can enable their interactions.

Cognitive Development. In kindergarten, emerging literacy skills include the growing recognition of letters, numbers, and words. Kindergartners develop the ability to represent their own ideas through the written word, and environments that foster literacy skills provide kindergartners a variety of opportunities to represent their thoughts. Journals, classroom pen pals, and writing workshops give children opportunities to write about things important to them, and their own interests provide kindergartners key motivation.

Developmental Considerations for Children in the Primary Grades. Children in the primary grades must independently regulate their work and function autonomously in groups. As in each of the previous stages, the primary grade environment needs to encourage students' independence and ability to take care of their own needs. Their ability to function autonomously as a member of a group also needs to be supported. Opportunities for exploration and experimentation are essential for children to make sense of the world around them.

Physical Development. Children in the primary grades continue to refine their gross and fine motor abilities. As many of their abilities to function effectively in the classroom environment are contingent on these abilities, teachers need to ensure that development is progressing and that challenges are addressed. For example, writing abilities are shaped in part by appropriate fine motor grasp, and the child's ability to function in physical games with rules requires attention to developing gross motor abilities.

TEACHING AND LEARNING CONNECTIONS

Creating Effective Physical Environments for Kindergartners

- Provide plenty of noncompetitive activities, including cooperative games and opportunities to work together toward classroom goals (such as starting recycling in the classroom or planting an indoor herb garden).

- Support children in meeting individual goals through direct instruction supporting appropriate pacing and organizational strategies, for example, teaching children how to monitor how effectively they are reaching a goal and how to organize their work in folders.

- Promote positive peer relationships through community building and constructing positive peer interactions.

- Provide opportunities to represent words through written means.

TEACHING AND LEARNING CONNECTIONS

Creating Effective Physical Environments for Children in the Primary Grades

- Ensure that developing skills are supported through materials and opportunities. For example, measuring skills are supported through easy access to rulers and graph paper, and literacy skills are supported through access to a variety of books.

- Provide a strength-based curriculum and support for self-esteem.

- Provide integrated curriculum supporting connections across and between content areas. For example, a project on exploring water wells integrates literacy, mathematics, and the arts.

- Support developing self-regulation skills through schedules and child-created lists.

Social-Emotional Development. The requirement that children function independently in a group becomes even more pronounced during the primary years. Ever-developing peer relationships require increasing social skills, and emotional self-regulation is a predictor of successful interactions. Attention to children's success at navigating the social environment is a key role of the teacher, and interventions, should they be needed, are targeted toward successful peer interaction. A strength-based curriculum, important throughout early childhood, can support acceptance for children's unique ways of viewing and interacting with their world.

Cognitive Development. Literacy skills continue to develop, and children in the primary grades benefit from an integrated curriculum that allows them to form connections between content areas and the larger world. Academic self-regulation becomes an important goal, concurrent with children's needs to function more independently in the environment. Similar to emotional self-regulation, these skills need to be taught. Teachers need to both break down tasks involved in mastery of a topic matter and support the ability to monitor one's own progress toward an academic goal. Physical reminders of daily tasks can support academic self-regulation, including child-created lists and schedules of daily topics presented and weekly task expectations.

Supporting Knowledge of Individual Children. Knowledge of children's development in general, although useful, cannot replace knowledge of individual children in particular. Information on ages and stages can provide useful guidelines. Knowledge of individual children, presented holistically and composed of the interrelationship between different areas of development, provides the cornerstone to effective practice.

How can knowledge of individual children be acquired? You've learned that observation and assessment strategies play an important role in knowing and understanding individual children. You've also learned that by building relationships with young children, professionals learn about their needs and preferences and build foundations of trust and security that developmental practices can build on. Further, reflective practices, such as the ones discussed in Chapter 7, support the evaluation of children's development. Together, assessment, relationships, and reflection provide tools to support knowledge of each child as a unique individual.

Supporting Knowledge of the Cultural Context. In addition to knowledge of ages, stages, and individual development, DAP includes knowledge of the child's cultural context. How can this knowledge be integrated into the early childhood environment? Knowledge of the cultural context emerges from knowledge of children's families. Space for teachers and families to conference, exchange information, and develop mutual relationships is important in environmental design.

Ensuring Simple and Intuitive Use

Simple and intuitive use ensures that the design of the environment is straightforward and intuitive for children and staff and that adopted design principles support children's development and learning.

Supporting Learning Through the Senses. You learned in Chapter 4 that the senses play a significant role in children's development and that a carefully designed environment supports children's exploration through their senses. In the field, the areas of visual and tactile development often receive the most attention. Brightly colored items and carefully selected objects meant for little hands to explore often adorn early childhood classrooms. Certainly, the senses of sight and touch are important, but attention to these senses should not eclipse inclusion of sound, smell, and taste in the environment. Lack of knowledge about what best engages children's senses leads to a misuse of visual and tactile objects.

When designing environments that accommodate children's senses, consider the following guidelines (Council on Rural Services, 2006):

- **Sight:** Brain research demonstrates that children respond to various colors in a variety of ways. When planning the colors for a classroom, think about the amount of time children might spend in the environment each day and the program objectives. Brightly colored walls, often a staple in early childhood environment because of the idea that primary colors communicate "kid space," serve to make children more alert. However, for children spending a long time in a brightly colored classroom, these colors might actually interfere with their ability to concentrate. More subdued colors such as beige, salmon, and gray can have an overall calming effect, harnessing children's attention and concentration.
- **Touch:** A sensory-rich environment gives children a variety of tactile experiences. These tactile experiences provide important information to children about their world. Incorporating a variety of textures accompanied by verbal labels can provide children with needed information. For example, placing contact paper sticky side up in an infant environment can provide a surprise for the crawling child. As the child touches the contact paper, using the word *sticky* can connect the sensory experience with a new vocabulary word.
- **Taste:** Allowing children to explore a variety of different tastes can give them information about likes and dislikes and augments their developing vocabularies. Young children learn about objects by placing them in their mouths, and infants and toddlers are likely to taste anything within reach. Because of this drive for mouth exploration, safety is paramount, and anything infants and toddlers can access needs to be safe for this exploration to occur. For older children, exposing them to a variety of different tastes can help develop a diverse palate. From tasting lemons, children can learn sour; raw potatoes can teach bland; nutmeg can provide a connection to the word *bitter*. Of course, allergies are an important consideration, and taste-learning experiences must take information about allergies into account.

TEACHING AND LEARNING CONNECTIONS

Creating a Supportive Sensory Environment

- Use subdued colors and tones on the walls and floor coverings to support children's attention and concentration.
- Provide plenty of opportunity for tactile stimulation.
- Allow children to explore a variety of different tastes and textures. (Note of caution: Be aware of potential allergies.)
- Support the sense of smell through subtle background odors.
- Encourage children to tune in to sounds of the environment and be sure noise levels, such as music in the background, are supportive of attention and concentration.

- **Smell:** Different smells stimulate the brain in different ways. For example, peppermint, orange, and cinnamon make us more alert, whereas chamomile, lavender, and rose have a calming effect. Incorporate the sense of smell into the environment by adding scents to play dough and paints, having potpourri (out of children's reach), and using slow cookers with apples or orange slices and spices in the environment.
- **Hearing:** There are a variety of sounds that can be included in the environment—child-created and/or recorded songs, rain pattering against the pavement, or the whistling of birds outdoors. Children can be taught to "tune in" to different sounds in the environment, and both the natural and teacher-created worlds provide endless opportunities. Be careful not to overstimulate. The sounds in the environment need to complement the activity—for example, calm, soothing music for nap time, catchy tunes for movement.

How can attention to these senses be included in the early childhood environment? An important balance must be struck. Overstimulation can interfere with the child's focusing ability; however, **multisensory** experiences—such as red, peppermint-scented play dough with kosher salt for texture—best enhance children's learning. Teachers must observe each child and make sure that the level of sensory stimulation meets his or her individual needs.

multisensory
Providing stimulation for a variety of the senses.

Supporting Play and the Learning Needs and Preferences of Each Child. How can environments support children's play and unique ways of interacting with materials and each other? The answer is as broad as the multitude of different needs children bring to the classroom but as simple as careful attention to design and selection of materials that allow children to interact with their surroundings. The ways children act on an environment and how they choose to experiment and process the material in it is determined by the individual child, based on his or her own needs. A good environment will provide children with a variety of options that encourage their varied explorations. The richer and more diverse the possibilities offered to children, the more children will gain in terms of knowledge, understanding, and the meaning of place and space in their own lives (Cosco & Moore, 1999). Careful attention to material selection, activity center design, and area placement (covered in more detail later in the chapter) ensures that the environment provides extensive options.

anti-bias
Curricular approach that nurtures each child by actively addressing issues of diversity and equity in the classroom.

ISSUES OF ACCESS AND EQUITY
An Environment Supporting Anti-Bias

Treating others with dignity, equity, and respect are important behaviors for society. Unfortunately, we live in a world of bias where people are discriminated against because of age, gender, ability, race, socioeconomic factors, and a myriad other differences and similarities among people. **Anti-bias** education not only embraces teaching children about the diverse world around them, but also advocates that individual members of society—including children—effectively stand up and work to eradicate biases.

Early childhood classrooms can demonstrate bias in a variety of ways—through how people and cultures are represented to the messages that are conveyed to children about person's differences and similarities to how children are taught to respond to diversity in society. The child who asks, for example, "Why is she in a wheelchair?" and is told to "Shhh!" gets a very clear message about things that are okay to talk about. She also gets the message that things that are different are perhaps construed as shameful and should be ignored.

According to the Anti-Defamation League (2006), "Anti-bias education takes an active, problem solving approach that is integrated into all aspects of an existing curriculum and a school's environment." To eliminate biases, careful attention must be paid to the formal curriculum. Evaluation includes examination of what is taught to children, how they are assessed, and what is expected regarding learning and behavior. The hidden curriculum includes more covert messages about bias. These messages are conveyed through what holidays are celebrated and how males and females are represented in the picture books around the room. All aspects of the early childhood curriculum, from holiday practices to classroom materials, need be examined and changed if teachers truly wish to implement anti-bias curriculum.

Hohensee and Derman-Sparks (1992) suggest a three-phase process, which begins with teachers examining their own biases and biases implicit in the program. Important in this process is not only learning more about yourself, but also becoming more aware of children's ideas of diversity. In addition, looking at the classroom environment and making changes that support anti-bias are important. Changes might include the pictures on the walls and toys and materials present in the classroom.

During the second phase, the focus becomes capitalizing on "teachable moments" or implementing teacher-initiated processes to address bias as it emerges. Again, this phase requires ongoing communication and self-reflection.

Finally, in the third phase ongoing, systematic anti-bias planning becomes a part of the overall curricular goals. To best support anti-bias practices and education, all members of the classroom community—children, families, and professionals—must be included in the process.

Providing Feedback. As the third teacher, what might be the environment's teaching role? Environments, although they are inanimate, can provide children with feedback for their actions. Consider again the work of Urie Bronfenbrenner—the ecological systems theory—regarding bidirectionality. The child affects his or her environment and is, in turn, affected by the environment.

Based on bidirectionality, for example, children's actions provide opportunities to learn about cause and effect. An 8-month-old who throws a rattle onto the floor from a high chair hears a crash and, peering over the edge, sees that the rattle is now on the floor. The environment naturally provides a lesson in object permanence, where children learn that an object exists even when out of their sight.

Consider the 3-year-old who pours sand through a funnel and watches the slow stream as the sand makes its journey through the narrow end. The funnel, in this case, serves as a conduit not only for the sand but also for the child's knowledge of the funnel's function.

Observe the first grader study the butterfly garden he and his classmates have developed. On one side of the black-eyed Susans that border the garden, the children, with the assistance of their teacher, have prepared a natural soap mixture to ward off June beetles. On the other side, nature has run its course without the interference of their natural bug treatment. The result? On the treated side, the plants' leaves appear sturdy and intact. On the untreated side, the leaves display a polka-dot pattern of holes where the bugs have eaten through the leaves.

TEACHING AND LEARNING CONNECTIONS

Tools in Early Childhood Environments

- Tools for exploration
  - Science set, including magnifying glasses, tweezers, containers, and pencils and paper for documentation
  - Blocks and building materials
  - Woodworking bench
  - Pottery wheel and clay
  - Musical instruments
  - Sociodramatic materials supporting exploration, such as scientist coat, explorer hat, camera, and butterfly net
- Tools for communication and representation
  - Writing materials, tape recorders, and cameras to document and support communication
  - Graphing materials
  - Materials to cut, glue, and create
  - Card and board games
  - Mail centers, including mailbox and envelopes for letter writing and delivery
  - Sociodramatic materials supporting communication play, including mail carrier outfit, bag for mail, and art smock
- Tools for numeracy and letter identification
  - Books, books, books!
  - Alphabet and number sequences posted in room and on tables supporting letter and number production (appropriate for older children)
  - Manipulatives and materials for use in counting, sequencing, and problem solving

Across the curriculum:
- Art area that includes wide variety of art and craft materials supportive of open-ended creation
- Literature that complements and extends children's interests

In each of the above cases, children learn from their actions, and the environment serves as a teacher. This learning requires that environments be designed to cultivate feedback. Just as a teacher needs to observe the effects of the environment on children, he or she also needs to teach children to pay careful attention to the feedback the environment gives them.

Including Tools and Supporting Skill Development. Tools are devices that support the achievement of the developmental task. Scissors, for example, are a tool. Language can also be thought of as a tool, as can pencils and crayons. Tools can provide a rich foundation for exploring, developing, and practicing the myriad skills children are expected to develop. These skills can include:

- How to physically navigate the environment
- How to get along with others
- How to communicate and be understood
- Different means of representation (including the written word)
- How to use these skills to communicate ideas
- Basic concepts of numeracy and letter identification

Ensuring Perceptible Use

The environment communicates information to children in a variety of ways. This information is perceptible, representing something the child can understand, process, and interact with. Supporting perceptible use means paying careful attention to how the child perceives things and designing the environment accordingly.

What strategies can be used to ensure perceptible use? Begin with consideration of the developmental needs of each individual child. All children present unique needs in the early childhood classroom, and focusing on these unique needs can lend insight into how the environment can meet those needs. Table 11.1 outlines different developmental needs and how these might be met through perceptible use.

The developmental needs and examples listed in Table 11.1 are an organizing tool for presenting information on perceptible use. The strategies suggested are not a representative discussion of what each child with a developmental need require, rather, the suggestions are intended to represent what all children might need.

Ensuring Tolerance for Error

The universal design application of tolerance for error means that the environment is safe and free from hazards. There are many sources of information about safety in early childhood environments. Each state has its own licensing requirements that ensure that basic health and safety principles are met. In addition, organizations such as the American Academy of Pediatrics and the National Consumer Product Safety Commission (CPSC) have instituted safety guidelines. Interest in guidelines that ensure the safety of all children emerged from data indicating that safety hazards are prevalent in child care programs (CPSC, 1999). Table 11.2 on page 334 summarizes broad considerations derived from the CPSC guidelines.

These issues represent a few considerations of safety in the early childhood environment. The National Program for Playground Safety publishes a list of requirements for outdoor programs. The National Child Care Information Bureau publishes a list of safety considerations for indoor programs.

TABLE 11.1 Individual Learning Needs Related to Developmental Need and Strategies for Supporting Perceptible Use		
Developmental Need	**Learning Need**	**Potential Accommodation to Support Perceptible Use**
Hearing impairment	Child's ability to process auditory stimuli and communicate verbally can be affected.	• Ensure that the child can see persons speaking and activities. • Include visual aids such as pictures and signing in environment. • Use physical prompts when appropriate to communicate.
English language learners	Child's ability to process verbal and written information in language other than the child's primary language.	• Include written materials in the child's primary language in and English. • Use pictures to communicate transitions, label objects, and assist in child choice.
Learning differences	Child's ability to process visual and auditory materials.	• Use audio, visual, and hands-on learning to communicate information. • Break down tasks in the environment and provide labels for each portion of a task.
Visual challenges	Child's ability to process visual stimuli in the environment.	• Consult with parents to determine what the child can see, for example, shadows, color, or large pictures. • Design environment to accommodate sight abilities: large pictures and labels, highly contrasting colors. • Use tactile stimuli such as floor colorings and mobiles to communicate different areas of the environment. • Check lighting where the teacher is sitting, the glare on materials, and the distance and size of items used.
Autism	Child's ability to relate to and process social and emotional environment and high need for environmental routine.	• Design environment that is well organized, with classroom areas well marked and labels used to mark areas and objects in the environment. • Use visual and auditory cues to signal transitions and environmental expectations.

Source: Based on Cook, R., Klein, M., & Tessier, A. (2004). *Adapting early childhood curricula for children in inclusive settings.* (6th Edition). Upper Saddle River, NJ: Merrill/Prentice Hall.

Ensuring safety means looking at the physical aspects of the environment and objects and materials placed in the environment. Teachers must have knowledge of poisonous items, including ammonia, bleach, furniture polish, rhubarb leaves, and azaleas and make sure these objects are not within children's reach. Teachers also need to know the location of and how to use emergency equipment, including electric fuse boxes, exits, fire extinguishers, and first-aid equipment.

Prevention is one of the most effective ways to ensure children's safety. Effective outdoor play supervision can ward off many injuries. Program staff needs to determine their own plan for outdoor supervision (Kern & Wakeford, 2007). The following should be considered when developing this plan:

• Establish a small work group or committee responsible for evaluating current issues and developing an appropriate plan.
• Use a democratic or collaborative process for developing the plan and making final decisions, ensuring that there is consensus about implementing the plan.

Selecting appropriate toys for children does not mean spending a good deal of money. There are a variety of inexpensive sources for good, safe toys; garage sales provide a good buying opportunity. However, buyers must be cautious to check for recalls, missing safety features, or broken pieces. In addition, homemade toys can be a wonderful addition to the environment.

Supporting Size and Space for Approach and Use

Environments that take into consideration size and space for appropriate use accommodate the needs of individual children. You have learned important information on how the environment can support children's learning. You will now explore how to design the environment to ensure that it meets the needs of each child in the classroom. Because of children's individual needs, what works effectively with one class may not be as effective in another. Like any work of art, the exact recipe can never be duplicated; however, well-applied skills and techniques can serve to strengthen each environmental creation. We will now look at the knowledge, skills, and techniques needed to create a vibrant indoor environment.

THE INDOOR LEARNING ENVIRONMENT

Since many children spend the bulk of their days indoors, this environment must serve many purposes. These purposes might include sleeping and eating, but also must include experiences that assist development and learning.

Room Arrangements and Floor Plans

Many factors are important when designing indoor environments. When considering room arrangements and floor plans, space, amount of choice, circulation patterns, and balance are important.

Space. Each state has its own requirements for the amount of space per child, but most have adopted an allocation of 35 sq ft per child (White & Stoeklin, 2003). The blanket adoption of 35 sq ft per child is directly contradicted by most research on classroom size, which stresses that 45 to 50 sq ft per child is most appropriate (Butin, 2000).

How does space affect children's behavior and learning? Crowded spaces with too many children invite conflict, whereas adequate space can support the child's positive interactions with both environment and peers. Fundamentals for thinking about space include the following:

- Space should be designed to fit the overall needs and goals of the classroom. Therefore, space should be allocated for interacting with materials and include opportunities for large and small group and individual play.

learning centers
Small defined areas of the classroom that support targeted learning or types of play.

- Each classroom space should be designed in smaller "learning areas," which are often referred to as **learning centers** or activity areas. These should offer specific areas of learning and types of play and should provide children with both adequate materials and clear definitions of where the space begins and ends.
- Spaces in the classroom should be flexible to encourage children's imaginations and need for exploration. It is important to avoid absolutes such as "all housekeeping materials stay in the housekeeping area" or "blocks can be used only in the block area." Rather, establishing guidelines such as "all materials need to be returned to their original places" allows children to freely explore and create but also addresses the need for overall organization.

Figure 11.1 provides a sample of a room arrangement.

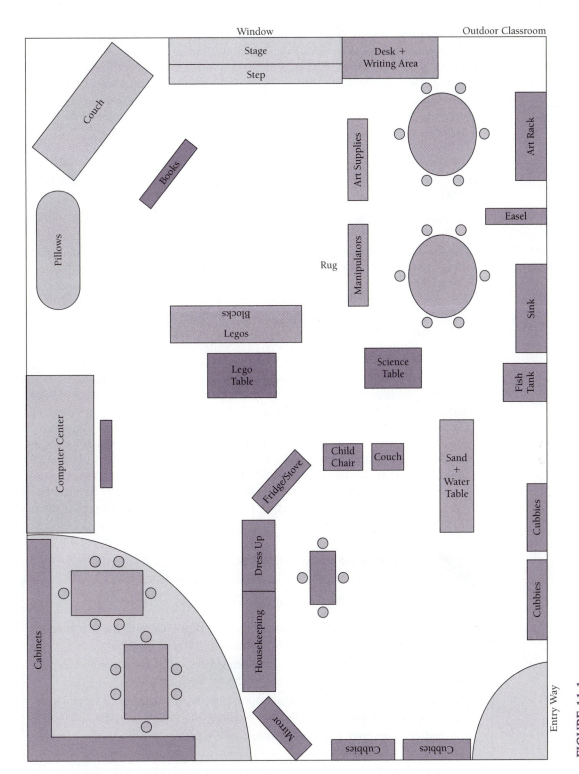

FIGURE 11.1
Room Arrangement for Toddlers

337

Amount of Choice. The amount of choice in a classroom includes the number of options children have for engagement at any particular point in time. Although there are some periods of time (such as lunch and nap) where choices might be limited, providing some choices, even during these periods of time, can have an overall positive impact on classroom transitions and children's behavior during these transitions. During nap, for example, quiet activities such as looking at books or coloring at the art table could be included. That many children are sleeping means that quiet activities need to occur; however, the environment also should accommodate those children who do not need a nap.

Choice affects engagement and children's interactions with one another. Too few choices can promote crowding in particular areas and can result in conflict instead of engagement. Conversely, too many choices can promote indecision. Some fundamentals for thinking about choice include the following:

- The number of choices in the classroom should be based on the number of children. At any given time, each child should have two to three choices.
- The choices in the environment should have natural boundaries. For example, if there is space for two children in the computer center, two chairs should be placed there.
- The choices presented in the classroom need to reflect overall classroom goals and children's individual needs and interests. Therefore, although a classroom might always have the block area and art center available as a choice, careful attention needs to be directed toward making sure materials provided in these areas are changed regularly to reflect children's changing needs, goals, and interests. Consider the art area. A well-stocked area would always include certain fundamentals such as art easels and drawing, coloring, cutting, and pasting tools. A wide variety of papers and materials for creations should also be a regular staple in the environment. Various other objects that engage children's creativity could be rotated in based on availability. The cardboard cylinder of a roll of toilet paper, empty film canisters, and the clear tops to yogurt are a few examples.
- Children need to be allowed to make their own choices. One child, for example, might spend most of her time at the manipulative table. Her family might express concerns about this by saying, "But I want my child to be well-rounded; make her

---

TEACHING AND LEARNING CONNECTIONS

Providing Appropriate Amounts of Choice

- Provide choices appropriate for the time of day, including quiet activities during nap time and engrossing activities during transition times.
- Consider the number of children in the classroom when determining choices, making sure that there are enough choices for each child.
- Provide choices that have natural boundaries, including physical boundaries for younger children and written and pictorial boundaries for older children.
- Provide choices that support individual development and learning goals for children in the classroom.
- Allow children opportunities and time to make and pursue their choices.

experience all the areas of the room." Teachers must help families understand that choices children make are based not only on their own interests but also on internal drives that enable the mastery of certain tasks at particular points in time (Froebel, 1826/1974). Therefore, teachers must make sure to integrate materials that support children's overall development in each domain in the child's area of choice.

Circulation Patterns. Circulation refers to the overall layout of the classroom, indicating how children are expected to move through it. Poorly designed classrooms leave children aimlessly wandering, which can impede self-directed exploration, engagement, and focused play. This lack of engagement, in turn, can result in an increase in aggressive behavior (Torelli & Durrett, 1996). Imagine the child who has just created an epic block structure and who is anxiously awaiting the picture that the teacher has promised to take of his creation. Suddenly, another child bursts through the center of the structure on her way to the water table. In this case, the circulation pattern was developed without attention to the kinds of activities that could occur in each area of the classroom. In turn, this leads to conflict ("You knocked down my tower") and quite a few tears.

What are factors to consider when developing circulation patterns? First, *circulation patterns need to provide clear pathways that do not run into activity areas or interest centers*. As the above example indicates, failure to develop clear pathways can create many challenges. In addition, *the overall circulation pattern should draw children to activities*. Children following the circulation pattern need to be able to easily move from one area to another. As they move through the classroom, they should encounter a variety of enticing choices, supporting their ability to make informed decisions.

Taking circulation patterns into account means incorporating special considerations for individual areas into your planning. A gross motor area might be best placed in a corner, as the highly physical activities that occur on the climber (were they not placed outside the main traffic patterns) might lead to many crashes. The placement of a high interest activity at the entryway to the classroom can encourage initial engagement in the classroom. A well-placed sand and water table could catch children's eyes and aid their transitioning into the classroom. High interest areas should also be placed throughout the room to support a circulation pattern that does not induce crowding. If computers, the sand and water table, and blocks are the most popular activities in the classroom, make sure that each is placed apart from one another.

Balance. Balance is equilibrium. Noisy activities in a classroom are tempered by quiet ones, active choices by ones that are passive. Balance means that the whole of the classroom experience meets a variety of needs and that each individual need a child might have is considered.

Balance in the classroom has been thought of in a variety of ways. This includes balance between noisy and quiet activities, and between quiet and active ones. In addition, classrooms have been thought of as **zones**, or groupings, where activities are placed with careful attention to the overall functions of the classroom. When walking into a classroom, for example, you might be taken aback if you enter a high activity zone where children are frantically dancing.

Within classroom zones, it is useful to think of the different dimensions of the classroom. The following guidelines support thinking of space in early childhood environments in terms of dimensions (Jones, 2003):

- The soft–hard dimension includes a balance of soft and hard surfaces and objects in the classroom.
- In the intrusion–seclusion dimension, novelty from the outside world is tempered by space for children to be alone.

zones
Classroom design that incorporates attention to the function of space.

myeducationlab

Go to MyEducationLab and select the topic "Guidance." Under Activities and Applications, watch the video *Arranging Furniture and Materials* and reflect on the role of the environment in supporting children's development and learning.

FIGURE 11.2
Toddler Classroom

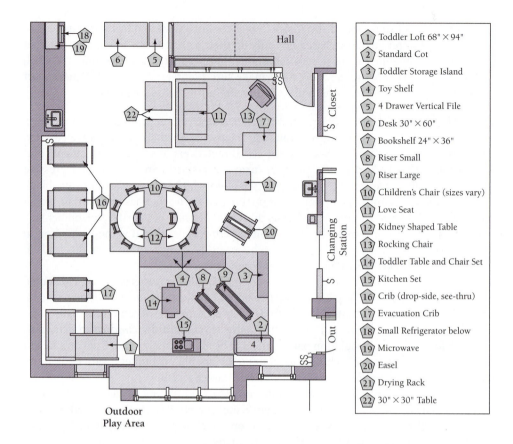

Legend:

1. Toddler Loft 68" × 94"
2. Standard Cot
3. Toddler Storage Island
4. Toy Shelf
5. 4 Drawer Vertical File
6. Desk 30" × 60"
7. Bookshelf 24" × 36"
8. Riser Small
9. Riser Large
10. Children's Chair (sizes vary)
11. Love Seat
12. Kidney Shaped Table
13. Rocking Chair
14. Toddler Table and Chair Set
15. Kitchen Set
16. Crib (drop-side, see-thru)
17. Evacuation Crib
18. Small Refrigerator below
19. Microwave
20. Easel
21. Drying Rack
22. 30" × 30" Table

- The mobility dimension provides children with adequate time for active movement and rest and quiet play.
- The open–closed dimension provides adequate opportunity to make choices in the environment.
- The simple–complex dimension provides opportunities for children to engage with their environment at different levels of complexity.

Each of the considerations presented for effective environmental design provides a template through which specific activities can be planned. Figures 11.2 and 11.3 provide examples of a toddler and preschool classroom. Note in each diagram how space, choice, circulation, and balance are enabled.

Learning Center Design

Learning centers, or activity areas as they are sometimes referred to, represent specific areas in the classroom that assist targeted learning and specific types of play. Learning centers are sometimes referred to by developmental domain, such as the gross motor area. However, children do not bring individual domains to each area and leave other areas of development behind. For example, a room might have an art center, but fine motor and creative skills are not the only ones being used in this area. Rather, the art area is a place where skills related to communication, interaction, processing, negotiation, and experimentation (to name a few) might occur. Therefore, the area needs to be designed in a way that supports these varied developmental tasks.

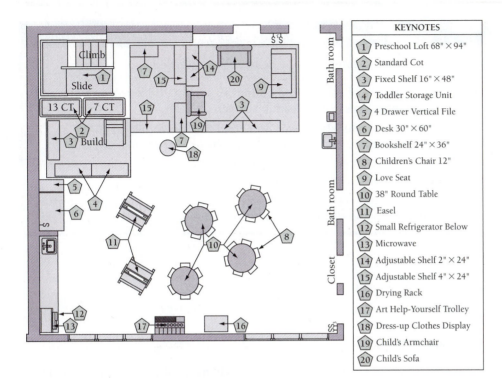

FIGURE 11.3
Preschool Classroom

KEYNOTES

1. Preschool Loft 68" × 94"
2. Standard Cot
3. Fixed Shelf 16" × 48"
4. Toddler Storage Unit
5. 4 Drawer Vertical File
6. Desk 30" × 60"
7. Bookshelf 24" × 36"
8. Children's Chair 12"
9. Love Seat
10. 38" Round Table
11. Easel
12. Small Refrigerator Below
13. Microwave
14. Adjustable Shelf 2" × 24"
15. Adjustable Shelf 4" × 24"
16. Drying Rack
17. Art Help-Yourself Trolley
18. Dress-up Clothes Display
19. Child's Armchair
20. Child's Sofa

An effective way to think about designing learning centers is to think about the kind of play that is likely to occur in the center boundaries. Learning centers not only encourage different kinds of play, such as **sociodramatic play**, but also facilitate various types of play, such as parallel and cooperative play.

How does a learning center design address engagement in the environment and interactions with peers? Think about these areas as places where children play, work, and learn, both independently and with one another. Learning centers must be designed to support child-directed learning. Based on this, learning centers need to provide *a variety of choices and options to support children's varied needs and interests.*

In addition to including a variety of choices, learning centers and the overall room organization should *promote activity within and between learning centers.* Children who are dressing up as construction workers in the sociodramatic play area might choose to extend their play to the block area. Classroom design (such as placing related areas near one another) and rules (including that children should return materials to their original area when finished with them) can assist children in making these choices and support experiencing and interacting with all the environment has to offer in a way that is self-directed.

Activity areas also need to be *well organized* and have *organizational and labeling strategies* that children can clearly understand. For younger children, labels might include pictures of the objects, and for older children, labels might consist of the written word. Labels will also take into account the needs of different children in the classroom. A child with a visual impairment might not be able to read standard-size labels, but making larger labels with big print and highly contrasting colors supports access to these organizational tools. Labels denote the appropriate space for certain objects and therefore create an atmosphere where children can take part in the responsibility of cleaning up and organizing items.

What learning centers are you likely to find in an early childhood environment? The following are examples of a few of the more common learning centers:

sociodramatic play

Type of play where children carry out action plans, take on roles, and transform objects.

Block area	Science and nature
Music and movement	Book area
Computers	Manipulative toys
Sensory materials	Writing and art center
Sociodramatic play	

Although each area might include some likely materials, creating child-centered, engaging environments requires that most of the materials included be based on the needs and interests of the individual children. Table 11.4 describes possible materials for individual areas and provides questions that can guide you in center design.

Attention to each of these factors is needed to create equitable indoor learning environments. Creating engaging, equitable outdoor learning environments requires attention to unique learning opportunities available outdoors as well as these same design principles.

THE OUTDOOR LEARNING ENVIRONMENT

All too often, planning for the outdoor environment consists of picking out a few pieces of playground equipment, arranging them in compliance with playground safety codes, and letting the children climb, swing, and slide while the teachers take a break. Limiting outdoor playgrounds to gross motor equipment fails to embrace the potential for outdoor areas to be enticing play and learning environments (White & Stoeklin, 2003). The outdoor environment provides several distinct opportunities for education, such as exploring nature, learning about how to care for the environment, and examining different ways of acquiring knowledge and interacting with the world.

Supporting the Exploration of Nature

As Mark Francis (1995) said, children's worlds are a "childhood of imprisonment." Within larger society, children are often ushered from one person-made activity to another without the freedom to explore the great outdoors, which has been largely abandoned due to concerns about safety. Because of this, outdoor environments in early childhood education programs might represent the only opportunity children have to safely explore and process natural settings.

TABLE 11.4   Learning Center Construction

Learning Center	Questions to Ask About Center Design	Potential Materials for Inclusion
Block area	Is there adequate space for children to create a variety of structures? Is the area away from traffic in order to sustain children's creations? What materials can be included that aid curricular goals and children's development?	Materials included in the block area can complement the overall curriculum. For example, zoo animals might accompany a project on animals and trucks might be included for a project on transportation.
Manipulative toys	Is the manipulative area located near a space that is large enough to—for example—construct puzzles, place beads on string, and count beans? Is adequate storage nearby so that if a table is employed that is also used for eating, materials can be easily cleaned up?	Materials in manipulative toys can serve to complement goals for children's fine motor needs and the overall curriculum. A toddler working on eye–hand coordination? Include large knobbed puzzles. A 5-year-old interested in graphing? Provide color-coded objects for representation.
Sensory materials	Does the space that the sensory materials are located in allow for easy clean up? Is there opportunity for easy transitions between the indoor and the outdoor environment?	Children need materials that support each of the five senses. For example, dirt with watering cans in a sand and water table to complement a project on plant life or measuring cups and cotton balls to extend a cooking activity.
The writing and art center	Does the space selected have adequate room for children's work and easy access to a variety of different materials? Are there numerous examples of written and pictorial materials nearby?	Children need access to a wide variety of tools, including paper, pencils, crayons, markers, scissors, glue, rulers, rubber shapes, stencils, stickers, and loose objects such as recyclables.
Sociodramatic play	Is the space selected adequate for both materials and involved play? Is the dramatic play area placed in an area of the room that allows connections with other areas, such as the book corner and writing center?	The basics of dress-up and housekeeping are often included in the dramatic play area; however, materials need to be rotated regularly and to encourage opportunities to explore a variety of different roles.
Science and nature	Is there room for storing a variety of materials? Does the space allocated allow for easy cleanup? Is there opportunity for easy transitions between the indoor and the outdoor environment? Are writing utensils for data collection nearby?	Materials included in the science and nature table are limited only by imagination and ability to collect different objects. To support exploration of the varied objects, be sure to include objects that encourage study, such as magnifying glasses, tweezers, and binoculars.
Music and movement	Is there adequate space for movement? Does the selected environment provide for ease of storage and access to varied materials? Are choices in this area available to children throughout the day?	A variety of instruments and objects that suggest movement, including such things as scarves and ribbons, should be available. Children should have access to tape recorders and cassettes to play music as they become inclined. An assortment of instruments, including child-made creations, should be available throughout the day.
Book area	Is there adequate, comfortable space for curling up with a good book? Does the selected area have space for both individuals and small groups? Is there space for organized and protective storage of the books?	The books selected should include many formats suitable to the full range of developing literacy skills for young children. In addition, books selected should complement children's interests and the overall classroom focus of study.
Computers	Does the space include opportunities for individual and small group interaction with the computer? Is use of the computer treated as a complement to the overall curriculum, as opposed to an addendum?	Does the software include a wide variety of age- and content-appropriate choices that complement the overall curriculum?

Exploring the natural environment is an endless source of learning.

Elements of nature—such as trees, shrubs, berms, plants, driftwood, water, and rocks—are all appropriate for young hands and minds to explore. The simple addition of birdfeeders, birdbaths, and some well-chosen plants that attract butterflies encourages wildlife to join your outdoor environment. By providing children with magnifying glasses, tweezers, and containers, opportunities for science and observation are endless. Chalk, paintbrushes, and easels may complement the outdoor environment and can help children to create representations of their encounters with the world.

Supporting the exploration of nature requires that children be taught how to participate in the outdoor environment. Basic principles that need to be included are respecting nature and preserving natural habitats. Children also need to learn that observation can occur without damaging natural environments. Over time, children will learn that time and patience are often rewarded with new knowledge.

In addition, children must be provided with tools that support their hypotheses, data gathering, and conclusions. Therefore, in addition to elements of nature, outdoor environments need to include a variety of tools for children to collect and record data, including well-placed clipboards, paper, and writing instruments.

The benefits of play in nature-rich environments have been well documented. One study focused on differences in children's behavior in an environment dominated by play structures as compared with one that was dominated by "vegetative rooms" (Herrington & Studtman 1998), or small garden areas. In the outdoor environment with play structures, children developed social hierarchies based on physical capabilities. In the "vegetative rooms," fantasy play and socialization was the norm, with hierarchies based on children's language, creativity, and inventiveness. This alternative environment provided rich opportunities for a variety of child strengths to flourish.

Supporting Children's Ways of Knowing

The outdoor environment provides children with (1) unending diversity, (2) the opportunity to interact in worlds not created by adults for children, and (3) a timeless quality created by the myths and fairy tales of old (Prescott, 1987). The same trees and landscapes that pepper stories can be found in children's own outdoor environment.

Given the opportunity, children learn to "know" the natural environment as a place of beauty, mystery, and wonder. Children are drawn to the hands-on experience of nature—the feel of the mud squishing through their fingers, the thrill of the hunt as they look for the worm that has burrowed into the dirt, the pleasurable anxiety caused by watching a bumble bee dart from flower to flower. Children tend to experience their world in a more hands-on way, unlike adults who are more likely to observe and process from a distance. Their knowledge of this world can be richer, more diverse, and more complete.

These general considerations for the overall goals of outdoor environments can be further refined into guidelines for space, amount of choice, circulation patterns, and balance. These guidelines vary from those of indoor environments based on the breadth of options presented and the need to preserve natural elements.

TEACHING AND LEARNING CONNECTIONS

Fundamentals of Outdoor Learning Environments

- Provide opportunities to explore nature.
- Ensure that there are appropriate tools to document and record data and explorations of the environment.
- Allow free exploration of the environment within the parameters of safety.
- Provide choices that support all areas of children's development and learning.
- Create clear boundaries that denote different areas, such as riding paths and spaces for building sand structures.
- Provide choices that mirror those in the indoor environment and expand on these indoor opportunities through incorporating nature.

Space. In the outdoor environment, assign space for varied types of environmental learning. Careful attention to square footage allocations and the needs of various vegetations, for example, allows for fruitful environment experiences in smaller outdoor areas.

Amount of Choice. As with indoor environments, at any given time outdoor environments should allow two to three choices in activities and types of play. Outdoor environments need to be designed with the same diverse opportunities to aid children's learning that the indoor environment provides. Outdoor areas must support all areas of children's development.

Circulation Patterns. Although children need freedom in outdoor environments, they also need to be presented with space that communicaties potential use. For example, the path for riding toys needs to be kept clear, just as the area for sand and water play should be placed near one another. Vegetation should be placed in accordance with growing needs, with boundaries that protect the developing wildlife, flora, and fauna.

Balance. A balanced indoor environment attends to the range of children's needs and provides an array of activities and materials. Such a range should not differ in the outdoor environment, where opportunities for children to swing freely should be offered along-side opportunities to lie on one's back and watch the clouds go by. Children may elect to form a large group and play tag just as easily as they may gather with dolls on a blanket under the climber. For children who wish to paint, easels may be placed on the grassy area, well away from the barreling of children on scooters.

All of these principles combine to create outdoor environments that assist children's learning. These environments have been referred to as **creative–comprehensive environments** (Malone & Tranter, 2003).

The time and attention spent on developing the indoor and outdoor environments has a direct impact on the quality of the program for young children. How program staff utilizes the environment as the third teacher is a highly individualized decision. This decision is based on the children in the class and on the whole staff's ways of viewing and interacting with the world.

creative–comprehensive environments
Outdoor environments that address all areas of development and all types of children's play.

CREATING SUPPORTIVE SOCIAL-EMOTIONAL ENVIRONMENTS

As you have been learning, Maslow's hierarchy of needs provides a template for understanding children's social-emotional needs in early childhood education. For people to reach self-actualization—where they make the most of their unique abilities and strive to be the best they can be—foundational physiological, safety, love and belonging, and self-esteem needs must be met. The classroom environment plays a key role in meeting these needs. Figure 11.4 provides an adaptation of Maslow's hierarchy to children's social-emotional environments.

Supporting Maslow's concepts of safety and security, social needs, and self-esteem in social-emotional environments for children are important professional goals. Table 11.5 describes how each of these factors influences environmental design.

Each of these needs builds on one another: If children do not feel safe and secure in an environment, relationships and a sense of community will be negatively affected. Further, without successful relationships and feelings of community, children will not have the confidence to tackle challenges, potentially having a negative impact on the respect they have for themselves and others.

FIGURE 11.4
Adaptation of Maslow's Hierarchy to Early Childhood Social-Emotional Environments

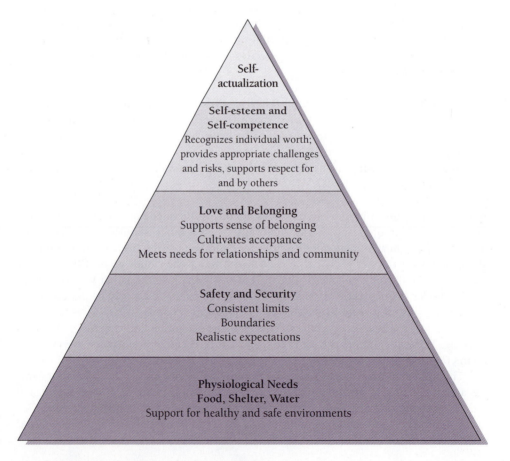

Self-actualization

Self-esteem and Self-competence
Recognizes individual worth; provides appropriate challenges and risks, supports respect for and by others

Love and Belonging
Supports sense of belonging
Cultivates acceptance
Meets needs for relationships and community

Safety and Security
Consistent limits
Boundaries
Realistic expectations

Physiological Needs
Food, Shelter, Water
Support for healthy and safe environments

TABLE 11.5   The Relationship Between Maslow's Hierarchy of Needs and the Social-Emotional Environment

Maslow's Need	Environmental Application	Outcome
Safety and security	Environments must not only meet needs for safety and health, but also provide children with consistent limits and boundaries and realistic expectations.	Self-regulation skills
Social needs	Environments must support children's sense of belonging, acceptance, and needs for relationships and community.	The ability to form successful relationships and act as a member of a community
Self-esteem	Environments must recognize individual worth, provide appropriate challenges and risks, and support respect both for and by others.	Self-acceptance and respect for self and others

Support for Safety and Security

Safety and security are supported in early childhood environments in a variety of ways. You have learned about the importance of supporting safety and security through effective health and safety practices. Safety and security in the social-emotional environments can also be supported through attention to children's developing self-regulation skills. Self-regulation refers to the ability to gain control of bodily functions, manage powerful emotions, and maintain focus and attention (Shonkoff & Phillips, 2000). Developmental goals for self-regulation differ by the child's age. Infants and toddlers rely most on external sources to help them regulate, whereas preschool through primary-aged children become more adept at employing internal controls. The role of the environment in supporting self-regulation skills varies by the age of the child. However, it is constant in terms of the supports needed: clear and consistent limits and boundaries and realistic expectations.

TEACHING AND LEARNING CONNECTIONS

Supporting Safety and Security

- Ensure healthy and safe practices.
- Provide clear and consistent boundaries.
- Provide realistic expectations and communicate those to children.
- Ensure that there is support for social needs and relationship building.
- Support belonging and acceptance through attention to individual needs and relationships.
- Provide opportunities for relationships through small groups and opportunities to gather in pairs.
- Build a sense of community through coaching, teaching respect, and cultivating relationships.

boundaries

Natural or constructed parts of the environment that give children physical limits regarding play.

Clear and Consistent Limits and Boundaries. An environment that supports self-regulation skills will provide clear and consistent limits and use **boundaries** that communicate to the children what is expected of them. Clear and consistent limits mean that what is expected of a child one day is an expectation that holds true everyday.

Limits are your expectations for children's behavior. Boundaries are a function of environmental design and can assist you in attaining limits. Boundaries can be concrete, such as a child-lock on a cabinet that communicates "not for children's use," or more abstract, such as classroom signs that indicate different areas of the classroom.

Infants and toddlers need boundaries that are concrete. For example, you might have an expectation that only children who are sleeping can be in the nap area. Posting a sign or stating the rule will do little to dissuade the enterprising 12-month-old from toddling into that area on a clear mission to wake up her sleeping peers. A small gate will provide a barrier to children and allow adult access.

For older children, increased representation and self-regulation skills means that both physical reminders and symbols can be employed to indicate limits. Signs are one way to help children regulate their behavior, the purposeful placement of objects another. A table easel used for children's artistic creations with paint easily accommodates two children. The placement of one chair, one set of brushes, and one set of paints on either side of the easel communicates boundaries. However, it also allows for flexibility based on child interest. For example, five children might be interested in the easel area and able to negotiate the space well, while three might need to problem solve about how to make more room. By not specifying a particular number of children in the area, flexibility allowing this negotiation and problem solving is supported. In the outdoor environment, arrows and signs indicating "one way" can be used to prevent crashes on the riding path, and a covered fishpond communicates that exploring hands are not welcome.

Realistic Expectations. An environment that is safe and secure to children takes their individual developmental needs into account. Knowing children's unique developmental patterns informs realistic expectations for behavior, and how you design the environment can play an important role in supporting individual developmental goals.

Realistic expectations for behavior are affected by the ages of the children and their developmental needs. One of the children in Mr. Gregory's class has Asperger's syndrome and has difficulty sustaining attention in large group activities. During these activities, Ella will often become distracted by the sand and water table located nearby. By redesigning the room and moving the sand and water table out of Ella's sight, Mr. Gregory has succeeded in reducing the source of Ella's distraction during this period. This, in turn, supports her success during large group activities.

Support for Social Needs

Humans are social beings who have a base need to form successful relationships with others. The success of any community is contingent upon its members: An environment of mutual respect and cooperation will support the social needs of those within. Environments can facilitate relationships and a sense of community through supporting children's sense of belonging and acceptance.

Belonging and Acceptance. A sense of belonging begins with feeling safe and secure in an environment and builds on safety and security through communicating to children that they are accepted for who they are. Environments support belonging through reflecting information about individual children and their lives.

TEACHING AND LEARNING CONNECTIONS

Creating an Anti-Bias Environment

- Expose children to diverse images, including artwork, book, toys, materials, and displays.
- Provide diverse experiences, including songs, plays, poetry, lessons, and games (Anti-Defamation League, 2006).

Diversity should reflect the classroom and larger community. Professionals must make sure that representations include people in real life, present-day situations.

Professionals can facilitate belonging by incorporating pictures of the children and families in the classroom. For younger children, child and family pictures should be placed in covered frames at eye level near the floor. For older children, pictures of children and families can be placed in prominent spots throughout the room. Children's work should also be displayed on the walls of the classroom. Their work can be collected to create a gallery of each child's creative efforts and/or to adorn shelves with projects and sculptural creations.

Books and toys should reflect the lives of children and families in the environment and those in the larger community. The same principles that guide the selection of diverse books and toys to support *anti-bias* and acceptance apply in the larger environment.

Relationships. Relationships develop in early childhood from a foundation of security, acceptance, and knowledge of self and others. Social skills play an important role in relationship development: Children need to learn how to act and interact with others. The environment can provide opportunities for skill and relationship development.

The environment supports relationships through provision of time and space for peer interactions. For infants and toddlers, opportunities for supervised parallel play should be provided with the teacher guiding and supporting children's awareness of each other. For preschoolers and primary grade children, the environment needs to provide opportunities for small and large group gatherings. This might include a cozy spot in the book corner, a blanket next to the outdoor butterfly garden, and/or a large space for kickball in the outdoor environment. In addition to supporting small and large groups, the environment must also support the needs of individual children.

Community. A successful early childhood classroom community values and respects the unique, individual contributions of each member. Messages about community can be conveyed through the classroom environment.

A sense of community builds from feelings of belonging and acceptance and is a big-picture representation of the relationships in the classroom. Each community has its own character, spirit, or guiding beliefs and values the contributions of individual members (Katz & Chard, 2000). The environment conveys community through reflection of not only the individual children, but also the group as a whole. The classroom walls can document community through pictures of the larger group and various class creations. For example, an infant and toddler classroom might have a painted mural on the wall of the children's hands and feet. A primary classroom might display the written and pictorial materials from the plays the children recently developed in small groups. Environmental representations of communities can document relationships, collaborations, and group efforts.

Supportive social and emotional environments provide space for relationships to develop.

Support for Self-Esteem

High self-esteem means that persons know and accept themselves and believe at a base level that they are worthy and worthwhile. Self-esteem affects interpersonal relationships, behavior, and learning (Egertson, 2006), and support for healthy self-esteem is an important goal in early childhood education. In addition to guidance, curricular, and teaching strategies that support the development of healthy self-esteem, the environment also plays a key role. Environmental strategies include supporting individual worth, providing appropriate challenges and risks, and supporting respect for and by others.

Individual Worth. Environments support individual worth through communicating belonging and acceptance and valuing the individual contributions of each child. Worth is conveyed in the environment not only through a reflection of the child's world and efforts, but also by allowing opportunities for each child to contribute.

Providing Appropriate Challenges and Risks. One of the teacher's primary responsibilities in early childhood education is to keep children safe. Safety is an important context through which children's development and learning can occur. However, an environment that provides children with challenges and risks is one that contributes to the healthy development of self-esteem. For children to know and understand their limits, testing their own capabilities and boundaries is an important developmental task.

Safety in the outdoor environment often translates into a series of rules: "Only slide down the slide feet first," "Swing on the swing, don't spin," "Climb off the climber, don't jump." Rules of safety for the children are often borne out of teacher needs—the more **teacher directed** the environment is in terms of how children use objects, the less chance risks will be taken.

teacher directed

An environment characterized by the teacher determining classroom curriculum activities and interactions.

Environments need to provide support for children's desire and capabilities in testing their own developmental skills and understandings of the world (New, Mardell, & Robinson, 2005). These "risk-rich" environments support thinking outside the box and allow children the freedom to explore their own capabilities.

Supports Respect for and By Others. Respect is often thought of as uni-directional, where a child "shows" an adult respect, or is respectful to objects in the environment by not damaging them, putting them back in their proper place, and/or using them appropriately. In this context, and throughout this text, respect is bi-directional, and the result of careful consideration of development and learning, the cultural context, and classroom community. Environments support respect for and by others when each of the other facets of Maslow's adapted hierarchy are in place. In other words, when the environment is healthy and children are safe, when safety and security is cultivated through consistent limits, boundaries, and realistic expectations, when there is a sense of belonging and acceptance in an environment that thrives on relationships and community, and when appropriate challenges and risks cultivate a sense of worth—the environment is being respectful of the child. An environment that respects and fosters children's development and learning is an environment that creates the conditions in which children's respect for the environment can be cultivated. It is important to note that child respect, therefore, is not a precursor to designing effective environments, but rather something that emerges from effective environmental design.

MOVING FORWARD

Learning environments—as they pertain to children—represent an important aspect of implementing quality early childhood education programming. Implementation is informed by theory, planning, and assessment. Through each of these stages, the common denominator is you, and your ability to meet the diverse and dynamic needs of children and families will have an impact on the effectiveness of the curriculum. Your teaching practices are therefore an essential aspect of implementation.

myeducationlab

Go to MyEducationLab and select the topic "Environments." Under Building Teaching Skills and Dispositions, complete the exercise *Developing a Preschool Room Arrangement.*

CASE STUDY

The Indoor Learning Environment

The Child Development Lab and Learning Center: Infant-Toddler Classroom (6 weeks to 3 years)

Filled with busy infants and toddlers who have different developmental needs, this classroom has a curriculum that supports the children's needs for security, autonomy, and independence. Inside, teachers have carefully organized specific materials and activities to support these needs.

When you open the door, the first thing you might notice is a couch, worn by use and adorned with a washable, floral cover. Many of the young children (and families) entering through the door need just a bit more time, a few more hugs before they are ready to venture out into other areas of the room. On this couch, families and teachers hold children in their laps and read to them from one of the many good books placed next to the couch in an inviting straw basket. Some children prefer an overview of the activities in the room, so the books are put aside in favor of conversation "Oh, look. Jessica is playing in the dirt table." "Looks like Juanita is enjoying painting." "John is pushing up on his elbows." From this point of security, physical contact and language prepare the children for the day ahead.

Other children enter the room ready to jump right in. For these children, the variety of inviting objects—scarves, rocks, an aquarium that is at their eye level, but securely attached to prevent fish-related disasters—are there to attract their attention and fulfill their need to explore. Families seem to appreciate the time to sign in, talk with the teachers about important information regarding their children, and hang up various belongings in their child's cubbies. The families can further guide the child into the classroom and devote time to saying goodbye.

One of the most unusual aspects of the environment is what you don't see: There are no playpens, swings, or bouncy seats for children to be placed in. The goal of the classroom is to fully include all children, and the choice in classroom furniture supports this goal. Children unable to sit up are either on the floor enjoying their tummy time or being held by one of the teachers. To safely support tummy time in a room that includes newly toddling (and often falling) children, flexible barriers are provided in the way of moveable risers. These allow the teachers to create "safe spaces" around the younger infants as they play.

One 2-year-old child in the classroom has a visual impairment, and the teachers created large picture labels for all plastic bins, activities, and learning areas. Physical prompts are also used to guide her: Shelving and tables define clear pathways, so that she can run her hand along and negotiate the room.

Teachers and staff encourage all children to participate in family-style lunch, obtaining their own food from the circulating bowls. Weighted pitchers are used to support pouring skills, and spoons with curves in the handle allow for children to successfully get food to their mouths (most of the time). The chairs placed around the table with graduated heights and depth provide needed support for the newly sitting-up 6-month-old and the firmly planted 2-year-old. Young infants on their way to developing the musculature control needed to sit in the chairs are helped by the teachers and allowed an excellent vantage point for observing and participating in mealtime.

CONSTRUCTED-RESPONSE QUESTIONS

1. In what ways does the infant-toddler classroom reflect using the environment as the third teacher?

2. How does the CDLLC's infant-toddler environment support children's developmental needs?

3. Describe child, family, and professional needs in the early childhood environment. How does the CDLLC's environment meet these needs?

CASE STUDY

The Outdoor Learning Environment

Mulberry School: Multiage Classroom

In the multiage classroom, the call has gone out to Reduce! Reuse! Recycle! The children have been spending their time outdoors learning about the natural environment; their burgeoning interest in how to preserve the environment has led to a project on recycling. This project has resulted in placement and labeling of recycling bins in the building. The children designed their own sign on the front door to the building to inform families of the importance of recycling.

In the outdoor environment, their attention has turned to sustaining life in the variety of gardens they have planted—butterflies, vegetables, and a garden of native plants. They are learning appropriate care of the environment: From the basics of watering and mulching has come an important development—the use of compost. Developing the compost pile is something that all the children have opted to participate in. The typical games of soccer and hide-and-go-seek have been replaced by hunts for the perfect spot for the compost pile. Once the children selected the spot, they brought a variety of potential compost materials from home to create their pile. After a few months of collecting materials, the children decided that they needed to adequately prop up the pile. They built and installed a small fence to ensure that the compost stayed in its designated spot. And toward the end of spring they were ready for their first application of compost. Under their tutelage, the growing plants thrived.

CONSTRUCTED-RESPONSE QUESTION

1. What are the developmental needs of primary-aged children in early childhood environments? What strategies does Mulberry School use to support these needs?

REFLECTING ON AND APPLYING EFFECTIVE PRACTICES (NAEYC AND CEC/DEC)

Ethics

• You are a new teacher in a second-grade classroom. You have noticed that one of the children in your class seems to have a difficult time sitting during morning meeting. During lunch time, she has a hard time sitting in her chair without balancing the chair on alternating legs. You consult with your school's occupational therapist, who suggests having the child sit on a pillow filled with air during these periods of time, which would give the child extra feedback when sitting and allowing some safe wiggle space. Your principal observes these accommodations, and comments "I think it is more important to teach the child how to sit still than to give her a pillow." How would you respond in this situation?

NAEYC Ideals: Ethical Responsibilities to Children

I-1.2. To base program practices upon current knowledge and research in the field of early childhood education, child development, and related disciplines, as well as on particular knowledge of each child.

I-1.8. To support the right of each child to play and learn in an inclusive environment that meets the needs of children with and without disabilities.

DEC: Professional and Interpersonal Behavior

3. We shall strive for the highest level of personal and professional competence by seeking and using new evidence based information to improve our practices while also responding openly to the suggestions of others.

6. We shall build relationships with individual children and families while individualizing the curricula and learning environments to facilitate young children's development and learning.

Standards for Professional Practice

- The environment plays a key role in the effectiveness of the early childhood environment. In two to three paragraphs, describe the theoretical rationale for using the learning environment as a tool in supporting young children's development and learning. Explain how you as a professional can translate this rationale into practice, and identify three ways that theory will guide your environmental design.

NAEYC: Promoting Child Development and Learning
1a. Knowing and understanding young children's characteristics and needs.

DEC: Instructional Planning
EC7K1: Theories and research that form the basis of developmental and academic curricula and instructional strategies for infants and young children.

- The early childhood environment plays an important role in welcoming and involving families. List five ways you can create an inviting environment for families, taking into account each family's unique characteristics. Then, explain how welcoming and involving families can affect the success of your early childhood environment.

NAEYC: Building Family and Community Relationships
2a. Knowing about and understanding family and community characteristics.

2c. Involving families and communities in their children's development and learning.

- Develop a list of five factors you feel are essential to effective learning environment design. Using this list as a guide, conduct a 1-hour observation in an early childhood environment of your choice. Evaluate the environment in terms of its ability to meet the five factors you identified. Consider how the environment, including its materials and equipment, meets the diverse needs of children and families.

NAEYC: Teaching and Learning
4b. Knowing, understanding, and using effective approaches, strategies, and tools for early education.

DEC: Learning Environments and Social Interactions
EC5S1: Select, develop, and evaluate developmentally and functionally appropriate materials, equipment, and environments.

DEVELOPING YOUR PHILOSOPHY

What is the role of the early childhood environment in supporting the development of young children? Does your response differ when comparing the outdoor and indoor environments? How can the environment support the needs of families? Professionals?

DEVELOPING YOUR PORTFOLIO

Focusing on infants, toddlers, preschoolers, kindergartners, or primary grade children, design both an outdoor and an indoor environment that you feel supports children's development and learning. Include in your environment the placement of furniture, learning centers, and the materials you included. Reflect on your diagrams and consider the factors you saw as essential components of your indoor and outdoor environment. In what ways would you adapt or modify your learning environments to support the social and emotional needs of children, families, and professionals?

CHAPTER REVIEW

• **In what ways is the early childhood learning environment considered the third teacher?**

Maria Montessori was one of the greatest advocates supporting the role of the environment and young children's development and learning. Careful attention to environmental design can serve to facilitate children's explorations of the environment. In turn, this careful attention can allow the teacher additional time to observe and interact with each child in the classroom.

• **How has universal design contributed to understanding how learning environments affect children, families, and professionals?**

Universal design, as it was originally conceptualized in the field of architecture, was based on seven principles that support access and equity buildings and products. Universal design has contributed to understanding the impact of learning environments on children, families, and professionals through advocating principles that affect the interactions of all people in the environment. Therefore, applying universal design to early childhood environments ensures that children, professionals, and families exist in physical and social environments that support their meaningful interaction.

• **What general environmental design principles need to be considered in the goal of supporting children's development and learning?**

Each of the universal design principles can be applied to design early childhood environments. These principles include ensuring that there is equitable use, flexibility in use, a simple and intuitive design, perceptible information, tolerance for error, low physical effort, and size and space for approach and use. These principles are equally applied to the physical and social-emotional environments and are designed to meet the needs of children, families, and professionals.

• **What specific environmental design principles need to be considered to support children's development and learning in the indoor environment? The outdoor environment?**

Both the indoor and the outdoor environment benefit from application of universal design principles. Factors to look at in the indoor environment include whether the environment is physically accessible in terms of access and organization. These factors are also relevant in the outdoor environment; however, careful attention must be paid to how children interact with the environment. For example, a transport system, where a child is carried from object to object in the outdoor environment, might serve to highlight differences and work against successful inclusion.

• **How does Maslow's hierarchy of needs contribute to conceptions of the social-emotional environment for young children, families, and professionals?**

Maslow's hierarchy of needs, adapted to early childhood environmental design, stresses that the physical and social environment for children, families, and professionals must meet needs of safety and security, social needs, and self-esteem. Each of these factors has implications for how the social and physical environment is arranged. For example, safety and security means attention not only to basic health and safety practices, but also to consistent limits, boundaries, and realistic expectations. Supporting social needs requires that belonging, acceptance, and the need for relationship and community are accommodated. Finally, environments—through attention to self-esteem—recognize individual worth, provide appropriate challenges and risks, and support respect for and by others.

12 Effective Teaching Practices

"Those that know, do. Those that understand, teach."

—ARISTOTLE

Tasia had heard this particular opinion expressed many times before but was surprised at how annoyed she felt after hearing a fellow student in her communications class comment, "Who couldn't teach preschool? Just a bit of singing, dancing, and wiping runny noses."

Now that Tasia had been in a preschool classroom for a month, she was beginning to feel like she was just getting a handle on all the complex skills she needed in the classroom. However, she still struggled with how to put what she knew into practice. Although, on any given day, she did sing, dance, and wipe runny noses, the scope of what she was trying to accomplish was great: Support the development and learning of 20 eager minds who had not read her college course books and who were, at their very core, totally driven to see and experience everything in their immediate world.

GUIDING QUESTIONS

- What are the general principles of curriculum, and how do these support children's development and learning?
- Identify teaching practices that support implementing curriculum. How do these strategies support children's engagement?
- Content areas identified in curriculum include literacy, mathematics, science, technology, social studies, health and safety, and the creative arts. What are important considerations for each of these content areas?
- What strategies can be used to support professional and family comfort with the curriculum?

Teaching is both an art and a science. The science emerges from historical philosophical debates, which are tempered by the findings of brain research and compelling data that demonstrate how children learn most effectively. The art represents a teacher's ability to apply this information in a way that brings out the best in each child and family. In this chapter, you will learn about effective teaching practices—strategies used to create early childhood environments that are alive with learning.

THE ART AND SCIENCE OF TEACHING

Effective teaching—teaching that inspires children, allows them to see and interact with the world in new and exciting ways, and enhances the children's view of their role in relationships—is the medium through which the art and science of teaching becomes a reality. You may have endless knowledge of how to design a math and science activity or develop a thriving outdoor environment with rich opportunities for exploration. However, without the ability to support children's connections and interaction with these activities in their environment, your efforts are limited.

The art and science of teaching is based on several general principles of effective curriculum:

- Taking a holistic approach to children's development and learning
- Supporting integrated learning
- Supporting children as active learners
- Taking the role as an interested supporter in learning
- Recognizing that children learn through interactions
- Recognizing play as the medium for learning (Nurturing Early Learners, 2007)

Taking a Holistic Approach

holistic approach
Focusing on the whole of children's learning as well as the interdependent parts.

Taking a **holistic approach**, which recognizes the interdependent relationship between different areas of development and learning, requires knowing and planning for all areas of children's development, with the recognition that each child's development is unique and that developmental domains are closely interrelated. For example, a child's social-emotional development affects her feelings of safety and security, which affects her confidence in exploring the environment. This confidence in exploration, in turn, influences cognitive development, as direct interaction with the environment supports knowledge. Curricular practices that acknowledge the interrelationship between different areas of development and learning support children's acquisition of knowledge, skills, and dispositions.

Holistic planning requires teachers to consider each area of development. Therefore, attention to physical, cognition, language and literacy, and social-emotional domains is essential.

In addition to developmental domains, the field typically divides learning into specific content areas. These include literacy, mathematics, science, technology, social studies, health and safety, and the creative and performing arts.

Content goals, or what children are expected to learn, might vary based on the individual needs of the children and their ages. For example, although the content area of technology is becoming an increasing focus for children preschool age and older, technology-related content goals are not appropriate for infant and toddler populations (American Academy of Pediatrics, 2001). Appropriate implementation of content can support all developmental domains; a preschool math activity, for example, can affect cognition, language, physical development, and social-emotional development. Further, that same activity can include goals related to other content areas. Children may, for example, explore literacy goals that complement math activities focused on learning one-to-one correspondence through reading the book *A Day at the Beach* by Sandy Seely Walling.

Taking a holistic approach to learning requires looking at the needs of the whole child.

In Cassandra's first-grade class, many of the children are invested in acquiring numeracy skills that include addition and subtraction. Their numeracy knowledge is supported and complemented by their development in differing areas. For example, one of the first graders, Jasper, learns best through interacting with objects in his environment. To support his needs in the area of numeracy skills, Cassandra provides a variety of manipulatives that allow him to explore addition and subtraction physically. She often finds him solving basic addition problems by lining up the counting rods or breaking Unifix® cubes into smaller chunks. Jerome, however, is adept at processing numeracy skills in his head. He responds well to paper and pencil exercises. Cassandra regularly assesses the progress of each child in accordance with the early learning standards of their state, ensuring that every student is mastering expected knowledge in a way that is individually appropriate. By focusing on how children learn best, Cassandra is looking not only at the content goal, but also how the child's individual strengths best support his or her learning.

Supporting Integrated Learning

integrated learning
Learning experiences that authentically combine knowledge, skills, and dispositions across curricular areas.

Integrated learning respects the interrelationships of content areas, recognizing that all areas of knowledge are complexly intertwined. Literacy skills, for example, can support knowledge of scientific concepts, and skills in mathematics can support technology learning. Learning experiences should mirror this presentation. Consider a group of preschoolers who are learning about plants. One approach to learning might include a teacher reading a book to children that describes plants. Another, more integrated approach, involves the teacher giving children a list of plant attributes (color, size, texture, shape) and taking the children on a nature walk to find plants that fit into each category. Upon their return to the classroom, the children count the plants they found that fit into each category and graph the most common attributes. In the first approach, literacy is presented as the main tool for learning about plants. In the second approach, children learn about plants through applying a variety of math (counting and graphing) and science (observation and classification) skills.

Although integrated learning has become a focus in the field, there are many misuses of this term. This misuse is particularly problematic when the term *integrated* is applied to practices that are piecemeal and not reflective of learning experiences that extend to real-life applications. For example, a prepackaged unit on fish might include a fishing game and a fish counting activity, neither of which, in combination, are likely to support knowledge of fish and how they live their lives. Consider the following:

> These misnamed integrated learning systems view a topic, such as dinosaurs or planets or fish, as only a series of superficially related activities and isolated skills linked casually together in sequence, much as a worm appears to be no more than a chain of loosely attached segments that can be severed and still function independently. Real knowledge is much more than a group of unrelated segments; each section supports a particular function, and all are related to one another. If the severed pieces are thrown into a box (brain) and shaken up without the support of their natural connections, neither the worm nor deep understanding will grow. (Davis & Shade, 1994, p. 7)

> Junie applied integrated learning concepts in her third-grade class during a project on the issues of hunger in their community. The class learned about their city government and how it provided resources for those living in poverty (such as availability of food supplies, shelters, and clothing resale stores) and examined issues such as access to healthy food, housing, and clothing that are faced by those who were impoverished. Knowledge and skill areas covered in the project included geography, social studies, science, and mathematics. By presenting the information in an integrated fashion, Junie supported the children's realistic knowledge of the world around them and helped them understand how a variety of factors intertwine to create varied outcomes.

Integrated learning, at its core, embraces teaching and learning within and between content areas. The key to appropriate learning experiences is that they are meaningful, reflective of real-world applications, and based on children's personal experiences.

Supporting Children as Active Learners

Knowledge stems from and is fed by *interaction*. Exploration and inquiry allows shaping our knowledge of the world around us and our role in this world. Active learning provides children with the opportunity to fully explore varied aspects of their environment, using their senses, skills, and cognitive abilities to create meaning. Children explore and process their environments based on their own developing preferences and abilities. Gardner's theory of multiple intelligences, introduced in Chapter 4, stresses that these developing preferences and abilities play an important role in understanding how children interact with the environment and how this interaction can be supported through active exploration. A classroom that embraces multiple intelligences presents information to children in a variety of ways.

> Margot is working on a project with her pre-K classroom, and the topic she and the children have chosen to focus on is pets. Margot works to ensure that each area of intelligence is well represented in the presentation of knowledge about pets. For example, the

linguistic intelligence
Ability to use words and language.

spatial intelligence
Ability to perceive the visual.

bodily-kinesthetic intelligence
Ability to control body movements and handle objects skillfully.

interpersonal intelligence
Ability to relate to and understand others.

logical-mathematical intelligence
Ability to use reason, logic, and numbers.

intrapersonal intelligence
Ability to self-reflect and be aware of one's own inner states.

naturalistic intelligence
Knowledge of the natural world.

musical intelligence
Ability to produce and appreciate music.

TEACHING AND LEARNING CONNECTIONS

Supporting Active Learning

- Allow children to fully explore their environment with their own preferences and abilities serving as a guide for their explorations.
- Ensure that the materials and activities in the classroom environment support each area of children's developing intelligences, such as extensive conversation supporting linguistic intelligence, puzzles and building materials supporting spatial intelligence, plenty of opportunity to explore the environment physically supporting bodily-kinesthetic intelligence, interactions in small groups and during class meetings supporting interpersonal intelligence, experimenting and graphing opportunities supporting logical-mathematical intelligence, opportunities to grow plants and care for living things (paying close attention to allergies) supporting naturalistic intelligence, and access to musical instruments and cassette tapes with songs supporting musical intelligence.

---

children in her classroom visited the pet store, where they learned about the care of various animals. To support **linguistic intelligence**, Margot prepared the children for what to expect on their visit to the store, and as a class they brainstormed possible questions to ask the store's owner. Each child came to the store equipped with a clipboard, where pictures, enhancing **spatial intelligence**, were drawn to document and summarize what they had learned on their trip. **Bodily-kinesthetic intelligence** was supported through direct interaction with the animals: Children learned how to hold the baby rabbits and the appropriate way to approach an eager puppy. To the children's surprise and delight, they were allowed to select a pet fish for the classroom. Upon returning to the classroom, the children had the opportunity to work in small groups with the objective of selecting a name for the pet. This activity allowed for the development of **interpersonal intelligence** skills. Each group then presented its choice for a name, and through a graphed representation of their voting (again supporting *spatial intelligence*), the name "Bubbles" was selected.

The children in Margot's class decided to outline a care plan for Bubbles, which stressed **logical-mathematical intelligence**. How often would the fish need to be fed? How could they ensure that this responsibility was carried out each day? Who would clean the fishbowl, and when would this be completed? Children developed individual plans, supportive of **intrapersonal intelligence**, and then presented their plans (supporting *linguistic intelligence*) to the larger group. The care of Bubbles supported **naturalistic intelligence**, and the project culminated with a presentation to the parents, complete with a song that allowed children to develop and exercise their **musical intelligence**.

Figure 12.1 illustrates Gardner's multiple intelligences.

Professionals as Interested Supporters of Learning

The role of the adult in supporting children's learning and development has changed significantly over the years. Once conceptualized as a "sage on the stage," where adults shared bits of knowledge with "eager" minds and inactive bodies, the teacher is now seen as a person who provides support for children's learning. This support is based on careful observation,

FIGURE 12.1
Gardner's Types of
Intelligence

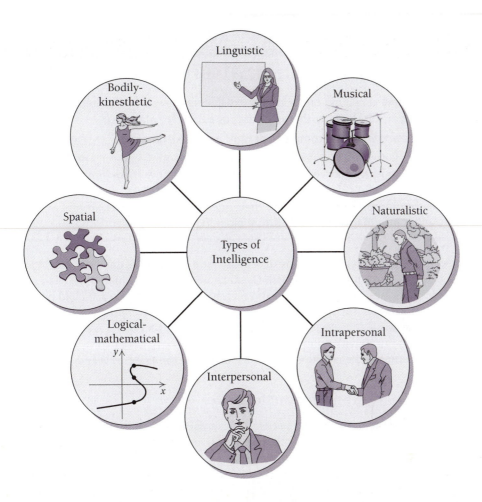

planning, interaction, assessment, and reflection and stems from the belief that children are the best informants as far as what and how they best learn. Professionals play an active role in supporting children's knowledge and learning, but this role places the child as the sage and the adult in a supporting, informed role.

The shift from adult-centered teaching practices is also represented through a current focus on child-centered teaching, which speaks to the need for children to be the controllers and catalysts of their learning experiences. Effective child-centered curriculum begins with attention to the child's individual interests and learning styles and is developed through creating experiences that honor those characteristics.

Planning for David's child-centered second-grade class begins with his review of the learning standards for second graders in his state. He uses this information to help establish a list of general goals for learning. These processes occur before

Child-centered teaching begins with following the interests of the children.

> ## TEACHING AND LEARNING CONNECTIONS
>
> ### Creating the Child-Centered Environment
>
> - Spend time reflecting on children's individual interests and development and learning needs, and use these interests as a basis for planning.
> - Provide activities that complement both interests and needs.
> - Allow children free exploration of provided activities, carefully observing to determine how children interact with objects and how these interactions support each child's development and learning goals. Take note of children's questions and comments during their interaction with the environment, and use this information to guide future planning.

he meets the children on the first day of school, but it is when the children first enter his class that the real planning begins. First, David figures out where children are with regard to their learning, and he then tries to gather information about how each child prefers to process information in the environment. As he gets to know the children, he carefully observes them at work and play, selecting curriculum topics that seem to be of interest to them. At that point, David is able to create a bridge between their interests and the classroom curriculum, and he uses this as a launch pad for learning projects and activities.

Children Learn from Interactions

Children bring their strengths and needs to the environment, and their interaction with the environment shapes learning. Both the physical and the social environment influence interactions.

Successful interactions in the early childhood classroom require careful attention and planning by the professional. Professionals begin with observation focused on children's interests and learning styles and further develop—or plan—experiences based on this information. They pay attention to the classroom community as well, with building nurturing, supportive relationships a primary goal.

> Zac spends a great deal of time focusing on relationships in his preschool class. He has worked extensively to ensure that the environment is filled with active learning experiences that support children's explorations. Also, Zac uses observations of relationships to ensure that safe and supportive communities are created. He has noticed that some children seem to bring out the best in one another, and their supportive interactions create effective partnerships and small groups. Other children seem more like oil and water. Zac's goals include providing support for their relationships to develop, while recognizing that until those relationships flourish, learning interactions are best minimized.

Play Is a Medium for Learning

With all of these foundational curricular practices in place, you can turn your attention to the kinds of experiences that support growth and development. As you have been learning, play—where a child directly interacts with the environment and other children—is the medium through which children grow and develop. Play is a dynamic, active, and constructive behavior that supports children in all developmental domains (Isenberg & Quisenberry, 2002) and provides an essential vehicle for development and learning across all ages and in all areas of learning.

How can play serve as a curricular tool? When planning for play in the environment, the following serve as broad guidelines:

- **Children need adequate time to engage in play.** Infants, toddlers, and young preschoolers need to explore the environment with minimal transitions and extensive opportunities for child-directed activity. As children become older, increased teacher-directed activity can be introduced based on the need to support academic goals; however, child-directed activity should predominate. For example, Noma's kindergarten class is working on a project on farm produce. The children have visited a farm, studied different types of produce, and planted a small vegetable garden in the back of the playground. One of the academic goals that Noma has for the children is knowledge of how living things grow. Although children are allowed ample time for observation and documentation, there is still academic information (such as natural fertilizing and the plant cycle) that the children are unlikely to discover on their own. Therefore, Noma presents the information to children in a variety of interesting and engaging ways, including books, labeled diagrams, and short presentations followed by observation. The time Noma allocates to each activity is based on the children's attention spans and recognition that their learning is best supported through direct interaction with the environment.

  A good rule of thumb regarding the use of time in the infant-toddler environment is to allow infants and toddlers free exploration of the environment and to provide at least an hour and a half of uninterrupted play time for children preschool to primary age.

- **Children need ample space for play to occur within.** Infants and toddlers thrive in environments that support their free exploration and minimize "nos." For children aged preschool and beyond, space for play needs is informed by observations of how children use the environment. For example, Noma found that many of her children were interested in playing in the housekeeping area, but the present arrangement could accommodate no more than four children comfortably. To support their interests, Noma enlarged the housekeeping area, which expanded play opportunities. Play spaces should be designed based on children's current interests and developmental needs, with space designated for small groups to gather and interact (Torelli & Durrett, 1996).

- **Children need interesting and engaging materials.** Materials provide the props for play. Infants and toddlers rely on concrete materials to represent their play: Toddlers, for example, usually need a specific phone prop to pretend they are speaking to Dad on the phone. As children age, various materials can represent objects—for example, a 4-year-old might use a block as a telephone. Through observation, teachers can see how children are using objects in the environment and can brainstorm ideas for the kinds of additional materials that would support play. Knowledge of child development affords information about how children are likely to use materials, which in turn can contribute to decisions about material selection.

From general principles of effective curriculum, specific teaching strategies emerge. Theory and universal approaches for supporting development and learning provide the foundation for effective teaching. How professionals translate this information into action is represented through the teaching strategies, or practices, they use.

TEACHING STRATEGIES

Planning involves focusing on what children need to learn and how to effectively teach it, including a foundational basis on children's interests. As individual children are vastly different and have unique learning needs, teachers need numerous practices and strategies tailored to each child. This is one way that curriculum is individualized: Teachers create environments for both individuals and the classroom community that create successful learning experiences.

Teaching practices are strategies that can be used to support development and learning. The following practices are foundational:

- Matching instructional resources and teaching activities to the developmental levels of the children
- Holding high expectations for all children and taking steps to ensure that they will be prepared for success at their next level of education
- Making sure that activities flow from previous activities and learnings into future ones and explaining these connections to the children as part of the activity
- Previewing lessons, giving clear directions, and checking student understanding
- Allowing children plenty of opportunity for guided and independent practice with new concepts and skills
- Monitoring student activities and providing help as needed
- Allocating and making use of time in ways that meet program goals (Cotton & Conklin, 2001)

Matching Instructional Resources, Teaching Activities, and Children's Developmental Levels

Supporting each child's development requires attention to a variety of questions: What are this child's needs? What resources do I have to support these needs? How can I structure the environment to best ensure child success?

The answers to these questions are as varied as each individual child; however, there is consensus on effective ways to structure children's learning. As you have learned, play is one strategy. Coupled with play is the need to support children's sensory engagement and to group children appropriately.

sensory engagement

The provision of active experiences that support stimulation of the senses.

Sensory Engagement. **Sensory engagement** provides active experiences in the environment that stimulate the senses (sight, smell, taste, touch, and hearing). Children use their senses to process their world. Sensory engagement supports child exploration, attention, and interaction. Commonly referred to as hands-on learning, this teaching strategy reflects the extensive research that connects active involvement, brain development, and children's overall learning and retention.

Chapter 11 introduced you to many strategies for developing learning environments that engage children's senses and can support an appropriate *sensory diet* for young children. Applying sensory engagement to teaching practices requires a focus on learning by doing, where children act on and interact with their environment.

In Korri's infant-toddler classroom, opportunities to learn through the senses are apparent the moment children enter the classroom. Next to the door is a basket filled with multicolored scarves. Next to the basket is a sheet of sticky tape (sticky side out) that enables children to attach the scarves to the tape in a variety of patterns. The floor is covered with pictures of animals and plants, with each picture covered with contact paper to protect it from prying hands. The carpeted area in the center of the classroom has a basket filled with bells, and the children love to experiment with the different sounds created. There are pictures throughout the room at the children's eye level, and the class is filled with objects that say "Touch Me!" This includes scrap baskets of varied materials,

TEACHING AND LEARNING CONNECTIONS

Supporting Appropriate Sensory Environments

- Ensure that each of the senses are supported through materials and activities in the environment.
- Pay careful attention to children's sensory needs, noting both overstimulation and understimulation.
- Structure the environment so that sensory stimulation reflects current classroom needs, including low levels of stimulation during quiet times and more active forms of stimulation during periods of exploration.

soft and hard objects for explorations, and endless opportunities to cuddle with adults and friends. When designing her classroom, Korri often reminds herself of the need to support each of the senses. She carefully watches the children to determine which objects they seek out and (in rare instances) which objects they tend to ignore.

Effective Grouping Practices. Many early childhood programs group children by their age. However, a child's best teacher is often his or her peers, creating a preference for grouping children in a nongraded, or mixed-age, fashion. Many programs, because of organization culture or perceived financial costs, are not able to develop these heterogeneous groups. In these cases, grouping should be designed in a way that allows children to learn from one another and supports equitable contributions from each group member (Katz, 1992). This kind of grouping directly contradicts practices where children are grouped by ability, with grouping designated in high, average, or low competencies.

In the context of infant and toddler groupings, teachers should group children based on their developmental needs. For example, primary caregivers should not have children of similar ages in one group. Imagine the challenges of meeting the needs of four children under the age of 6 months! Staggering ages in a group is more likely to support their development and professionals' ability to provide responsive care.

For children of preschool, kindergarten, and primary grades, grouping should be based on the needs of the children, the task at hand, and how individual children's strengths will complement the strengths of other children. The size of the group will vary based on activity objectives. Sometimes, children might form small groups; other times, they may be paired or grouped into a triad for learning or divided individually.

When considering how to group children, there are many factors to consider:

- What will children be learning?
- What grouping will facilitate learning for all the children?
- What grouping will support positive self-esteem for each child?
- What grouping will support overall classroom community? (North Central Regional Education Laboratory, 1999)

Groupings should support child engagement.

TEACHING AND LEARNING CONNECTIONS

Effective Grouping Practices

- Infants and toddlers
  - Use primary groupings that include varied ages.
  - Large-group activities are not appropriate for infants and toddlers.
- Preschoolers, kindergarten, and primary-age children
  - Group children based on complementary strengths.
  - Create small groups with support for developing relationships.
  - Minimize large-group activities; include opportunity for class meetings.

Grouping needs to be flexible in response to children's changing developmental needs and varied learning tasks or objectives. Successful grouping begins with supporting effective group behaviors such as collaboration and placing value on each child's contributions.

In Guptah's third-grade class, children are divided into groups for the duration of various class projects. Before placing children into groups, she reviews the overall objectives of the project and considers her observations and assessments of children's areas of strength and need. For the upcoming class project on bird migration patterns, Guptah makes sure that each group has a child who enjoys writing, another who enjoys drawing, and a third who is drawn to problem solving and scientific thinking. Once she structures the groups, she designs questions and prompts that will not only capitalize on each child's strengths, but also support collaboration and learning from one another.

Holding High Expectations for All Children

The knowledge, skills, and dispositions children are expected to master today lay a foundation for skills children need to acquire down the road (Epstein, 2003). Holding high expectations for all children recognizes that children, as learners, should play an integral role in planning, investigating, and reflecting on their learning. Promoting children's thinking abilities—which form the foundation for making decisions, regulating behavior, meeting complex challenges, and taking responsibility for their actions—is an important way these high expectations can be conveyed (Epstein, 2003).

Compare the following class investigations, or focused areas of study, examining the metamorphosis of a caterpillar to a butterfly.

The children in Tamika's kindergarten class were surprised to return to school on a Monday morning to find a mesh caterpillar habitat in the corner of the room. Inside, a caterpillar is eating a leaf while he lies on one of the wooden branches. Next to the habitat are several clipboards with notepaper and pencils, ready for the children to document the changes they observe in the caterpillar over time.

Now consider Darin's kindergarten class: They, too, returned to school on a Monday morning to find a mesh caterpillar habitat in the corner of the room. For this group, the arrival of the habitat was no surprise, as they had been planning the caterpillar's arrival, and its subsequent care, for weeks. Next to the habitat were clipboards, notepaper, pencils, and binoculars, which the children had gathered and placed there before they left school Friday afternoon. Darin had made preparing for the caterpillar an ongoing project in the classroom, with children deciding what

• • • BECOMING A PROFESSIONAL • • •

Career Pathways

Licensed Home Child Care Provider

Angela's family child care home has an important distinction from others in her rural community in Wisconsin—it is the only one that is licensed. Serving children between birth and the age of 12, her program is the only legal option, with the nearest early childhood center 25 miles away.

Angela's program is in high demand and not without its challenges. "One of the main challenges of my work is that I am the nurse, janitor, cook, and teacher. This can make it hard to make sure that each child in the environment is getting what he or she needs." In addition to these challenges, Angela feels that the pay and the fact that there is no health insurance are other cons and feels she is fortunate in that her spouse has insurance.

These cons are far outweighed by the pros, where Angela can be her own boss, set the curriculum for the children, and design the whole program in a way that she feels best supports each child's development and learning. Angela's catalyst for starting her program was the desire to stay home with her own three children, and the home child care allowed her to have income while doing so. She is currently a junior pursuing her bachelor's degree. Taking courses in an online program meets both her needs to work during the day and her desire to further her education. She takes part in the T.E.A.C.H. program in her state, which supplements her income and provides monies to help her pursue her education. Angela comments: "It is fun to see my income go up and feel like I am making progress toward an important goal."

Where does Angela see herself 5 years from now? "I could see myself getting a master's in early childhood education. There are so many changes in what we know and do about preschool children—I really want to be a part of that."

The outlook for family child care professionals is very good and is anticipated to increase by 18% between 2006 and 2016 (U.S. Department of Labor, Bureau of Labor Statistics, 2007). One factor that might detract from this increase is the increasing focus on universal preschool programs in the state of Illinois, which places a priority on center-based care. The wages of family child care providers tend to be lower than those in center-based care, as these providers almost exclusively rely on parent fees (U.S. Department of Labor, Bureau of Labor Statistics, 2007).

kinds of tasks needed to be completed and how these would be accomplished. The children also developed a plan for the caterpillar's ongoing care, which they would revisit on a regular basis to ensure that no accommodations to the plan were needed.

The approach to the butterflies that Darin used supported the curricular component of planning (Epstein, 2003). Planning is the process through which children make choices with intention, requiring the child to identify her or his own goals and consider what options exist to fulfill those goals. Seven strategies can specifically support planning:

1. *Make planning a regular part of the day,* encouraging children to think in terms of what they need to do and how they can accomplish needed tasks.
2. *Make sure children can see areas of the room when they are planning* to support their generation of different possibilities.
3. *Ask children questions* to help them identify their objectives and how they might pursue these.

4. *Listen attentively to their plan*, with the idea of both understanding their objectives and supporting their ability to consider alternatives and fully plan.

5. *Support, accept, and extend all the ways children express their plans* by valuing their unique ways of presenting and engaging with information and providing opportunities for connections and integration.

6. *Encourage all children to elaborate on their plans* by using questioning and brainstorming to help them extend their ideas.

7. *Write down children's plans.* This supports child consciousness of the process involved in planning and the overall value (Epstein, 2003).

Planning can become a part of many different aspects of the curriculum. Children, for example, can plan what they are going to do that day, the next steps on a class project they are working on, or how to resolve an ongoing challenge in the classroom. Throughout the planning process, language serves as an important curricular tool. The following strategies facilitate children's planning and their investigations (Sietz, 2006):

sparks

Provocations designed to generate children's interests, hold conversations, and provide a launch pad for sharing and participating in experiences.

1. **Sparks** ("What could possibly happen next!" "How will that caterpillar grow wings?") are provocations designed to generate children's interests, hold conversations, and provide a launch pad for both sharing and participating in experiences.

2. *Conversations with interested participants* (including children, teachers, and parents) are used to brainstorm and explore. Conversations may include such questions as "What do we already know about how to care for caterpillars?" "What do we wonder about?" "How can we learn more?" "What is the plan?"

3. *Opportunities and experiences encourage further investigation.*

4. *More questions and more theories* allow children to delve further and further into the learning process.

Connecting Past and Future Activities

One of the goals of children's learning is to create continuity across subject matters, time, and areas of exploration, where new areas of knowledge build on existing areas and understanding grows and develops over time. Teaching practices that support this continuity embrace children's existing knowledge base and create mental space and motivation for new connections to form.

Supporting child engagement in learning is a useful way to create continuity (Jablon & Wilkinson, 2006). Engagement creates investment in the overall process and supports

---

TEACHING AND LEARNING CONNECTIONS

Tools for Conversing with Young Children

- Get on the child's level, squatting or using a chair to ensure eye contact. (Note: Be sure to respect the child's preferences for eye contact and other nonverbal communication strategies.)

- Focus on the individual child, being sure—if you need to be interrupted—to excuse yourself and continue the conversation after you have tended to the interruption.

- Let the child lead the conversation, with the adult using questioning to scaffold learning and reflections to convey interest.

maintained interest and investment among the children. Strategies supporting engagement across learning contexts and over time include:

- **KWL**–Investigations of any topic of learning begin with "What do you already *know*, what do you *wonder* about, and what do you want to *learn*?" This strategy conveys that previous learning is a valued and an important part of the continued learning process.
- **Think, pair, share**–In this strategy, children are asked a question, told to think about it, and then encouraged to discuss their response with a partner. Think, pair, share supports collaboration and learning continuity, as questions can focus on experiences and ideas about the present learning activity.
- See what you can find out–This approach, easily used along with the other approaches, supports children's engagement in the learning process by challenging them to discover information. This supported discovery causes them to rely on existing knowledge and carry over ideas to new investigations through collaboration. Further, children are provided with choice regarding how to proceed, which places their own ideas as a top priority (Jablon & Wilkinson, 2006).

In addition to engagement strategies, many other teaching practices support continuity. For example, transcribing children's ideas and reflections over time and posting them in a visible spot in the room provide a past and present context for learning. Teachers can also take pictures and collect samples representing areas of children's learning and explain to children verbally, visually, and through demonstrations how materials and learning connect.

Previewing Lessons, Giving Clear Directions, and Checking Student Understanding

Children, similar to adults, need to understand the context of learning. What are they expected to master? What skills will they need to carry out their plans? How does their learning fit with their overall lives?

There are many teaching practices that can provide children with the knowledge they need to process, understand, and apply their learning. These include providing children with **motivations**, which inform children as to why particular information might be important to them. Teachers can also **preview lessons** by telling children about the importance and goals of the activity and how it complements their motivations. **Directives** can also be a useful teaching practice, as they provide children with the verbal, written, and pictorial information they need to successfully participate in an activity. Finally, using **open-ended questions** can help determine the child's present level of understanding and potential future directions.

Each of these practices can be provided at various points in time. Casey begins each new topic of investigation in her kindergarten classroom with a *motivation*—for her exploration of

KWL
Learning strategy that focuses on what children already **k**now, what they **w**onder about, and what they want to **l**earn.

think, pair, share
Children think about the question, pair with partner, and share their response.

motivations
Process of informing children the reasons that information may be important to them.

preview lessons
Telling children about the importance and goals of an activity and how it complements their motivations.

Questions provide feedback on children's present level of understanding.

directives
Verbal, written, and pictorial information children need to successfully participate in an activity.

open-ended questions
Questions that have multiple responses used to determine child's present level of understanding and potential future directions.

task analysis
Examination of a multistep task and the process of breaking the task into finite chunks that the child can understand and apply.

picture schedules
Pictorial tool used to break tasks or events into understandable chunks.

the body, the motivation was to learn how we grow and develop. For each topic introduced and covered, *previewing* consisted of an overview of the topic and its relative importance. The digestive system, for example, was begun by "We are going to learn about what happens to our food once we eat it! We'll begin with what we put in our mouths, learn about where it goes and what happens to it, and then when, why, and in what form it comes out." The children are given *directives* throughout their investigations. These directives tell them what a particular chart means or what they are looking at on the school field trip to the "Our Body Ourselves" section of the children's museum. *Open-ended questions* are used continually as an informal assessment tool to check children's understanding and to serve as a catalyst for clarifications or future activities.

Opportunities for Guided and Independent Practice

One of the keys to children's mastery of information is their ability to independently apply new knowledge and skills. This process begins with teacher guidance, where children are supported in their acquisition. Next, teachers need to provide children with adequate time and materials to practice these developing abilities independently. **Task analysis**, where teachers look at a multistep task and break the task into finite chunks that the child can understand and apply is an initial step in this process (Kostelnik & Soderman, 1999).

The number of steps a child can retain and apply will vary by the child's age. A toddler who is asked to go to the sink and wash his hands before lunch, for example, is likely to require behavioral reflections that also serve as reminders every step of the way ("I see you are walking to the sink." "There you go, walking over to the sink."). A first grader, however, might be able to carry out the task based on the schedule in the room alone and merely need a chart posted next to the sink that outlines the steps involved in carefully washing hands. For children experiencing challenges in task analysis, **picture schedules** can be a useful tool. These illustrate each step in the process to give children visual guidance.

After a child has mastered a task with guidance, the teacher needs to be sure that the environment provides ample opportunities. A toddler learning to use scissors, for example, should have easy access to scissors and objects for cutting that support her developing skills. Play dough provides an easy target for developing cutting skills and provides children with visual and tactile feedback. As these skills develop, the toddler can apply them to more challenging mediums, such as small strips of paper.

Monitoring Student Activities and Providing Help as Needed

Learning targeted in Vygotsky's zone of proximal development (ZPD) requires attention to the child's present level of mastery and support for the attainment of skills and knowledge that are beyond his present level. A useful way to think of this is that the zone represents abilities that the child can master with the assistance of adults or more experienced peers.

Vygotsky argues that there are two processes that contribute to children's development in the ZPD: scaffolding and reciprocal teaching. Scaffolding includes careful attention to the child's present level of knowledge and the design of clear, attainable, relevant goals. Using children's interests and existing knowledge as the base, teachers develop discovery experiences and emotional and informational supports as children work toward their goal. Again, return to the image of the ladderlike progression of knowledge: When a child is struggling, more assistance is provided; as the child masters materials, assistance is decreased to ensure challenge.

TEACHING AND LEARNING CONNECTIONS

Scaffolding Children's Learning

- Pay close attention to how children process activities and interact with their environment.
- Provide modeling and coaching for the completion of difficult tasks.
- Decrease assistance (referred to as fading) as the child becomes increasingly competent.

Reciprocal teaching represents a two-way dialogue between child and teacher or a more experienced peer. Through reciprocal teaching, children are encouraged to move beyond a rote answering of questions and to engage in meaningful discourse that supports in-depth knowledge of a topic area. Problem solving is a key component of reciprocal teaching, and the process of sharing and interacting with material is considered far more important than the product.

Related to reciprocal teaching is the concept of intentional teaching, which is based on the idea that children and adults are partners in the learning process. In this partnership, children have active, significant roles in adult-guided experiences. Adults also play intentional roles in child-guided experiences (High/Scope, 2007).

With intentional teaching, adults take advantage of learning opportunities that are both planned and unexpected. Capitalizing on unexpected learning opportunities requires openness to children's explorations and unique connections with their world and the ability to embrace teachable moments. This requires a focus on what is happening in the present sense and an awareness of your overall goals for children's learning. A preschooler who states "Only boys can be doctors," for example, has just provided a teachable moment in the area of gender roles.

reciprocal teaching
Bidirectional process of knowledge construction between child and more experienced member of society.

Allocating and Making Use of Time Meaningfully

One of the most precious tools available to teachers is time. Using time appropriately requires respect for program goals and children's needs. Many of the guidelines for effectively supporting play can be carried over to developing a daily schedule. In general,

TEACHING AND LEARNING CONNECTIONS

Capitalizing on Teachable Moments

- Observe children's interactions with the environment, and listen to their conversations with one another.
- Take notes on their present level of understanding, including connections and misconceptions.
- Look for opportunities to use children's processing and exploration of their environment as a catalyst for conversations, activities, and materials in the environment.
- Plan to revisit concepts introduced through teachable moments and monitor new levels of understanding.

TEACHING AND LEARNING CONNECTIONS

Developing Effective Schedules

- Young infants
  - Create schedules based on each child's caregiving needs.
- Older infants and toddlers
  - Use more structure in scheduling eating, diapering, and play.
  - Ensure flexibility for changing developmental needs.
  - Provide a wide variety of activities, suited to shorter attention spans.
  - Create a limited number of small group activities and provide extensive support for social skill development.
  - Minimize transitions.
- Preschoolers
  - Include large blocks of uninterrupted play in daily schedule.
  - Provide opportunities to gather in small groups.
  - Include minimal opportunities for large group activities, such as class meetings.
  - Minimize transitions.
  - Create flexible, predictable schedules.
- Kindergarten and primary-age children
  - Provide structure and flexibility.
  - Ensure large blocks of time for activity exploration.
  - Support child planning in the schedule.
  - Provide supports for transitions between rooms.

children need large blocks of uninterrupted time to explore and interact with their environment. What that looks like in terms of a schedule will vary by the age of the child. The following are some general guidelines:

- **Young infants require a schedule that is driven by their caregiving needs.** Feeding, diapering, and sleeping should be established in accordance with the child's own clock, and caregiving routines developed accordingly. To support group care, scheduling should be a factor in developing primary caregiving groups.
- **Older infants and toddlers start responding to more structured schedules of eating, sleeping, diapering, and play.** However, individual needs must be taken into account. Some children will still be napping twice a day, others taking one long nap at midday. A toddler who arrives at the environment early, for example, might require an earlier lunch and nap than a child of the same age who arrives later in the morning. Activity schedules should be based on children's interests and needs and should consider shorter attention spans and interests in a wide variety of activities. Children in this age group might be able to spend short amounts of time in small group activities. However, because of extensive needs for individualized attention, autonomy, and their shorter attention spans, large group activities are not appropriate. Caregiving routines must be embraced as a part of the curriculum, as it is during these times that children are primed to learn about trust, security, and the importance of caregiving relationships. See Figure 12.2 for a sample toddler schedule.
- **Preschoolers require schedules that allow opportunities to explore both their environments and relationships with one another.** Therefore, the daily schedule

FIGURE 12.2
Sample Toddler
Schedule

7:15–8:00	Arrival, breakfast available
8:00–10:00	Environment exploration
	Self-serve snack available from 9:20 to 10:00
10:00–10:15	Prepare to go outdoors* or to gross motor room
10:15–11:00	Outdoor time
11:00–11:20	Clean up and transition to lunch
11:20–11:45	Lunch
11:45–12:00	"Puddling" time, where children sit on teacher laps, read, and have hands washed in preparation for quiet time
12:00–2:00	Quiet/rest time
2:00–2:15	Bathroom, hand washing
2:15–5:30	Environment exploration
	Self-serve snack available from 2:30 to 3:30
	Outdoor option* from 3:30 to 4:30

*Ideally, children are in classroom environments where they can make the choice to go to the outdoor environment at any time. This schedule assumed a balance of other classroom outdoor environment needs.

should be arranged in large blocks of uninterrupted play. Although large group meetings often become standard practice in preschool settings, teachers need to keep children's developmental and learning needs in mind when developing activities such as circle time. For example, standard practice often includes a circle time focusing on activities such as the calendar and weather. Preschoolers are unlikely to grasp concepts such as time and are far better suited to learning about the weather by active exploration of these concepts outdoors. Therefore, much of what is considered standard practice is not developmentally appropriate. Based on this, small group activities are well suited to preschooler needs. With all children preschool age and younger, transitions should be minimized, requiring the teacher to organize the day in large blocks with transitions centered on absolutes, including transitioning to lunch or outdoors. Preschoolers need a schedule that is predictable and that is flexible to accommodate changing needs and diverse activities. See Figure 12.3 for a sample preschool schedule.

- **Kindergarten and primary-age children benefit from structure and flexibility.** Although content learning often becomes more of a standards-driven priority in these age groups, children benefit most from learning that is presented in an integrated, hands-on fashion. Therefore, large blocks of time for activity exploration are still an essential scheduling component. As children age, activities such as music and physical education might require children moving to a different classroom. Teachers must guide these transitions and give children ample time and opportunity to plan and respond to needed transitions in the environment. Figure 12.4 provides a sample schedule for first grade.

Using time effectively requires teaching strategies that support child success. To help children adjust to the daily schedule and its requirements, teachers can use a variety of scheduling and transition supports.

FIGURE 12.3
Sample Preschool
Schedule

7:15–8:00	Arrival, breakfast available
8:00–9:30	Environment exploration
9:30–9:45	Morning meeting
9:45–10:15	Environment exploration
	Self-serve snack available from 9:45 to 10:15
10:15–10:30	Prepare to go outdoors* or to gross motor room
10:30–11:15	Outdoor time
11:15–11:20	Clean up and transition to lunch
11:20–11:45	Lunch
11:45–12:00	Drop Everything and Read (D.E.A.R.)
12:00–2:00	Quiet/rest time
2:00–2:15	Bathroom, hand washing
2:15–5:30	Environment exploration
	Self-serve snack available from 2:30 to 3:30
	Outdoor option* from 3:30 to 4:30

*Ideally, children are in classroom environments where they can make the choice to go to the outdoor environment at any time. This schedule assumed a balance of other classroom outdoor environment needs.

Scheduling supports include *written and pictorial representations* of the daily schedule that inform children of what has happened in the day and what is coming next. These should be posted in a prominent place in the classroom or provided to children on an individual basis. *Using verbal reminders of when children will need to transition*, including ample warning, is also a useful strategy. Verbal reminders must be based on the developmental

FIGURE 12.4
Sample First-Grade
Schedule

8:00–8:15	Arrival, table games and manipulatives available
8:15–8:30	Morning meeting
8:30–9:30	Language arts block/cooperative learning groups
9:30–10:15	Scientific explorations (integrated learning block)/cooperative learning groups
10:15–10:40	Outdoor environment/snack
10:45–11:45	Math and manipulatives/Drop Everything and Read (D.E.A.R.)
11:45–12:15	Lunch
12:15–12:40	Outdoor environment
12:45–1:00	Project planning meeting
1:00–2:00	Project work
2:00–2:30	Selective*
2:30–3:00	Music/Art (alternating days)
3:00–3:10	Group dismissal

*Include child-selected course of study, such as yoga, swimming, karate, gymnastics paper maché, gardening, rocket building, or theater.

level of the child. For example, a third grader might comprehend "5 minutes till clean up time," but a preschooler might need time-related words such as "a short time till clean up" to understand that a transition is coming up. Teachers must have *respect for children's activities*, allowing children to leave out objects they are working on and want to return to later. For example, children who have been working all morning on a block structure should be allowed to leave their structure intact to continue their labors at a later time.

Supporting transitions requires taking into consideration that waiting can be challenging for children (and adults as well). Teachers should *minimize transitions* in the environment. When the transition is necessary, teachers should *provide children with engaging activities during the transition*. These can include, but are not limited to, songs, finger plays, and strategically placed objects that children can play with while they wait.

The effectiveness of teaching practices is measured by the value of the information taught; even the most effective practices are lost in the face of poor content. Therefore, professionals must evaluate the value of the content they are teaching.

CONTENT LEARNING

Content areas in early childhood education are typically divided into distinct subject categories, which can include:

1. Literacy
2. Mathematics
3. Science
4. Technology
5. Social Studies
6. Health and Safety
7. Creative and Performing Arts

These subjects are often presented and discussed individually. However, learning in each of these areas does not occur in isolation: Real-world applications require a (1) holistic view of knowledge that is (2) presented in an integrated, active manner that uses (3) play as a primary vehicle for learning. The following information supports general knowledge of effective teaching practices for each of these curricular areas.

literacy
The ability to read, write, speak, and listen.

Literacy

In its broadest sense, **literacy** refers to the ability to read, write, speak, and listen. There is a strong focus on developing literacy skills at the national, state, and local levels, as skills in this area are strongly predictive of student and life success.

Literacy learning is typically divided into five main categories (often referred to as the "Big Five"):

- Phonemic awareness, which is the ability to hear and manipulate the sounds in words
- Alphabetic principle, reflecting the ability to associate sounds with letters and use these sounds to form words
- Fluency with text, which represents the ability to read words in connected text in a way that is automatic and effortless
- Vocabulary, which is the ability to understand (receptive) and communicate (expressive) words to acquire and convey meaning
- Comprehension, which represents meaning derived from the interaction between reader and text

myeducationlab

Go to MyEducationLab and select the topic "Emergent Literacy and Language Arts." Under Activities and Applications, watch the video *Literacy* and reflect on how you can apply this information to your early childhood environment.

> ## TEACHING AND LEARNING CONNECTIONS
>
> ### Creating Supportive Literacy Environments: Preschool, Kindergarten, and Primary-Age Children
>
> - Provide a wide variety of experiences to practice listening, oral comprehension, expressive language, and phonological awareness.
> - Create links between prior experiences and stories, listen to and comment on stories.
> - Use questions liberally in the classroom environment.
> - Provide extensive opportunities to explore print and language.
> - Ask children to tell and write stories about their ideas.
> - Share children's first languages with other children.
> - Encourage children to experiment with their second language.
> - Provide books and materials that reflect children's first and second languages.
> - Provide opportunities for shared reading.
> - Create daily writing opportunities.
> - Post selected writings on the walls and in portfolios.
>
> *Source:* Based on *The Early Language and Literacy Classroom Observation,* by M. W. Smith, D. K. Dickinson, and A. Sangeorge, 2002, Baltimore, MD: Brookes Publishing.

Literacy learning begins at birth! As a mental tool, literacy provides an essential form of connecting with our world: Through written and spoken language, our internal worlds become an external reality, allowing us to represent our thoughts and connect to other worlds.

How can infant and toddler literacy learning be supported? The tools of literacy (Knapp-Philo, Notari-Syverson, & Stice, 2005) provide a framework for identifying tools and related strategies (see Table 12.1 on the next page).

Teaching children to read and write competently is both essential and urgent to support each child's achievement in today's high standards of literacy (NAEYC/IRA, 1998). The following practices area identified by NAEYC and the International Reading Association (IRA) as essential tools supporting literacy development. Please see Figures 12.5 through 12.7 for practices identified by NAEYC and the International Reading Association (IRA) as essential tools supporting literacy development.

Mathematics

Children's mathematical understanding is an important precursor to understanding and processing the world around them. At a societal level, concerns regarding the mathematical achievements of young children emerged during the 1970s and remain today. Mathematics education in the early years has been embraced as one strategy to support mathematical achievement. Important knowledge areas young children need to master include:

- Number and operations
- Geometry and spatial relationships
- Measurement
- Patterns and algebra
- Displaying and analyzing data

myeducationlab

Go to MyEducationLab and select the topic "Math and Science." Under Activities and Applications, watch the video *Mathematics* and reflect on engaging math activities that provide children with foundational knowledge.

TABLE 12.1 Tools of Literacy

Tools of Literacy	Related Strategies
Nurturing relationships	• Support and respond to infant communication. • Provide behavioral reflections and labels.
Listening and talking	• Respond to infant and toddler communications by giving words to the children's experiences ("you want milk now"). • Encourage children to use new words and sounds, providing encouragement for their efforts.
Discovering the world through words and experiences	• Provide opportunities for babies to see, hear, touch, taste, and feel objects and people. • Provide novel and familiar experiences and repeat them often.
Adults modeling the value of literacy	• Communicate the value of literacy by reading and writing in children's presence.
Using symbols to communicate meaning	• Use and talk about symbols such as photos, pictures, science, books, calendars, and writing materials. • Explain the meaning of environmental signs.
Using sounds (rhymes, rhythms, and songs)	• Play some games with babies by repeating sounds they make and varying the sounds slightly. • Sing songs, use finger plays, recite nursery rhymes together.
Providing experiences with print and writing	• Provide opportunities for children to explore materials including sand, finger paint, water, and writing utensils. • Talk about writing while you do it.
Providing enjoyable experiences with stories and books	• Tells stories about yourself, the child and his or her experiences, things that you've read or seen, things that happened at work. • Engage in shared conversations about books. • Introduce new words, summarize previous events, discuss predictions, make elaborations, and link ideas to previous experiences during mealtime and while you're reading.

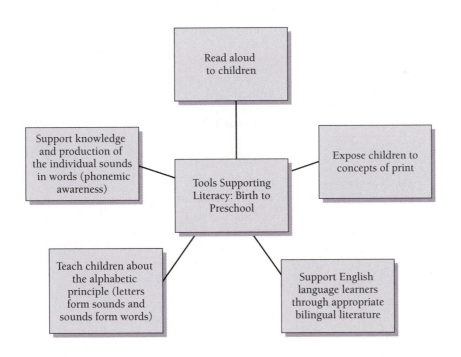

FIGURE 12.5
Tools Supporting Literacy: Birth to Preschool

FIGURE 12.6
Tools Supporting
Literacy: Kindergarten

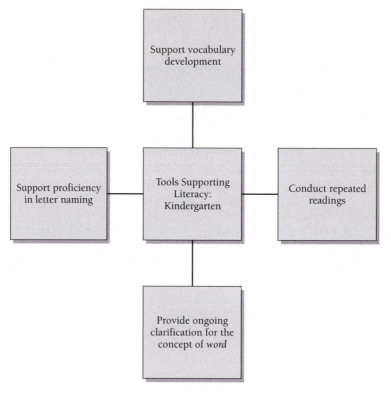

FIGURE 12.7
Tools Supporting
Literacy: Primary
Grades

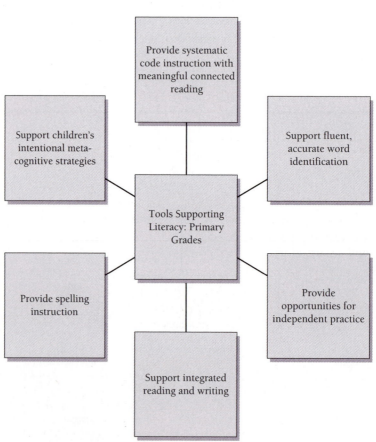

To support learning in these areas, the joint position statement of NAEYC/NCTM (2002) supporting appropriate early childhood mathematics education identified 10 effective teaching practices in mathematics. These practices include *enhancing children's natural interest in mathematics and their disposition to use it to make sense of their physical and social worlds*. Math is a tool that supports understanding of our daily world and should be presented and celebrated as such. In addition, *children have rich experiences that can be built upon*. These include family, linguistic, cultural, community backgrounds, informal knowledge, and individual approaches to learning. Mathematics curriculum and teaching practices, just like effective practice in any content area, *should be based on knowledge of children's development and learning needs*.

Effective mathematics curriculum and teaching practices serve to *strengthen children's problem-solving and reasoning practices* and provide for *deep and sustained interaction with key mathematical ideas*. Mathematics should be *integrated across the curriculum*, with *ample time, materials, and teacher support provided for meaningful exploration of mathematical ideas*. Mathematics curriculum must be *coherent and compatible with known relationships and sequences of mathematical ideas* and *introduced as a range of appropriate experiences and teaching strategies*. Finally, mathematical learning is *informed by assessment that focuses on children's knowledge, skills, and strategies*.

Science

Knowledge of science for young children begins with **scientific inquiry**, where children develop skills needed to process the world around them. Important skills supportive of inquiry include the child's ability to (Westminster College, 2007):

- Raise questions about objects and events around them.
- Explore objects, materials, and events by acting on them and noticing what happens.
- Make careful observation of objects, organisms, and events using all of their senses.
- Describe, compare, sort, classify, and order in terms of observable characteristics and properties.
- Use a variety of simple tools to extend their observations (e.g., hand lenses, measuring tools, eyedroppers, a balance).
- Engage in simple investigations including making predictions, gathering and interpreting data, recognizing simple patterns, and drawing conclusions.
- Record observations, explanations, and ideas through multiple forms of representation, including drawings, simple graphs, writing, and movement.
- Work collaboratively with others.
- Share and discuss ideas and listen to new perspectives.

Although children are often referred to as "natural scientists," adult guidance is critical to developing successful inquiry skills. Specific scientific processing skills that require adult guidance include observation, communication, classification, measurement, inference, and prediction. Table 12.2 on the next page summarizes and describes science process skills.

Technology

The recent cultural focus on technology as a tool for learning, problem solving, and communicating has resulted in an increased focus on supporting **technological literacy** in the early childhood curriculum. Although technological literacy is a key factor in children's present and future educational success, there are many inequities that impede the successful development of technological literacy. One of these inequities is a lack of equal

scientific inquiry
The process of asking a question, conducting an investigation, answering the question, and presenting the results to others.

Go to MyEducationLab and select the topic "Math and Science." Under Activities and Applications, watch the video *Science* and consider how to apply this information to create an environment that is rich with scientific learning.

technological literacy
The ability to process and communicate through use of technology.

TABLE 12.2 Science Process Skills		
Process Skill	**Description**	**Example**
Observation	Noting the attributes of objects and situations through the senses.	Encouraging children to look at, touch, listen to, and (when appropriate) taste and smell.
Classification	Grouping objects based on shared attributes.	How are objects and situations similar? How do they differ?
Measurement	Using quantitative ways to express physical characteristics.	What do the objects weigh? How long are they? Would they sink or float?
Communication	Reporting what has been found through observing, classifying, and measuring objects.	Graphing results, creating charts, and/or giving verbal reports to summarize findings.
Inference	Making an educated guess based on what you have observed.	X happened because of Y.
Prediction	Making an educated guess about the outcome of future events.	In the future, if X happens, we expect Y to occur.

myeducationlab

Go to MyEducationLab and select the topic "Technology." Under Activities and Applications, watch the video *Technology in Classrooms* and consider the various roles technology plays within the early childhood curriculum.

access, referring to the fact that many children from families with low income have limited access to technology. These children are also more likely to be exposed to drill-and-practice uses of technology (Northwestern Regional Education Laboratory, 2001) rather than to project-based inquiry and collaborative learning uses. In addition, there can be great variance in the quality and availability of technology programs and materials, which in turn introduces bias and inequity (Northwestern Regional Education Laboratory, 2001).

Addressing inequities requires attention to several factors. First, equal access should be planned for all children, regardless of their gender, ability level, race, or socioeconomic status. Teachers need to select software programs that make children feel represented and that allow for different learning styles and varying ability levels. Computer use must complement what is occurring in the early childhood environments and not be treated as an unrelated addendum to the curriculum. Finally, teachers must treat all students as capable and worthy of equal access to educational opportunities (Northwestern Regional Education Laboratory, 2001).

In addition to the use of technology as a curriculum tool, it can also be used to support access to the environment. Table 12.3 on the next page provides information on forms of assistive technology and their potential use.

Social Studies

The early childhood social studies curriculum is based on the need to teach children about how to act and interact in a larger society. Social studies education begins with knowledge of self and is complemented by knowledge of others, one's role in community, and one's role as an active participant in a democratic society.

The National Council for the Social Studies provides a list of 10 content themes that comprise the social studies curriculum (1994):

- Culture
- Time continuity and change
- People, places, and environments
- Individual development and identity

TABLE 12.3   Types and Uses of Assistive Technology

Type of Assistive Technology	Usage
Alternative keyboards	Can be adapted to be larger or smaller or used with one hand.
Assistive listening devices	Transmits and amplifies sound to children with hearing impairments.
Augmentative communication materials	Provides alternative communication strategies for children who are unable to speak.
Braille	Allows children who are visually impaired to read.
Captioning and video descriptions	Uses visual or auditory accompaniments to video presentations.
Electronic pointing devices	Controls the cursor on a screen without need for hands.
Large print/screen magnification hardware and software	Functions like a magnifying glass and automatically moves over the page.
Personal reading machines	Scans and reads printed pages.
Picture cards	Provides pictorial representation of activities or daily schedule as an alternative to written and spoken communication.
Sip and puff systems	Allows students to control computers or other technology devices through inhaling or exhaling.
Speech recognition systems	Allows students to control computers or other technology devices through their voice.
Switches	Can be used to trigger battery-operated toys.
Talking calculators	Recites numbers, symbols, and functions as keys are pressed, as well as reads back answers to completed problems.
Word prediction software programs	Presents words based on first letters typed—allows for fast, supported transcription.

- Individuals, groups, and institutions
- Power, authority, and governance
- Production, distribution, and consumption
- Science, technology, and society
- Global connections
- Civic ideals and practices

These broad themes are interwoven in the social studies curriculum in a variety of ways. The scope and sequence of social studies learning in the primary grades include (Mindes, 2005):

- Kindergarten—awareness of self in the social setting
- First grade—the individual in school and family life
- Second grade—the neighborhood
- Third grade—sharing the earth with others in the community

The foundation for each of these themes begins in the infant-toddler and preschool years, where children learn important information about themselves (infant through preschool), their relationship to others in their classroom community (toddler through preschool), and how to effectively participate as a member of the community (preschool). Learning in kindergarten and the primary grades builds on and extends this foundation.

There are many ways to support the arts and creative development in early childhood environments.

Multicultural Curriculum. Diversity is one of the most common characteristics shared by children and families in the United States and the world. Although we all share common characteristics, we differ in a wide array of characteristics, including age, gender, sexual orientation, social class, cultural practices, religiosity, and native language. Historically, the United States has been conceptualized as a "melting pot," where diversity combines and creates one larger representation of humanity. However, historically, politically, and socially the concept of a melting pot has not borne true. Much of society values certain characteristics, ways of living one's life, and ways of interacting with others, to the exclusion, or devaluing, of other practices.

Early childhood is thought to be a prime time for supporting children's acceptance and re-

multicultural education

Curricular strategy that supports children's knowledge of diversity and promotes respect for others.

spect for others. There are many tools to support this larger goal, one of which is **multicultural education**. At its core, multicultural education provides children with knowledge of diversity and supports respect for the many ways that individuals choose to live their lives. Historically, multicultural education has been conceptualized in a variety of ways in the field, from developing activities that educate children about diversity through holiday celebrations or taking children on "tours" of other cultures. Each of these practices, though well intended, can actually serve to highlight differences that may not accurately reflect people's lives.

Consider an activity designed to support knowledge of the Christmas holiday in the United States for children in Iraq. The Iraqi children learn about such things as the anticipation of a large, jolly man in a red suit coming down the chimney and placing gifts under a decorated tree. That lesson would not only promote a skewed vision of what Christmas means for many people in the United States, but also fail to acknowledge that Christmas is not a holiday that is universally celebrated or meaningful in the United States.

Tourist curricula achieve similar results. Again, consider the lesson of a well-intentioned teacher in Iraq. To support knowledge of how children live their lives in the United States, the Iraqi children explore various activity centers that include descriptions of video games and a Game Boy and a food-sampling table that includes hot dogs and pizza. Although certainly many children in the United States might play Game Boys and eat hot

---

TEACHING AND LEARNING CONNECTIONS

Supporting Multiculturalism

- Take note of diversity in the classroom community, families, and the surrounding community.
- Ensure that the physical environment reflects this diversity, including pictures, books, and material selections.
- Make sure that diversity is portrayed as present-day representations of real people in real situations.

dogs and pizza, this is neither an accurate nor a holistic picture of the overall culture or the diversity in how individuals live their lives.

The foundations of multicultural education include learning about our similarities and our differences and embracing the fact that we are all human. The best place to begin is with the children in your class: Where do you live? What does your family do when they gather together? What foods do you eat? This focus on how individuals live their lives provides a template for rich discussion of each child's world.

The Anti-Bias Curriculum. An unfortunate societal truth is that the world we live in is rife with prejudice, bias, and discrimination. The sources of these are varied, from policies and practices that support access and equity for some, but not all, to attitudes and ways of interacting with people that are reflective of these underlying biases. Many of our own personal biases go unnoticed; however, we must recognize that as a product of a society with inherent inequities, we are each likely to have biases. Whether these biases are acted on in the form of prejudice and discrimination, however, will vary with our own levels of awareness.

The goal of the **anti-bias curriculum** is to support children's appreciation of diversity and to support equity in the early childhood classroom and larger community. Anti-bias goes beyond the recognition of bias to advocate an active approach for eradicating bias and its outcomes. Goals of the anti-bias curriculum include (Hohensee & Derman-Sparks, 1992):

- Construction of a knowledgeable, confident self-identity
- Comfortable, empathic interaction with people from diverse backgrounds
- Critical thinking about bias
- Support for the ability to stand up for yourself, and for others, in the face of bias

anti-bias curriculum

An active, activist curricular approach that seeks to address issues of social inequity at the individual and classroom level.

ISSUES OF ACCESS AND EQUITY FOR YOUNG CHILDREN

The Anti-Bias Curriculum

The anti-bias curriculum supports children's critical thinking about bias and the ability to stand up for themselves and others in the face of bias. Through this process, children develop a confident self-identity and develop empathy for and comfort with persons from diverse backgrounds (Hohensee & Derman-Sparks, 1992). Access and equity is supported, therefore, as children learn about themselves and others and how to act in and have an impact on a democratic society.

There are four phases involved in the successful implementation of the anti-bias curriculum. Phase one, which pertains to *creating the climate*, includes:

- Learning about oneself, one's own biases, and anti-bias issues in the classroom and community. Developing a support group, where ideas, concerns, and issues related to anti-bias can be presented and discussed in a safe and supportive classroom community, can support this phase (Hohensee & Derman-Sparks, 1992).

- Exploring children's concepts of diversity. This can be accomplished through observation and direct questioning. Questions can be based on existing areas of societal bias, such as "What kinds of jobs can boys and girls do?" or "What do you know about Indians?" Both questioning and observation can provide information about children's discomfort or misconceptions about their world.

- Evaluating the environment and making changes supportive of diversity and anti-bias. This can include making sure diversity is represented in books, toys, and material.

- Identifying families who are interested and willing to participate in the process.

Phase two, *nonsystematic implementation*, consists of:

- Exploring the anti-bias activity process, including capitalizing on teachable moments and using ideas gleaned from observation and questioning to shape the curriculum.

- Developing and implementing teacher-initiated activities that highlight key concepts in the anti-bias curriculum. For example, if a child in the class expresses "only boys can be doctors," the teacher can initiate an activity exploring gender representation in different occupations.

- Continuing to participate in support group to explore and discuss issues as they arise.

Phase three, *systematic implementation,* involves:

- Developing long-term planning based on issues that have arisen, including goals for learning and activities supportive of these goals.

- Continuing to involve families.

- Participating in support group.

Phase four, *ongoing integration,* includes:

- Embracing diversity and equality as key aspects of the curriculum.

- Continuing to integrate diversity and equality concepts in the curriculum.

Phase four does not represent an endpoint, but rather represents the anti-bias curriculum's full integration into the program. Based on this, each phase is repeated and returned to as necessary, with ongoing support and communication foundational characteristics.

Health and Safety

Curriculum targeting health and safety focuses on both prevention and intervention. Teaching children about good nutrition and physical fitness serves as a tool to support overall health and the prevention of illness. Teaching children to wear helmets, use seat belts, and have a fire safety plan in place can serve to prevent serious injuries. Two topics that have recently received a great deal of attention in the field include childhood obesity and sexuality education.

Childhood Obesity. **Childhood obesity** has reached epidemic proportions in the United States, with rates of obesity doubling for children between the ages of 6 and 11 (Mayo Clinic, 2007). The physical health risks of obesity are dramatic, with children who are overweight and obese being at higher risk for developing:

childhood obesity
Excess body fat that places overall health in danger.

- Type 2 diabetes
- Metabolic syndrome
- High blood pressure
- Asthma and other respiratory problems
- Sleep disorders
- Liver disease
- Early puberty or menarche
- Eating disorders
- Skin infections

In addition to health risks, there are many psychological risks associated with being overweight or obese. These include victimization by other children, which can lead to depression and behavioral problems.

The most effective solution to childhood obesity is the prevention of its occurrence. Prevention efforts include educating children about proper nutrition and the importance of exercise. Childhood obesity prevention is a family affair, as poor eating and exercise habits often develop in the family environment. Therefore, efforts targeted toward prevention need to include attention to the family system. Many children are beyond the point of prevention and require intervention to address the fact that they are overweight or obese. For these children, nutrition and exercise remain important strategies.

In both prevention and intervention, it is important that children's healthy self-concept and self-esteem are supported. One of the challenges facing professionals is trying to help children develop healthy lifestyles and eating habits without hurting their social-emotional development. Therefore, support for healthy body image must be coupled with support for a healthy lifestyle.

Sexuality Education. Although many early childhood professionals recognize the role they play in children's cognitive, physical, and social-emotional development, the role played in children's **sexuality education** is often less recognizable. Sexuality education is not information on specific sex acts or STD for pregnancy prevention strategies, it is actually a broad term that encompasses the whole of individual sexuality, including relationships, responsibility, and respect.

Cultural values communicated through larger society include that specific information about sex education is communicated in the home environment. Although an individual

sexuality education
Broad term that refers to curricular approach supporting relationships, responsibility, and respect.

teacher or program might subscribe to this viewpoint, sexuality education is something that is likely to continuously come up in the early childhood environment. This might include a child asking what the word *penis* means or another child questioning a slang term she heard used. Professionals need to respect the rights of families to communicate their own morals and ethics regarding sexuality to children, but they also need to respond to children's inquiries in a factual and respectful manner.

How can relationships, responsibility, and respect for one's own body and those of others be incorporated into the early childhood curricula? Relationships are a core part of the curriculum, and the skills children learn in developing and maintaining friendships are important life skills. Responsibility includes a focus on one's own body. Children must learn to take care of themselves and take responsibility for their interactions with others. Finally, respect means an embracing of one's own self and being able to acknowledge, empathize, and support the needs of others.

The Sexuality Information and Education Council of the United States (2004) developed guidelines for the appropriate inclusion of sexuality education from kindergarten through 12th grade. These guidelines include the following areas:

- Human development
- Relationships
- Personal skills
- Sexual behavior
- Sexual health
- Society and culture

Table 12.4 provides a partial overview of the guidelines as they apply to human development.

TABLE 12.4 Examples of Sexuality Education Topics as They Relate to Human Development

Human Development Topic	Related Knowledge
Reproductive and sexual anatomy and physiology	• Each body part has a correct name and a specific function. • A person's genitals, reproductive organs, and genes determine whether the person is male or female.
Reproduction	• Men and women have reproductive organs that enable them to have a child. • Men and women have specific cells in their bodies (sperm cells and egg cells) that enable them to reproduce.
Body image	• Individual bodies are different sizes, shapes, and colors. • All bodies are equally special. • Differences make us unique. • Good health habits, such as eating well and exercising, can improve the way a person feels about his or her body. • Each person can be proud of his or her body.

Source: Based on *Guidelines for Comprehensive Sexuality Education,* 3rd ed., by Sexuality Information and Education Council of the United States, 2004. Retrieved April 1, 2008, from http://www.siecus.org/pubs/guidelines/guidelines.pdf

Creative and Performing Arts

Arts education supports children's development in all areas of learning and—similar to reading, writing, and arithmetic—should be viewed as an essential component of education. Unfortunately, the arts are often viewed as supplementary and not integral to children's learning. Because of this, the arts are often passed over in designing and implementing effective curriculum.

Arts education supports critical knowledge, skills, and dispositions (Eisner, 2007), such as:

1. The ability to make judgments in the absence of rules.
2. Problems can have more than one solution.
3. Flexibility in problem solving.
4. Neither words nor numbers define the limits of our cognition.
5. Joy, through the experience of being moved, having one's life enriched, and discovering our capacity to feel.

Go to MyEducationLab and select the topic "Creative Arts." Under Activities and Applications, watch the video *Technology in Creative Arts* and reflect on the role of technology in the creative arts.

How can the arts be successfully incorporated into the curriculum? As stated earlier, arts education should be viewed as equally important when compared with all other areas of the curriculum. Further, the arts—like reading and writing—should be viewed as a tool for communication and embraced as another means for children to process, experiment with, and represent their world.

Effective teaching practices provide the medium through which the intentional curriculum is communicated. In other words, it is your teaching that brings the curriculum to life! Putting each of the processes of theory, planning, implementation, and assessment together requires a format for organizing and processing this information. Development and learning plans can provide such an opportunity.

Families can provide knowledge of their own cultural practices.

Putting It All Together: Development and Learning Plans

The field has historically relied on lesson plans for outlining curricular activities and strategies. Development and learning plans are similar to lesson plans in that they provide information needed to plan, carry out, and assess an individual activity. However, they are broader in that they encompass the whole of the curricular process and provide a format that synthesizes each aspect of the process needed for consideration. Development and learning plans synthesize each aspect of curriculum into one coherent, holistic document that includes children's individual needs, classroom community needs, social and physical environment needs, and specific objectives for learning and ongoing assessment. Further, the focus extends beyond the individual lesson to support for each child, the whole of the classroom community, and families.

Figure 12.8 provides an example of a development and learning plan that incorporates aspects of theory, planning, implementation, and assessment.

FIGURE 12.8
An example of a development and Learning Plan

Teacher: Date:

Age Range/Grade Level: Lesson/Activity:

Duration:

Developmental Domain:

Curricular Area or Topic of Investigation:

Relevant Standards:

Planning:

Needs of individual learners informed by developmental domains

Child	Developmental Need	Suggested Accommodation

Needs of Classroom Community:

Community Strength	Community Challenge	Suggested Accommodation

Structure Provided Through Physical and Social-Emotional Environment:

Needs in the Physical Environment	Strategy to Support Need

Needs in the Social-Emotional Environment	Strategy to Support Need

Grouping Structure:

Implementation:

Learning Objectives:
• X
• X
• X

Learning Objectives Represented Through Areas of Learning:

Area of Learning	Teaching Strategy	Assessment
Knowledge		
Skills		
Dispositions		
Feelings		
Materials/Equipment/Resources		

Procedures:
Outline of activity
Teaching strategies
Simplifications
Extensions
Accommodations

Opportunities for Family Involvement:

Ongoing Assessment Strategies:

Development and learning plans provide a comprehensive view of classroom needs. Over time, as you familiarize yourself with each of these variables, you can adapt the plan for individual activities. Starting with this comprehensive format, however, can help you ensure that you consider each of the factors needed for the success of individual children and the classroom community.

PROFESSIONAL AND FAMILY COMFORT WITH CURRICULUM

As you are planning, implementing, and evaluating curriculum, your comfort with different curricular areas may vary. For example, you might find yourself feeling very comfortable supporting children's mathematical skills and less sure of yourself in the creative arts.

Just like children, you must actively work to support your knowledge, skills, dispositions, and feelings regarding curricular content. Table 12.5 provides an overview of strategies supporting these goals.

Just as your comfort might vary with different aspects of the early childhood curriculum, families may question their ability to support their children's learning and development. The

TABLE 12.5 A Focus on Supporting Professional Comfort with Curriculum		
Type of Learning Goal	**Relevant Knowledge and Skills**	**Strategies Supporting Your Professional Development**
Knowledge	• Information • Concepts • Relations • Meaning	• Reviewing information provided through content area organizations. • Consulting with content experts (parents, other teachers). • Using local "experts" as teaching assistants.
Skills	• Basic academic skills • Social and personal skills	• Practicing new and acquired skills. • Seeking out training on new areas of knowledge and skills. • Participating in mentoring relationships where feedback is provided on social and relationship skills.
Dispositions	• Habits of mind • Approaches to work • Preferences for learning	• Embracing lifelong learning. • Remaining open to new experiences and areas of knowledge. • Learning about your own preferences for processing and interacting with the world.
Feelings	• Realistic expectations • Dealing with success and failure, learning from mistakes • Coping with challenges • Emotional self-regulation • Dealing effectively with personal problems	• Setting attainable goals. • Embracing both success and failure as important learning tools. • Learning to feel and learn from challenging emotions. • Listening and seeking to understand your reactions to the world. • Building a strong, supportive social network.

Source: Based on *Engaging Children's Minds: The Project Approach,* 2nd ed., by L. G. Katz and S. C. Chard, 2000, Stamford, CT: Ablex.

strategies for supporting and cultivating the family's role as their child's first and most important teacher relate to supporting children's curricular development as well. Further, families can benefit from sharing knowledge and resources that will help them support their child.

Resources shared with families might include information on the importance of children's play and work and strategies that families can use in the home environment to support their child's development and learning. Teachers can also provide families with "primers" that relate to specific content areas and strategies that they can use in the home environment to support targeted development in each area.

PEARSON myeducationlab

Go to MyEducationLab and select the topic "Curriculum/Program Models." Under Building Teaching Skills and Dispositions, complete the exercises *Developing an Integrated Curriculum* and *Activity and Child-Centered Learning.*

MOVING FORWARD

Teaching practices, as an implementation tool, communicate the larger curriculum. Planning and implementing the early childhood curriculum are shaped by theory, and assessment provides the next step in the ongoing loop designed to support the learning and development of individual children. Chapter 13 of your text focuses on assessment at both the curricular and the program level and completes chapters 13 and 14 focus on supporting the intentional curriculum.

CASE STUDY

Infant and Toddler Curriculum

The Child Development Lab and Learning Center (6 weeks to 6 years)

Many of the families who attend Marian and Korissa's Welcome Night at the beginning of each semester at the CDLLC are surprised to learn that there is a formal curriculum in their infant and toddler classroom. Last year, one parent asked, "Curriculum? What are you doing other than feeding, changing, and getting them to sleep?"

Actually, the routines surrounding meeting the child's basic needs represent one of the most important pieces of the curriculum. During these periods of time, the children are spoken with and nurtured and gain important information about themselves, relationships, and those around them.

In addition to caregiving routines providing a curricular foundation, the CDLLC uses an approach they call project experiences with the young children in the classroom. Most recently, a project focused on cotton balls, and the children explored these fluffy objects in a variety of different ways. Each of the child's senses was involved in exploration. For example, the children were encouraged to use the cotton balls as an expressive tool, including mediums for painting, sculpture, and experimentation with water and shaving cream.

Through careful observation, Marian and Korissa were able to note how the children were interacting with materials and made appropriate environmental accommodations. One day, one of the children in the classroom brought cotton balls over to the sand and water table, which was filled with dirt. The next day, the children were surprised and pleased to see the table was filled with cotton balls and dirt. The teachers had also added a pitcher of water supporting of new directions in exploration.

CONSTRUCTED-RESPONSE QUESTIONS

1. Describe the role of daily routines in supporting children's development and learning. What strategies are used in the CDLLC's infant-toddler environment to support children's development and learning?

2. How are the project experiences employed by Marian and Korissa similar to the project approach? In what ways are these experiences modified to reflect infant and toddler needs?

3. How would you respond to the question, "What are essential pieces of the infant-toddler curriculum?" How does Marian and Korissa's room align with your expectations? Are there any differences? If so, what are these?

CASE STUDY

Effective Teaching Strategies

Myrna's Children's Village (6 weeks to 6 years)

"It is a sad day for us, but a happy day, too! It is Bella's last day, but we will make it the BEST DAY EVER to say farewell to her."

With that opening, Sergio begins group-time activities for the children in his bilingual preschool classroom. First, each child is assigned a role as helper for the day. The children's names are on separate cards, and Sergio hides them in his hand as he reveals "clues" before each child's name is called. "And this is a boy. A boy whose name starts with the sound *ka*. And here is a girl, a girl who is wearing red today. Now look at my lips and see if you can guess who this is." Silently, Sergio's lips mouth a *w*. "AND she has the same letter at the end of her name *TWICE!*"

The activity moved to reviewing the days of the week, singing the days first in English and then in Spanish. Sergio then places puzzle pieces in the middle of the floor, arranging them so all the children can see them. Co-teacher April, puts a song about the vowels A, E, I, O, U on in the background, and Sergio and the children sing the songs together. While they sing the different vowels, Sergio points to each of them. The process is repeated in both English and Spanish.

Their group time lasts for about 20 minutes, but there are so many changes and activities and engaging strategies that the time just seems to fly by. In their brief 20-minute block of time, children are singing, dancing, writing, reading, and communicating.

CONSTRUCTED-RESPONSE QUESTIONS

1. What strategies support literacy development in preschool? How do practices in Sergio and April's classroom reflect those strategies?

2. Describe components of effective bilingual education. What strategies do Sergio and April use to support bilingual development?

REFLECTING ON AND APPLYING EFFECTIVE PRACTICES (NAEYC AND CEC/DEC)

Ethics

You are a new teacher in a toddler classroom. Your co-teacher has been working to make sure all of the children follow the same daily schedule. You have noticed that two of the toddlers become very tired mid-morning, and that they each nod off as soon as lunch is served. When you suggest to her that perhaps they can be served lunch a bit earlier than the other children and go down for an early nap, she responds "Routine is important at this age, and they are old enough to all be on the same schedule. Besides, we don't have the staff to support serving lunch at different times and have the children awake at all different points in the day." What would you do in this situation?

NAEYC Ideals: Ethical Responsibilities to Children
I-1.2. To base program practices upon current knowledge and research in the field of early childhood education, child development, and related disciplines, as well as on particular knowledge of each child.

NAEYC Ideals: Ethical Responsibilities to Colleagues
I-3A.2. To share resources with co-workers, collaborating to ensure that the best possible early childhood care and education program is provided.

DEC: Professional and Interpersonal Behavior

6. We shall build relationships with individual children and families while individualizing the curricula and learning environments to facilitate young children's development and learning.

• •

- Schedules play an important role supporting children's development and learning through classroom activities and interactions. Review the schedules provided in this chapter. Are there any adaptations you would suggest? In addition, identify three teaching strategies that you feel would complement the successful implementation of the daily schedule.

Standards for Professional Practice

NAEYC: Teaching and Learning

4d. Using own knowledge and other resources to design, implement, and evaluate meaningful, challenging curriculum to promote positive outcomes.

DEC: Learning Environments and Social Interactions

EC5S2: Organize space, time, materials, peers, and adults to maximize progress in natural and structured environments.

EC5S3: Embed learning in everyday routines, relationships, activities, and places.

DEVELOPING YOUR PHILOSOPHY

The art and science of effective teaching was introduced in this chapter. In what ways do you see teaching as an art? In what ways does it reflect science? How will you use these factors together to support your development as a professional?

DEVELOPING YOUR PORTFOLIO

Utilizing a fictional classroom that you create and your own state's standards, develop a comprehensive lesson plan based on the template provided in this chapter. In what ways did you find completing this comprehensive plan beneficial? How might you use or adapt this plan in the future?

CHAPTER REVIEW

- **What are the general principles of curriculum, and how do these support children's development and learning?**

  Effective the curriculum is based on several general principles. One principle is the need to take a holistic approach to children's development and learning, where all developmental and curricular areas are supported. Further, learning should be integrated, reflecting the presentation of the world in the natural environment.

Children need to be supported as active learners and allowed to act and interact with their environment. Professionals take the role of interested supporters in learning, acting as children's guides with the environment. Recognition that children learn through interactions is paramount, and appropriate experiences that serve as a medium for learning provide environments in which development and learning can occur.

- **Identify teaching practices that support implementing curriculum. How do these strategies support children's engagement?**

There are many teaching practices that support implementing curriculum. Each of these practices support children's engagement through careful attention to the child's individual learning needs and the creation of a context that supports these needs. Teaching practices that need to be included are matching instructional resources and teaching activities to the developmental level of the child; holding high expectations for all children and ensuring that they will be prepared for the next level of education; making sure that activities flow from previous activities and learning into future ones, where connections are explained to children as part of the activity; previewing lessons, giving clear directions, checking for student understanding; allowing children plenty of time and opportunity for practice with new concepts and skills; monitoring student activities and providing help as needed; and allocating and making use of time in ways that make program goals.

- **Content areas identified in curriculum include literacy, mathematics, science, technology, social studies, health and safety, and the creative arts. What are important considerations for each of these content areas?**

There are many important guidelines to consider for successful teaching in each of the content areas. First, teachers must take a holistic view of children's development and learning, where all areas of children's development are assessed and planned for. Integrated learning is key, with the recognition that each content area does not exist in isolation but exists in meaningful intersections. Children are active learners who construct knowledge based on their interactions with the environment. Interactions are central to development and learning and are represented through experiences with both adults and other children. Finally, play—where children design their own experiences and interact with the environment based on their own interests and abilities—provides the medium for learning in early childhood.

- **What strategies can be used to support professional and family comfort with the curriculum?**

Both professionals and families may feel different levels of comfort with early childhood curriculum. Professionals might experience discomfort in areas they feel less equipped to teach, and some families may experience discomfort supporting their child's development and learning. Professional comfort can be supported through ongoing training and professional development, consulting and collaborating with other professionals and parents, practicing new skills, learning about preferred methods of processing and applying new information, setting goals toward pursuing and applying new information; recognizing there will be success and challenges along the way, and embracing lifelong learning. Family comfort in the curriculum can be supported through sharing knowledge and resources; providing activities to link home and school learning; and providing specific information on content areas and teaching strategies that can be used in the home environment.

13 Program Planning and Evaluation

"One test of the correctness of educational procedure is the happiness of the child."

—MARIA MONTESSORI

Marie looked forward to her second year of teaching 4-year-olds at a local child care program. She felt that she made great gains as a professional in her first year. As the year went on, she felt increasingly able to plan activities based on children's interests and developmental needs. Each of the three early childhood education classes she took at the local college contributed greatly to her development. The class on guidance was of particular interest, as supporting positive behaviors in the early childhood environment was what she had struggled with the most.

For the coming year, one of Marie's goals was to learn more about how effectively her classroom was operating. Although Marie felt competent in her ability to support individual children, she was less sure of how effectively she was meeting the program's overall goals. Marie relied on her state's Early Learning Standards for classroom-based assessment and curriculum, but also knew that the program had a whole other set of standards—related to such things as health, safety, and overall program quality—to adhere to, which affected her performance in the classroom. Marie felt that understanding these standards and their evaluation would strengthen her overall performance.

GUIDING QUESTIONS

- How do standards inform program evaluation?
- In what ways can program evaluation practices support equity and accountability for all children?
- What standards gaps exist in the field?
- What role do standards play in program planning?
- What factors need to be considered when assessing program effectiveness?
- What is the role of the family and the professional in determining program effectiveness?

● ● ●

You have been learning about the scope of curriculum in early childhood programs, including assessment, enriched and engaging learning environments, and effective and respectful teaching practices. At this point, our attention turns to program planning and evaluation, which represent the composite of all the different curricular pieces. Whether you are presently teaching in a classroom or will in the future, as a professional you must know how to evaluate programs and constantly strive for high quality. This examination is vital because all aspects of the early childhood curriculum are interrelated, just as all domains of development are interrelated. Therefore, knowledge of the individual parts is only useful when we understand how these parts come together in a coherent whole. Having program goals and striving to meet them translates into effective practices.

What are appropriate early childhood program goals? The NAEYC (2005) Code of Ethical Conduct identifies one of the ideals of professionals in the field as providing communities with high-quality care and education programs and services. As you have been learning, one of the main challenges facing the field is the lack of consistency in meeting quality goals. On the one hand, there is extensive research demonstrating the important role that quality programming plays in the lives of young children and their families (Cotton & Conklin, 2001; American Federation of Teachers, 2002). On the other hand, there is incredible variance in how or if this knowledge is applied in terms of public policy, standards, and requirements for early childhood programs (National Association of Child Care Resource and Referral Agencies [NACCRRA], 2007). This is essentially a gap between what we know and what we do.

Standards and assessment that guide program practice represent an important foundation of early childhood programs. High standards and solid assessment inform effective, quality programming that supports the development and learning of each child. Poorly developed and implemented standards and assessment, on the other hand, create programming and practice that is variable in their quality and potentially damaging to young children's healthy development and learning.

397

STANDARDS AT THE FOREFRONT

In Chapter 9, you learned about content standards and their role in guiding learning and development in specific content areas such as mathematics, technology, and language arts. This chapter focuses on standards that guide the development of a solid, effective infrastructure from which quality programming and practices can be built. How do standards relate to **program planning and evaluation**? First, standards provide information about quality and address the question: What should my program include to support children's development and learning? In turn, the standards informing program planning become the same factors that are evaluated, addressing the question: How effectively is my program supporting development and learning? As you have learned, program effectiveness is not limited in its impact on children alone, but also affects families, professionals, and the larger community.

The standards affecting early childhood programming vary. For example, state early learning standards provide information on what children should know and be able to do. These, in turn, affect professional teaching standards that guide the knowledge, skills, and dispositions professionals need to support children in meeting the early learning standards. As development and learning occur in early childhood programs, standards also provide guidelines for program operation. Figure 13.1 illustrates standards affecting early childhood programming.

Program standards vary in the kinds of programs they influence as well as who is affected. For example, some standards are legal and must be adhered to for operation. These standards include licensing standards, the Department of Defense's military child care standards, National Fire Protection Association standards, and Child and Adult Care Food Program standards. Other standards are linked to funding and represent requirements programs must meet to receive or continue to receive money from the funding source. These include, for example, standards provided through the No Child Left Behind Act, Head Start Performance Standards, and **tiered reimbursement strategies** (Alliance for Early Childhood Finance, 2006). Other standards are based on **community norm standards** or quality standards determined by organizations in the field or those decided on by individual schools or school districts.

The largest organizations that have quality standards include the NAEYC, the National Association for Family Child Care (NAFCC), and the National AfterSchool Association (NAA). These standards are reinforced by consumer behavior. For example, parents who

program planning and evaluation
Focus on the whole of the early childhood curriculum in terms of effective planning and assessment of program effectiveness.

tiered reimbursement standards
Funding standards linked to the quality of care children receive.

community norm standards
Standards such as accreditation that are supported through consumer behavior.

FIGURE 13.1
Standards Affecting Early Childhood Programming

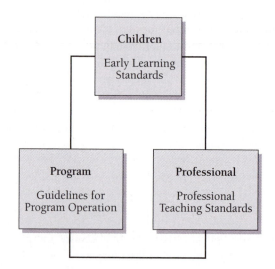

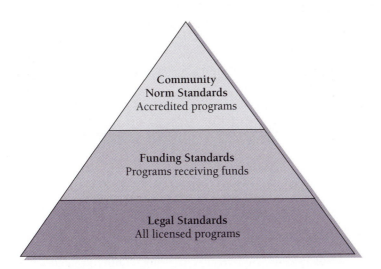

FIGURE 13.2
Impact of Program
Standards on a
Program Meeting
Legal, Funding, and
Community Norm
Standards

are educated about the importance of NAEYC accreditation might choose to place their children only in accredited programs, reflective of consumers making choices based on these quality standards. Figure 13.2 illustrates the potential impact of program standards.

Depending on your job or role in early childhood education, some of these standards are more likely to affect you than others. All professionals in early childhood programs need to be aware of **legal standards** as they relate to their classroom environment. For example, you need to be aware of hand-washing practices, fire safety, staff–child ratio, and food service requirements. **Funding standards**, however, are more likely to affect the directors of programs or the superintendents or principals of schools that receive funding from the organization issuing the standards. For example, Head Start Performance Standards are only applicable to Head Start programs. Community norm standards are elective standards and relevant if you are in a program that is pursuing or has pursued accreditation. These standards will affect your daily role in the environment and specific classroom policies and practices.

Standards need to work together to create a coherent composite of quality that is greater than the sum of its parts (Stoney, Mitchell, & Warner, 2006). All programs (with the exclusion of those that are licensed-exempt, such as preschool or after-school programs operated by public schools, drop-in programs, and private school programs) are required to meet minimal health and safety standards established through licensing standards. Then, programs must ensure that they are meeting requirements, if applicable, of their funding source. From this point, quality standards established in the field, such as accreditation standards, can be met.

legal standards
Program standards that must be adhered to for program operation.

funding standards
Standards programs must adhere in order to meet requirements of external funders.

TEACHING AND LEARNING CONNECTIONS

Learning About Your Program's Standards

- What kinds of standards does your program or school have to follow?
- Do the standards your program or school uses reflect quality recommendations?
- How are standards assessed at the program level?
- What is your role in carrying out program standards?
- How can you ensure that standards are incorporated daily?

FIGURE 13.3
Variation in State Infant–Caregiver Ratios

Source: From National Association of Child Care Resource and Referral Agencies (2006).

Number of Infants per Caregiver

- NAEYC
- Georgia
- Louisiana
- Oregon

Legal Standards: Licensing

licensing standards

Legal standards that reflect the meeting of basic health and safety requirements.

Licensing standards provide requirements regarding minimum standards of health and safety that must be in place for programs to operate. All fifty states have child care licensing statutes, which provide standards for safe and legal operation of a child care facility (National Resource Center for Health and Safety in Child Care, 2002). Each state, however, can develop its own standards, leading to great variance between states. Staff–child ratio is one example where there is great discrepancy. Because of the need for nurturing and supportive relationships, NAEYC standards recommend a staff–child ratio of 1:3 for infants in child care settings. The state of Georgia allows a 1:6 ratio, Louisiana a 1:5 ratio, and Oregon a 1:4 ratio (National Child Care Information and Technical Assistance Center, 2006). Figure 13.3 shows the variation of infant-caregiver ratios in these states.

Family child care homes also have great variance in group size and staff–child ratio. Oklahoma, for example, allows a group size of seven, with no more than two children under the age of 5 in the care environment. Maine allows no more than four infants and toddlers total in a child care environment, whereas California requires no more than two infants when up to six children are being cared for (National Child Care Information and Technical Assistance Center, 2006).

Although the existence of these standards and a regulating agency responsible for making sure the standards are met is universal, there is great variance in who is exempted, or not regulated, by the standards. For example, some states exempt part-time day centers, school-age child care, care provided in summer camps or group homes, and care provided by religious organizations (National Resource Center for Health and Safety in Child Care, 2002). All entities that provide care to children, with the exception of close relatives, should be regulated, as any kind of exemption could put children at risk (National Resource Center for Health and Safety in Child Care, 2002).

What kinds of standards are important for programs? Standards should provide guidance in the following areas (National Resource Center for Health and Safety in Child Care, 2002):

- Staffing, including the overall qualifications of staff working with young children
- Programming, including activities for healthy development

Healthy and safe environments allow children to thrive.

- Health promotion and protection in child care
- Nutrition and food service
- Facilities, supplies, equipment, and transportation
- Infectious diseases, including prevention and dealing effectively with chronic and emerging illness
- Children who are eligible for services under IDEA
- Administration of the overall program
- Licensing and community action

Professionals need to look first to their state standards for health and safety to ensure that these are being met. However, standards for health and safety are designed to be minimal standards. Additional program planning and evaluation standards provide a guide for achieving quality.

Funding Standards

Funding standards are requirements that must be met by programs in order for them to receive or continue to receive monies from their funders. Funding standards are in addition to licensing standards. These standards can also overlap with community norm standards, as some funders (such as the Department of Defense's military child care) require NAEYC accreditation as a prerequisite for continued funding.

Head Start Performance Standards. The Head Start Performance Standards are mandatory requirements that all grantees must abide by to operate a Head Start or Early Head Start program. These standards include attention to defining the objectives and features of Head Start programs in concrete and measurable terms. The standards also communicate a vision of services for children and families. Finally, the standards provide a regulatory structure for the monitoring and enforcement of quality standards (U.S. Department of Health and Human Services, 2007).

Tiered Quality Strategies. Thirty-five states and the District of Columbia have instituted forms of **tiered quality strategies** (TQS) (National Child Care Information and Technical Assistance Center, 2005). TQS systems can be linked to licensing, funding, and/or consumption. For example, some states have adopted a quality star rating system where programs are assessed through the local **Child Care Resource and Referral Agency** and provided with a star rating based on quality in the center. A program earning three stars will be reimbursed at a higher level per child than a program earning two stars, creating a link between TQS and funding strategies. Consumer strategies include the provision of a "report card" that informs families of the program's performance in varied quality standards. In turn, these strategies will ideally affect family choice to participate in the program.

The overall goal of TQS standards is moving subsidized child care to higher levels of quality, where state licensing provides a baseline index of quality. The components of tiered reimbursement include the following (National Child Care Information and Technical Assistance Center, 2005):

- States establish a formal system of more than one level of quality, based on specified criteria that the state believes to be associated with improved child development, learning, and well-being.
- Different rating levels are used for establishing reimbursement rates for child care centers and family child care homes.
- Tiered reimbursement is a part of the state's consumer education or parent outreach activities. The system includes a way of informing parents about the rating of each provider and thus the quality of care.

tiered quality standards
Quality standards linked to licensing, funding, and/or consumption.

Child Care Resource and Referral Agencies
State and local organizations that work with parents, providers, and communities to improve access to child care for families.

ISSUES OF ACCESS AND EQUITY
Head Start Performance Standards

The Head Start Performance Standards provide quality assurances. Head Start and Early Head Start serve the most vulnerable children and families in the country, with 90% of the incomes of Head Start families falling below the federal poverty guideline (NAEYC, 2007). Ensuring that the needs of these children and families are met requires careful attention to program planning and evaluation. Programming standards designed to support these goals include:

- Child health and developmental services
- Education and early childhood development
- Child health and safety
- Child nutrition
- Child mental health
- Family partnerships
- Community partnerships
- Program governance
- Management systems and procedures
- Human resources management
- Facilities, materials, and equipment

For Head Start programs to continue receiving funding, criteria in each area must be met. The criteria are not static and were recently reviewed as a part of the 2008 Head Start Reauthorization. Some of the goals or recommendations made in the reauthorization included supporting a continuous transition between preschool and elementary school; however, these changes might come with costs (Stipek, 2005). Stipek argues that although alignment is a goal in the field, the alignment can occur in the wrong direction. Specifically, as opposed to the elementary grades becoming more child and family centered and developmentally appropriate, preschool would become more like elementary schools, with formal instruction and a de-emphasis on family partnerships.

- Differential reimbursement rates are linked to accreditation by a national organization. Thirty-one states have linked differential reimbursement rates to child care programs that have achieved accreditation.

Research on the link between TQS and quality has indicated a positive impact (National Child Care Information and Technical Assistance Center, 2005). However, there is great variance in how states define quality and which populations of children and families are affected by TQS strategies. For example, TQS exclusively affects children who are in nonexempt programs, meaning programs that require licensing. Therefore, not all programs are eligible to participate in the rating system. In Illinois, for example, the TQS of a quality rating system only applies to programs where children are receiving subsidized child care services. Only programs that provide these subsidies will receive a quality rating. Therefore, only the families of children who are receiving child care subsidies can use the quality rating system as an assessment tool.

Community Norm Standards

The accreditation processes of the NAFCC, the NAA, and the NAEYC were designed to create continuity between early childhood programs by providing guidance for how to attain high-quality care and through a process that recognizes program excellence. Accreditation through each of these agencies is a voluntary process—programs must opt to pursue the accreditation. Therefore, although the goal of accreditation is supporting uniform standards that represent high-quality programming, not every program elects or is able to participate in the process. Potential obstacles include the time involved in accreditation; the costs associated with pursuing, attaining, and maintaining accreditation; and knowledge of the accreditation process (Center for Early Childhood Leadership, 2001).

• • • BECOMING A PROFESSIONAL • • •

Career Pathways

Director of Intergenerational Program

The Hildebrandt Learning Center is an intergenerational program located on the residence of a life care facility. This large campus of 1,400 acres provides independent and assisted-living services and a full health-care facility. The children at the learning center have daily contact with program residents.

Rose's job is to oversee the operations of the center, manage the quality of the program, and collaborate with families and teachers. Related responsibilities include overseeing licensing, accreditation, the development of the center's portfolio, staffing, and working with teachers on their professional development plan. Rose embraces her advocacy role as the center's director and spends a good deal of her time working on community action and state initiatives related to quality care.

"One of the main things that I like about my job is that no two days are alike. I have a lot of autonomy to make professional judgments, and I have a great deal of support from my company. I just love working with teachers and families and doing what's best for kids, and I have the freedom to interact with the kids on a daily basis."

The job does not come without its challenges. One of the main challenges Rose identifies is that the job has a very high stress level. "I have ethical responsibilities to children, families, and staff. Sometimes, these can pull me in many different directions. This is one reason why the job is one of the most rewarding and frustrating things that I have ever done. Some things that have helped me resolve issues that have arisen include having a clear understanding of my own values and vision and really taking the time to think and reflect."

Rose has her associate's degree in early childhood education and is taking courses pursuing her bachelor's degree. She also has a certificate in Management and Organizational Development, which she feels helps her greatly in the daily challenges of her position.

The occupational outlook for educational administrators is very good—this role is expected to grow as fast as the average for all occupations through 2014. Particularly as more states begin sponsoring public preschool programs, an increased number of preschool program directors will be needed (Onveon, 2008). Successful preparation for this career includes knowledge of early childhood development and programming and effective management and organizational skills.

CHALLENGES OF STANDARDS: EQUITY AND ACCOUNTABILITY

Strategies based on legal issues, funding, and/or community norms share many common characteristics. Each standard set includes criteria that guide program development and provide concrete factors for evaluation. In addition, each set of standards is based on research and extensive professional development and input.

There are, however, differences between the standard sets. An obvious difference is the ages that the standards cover. For example, NAEYC accreditation covers children from birth through kindergarten, whereas Head Start standards cover preschool-age children. The NAA standards cover children in after-school programs between the ages of 5 and 14. The standards also differ in who is affected. For example, NAEYC standards are voluntary, the Head Start standards are mandatory only for grantees, and Department of Defense standards are applicable exclusively to military child care. Legal operation exclusively requires that programs meet legal standards, resulting in great variance in quality: For example, although NAEYC standards for accreditation advocate a 1:3 ratio for professionals to infants and young toddlers, states can vary in their ratio requirements for this age group from 1:3 to 1:8 (NACCRRA, 2007).

For universal quality in the field, uniform standards that apply to all programs are essential. Ideally, these standards would be continuous from infancy through third grade, supporting children's development within and across a variety of care and education settings and reflecting what is known about effective practice for children from birth to age 8 and their families. Presently, a model supportive of such continuity is lacking. In fact, the only monitoring system that presently exists across states is the minimum requirements set forth through licensing standards. Improving licensing standards at the national level, therefore, has been viewed as a tool to ensure programmatic equity and quality (NACCRRA, 2007).

NACCRRA'S Program Benchmarks

For standards to be effective, they need to exist on a continuum that begins with meeting basic licensing requirements and proceeds to ensure that additional standards provided through funders and community norms are met (Stipek, 2005). Ideally, all programs would strive to meet standards at each level, thereby ensuring that basic licensing requirements are met and exceeded. The NACCRRA has provided a list of 10 benchmarks applying to quality programming and professionals that take each of these levels into account. Their assessment of how well states meet these standards, however, indicates that most states are sorely lacking (NACCRRA, 2007).

NACCRRA (2007) identifies quality standards as essential in the licensing system. If quality standards were included in licensing, they would be most likely to affect the largest population of children, as licensing is required in states for the legal operation of programs. This will require that the present system move from assurances of health and safety to assurances of quality in a healthy and safe environment. The standards NACCRRA (2007) examined, related benchmarks of quality, and the number of states that meet these benchmarks are summarized in Table 13.1.

The Department of Defense's military child care system ranked first in quality assurances, and the state of Idaho ranked last. Regarding program standards, NACCRRA (2007) recommended that states *meet NAEYC staff–child ratios and limit overall group size*. It is also identified as *essential that states are required to include health and safety standards in all 10 basic areas*. Their third recommendation stressed that *parent involvement and at-will access to centers during normal business hours be required*.

Standard	Benchmark	States in Full Compliance
TABLE 13.1 NACCRRA Standards, Benchmarks of Quality, and States in Full Compliance		
Staff–child ratio	Based on NAEYC Accreditation Standards Birth to 15 months: 1:3–1:4 12 to 28 months: 1:3–1:4 21 to 36 months: 1:4–1:6 2 to 3 years: 1:6–1:9 4 years: 1:8–1:10 5 years: 1:8–1:10	0
Group size requirements	Based on NAEYC Accreditation Standards Birth to 15 months: 6–8 children 12 to 28 months: 6–8 children 21 to 36 months: 8–12 children 2 to 3 years: 12–18 children 4 years: 16–20 children 5 years: 16–20 children	0
Criminal background check requirements	Center staff must undergo a criminal history background check, a check of child abuse and neglect registries, a state fingerprint check, a federal fingerprint check, and a check of sex offender registries.	3
Developmental domains that programs must address	Center programs must address six areas of child development, including social, physical, language-literacy, cognitive-intellectual, emotional, and cultural.	13
Health and safety requirements	Center procedures must address each of the following 10 areas and explicitly prohibit corporal punishment: • Guidance and discipline • Immunizations • Sudden Infant Death Syndrome • Fire evacuation • Administration of medicine • Incident reporting • Hand washing/diapering • Hazardous materials • Surfaces under playground equipment • Emergency preparedness	8 states and the Department of Defense (military child care)
Parent involvement, communication, and parental access	Centers must involve and communicate with parents and allow parental visits.	22 states and the Department of Defense (military child care)

Source: From National Association of Child Care Resource Referral Agencies (2007).

Incorporating quality standards into licensing requirements supports high-quality early childhood programming. However, high-quality early childhood programming is not necessarily reflective of high-quality *inclusive* early childhood programming (Buysse, Wesley, Bryant, & Gardner, 1999). Further, children in kindergarten and the primary grades are not likely to be affected by the standard sets ensuring quality in early childhood programs, as the regulations affecting programming and practice are determined in another standard set. Therefore, at present, the whole of the early childhood population would not be affected by NACCRRA's recommendations.

STANDARDS GAPS: CHILDREN WITH DISABILITIES AND PRIMARY GRADES

Early childhood education must support the diversity of child, family, professional, and community needs. As you will remember, part of the challenge in early childhood education today is the synthesis of the five disparate historical strands of the field. These strands include child care, preschool, kindergarten, primary grade education, and the education of children with disabilities. The standards summarized to this point reflect these disparate origins. Specifically, these standards fail to apply to the breadth of the field in terms of (1) ages included and (2) attention to the inclusion of children with disabilities. Although NACCRRA's indicators represent quality benchmarks for children between birth and the age of 5, adaptation is required to support children with disabilities and children in the primary grades. In addition, research has demonstrated that quality early childhood program and quality inclusion are not synonymous—in other words, just because a program is high quality does not mean that it is reflective of high-quality practices that support inclusion (Buysse et al., 1999).

As you learned in Chapter 3, the 2008 Field Review Draft of the Joint Position Statement of Early Childhood Inclusion developed by the Division for Early Childhood (DEC) and the National Association for the Education of Young Children (NAEYC) identifies the defining features of inclusion in high-quality early childhood programs and services. These include (1) access, supporting children's active engagement in a wide range of learning opportunities, activities, environments, and settings; (2) participation, supporting belonging, participation, and engagement of children with disabilities and their typically developing peers through intentional strategies matched to the child's development and learning needs; and (3), supports, reflecting ongoing professional development and support provided to families, practitioners, administrators, and specialists to ensure the development and implementation of high-quality inclusive programming. For programming to be high-quality and inclusive, each of these factors must be in place.

Standards are one tool that can have an impact on each of these factors, as they can be utilized to ensure access, promote active participation, and serve as a catalyst for needed supports. Therefore, standards represent a guidance tool that can contribute to whether universal high-quality inclusive programs become a reality.

High-quality environments support each child's developing strengths.

Children with Disabilities

Through IDEA, the federal government provides specific legal requirements for inclusive practices. Most relevant is the requirement that all children are entitled to a free and appropriate public education in the least restrictive environment and, for infants and toddlers, early intervention services in natural environments.

In 2002, NAEYC and the National Association of Early Childhood Specialists in State Departments of Education (NAECS/SDE) published a joint position statement entitled *Early Learning Standards: Creating the Conditions for Success*. In this position statement, four essential features of early learning standards that have to be developmentally effective are described:

- Significant, developmentally appropriate content and outcomes are emphasized.
- Informed, inclusive processes are used for development and review.
- Implementation and assessment strategies that are ethical and appropriate for young children are used.
- Strong supports for early childhood programs, professionals, and families accompany the standards.

In 2007, the Division for Early Childhood of the Council for Exceptional Children developed a companion document to the NAEYC/NAECS/SDE position statement, with the goal of considering the general recommendations in light of specific issues for programs serving young children with disabilities and their families.

DEC Indicators of Program Effectiveness. The main goal of program effectiveness as articulated by the DEC includes that *all learners have the opportunity to participate in the curriculum through multiple means of expression, engagement, and representation.* Table 13.2 summarizes DEC's major recommendations and their applications in the early childhood environment.

TABLE 13.2   DEC Indicators of Program Effectiveness and Their Applications

DEC Indicator	Application
Multiple means of representation are provided so that the curriculum is accessible to all children regardless of ability, needs, or background.	Effective participation of all children is supported through the: • Presentation of instruction • Interactions between adults and children • Materials and toys • Environment
Multiple means of engagement are available so that children fully participate in the curriculum regardless of ability, needs, or background.	The curriculum provides flexible options that support and appeal to children with different abilities, developmental levels, preferences, and cultural backgrounds.
Multiple means of expression are supported so that children can demonstrate what they know and are able to do regardless of ability, needs, or background.	The curriculum provides children with many options to communicate their knowledge and skills and supports this communication through children using their preferred mode of communication.
Programs adopt curriculum goals that are clear and shared by all.	Common goals (provided through standards or outcomes) are derived from knowledge and skills deemed appropriate for all children. Developing individual goals will support children in acquiring this knowledge and skills.
Curriculum is comprehensive.	The curriculum provided is clearly understood by all stakeholders and covers all areas of development and learning. In addition, the curriculum covers federal, state, or agency standards and exposes children to a wide variety of experiences through a continuum of teaching strategies.
Programs strive to build and maintain successful partnerships as curriculum is implemented.	Children should be served by community, schools, and families that are working toward a common vision and goals supportive of children's healthy learning and development. Open communication, mutual trust, and shared values are essential for this common vision and related goals to develop.

Source: From Division for Early Childhood/Council for Exceptional Children (2007).

The DEC recommendations (2007) advocate for a universally designed curriculum that incorporates and supports the individual needs of children and families, provides sensitive and appropriate assessment processes; , and includes meaningful program evaluation. For curriculum to be fully supportive of children between birth and the age of 8, however, attention to primary grade populations is essential.

Children in the Primary Grades

The No Child Left Behind Act, passed by President George W. Bush in 2001, has had a dramatic impact on standards and accountability for children in the primary grades. NCLB represented a reauthorization of the Elementary and Secondary School Act, which was the main law affecting students in kindergarten through high school. The four guiding principles of the act consist of:

- Accountability for results
- More choices for parents
- Greater local control and flexibility
- An emphasis on actions based on scientific results

Figure 13.4 defines some of the important NCLB terms.

NCLB has been controversial since its inception and the target of wide criticism. Criticisms fall into three main categories: (1) The NCLB isn't adequately funded, (2) NCLB unfairly holds schools accountable for student performance, and (3) NCLB relies extensively on assessment (Brookings Institution, 2008). Educational theorist and writer Alfie Kohn (2007) believes that there are dangers in these shortcomings. One of his main concerns centers on reductions in funding for schools that do not meet requirements for adequate yearly progress (AYP). In Schools Matter, a blog on educational policy, he notes the following:

> The No Child Left Behind Act (NCLB) places an overwhelming emphasis on standardized testing as a route to success in school. However, it is also designed to humiliate and hurt the schools that, according to its own warped standards, most need help. Families at those schools are given a green light to abandon them—and, specifically, to transfer to other schools. This, it quickly becomes clear, is an excellent way to sandbag the "successful" schools, too. (Kohn, 2007)

FIGURE 13.4
Important NCLB
Terms to Know

- *Title I:* Provides support for children of families with low income.
- *State assessments:* Tests developed by each state to be administered in grades 3 through 8 and once in high school.
- *Adequate yearly progress (*AYP*):* Term reflecting a school's ability to meet defined reading and math goals.
- *School in need of improvement:* Term used for schools receiving Title I funds that have not met AYP for at least 2 years.
- *Supplemental educational services:* Tutoring and extra help that children from families with low income may be able to receive, which is offered to families free of charge.
- *Highly qualified teacher (*HQT*):* Term used to represent a teacher who has demonstrated knowledge and skills in the subject he or she is teaching, has a college degree, and is state certified. Children must be taught by HQTs in core subject matters.

Accountability measures in the NCLB begin during grade 3, placing increasing pressure on early childhood teachers to emphasize more basic academic skill acquisition (Stipek, 2005). Should this increased focus on academic skills come at the expense of attention to social and emotional skills, the ability to support young children's development and learning through effective practice is likely to be affected (Stipek, 2005). NCLB, therefore, represents an important standard set affecting early childhood.

STANDARDS: THE FOUNDATION FOR PLANNING AND EVALUATION

Standards are only effective if they are used as a tool in planning and evaluation. The quality of underlying standards, therefore, has the potential to greatly affect the quality of programming in the field. For example, imagine an early childhood program that takes its state's minimum standards of health and safety as the bar of quality to aspire to—the programming and practices in this program are likely to differ significantly from a program that uses accreditation guidelines as its bar. In addition, a program may have quality practices in place, but not reflect quality factors supportive of inclusion. Standards, as they exist in the field, are not always reflective of the full range of ages included in the field and diversity of child and family populations.

How do we synthesize these standards and create one system of quality supportive of all children and families? NACCRRA recommends that its program benchmarks be included as standard licensing requirements. However, NACCRRA benchmarks apply only to early childhood care and education programs and not to kindergarten and primary grades. Further, although the NACCRRA standards include information on programming related to six developmental domains, they don't include how these standards translate into effective programming. The NAEYC Accreditation Programming Criteria, designed to represent community norms once licensing has been attained, provide specific information on what variables are important in planning and evaluating effective programming. Again, this standard set is limited in its lack of specific attention to primary grades. Further, although each of these standard sets is designed to support diversity in child and family learning and development, expansion to specifically include inclusive program factors fits within the goals of inclusion and flexibility that reflect current goals in the field.

What standards are effective for program planning and evaluation? Figure 13.5 represents an organizing structure for NAEYC Accreditation Standards, NACCRRA benchmarks, and the DEC's Indicators of Program Effectiveness. As success and equity for all children and families are based on access to programs and successfully meeting the varied components of the intentional curriculum—including knowledge of theory, planning, implementation, and assessment—these categories are used as a template for organizing relevant standards.

From Standards to Program Planning

Standards shape program practice. Therefore, effective planning and evaluation require knowledge of underlying standards. Taking a holistic view of the program similar to the one advocated for child, family, and professional development requires looking at the varied program components. Figure 13.6 provides a template that can serve as a guide in program planning and evaluation.

FIGURE 13.5
Standards for
Program Planning
and Evaluation

Standards

Access for Children and Families

- The program provides opportunities for equitable participation amongst children, families, and professionals.

- The individual needs of children, families, and professionals are considered in the program's infrastructure, including appropriate staff–child ratios, professional development, and group size.

- Children are served by community, schools, and families that are working toward a common vision and goals supportive of children's healthy development and learning. Open communication, mutual trust, and shared values are essential for this common vision and related goals to develop.

- The program promotes the nutrition and health of children and protects children and staff from illness and injury. Health and safety standards must address each of the following 10 areas and explicitly prohibit corporal punishment:

  - Guidance and discipline
  - Immunizations
  - Sudden Infant Death Syndrome
  - Fire evacuation
  - Administration of medicine
  - Incident reporting
  - Hand washing/diapering
  - Hazardous materials
  - Surfaces under playground equipment
  - Emergency preparedness

- The program employs and supports a teaching staff that has the educational qualifications, knowledge, and professional commitment necessary to promote the development and learning of each and every child and to support families' diverse needs and interests.

- The program establishes and maintains collaborative relationships with each child's family to foster children's development in all settings. These relationships are sensitive to family composition, language, and culture. Programs must involve and communicate with families and allow open family access to the program.

Program Theory and Planning

- The program has a clearly articulated philosophy that presents overall goals and communicates expected outcomes.

- There is measurable continuity between the program's philosophy and goals, curricular environment, and outcomes for children, families, and professionals.

- Common goals (provided through standards or outcomes) are derived from knowledge and skills deemed appropriate for all children. Developing individual goals and instruction designed to meet these goals supports children in acquiring this knowledge and skills.

Program Implementation

- The curriculum provides flexible options that support and appeal to children with different abilities, developmental levels, preferences, and cultural backgrounds.
- Effective participation of all children is supported through the:
  - Presentation of instruction, ensuring multiple means of expression, engagement, and representation
  - Interactions between adults and children
  - Materials and toys
  - Environment
- The curriculum provided is clearly understood by all stakeholders and covers all areas of development and learning, including social, emotional, physical, language, and cognitive. In addition, the curriculum covers federal, state, or agency standards and exposes children to a wide variety of experiences through a continuum of teaching strategies.
- Positive relationships are supported among children and adults encouraging each child's sense of individual worth and belonging as a part of a community.
- The program uses developmentally, culturally, and linguistically appropriate and effective teaching approaches that enhance each child's development and learning in the context of the program's curricular goals.
- The program has a safe and healthful environment that provides appropriate and well-maintained indoor and outdoor physical environments. The environment includes facilities, equipment, and materials to facilitate child and staff learning and development.

Program Assessment

- The curriculum provides children with many options to communicate their knowledge and skills and supports this communication through children using their preferred mode of communication.
- The program is informed by ongoing, systematic, formal, and informal assessment approaches to provide information on children's development and learning. These assessments occur in the context of reciprocal communications with families and sensitivity to the cultural contexts in which children develop. Assessment results are used to benefit children by informing sound decisions about children, teaching, and program improvement.
- The program effectively implements policies, procedures, and systems that support stable staff and strong personnel, fiscal, and program management so that all children, families, and staff have high-quality experiences.

How can these program standards be put into practice? You will recall that Marie, presented in the vignette at the beginning of the chapter, was searching for strategies to help her examine the "big picture" of her early childhood classroom. Marie recognized that understanding the "big picture" would require examining individual parts. One of the first steps she took was to learn more about her program through examining the program's **mission statement**, which reflected the underlying goals of the program.

Identifying the Program's Mission. Once programs have formally defined what standards are included in their program and how these standards inform practice, a mission statement can be developed. Mission statements provide a clear depiction of the program's

mission statement
Clear depiction of program goals and reason for being.

FIGURE 13.6
Template for
Program Planning
and Evaluation

Access

- How is access supported for children and families?
- How does the program ensure that all children and families are included and have access to the early childhood program? Defining this factor includes articulating information about:
  - Who is the targeted population? This might include the number of children served, whether the program is inclusive, and whether the program is designed to support specific diverse student needs.
  - Where is the targeted population drawn from, such as the larger community or a specific subset of the community?
  - How are children, families, professionals, and the community served by the program's goals?
  - How does the program ensure children's basic health and safety?
  - Who is the teaching staff?
  - How is collaboration supported?

- **Theory and Planning**
  - What is the program philosophy? You learned in Chapter 7 that professional philosophies provide information on your personal goals and beliefs regarding children's learning. Program philosophies are similar, but based on the goals of the whole program. Because of their similarities, Chism's (1998) guidelines for the development of a professional portfolio can be adapted to the early childhood program. These include:
    - *The program's conceptualization of learning,* which includes beliefs about how children learn and develop. Effective philosophies include a synthesis of current literature on children's learning and the role of families, professionals, and the field in supporting learning.
    - *The program's conceptualization of effective teaching,* which includes curricular models (if applicable) and teaching strategies used to support the development of children and families.
    - *The goals of the program in supporting the development of children, families, and professionals,* including the knowledge, skills, and dispositions that the program seeks to support.
    - *How the philosophy is implemented,* including the environmental design, community building, and teaching practices that would be observable in the program, as well information on family and community partnerships and support for ongoing professional development.
    - *Long-term goals of the program,* including a statement of how these goals will be attained.
  - How does the program philosophy translate into measurable goals, the curricular environment, and outcomes for children and families?

- **Implementation**
  - How does the curriculum provide flexible options and support for:
    - Children with varying abilities and developmental levels.
    - Children's varied learning styles and interaction preferences.
    - Child and family culture.

- What knowledge, skills, dispositions, and feelings does the program work to cultivate? What strategies support each of these areas?
- How does the curriculum meet learning and development goals in each of the following areas:
  - Social-emotional
  - Cognitive-language and literacy
  - Physical
- What teaching practices are utilized in the curriculum? How do these practices support developmental, cultural, and linguistic diversity?
- How does the curriculum align with local, state, and national standards?
- How are positive relationships cultivated in the program?
- How does the environment support children's learning?

- **Assessment**
  - What opportunities do children have to communicate their knowledge and skills? How do these opportunities accommodate individual differences in communication abilities and preferences?
  - What ongoing, systematic, formal, and informal assessment strategies are used in the program? How do these assessment strategies benefit children, inform teaching, and provide information for program improvement?
  - What policies and procedures does the program have in place, and how do these support stable staff and strong personnel and fiscal and program management?

goals and summarize the program's reason for being. They are used in public schools, centers, family child care homes, and Head Start programs. Any program with goals affecting young children and their families can benefit from providing these in a mission statement. In general, effective mission statements provide the following information (Radtke, 1998):

- What is the purpose of the organization?
- How does the organization meet its purpose?
- What principles of our beliefs guide the program?

With this information provided, effective mission statements should (Radtke, 1998):

- Express the program's purpose in a way that inspires support and ongoing commitment.
- Serve to motivate those who are connected to the organization.
- Be communicated in a way that is convincing and easy to grasp.
- Use proactive verbs to describe what the program does.
- Be free of jargon.
- Be short enough that anyone from the organization can read and repeat it.

The mission statement provides a written representation of a program's goals. Program implementation starts with determination of each child's strengths, challenges,

A program's mission statement serves as a guide to effective practice.

and goals and continues with effective curricular practices (pertaining to the physical and social environment, support for social-emotional development, effective assessment, and appropriate curricular models and teaching practices) that support these goals. Assessing a program's effectiveness is an ongoing need and ensures that there is alignment between standards, mission, and practices.

ASSESSING PROGRAM EFFECTIVENESS

Effective program planning begins with looking at the relevant standards and determining how these will be met. How the standards will be met is linked closely to planning, as the standards, in turn, inform program practices. Addressing the question "How effective is the program in meeting its goals?" is provided through evaluation. Program evaluation is not an endpoint, but rather, evaluation serves as a tool that in turn informs planning.

Program effectiveness can be evaluated in a variety of ways. One evaluation strategy is to look within the program through observation and assessment. Another is to look at the effectiveness of the program externally, through the eyes of its stakeholders.

Observation and Assessment

Professionals can look can look within programs to determine how effectively the programs are meeting their targeted goals. They can evaluate many standards through documentation review, where they examine programs to make sure that policies, data collection procedures, and finances are in order. Much of this work would be relevant to a program director or school principal. At the teacher's level, determining how effectively developmental and educational goals are being met is essential and requires substantive knowledge and skills in program planning and evaluation.

Some of the same methods used to observe and assess children's development and learning can be used for program evaluation. These include:

Go to MyEducationLab and select the topic "Observation and Assessment." Under Activities and Applications, watch the video *Observing Children in Authentic Contexts* and consider the importance of observation within authentic environments.

- Time sampling, where data can be collected on where children are at in the room at varying points in time to determine room usage.
- Tallies, to determine the frequency of events occurring in the classroom environment.

Marie is interested in knowing how well the different areas of her room are being used and if redesign is needed. She decides to use a combination of time sampling and tallying strategies. First, she prepares a sheet that includes a listing of every area in her classroom and the different periods of time during the day. Every 15 minutes, Marie notes where children are in the room and records her findings on the prepared sheet. At the end of a week, she is able to look at areas of the room that seem to be used the most. Marie is very surprised at her findings, as it appears that the housekeeping area is underutilized and that there is a continuous rush of children in the block area. Marie decides to expand the block area and try to redesign the housekeeping area to be more inviting.

Formal Observation and Assessment Tools. One of the most challenging aspects of determining program effectiveness is evaluating how well the curriculum engages children and cultivates connections with the environment. Assessing these areas presents such questions as:

- What is the observable relationship between program goals, curriculum, and outcomes?
- Does the curriculum support the needs of all children?

- Are children engaged in the early childhood environment?
- Are the development and learning goals of the classroom as a whole being supported?
- Is the breadth of child development and learning diversity supported through the curriculum?
- How effective are the assessment strategies being utilized?

Fortunately, many of the curricular models presented in Chapter 8 include program evaluation strategies. For example, the Creative Curriculum, High/Scope, Bank Street, and Montessori models have instruments that determine program effectiveness. Further, accreditation organizations provide specific information about what factors need to be present in the program. However, not all programs follow a curricular model, and many are not accredited. For many programs, this means that the minimal standards enforced through licensing are their only form of program evaluation.

There are reliable, valid evaluation tools on the market that can be used to determine the effectiveness of programs in supporting access, representation, engagement, and expression: the Early Childhood Environment Rating Scales.

Early Childhood Environment Rating Scales. The **Early Childhood Environment Rating Scales** (ECERS) were developed by Frank Porter Graham Child Development Institute researchers Thelma Harms, Richard Clifford, and Debbie Cryer. The scales are composed of four different instruments:

- The Early Childhood Environment Rating Scale-Revised (ECERS-R) is applicable to early childhood group programs serving children between the ages of 2.5 and 5 (Harms, Clifford, & Cryer, 2005).
- The Infant/Toddler Environment Rating Scale-Revised (ITERS-R) is applicable to center-based child care programs serving children between infancy and 30 months (Harms, Clifford, & Cryer, 2003).
- The Family Child Care Environment Rating Scale-Revised (FCCERS-R) is applicable to family child care programs conducted in a provider's home serving children between infancy and school age (Harms, Clifford, & Cryer, 2007).
- The School-Age Care Environment Rating Scale (SACERS) is applicable to group care programs for children between the ages of 5 and 12 (Harms, Clifford, & Cryer, 1995).

Each of the rating scales includes items relevant to the physical environment, basic care, curriculum, interaction, schedule and program structure, and parent and staff education. Core values included in the design of each scale indicate that quality programs must support three basic needs that all children have:

- Protection of health and safety
- Building positive relationships
- Opportunities for stimulation and learning from experience

Table 13.3 provides a brief overview of each of the scales.

Early Childhood Environment Rating Scales

Developed by Harms, Clifford, and Cryer, the rating scales focus on early childhood, infant-toddler, family child care, and school-age environments. The scales consist of items relevant to the physical environment, basic care, curriculum, interaction, schedule and program structure, and parent and staff education.

Classroom activities represent one important aspect of the early childhood environment.

Scale	Targeted Components
TABLE 13.3	**Early Childhood Environment Scales and Their Targeted Components**
ECERS-R	43 items divided into 7 subscales, which include: • Space and Furnishings • Personal Care Routines • Language-Reasoning • Activities • Interaction • Program Structure • Parents and Staff
ITERS-R	39 items divided into 7 subscales, including: • Space and Furnishings • Personal Care Routines • Listening and Talking • Activities • Interaction • Program Structure • Parents and Staff
FCCERS-R	37 items divided into 7 subscales, including: • Space and Furnishings • Personal Care Routines • Listening and Talking • Activities • Interaction • Program Structure • Parents and Provider
SACERS	49 items, including 7 supplementary items for programs serving children with disabilities, including: • Space and Furnishings • Health and Safety • Activities • Interactions • Program Structure • Staff Development • Special Needs

The scales have been used in extensive and varied ways at the national level. A number of states, for example, have used the scales as research and evaluation tools. In some states, the government uses the tools *as a means of assessing quality* and in some cases ties scores to *tiered reimbursement*. Many programs use the scales for *teacher training and mentoring* and as tools supportive of *program improvement*, as the scales can provide specific information about a program's strengths and areas needing improvement.

After looking at the program's mission, Marie has decided that a specific tool might assist her in learning more about her program environment and how different factors combine to support quality programming. One of her colleagues mentioned learning about the ECERS-R at a local conference, and Marie elects to use that in her program.

Marie reviews the instrument, familiarizing herself with what she will be observing for. During her observation, she takes careful notes, and after she has observed long enough to get a sufficient picture of the environment, she scores the items, which

TABLE 13.4	Methods of Data Collection Evaluating Stakeholder Satisfaction	
Method	**Description**	**Potential Uses**
Questionnaires and surveys	Series of questions designed to gather information on specific program factors. When compiled, surveys and questionnaires can provide information about program strengths and weaknesses.	Data can be gathered from a large group and can be done anonymously, if needed.
Interviews	In-depth format that allows for deeper understanding of perspectives. Can be used along with questionnaires and surveys.	As interviews are more time-consuming, small sample sizes are generally most effective. Combining interview and questionnaire/survey data can present a holistic view of programming.
Focus groups	Small-group forum that allows for in-depth investigation of program's operations, goals, and areas of strength and challenges.	Focus groups allow for group processing. They can be used along with each of the other data collection techniques to determine program effectiveness.

are arranged on a Likert scale from inadequate to excellent. She then asks a coworker to separately complete one for her. The results are very informative: Marie can see her classroom's strengths and focus on areas that need additional support. Further, the organization of the scales gives Marie specific information about factors she needs to target for program effectiveness, and she uses these to help her set program goals.

Stakeholder Input

Stakeholders are persons who are affected by the early childhood programs. These persons might include, but are not limited to, children, families, professionals, and the larger community. Each of these groups must evaluate whether goals for access have been supported; once each party has access to the program, they can evaluate whether the overall goals are met. Because of variance in populations served and professional and community goals, each program will need to tailor its evaluation process to its program's specific goals and needs. Tools that can be used to evaluate stakeholder's perceptions of program effectiveness are summarized in Table 13.4.

For stakeholder assessment to be most effective, it needs to include both populations that the program presently serves and those who might be excluded from the present population. For example, at the college where I teach, we have an inclusive early childhood program. One of the main goals of the college is supporting access to the college courses for parents of students, and the provision of early education services to children of students is collectively viewed as a means of attaining access goals. For access to be

stakeholders
Persons who are affected by early childhood programs.

TEACHING AND LEARNING CONNECTIONS

Learning About Your Program's Stakeholders

- Who are the people most invested in the program, including those who are directly affected by services provided?

- What populations are indirectly affected by the program, including community members and programs?

- What messages are most likely to be heard by these populations relevant to their own personal and program mission?

evaluated, however, we have to examine data on those who have successfully made it to the college and those who would like to attend but have not been able to. Focusing on this population can provide useful information about continued obstacles and the early childhood program's potential role in addressing these obstacles.

THE ROLES OF FAMILIES AND PROFESSIONALS

Families and professionals each play an important role in program planning and evaluation. These roles, and their contributions, are not isolated from one another but are created in the context of a collaborative partnership. In this partnership, professionals are responsible for recognizing the value of family involvement and cultivating opportunities for meaningful participation.

The Role of the Family

What role do families play in program planning and evaluation? Families should be involved in each aspect of the planning, implementation, and evaluation process. Along with children, families can provide some of the most important information about program effectiveness, as supporting children and families comprises the main mission of the field.

Families can be involved in program planning, implementation, and evaluation in a variety of ways. Programs such as Head Start require family involvement in program planning and design their involvement into committee decision-making infrastructures. For families to effectively participate in all aspects of the programming process, their voice as their child's first and most important teacher must be both heard and respected.

The relationship between families and programming is bidirectional—just as families should have a role in the overall process, an ideal outcome would be that families are educated about how to effectively support and advocate for their child's education. Advocacy experiences that families gain in a safe, supportive atmosphere can carry over to other educational environments affecting the child. In turn, these environments can be influenced by the families existing and developing expertise about their child's needs and how these needs can effectively be met.

How can the professional cultivate family involvement? In addition to family involvement in their child's assessment and evaluation and classroom environment, families should be provided with an opportunity for program decision making. This can include formal measures such as those adopted by Head Start, or informal measures such as questionnaires, surveys, and focus groups.

Family education about the program's goals and the role of early childhood education can take many forms. All families should be provided with the program's mission statement and information on how this mission translates into program and classroom practices. Further, families benefit from information about the "why" of early childhood education, supporting knowledge of the vast amount of research pointing to the incredible importance of the early years. Successfully educating families means that the program's goals can have an impact far beyond those served directly, as family members can

Professional input is vital to whole-program assessment processes.

communicate important information on selecting quality care and advocating for appropriate environments to members of their social network.

The Role of the Professional

Professionals have many roles in program planning and evaluation. Teachers are responsible for the quality of practice in their classroom and ensuring that child and family development and learning are supported in the context of standards. Administrators (e.g., directors of centers or preschools and school principals) are responsible for ensuring that the overall program meets program goals and standards. Administrators also must ensure that effective evaluation practices support these goals. Both parties are responsible for ensuring that the planning and assessment practices are conducted in a collaborative manner.

In addition, many standards apply exclusively to professionals. Increasingly, standards are mandating that professionals attain higher levels of education, as education is strongly linked to program quality (Spodek & Saracho, 1990; Whitebook, 2003). As you have been learning, national community norm standards are increasingly requiring at least an associate's degree and many require a bachelor's degree.

For example, NACCRRA (2007) recommends that center directors have at least a bachelor's degree and that teachers in early childhood programs have a CDA or associate's degree. Further, training in specific areas such as CPR and ongoing education is mandated.

Professional support for program planning and evaluation requires attention to programming and ongoing professional development. It is the responsibility of each professional, therefore, to invest in child and family development and his or her own changing developmental needs. Commitment to lifelong learning, therefore, is essential.

MOVING FORWARD

Effective curriculum for early childhood education begins with program planning and is informed by ongoing evaluation. Attention to the whole program ensures that child and family development is effectively supported and that the goals of communities and larger society are met. Programs must operate based on standards of quality and surpass minimum licensing standards.

Program planning and evaluation provide a composite of all curriculum practices, including child and professional assessment, learning environments, and teaching practices. The total impact of the field, and its related responsibilities, can be summarized as follows (Shonkoff, 2004, p. 4):

> As for children, the healthy development of the early childhood field requires a safe and nurturing environment that provides opportunities for exploration, builds on previous experiences, promotes judicious risk taking, and learns from mistakes. This kind of environment would promote a spirit of collaboration and partnership among parents, service providers, evaluators, and funders. And it would lead to broad-based agreement about the need for unbiased and honest investigation to learn as much as possible about how to get the highest achievable return on the investment of finite resources in high-quality programs that are well implemented by skilled providers.

Access and the theory, planning, implementation, and assessment that guide the intentional curriculum are each vital factors to be tended to in early childhood programs. Supporting each of these factors ensures that the field is accountable to the needs of all stakeholders and that, ultimately, success and equity for all members of the early childhood field are supported.

Go to MyEducationLab and select the topic "Special Needs/Inclusion." Under Activities and Applications, view the simulation *RTI: Considerations for School Leaders* and think about how RTI can be supported in school policy and practice.

Go to MyEducationLab and select the topic "Professionalism/Ethics/Standards." Under Building Teaching Skills and Dispositions, complete the exercise *Comparing State Licensing and NAEYC Accreditation Standards.*

CASE STUDY

Supporting Stakeholders

Myrna's Children's Village (6 weeks to 6 years)

The stakeholders of the Children's Village are numerous and extend far beyond the children and families served by the program. These additional stakeholders include the college community, local school districts, and the community as a whole. The Children's Village not only provides high-quality services to young children and their families, but also serves as a tool supporting access to continuing education for nontraditional students. Access, in this respect, has a direct impact on the community through the preparation of well-qualified members of the workforce.

How does the Children's Village convey the importance of its programming to its stakeholders? Throughout the year, the program engages in a variety of advocacy efforts. These include Week of the Young Child activities, participation in the college's homecoming parade, family participation days, and tours for potential beneficent donors. In addition, local politicians and policy makers are regularly invited to the program's activities. The goal of including these groups is to educate them about the program's practices and the impact that the activities have on children, families, and the community.

The Children's Village has had extensive success in communicating its message to stakeholders, as measured through the dramatic recent expansion of the program and the continued support provided through beneficent donors. In addition, the Children's Village has received extensive support and funding through various grant opportunities and has been very successful at combining resources from the various programs housed in the Village.

CONSTRUCTED-RESPONSE QUESTION

1. What role do stakeholders play in early childhood education? Describe how to support stakeholder investment, and identify various stakeholders in the Myrna's Children's Village. What strategies does the Village use to convey the importance of their services to their varied stakeholders?

CASE STUDY

Families as Stakeholders

Mulberry School (preschool through 3rd grade)

As a parent cooperative, the Mulberry School is reliant on stakeholder input from families and their participation in whole program assessment. Families are involved in the process in a variety of ways. For example, the board is composed of families, and each family is required to participate in 50 hours of service to the school a year. Families also have feedback and input opportunities into each aspect of the program.

As stakeholders in the program who are direct contributors to the educational system, families are educated about the program itself and what represents quality pre-K through primary education. Families are also surveyed about their own needs, and there is extensive discussion about existing and potential overlap. The goal is for program families to make informed choices and decisions about the program. This includes each aspect of programming. Family members who volunteer during the lunch period, for example, participate in training on guidance, community building, and social coaching prior to their placement. Family members who volunteer directly in the classroom are educated about classroom needs and goals, including the most effective strategies for working with each individual child.

CONSTRUCTED-RESPONSE QUESTION

1. What role do stakeholders play in early childhood education? Describe how to support stakeholder investment, and identify the various stakeholders in the Mulberry School.

REFLECTING ON AND APPLYING EFFECTIVE PRACTICES (NAEYC AND CEC/DEC)

Ethics

- You are a new teacher in a community child care program. During your second week of employment, your director tells you to review the state licensing standards and make sure your classroom meets all requirements, as the licensing representative will be coming for a visit in a few days. Upon reviewing the requirements and classroom practices, you notice several instances where your environment does not meet the minimal requirements. When you bring this to your director's attention, she responds, "Well, that's why I had you review the standards. Just get everything together for the visit." What would you do in this situation?

NAEYC Ideals: Ethical Responsibilities to Children
I-1.5. To create and maintain safe and healthy settings that foster children's social, emotional, cognitive, and physical development and that respect their dignity and their contributions.

NAEYC Ideals: Ethical Responsibilities to Colleagues
I-3A.2. To share resources with co-workers, collaborating to ensure that the best possible early childhood care and education program is provided.

DEC: Professional and Interpersonal Behavior

2. We shall demonstrate the highest standards of personal integrity, truthfulness, and honesty in all our professional activities in order to inspire the trust and confidence of the children and families and of those with whom we work.

Standards for Professional Practice

- Provide a brief list of factors that need to be considered when assessing program effectiveness. In what ways would a lack of attention to these factors negatively affect child benefits from the curriculum and program?

NAEYC: Teaching and Learning
4b. Students know, understand, and use a wide array of effective approaches, strategies, and tools to positively influence children's development and learning.

Accountability refers to the field's ability to deliver positive outcomes for children, families, and professionals. Positive outcomes are determined by each of these constituents and larger society. At its base level, accountability requires the field as a whole to demonstrate that early childhood education achieves its intended results. Accountability also requires the community at large to embrace the goals of the field as essential to a thriving society.

Developing systems and processes that provide accountability—through a focus on proven results—is particularly important in the present cultural climate. Commonly referred to as the "age of accountability," the focus on demonstrated results currently crosses all sectors of private and public human services and education programs. According to Robert Pianta (2007), Professor of Education at the University of Virginia, the field's current focus and challenge centers on "developmentally accountable practices."

Extensive research and data demonstrate that early childhood education can and does make a difference in the lives of young children and their families. The field's successes are marred by the lack of comprehensive accountability systems demonstrating that the field as a whole is achieving its intended results (National Early Childhood Accountability Task Force, 2007). Accountability efforts must attain, respond to, and document:

- Quality care and education for all children.
- High-quality experiences that make a difference in children's lifelong academic and social success.
- Programs that are accessible to all families.
- Excellent preparation of early childhood professionals, including a system that supports ongoing development and is responsive to needs for compensation that reflect qualifications and experience.
- Educational experiences that are challenging and appropriate to young children's ages, diverse individual needs, and culture.
- A system of early childhood education that is responsive to and represents the needs of children, families, professionals, community, and society.

At the center of accountability is the question, How do we support children's early learning and development? This seemingly simple question is particularly complex when coupled with the reality that the United States lacks a national policy supporting the learning and development of our youngest citizens.

The Lack of a Cohesive Vision in the United States

According to Anne Mitchell (2007), past president of the NAEYC, the lack of a national policy for the field of early childhood education leads to great disparity in how states define the field, success for children and families in the field, professional preparation, and the funding for the development, implementation, and evaluation of such efforts. As a result, defining and evaluating accountability becomes a daunting task, as this lack of cohesive vision makes accountability measures difficult to determine and apply.

A notable exception to the variance between states is the nationally defined and funded program of Head Start and Early Head Start. Head Start programs, however, are limited in the populations affected, as children from families with low income are predominantly targeted. This creates issues of access for these high-quality services, which are further confounded by the fact that Head Start programs are not sufficiently funded to reach all the children and families who qualify. Also, the effectiveness of spending dollars on Head Start services is often of great political debate, as funding fluctuations during the G. W. Bush administration demonstrated. It is important to note that Head Start funding

• • • BECOMING A PROFESSIONAL • • •

Career Pathways

Early Childhood Special Education Teacher

Sergio's commitment to supporting the needs of *all* children led him to his career in early childhood special education. His commitment to supporting these needs in a way that was most beneficial to children led him to his passionate investment in inclusion. This investment was the catalyst behind his creation of a blended early childhood Head Start and special education classroom.

"I just felt as if something was missing." Most of the children in Sergio's classroom had diagnosed delays in speech and language, and what Sergio felt these children most needed were appropriate models. His classroom was right next to a Head Start class, and daily he was struck by the rich language interactions that occurred between children. He felt his children could benefit from being in an environment with those experiences. Becoming invested in creating a collaborative classroom, he set about making this work.

His first steps were to talk with support staff: Could the cook prepare food for more children? Would the bus driver be able to accommodate their schedule? He then approached the Head Start teacher and presented his idea: Would she be willing to collaborate? When he took his idea to administration, he was greeted with "Great idea, but . . ." followed by a list of potential obstacles. Sergio's groundwork paid off, as he was able to report that he had already addressed those obstacles.

There was a good amount of red tape—different funding streams to blend, different reporting requirements, and different teaching expectations. But at the core of all of this was that good teaching is best for all children, and keeping his eye on that core, Sergio was able to make his dream a reality.

It is now Sergio's fourth year of this collaborative, inclusive model, and he is working to extend his work beyond his school community. When asked about the biggest obstacle, Sergio replied, "It is difficult to get past the way things have always been done."

For positions like Sergio's, the job outlook is excellent and is expected to increase faster than average (U.S. Bureau of Labor Statistics, 2007). According to the Bureau of Labor Statistics, many districts report challenges in finding adequate numbers of certified special education teachers, and finding ones who are bilingual is a particular challenge. Further, extensive research demonstrating the benefits of intervening early, coupled with increased early identification efforts, translates into early childhood special education, in particular, experiencing dramatic staffing needs. With regards to compensation, the middle 50% of special education teachers earn between $37,500 and $59,320. All states require teachers to be licensed, including completion of a special education teacher training program and at least a bachelor's degree. Many states require a master's degree.

cuts during the previous Bush administration were dramatically reversed under the **American Recovery and Reinvestment Act of 2009**, which allocated 2.1 billion dollars in grants to Head Start and Early Head Start services (National Governors Association, 2009).

Presently, there is no nationally enacted and supported vision for services and accountability, and the field as a whole consists of a great variety of programs and services. Berkeley Professor of Public Policy David Kirp (2007) called the variety of programs and

American Recovery and Reinvestment Act of 2009
Economic stimulus package signed into law by President Barack Obama on February 17, 2009.

services in the early childhood education field "education's version of the Wild West" (p. 25). This "hodgepodge" of programs, as Kirp refers to it, emerged due to the origins of the disparate areas of the field, where services caring for children occurred in schools, social service agencies, church basements, and people's homes. Services considered more "educational" in nature were associated with universities or public programs, and more recently, the public school settings. Recall too that special education as a field did not exist before the 1960s and, as an "add on" to existing services extended to children, developed a completely different infrastructure and service delivery system.

Accountability measures in the United States are contingent upon the development of a clearly defined, cohesive system of early childhood care and education. NAEYC's Vision for Excellence, discussed next, provides an image of what the field of early childhood education could look like were such a system in place.

NAEYC'S Vision for Excellence

The field of early childhood education comprises many constituents and mandates. At the core, however, the field's success depends on its ability to meet the needs of children, families, professionals, and communities. NAEYC (2000) argues that if the field is to be successful in meeting these needs, the following is critical:

> **All Children** have access to a safe and accessible, high quality early childhood education that includes a developmentally appropriate curriculum, knowledgeable and well-trained program staff and educators, comprehensive services that support their health, nutrition, and social well-being, in an environment that respects and supports diversity.
>
> **All Early Childhood Professionals** are supported as professionals with a career ladder, ongoing professional development opportunities, and compensation that will attract and retain high quality educators.
>
> **All Families** have access to early care and education programs that are affordable and of high quality, and are participants in the education and well being of their children through family involvement in programs and schools, as well as opportunities to increase their educational attainment.
>
> **All Communities** are accountable for the quality of early childhood programs provided to all children, backed by the local, state, and federal funding needed to deliver quality programs and services.

See Figure 14.1 for how these goals can be supported at the national, state, and local levels (NAEYC, 2000).

The field's ability to support equity and success for all those it affects depends on effectively meeting each of these guidelines. However, accountability for equity and success, or the field's ability to meet these goals, is hampered by the lack of a clear and cohesive vision of what the field is and how it can most effectively support children and families. This lack of clarity and cohesiveness is marked by:

- **Varied emphasis on the importance of services for children between birth and the age of 3 and for children in pre-kindergarten, kindergarten, and primary grades,** leading to varied definitions of the ages of children included in the field and levels of societal investments.
- **A lack of support and monitoring of quality in the field,** resulting in many children spending their days in environments that are substandard, hampering their healthy development and learning.

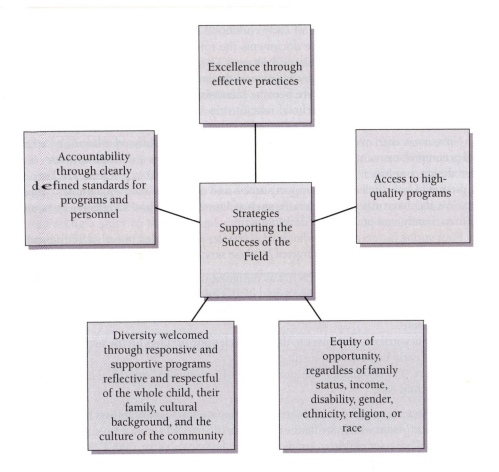

FIGURE 14.1
Strategies Supporting the Success of the Field

Source: From *A Call for Excellence in Early Childhood Education,* by the National Association for the Education of Young Children, 2000. Retrieved April 12, 2007, from http://www.naeyc.org/policy/excellence.asp

- **The historical segregation of children with disabilities,** leading to disparate fields of early childhood general and special education and the lack of universal application of identified strategies, policies, and practices supporting the development and learning of each and every child in high-quality, inclusive environments.
- **Emerging recognition of the diverse cultural and linguistic needs of children and families,** leading to inconsistent practices, policies, and standards supporting children and families who are culturally and linguistically diverse.
- **Emerging realization of the essential role families play in supporting young children's development,** leading to disparity in how families are welcomed and embraced in the field.
- **Emerging realization of the importance of professionals in supporting young children's development,** leading to substandard pay and high staff turnover.

The field of early childhood education supports present and future development.

Present-Day Impact. In the past 5 years, efforts to support professional preparation that are linked to professional salary have emerged. In general, these models link formal education and salary supplements. Retention is addressed through requiring participants to have worked in their program for a certain period of time and make a commitment to remain there for a specific time period as well (NAEYC, 2002).

Two of the most developed programs targeting under-education, increased compensation, and increased retention are the Teacher Education and Compensation Helps (T.E.A.C.H.) Early Childhood Project and the **Child Care WAGE$** Project. In 2006, 22 states provided T.E.A.C.H. scholarships, with 64% of recipients working on their associate's degree; 14% of recipients working in Head Start programs; 60% of recipients working with 3- and 4-year-olds; 36% of the programs offered in family child care homes; and 47% of the recipients persons (women) of color (T.E.A.C.H., 2006). The Child Care Wage$ Project was provided in 4 states, with all recipients providing care and education to children between the ages of birth and 5.

Efforts designed to address issues of compensation and affordability cannot exist in isolation. Rather, a contextual approach reflecting connections between the early childhood community and larger society that supports each of these factors must be developed. One such example is the career lattice.

Supporting a skilled and stable workforce requires that the early childhood profession is viewed as a career choice and not just a job (Center for Early Childhood Leadership, 2003). Careers include opportunities for advancement and compensation that is differentiated by level of education and experience. Career lattices provide a structure to support the ongoing development of early childhood professionals. When lattices are tied to compensation, as they are in many states, the retention and the overall quality of services provided to children and families can be positively affected.

Ongoing career development, compensation, and retention are professional development issues that have been supported by advocacy efforts. Each of these efforts certainly affects you as

Child Care WAGE$

National initiative designed to support equitable compensation and professional preparation for early childhood professionals.

Early childhood education makes a difference in the lives of our youngest citizens.

a professional. In addition, these efforts are bidirectional: You play a key role in their success. Specifically, your ability to develop and present yourself as a professional affects both you and the field as a whole.

Effective advocacy has many challenges. One of these is creating a clear, concise message that can be heard and responded to by your targeted audience. Other early childhood professionals are one of the most likely audiences to recognize the importance of the field. However, the advancement of the field depends on communicating its importance to larger audiences.

Advocacy as a Tool for Moving Forward

One of the central questions addressing advocacy efforts outside of the field of early childhood education is: What message is most likely to be effective? I believe, for example, that inclusive, quality early childhood education is a moral issue, and one that a just, equitable society that supports the development of all its members would embrace. This message might be effective with some groups, depending on whether they share values and a belief system similar to mine and a willingness to support such a cause and its related needs. At the same time, this message can be ineffective as a whole, as many might not share the same values and beliefs that I do regarding the important role early childhood education plays in ensuring a just and equitable society. Further, even if value and belief systems are similar, vast discrepancies might exist regarding how to proceed in supporting and attaining such goals.

The language used to communicate the effectiveness of early childhood education to the larger context, therefore, must be one that is likely to be heard. Communication requires not only a clear articulation of our own message, but also an understanding of the language of our stakeholders. Many believe an economic argument, based on dollars saved down the road by investing in services now, is most effective.

Consider the following quote by Arthur Rolnick and Rob Grunewald (2003), who are respectively the Director of Research and the Regional Economic Analyst at the Federal Reserve Bank of Minnesota:

> Early childhood development programs are rarely portrayed as economic development initiatives, and we think that is a mistake. Such programs, if they appear at all, are at the bottom of the economic development lists for state and local governments. They should be at the top. Most of the numerous projects and initiatives that state and local governments fund in the name of creating new private businesses and new jobs result in few public benefits. In contrast, studies find that well-focused investments in early childhood development yield high public and private returns. (p. 2)

These leaders argue that our conventional view of investment in economics, which includes "company headquarters, office towers, entertainment centers, and professional sports stadiums and arenas," is misguided (Rolnick & Grunewald, 2003, p. 9).

What data in the field support economic investment? Consider the following:

- High-quality early childhood education helps prepare young children to succeed in school and become better citizens; they earn more so they pay more taxes, and they commit fewer crimes.
- Every dollar invested in quality early care and education saves taxpayers up to $13 in future costs.
- The early care and education industry is economically important—often much larger in terms of employees and revenues than other industries that receive considerable government attention and investment.

TEACHING AND LEARNING CONNECTIONS

Creating Advocacy Messages

- Learn about the needs of the group you are communicating with.
- Tailor your message to reflect those needs, as appropriate.
- Be clear and concise in articulating your message.
- Use both verbal and written strategies.
- Back up your message with clear, compelling data.
- Always act professionally and remember that you are a representative of the field.

- Failure to invest sufficiently in quality early care and education shortchanges taxpayers because the return on investment is greater than many other economic development options.
- Access to available and affordable choices of early childhood learning programs helps working parents fulfill their responsibilities.
- Quality early education is as essential for a productive 21st century workforce as building roads or maintaining the Internet; investing in it grows the economy (Calman & Tarr-Whelan, 2005).

The success of the field depends on its effectiveness in communicating this message and providing concrete information on how to most effectively support positive developmental outcomes for children and families. The message that the early years matter must be accompanied, therefore, by a clear vision of how to support these years.

The early childhood professional plays an important role in the implementation of this vision. Professionals must advocate in their immediate environment and have knowledge of the larger context and how these various parts work together. In the classroom, professionals must develop effective learning and teaching environments that support children and families, while concurrently representing themselves as a part of a larger professional system. How you present yourself, both in your interactions and ability to communicate professionalism, represents your own personal, direct contribution to the field. Beyond the classroom, the language you use to communicate the goals of the field needs to be directed toward the larger audience and supportive of the development of an overall system of early childhood education.

How do we get from here—a time of great opportunity for the advancement of the field—to there—represented by a supported system of early childhood education that reflects the goals of children, families, and professionals? Before moving forward and looking at statewide efforts supportive of such a system, let's take a few steps back and review where the field has been, its remaining challenges, and its great opportunities for growth.

GETTING THERE FROM HERE

How do you use the field's rich history and incredible strength as a tool to inform effective practices supporting children, families, and professionals at present and in the future? First, let's explore where the field has been.

First, A Few Steps Back

The importance of the field and its remaining challenges were effectively summarized in *From Neurons to Neighborhoods*: *The Science of Early Childhood Development* (Shonkoff & Phillips, 2000). This report identified four overarching themes:

- All children are born wired for feelings and ready to learn.
- Early environments matter and nurturing relationships are essential.
- Society is changing and the needs of young children are not being addressed.
- Interactions among early childhood science, policy, and practice are problematic and demand dramatic rethinking.

From this report, the National Research Council and Institute of Medicine made several conclusions (Haflon, Uyeda, Inkelas, & Rice, 2004):

- Brain development can be optimized by early experiences.
- Early experiences set the foundation for learning throughout life.
- For optimal development and learning, how young children feel is as important as how they think.
- Many U.S. children enter school without the competencies they need to succeed.
- Service systems are not adequately organized to promote optimal childhood development and readiness for school.

Further, gaps exist in the current system, leading to the system's failure to adequately address children's needs. These gaps include that *the capacity of high-quality care, despite better developmental outcomes, is not available to the majority of children.* For example, only 24% of preschool classrooms provide good or excellent quality. In addition, *over half of American parents of young children do not receive guidance about important developmental topics, despite their wanting more information on how to help their child learn, behave appropriately, and be ready for school.* Another major gap is that *many of children least likely to receive services are the most needy, and from low-income and ethnic minority families.* (Haflon et al., 2004). Effectively dealing with diversity is one of the central challenges of 21st century education (Darling-Hammond & Garcia-Lopez, 2002), and one that we have not yet effectively met.

In addition to these gaps, the National Professional Development Center on Inclusion, housed at Frank Porter Graham, Child Development Institute at the University of North Carolina at Chapel Hill identifies that while most early childhood programs have at least one child with a disability, most teachers are ill prepared to support their individual needs (Chang, Early, & Winton, 2005).

Gaps in program quality, access, family knowledge of how to advocate for and secure high-quality care, appropriate policies and practices supporting children who are culturally and linguistically diverse, and appropriate supports for high-quality, inclusive practices are further compounded by the gaps that exist in the attention devoted to various areas of the field. These are based on the history of the field and its ambiguity regarding who is included in the definition of *early childhood*. This disparity has resulted in a lack of focus on infants and toddlers, resulting in emerging standards, assessment, and accountability efforts targeted toward this group. Further, there is a lack of continuity as measured by standards, quality, and public investments between birth and the age of 8. In addition, systematic attention to developing policies and practices, including professional development standards, supporting children who are culturally and linguistically diverse, has been lacking. Finally, children with disabilities have historically been segregated from environments with their typically developing peers, including traditional early childhood education programs.

In addition to disparity between knowledge and practice for children, the field has struggled with creating continuity between research and practice regarding professionals and families.

The heading of this section—Getting There from Here: First, a Few Steps Back—implies that these challenges are in the past. Although these challenges certainly remain today, there is great movement in many parts of the country that reflects NAEYC's Vision for Excellence. These programs and practices are pushing the edges of where the field has been and presently is and slowly but surely making advancements.

Now, A Few Steps Forward

The promise and potential of the field described at the beginning of this chapter are affected by practices and programs emerging throughout the country, reflecting that the field now knows where it has been, where it is going, and what it needs to do to get there. You have learned about nationally funded programs such as Head Start and Early Head Start. Although these programs represent goals of inclusion and flexibility, national support and sponsorship of programs are unique to these programs and the military child care system. More common in the field are initiatives, many of which are developed in communities by dedicated professionals. There are also many initiatives at the national level, which serve to coordinate and support efforts in the states. The following provides a sampling of just some of the national programs and initiatives; to provide a complete listing would be exhaustive.

North Carolina's Smart Start

North Carolina early childhood initiative designed to ensure all children enter school healthy and ready to succeed.

Creating a Continuum of Early Childhood Education Services. North Carolina's Smart Start is an example of a local solution to early childhood systems that has extended to the national level. The goals of Smart Start in North Carolina included ensuring that each child in the state entered school healthy and ready to succeed. In support of this goal, the vision of Smart Start includes developing collaborative programs and services between state and community as well as developing accessible, inclusive programs and services. Smart Start pays careful attention to developing the infrastructure needed for success, including supporting accessible, affordable, quality child care; improving child health outcomes; and strengthening families. To accomplish these goals, extensive attention is paid to developing the infrastructure needed for success through proactive, cutting-edge, and innovative programs and services, including public–private partnerships funding early childhood programming.

In addition, Smart Start has expanded its goal of supporting the development of an effective early childhood system by supporting system development in other states. Through their National Technical Assistance Center, they provide support to states and localities by ensuring the health and readiness of each child.

National programs have also supported early childhood initiatives at the community level. For example, United Way's Success by Six relies on coalitions of business, education, and community leaders to develop unique systems of early childhood education reflective of the needs of individual communities. The goals of Success by Six include:

United Way's Success by Six

National system supportive of community coalitions that develop programs to meet unique early childhood education needs.

- Helping parents, grandparents, and informal caregivers to understand how to encourage and support early learning through public service advertising and research-based educational material and community mobilization efforts.
- Improving the quality of care children receive by supporting Quality Star Rating Systems and support for Head Start and universal preschool initiatives.
- Strengthening communities by supporting local early childhood initiatives.

In this case, change is supported at both the community and national level, as the United Way system serves as a national conduit for information exchange.

Another great example of a national initiative supporting change in communities is **School of the 21st Century** (21C), developed by Edward Zigler of the Yale Child Study Center. 21C is a community school model that incorporates child care and family support services into the school system, thereby extending the public schools' ability to meet the needs of diverse populations. 21C schools, numbering over 1,300 in the United States, have six program components:

- Guidance and support for parents through education and outreach.
- High-quality, developmentally appropriate child care services for children between the ages of 3 and 5 at the school or a school-linked site.
- Before- and after-school programs and vacation programs for school-age children.
- Health education and services, including health, nutrition, and fitness education, physical health services, care for children with special needs, developmental and dental assessments, and mental health services.
- Networks and training for child care providers, including workshops, training opportunities, support groups, and newsletters for community early childhood professionals.
- Information and referral services designed to inform families about child care options, health care, financial assistance, social services, and other needed family support services.

The 21C model, originally developed in 1988, was a pioneer in creating links between home and school systems.

In addition to supporting community change, national initiatives have also supported change for individual children, teachers, and programs. A good example of this is **Jumpstart**, which is a national organization whose goals include building language, literacy, social, and initiative skills in young children. The goals of the model include promoting school success through literacy and social-emotional readiness. This is accomplished through supporting three areas of family involvement: building strong relationships, ongoing and consistent communication, and the Jumpstart home-learning connection. Jumpstart also focuses on supporting future teachers through building their excitement about the field of early childhood education and providing them with skills to carry out their passions.

The creation of a continuum of early childhood services depends on the field providing equal recognition of each aspect of early childhood education affecting children between birth and the age of 8. Infant and toddler populations have historically lacked the attention afforded to other age groups in the field. Several national initiatives have been designed to support quality care and education for this population.

Support for Early Learning Guidelines for Infants and Toddlers. The **National Infant and Toddler Child Care Initiative**, for example, is working along with Child Care Development and Fund administrators and other partners to support, develop, and improve the quality of infant and toddler child care. As part of this initiative, states are being supported in their development of early

School of the 21st Century
Community school model supportive of child care and family support systems in the school system.

jumpstart
National program supporting language, literacy, social, and skill-building initiatives in communities.

National Infant and Toddler Child Care Initiative
Zero to Three's national initiative designed to develop systems of support for infant and toddler education.

High-quality programs support children's knowledge, skills, and positive dispositions.

learning guidelines (ELG) for the infant–toddler population. Currently, 17 states had either completed guidelines or have drafted guidelines that are currently under review (Zero to Three Policy Center, 2008).

Support for Statewide Infant-Toddler Systems.   In the Child Care and Development Fund managed through the U.S. Department of Health and Human Services, targeted funds have been set aside specifically addressing the quality of infant and toddler care. The goal of these funds, reaching 100 million dollars in 2007, is to help states develop quality programming based on the state's unique needs. In 2009, an additional $93,587 was allocated toward infant and toddler care quality through the American Recovery and Reinvestment Act (U.S. Department of Health and Human services, 2009). These monies have been used for:

- Professional development, in the form of scholarships, credential development, technical assistance through infant-toddler specialists, and support for infant-toddler professional development through an articulated career lattice.
- Facilities, including higher reimbursement for the care of infants and toddlers, technical assistance supporting quality in infant-toddler environments, and grants to providers for equipment and materials supportive of the needs of infants and toddlers.
- Child care settings and evaluation supporting demonstration sites for high-quality programming in the state.
- Planning, research, and evaluation focused on examination of and improvement for state efforts in supporting infant-toddler education.
- Development of program standards, supporting state ability to meet standards, including funding, quality, and accreditation standards.

In addition to these monies, several initiatives have emerged nationally designed to develop systems of support for infant and toddler education. For example, the National Infant and Toddler Initiative at Zero to Three provides planning, resources, and development services to planning teams in the United States and its territories. In addition, the project disseminates information about the initiatives nationally, working toward a broader impact.

Supporting Infant-Toddler Professional Preparation.   States have elected to support quality in infant-toddler programs in different ways. One way is through developing course offerings in infant and toddler education. Another strategy centers on recognizing professional achievement in infant and toddler development and learning through awarding infant-toddler credentials, certificates, certification, or endorsements. Twelve states presently have a fully developed credential in place, and five more are in the process of developing credentials (Zero to Three Policy Center, 2008). Each credential is developed based on the unique professional development systems in states and specific infant and toddler needs.

Ensuring That Children Are Physically and Mentally Healthy.   Children's development and learning depend on their physical and mental health. **Healthy Child Care America** (HCCA) is a collaborative effort of families and health and child care professionals. The overall goal of HCCA is to improve the health and safety of children in child care environments. The program is coordinated through the American Academy of Pediatrics (AAP) and includes the following information and services:

- A national speakers bureau of health and safety experts
- National health and tribal safety performance standards
- Educational materials and presentations
- Networking, mentorship, and technical assistance opportunities
- Health and safety fact sheets

Healthy Child Care America

National program providing information and application strategies to ensure health and safety.

- AAP policies on early care and education
- Resource materials

In addition to physical health needs, children's mental health needs must be met in order to ensure successful development. At the national level, the Office of Special Education Programs in the U.S. Department of Education has funded the **Technical Assistance Center on Social Emotional Intervention for Young Children**. The mission of the center is to support the use of evidence-based practices in meeting the needs of young children who are demonstrating, or are at risk for, challenging behaviors. In support of this mission, the center works to determine effective policies and practices for the prevention and/or addressing of challenging behavior and to develop materials and training opportunities that support these practices. The center provides PowerPoint presentations and policy briefs and works to affect state and national policy supportive of children with challenging behaviors.

In addition, the **National Technical Assistance Center for Children's Mental Health** is dedicated to helping states, tribes, territories, and communities meet the mental health needs of children and their families. Housed in Georgetown University's Center for Child and Human Development, the center offers varied activities throughout the nation with the goal of transforming systems of support based on the needs of children and families. Specific to early childhood, the center coordinates the Early Childhood System of Mental Health project, whose goals include:

- Promoting mental health.
- Preventing mental health problems in children and families.
- Intervening on behalf of children and families affected by mental health disorders.

To support these goals, the project offers training and technical assistance; presentations at the national, state, and local levels; the development of articles, chapters, and issues briefs; and an Early Childhood Mental Health Academy. The goals of this academy include assisting states, tribes, and territories to develop public policies supportive of an integrative, collaborative approach to ensuring mental health.

Embracing Families as Their Child's First and Most Important Teacher. **Parents as Teachers** is a national organization that coordinates programs throughout the United States and abroad. The program was started in the 1970s in response to growing concerns about children entering school lacking essential readiness skills. This concern was coupled with recognition that one of the most important players in remedying this concern was the child's family. Originating in Missouri, the program now operates in all 50 states and several other countries.

The program provides the agencies it serves with curriculum and training, scientific research, and evidence-based practice. Professionals are trained to use the curriculum with parents, supporting parental confidence and skills and creating vital support systems.

Another example of a national initiative supporting families and representing a well-developed public–private partnership is the **Toyota Family Literacy Program**. In partnership with the National Center for Family Literacy, Toyota has funded 211 family literacy sites in 38 cities in 26 states (National Center for Family Literacy, n.d.). The program started with supporting family literacy skills for the families of preschool-aged children and has since expanded to school-aged children and children in families who are Hispanic. The model supports parental involvement and education and uses literacy as a tool to improve the lives of children and families.

Technical Assistance Center on Social Emotional Intervention for Young Children
National program providing research-based resources designed to improve the social-emotional outcomes for children who have, or are at risk for developing, challenging behaviors.

National Technical Assistance Center for Children's Mental Health
Focused on supporting professionals in meeting the mental health needs of children and families.

Parents as Teachers
National project dedicated to supporting parents as their child's first and most important teacher.

Toyota Family Literacy Program
National effort supportive of family literacy in early childhood and, most recently, in Hispanic families.

Parent Empowerment Project

National Black Child Development Institute project supporting families in their roles as their child's first and most important teacher through a parent-driven, culturally-based education program.

National Professional Development Center on Inclusion

National program designed to support states in developing systems designed to prepare professionals to successfully include all children in early childhood education environments.

CONNECT: The Center to Mobilize Early Childhood Knowledge

Provides online, interactive modules to help practitioners to develop confidence and competence needed to work with young children with disabilities.

Special Quest Birth-Five

National project designed to enhance and sustain high-quality, inclusive services for children with disabilities age birth through 5 and their families.

The **Parent Empowerment Project** of the National Black Child Development Institute also works to support families in their role as their child's first and most important teacher. The "parent-driven" curriculum, where families select the topics they will study based on their unique needs, supports parenting practices identified by research as improving child outcomes. The project also supports and enables families to adapt their cultural values to these parenting practices. Through this model, culture, individuality, and research are interwoven, respecting the unique lens that each participant brings to their parenting (National Black Child Development Institute, 2007), and working to form a partnership that educates, motivates, and inspires parents.

Supporting Inclusion. One of the national leaders in supporting inclusive education is the Frank Porter Graham **National Professional Development Center on Inclusion**. The goal of the center is to support states in developing systemic, professional development supportive of the knowledge, skills, and dispositions that early childhood professionals need to successfully include all children in early childhood education environments.

To succeed in this goal, the project began its work in 2007 with four states: Oregon, Minnesota, Georgia, and Pennsylvania. The second cohort of states was selected in 2008 and includes Illinois, New Mexico, North Carolina, and Virginia. With each targeted state, the center provides support for:

• Policy needs, supporting states in their alignment of personnel standards between general and early childhood special education. In turn, these standards will serve as the foundation for building, implementing, and evaluating a cross-agency professional development system.
• Resource issues, helping states identify and obtain fiscal, human, and materials resources needed to develop a state plan for professional development that is integrated and reflective of cross-agency collaboration.
• Practice concerns, supporting the identification and training of states on the most promising professional development approaches.

Also at Frank Porter Graham, **CONNECT: The Center to Mobilize Early Childhood Knowledge** provides interactive modules designed to help early childhood practitioners develop the confidence and competence needed to work effectively with young children with disabilities. The modules are delivered in an online format, and include content related to young children with disabilities and support for developing evidence-based decision-making skills.

Special Quest Birth-Five also represents a leading national initiative supporting inclusion. Funded through the U.S. Department of Health and Human Services, Administration for Children and Families, Office of Head Start, the focus of Special Quest Birth-Five is to use a collaborative, relationship, and team-based approach to enhance and sustain high-quality, inclusive services for children with disabilities age birth through 5 and their families. Their specific focus includes improving practices in Head Start and Early Head Start programs.

Supporting Children and Families Who Are Culturally and Linguistically Diverse. Increasingly, national efforts have targeted children from diverse populations, including English language learners. For example, the **National Task Force on Early Childhood Education for Hispanics** brings together public and private leaders, strategists, early childhood educators, and researchers to develop creative, collaborative solutions supporting the school readiness of children from Hispanic backgrounds, with a focus on supporting their language and literacy needs.

The **National Black Child Development Institute** (NBCDI) works to create a society that ensures a successful future for all children, with the mission of improving and advancing the quality of life for black children and their families through education and advocacy (NBCDI, 2009). Recommendations made in 2009 to President-elect Barack Obama's Transition Team included the need to build the capacity to produce culturally competent graduates of higher education who are as culturally and linguistically diverse at all levels as the population of children in early childhood care and education.

One initiative several states (Illinois, Michigan, New Jersey, Ohio, Minnesota, Pennsylvania, and Washington) have taken advantage of is **Build Strong Foundations for Our Youngest Children**, which focuses on developing comprehensive policies responding to the needs of families, the wise use of public and private resources, and the effective preparation of young children for the future. An essential part of Build's work focuses on early childhood systems that reflect and support a multiethnic society (Build, n.d.). As Build has defined gaps for children in culture and language as resulting from a readiness gap, participation gap in formal services, cultural awareness and recognition gap, workforce diversity gap, and stakeholder planning and decision making gap (Build, n.d.), careful attention is paid in early childhood system development to remedy these gaps. This includes the development of culturally and linguistically responsive early learning standards, the development of culturally competent quality rating systems, and the development of an early childhood planning and decision-making infrastructure that reflects the diversity of the field.

Providing Early Identification and Support. Respecting the diverse learning needs of all children requires careful attention to children's individual needs and high-quality educational approaches tailored to meet these needs. Two recent national identification and intervention approaches in the United States are Response to Intervention (RTI) and Recognition and Response. RTI targets school-aged children with learning challenges and is designed to support the success of all learners. RTI is based on a three-tiered model, similar to the teaching pyramid introduced in Chapter 10. The tiers consist of (Kovaleski, 2007):

- **Tier 1 (universal prevention):** All children receive high-quality, evidence-based instruction tailored to their individual development and learning needs. All children are screened regularly to identify learners who need additional support. Tier 1 is a universal preventive measure, and it is anticipated that 80% of students will respond at this level and not require additional intervention.
- **Tier 2 (secondary prevention or strategic intervention):** Children in the second tier of RTI have been identified as needing additional supports and receive supplemental and/or targeted group interventions.
- **Tier 3 (intensive, individual intervention):** In the third tier, additional intensive, individual supports are implemented for students who are experiencing challenges and to prevent the development of more severe challenges.

The benefits of RTI include its focus on universal practices and high-quality education for all.

At the pre-K level, Recognition and Response focuses on supporting school success for all children, including those who are at risk for learning challenges (Coleman, Buysse, & Neitzel, 2006). The components of Recognition and Response include the following:

- An intervention hierarchy that responds to children's needs for support
- Appropriate and universal screening, assessment, and progress monitoring
- Research-based curriculum, instruction, and focused intervention
- A collaborative problem-solving process for decision making

National Task Force on Early Childhood Education for Hispanics

National organization designed to support school readiness of children from Hispanic backgrounds.

National Black Child Development Institute

Advocacy and education group focused on enhancing and improving the quality of life for black children and their families.

Build Strong Foundations for Our Youngest Children

National initiative to develop early childhood systems that reflect and support a multiethnic society.

Go to MyEducationLab and select the topic "Special Needs/ Inclusion." Under Activities and Applications, view the simulation *RTI Part 1: An Overview* and consider the role of RTI in ensuring that the development and learning needs of all children are met.

ISSUES OF ACCESS AND EQUITY
Why I Wrote This Book

My drive to write this book was both professional and very personal. As a professional, my passion for the field has been shaped by my students, colleagues, and the work of many I have never met. To those people I add the children I have taught, observed, and interacted with over the years—seeing their joy and connection with the world has served as a continuous, wonderful reminder of why we are all here.

As for the personal . . . I am the parent of two amazing children: My son is 11 years old; my daughter 9. To say that their disabilities and struggles—my son with a reading and writing disability, and my daughter with a rare genetic disorder that has resulted in a host of medical, learning, and social challenges—were the catalyst behind this text would be accurate on some level, but a gross oversimplification on another.

Although both my children fit federal disability categories, my daughter has seemed to develop a talent for fitting into multiple categories simultaneously. Both are children of amazing, wonderful abilities, and I am honored, humbled, and filled with joy to see the ongoing zest with which they tackle their lives. My son's challenges are addressed in our school system and the home environment; my daughter requires a team of medical specialists whose areas of expertise I can, at times, barely pronounce. Together, she and I have spent hours upon hours at medical appointments and therapy sessions, which I try to make a thrilling adventure. Alone, I have spent a similar amount of time trying to decipher and determine how to meet and exceed her needs, while I try not to succumb to anxiety.

My interest in inclusion predated my daughter's birth; however, it was after she was born that I learned—in a very concrete sense—just what social segregation for children with disabilities meant. She and I existed in a well-defined system, where there were few alternatives outside the ones offered to us, most of which did not fit my definition of a least restrictive environment. The system, as opposed to offering choices and valuing our voice, seemed not unique.

And so, we have forged our own path. Meg has always been in public programs serving all children, and, did they not consider themselves inclusive before our enrollment, I am sure they considered themselves so afterwards. I have learned on an anecdotal and research-based level that my struggles in securing inclusive placements for Meg are not unique to us. Families want high-quality, inclusive placements for their children, and teachers want to be prepared, and to have the supports needed, to meet a diverse range of children's needs.

The underlying premise of this book—supporting inclusion and flexibility—started as a framework supporting inclusion for all children and, over time and conversations with colleagues and students, developed into a framework encompassing the field. It is interesting to me that what I want for my children on a personal level does not differ from what this text offers at its core—compassion for self and others, connection with the world around us, and belief in and acceptance of ourselves, our capabilities, and our potential to create change. No matter how you examine the framework and no matter how you dissect and examine the individual components, that core remains intact. And for me, that is the swirling overlap between the personal and the professional, and the catalyst for this book.

Both RTI and Recognition and Response reflect fundamental changes in identification and intervention strategies. One of the main advantages of each model is that all children are accepted as belonging, and teaching strategies are differentiated based on the child's individual needs.

Professionals need support and recognition for the role they play in supporting children's development and learning.

Developing Systems of Professional Development. Many initiatives are supportive of professional development in the field. Two of the most far-reaching programs—T.E.A.C.H. and Child Care WAGE$—are coordinated through the Child Care Services Association. The goals of each of these projects include:

- Creating access to education.
- Increasing the quality of services provided in the early childhood field.
- Supporting ongoing education and professional development.
- Addressing issues of turnover and quality through increased staff compensation.

The T.E.A.C.H. early childhood project offers educational scholarships, which in turn create a link between education and compensation for the early childhood workforce. During 2005-2006, there were 20,299 T.E.A.C.H. scholarships awarded in 22 participating states (T.E.A.C.H., 2006). The goal of Child Care WAGE$ is to provide education-based salary supplements to low-paid teachers, directors, and family child care providers. Four states are participating in the program, and the average 6-month supplement in these programs was $579. In each of these programs, the turnover rate for participants was significantly less when compared with state turnover rates.

In addition to these initiatives supporting professional compensation and education, many states have adopted a career lattice approach. This approach provides professional development opportunities that are accessible and based on a clearly articulated framework. Included in this framework is a continuum of training and ongoing supports, defined pathways that are tied to licensure and lead to qualifications and credentials, and programs that address the needs of individual, adult learners (NCCIC, 2006). States vary in their funding sources, core knowledge requirements, articulation systems, and forums that education is offered through.

CREATING UNIVERSAL OPTIONS

Universal options means that quality, affordable, accessible early childhood programming that supports the development and learning of each child is an option for *all* children and families. Universal preschool programs, which embrace at the core of their philosophy voluntary, universal access to preschool services, are increasingly becoming a social and political force in the United States. As of 2009, six states (Florida, Oklahoma, Georgia, West Virginia, New York, and Illinois) have passed legislation guaranteeing preschool for all, and 40 states are subsidizing some kind of preschool education (National

Institute for Early Education Research, 2007). This support is born out of increasing recognition for the role preschool can play in the lives of young children and the fact that quality preschool programs are financially inaccessible to many.

At present, 80% of 4-year-olds and 97% of 3-year-olds are not enrolled in state-initiated preschool programs in the United States. When enrollment in Head Start and special education programs is considered, a full 57.5% of 3-year-olds and 34.7% of 4-year-olds are not in any kind of center-based preschool program (National Institute for Early Education Research, 2007). These statistics indicate that many children are not benefiting from state pre-K.

States vary not only in access, ranging from full to no availability, but also in quality standards, ranging from excellent to poor (National Institute for Early Education Research, 2008). These data reflect that, although universal preschool is growing as an option across the United States, the term *universal*—applying to access and quality—is a misnomer.

The transformation of preschool as an important part of children's education is similar to the transformation kindergarten education underwent several years ago. The impact could be quite similar, where preschool eventually becomes as commonplace as kindergarten education in the lives of young children. For this transformation to be successful, however, the preschool experiences children have *must* be of high quality: Merely giving children access will do little to attain positive results.

Currently, early childhood education is ripe with opportunity and promise, but with this opportunity comes great responsibility. As a professional, you are an ambassador of the field, serving to carry out the mission of the field and communicate and advocate for its importance to others. A large part of your ambassadorship is ensuring that you provide children and families with high-quality experiences that support their individual goals and the goals of the larger context. Another part of your role is recognizing and advocating for the potential of the field. This is accomplished through both embracing and supporting the field today and looking to how the field needs to continue to grow and develop.

The term *universal preschool*, in both its promise and practice, represents one small component of the larger system of early childhood education. High-quality preschool experiences that are accessible to all children would be, and is on its way to being, an incredible accomplishment resulting from the passions and hard work of many. A truly universal system, however, would support the continuum of children's learning and development needs between birth and the age of 8, the needs of their families, and the needs of professionals. We are a long way from attaining this goal, but what was once the stuff of dreams is slowly but surely taking on the defined outline of a potential reality.

Vision for the Future: Ensuring Universal Options

In the book *The Sandbox Investment*, Kirp (2007) argues that high-quality universal preschool programs throughout the United States will be a major step in improving children's lives. However, this move is just a step, and he advocates that:

> If the aspiration is to have a marked and sustained impact on children, especially poor children, preschool for all is much too narrow a vision. Its benefits come too late, since so much has already happened to children by the time they are four years old. And they end too early, because primary schools are going to have to improve if their impact is going to last. (Kirp, 2007, p. 9)

Kirp's argument points to the need for quality early childhood programming that supports the continuum of the field of early childhood education from birth through age 8. Further, the diverse needs of children and families in this continuum must be accommodated and supported.

You have explored what access to the field means for children, families, and professionals and how quality practices in the overall field can promote accountability for equity and success for each of these groups. The interactions between each of these groups and larger society are complex and interdependent, where supports, strengths, and resources interact with and can counteract challenges. Through examination of each piece of this complex, dynamic puzzle, the goal is to support change through a systemwide perspective.

What are the obstacles to the field achieving its full potential? The barriers to systemic change are plentiful (Gallagher & Clifford, 2000), and your knowledge of them as a professional supports your development of strategies to overcome them.

Barriers to Attaining Universal Options

The potential impact of early childhood education on society is well documented. In a perfect world, this substantive evidence might conflate into a maelstrom of policies and practices that support and enhance the development of all children and their families. Professionals would receive recognition and appropriate compensation for their essential role, and the field of early childhood education overall would be embraced as an important ingredient in a potential anecdote to many of society's ills. The fact that we don't live in a perfect world where evidence and practice are in perfect unison can present daunting—and at times, invigorating—challenges. Challenges associated with changing early childhood education can be divided into the following categories (Gallagher & Clifford, 2000):

- Institutional, where proposed change might conflict with widely adhered to practices in social and political institutions
- Psychological, representing individual, personal responses to proposals for change
- Sociological, where policies and practices might not be reflective of cultural norms at the familial level
- Economic, where the price tag in terms of dollars saved in the future does not offset the fears of spending resources now
- Geographic, as many parts of the country have varied access to comprehensive systems

Despite visions of how to change the field and larger society, these obstacles are real and likely ones professionals will experience. In addition, change always requires more energy and attention than maintaining the status quo, and that factor alone can derail substantive research, a clear vision of future potential, and an articulated pathway for how to get there.

Support for Universal Options

You have learned how to view the field, assisting you in understanding your potential impact on each aspect of the field. Supporting universal options in early childhood education requires attention to the overall framework and the components in it. These components begin with ensuring access for children, families, and professionals. Providing varied programs, curricular approaches, and philosophies is essential to supporting universal options, as is providing children with curriculum that is intentional. Children, professionals, and programs benefit from meaningful assessment practices, and each of these factors in turn supports accountability for equity and success.

The field of early childhood education and your role in it is supported by examining the bidirectional impact of the environment on the developing child, which embraces the diverse needs of children, families, professionals, classroom communities, the field as a whole, and society and culture. Adopting an ecological systems perspective acknowledges the changing nature and needs of each of these components and their complex interactions. Through examination of these interrelated parts, professionals are able to understand their impact on individual children and families and how these interactions affect the field, community, society, and culture as a whole. Further, you have explored the tools for developing a supportive infrastructure—building the knowledge, skills, dispositions, and supports necessary for the field to be effective. The effectiveness of inclusion and flexibility as catalysts for change and the field's capacity in general to meet and support today's challenges depend on each professional in the field. You, as a present or future professional, are an essential piece of this puzzle.

MOVING FORWARD

myeducationlab

Go to MyEducationLab and select the topic "Professionalism/Ethics/Standards." Under Building Teaching Skills and Dispositions, complete the exercise *My Plan for Success.*

With knowledge and skills needed to create effective programs, dispositions supportive of advocacy, and the passion to make your message heard, you can play a vital role in supporting the learning and development of young children and their families, supporting and enhancing your own professional development, and advancing the field. In turn, your actions and interactions can affect both the present *and* the future.

Access and Equity for All: Education as a Tool of Change

Fundamentally, education is about change, whether it be changing your present way of viewing the world, your interactions with that world, or how you feel about those interactions. And as was conveyed in this chapter's opening vignette, you are a catalyst for change.

Throughout this text, many ideas and strategies have been shared for supporting the field of early childhood education, the children and families in it, and the community and society it affects. All of this begins with you—your belief in yourself and your ability to use this belief to have a positive impact on others. I have chosen to end this text with quotes and have selected each of these because I feel they reflect some kernel of truth, not only of the world around us, but also of what we can find within ourselves.

"Education is the most powerful weapon you can use to change the world."
—Nelson Mandela, the first democratically elected president of South Africa

"How wonderful it is that nobody need wait a single moment before starting to improve their world."
—Anne Frank, German-Jewish teenager forced to go into hiding during the Holocaust

"Never doubt that a small group of thoughtful, committed citizens can change the world. Indeed, it is the only thing that ever has."
—Margaret Mead, internationally renowned American anthropologist

"If you don't like the way the world is, you change it. You have an obligation to change it. You just do it one step at a time."
—Marian Wright Edelman, president
of Children's Defense Fund

"With realization of one's own potential and self-confidence in one's ability, one can build a better world."
—Dalai Lama, the head of state and
spiritual leader of the Tibetan people

"You give but little when you give of your possessions. It is when you give of yourself that you truly give."
—Kahlil Gibran, Lebanese writer and poet

"Yes, we can!"
—Barack Obama, 44th president of the United States

CASE STUDY

Your Role in Moving the Field Forward

In this book's final case study the material will be written by you. Consider the various topics we've discussed, as well as any experience you may already have working with young children. How will you support the development and learning of all children and families? How will you work to support your own professional development over time? What will you do to make sure that the practices you put in place are reflective of effective practices in the field and respectful and responsive to the needs of children and families in your care? And, what will you do to move the field forward?

CONSTRUCTED-RESPONSE QUESTION

1. What are the components of effective advocacy? What strategies will you use to support the development and learning of all children and families and advance the vital mission of the field of early childhood education?

REFLECTING ON AND APPLYING EFFECTIVE PRACTICES (NAEYC AND CEC/DEC)

Ethics

- You are working in the field of early childhood education. Perhaps you are a teacher in a preschool classroom, a director of a center-based program, an owner of a family child care home, a first-grade teacher, or a developmental therapist. On a daily basis, you are confronted with reminders that the field, the profession, your work and the people you work with, the lives of young children and families, are perhaps not viewed with the same value you have for the field, the professionals, and the children and families it serves. Perhaps a casual comment is made about "babysitting" services, or a disparaging comment about "families who don't know anything about kids," or a comment about "babies needing little more than a bottle and a clean diaper." Maybe someone makes a comment about "disabled kids" or claims "we'd all be better off if we made everyone speak English exclusively." Think about what you have learned in this course, your own values, your hopes for the field, yourself as a professional, for those you work with, for families, and for children. How would you respond to these comments?

NAEYC Ideals: Ethical Responsibilities to Community and Society
I-4.7. To further the professional development of the field of early childhood care and education and to strengthen its commitment to realizing its core values as reflected in this Code.

DEC: Professional and Interpersonal Behavior
1. We shall demonstrate in our behavior and language respect and appreciation for the unique value and human potential of each child.

PHILOSOPHY DEVELOPMENT ACTIVITY

Reflect on the philosophy development activities you've completed throughout this course. Based on these, develop a collective statement reflective of your future pathway as a professional.

PORTFOLIO DEVELOPMENT ACTIVITY

Develop an action plan for your next steps as a professional. Specifically, what will you do to support the further development of your knowledge, skills, and dispositions? How will you assess whether you are meeting your goals? What strategies will you use to ensure your success in the field?

CHAPTER REVIEW

- **What role does accountability play in answering the field's call to excellence?**

  Accountability refers to the field's ability to deliver positive outcomes for children, families, and professionals. One of the major challenges in attaining accountability is that the United States lacks a clear and cohesive vision and policies and practices that support the whole of the field of early childhood education.

  Attention to excellence in services provided; access to the field for children, families, and professionals; equity, reflected in opportunities for all children to attend high-quality programs; diversity, reflective of the fields ability to meet the needs of children, families, and professionals regardless of ability and/or cultural and linguistic diversity; and accountability, reflected through clearly defined standards for program quality and personnel are each needed components for attaining NAEYC's Vision for Excellence.

- **What is the role of advocacy in advancing the field of early childhood education?**

  Advocacy plays an important role in advancing the field of early childhood education. Advocacy supports the creation of a shared vision of the importance of the field and the incredible impact it can have on children, families, and society. To date, advocacy has played an essential role in the dramatic changes in the field over the past two decades. For the field to continue to advance, and attain its incredible promise, targeted advocacy is essential.

- **What present-day strategies, systems, and initiatives contribute to the advancement of the field?**

  The present-day strategies, systems, and initiatives that contribute to the advancement of the field include creating a continuum of early childhood services, supporting early learning guidelines for infants and toddlers, supporting statewide infant and toddler systems, supporting infant and toddler professional preparation, ensuring that all children are physically and mentally healthy, embracing families as the child's first and most important teacher; supporting inclusion, developing systems of professional development; and creating universal options.

- **What are present-day barriers to achieving universal options?**

  Barriers to attaining universal options include institutional, psychological, sociological, economic, and geographic factors. Each of these present challenges that education and advocacy can work to overcome. Further, the development of early childhood systems that meet the needs of children, families, professionals, and larger society can work to address these barriers.

Appendix A

NAEYC Code of Ethical Conduct and Statement of Commitment

PREAMBLE

NAEYC recognizes that those who work with young children face many daily decisions that have moral and ethical implications. The NAEYC Code of Ethical Conduct offers guidelines for responsible behavior and sets forth a common basis for resolving the principal ethical dilemmas encountered in early childhood care and education. The Statement of Commitment is not part of the Code but is a personal acknowledgement of an individual's willingness to embrace the distinctive values and moral obligations of the field of early childhood care and education. The primary focus of the Code is on daily practice with children and their families in programs for children from birth through 8 years of age, such as infant/toddler programs, preschool and prekindergarten programs, child care centers, hospital and child life settings, family child care homes, kindergartens, and primary classrooms. When the issues involve young children, then these provisions also apply to specialists who do not work directly with children, including program administrators, parent educators, early childhood adult educators, and officials with responsibility for program monitoring and licensing. (Note: See also the "Code of Ethical Conduct: Supplement for Early Childhood Adult Educators," online at http://www.naeyc.org/about/positions/asp/ethics04.)

Core Values

Standards of ethical behavior in early childhood care and education are based on commitment to the following core values that are deeply rooted in the history of the field of early childhood care and education. We have made a commitment to

- Appreciate childhood as a unique and valuable stage of the human life cycle
- Base our work on knowledge of how children develop and learn
- Appreciate and support the bond between the child and family
- Recognize that children are best understood and supported in the context of family, culture,[1] community, and society
- Respect the dignity, worth, and uniqueness of each individual (child, family member, and colleague)
- Respect diversity in children, families, and colleagues
- Recognize that children and adults achieve their full potential in the context of relationships that are based on trust and respect

Conceptual Framework

The Code sets forth a framework of professional responsibilities in four sections. Each section addresses an area of professional relationships: (1) with children, (2) with families, (3) among colleagues, and (4) with the community and society. Each section includes an introduction to the primary responsibilities of the early childhood practitioner in that context. The introduction is followed by a set of ideals (I) that reflect exemplary professional practice and by a set of principles (P) describing practices that are required, prohibited, or permitted.

The **ideals** reflect the aspirations of practitioners. The **principles** guide conduct and assist practitioners in resolving ethical dilemmas.[2] Both ideals and principles are intended to direct practitioners to those questions which, when responsibly answered, can provide the basis for conscientious decision making. While the Code provides specific direction for addressing some ethical dilemmas, many others will require the practitioner to combine the guidance of the Code with professional judgment.

The ideals and principles in this Code present a shared framework of professional responsibility that affirms our commitment to the core values of our field. The Code publicly acknowledges the responsibilities that we in the field have assumed, and in so doing supports ethical behavior in our work. Practitioners who face situations with ethical dimensions are urged to seek guidance in the applicable parts of this Code and in the spirit that informs the whole.

Source: NAEYC. *Position Statement. Code of Ethical Conduct and Statement of Commitment.* 2005 rev. Washington, DC: Author. www.naeyc.org/about/positions/pdf/PSETH05.pdf. Reprinted with permission from the National Association for the Education of Young Children.

---

[1]*Culture* includes ethnicity, racial identity, economic level, family structure, language, and religious and political beliefs, which profoundly influence each child's development and relationship to the world.

[2]There is not necessarily a corresponding principle for each ideal.

453

Often "the right answer"—the best ethical course of action to take—is not obvious. There may be no readily apparent, positive way to handle a situation. When one important value contradicts another, we face an ethical dilemma. When we face a dilemma, it is our professional responsibility to consult the Code and all relevant parties to find the most ethical resolution.

SECTION I: ETHICAL RESPONSIBILITIES TO CHILDREN

Childhood is a unique and valuable stage in the human life cycle. Our paramount responsibility is to provide care and education in settings that are safe, healthy, nurturing, and responsive for each child. We are committed to supporting children's development and learning; respecting individual differences; and helping children learn to live, play, and work cooperatively. We are also committed to promoting children's self-awareness, competence, self-worth, resiliency, and physical well-being.

Ideals

I-1.1—To be familiar with the knowledge base of early childhood care and education and to stay informed through continuing education and training.

I-1.2—To base program practices upon current knowledge and research in the field of early childhood education, child development, and related disciplines, as well as on particular knowledge of each child.

I-1.3—To recognize and respect the unique qualities, abilities, and potential of each child.

I-1.4—To appreciate the vulnerability of children and their dependence on adults.

I-1.5—To create and maintain safe and healthy settings that foster children's social, emotional, cognitive, and physical development and that respect their dignity and their contributions.

I-1.6—To use assessment instruments and strategies that are appropriate for the children to be assessed, that are used only for the purposes for which they were designed, and that have the potential to benefit children.

I-1.7—To use assessment information to understand and support children's development and learning, to support instruction, and to identify children who may need additional services.

I-1.8—To support the right of each child to play and learn in an inclusive environment that meets the needs of children with and without disabilities.

I-1.9—To advocate for and ensure that all children, including those with special needs, have access to the support services needed to be successful.

I-1.10—To ensure that each child's culture, language, ethnicity, and family structure are recognized and valued in the program.

I-1.11—To provide all children with experiences in a language that they know, as well as support children in maintaining the use of their home language and in learning English.

I-1.12—To work with families to provide a safe and smooth transition as children and families move from one program to the next.

Principles

P-1.1—Above all, we shall not harm children. We shall not participate in practices that are emotionally damaging, physically harmful, disrespectful, degrading, dangerous, exploitative, or intimidating to children. *This principle has precedence over all others in this Code.*

P-1.2—We shall care for and educate children in positive emotional and social environments that are cognitively stimulating and that support each child's culture, language, ethnicity, and family structure.

P-1.3—We shall not participate in practices that discriminate against children by denying benefits, giving special advantages, or excluding them from programs or activities on the basis of their sex, race, national origin, religious beliefs, medical condition, disability, or the marital status/family structure, sexual orientation, or religious beliefs or other affiliations of their families. (Aspects of this principle do not apply in programs that have a lawful mandate to provide services to a particular population of children.)

P-1.4—We shall involve all those with relevant knowledge (including families and staff) in decisions concerning a child, as appropriate, ensuring confidentiality of sensitive information.

P-1.5—We shall use appropriate assessment systems, which include multiple sources of information, to provide information on children's learning and development.

P-1.6—We shall strive to ensure that decisions such as those related to enrollment, retention, or assignment to special education services, will be based on multiple sources of information and will never be based on a single assessment, such as a test score or a single observation.

P-1.7—We shall strive to build individual relationships with each child; make individualized adaptations in teaching strategies, learning environments, and curricula; and consult with the family so that each child benefits from the program. If after such efforts have been exhausted, the current placement does not meet a child's needs, or the child is seriously jeopardizing the ability of other children to benefit from the program, we shall collaborate with the child's family and appropriate specialists to determine the additional services needed and/or the placement option(s) most likely to ensure the child's success. (Aspects of this principle may not apply in programs that have a lawful mandate to provide services to a particular population of children.)

P-1.8—We shall be familiar with the risk factors for and symptoms of child abuse and neglect, including physical, sexual, verbal, and emotional abuse and physical, emotional, educational, and medical neglect. We shall know and follow state laws and community procedures that protect children against abuse and neglect.

P-1.9—When we have reasonable cause to suspect child abuse or neglect, we shall report it to the appropriate community agency and follow up to ensure that appropriate action has been taken. When appropriate, parents or guardians will be informed that the referral will be or has been made.

P-1.10—When another person tells us of his or her suspicion that a child is being abused or neglected, we shall assist that person in taking appropriate action in order to protect the child.

P-1.11—When we become aware of a practice or situation that endangers the health, safety, or well-being of children, we have an ethical responsibility to protect children or inform parents and/or others who can.

SECTION II: ETHICAL RESPONSIBILITIES TO FAMILIES

Families[3] are of primary importance in children's development. Because the family and the early childhood practitioner have a common interest in the child's well-being, we acknowledge a primary responsibility to bring about communication, cooperation, and collaboration between the home and early childhood program in ways that enhance the child's development.

Ideals

I-2.1—To be familiar with the knowledge base related to working effectively with families and to stay informed through continuing education and training.

I-2.2—To develop relationships of mutual trust and create partnerships with the families we serve.

I-2.3—To welcome all family members and encourage them to participate in the program.

I-2.4—To listen to families, acknowledge and build upon their strengths and competencies, and learn from families as we support them in their task of nurturing children.

I-2.5—To respect the dignity and preferences of each family and to make an effort to learn about its structure, culture, language, customs, and beliefs.

I-2.6—To acknowledge families' childrearing values and their right to make decisions for their children.

I-2.7—To share information about each child's education and development with families and to help them understand and appreciate the current knowledge base of the early childhood profession.

I-2.8—To help family members enhance their understanding of their children and support the continuing development of their skills as parents.

I-2.9—To participate in building support networks for families by providing them with opportunities to interact with program staff, other families, community resources, and professional services.

Principles

P-2.1—We shall not deny family members access to their child's classroom or program setting unless access is denied by court order or other legal restriction.

P-2.2—We shall inform families of program philosophy, policies, curriculum, assessment system, and personnel qualifications, and explain why we teach as we do—which should be in accordance with our ethical responsibilities to children (see Section I).

P-2.3—We shall inform families of and, when appropriate, involve them in policy decisions.

P-2.4—We shall involve the family in significant decisions affecting their child.

P-2.5—We shall make every effort to communicate effectively with all families in a language that they understand. We shall use community resources for translation and interpretation when we do not have sufficient resources in our own programs.

P-2.6—As families share information with us about their children and families, we shall consider this information to plan and implement the program.

P-2.7—We shall inform families about the nature and purpose of the program's child assessments and how data about their child will be used.

P-2.8—We shall treat child assessment information confidentially and share this information only when there is a legitimate need for it.

P-2.9—We shall inform the family of injuries and incidents involving their child, of risks such as exposures to

[3]The term *family* may include those adults, besides parents, with the responsibility of being involved in educating, nurturing, and advocating for the child.

communicable diseases that might result in infection, and of occurrences that might result in emotional stress.

P-2.10—Families shall be fully informed of any proposed research projects involving their children and shall have the opportunity to give or withhold consent without penalty. We shall not permit or participate in research that could in any way hinder the education, development, or well-being of children.

P-2.11—We shall not engage in or support exploitation of families. We shall not use our relationship with a family for private advantage or personal gain, or enter into relationships with family members that might impair our effectiveness working with their children.

P-2.12—We shall develop written policies for the protection of confidentiality and the disclosure of children's records. These policy documents shall be made available to all program personnel and families. Disclosure of children's records beyond family members, program personnel, and consultants having an obligation of confidentiality shall require familial consent (except in cases of abuse or neglect).

P-2.13—We shall maintain confidentiality and shall respect the family's right to privacy, refraining from disclosure of confidential information and intrusion into family life. However, when we have reason to believe that a child's welfare is at risk, it is permissible to share confidential information with agencies, as well as with individuals who have legal responsibility for intervening in the child's interest.

P-2.14—In cases where family members are in conflict with one another, we shall work openly, sharing our observations of the child, to help all parties involved make informed decisions. We shall refrain from becoming an advocate for one party.

P-2.15—We shall be familiar with and appropriately refer families to community resources and professional support services. After a referral has been made, we shall follow up to ensure that services have been appropriately provided.

SECTION III: ETHICAL RESPONSIBILITIES TO COLLEAGUES

In a caring, cooperative workplace, human dignity is respected, professional satisfaction is promoted, and positive relationships are developed and sustained. Based upon our core values, our primary responsibility to colleagues is to establish and maintain settings and relationships that support productive work and meet professional needs. The same ideals that apply to children also apply as we interact with adults in the workplace.

A—Responsibilities to co-workers

Ideals

I-3A.1—To establish and maintain relationships of respect, trust, confidentiality, collaboration, and cooperation with co-workers.

I-3A.2—To share resources with co-workers, collaborating to ensure that the best possible early childhood care and education program is provided.

I-3A.3—To support co-workers in meeting their professional needs and in their professional development.

I-3A.4—To accord co-workers due recognition of professional achievement.

Principles

P-3A.1—We shall recognize the contributions of colleagues to our program and not participate in practices that diminish their reputations or impair their effectiveness in working with children and families.

P-3A.2—When we have concerns about the professional behavior of a co-worker, we shall first let that person know of our concern in a way that shows respect for personal dignity and for the diversity to be found among staff members, and then attempt to resolve the matter collegially and in a confidential manner.

P-3A.3—We shall exercise care in expressing views regarding the personal attributes or professional conduct of co-workers. Statements should be based on firsthand knowledge, not hearsay, and relevant to the interests of children and programs.

P-3A.4—We shall not participate in practices that discriminate against a co-worker because of sex, race, national origin, religious beliefs or other affiliations, age, marital status/family structure, disability, or sexual orientation.

B—Responsibilities to employers

Ideals

I-3B.1—To assist the program in providing the highest quality of service.

I-3B.2—To do nothing that diminishes the reputation of the program in which we work unless it is violating laws and regulations designed to protect children or is violating the provisions of this Code.

Principles

P-3B.1—We shall follow all program policies. When we do not agree with program policies, we shall attempt to effect change through constructive action within the organization.

P-3B.2—We shall speak or act on behalf of an organization only when authorized. We shall take care to acknowledge when we are speaking for the organization and when we are expressing a personal judgment.

P-3B.3—We shall not violate laws or regulations designed to protect children and shall take appropriate action consistent with this Code when aware of such violations.

P-3B.4—If we have concerns about a colleague's behavior, and children's well-being is not at risk, we may address the concern with that individual. If children are at risk or the situation does not improve after it has been brought to the colleague's attention, we shall report the colleague's unethical or incompetent behavior to an appropriate authority.

P-3B.5—When we have a concern about circumstances or conditions that impact the quality of care and education within the program, we shall inform the program's administration or, when necessary, other appropriate authorities.

C—Responsibilities to employees

Ideals

I-3C.1—To promote safe and healthy working conditions and policies that foster mutual respect, cooperation, collaboration, competence, well-being, confidentiality, and self-esteem in staff members.

I-3C.2—To create and maintain a climate of trust and candor that will enable staff to speak and act in the best interests of children, families, and the field of early childhood care and education.

I-3C.3—To strive to secure adequate and equitable compensation (salary and benefits) for those who work with or on behalf of young children.

I-3C.4—To encourage and support continual development of employees in becoming more skilled and knowledgeable practitioners.

Principles

P-3C.1—In decisions concerning children and programs, we shall draw upon the education, training, experience, and expertise of staff members.

P-3C.2—We shall provide staff members with safe and supportive working conditions that honor confidences and permit them to carry out their responsibilities through fair performance evaluation, written grievance procedures, constructive feedback, and opportunities for continuing professional development and advancement.

P-3C.3—We shall develop and maintain comprehensive written personnel policies that define program standards. These policies shall be given to new staff members and shall be available and easily accessible for review by all staff members.

P-3C.4—We shall inform employees whose performance does not meet program expectations of areas of concern and, when possible, assist in improving their performance.

P-3C.5—We shall conduct employee dismissals for just cause, in accordance with all applicable laws and regulations. We shall inform employees who are dismissed of the reasons for their termination. When a dismissal is for cause, justification must be based on evidence of inadequate or inappropriate behavior that is accurately documented, current, and available for the employee to review.

P-3C.6—In making evaluations and recommendations, we shall make judgments based on fact and relevant to the interests of children and programs.

P-3C.7—We shall make hiring, retention, termination, and promotion decisions based solely on a person's competence, record of accomplishment, ability to carry out the responsibilities of the position, and professional preparation specific to the developmental levels of children in his/her care.

P-3C.8—We shall not make hiring, retention, termination, and promotion decisions based on an individual's sex, race, national origin, religious beliefs or other affiliations, age, marital status/family structure, disability, or sexual orientation. We shall be familiar with and observe laws and regulations that pertain to employment discrimination. (Aspects of this principle do not apply to programs that have a lawful mandate to determine eligibility based on one or more of the criteria identified above.)

P-3C.9—We shall maintain confidentiality in dealing with issues related to an employee's job performance and shall respect an employee's right to privacy regarding personal issues.

SECTION IV: ETHICAL RESPONSIBILITIES TO COMMUNITY AND SOCIETY

Early childhood programs operate within the context of their immediate community made up of families and other institutions concerned with children's welfare. Our responsibilities to the community are to provide programs that meet the diverse needs of families, to cooperate with agencies and professions that share the responsibility for children, to assist families in gaining access to those agencies and allied professionals, and to assist in the development of community programs that are needed but not currently available.

As individuals, we acknowledge our responsibility to provide the best possible programs of care and education for children and to conduct ourselves with honesty and integrity. Because of our specialized expertise in early childhood development and education and because the larger society shares responsibility for the welfare and protection of young children, we acknowledge a collective obligation to advocate for the best interests of children within early childhood programs and in the larger community and to serve as a voice for young children everywhere.

The ideals and principles in this section are presented to distinguish between those that pertain to the work of the individual early childhood educator and those that more typically are engaged in collectively on behalf of the best interests of children—with the understanding that individual early childhood educators have a shared responsibility for addressing the ideals and principles that are identified as "collective."

Ideal (Individual)

I-4.1—To provide the community with high-quality early childhood care and education programs and services.

Ideals (Collective)

I-4.2—To promote cooperation among professionals and agencies and interdisciplinary collaboration among professions concerned with addressing issues in the health, education, and well-being of young children, their families, and their early childhood educators.

I-4.3—To work through education, research, and advocacy toward an environmentally safe world in which all children receive health care, food, and shelter; are nurtured; and live free from violence in their home and their communities.

I-4.4—To work through education, research, and advocacy toward a society in which all young children have access to high-quality early care and education programs.

I-4.5—To work to ensure that appropriate assessment systems, which include multiple sources of information, are used for purposes that benefit children.

I-4.6—To promote knowledge and understanding of young children and their needs. To work toward greater societal acknowledgment of children's rights and greater social acceptance of responsibility for the well-being of all children.

I-4.7—To support policies and laws that promote the well-being of children and families, and to work to change those that impair their well-being. To participate in developing policies and laws that are needed, and to cooperate with other individuals and groups in these efforts.

I-4.8—To further the professional development of the field of early childhood care and education and to strengthen its commitment to realizing its core values as reflected in this Code.

Principles (Individual)

P-4.1—We shall communicate openly and truthfully about the nature and extent of services that we provide.

P-4.2—We shall apply for, accept, and work in positions for which we are personally well-suited and professionally qualified. We shall not offer services that we do not have the competence, qualifications, or resources to provide.

P-4.3—We shall carefully check references and shall not hire or recommend for employment any person whose competence, qualifications, or character makes him or her unsuited for the position.

P-4.4—We shall be objective and accurate in reporting the knowledge upon which we base our program practices.

P-4.5—We shall be knowledgeable about the appropriate use of assessment strategies and instruments and interpret results accurately to families.

P-4.6—We shall be familiar with laws and regulations that serve to protect the children in our programs and be vigilant in ensuring that these laws and regulations are followed.

P-4.7—When we become aware of a practice or situation that endangers the health, safety, or well-being of children, we have an ethical responsibility to protect children or inform parents and/or others who can.

P-4.8—We shall not participate in practices that are in violation of laws and regulations that protect the children in our programs.

P-4.9—When we have evidence that an early childhood program is violating laws or regulations protecting children, we shall report the violation to appropriate authorities who can be expected to remedy the situation.

P-4.10—When a program violates or requires its employees to violate this Code, it is permissible, after fair assessment of the evidence, to disclose the identity of that program.

Principles (Collective)

P-4.11—When policies are enacted for purposes that do not benefit children, we have a collective responsibility to work to change these practices.

P-4.12—When we have evidence that an agency that provides services intended to ensure children's well-being is failing to meet its obligations, we acknowledge a collective ethical responsibility to report the problem to appropriate authorities or to the public. We shall be vigilant in our follow-up until the situation is resolved.

P-4.13—When a child protection agency fails to provide adequate protection for abused or neglected children, we acknowledge a collective ethical responsibility to work toward the improvement of these services.

Glossary of Terms Related to Ethics

Code of Ethics: Defines the core values of the field and provides guidance for what professionals should do when they encounter conflicting obligations or responsibilities in their work.

Core Values: Commitments held by a profession that are consciously and knowingly embraced by its practitioners because they make a contribution to society. There is a difference between personal values and the core values of a profession.

Ethical Dilemma: A moral conflict that involves determining appropriate conduct when an individual faces conflicting professional values and responsibilities.

Ethical Responsibilities: Behaviors that one must or must not engage in. Ethical responsibilities are clear-cut and are spelled out in the Code of Ethical Conduct (for example, early childhood educators should never share confidential information about a child or family with a person who has no legitimate need for knowing).

Ethics: The study of right and wrong, or duty and obligation, that involves critical reflection on morality and the ability to make choices between values and the examination of the moral dimensions of relationships.

Morality: Peoples' views of what is good, right and proper; their beliefs about their obligations; and their ideas about how they should behave.

Professional Ethics: The moral commitments of a profession that involve moral reflection that extends and enhances the personal morality practitioners bring to their work, that concern actions of right and wrong in the workplace, and that help individuals resolve moral dilemmas they encounter in their work.

Values: Qualities or principles that individuals believe to be desirable or worthwhile and that they prize for themselves, for others, and for the world in which they live.

Sources for Glossary Terms and Definitions

Feeney, S., & N. Freeman. 1999. *Ethics and the early childhood educator: Using the NAEYC code.* Washington, DC: NAEYC.

Kidder, R. M. 1995. *How good people make tough choices: Resolving the dilemmas of ethical living.* New York: Fireside.

Kipnis, K. 1987. How to discuss professional ethics. *Young Children* 42 (4): 26–30.

Statement of Commitment[4]

As an individual who works with young children, I commit myself to furthering the values of early childhood education as they are reflected in the ideals and principles of the NAEYC Code of Ethical Conduct. To the best of my ability I will

- Never harm children.
- Ensure that programs for young children are based on current knowledge and research of child development and early childhood education.
- Respect and support families in their task of nurturing children.
- Respect colleagues in early childhood care and education and support them in maintaining the NAEYC Code of Ethical Conduct.
- Serve as an advocate for children, their families, and their teachers in community and society.
- Stay informed of and maintain high standards of professional conduct.
- Engage in an ongoing process of self-reflection, realizing that personal characteristics, biases, and beliefs have an impact on children and families.
- Be open to new ideas and be willing to learn from the suggestions of others.
- Continue to learn, grow, and contribute as a professional.
- Honor the ideals and principles of the NAEYC Code of Ethical Conduct.

[4]This Statement of Commitment is not part of the Code but is a personal acknowledgment of the individual's willingness to embrace the distinctive values and moral obligations of the field of early childhood care and education. It is recognition of the moral obligations that lead to an individual becoming part of the profession.

Appendix B

Division for Early Childhood of the CEC Code of Ethics

The Code of Ethics of the Division for Early Childhood (DEC) of the Council for Exceptional Children is a public statement of principles and practices guidelines supported by the mission of DEC.

The foundation of this Code is based on sound ethical reasoning related to professional practice with young children with disabilities and their families and with interdisciplinary colleagues. Foremost, is our value of respecting the autonomy of families as they make decisions for their young children with disabilities while also practicing a mutual respect for our colleagues in the field. We, as early childhood professionals, practice within the principles and guidelines outlined below as well as uphold the laws and regulations of our professional licensure standards.

The Code's purpose is to: (1) identify the key principles guiding our professional conduct; and (2) provide guidance for practice and personal dilemma in our conduct of research and practice. The Code is intended to assist professionals in resolving conflicts as they arise in practice with children and families and with other colleagues.

The following principles and guidelines for practice include:

Professional Practice

Professional Development and Preparation

Responsive Family Centered Practices

Ethical and Evidence Based Practices

PROFESSIONAL PRACTICE

Professional Practice encompasses the practice principles to promote and maintain high standards of conduct for the early childhood special education professional. The early childhood special education professional should base his or her behaviors on ethical reasoning surrounding practice and professional issues as well as an empathic reflection regarding interactions with others. We are committed to beneficence acts for improving the quality of lives of young children with disabilities and

Source: Council for Exceptional Children/Division for Early Childhood. *DEC Code of Ethics* (draft version). Retrieved April 28, 2009 from: http://www.dec-sped.org/uploads/docs/about_dec/position_concept_papers/Code%20of%20Ethics_Field%20Review%2011_08.pdf. Reprinted with permission from the Division for Early Childhood of the Council for Exceptional Children.

their families. The guidelines for practice outlined below provide a framework for everyday practice when working with children and families and with other professionals in the field of early childhood special education.

Professional and Interpersonal Behavior

1. We shall demonstrate in our behavior and language respect and appreciation for the unique value and human potential of each child.
2. We shall demonstrate the highest standards of personal integrity, truthfulness, and honesty in all our professional activities in order to inspire the trust and confidence of the children and families and of those with whom we work.
3. We shall strive for the highest level of personal and professional competence by seeking and using new evidence based information to improve our practices while also responding openly to the suggestions of others.
4. We shall serve as advocates for children with disabilities and their families and for the professionals who serve them by supporting both policy and programmatic decisions that enhance the quality of their lives.
5. We shall use individually appropriate assessment strategies including multiple sources of information such as observations, interviews with significant caregivers, formal and informal assessments to determine children's learning styles, strengths, and challenges.
6. We shall build relationships with individual children and families while individualizing the curricula and learning environments to facilitate young children's development and learning.

Professional Collaboration

1. We shall honor and respect our responsibilities to colleagues while upholding the dignity and autonomy of colleagues and maintaining collegial interprofessional and intraprofessional relationships.
2. We shall honor and respect the rights, knowledge, and skills of the multidisciplinary colleagues with whom we work recognizing their unique contributions to children, families, and the field of early childhood special education.
3. We shall honor and respect the diverse backgrounds of our colleagues including such diverse characteristics as

sexual orientation, race, national origin, religious beliefs, or other affiliations.

4. We shall identify and disclose to the appropriate persons using proper communication channels errors or acts of incompetence that compromise children's and families' safety and well being when individual attempts to address concerns are unsuccessful.

PROFESSIONAL DEVELOPMENT AND PREPARATION

Professional Development Preparation is critical to providing the most effective services for young children with disabilities and their families. Professional development is viewed and valued as on ongoing process guided by high standards and competencies for professional performance practice. Professionals acquire the knowledge, skills, and dispositions to work with a variety of young children with disabilities and their families within natural and inclusive environments promoting children's overall growth, development and learning, and enhancing family quality of life. Finally, professionals continually should seek and interpret evidence based information for planning and implementing individually appropriate learning environments linked to ongoing assessment and collaboration with parents and professional team members.

1. We shall engage in ongoing and systematic reflective inquiry and self-assessment for the purpose of continuous improvement of professional performance and services to young children with disabilities and their families.
2. We shall continually be aware of issues challenging the field of early childhood special education and advocate for changes in the laws, regulations, and policies leading to improved outcomes and services for young children with disabilities and their families.
3. We shall be responsible for maintaining the appropriate national, state, or other credential or licensure requirements for the services we provide while maintaining our competence in practice and research by ongoing participation in professional development and education activities.
4. We shall support professionals new to the field by mentoring them in the practice of evidence and ethically based services.

RESPONSIVE FAMILY CENTERED PRACTICES

Responsive Family Centered Practices ensure that families receive individualized, meaningful, and relevant services responsive to their beliefs, values, customs, languages, and culture. We are committed to enhancing the quality of children's and families' lives buy promoting family well-being and participation in typical life activities. The early childhood special education professional will demonstrate respect for all families, taking into consideration and acknowledging diverse family structures, culture, language, values, and customs. Finally, families will be given equal voice in all decision making relative to their children. The following practice guidelines provide a framework for enhancing children's and families' quality of lives.

Enhancement of Children's and Families' Quality of Lives

1. We shall demonstrate our respect and concern for children, families, colleagues, and others with whom we work, honoring their beliefs, values, customs, languages, and culture.
2. We shall recognize our responsibility to improve the developmental outcomes of children and to provide services and supports in a fair and equitable manner to all families and children.
3. We shall recognize and respect the dignity, diversity, and autonomy of the families and children we serve.
4. We shall advocate for equal access to high quality services and supports for all children and families to enhance their quality of lives.

Responsive Family Centered Practices

1. We shall demonstrate our respect and appreciation for all families' beliefs, values, customs, languages, and culture relative to their nurturance and support of their children toward achieving meaningful and relevant priorities and outcomes families desire for themselves and their children.
2. We shall provide services and supports to children and families in a fair and equitable manner while respecting families' culture, race, language, socioeconomic status, marital status, and sexual orientation.
3. We shall respect, value, promote, and encourage the active participation of ALL families by engaging families in meaningful ways in the assessment and intervention processes.
4. We shall empower families with information and resources so that they are informed consumers of services for their children.
5. We shall collaborate with families and colleagues in setting meaningful and relevant goals and priorities throughout the intervention process including the full disclosure of the nature, risk, and potential outcomes of any interventions.
6. We shall respect families' rights to choose or refuse early childhood special education or related services.

7. We shall be responsible for protecting the confidentiality of the children and families we serve by protecting all forms of verbal, written, and electronic communication.

ETHICAL AND EVIDENCE BASED PRACTICES

Ethical and Evidence Based Practices in the field of early childhood special education relies upon sound research methodologies and research based practices to ensure high quality services for children and families. As professionals researching and practicing within the field, it is our responsibility to maintain ethical conduct in building a cadre of practices based on evidence. Establishing an evidence base not only involves critically examining available research evidence relative to our professional practices, it also involves continually engaging in research to further refine our research-based or recommended practices.

Sound ethical research strategies always should be used including adherence to institutional review board procedures and guidelines prior to the conduct of research and use of peer-reviewed venues for published dissemination of findings. Honoring and respecting the diversity of children and families should guide all research activities.

Evidence Based Practices

1. We shall rely upon evidence based research and interventions to inform our practice with children and families in our care.

2. We shall use every resource, including referral when appropriate, to ensure high quality services are accessible and are provided to children and families.
3. We shall include the diverse perspectives and experiences of children and families in the conduct of research and intervention.

Ethical Practice in Research

1. We shall use research designs and analyses in an appropriate manner by providing a clear rationale for each. We shall provide enough information about the methodologies we use so that others can replicate the work.
2. We shall maintain records of research securely; no personal information about research participants should be revealed unless required by law.
3. We shall conduct on-going research and field work that is consistent with and builds upon the available cadre of evidence based practices.
4. We shall utilize collaboration and interdisciplinary research for strengthening linkages between the research and practice communities, as well as for improving the quality of life of children with disabilities and their families.

Glossary

A

Academic English: Language necessary for success in school.

Access: The ability of children and families to participate in high-quality programs that support individual development and learning needs.

Accommodation: Altering existing schemes as a result of new information or experiences.

Accommodations: The provision of equipment, conditions, or an environment that support the child's effective interactions with the environment.

Accountability: Requirement that schools, teachers, and students meet external standards of individual and program performance.

Accountability for equity and success: Attention to the outcomes of early childhood policies, programs, and practices with the overall goal of supporting each child's success within his or her larger world.

Accreditation standards: Series of standards developed by NAEYC to ensure quality in early childhood programs and teacher preparation institutions.

Achievement gap: Disparity in academic performance between children from economically impoverished backgrounds and their more affluent peers.

Adaptations: Adjustments to the classroom environment, curriculum, and/or assessment.

Advocacy: An active role in supporting an idea or cause.

AEYC affiliate: Local chapter of the National Association for the Education of Young Children.

Affective reflections: Simple statements identifying your perceptions of a child's emotions.

Alignment: Process through which standards at various age levels and in varied content areas are matched, ensuring that children can make a seamless transition between sets of standards.

American Association on Intellectual and Developmental Disabilities: Called the American Association on Mental Retardation until 2007, the AAIDD is the oldest organization in the United States focusing on the intellectual disabilities of children and adults.

American Recovery and Reinvestment Act of 2009: Economic stimulus package signed into law by President Barack Obama on February 17, 2009.

Americans with Disabilities Act: Passed in 1990, the ADA required public barriers be eliminated for persons with disabilities.

Anti-bias: Curricular approach that nurtures each child by actively addressing issues of diversity and equity in the classroom.

Anti-bias curriculum: An active, activist curricular approach that seeks to address issues of social inequity at the individual and classroom level.

Assessment: Means of determining how effectively knowledge, skills, and dispositions are developing.

Assimilation: Incorporating new concepts into existing schemes.

Association for Childhood Education International: Organization focused on the education and development of children between birth and adolescence at the international level.

At-Risk Child Care Program: Enacted in 1990, the ARCCP is designed to fund child care services for children of families with low income who do not receive Aid to Families with Dependent Children monies.

Attachment relationship: Quality of interactions and resulting relationship between a child and the primary caregiver.

Attachment theory: Ethological theory of development that posits that the quality of the caregiver–child relationship in the first 18 months of life will have a lifelong impact on the child's future relationships.

Attention deficit disorder: Disorder marked by challenges in maintaining attention and impulse control.

Attention-deficit/hyperactivity disorder: Disorder marked by challenges in maintaining attention, impulse control, and hyperactivity.

Authentic assessment: Assessment practices that reflect expectations for development as demonstrated in the natural environment and that include a focus on how the child would use assessed knowledge, skills, and dispositions.

Autism: Specific diagnosis within pervasive developmental disorders that includes deficits in communication, social interaction, or creative and imaginative play.

Auto-educate: Montessori concept stressing that children actively construct knowledge based on their interactions with the environment.

B

Bank Street Approach: Curricular approach that inspired both a child- and teacher-training program.

Behavior modification: Process of replacing undesired behaviors with more desirable ones.

Behavioral disorders: Diagnostic category reflecting that the child's behaviors deviate significantly from the expectations of others.

Behavioral reflections: Simple statements identifying a child's behavior.

Biased: Assessment instruments that have prejudice, toward either a particular learning style or a content area, inherent in their design.

Bilingual education: Approach within educational settings that uses the home language of English language learners (ELL) for instruction.

Bilingualism: Ability to fluently speak two languages.

Bodily-kinesthetic intelligence: Ability to control body movements and handle objects skillfully.

Boundaries: Natural or constructed parts of the environment that give children physical limits regarding play.

Brown v. Board of Education: Landmark case within the U.S. Supreme Court that outlawed racial segregation in schools.

Build Strong Foundations for Our Youngest Children: National initiative to develop early childhood systems that reflect and support a multi-ethnic society.

C

Challenging behavior: Repeated pattern or perception of behaviors that interferes with children's interactions with others and/or the learning environment.

Checklist: Assessment based on whether a child can complete particular age-related skills.

Child Care and Development Block Grant: Federal source of funding targeted toward supporting the financial independence of families who are low income.

Child Care Resource and Referral Agencies: State and local organizations that work with parents, providers, and communities to improve access to child care for families.

Child care trilemma: Interrelated issues of quality, accessibility, and affordability that affect a parent's ability to find care.

Child Care WAGE$: National initiative designed to support equitable compensation and professional preparation for early childhood professionals.

Child-centered curriculum: Curricular approach characterized by children's independent exploration of the classroom accompanied by appropriate teacher guidance and support.

Child Development Associate (CDA): Awarded through the Council of Professional Recognition, the credential recognizes competencies in all areas of child development.

Child Find: Services that focus on early identification, screening, referral, and initial service coordination.

Child study movement: The initial recognition and exploration of the child as an object of study.

Childhood obesity: Excess body fat that places overall health in danger.

Children with disabilities: Disabilities refer to physical, cognitive, social and emotional, or genetic factors that have an impact on a child's ability to interact within the environment.

Choices: Statements that identify a choice between a or b.

Chronosystem: The dimension of time.

Co-constructed: Shared power between families and the educational system that support a mutual vision of children's education.

Code of Ethical Conduct: NAEYC's guide to help professionals resolve ethical dilemmas.

Cognitive development: The ability to take in, process, and make sense of the environmental world.

Communication disorders: Speech, language, or hearing disorders that impair a child's abilities to communicate thoughts and ideas to others.

Community norm standards: Standards such as accreditation that are supported through consumer behavior.

Compensation: The amount of money earned for professional activity.

Compensatory education: Movement to provide children from low-income backgrounds with educational experiences designed to compensate for potential challenges in learning and development.

Confidential: Ensuring that information about individual children and their families remains private and is shared only with family consent.

Conflict management: Series of strategies designed to help children respond to and resolve interpersonal conflicts.

CONNECT: The Center to Mobilize Early Childhood Knowledge: Provides online, interactive modules to help practitioners develop confidence and competence needed to work with young children with disabilities.

Constructivism: Theoretical perspective that emphasizes the interaction between child and environment.

Content standards: Broad expectations of knowledge, skills, and dispositions that individual children should have at a particular age in a specified subject.

Context: External environments in which children grow and develop, such as the family, neighborhood, and community.

Continuity of care: Minimal transitions between caregivers, supporting development of ongoing relationships.

Council for Exceptional Children: The largest international professional organization dedicated to the improvement of educational outcomes for children with disabilities.

Creative–comprehensive environments: Outdoor environments that address all areas of development and all types of children's play.

Credentialing: Process that verifies a practitioner's professional qualifications.

Cultural continuity: Creation of a bridge between home and early childhood environments and child-rearing practices.

Cultural transmissionists: Also known as behaviorists, these theorists viewed the environment as the causal factor in children's development.

Culturally and linguistically diverse: Term used by the Department of Education to describe children who are non-English proficient or have limited English proficiency.

Culturally and linguistically sensitive: Assessment practices based on the individual cultural and linguistic backgrounds of each child.

Culture-bound: Assessment practices that assume a child has particular areas of knowledge related to overall culture. Assessment should be culture-free, where children's abilities can be highlighted without test bias.

Curricular approaches: Generalized approaches that provide guidelines for effective practice.

Curriculum models: Conceptual frameworks and organizational structures for program planning, implementation, and evaluation.

D

Developmental disability: Assortment of severe, chronic, or ongoing conditions caused by physical and/or mental impairment.

Developmentally appropriate practices: Series of practices that are age, individually, and culturally appropriate.

Direct instruction: Behaviorist curricular model utilizing shaping and behavior modification. Formal, teacher-directed curricular approach.

Directives: Verbal, written, and pictorial information children need to successfully participate in an activity.

Disabilities: Disabilities refer to physical, cognitive, social and emotional, or genetic factors that have an impact on a child's ability to interact within the environment.

Disequilibrium: Cognitive conflict resulting from a mismatch of interpretation and information presented in the environment.

Dispositions: Habits of mind or ways of responding to situations that focus on the *how* of applying the skills and knowledge that individuals have.

DISTAR: Commonly known as direct instruction, DISTAR is based on behaviorist principles that support teacher-directed learning.

Division for Early Childhood Education (DEC): Division of the Council for Exceptional Children for individuals who work with or on behalf of young children with disabilities and other special needs.

Documentation: A strategy used to record children's development and learning over time.

Domains: General categories of development.

Dual-earner families: Families where both parents are working outside the home.

Dual language learners: Children who are learning a second language while developing a basic competency in their first language.

Dysgraphia: Challenges in expressing thoughts through the written word.

E

Early Childhood Environment Rating Scales: Developed by Harms, Clifford, and Cryer, the rating scales focus on early childhood, infant-toddler, family child care, and school-age environments. The scales consist of items relevant to the physical environment, basic care, curriculum, interaction, schedule and program structure, and parent and staff education.

Early childhood intervention: Practices designed to have an impact on both children's development and risk factors within children's environments.

Early Head Start: Federal program designed to support economic and social well-being of pregnant women and children between the ages of birth and 3 and their families.

Early intervention: Practices designed to have an impact on both children's development and risk factors within children's environments.

Early learning standards: Expectations of knowledge, skills, and dispositions that children should have at a particular age.

Ecological systems theory: Theoretical model developed by Urie Bronfenbrenner that describes the interrelationship between children and the contexts of their development.

Educarer: Gerber's term for infant-toddler caregivers who implement a philosophy based on respect and support for relationships.

Education for All Handicapped Children Act: Also called P.L. 94-142, the act ensured a free and appropriate education (FAPE) to all children with disabilities between the ages of 3 and 21.

Egocentrism: Piagetian term referring to a young child's inability to understand a perspective other than his/her own.

Emergent curriculum: Curriculum based on the interests of the child.

Emotional development: The ability to identify and understand emotions within oneself and to respond appropriately to the emotions of others.

Empathy: The capacity to share and understand the emotions of others.

Empowerment: The expansion of individuals' capacities to negotiate with, influence, and control facets of their world.

Encouragement: Statements that reflect a child's efforts or progress and that are supportive of intrinsic motivation.

English language learners: Term used to describe children who are acquiring English proficiency.

Equitable compensation: Fair wages based on the professional requirements of employment.

Evidence-based practice: Process through which research and effective practices are evaluated and applied to support children's development and learning.

Exceptionalities: Differences in development including syndromes, impairments, disorders, and disabilities.

Exosystem: The larger social system that affects the child, but that the child does not directly participate in.

External motivation: Behavior that is produced and repeated based on rewards.

Extreme poverty: Families who earn less than one-half the federal poverty level.

Extrinsic motivation: Factors outside the child that serve to motivate behavior.

F

Family friendly: Policies and practices that support families.

Family involvement: Strategies designed to support the familial goal of involvement in the early childhood community.

Family structure: Descriptive characteristics of a family.

Family systems theory: View of the family as a complex emotional unit that uses systems to describe the interaction among members.

Federal Child Abuse Prevention and Treatment Act: Public Law 93-247, which provides federal monies to the states to support prevention, assessment, investigation, prosecution, and treatment activities.

Field of early childhood education: Educational programs serving children between birth and the age of 8 and their families and the field of study that prepares professionals to work with children and families in this age group.

Flexibility: Policies, programs, and practices are designed to respond to the unique needs of children, families, and professionals.

Formal assessment: Standardized strategies used to determine how children are developing based on the development of their peers.

Foster Families: Certified "parents" or families who care for minor children who have been removed from birth or custodial parents by state authority.

Free and appropriate education: Outcome of federal law ensuring that all children within the jurisdiction of the school district receive an education that meets their individual needs in an educational setting reflective of least restrictive environment law.

Functional assessment: Five-step process designed to identify, intervene, and evaluate children's persistent challenging behaviors.

Funding standards: Standards programs must adhere to in order to meet requirements of external funders.

G

Giftedness: Significant difference in ability in academics, aptitudes or talents, creative and productive thinking skills, and leadership abilities.

Gifts and occupations: Series of specific instructional materials designed by Frederick Froebel supporting children's experimentation within their environment.

Good Start Grow Smart: A federal early childhood initiative that focuses on strengthening Head Start; partnering with states to improve early learning; and providing information on early learning.

Goodness of fit: Term coined by Thomas and Chess to describe the match between the environment and a child's temperament.

Guidance: Series of practices that support children's social-emotional development.

H

Head Start: An intervention program that includes the provision of high-quality care and education to children from at-risk backgrounds, access to health care and social services, and parent education.

Health impairments: Health issues that require special health or educational services.

Healthy Child Care America: National program providing information and application strategies to ensure health and safety.

Hierarchy of needs theory: Abraham Maslow's hierarchy of five levels of basic needs, culminating with attaining self-actualization.

High/Scope Curriculum: Curriculum model derived from Piaget's theory that served as the underlying model for the Perry Preschool Project.

High-stakes testing: Assessment practices that have important consequences for children, families, professionals, or programs.

Holistic approach: Focusing on the whole of children's learning as well as the interdependent parts.

I

Ideals: The aspirations of practitioners as represented through the NAEYC Code of Ethical Conduct.

Immersion strategies: Expectation that children will acquire a second language through exposure alone.

Inclusion: Philosophical and practical approach emphasizing that children of varying needs and abilities should be educated in the same environment.

Inclusion: The individual needs of each child, family, and professional are embraced and supported.

Individualized education: Care and education based on children's individual needs.

Individualized Education Program: A team-developed, written program identifying goals and objectives to support the development of a child between the ages of 3 and 21 who has a disability.

Individualized Family Service Plan: Written plan outlining family-centered individual supports and services to enhance development of a qualified child between birth and 3 years.

Individuals with Disabilities Education Act: Also called P.L. 94-142, IDEA is a federal program that provides funds to states and local education agencies to provide education services for children between the ages of 3 and 21. Passed in 1990, IDEA was the new name for the Education of the Handicapped Act.

Informal assessment: Strategies used daily to gain knowledge of each individual child's development.

Integrated learning: Learning experiences that authentically combine knowledge, skills, and dispositions across curricular areas.

Intellectual disability: Impairments in a child's overall intelligence and adaptive behavior.

Intellectual goals: Dispositions or habits of mind that children use to interpret experiences.

Intelligence quotient: Measure of intellectual functioning based on performance and verbal scales and evaluated through standardized tests.

Intentional curriculum: Content-driven, research-based curriculum reflecting active engagement with children, purposeful decision making, and attention to the consequences of decisions.

Interpersonal intelligence: Ability to relate to and understand others.

Intrapersonal intelligence: Ability to self-reflect and be aware of one's own inner states.

Intrinsic motivation: Internal motivation to act in a particular way.

J

Jumpstart: National program supporting language, literacy, social, and skill-building initiatives in communities.

K

Kamii-DeVries Approach: Curricular approach based on Piaget's theory.

Kindergarten education: Founded in the mid-1800s in the United States by Elizabeth Peabody, the original intent of kindergarten was to support social and emotional preparedness for education.

Kith and kin care: The care of children by relatives and neighbors who are considered exempt from licensing.

KWL: Learning strategy that focuses on what children already know, what they wonder about, and what they want to learn.

L

Labels: Term applied to describe a particular set of characteristics.

Lanham Act of 1940: Provided funds for the maintenance and operation of public works, including child care facilities in war-impacted areas.

Learning centers: Small defined areas of the classroom that support targeted learning or types of play.

Learning disabilities: A significant gap in children's abilities and their performance.

Learning environment's role as the third teacher: As part of a triad based on the child and the professional, the learning environment's role is thought to be equally important in supporting children's development and learning.

Least restrictive environment: Term referring to the right for all children, regardless of individual ability and to the greatest extent possible, to be educated within environments with typically developing peers.

Legal standards: Program standards that must be adhered to for program operation.

Legally blind: Visual acuity less than 20/200.

Licensing requirements: Rules established through state licensing agencies that mandate minimum standards of health, safety, and practice for the field of early childhood care and education.

Licensing standards: Legal standards that reflect the meeting of basic health and safety requirements.

Lifelong learners: Those with a passionate commitment to acquiring new knowledge across the lifespan.

Linguistic intelligence: Ability to use words and language.

Literacy: The ability to read, write, speak, and listen.

Logical consequences: Reasonable, related, and respectful teacher-initiated consequences that respond to challenging behaviors.

Logical-mathematical intelligence: Ability to use reason, logic, and numbers.

Looping: Arrangement designed to support continuity of care through professionals transitioning to a new classroom with the children.

Low vision: Partial sight that cannot be corrected through use of corrective lenses or contacts.

M

Macrosystem: The outermost layer of the child's environment, which includes cultural values, customs, and laws.

Mainstreaming: Designed to integrate children with disabilities into the regular classroom environment, mainstreaming referred to strategies to support this goal.

Mandated reporters: Professionals who must issue a report should child abuse or neglect be suspected.

Maria Montessori: Italian educator who founded the first children's school and developed materials and a training program based on her philosophy for educating children.

Maturationists: Theorists who view the child's natural development as being the causal factor in their development.

McKinney-Vento Homeless Assistance Act: Passed in 1987, the act provides federal funds for shelter programs and related services to populations who are homeless.

Media engagement: Using the media to convey a message.

Medicaid: Federal-state health care program for persons who are low income, including children who have disabilities.

Mental health disorders: Broad range of issues that affect children's conception of themselves and their interactions with others. Can include depression, anxiety, conduct disorders, and eating disorders.

Mesosystem: The connections between different structures of the microsystem.

Microsystem: The immediate surroundings and relationships of a child's world.

Mirroring: Guidance strategy where language and emotion are used to match a child's emotional response to a situation.

Mission statement: Clear depiction of program goals and reason for being.

Mixed-age grouping: The placement of children of varying ages (usually a 2- to 3-year span) in one classroom environment.

Modifications: A change in what is being taught or expected of a student.

Motivations: Process of informing children the reasons that information may be important to them.

Multicultural education: Curricular strategy that supports children's knowledge of diversity and promotes respect for others.

Multisensory: Providing stimulation for a variety of the senses.

Musical intelligence: Ability to produce and appreciate music.

N

National Association for Family Child Care (NAFCC): An organization whose mission is to strengthen the profession of family child care.

National Association for the Education of Young Children (NAEYC): The largest association of early childhood professionals, NAEYC is concerned with education, advocacy, and the provision of high-quality early childhood environments for young children.

National Black Child Development Institute: Advocacy and education group focused on enhancing and improving the quality of life for black children and their families.

National Council on Disability: Independent council that makes recommendations to the president and Congress on issues affecting Americans with disabilities.

National Fatherhood Initiative: Sponsored through the federal government, the goal of the initiative is to strengthen the role of fathers in families.

National Infant and Toddler Child Care Initiative: Zero to Three's national initiative designed to develop systems of support for infant and toddler education.

National Professional Development Center on Inclusion: National program designed to support states in developing systems designed to prepare professionals to successfully include all children in early childhood education environments.

National Task Force on Early Childhood Education for Hispanics: National organization designed to support school readiness of children from Hispanic backgrounds.

National Technical Assistance Center for Children's Mental Health: Focused on supporting professionals in meeting the mental health needs of children and families.

Natural consequences: Consequences that occur naturally in the environment and do not require teacher intervention.

Natural environment: Under Part C of IDEA, the term *natural environment* stresses that early intervention services for infants and toddlers should be provided in settings in which children without disabilities participate.

Naturalistic intelligence: Knowledge of the natural world.

Nature: Genetic propensities and capabilities that represent internal qualities.

No Child Left Behind Act: Signed into law by President George W. Bush in 2002, the NCLB Act promised sweeping reforms to the educational system focusing on standards of accountability, parent participation, and student performance.

Nongraded classrooms: Blend of first and second, or, less commonly, second and third grades.

Normed: Assessment tests used as a basis of comparison, where the norm is considered a representation of typical expectations.

North Carolina's Smart Start: North Carolina's early childhood initiative designed to ensure all children enter school healthy and ready to succeed.

Nurture: Personal experiences.

O

Objectivity: Representation of observed facts, without the insertion of opinion.

Open-ended questions: Questions that have multiple responses used to determine child's present level of understanding and potential future directions.

Out-of-school time: Time spent and services provided to children when not in school settings.

P

Parent education: Training and information designed to support parents in attaining goals relative to child rearing.

Parent Empowerment Project: National Black Child Development Institute project supporting families in their roles as their child's first and most-important teacher through a parent-driven culturally-based education program.

Parents as Teachers: National project dedicated to supporting parents as their child's first and most important teacher.

Part C of IDEA: Federal regulations targeted toward infants and toddlers with disabilities.

PDD-not otherwise specified: Diagnostic category for children who have significant impairments in social, cognitive, language, and/or motor functioning, but don't meet the criteria for an existing specified category.

Peer competence: Ability to interact successfully and independently with peers.

People-first language: Use of language that places the child before the disability, as opposed to defining the child by the disability. Example: child with special needs versus special-needs child.

Performance assessment: Form of assessment that requires children to perform tasks in order to demonstrate knowledge, skills, and dispositions.

Perry Preschool Project: The project provided high-quality preschool education services to African American children who were living in poverty. Follow-up studies have been conducted when the original children were 27 and 40.

Pervasive developmental delay: Broad category that includes children who have a significant delay or deviance in social, cognitive, language, and/or motor functioning.

Physical disabilities: Impairments that include orthopedic, neuromuscular, cardiovascular, and pulmonary disorders.

Picture schedules: Pictorial tool used to break tasks or events into understandable chunks.

Play value: How effectively a toy meets development and play goals.

Play-based assessment: Tool focusing on how children demonstrate development in their natural interactions with the environment.

Positive stress: Daily stressors resulting from not being able to engage in a desired activity.

Praise: Statements that focus on a child's product and are supportive of extrinsic motivation.

Preview lessons: Telling children about the importance and goals of an activity and how it complements their motivations.

Prime: The process of preparing children for upcoming social interactions.

Principles: Guides for conduct and assistance in resolving ethical dilemmas.

Private speech: Self-directed language children engage in to assist in problem solving.

Profession: The body of people in an occupation that is learned.

Professional development plan: Systematic plan designed to support ongoing professional development based on individual needs and goals.

Professional philosophy: Statement of one's beliefs and values regarding the field of early childhood education and one's role within it.

Program planning and evaluation: Focus on the whole of the early childhood curriculum in terms of effective planning and assessment of program effectiveness.

Project Approach: Developed by Sylvia Chard and Lilian Katz, the Project Approach represents an investigation of a real-world topic worthy of children's attention and effort.

Project Follow Though: Largest and most comprehensive federally funded experiment to determine the effectiveness of various early childhood curricula. The project examined the effectiveness of child-centered vs. direct instruction teaching strategies.

Psychoanalytic theory: As part of the relevant application to young children, psychoanalytic theory stresses that what happens to you as a child affects you as an adult.

Public engagement: Advocacy strategies targeted toward the general public and designed to build awareness and support.

Public policy: Attempt by the government to address a public issue.

Punishment: Intervention strategy focused on extinguishing behaviors perceived as challenging.

Push-down: Used to describe increased expectations for knowledge of young children.

R

Readiness: Social and academic skills children need to succeed in school.

Reciprocal teaching: Bidirectional process of knowledge construction between a child and a more experienced member of society.

Red flags: Developmental indicators that reflect atypical patterns of development.

Redshirting: Holding out of kindergarten entry for an extra year, despite their meeting age requirements for entry.

Reflection: The ability of professionals to recursively evaluate their own actions, interactions, and development.

Reggio Emilia: Town in Italy whose pedagogical approach to caring for and educating young children has been widely studied in the United States.

Reinforcement: Encouragement coupled with behavioral reflections that are provided following a play episode.

Reliability: Measurement of how likely assessment data are repeatable with similar results.

Resilience: The ability to overcome risk factors in the environment.

Retention: Practice of holding children back from promotion to the next grade because they have not met expected milestones.

S

Schemes: Logical mental structures that change based on the stage of cognitive development children are in.

School Breakfast Program: Government program providing cash assistance to states to operate nonprofit breakfast programs.

School of the 21st Century: Community school model supportive of child care and family support systems in the school system.

Scientific inquiry: The process of asking a question, conducting an investigation, answering the question, and presenting the results to others.

Screening: Assessment practice used to determine if children require additional assessment or services designed to support development and learning.

Self-advocacy: The ability of professionals to articulate and advance the public perceptions of their work.

Self-awareness: Understanding and recognizing one's own feelings.

Self-esteem: The belief that one can have a positive impact on his or her environment.

Self-regulation: Being able to effectively control and communicate one's emotions.

Sensory diet: Personalized activity schedule that matches the unique nervous system needs of each child.

Sensory engagement: The provision of active experiences that support stimulation of the senses.

Sensory processing disorders: Difficulties processing information in the environment, including touch, sound, and movement.

Sexuality education: Broad term that refers to curricular approach supporting relationships, responsibility, and respect.

Shaping: Providing feedback or rewards for successive behaviors that bring a child closer to a desired outcome.

Single-parent families: Families in which one parent cares for one of more children without the assistance of another adult in the household.

Social class: Hierarchal distinctions between social groups, often determined by income.

Social development: How effectively the child navigates interactions and relationships.

Social-emotional adjustment: The child's ability to socially and emotionally adapt to new situations.

Social English: Language of everyday oral and written communications.

Social equity: The just treatment of all members of society.

Social prompts: The provision of verbal or physical cues to guide children in social situations.

Social skills: Skills needed to establish and maintain relationships.

Social skills curricula: Series of practices designed to support children's social skills.

Social support: Strategies designed to support the child's family system.

Social support theory: Theory stating that the support provided by other humans is predictive of mental and physical health.

Socially isolated: Lack of social support and a social network.

Socially mediated process: Children's learning is based on their interactions with other members of society.

Sociocultural context: A combination of both social and cultural factors—such as politics and societal values—that affect the field.

Sociodramatic play: Type of play where children carry out action plans, take on roles, and transform objects.

Sparks: Provocations designed to generate children's interests, hold conversations, and provide a launch pad for sharing and participating in experiences.

Spatial intelligence: Ability to perceive the visual.

Special Quest Birth–Five: National project designed to enhance and sustain high-quality inclusive services for children with disabilities ages birth through five and their families.

Stages of teacher development: Conceptual framework of four stages that Katz (1972) argues teachers move through in their professional development.

Stakeholders: Persons who are affected by early childhood programs.

Standardized tests: A testing instrument that is administered, scored, and interpreted in a standard manner.

Standards: Generalized goals for children who are learning at varying ages of development.

Strength-based assessment: Assessment practices that focus on what a child *can* do and that provide a holistic picture based on the child's capabilities.

Subjectivity: Reporting of assessment data that includes professional opinion.

T

Task analysis: Examination of a multistep task and the process of breaking the task into finite chunks that the child can understand and apply.

Task-based assessment: Assessment practices that require a child to perform a particular task at a given point in time.

T.E.A.C.H. scholarship: Scholarship opportunity that links education to compensation. As of early 2009, T.E.A.C.H. scholarships were offered in 23 states.

Teacher directed: An environment characterized by the teacher determining classroom curriculum activities and interactions.

Teacher licensure and certification exams: Educational tests used to determine if candidate has academic and general knowledge and teaching skills needed to earn a state-issued license or certification.

Technical Assistance Center on Social Emotional Intervention for Young Children: National program providing research-based resources designed to improve the social-emotional outcomes for children who have, or are at risk for developing, challenging behaviors.

Technological inquiry: The ability to process and communicate through use of technology.

Teen parents: Persons age 19 and under who become parents.

Temporary Assistance for Needy Families: A 1996 block grant program designed to move recipients into work and make welfare support temporary.

Theory: Body of knowledge used to describe, explain, and predict behavior.

Theory of cognitive development: Piaget's theory that presented children's cognitive development in a series of four stages.

Theory of psychosocial development: Erikson's theory that development occurs based on internal psychological factors and external social factors.

Think, pair, share: Children think about the question, pair with partner, and share their response.

Tiered quality standards: Quality standards linked to licensing, funding, and/or consumption.

Tiered reimbursement standards: Funding standards linked to the quality of care children receive.

Time-in: Guidance strategy used as a replacement for, or in conjunction with, time-out. The focus of time-in is to help children regulate their own emotions.

Timescape: Planned sequence of activities for a topic of investigation.

Tolerable stress: Stress responses that can be overcome by warm and consistent caregiving.

Toxic stress: Ongoing stress that is not buffered by adult support for extended periods.

Toyota Family Literacy Program: National effort supportive of family literacy in early childhood and, most recently, in Hispanic families.

Transdisciplinary: Collaborative efforts of persons with specialized knowledge from many different professional and personal arenas.

Trichotimized: Curricular strategy advocated by Katz that focuses on social-emotional and intellectual learning and support for meaningful and useful academic skills.

Turnover rate: Statistical measure of number of professionals who leave the field.

Turtle technique: Series of strategies designed to help children deal with overwhelming feelings.

Types of stress: Stress includes positive, tolerable, and toxic levels of intensity.

U

United Way's Success by Six: National system supportive of community coalitions that develop programs to meet unique early childhood education needs.

Universal design: Developed in the field of architecture, it ensures that all buildings are designed to meet the diverse needs of the populations using them.

Universal Design for Learning: Framework for applying universal design principles to instructional materials, curricula, and educational activities so that they are engaging and accessible to each and every learner.

Universal preschool programs: Also referred to as Preschool for All, these programs work to ensure that preschool is accessible for all children.

University laboratory schools: Demonstration schools located in colleges and universities used for research, child education, and family—teacher training.

V

Validity: Measure of how effectively assessment data are measuring the concepts they were designed to measure.

Visual impairments: Impairments ranging in diagnosis from low vision to legally blind.

W

War on Poverty: Programs designed to eliminate poverty, including Job Corps, Head Start, Medicaid and Medicare, and the expansion of public housing and welfare programs.

Week of the Young Child: Annual celebration sponsored by the National Association for the Education of Young Children.

Windows of opportunity: Prime times for particular areas of brain development to occur.

Women, Infants, and Children: The mission of this government program is to provide support to women with low income and children under 5 who are at nutritional risk.

Women's Suffrage Movement: Political campaign designed to support women's right to vote.

Work Sampling System: Assessment process consisting of developmental guidelines and checklists, portfolios, and summary reports.

Works Progress Administration: Federal relief program designed to ease the hardships of the Great Depression by offering jobs to the unemployed.

Worthy Wage Campaign: Grassroots advocacy effort designed to increase awareness for issues of compensation and professionals in the field.

Z

Zone of proximal development: Vygotskian concept that refers to the distance between what a child can accomplish on his or her own and what he or she can do with assistance.

Zones: Classroom design that incorporates attention to the function of space.

References

Chapter 1

American Federation of Teachers. (2002). *Early childhood education: Building a strong foundation for the future* (Policy Brief No. 15). Retrieved January 20, 2006, from www.eric.ed.gov/ERICWebPortal/contentdelivery/servlet/ERICServlet?accno=ED478657

Children's Defense Fund. (2005). *Child care basics.* Retrieved September 1, 2006, from http://www.childrensdefense.org/site/DocServer/child_care_basics_2005.pdf?docID=282

Clinton, B. (2007). *Giving: How each of us can change the world.* New York: Knopf.

Copple, C., & Bredekamp, S. (Eds.). (2009). *Developmentally appropriate practice in early childhood programs* (3rd ed.). Washington, DC: National Association for the Education of Young Children.

Cotton, K., & Conklin, N. (2001). *Research on early childhood education.* Retrieved June 1, 2007, from http://www.nwrel.org/scpd/sirs/3/topsyn3.html

Council for Exceptional Children, Division for Early Childhood. (1996). *Code of ethics.* Retrieved March 15, 2007, from http://www.dec-sped.org/pdf/positionpapers/PositionStatement_CodeofEthics.pdf

Freeman, N., & Feeney, S. (2004). The NAEYC code is a living document. *Beyond the Journal.* Retrieved January 15, 2007, from http://www.journal.naeyc.org/btj/200411/freeman.asp

Galinsky, E. (2006). *The economic benefits of high-quality early childhood programs: What makes the difference?* Families and Work Institute. Retrieved March 25, 2007, from http://www.ced.org/docs/summary/summary_prek_galinsky.pdf

Government of Saskatchewan. (1997). *Equity in education: A policy framework.* Retrieved June 21, 2008, from http://www.sasked.gov.sk.ca/equity/

Guralnick, M. (2001). A framework for change in early childhood inclusion. In M. J. Guralnick (Ed.), *Early childhood inclusion: Focus on change* (pp. 3–35). Baltimore: Brookes.

Joint Economic Committee of the Congress. (1996). *The impact of the welfare state on America's children.* Retrieved October 1, 2008, from http://www.house.gov/jec/welstate/vg-3/vg-3.htm

Kennedy, R. (1966). "Day of Affirmation." University of South Africa, Cape Town. June 6, 1966. Retrieved May 1, 2008, from http://www.jfklibrary.org/Historical+Resources/Archives/Reference+Desk/Speeches/RFK/Day+of+Affirmation+Address+News+Release.htm

National Association for Child Care Resource and Referral Agencies. (2008). *Supporting the child care workforce: Education and compensation initiatives.* Retrieved October 1, 2008, from http://www.naccrra.org/policy/background_issues/supporting_ccwf.php

National Association for the Education of Young Children. (2005). *Code of ethical conduct.* Retrieved June 1, 2008, from http://www.naeyc.org/about/positions/pseth98.asp

National Association for the Education of Young Children. (2006a). *New TANF work rules increase need for child care assistance for TANF and low-income working families.* Retrieved June 25, 2008, from http://www.naeyc.org/about/releases/20060629.asp

National Association for the Education of Young Children. (2006b). *NAEYC mission and goals.* Retrieved June 25, 2008, from http://www.naeyc.org/about/mission.asp

National Coalition on Health Care. (2008). *Health insurance coverage.* Retrieved August 1, 2008, from http://www.nchc.org/facts/coverage.shtml

Raines, S., & Johnston, J. (2003). Developmental appropriateness: New contexts and challenges. In J. P. Isenberg & M. R. Jalongo (Eds.), *Major trends and issues in early childhood education: Challenges, controversies and insights* (2nd ed., pp. 85–96). New York: Teachers College Press.

Spodek, B., & Saracho, O. (2005). *Handbook of research on the education of young children.* London: Routledge.

Whitebook, M., & Sakai, L. (2004). *By a thread: How child care centers hold on to teachers, how teachers build lasting careers.* Kalamazoo, MI: W. E. Upjohn Institute for Employment Research.

Chapter 2

Bailey, D., Scarborough, A., Hebbeler, K., Spiker, D., & Mallik, S. (2004). *National early intervention longitudinal study: Family outcomes at the end of early intervention.* Menlo Park, CA: SRI International.

Banks, R. (2001). *The early childhood curriculum debate: Direct instruction vs. child-initiated learning.* Clearinghouse on Early Education and Parenting. Retrieved January 30, 2007, from http://ceep.crc.uiuc.edu/poptopics/preschoolcurr.html

Bellm, D., & Whitebrook, M. (2006). *The roots of decline: How government policy has de-educated teachers of young children.* Center for the Study of Child Care Employment, University of California at Berkeley. (ERIC Document Reproduction Service No. ED495838)

Belsky, J. (1994). *The effects of infant day care: 1986–1994.* Invited plenary address to the British Psychological Association Division of Developmental Psychology, University of Portsmouth, U.K.

Belsky, J., & Eggebeen, D. (1991). Early and extensive maternal employment and young children's socio/emotional development: Children of the National Longitudinal Survey of Youth. *Journal of Marriage and Family, 53,* 1083–1100.

Bergen, D. (2003). Perspectives on inclusion in early childhood education. In J. P. Isenberg & M. R. Jalongo (Eds.), *Major trends and issues in early childhood education: Challenges, controversies, and insights* (pp. 47–69). New York: Teachers College Press.

Bloch, M., & Choi, S. (1990). Conceptions of play in the history of early childhood education. *Child and Youth Care Forum, 19*(1), 31–48.

Bloom, B. 1964. *Stability and change in human characteristics.* New York: Wiley.

Bock, G., Stebbins, L., & Proper, E. (1977). *Education as experimentation: A planned variation model: Vol. IV-B. Effects of follow-through models.* Cambridge, MA: Apt Associates. [Also issued by U.S. Office of Education as National Evaluation: Detailed Effects Volume II-B of the Follow Through Planned Variation Experiment Series.]

Cahan, C. (1989). *Past caring: A history of U.S. preschool care and education for the poor, 1820–1965.* New York: National Center for Children in Poverty.

California Council of Parent Participation Nursery Schools. (1996). *Program overview.* Retrieved March 2, 2007, from http://www.ccppns.org/pdf/calbroch.pdf

Children's Defense Fund. (2005). *Child care basics.* Retrieved January 12, 2007, from http://www.childrensdefense.org/site/DocServer/child_care_basics_2005.pdf?docID=282

Cohen, A. (1996). A brief history of federal financing in the United States. *Financing Child Care, 6*(2). Retrieved February 16, 2007, from http://www.futureofchildren.org/information2827/information_show.htm?doc_id=73258

Commission on Behavioral Social Sciences and Education. (1982). *Learning from experience: Evaluating early childhood demonstration programs.* Washington, DC: National Academies Press.

CQO Study Team. (1995). *Cost, quality, and child outcomes in child care centers: Public report.* University of Colorado at Denver.

DeStefano, L., & Snauwaert, D. (1989). *A value-critical approach to transition policy analysis.* Champaign, IL: University of Illinois, Secondary Transition Intervention Effectiveness Institute.

Downs, J., Blagojevic, B., Labas, L., Kendrick, M., & Maeverde, J. (2005). Let's grow together: Laws that support early childhood education for all. In *Growing ideas toolkit* (pp. 11–12). Orono, ME: The University of Maine Center for Community Inclusion and Disability Studies. Retrieved June 8, 2008, from http://www.ccids.umaine.edu/ec/growingideas/inclawtip.htm

DuCharme, C. (1993). *Historical roots of the project approach in the United States: 1850–1930.* Paper presented at the National Association for the Education of Young Children in Anaheim, CA, November 10–13, 1993. Retrieved February 20, 2007, from http://eric.ed.gov/ERICDocs/data/ericdocs2/content_storage_01/0000000b/80/25/db/80.pdf

Education Commission of the States. (1995). *Making quality count in undergraduate education.* Washington, DC: U.S. Government Printing Office.

Fagan, J. (1999). *Predictors of father and father figure involvement in pre-kindergarten Head Start.* National Center on Children and Families. Retrieved July 12, 2007, from http://fatherfamilylink.gse.upenn.edu/org/ncoff/wrkppr/faganpaper.pdf

Forte Fast, E., & Hebbler, S. (2004). *A framework for examining validity in state accounting systems.* Retrieved June 4, 2007, from http://www.ccsso.org/projects/Accountability%5FSystems/Accountability%5FModels/

Froebel, F. (1826). *On the education of man (Die Menschenerziehung).* Keilhau/Leipzig: Wienbrach.

Furney, K., & Salembrier, G. (2000). Rhetoric and reality: A review of the literature on parent and student participation in the IEP and transition planning process. In D. R. Johnson & E. J. Emmanuel (Eds.), *Issues influencing the future of transition programs and services in the United States* (pp. 111–126). Minneapolis: University of Minnesota, Institute on Community Integration, National Transition Network.

Goffin, S., & Wilson, C. (2001). *Curriculum models and early childhood education: Appraising the relationship* (2nd ed.). Upper Saddle River, NJ: Merrill/Prentice Hall.

Gottlieb, J. (1981). Mainstreaming: Fulfilling the promise? *American Journal of Mental Deficiency, 86,* 115–126.

Hancock, L., & Wingert, P. (1997). The new preschool [Special Issue]. *Newsweek, 129,* 36–37.

Hawes, J. (1999). The great IQ wars: Struggles behind the ideas that supported project Head Start. *Connect for Kids.* Retrieved February 28, 2007, from http://www.connectforkids.org/node/137

Illinois Facility Fund. (2000). *A century of caring for children.* Retrieved January 30, 2007, from http://www.iff.org/resources/content/2/6/documents/Century_of_Caring.pdf

Katz, L. (1999a). *Another look at what young children should be learning* (ERIC Digest). Champaign, IL: ERIC Clearinghouse on Elementary and Early Childhood Education. (ERIC Document Reproduction Service No. ED430735)

Katz, L. (1999b). *Curriculum disputes in early childhood education* (ERIC Digest). Champaign, IL: ERIC Clearinghouse on Elementary and Early Childhood Education. (ERIC Document Reproduction Service No. ED436298)

Kunesh, L. (1990). *A historical review of early intervention* (Eric Digest). Champaign, IL: ERIC Clearinghouse on Elementary and Early Childhood Education. (ERIC Document Reproduction Service No. ED326328)

Marcon, R. A. (1992). Differential effects of three preschool models on inner-city 4-year-olds. *Early Childhood Research Quarterly, 7*(4), 517–530. (ERIC Document Reproduction Service No. ED EJ458104)

McBride, B., & McBride, R. (1993). Parent education and support programs for fathers. *Childhood Education, 70,* 63–84.

McLaughlin, M. W. (1990). The Rand change agent study: Macro perspectives and micro realities. *Educational Researcher, 19*(6), 11–16.

McLaughlin, M. W., & Shields, P. M. (1987). Involving low-income parents in the schools: A role for policy? *Phi Delta Kappan, 69,* 156–160.

McVicker, J. (1961). *Intelligence and experience.* New York: Ronald Press.

McWilliams, R. (2000). It's only natural . . . to have early intervention in the environments where it's needed. In S. Sandall & M. Ostrosky (Eds.), *Natural environments and inclusion.* Young Exceptional Children Monograph Series (2).

Meyer, L. (1984). Long-term academic effects of the Direct Instruction Project Follow Through. *Elementary School Journal, 84,* 380–394.

Mulligan, S., Morris, S., Green, K., & Harper-Whelan, S. (1999). *Child care plus curriculum on inclusion.* University of Montana-Missoula: Rural Institute on Disabilities.

National Association of Nursery School Educators. (1929). *Minimum essentials for nursery school education.* National Committee on Nursery Schools.

National Early Childhood Technical Assistance Center. (2007). *History of OSEP-funded early childhood projects.* Retrieved October 12, 2007, from http://www.nectac.org/ecprojects/history.asp

National Information Center for Children and Youth with Disabilities. (1996). *The education of children and youth with special needs: What do the laws say?* Retrieved February 2, 2007, from http://eric.ed.gov/ERICDocs/data/ericdocs2sql/content_storage_01/0000019b/80/23/0a/8f.pdf

Office for Civil Rights. (2005). *Protecting students with disabilities.* Retrieved October 1, 2008, from http://www.ed.gov/about/offices/list/ocr/504faq.html

Osgood, R. L. (2005). *The history of inclusion in the United States.* Washington, DC: Gallaudet University Press.

Palmaffy, T. (2001). Head Start: The war on poverty goes to school. *Education Next, 1*(2), 10–11.

Pardini, P. (2002). The history of special education. *Rethinking Schools Online, 16*(3). Retrieved January 30, 2007, from http://www.rethinkingschools.org/archive/16_03/Hist163.shtml

Piesner-Feinberg, E., Burchinal, M., Clifford, R., Culkin, M., Howes, C., Kagan, S., Yazejian, N., Byler, P., Rustici, J., & Zelazo, J. (1999). *The children of the cost, quality, and outcomes study go to school: Executive summary.* Chapel Hill, NC: University of North Carolina.

President's Panel on Mental Retardation. (1962). *A proposed program for national action to combat mental retardation.* Washington, DC: U.S. Government Printing Office.

Rose, E. (1999). *A mother's job: The history of day care 1890–1960.* New York: Oxford University Press.

Schweinhart, L. (1997). *Child-initiated learning activities for young children living in poverty* (ERIC Digest). Champaign, IL: ERIC Clearinghouse on Elementary and Early Childhood Education. (ERIC Document Reproduction Service No. ED413105)

Schweinhart, L., & Weikart, D. (1997a). The High/Scope preschool curriculum comparison study through age 23. *Early Childhood Research Quarterly, 12*(2), 117–143. (ERIC Journal No. EJ554350)

Schweinhart, L., & Weikart, D. (1997b). *Lasting differences: The High/Scope preschool curriculum comparison study through age 23* (High/Scope Educational Research Foundation Monograph No. 12). Ypsilanti, MI: High/Scope Press. (ERIC Document Reproduction Service No. ED410019)

Schweinhart, L., Weikart, D., & Lamer, M. (1986). Consequences of three preschool models through age 15. *Early Childhood Research Quarterly, 1*(1), 15–45.

Shaw, G. (2008). In *Encyclopædia Britannica.* Retrieved May 31, 2008, from http://www.britannica.com/EBchecked/topic/539048/George-Bernard-Shaw

Shonkoff, J., & Phillips, D. (2000). *From neurons to neighborhoods: The science of early childhood development.* Washington, DC: National Academies Press.

Skeels, H. (1966). Adult status of children with contrasting early life experiences: A follow-up study. *Monographs of the Society for Research in Child Development 31*(3), 1–65.

Stebbins, L., St. Pierre, R., Proper, E., Anderson, R., & Cerva, T. (1977). *Education as experimentation: A planned variation model: Vol. IV. An evaluation of follow through.* Cambridge, MA: Apt Associates.

U.S. Department of Education. (1999). *Impact of the Civil Rights laws.* Office for Civil Rights. Retrieved June 8, 2007, from http://www.ed.gov/about/offices/list/ocr/docs/impact.html

U.S. Executive Branch. (2006). *Head Start policy book: Executive summary.* Retrieved June 1, 2006, from http://www.whitehouse.gov/infocus/earlychildhood/hspolicybook/summary.html

Walsh, S., Rous, B., & Lutzer, C. (2000). The federal IDEA natural environments provisions. In S. Sandall & M. Ostrosky (Eds.), *Natural environments and inclusion.* Young Exceptional Children Monograph Series (2).

Weikart, D., Bond, J., & McNeil, J. (1978). *The Ypsilanti Perry Preschool Project: Preschool years and longitudinal results through fourth grade.* Ypsilanti, MI: High/Scope Press.

Chapter 3

Anderson, R., & Pavan, B. (1993). *Nongradedness: Helping it to happen.* Lancaster, PA: Technomic Press.

Bailey, D., Scarborough, A., Hebbeler, K., Spiker, D., & Mallik, S. (2004). *National early intervention longitudinal study: Family outcomes at the end of early intervention.* Menlo Park, CA: SRI International.

Bales, S. (2002). *Talking school readiness and early child development: A frameworks message memo.* Washington, DC: FrameWorks Institute.

Baum, R. (1999). Putting the millennium in perspective. *Millennium Special Report, 77*(49). Retrieved May 31, 2008, from http://pubs.acs.org/hotartcl/cenear/991206/7749spintro2.html

Beavers, L. & D'Amico, J. (2005). Children in Immigrant Families: U.S. and State-Level Findings From the 2000 Census. Retrieved March 20, 2009 from: http://www.prb.org/pdf05/ChildrenInImmigrant.pdf

Blaustein, M. (2005, July). See, hear, touch! The basics of learning readiness. *Beyond the Journal,* 1–10.

Bodilly, S., & Beckett, M. (2005). *Making out-of-school time matter: Evidence for an action agenda.* The RAND Corporation. Retrieved June 2, 2007, from http://www.rand.org/pubs/monographs/2005/RAND_MG242.sum.pdf

Bowman, B., Donovan, M. S., & Burns, M. S. (2000). *Eager to learn.* National Research Council. Washington, DC: National Academies Press.

Boyd-Zaharias, J. (1999). Project STAR: The story of the Tennessee class-size study. *American Educator, 23*(2), 30–36.

Brown-Lyons, M., Robertson, A., & Layzer, J. (2001). *Kith and kin—informal child care: Highlights from recent research.* New York: National Center for Children in Poverty. Retrieved July 1, 2008, from http://cpmcnet.columbia.edu/dept/nccp/kithkin.html

Calman, L., & Tarr-Whelan, L. (2005). *Early childhood education for all: A wise investment.* Legal Momentum's Family Initiative & MIT Workplace Center. Retrieved May 20, 2006, from http://web.mit.edu/workplacecenter/docs/Full%20Report.pdf

Center for Public Education. (2006). *Pre-K programs. What are they, and who benefits?* Retrieved March 26, 2007, from http://www.centerforpubliceducation.org/site/c.kjJXJ5MPIwE/b.2556325/k.B34F/Research_QA_Prek_programs_what_are_they_and_who_benefits.htm

Center for the Child Care Workforce. (2002). *Estimating the size and components of the U.S. childcare workforce and caregiving population.* Retrieved June 1, 2007, from http://www.ccw.org/pubs/workforceestimatereport.pdf

Child Care Law Center. (2004). *All children have individual needs: Building an inclusive preschool for all. Program principles and considerations for planning and implementation.* Retrieved May 28, 2008, from: http://www.cainclusivechildcare.org/camap/pdfs/CCLC0904.pdf

Children's Defense Fund. (2003). *School-age child care: Keeping children safe and helping them learn while their families work.* Retrieved March 19, 2007, from http://www.childrensdefense.org/site/DocServer/keyfacts2003_schoolagecare.pdf?docID=593

Children's Defense Fund. (2005). *Head Start basics.* Retrieved March 31, 2007, from http://www.childrensdefense.org/site/DocServer/headstartbasics2005.pdf?docID=616

Collins, A., & Carlson, B. (1998). *Child care by kith and kin: Supporting family, friends, and neighbors caring for children.* New York: National Center for Children in Poverty.

Conn-Powers, M., Cross, A., Traub, E., & Hutter-Pishgahi, L. (2006, September). The universal design of early education: Moving forward for all children. *Beyond the Journal*. Retrieved October 12, 2007, from http://www.journal.naeyc.org/btj/200609/

CQO Study Team. (1995). *Cost, quality, and child outcomes in child care centers: Public report*. University of Colorado at Denver.

Crosser, S. (1991). Summer birth date children: Kindergarten entrance age and academic achievement. *Journal of Educational Research, 84*(3), 140–146.

Darragh, J. (2007). Universal design for early childhood education: Ensuring access and equity for all. *Early Childhood Education Journal, 35*(2), 167–171.

Division for Early Childhood and National Association for the Education of Young Children. (2008). *Field review draft of draft position statement regarding early childhood inclusion*. Retrieved October 19, 2008, from http://community.fpg.unc.edu/resources/articles/Position-Statement-on-EC-Inclusion-draft-10-2008.pdf/view

Duncan, G. & Rodgers, W. (1988). Longitudinal aspects of childhood poverty. *Journal of Marriage and the Family* (November) 50,4:1007–21.

Education Commission of the States. (2007). *Kindergarten quick facts*. Retrieved March 11, 2007, from http://www.ecs.org/html/Issue.asp?issueID=77

Essential Information for Education Policy. (2005). *Early childhood education: Investing in quality makes sense*. 3(2), 2–6.

Evans, G. & Rosenbaum, J. (2008). Self-regulation and the income-achievement gap. *Early Childhood Research Quarterly*, 23(4): 504–514.

Ferguson, H. Bovaird, S., & Mueller, M. (2007). The impact of poverty on educational outcomes for children. *Paediatr Child Health*; 12(8): 701–706.

Goffin, S. G., & Wilson, C. (2001). *Curriculum models and early childhood education: Appraising the relationship* (2nd ed.). Upper Saddle River, NJ: Merrill/Prentice Hall.

Guo, G., & Harris, K. M. (2000). The mechanisms mediating the effects of poverty on intellectual development. *Demography, 37*(4), 431–447.

Hamm, K. (2006). *More than meets the eye: Head Start programs, participants, families, and staff in 2005*. Retrieved March 28, 2007, from http://www.clasp.org/publications/hs_brief8.pdf

Hamm, K., & Ewen, D. (2006). *From the beginning: Early Head Start children, families, staff, and programs in 2004* (CLASP Policy Brief). Retrieved March 28, 2007, from http://www.clasp.org/publications/headstartbrief_7.pdf

Hart, B., & Risley, T. (2003, Spring). The early catastrophe: The 30 million word gap by age 3. *American Educator*. Retrieved August 11, 2006, from http://www.aft.org/pubs-reports/american_educator/spring2003/catastrophe.html

Haveman, R., & Wolfe, B. (1995). The determinants of children's attainments: A review of methods and findings. *Journal of Economic Literature, 33*, 1829–1878.

Hong, G., & Raudenbush, S. W. (2003). Causal inference for multi-level observational data with application to kindergarten retention study. *2003 Proceedings of the American Statistical Association,* Social Statistics Section, Alexandria, VA: American Statistical Association, 1849–1856.

Illinois Gateways to Opportunities (2009), Careers in Early Care and Education. Retrieved March 3, 2009, from http://spanish.ilgateways.com/careers/careersavailable.aspx.

Jefferson, T. (2002). The Declaration of Independence. *Key Readings*. Ed. Temple University Intellectual Heritage Department. Boston: Pearson Custom Publishing. (Original work published 1776)

Kagan, S. L., Moore, E., & Bredekamp, S. (Eds.). (1995). *Reconsidering children's early development and learning: Toward common views and vocabulary*. Report of the National Education Goals Panel, Goal 1 Technical Planning Group. Washington, DC: U.S. Government Printing Office.

Karoly, L., Kilburn, M., & Cannon, J. (2005). *Early childhood interventions: Proven results, future promise*. The RAND Corporation. Retrieved October 5, 2007, from http://rand.org/pubs/monographs/2005/RAND_MG341.pdf

Katz, L. (1995). *The benefits of mixed-age grouping* (ERIC Digest). Champaign, IL: ERIC Clearinghouse on Elementary and Early Childhood Education. (ERIC Document Reproduction Service No. ED382411)

Kauerz, K. (2005). State kindergarten policies: Straddling early learning and early elementary school. *Beyond the Journal*. Retrieved March 1, 2007, from http://www.journal.naeyc.org/btj/200503/01Kauerz.asp

Kirk, S., Gallagher, J., Anastasiow, N., & Coleman, M. (2006). *Educating exceptional children* (11th ed.). Boston, MA: Houghton Mifflin.

Lee, V., & Burkam, D. (2002). *Inequality at the starting gate: Social background differences in achievement as children begin school*. University of Michigan Economic Policy Institute.

Lee, V., Burkham, D., Honigman, J. & Meisels, S. (2006). Learning in full- and half-day kindergarten. *American Journal of Education, 112*(2), 163–208.

Lynch, R. (2004). Preschool pays: High quality education would save billions. *American Educator* (Winter 2004–2005). Retrieved May 3, 2009, from http://www.aft.org/pubs-reports/american_educator/issues/winter04-05/preschoolpays.htm

Magliacano, K. (1994). *The effect of a child's age at school entrance on reading readiness and achievement test scores*. Champaign, IL: ERIC Clearinghouse on Elementary and Early Childhood Education. (ERIC Document Reproduction Service No. ED366935)

NASBE Task Force on Early Childhood Education. (1988). *Right from the start: A report of the NASBE Task Force on Early Childhood Education*. Champaign, IL: ERIC Clearinghouse on Elementary and Early Childhood Education. (ERIC Document Reproduction Service No. EJ382654)

National Association for the Education of Young Children. (1996). *Developmentally appropriate practice in early childhood programs serving children from birth through age 8*. Retrieved March 2, 2007, from http://www.naeyc.org/about/positions/dap6.asp

National Association for the Education of Young Children. (2008). *Using research on early development and education*. Retrieved June 10, 2008, from http://www.naeyc.org/resources/research/

National Center for Children in Poverty. (2006). *Promoting effective early learning: What every policy maker and educator should know*. Retrieved March 2, 2007, from http://www.nccp.org/pub_pes07a.html

National Center for Early Development and Learning. (1997). *Quality in child care centers*. Retrieved June 1, 2007, from http://www.fpg.unc.edu/~ncedl/PDFs/facts1_1.pdf

National Center for Early Development and Learning. (1998). *Kindergarten transitions*. Retrieved March 3, 2007, from http://www.fpg.unc.edu/~ncedl/pages/spotlt.htm

National Center for Education Statistics. (2000). *Entering kindergarten: Findings from the condition of education 2000.* Retrieved April 12, 2007, from http://nces.ed.gov/pubs2001/2001035.pdf

National Center for Education Statistics. (2007). *The condition of education 2007.* Retrieved June 3, 2007 from http://nces.ed.gov/pubs2007/2007064.pdf

National Institute for Early Education Research. (2006). Initiative to give teachers tools for high-quality inclusive classrooms. *Preschool Matters, 4*(6). Retrieved March 1, 2007, from http://nieer.org/psm/index.php?article=184

National Institute for Early Education Research. (2006). Initiative to give Pre-K teachers tools for high quality inclusive classrooms. *Preschool Matters,* Vol. 4(6).

National Institute on Out-of-School Time. (2003). *Making the case: A fact sheet on children and youth in out-of-school time.* Retrieved May 5, 2007, from http://www.niost.org/publications/Factsheet_2003.pdf

Ounce of Prevention Fund. (2005). *Invest in the early years.* Retrieved May 22, 2006, from http://www.ounceofprevention.org/index.php?section=publications&category=3#31

Pang, V. O., & Sablan, V. A. (1998). Teacher efficacy: How do teachers feel about their abilities to teach African American students? In M. E. Dilworth (Ed.), *Being responsive to cultural differences–how teachers learn* (pp. 39–58). Thousand Oaks, CA: Corwin Press.

Pavan, B. N. (1992). The benefits of non-graded schools. *Educational Leadership, 50*(2), 22–25.

Perry, B. D. (2001). *Violence and childhood: How persisting fear can alter the developing child's brain* [online]. Retrieved July 1, 2001, from www.childtrauma.org/CTAMATERIALS/Vio_child.asp

Porter, T., & Kerns, S. (2006). Family, friend, and neighbor care: Crib notes on a complex issue. *Perspectives on Family, Friend, and Neighbor Child Care: Research, Programs, and Policy.* Retrieved March 13, 2007, from http://www.bankstreet.edu/gems/ICCC/OPS15.pdf

Pre-Elementary Educational Longitudinal Study. (2006). *Preschoolers with disabilities: Characteristics, services, and results, wave 1 overview report from the Pre-Elementary Education Longitudinal Study (PEELS).* Retrieved May 31, 2008, from http://www.peels.org/reports.asp

Ray, A., & Bowman, B. (2003). *Learning multi-cultural competence: Developing early childhood practitioners' effectiveness in working with children from culturally diverse communities.* Final Report to the A. L. Mailman Family Foundation. Center for Race, Class, and Culture in Early Childhood, Erikson Institute, Chicago, IL.

Ray, A., Bowman, B., & Robbins, J. (2006). *Preparing early childhood teachers to successfully educate all children: The contribution of four-year undergraduate teacher preparation programs, A project of the initiative on race, class and culture in early childhood.* Final Report to the Foundation for Child Development, New York, NY.

Schanen, L. (2008). *The Internet and the early childhood classroom.* PBS Teachers. Retrieved June 10, 2008, from http://www.pbs.org/teachers/earlychildhood/articles/internet.html

Schweinhart, L. J. (1985). *Early childhood development programs in the eighties: The national picture.* Ypsilanti, MI: High/Scope Early Childhood Policy Papers, No. 1. (ERIC Document Reproduction Service No. ED262902)

Schweinhart, L. J., Berrueta-Clement, J. R., Barrett, W. S., Epstein, A. S., & Weikart, D. P. (1985). The promise of early childhood education. *Phi Delta Kappan, 66,* 548–553.

Schweinhart, L. J., & Weikart, D. P. (1985). Evidence that good early childhood programs work. *Phi Delta Kappan 66,* 545–551.

Shepard, L. A., & Smith, M. L. (1985). *Boulder Valley kindergarten study: Retention practices and retention effects.* Boulder, CO: Boulder Valley Public Schools.

Shonkoff, J., & Phillips, D. (2001). *From neurons to neighborhoods: The science of early childhood development.* Washington, DC: National Academies Press.

Shore, R. (1997). Rethinking the brain: New insights into early development. New York, NY: Families and Work Institute.

U.S. Census Bureau. 2000. "Race and Hispanic or Latino: 2000." In Census 2000 (Summary File 1), 8. Washington DC: Bureau of Census. Retrieved March 20, 2009 from: http://factfinder.census.gov

U.S. Department of Commerce. (2002). *Who's minding the kids? Child care arrangements winter 2002.* Retrieved March 11, 2007, from http://www.census.gov/population/www/socdemo/child/ppl-177.html

U.S. Department of Education, National Center for Education Statistics. (2001). *Entering kindergarten: A portrait of American children when they begin school: Findings from the condition of education 2000.* Washington, DC: Author.

U.S. Department of Labor, Bureau of Labor Statistics. (2003). *Teachers: Preschool, kindergarten, elementary, and secondary.* Retrieved June 1, 2007, from http://stats.bls.gov/oco/ocos069.htm#emply

U.S. Department of Labor, Bureau of Labor Statistics. (2009). Occupational Outlook Handbook: Teachers-Special Education. Retrieved March 3, 2009 from: http://www.bls.gov/oco/ocos070.htm#related

Valli, L., & Rennert-Ariev, P. (2000). Identifying consensus in teacher education reform documents: A proposed framework and action implications. *Journal of Teacher Education, 51*(1), 5–17.

Verzaro-Lawrence, M. (1981). Early childhood education: Issues for a new decade. *Childhood Education, 57*(2), 104–109.

Xiang, Z., & Schweinhart, L. J. (2002). *Effects five years later: The Michigan school readiness program evaluation through age 10.* Prepared for the Michigan State Board of Education. Ypsilanti, MI: High/Scope Educational Research Foundation.

Chapter 4

Agency for Health Care Research and Quality. (2006). *Screening for visual impairment in children under the age of five: Recommendation statement.* Retrieved June 10, 2006, from http://www.guideline.gov/summary/summary.aspx?doc_id=4822

Ainsworth, M. D. S. (1982). Attachment: Retrospect and prospect. In C. M. Parkes & J. Stevenson-Hinde (Eds.), *The place of attachment in human behavior* (pp. 3–30). New York: Basic Books.

Bergen, D. (2002). The role of play in children's cognitive development. *Early Childhood Research and Practice, 4*(1). Retrieved January 1, 2007, from http://ecrp.uiuc.edu/v4n1/bergen.html

Berk, L. (2007). *Infants, children and adolescents.* Boston: Allyn & Bacon.

Bodrova, E., & Leong, D. (2003). *Play: A Vygotskian approach.* San Luis Obispo, CA: Davidson Films.

Bowen, M. 1978. *Family therapy in clinical practice*. New York: Jason Aronson.

Bowlby, J. (1972). *Attachment and loss. Vol. 1: Attachment* (2nd ed.). New York: Basic Books. (New printing, 1999, with a foreword by Allan N. Schore; originally published in 1969)

Bronfenbrenner, U. (1979). *The ecology of human development*. Cambridge, MA: Harvard University Press.

Brooks-Gunn, J., & Duncan, G. J. (1997). The effects of poverty on children. *Future of Children, 7*, 55–71.

Carnegie Task Force on Meeting the Needs of Young Children. (1994). *Starting points: Meeting the needs of our youngest children*. New York: Carnegie Corporation of New York.

Chibucos, T., Randall W., & Weis, D. (Eds.). (2005). *Readings in family theory*. Thousand Oaks, CA: Sage Publications.

Christian, L. (2006). Understanding families: Applying family systems theory to early childhood practice. *Beyond the Journal*. Retrieved January 10, 2007, from http://journal.naeyc.org/btj/200601/ChristianBTJ.pdf

Cummins, J., & Wong Fillmore, L. (2000). *Language and education: What every teacher (and administrator) needs to know*. Dallas, TX: CopyCats.

Eastern Stream Center on Resources and Training. (2003). *Help! They don't speak English. Starter kit*. Oneonta, NY: State University College.

ERIC Development Team. (1996). *Multiple intelligences theory*. Retrieved January 5, 2007, from http://www.eric.ed.gov/ERICDocs/data/ericdocs2/content_storage_01/0000000b/80/2a/29/0c.pdf

Erikson, E. (1950). *Childhood and society*. New York: Norton.

Gabbard, C. (1998). Windows of opportunity for early brain and motor development. *Journal of Physical Education, Recreation, and Dance, 69*. Retrieved October 3, 2008, from http://www.highbeam.com/doc/1G1-21232030.html

Gardner, H. (1983). *Frames of mind: The theory of multiple intelligences*. New York: Basic Books.

Glass, P. (2002). Development of the visual system and implications for early intervention. *Infants and Young Children, 15*(1), 1–10.

Gonzalez-Mena, J. (2005). *Diversity in early care and education programs* (4th ed.). New York: McGraw-Hill Higher Education.

Head Start Policy Book: Executive Summary. (2006). Retrieved January 12, 2007, from http://www.whitehouse.gov/infocus/earlychildhood/hspolicybook/summary.html

Hughes, F., Noppe, L., & Noppe, I. (1988). *Child development*. St. Paul, MN: West Publishing.

Huttenlocher, J., Haight, W., Bryk, A., Seltzer, M., & Lyons, T. (1991). Early vocabulary growth: Relation to language input and gender. *Developmental Psychology, 27*, 236–248.

Hyson, M. (2008). *Enthusiastic and engaged learners: Approaches to learning in the early childhood classroom*. New York: Teachers College Press.

Isenberg, J. P., & Quisenberry, N. (2002). *Play: Essential for all children: A position paper*. Association for Childhood Education International. Retrieved April 2, 2008, from http://www.acei.org/playpaper.htm

Kamii, C., & DeVries, R. (1993). *Physical knowledge in preschool education*. New York: Teachers College Press.

Katz, L. (1972). Development stages of preschool teachers. *Elementary School Journal, 73*(1), 50–54. (ERIC Document Reproduction No. EJ064759)

Kornhaber, M. L. (2001). Howard Gardner. In J. A. Palmer (Ed.), *Fifty modern thinkers on education: From Piaget to the present*. London: Routledge.

Madson, K. (2007). *Play in the multilingual classroom*. Learn NC. Retrieved November 22, 2008, from http://www.learnn3c.org/lp/pages/1977

Maslow, A. (1998). *Toward a psychology of being*. New York: Wiley.

National Association for the Education of Young Children. (1998). *Self-esteem and young children: You are the key. Early years are learning years*. Retrieved November 25, 2008, from http://www.naeyc.org/ece/1998/15.asp

National Association for the Education of Young Children. (2008). *Developmentally appropriate practice in early childhood programs serving children from birth through age 8*. Washington, DC: Author.

National Association for Music Education. (2000). *Spotlight on early childhood music education*. Landham, MD: Rowan & Littlefield Education.

National Clearinghouse for English Language Acquisition. (2006). *Resources about early childhood education*. Washington, DC: Author. Retrieved March 1, 2007, from http://www.ncela.gwu.edu/resabout/ecell/index.html

National Conference of State Legislatures. (2006). *50 state summary of newborn hearing screening laws*. Retrieved February 1, 2007, from http://www.ncsl.org/programs/health/hear50.htm

Olson, M., & Hyson, M. (2003). *Early childhood educators and child abuse prevention*. Booklet. Washington, DC: National Association for the Education of Young Children.

Owen, M. (1998). *The effects of disabilities on play skills*. Pediatric Services. Retrieved November 1, 2008, from http://www.pediatricservices.com/parents/pc-28.htm

Peth-Pierce, R. (1998). *NICHD study of early child care*. Washington, DC: National Institute of Child Health and Human Development.

Piaget, J. (1972). Intellectual evolution from adolescence to adulthood. *Human Development, 15*(1), 1–12.

Rauscher, F., Shaw, G., Ky, K., & Wright, E. (1994). *Music and spatial task performance: A casual relationship*. Paper presented at the American Psychological Association 102nd Annual Convention, Los Angeles, CA.

Raver, C. (2002). Emotions matter: Making the case for the role of young children's emotional development for early school readiness. *Social Policy Report of the Society for Research in Child Development, 16*(3), 1–20.

Riddle, E. M., & Dabbagh, N. (1999). *Lev Vygotsky's social development theory*. Retrieved October 7, 2004, from http://chd.gse.gmu.edu/immersion/knowledgebase/theorists/constructivism/vygotsy.htm

Scarr, S., & McCartney, K. (1983). How people make their own environments: A theory of genotype-environment effects. *Child Development, 54*, 424–435.

Sireteanu, R. (1999). Switching on the infant brain. *Science, 286*(5437), 59–61.

Texas School for the Blind and Visually Impaired. (2007). *Early development*. Retrieved March 1, 2008, from http://www.tsbvi.edu/Education/infant/page3.htm

Thomas, A., & Chess, S. (1977). *Temperament and development*. New York: Brunner/Mazel.

Vygotsky, L. (1978). *Mind in society*. Cambridge, MA: Harvard University Press.

Zero to Three. (2001). *Brain wonders*. Retrieved January 22, 2007, from http://www.zerotothree.org/brainwonders/FAQ.html

Chapter 5

American Academy of Child and Adolescent Psychiatry. (1999). *Children with oppositional defiant disorder.* Retrieved March 2, 2007, from http://aacap.org/page.ww?name=Children+with+Oppositional+Defiant+Disorder&section=Facts+for+Families

Beauchaine, T. P., Hong, J., & Marsh, P. (2008). Sex differences in autonomic correlates of conduct problems and aggression. *Journal American Academy Child Adolescent Psychiatry, 47*(7), 788–796.

Beck, I., McKeown, M., & Kucan, L. (2002). *Bringing words to life: Robust vocabulary instruction.* New York, NY: Guilford Press.

Bernard, B. (1995). *Fostering resilience in children.* Urbana, IL: ERIC Clearinghouse on Elementary and Early Childhood Education. (ERIC Document Reproduction Service No. ED 386327)

Bhavnagri, N., Krolikowski, S., & Vaswani, T. (2000). *A historical case study on interagency collaboration for culturally diverse immigrant children and families.* Katz Symposium. Retrieved April 1, 2007, from http://ceep.crc.uiuc.edu/pubs/katzsym/bhavnagri.html

Bronfenbrenner, U. (1979). *The ecology of human development.* Cambridge, MA: Harvard University Press.

Buysse, V., & Wesley, P. (2006). *Evidence-based practice in the early childhood field.* Washington, DC: Zero to Three Press.

Centers for Disease Control and Prevention. (2007). *Learn the signs. Act early.* Retrieved March 18, 2007, from http://www.cdc.gov/ncbddd/autism/actearly/

Child Welfare Information Gateway. (2006). *Mandatory reporters of child abuse and neglect.* Retrieved March 2, 2007, from http://www.childwelfare.gov/systemwide/laws_policies/statutes/manda.pdf

Child Welfare Information Gateway. (2007). *Caregivers of young children: Preventing and responding to child maltreatment.* Retrieved June 1, 2007, from http://www.childwelfare.gov/pubs/usermanuals/caregive/caregived.cfm

Children's Defense Fund. (2004). *Defining poverty and why it matters for young children.* Retrieved November 3, 2007, from http://www.childrensdefense.org/site/DocServer/definingpoverty.pdf?docID=390

Clark, B. (2008). *Growing up gifted* (7th ed.). Upper Saddle River, NJ: Merrill/Prentice Hall.

Council for Exceptional Children. (2006a). *Autism.* Retrieved March 25, 2007, from http://www.cec.sped.org/AM/Template.cfm?Section=Autism_Asperger_s_Syndrome&Template=/TaggedPage/TaggedPageDisplay.cfm&TPLID=37&ContentID=5598

Council for Exceptional Children. (2006b). *Behavior disorders/emotional disturbances.* Retrieved March 21, 2009, from http://www.cec.sped.org/AM/Template.cfm?Section=Behavior_Disorders_Emotional_Disturbance

Council for Exceptional Children. (2007a). *Blindness and visual impairments.* Retrieved December 12, 2007, from http://www.cec.sped.org/AM/Template.cfm?Section=Blindness_Visual_Impairments&Template=/TaggedPage/TaggedPageDisplay.cfm&TPLID=37&ContentID=5625

Council for Exceptional Children. (2007b). *Learning disabilities.* Retrieved December 12, 2007, from http://www.cec.sped.org/AM/Template.cfm?Section=Learning_Disabilities&Template=/TaggedPage/TaggedPageDisplay.cfm&TPLID=37&ContentID=5629

Edinberg, M. (2000). *Talking with children about death.* Retrieved March 1, 2007, from http://www.ec-online.net/knowledge/Articles/deathchildren.html

Espinosa, L. (2010). *Getting it RIGHT for young children from diverse backgrounds: From research to practice.* Upper Saddle River: NJ: Pearson.

Federal Emergency Management Agency. (2006). *Helping children cope with disaster.* Retrieved April 11, 2007, from http://www.fema.gov/rebuild/recover/cope_child.shtm

Fitzgerald, H. (1992). *The grieving child: A parent's guide.* New York: Simon & Schuster.

Future of Children. (1995, Summer/Fall). Immigrant children and their families: Issues for research and policy. *Critical Issues for Children and Youths, 5*(2), pp. 72–89.

Greenspan, S. (2007). Helping special needs kids. *Scholastic.* Retrieved April 12, 2007, from http://content.scholastic.com/browse/article.jsp?id=10209

Gunnar, M. R. (2000). Early adversity and the development of stress reactivity and regulation. In C. A. Nelson (Ed.), *Minnesota Symposia on Child Psychology: Vol. 31. The effects of adversity on neurobehavioral development* (pp. 163–200). Mahwah, NJ: Erlbaum.

Hart-Shegos, E. (1999). *Homelessness and its effects on children.* Retrieved April 27, 2006, from http://www.fhfund.org/_dnld/reports/SupportiveChildren.pdf

Horn, E., & Jones, H. (2004). Collaborative teams. In E. Horn & H. Jones (Eds.), *Young exceptional children Monograph Series No. 6: Multidisciplinary teams* (pp. 4–16). Longmont, CO: Sopris West.

Hourcade, J. (2002). *Mental retardation.* Retrieved October 4, 2007, from http://www.clsf.info/Articles/mental_retardation_definition.htm

Hughes, R. (2005). The effects of divorce on children. *Menweb.* Retrieved June 1, 2008, from http://www.menweb.org/divorcekids.htm

Klein, L., & Knitzer, J. (2007). *Promoting effective early learning: What every policymaker and educator should know.* New York: National Center for Children in Poverty, Columbia University Mailman School of Public Health.

Knitzer, J. (2007). *Testimony on the economic and societal costs of poverty.* Testimony before the House Ways and Means Committee. January 24, 2007.

Kruse, S., Louis, K. S., & Bryk, A. S. (1994). Building professional community in schools. *Issues in Restructuring Schools.* Madison, WI: Wisconsin Center for Education Research. Retrieved September 12, 2008, from http://www.wcer.wisc.edu/archive/cors/Issues_in_Restructuring_Schools/ISSUES_NO_6_SPRING_1994.pdf

Ladner, M., & Hammons, C. (2001). Special but unequal: Race and special education. In C. Finn, A. J. Rotherham, & C. R. Hokanson (Eds.), *Rethinking special education for a new century* (pp. 85–110). Washington, DC: Thomas B. Fordham Foundation: Progressive Policy Institute.

Myers, M., & Popp, P. (2003, Fall). What educators need to know about homelessness and special education. *Project Hope Virginia* (Information Brief No. 7). Retrieved March 2, 2007, from http://www.wm.edu/hope/infobrief/personnel-complete.pdf

Myers-Walls, J. A. (2003). Children as victims of war and terrorism. In J. Mullings, J. Marquart, & D. Hartley (Eds.), *The victimization of children: Emerging issues* (pp. 41–62). New York: Haworth Press.

National Association for the Education of Young Children. (1995). *Responding to linguistic and cultural diversity recommendations for effective early childhood education.* A position statement of the

National Association for the Education of Young Children. Retrieved June 9, 2008, from http://www.naeyc.org/about/positions/pdf/psdiv98.pdf

National Association for the Education of Young Children. (1996a). Responding to linguistic and cultural diversity—Recommendations for effective early childhood education. *Young Children*. Retrieved March 12, 2007, from http://www.naeyc.org/ece/1996/03.asp

National Association for the Education of Young Children. (2003). *Supporting young children during war and conflict*. Retrieved February 18, 2007, from http://www.naeyc.org/ece/2003/06.asp

National Center on Family Homelessness. (2004). *The PEACH initiative: Physical and emotional awareness for children who are homeless*. Retrieved October 1, 2007, from http://www.familyhomelessness.org/work_program_peach.php

National Center on Family Homelessness. (2009). *America's youngest outcasts: State report card on child homelessness*. Executive Summary. Retrieved March 21, 2009, from http://www.homelesschildrenamerica.org/about_executive-summary.php

National Conference of State Legislatures. (2002). *Demographics and the 2000 census: A quick look at U.S. immigrants*. Retrieved March 20, 2007, from http://www.ncsl.org/programs/immig/demographics2000census.htm

National Dissemination Center for Children with Disabilities. (2008). *Supports, modifications, and accommodations for students*. Retrieved December 21, 2008 from http://www.nichcy.org/EducateChildren/Supports/Pages/default.aspx

National Mental Health Information Center. (2003). *Child and adolescent mental health*. Retrieved October 22, 2007, from http://mentalhealth.samhsa.gov/publications/allpubs/Ca-0004/default.asp

National Scientific Council on the Developing Child. (2005). *Excessive stress disrupts the architecture of the developing brain*. Working Paper No. 3. Cambridge, Massachusetts: Centre on the Developing Child, Harvard University. Retrieved March 5, 2007, from: www.developingchild.net/pubs/wp/excessive_stress.pdf

National Scientific Council on the Developing Child. (2007). How early child care affects later development. *Science Briefs*. Retrieved May 28, 2008, from http://www.developingchild.net/pubs/sb/Early_Child_Care/Early_Child_Care.html

Noddings, N. (1988). Schools face crisis in caring. *Education Week*, 8(14), 32.

Nunez, R. D. (1996). *The new American poverty*. New York: Plenum Press.

Perry, B. D., Conrad, D. J., Dobson, C., Schick, S., & Runyan, D. (2000). *The children's crisis care center model: A proactive, multidimensional child and family assessment process*. The Child Trauma Academy. Retrieved March 1, 2007, from http://www.bcm.tmc.edu/cta/cccc_paper.htm

Perry, B. D., Pollard, R., Blakely, T., Baker, W., & Vigilante, D. (1995). *Childhood trauma, the neurobiology of adaptation and "use-dependent" development of the brain: How "states" become "traits"* [online]. Retrieved June 1, 2008, from http://www.childtrauma.org/states_traits.htm

Reed-Victor, E., Popp, P., & Myers, M. (2003). *Using the best that we know: Supporting young children experiencing homelessness*. Retrieved on May 1, 2006, from http://www.wm.edu/hope/infobrief/ECSE-educ.pdf

Rice, P. F. (1996). *Intimate relationships, marriages, and families*. Mountain View, CA: Mayfield Publishing.

Richards, J. C., & Lockhart, C. (1994). Cambridge, UK: Cambridge University Press.

Saunders, W., & Goldenberg, C. (1999). *The effects of instructional conversations and literature logs on the story comprehension and thematic understanding of English proficient and limited English proficient students*. Retrieved June 1, 2007, from http://www.cal.org/crede/pubs/research/RR6.pdf

Sensory Processing Disorders Network. (2006). *What is sensory processing disorder?* Retrieved March 11, 2007, from http://www.sinetwork.org/faq/index.html

Shonkoff, J., & Richmond, J. (2007). *The science of early childhood development: Closing the gap between what we know and what we do*. Seed Sower Public Lecture, February 8, 2007. Retrieved March 19, 2007, from http://tulsa.ou.edu/outulsa/Shonkoff%20PP.ppt#358,1

Suarez-Orozco, C., & Suarez-Orozco, M. (2002). *Children of immigration (The developing child)*. Cambridge: Harvard University Press.

thesoni.com (n.d.). *Bell curve (Average IQ)*. Retrieved December 12, 2008, from http://images.google.com/imgres?imgurl=http://thesoni.com/Intelligence1.jpg&imgrefurl=http://thesoni.com/&usg=__wJad4_4yd1dAMDdr0pg695DTqsA=&h=396&w=773&sz=45&hl=en&start=1&sig2=qvGvkPhIJqNT1XVyhS7f9g&tbnid=O8opCCzcOhAFDM:&tbnh=73&tbnw=142&ei=QDZPSavVHYL0MOWusMkP&prev=/images%3Fq%3Dbell%2Bcurve%2Bthesoni%26gbv%3D2%26hl%3Den

Thorp, E. K., & Sánchez, S. Y. (2008). Infusing cultural and linguistic diversity into preservice and inservice preparation. In P. J. Winton, J. A. McCollum, & C. Catlett (Eds.), *Preparing effective professionals: Evidence and applications in early childhood and early intervention* (p. 81–97). Washington, DC: Zero to Three Press.

U.S. Department of Health and Human Services. (1999). *Mental health: A report of the surgeon general*. Rockville, MD: Author.

Venn, J. (1989). *Students with physical disabilities and health impairment*. ERIC Clearinghouse on Handicapped and Gifted Education. (ERIC Document Reproduction Service No. ED314915)

Waddell, D., & Thomas, A. (1992). *Children and fear of war and terrorism tips for parents and teachers*. Retrieved February 15, 2007, from http://www.nasponline.org/resources/crisis_safety/children_war_general.aspx

Weasmer, J., & Woods, A. M. (1998). I think I can: The role of personal teaching efficacy in bringing about change. *The Clearing House, 71*, 245–247.

Women's History Quotes. (2007). Marian Wright Edelman. Retrieved June 1, 2007, from http://womenshistory.about.com/od/quotes/a/marian_edelman_2.htm

Chapter 6

Acs, G., & Nichols, A. (2007). *Low income workers and their employers: Characteristics and challenges*. Urban Institute. Retrieved June 27, 2008, from http://www.urban.org/publications/411532.html

American Youth Policy Forum. (2006). *Helping youth succeed through out-of-school time programs*. Retrieved March 12, 2007, from http://www.aypf.org/publications/HelpingYouthOST2006.pdf

Barnett, W. S., Brown, K. C., Finn-Stevenson, M., & Henrich, C. (2006). From visions to systems of universal pre-kindergarten.

In J. L. Aber, S. J. Bishop-Josef, S. M. Jones, K. T. McLearn, & D. A. Phillips (Eds.), *Child development and social policy: Knowledge for action* (pp. 113–128). Washington, DC: American Psychological Association.

Breidenbach, M. (2003). *A family impact analysis of the Family and Medical Leave Act of 1993.* (Wisconsin Family Impact Analysis Series). Madison, WI: University of Wisconsin Center for Excellence in Family Studies.

Bureau of Labor Statistics. (1988). *Employer-sponsored childcare benefits.* Retrieved April 12, 2007, from http://www.bls.gov/opub/ils/pdf/opbils24.pdf

Buysse, V., & Wesley, P. (2006). *Evidence-based practice in the early childhood field.* Washington, DC: Zero to Three Press.

Calman, L., & Tarr-Whelan, L. (2005). *Early childhood education for all: A wise investment.* Legal Momentum's Family Initiative & MIT Workplace Center. Retrieved May 20, 2006, from http://web.mit.edu/workplacecenter/docs/Full%20Report.pdf

Children's Defense Fund. (2003). *School-age child care: Keeping children safe and helping them learn while their families work.* Retrieved March 11, 2007, from http://www.childrensdefense.org/site/DocServer/keyfacts2003_schoolagecare.pdf?docID=593

Children's Defense Fund. (2005). *Head Start basics.* Retrieved March 31, 2007, from http://www.childrensdefense.org/site/DocServer/headstartbasics2005.pdf?docID=616

Cotton, K., & Wikelund, K. (2001). *Parent involvement in education.* Retrieved July 2, 2008, from http://www.nwrel.org/scpd/sirs/3/cu6.html

CQO Study Team. (1995). *Cost, quality, and outcomes in child care centers.* Public report. University of Colorado at Denver.

Culkin, M., Helburn, S., & Morris, J. (1990). *Current price versus full cost: An economic perspective. Reaching the full cost of quality in early childhood programs.* Washington, DC: National Association for the Education of Young Children.

Culp, R., Appelbaum, M., Osofsky, J., & Levy, J. (1988). Adolescent and older mothers: Comparison between prenatal maternal variables and newborn interaction measures. *Infant Behavior and Development, 11*(3), 353–362.

Disability Rights Center. (2006). *Parents as advocates handbook.* Retrieved January 31, 2007, from http://www.drcme.org/publications.asp?pubid=35&secid=185

Epstein, J. L. (1994). Theory to practice: School and family partnerships lead to school improvement and student success. In C. L. Fagnano & B. Z. Werber (Eds.), *School, family and community interaction: A view from the firing line* (pp. 39–52). Boulder, CO: Westview Press.

Federal Interagency Forum on Child and Family Statistics. (2008). *America's children in brief: Key national indicators of well-being, 2008.* Retrieved December 1, 2008, from http://www.childstats.gov/index.asp

Friedman, M. (2006). Child care. *Almanac of Policy Issues.* Retrieved April 2, 2007, from http://www.policyalmanac.org/social_welfare/childcare.shtml

FSU Center for Prevention and Early Intervention Policy. (2005). *Adolescent parenting research.* Retrieved April 11, 2007, from http://www.cpeip.fsu.edu/resourceFiles/resourceFile_75.pdf

Galinsky, E., Bond, J. T., & Friedman, D. E. (1993). *The changing workforce: Highlights from the national study.* New York: Families and Work Institute.

Giannarelli, L., & Barsimantov, J. (2000). *Child care expenses of America's families.* Urban Institute. Retrieved March 12, 2007, from http://childcare.about.com/gi/dynamic/offsite.htm?zi=1/XJ/Ya&sdn=childcare&cdn=parenting&tm=1065&gps=90_2_1020_569&f=00&tt=14&bt=0&bts=0&zu=http%3A//www.urban.org/Template.cfm%3FNavMenuID%3D24%26template%3D/TaggedContent/ViewPublication.cfm%26PublicationID%3D7496

Great Inspirational Quotes. (2007). Parenting quotes. Retrieved August 31, 2007, from http://www.great-inspirational-quotes.com/parenting-quotes.html

Hewitt Associates. (2003). SpecSummary: United States salaried work/life benefits, 2003–2004. Lincolnshire, IL: Author.

Hickman, C., Greenwood, G., & Miller, M. (1995). High school parent involvement: Relationships with achievement, grade level, SES, and gender. *Journal of Research and Development in Education, 28,* 125–134.

Hofferth, S., & Collins, N. (2000). Child care and employment turnover. *Population Research and Policy Review, 19*(4), 357–395.

Hughes, R., Jr. (1994). A framework for developing family life education programs. *Family Relations, 43,* 74–80.

Karoly, L., Kilburn, M., & Cannon, J. (2005). *Early childhood interventions: Proven results, future promise.* The RAND Corporation. Retrieved October 5, 2007, from http://rand.org/pubs/monographs/2005/RAND_MG341.pdf

Kinch, A., & Schweinhart, L. (2004). *Achieving high quality child care: How ten programs deliver excellence parents can afford.* Washington, DC: National Association for the Education of Young Children.

Lincoln, K. D., Chatters, L. M., & Taylor, R. J. (2005). Social support, traumatic events and depressive symptoms among African Americans. *Journal of Marriage and Family 67*(3), 754–766.

Lopez, E., Kreider, H., & Caspe, M. (2004). Co-constructing family involvement. *The Evaluation Exchange, X*(4), 2–3.

Lucas, M. (2001, Spring/Summer). Reports from the field: The military child care connection. *Caring for Infants and Toddlers, 11*(1). Retrieved March 3, 2007, from http://www.futureofchildren.org/information2826/information_show.htm?doc_id=79401

Minnes, P., Nachen, J., & Woodford, L. (2003). The role of families. In I. Brown & M. Percy (Eds.), *Developmental disabilities in Ontario* (2nd ed., pp. 673–676). Toronto: Ontario Association on Developmental Disabilities.

Moll, L. (1992). Funds of knowledge for teaching: Using a qualitative approach to connect homes and classrooms. *Theory Into Practice, 31*(2), 132–141.

National Association of Child Care Resource and Referral Agencies. (2006). *Breaking the piggy bank: Parents and the high price of child care.* Retrieved April 10, 2007, from http://www.naccrra.org/docs/policy/breaking_the_piggy_bank.pdf

National Association for the Education of Young Children. (2000). *A call for excellence in early childhood education.* Retrieved April 12, 2007, from http://www.naeyc.org/policy/excellence.asp

National Association for the Education of Young Children. (2001). *Lessons from military child care.* Retrieved March 12, 2007, from http://www.naeyc.org/ece/2001/03.asp

National Association of Elementary School Principals. (2001). *Principals and after-school programs: A survey of pre K–8 principals, executive summary.* Retrieved March 7, 2007, from http://www.naesp.org/afterschool/aspexecsum.htm

National Campaign to Prevent Teen Pregnancy. (2005). *What docs should know about the impact of teen pregnancy on young children.*

Retrieved April 2, 2007, from http://teenpregnancy.org/resources/reading/pdf/tots.pdf

National Center for Education Statistics. (2004). *Contexts of elementary and secondary education.* Retrieved July 2, 2008, from http://nces.ed.gov/programs/coe/2004/section4/indicator33.asp

National Education Goals Panel. (1997). *The national education goals panel report: Building a nation of learners, 1997.* Washington, DC: U.S. Government Printing Office.

North Central Regional Laboratory. (1995). *National education goals panel.* Retrieved October 19, 2007, from http://www.ncrel.org/sdrs/areas/issues/envrnmnt/go/go4negp.htm

Organisation for Economic Cooperation and Development. (2006). *Starting strong II: Early childhood education and care.* Retrieved October 19, 2006, from http://www.oecd.org/dataoecd/16/16/37423778.pdf

Osofsky, J., Hann, D., & Peebles, C. (1993). Adolescent parenthood: Risks and opportunities for mothers and infants. In C. H. Zeanah (Ed.), *Handbook of infant mental health* (pp. 106–119). New York: Guilford.

Perkins, D., & Zimmerman, M. (1995). Empowerment theory, research, and application. *American Journal of Community Psychology, 23*(5), 569.

Pre-K Now. (2008). *Mapping pre-K.* Retrieved March 1, 2009, from http://www.preknow.org/resource/mapping/accessmap.cfm

Rothstein, R. (2004). *Class and schools: Using social, economic and educational reform to close the black-white achievement gap.* Washington, DC: Economic Policy Institute.

Stegelin, D. (2004). Early childhood education. In F. P. Schargel & J. Smink (Eds.), *Helping students graduate: A strategic approach to dropout prevention* (pp. 115–123). Larchmont, NY: Eye on Education.

Stipek, D. (2005, July/August). Early childhood education at a crossroads. *Harvard Education Letter.* Retrieved April 6, 2007, from www.edletter.org/current/crossroads.shtml

U.S. Army MWR. (2005). *Child and youth services.* Retrieved April 12, 2007, from http://www.armymwr.com/portal/family/childandyouth/

U.S. Census Bureau. (2002). *Who's minding the kids? Child care arrangements: Winter 2002.* Retrieved March 21, 2007, from http://childcare.about.com/gi/dynamic/offsite.htm?zi=1/XJ/Ya&sdn=childcare&cdn=parenting&tm=19&gps=189_7_1020_569&f=00&tt=14&bt=0&bts=0&zu=http%3A//www.census.gov/population/www/socdemo/childcare.html

U.S. Department of Health and Human Services. (2006). *Child care and development fund fact sheet.* Retrieved October 19, 2007, from http://www.acf.hhs.gov/programs/ccb/ccdf/factsheet.htm

U.S. Department of the Treasury. (1998). *Investing in child care: Challenges facing working parents and the private sector response.* Washington, DC: Author.

U.S. Department of the Treasury. (2008). *Claiming the child and dependent care credit.* Retrieved October 22, 2008, from http://www.irs.gov/newsroom/article/0,,id=106189,00.html

Vygotsky, L. (1978). *Mind in society.* Cambridge MA: Harvard University Press.

Zellman, G., Johansen, A., Meredith, L., & Selvin, M. (1994). *Improving the delivery of military child care.* Rand Corporation Report. Retrieved June 1, 2007, from http://www.rand.org/pubs/reports/R4145/R4145.appa.html

Chapter 7

Administration for Children and Families. (2008). Head Start Reauthorization: P.L. 110–134. Retrieved June 27, 2008, from http://eclkc.ohs.acf.hhs.gov/hslc/Program%20Design%20and%20Management/Head%20Start%20Requirements/IMs/2008/resour_ime_001a_010308.html

American Federation of Labor-Congress of Industrial Organizations. (2007). *Child care and early childhood education.* Retrieved June 1, 2007, from http://www.aflcio.org/issues/workfamily/childcare.cfm

Bailey, D., Scarborough, A., Hebbeler, K., Spiker, D., & Mallik, S. (2004). *National early intervention longitudinal study: Family outcomes at the end of early intervention.* Menlo Park, CA: SRI International.

Belsky, J., Vandell, D. L., Burchinal, M., Clarke-Stewart, K. A., McCartney, K., Owen, M. T., & The NICHD Early Child Care Research Network. (2007). Are there long-term effects of early child care? *Child Development, 78,* 681–701.

Burchinal, M. R., Cryer, D., Clifford, R. M., & Howes, C. (2002). Caregiver training and classroom quality in child care centers. *Applied Developmental Science, 6*(1), 2–11.

Center for the Child Care Workforce. (2004). *Current data on the salary and benefits of the U.S. early childhood education workforce.* Retrieved May 11, 2007, from http://ccw.cleverspin.com/pubs/2004Compendium.pdf

Chism, N. (2005). *Developing a philosophy of teaching statement.* The Professional & Organizational Development Network in Higher Education. Retrieved June 2, 2007, from http://teaching.uchicago.edu/pod/chism.html

Cunningham, B., & Watson, L. (2002). Recruiting male teachers. *Beyond the Journal.* Retrieved December 4, 2007, from http://journal.naeyc.org/btj/200211/PrinterFriendly_RecruitingMaleTeachers.pdf

Early, D. M., Bryant, D. M., Pianta, R. C., Clifford, R. M., Burchinal, M. R., Ritchie, S., Howes, C., & Barbarin, O. (2006). Are teachers' education, major, and credentials related to classroom quality and children's academic gains in pre-kindergarten? *Early Childhood Research Quarterly, 21,* 174–195.

Egertson, H. A. (2004). Achieving high standards and implementing developmentally appropriate practice—Both ARE possible. *Dimensions of Early Childhood, 32*(1), 3–9.

Fleet, A., & Patterson, C. (2001). Professional growth reconceptualized: Early childhood staff searching for meaning. *Early Childhood Research and Practice, 3*(2). Retrieved June 4, 2007, from http://ecrp.uiuc.edu/v3n2/fleet.html

Grossman, S., & Williston, J. (2001). Strategies for teaching early childhood students to connect reflective thinking to practice. *Childhood Education, 77*(4), 236–240.

Katz, L. (1993). *Dispositions: Definitions and implications for early childhood practice.* Retrieved January 7, 2009, from http://ceep.crc.uiuc.edu/eecearchive/books/disposit.html

Katz, L. (1995). Dispositions in early childhood education. In L. G. Katz (Ed.), *Talks with teachers of young children. A collection.* Norwood, NJ: Ablex. (ERIC Document Reproduction Service No. ED380232)

Katz, L. (1999). *Curriculum disputes in early childhood education* (ERIC Digest). Champaign, IL: ERIC Clearinghouse on Elementary and Early Childhood Education. (ERIC Document Reproduction Service No. ED436298)

McCormick Tribune Center for Early Childhood Leadership. (2005). *Research notes: A focused look at program directors.* Retrieved May 12, 2007, from http://cecl.nl.edu/research/issues/rnsu05.pdf

National Association for the Education of Young Children. (1993). *A conceptual framework for early childhood professional development.* Retrieved May 15, 2007, from http://www.naeyc.org/about/positions/pdf/psconf98.pdf

National Association for the Education of Young Children. (2005). *NAEYC early childhood program standards and accreditation criteria: The mark of quality in early childhood education.* Washington, DC: Author.

National Association for the Education of Young Children. (2007). *Professional development: Educational qualifications of program administrators and teaching staff.* Retrieved June 11, 2007, from http://www.journal.naeyc.org/btj/200703/BTJProfDev.asp

National Center for Early Development and Learning. (2000). Teacher education, wages key to outcomes. *Spotlight, 18.* Retrieved June 1, 2007, from http://www.fpg.unc.edu/ncedl/PDFs/spot18.pdf

National Center for Early Development and Learning. (2001). *Preparing the workforce.* Retrieved May 1, 2007, from http://www.fpg.unc.edu/~ncedl/PDFs/spot33.pdf

Nelson, B. (2006). Recruiting male teachers for education. *MenTeach.* Retrieved March 2, 2007, from http://www.menteach.com/news/editorial_recruiting_more_men_to_teach

North Carolina Institute for Early Childhood. (2001). *Recruitment, retention, and compensation of the early childhood workforce.* Retrieved May 15, 2007, from http://www.nccic.org/forum/ecwaudioconf2.pdf

Patterson, K., Grenny, J., McMillan, R., Switzler, R., & Covey, S. (2002). *Crucial conversations: Tools for talking when the stakes are high.* New York: McGraw-Hill.

Piesner-Feinberg, E., Burchinal, M., Clifford, R., Culkin, M., Howes, C., Kagan, S., Yazejian, N., Byler, P., Rustici, J., & Zelazo, J. (1999). *The children of the cost, quality, and outcomes study go to school: Executive summary.* Chapel Hill, NC: University of North Carolina.

Ros-Voseles, D., & Moss, L. (2007, September). The role of dispositions in the education of future teachers. *Young Children* 62(5): 90–98.

Taylor, R., & Wasicsko, M. (2000). *The dispositions to teach.* Retrieved June 1, 2007, from http://www.educatordispositions.org/dispositions/The%20Dispositons%20to%20Teach.pdf

Third World Traveler. (2006). Martin Luther King Jr. quotes. Retrieved October 19, 2007, from http://www.thirdworldtraveler.com/Authors/MLK_quotes.html

U.S. Department of Labor, Bureau of Labor Statistics. (2007). *Teachers: Preschool, kindergarten, elementary, and secondary.* Retrieved June 1, 2007, from http://stats.bls.gov/oco/ocos069.htm#emply

Usher, D. (2004). *Disposition-centered, programs for teacher education.* Paper presented at the Third symposium on Educator Dispositions. Richmond, KY: Eastern Kentucky University.

Whitebook, M., & Eichberg, A. (2002). Finding a better way: Defining policies to improve child care workforce compensation. *Young Children, 57*(3), 66–72.

Whitebook, M., Howes, C., & Phillips, D. (1990). *Who cares? Child care teachers and the quality of care in America.* Final report of the National Child Care Staffing Study. Oakland, CA: Child Care Employee Project.

Chapter 8

Aaron, R. (1971). *John Locke.* Oxford: The Oxford University Press.

Almy, M. (2000). What wisdom should we take with us as we enter the new century? *Young Children, 55*(1), 6–10.

Altenbaugh, R. (1999). *Historical dictionary of American education.* New York: Greenwood Publishing.

Ames, L. (1989). *Arnold Gesell: Themes of his work.* New York: Human Sciences Press.

Bank Street. (2006). *Curriculum: Educational philosophy.* Retrieved June 28, 2008, from http://www.bankstreet.edu/sfc/educ_philosophy.html

Banks, R. (2003). *The early childhood education curriculum debate: Direct instruction vs. child-initiated learning.* Champaign, IL: Clearinghouse on Elementary and Early Childhood Education. (ERIC Document Reproduction Service No. ED413106)

Barton, B., & Booth, D. (1990). *Stories in the classroom.* Markham, ON: Pembrode.

Bowlby, J. (1988). *A secure base: Parent-child attachment and healthy human development.* New York: Basic Books.

Bredekamp, S., & Rosegrant, T. (Eds.). (1995). *Reaching potentials: Transforming early childhood curriculum and assessment, Vol. 2.* Washington, DC: National Association for the Education of Young Children.

CAST. (2008). *Universal design for learning guidelines 1.0.* Wakefield, MA: Author. Retrieved July 1, 2008, from http://www.cast.org/publications/UDLguidelines/version1.html

Dewey, J. (2004). *Democracy and education.* New York: Macmillan. (Original work published 1916)

Division for Early Childhood of the Council for Exceptional Children. (2007). *Promoting positive outcomes for children with disabilities: Recommendations for curriculum, assessment, and program evaluation.* Retrieved October 1 2007, from http://www.dec-sped.org/pdf/positionpapers/prmtg_pos_outcomes_comparison_paper.pdf

Doyle, M., & Smith, M. (2007). *Jean-Jacques Rousseau on education, the encyclopaedia of informal education.* Retrieved May 31, 2008, from http://www.infed.org/thinkers/et-rous.htm

Edwards, C. (2002). Three approaches from Europe: Waldorf, Montessori, and Reggio Emilia. *Early Childhood Research and Practice, 4*(1). Retrieved May 11, 2007, from http://ecrp.uiuc.edu/v4n1/edwards.html

Edwards, C., Gandini, L., & Forman, G. (Eds.). (1993). *The hundred languages of children: The Reggio Emilia approach to early childhood education.* Norwood, NJ: Ablex.

Elkind, D. (1981). *The hurried child.* New York: Perseus Books.

Elkind, D. (1991). *Perspectives on early childhood education: Growing with young children toward the 21st century.* Washington DC. National Education Association.

Elkind, D. (2001). Much too early. *Education Matters, 1*(5). Retrieved December 12, 2007, from http://www.hoover.org/publications/ednext/3385081.html

Family and Child Experiences Study. (2006). *Research brief: Children's outcomes and program quality in Head Start, December 2006.* Retrieved March 1, 2007, from http://www.acf.hhs.gov/programs/opre/hs/faces/reports/research_2003/research_2003_title.html

Frost, J. L. (2006). *The dissolution of children's outdoor play: Causes and consequences.* Presentation to the Value of Play: A Forum on Risk, Recreation and Children's Health, May 31, 2006. Retrieved

April 22, 2008 from http://cgood.org/assets/attachments/Frost_-_Common_Good_-_FINAL.pdf

Gerber, M. (2002). *Educaring. Resources for infant educarers.* Retrieved September 15, 2007, from http://www.childsday.com/RIE.htm

Goffin, S. G., & Wilson, C. (2001). *Curriculum models and early childhood education: Appraising the relationship* (2nd ed.). Upper Saddle River, NJ: Merrill/Prentice Hall.

Hall, G. S. (1923). *The life and confessions of a psychologist.* New York: Appleton-Century-Crofts.

High/Scope Educational Research Foundation. (2009). *The classroom.* Retrieved April 1, 2009, from http://www.highscope.org/Content.asp?ContentId=181

Hohmann, M., & Weikart, D. P. (1995). *Educating young children.* Ypsilanti, MI: High/Scope.

Itard, J. M. (1962). *The wild boy of Aveyron.* Stamford, CT: Appleton and Lange.

Kamii, C. (1985). *Young children reinvent arithmetic: Implications of Piaget's theory.* New York: Teachers College Press.

Katz, L. (1999). *Curriculum disputes in early childhood education* (ERIC Digest). Champaign, IL: ERIC Clearinghouse on Elementary and Early Childhood Education. (ERIC Document Reproduction Service No. ED436298)

Katz, L., & Chard, S. (1989). *Engaging children's minds: The project approach.* Norwood, NJ: Ablex. (ERIC Document Reproduction Service No. ED407074)

Klein, L., & Knitzer, J. (2007). *Promoting effective early learning: What every policymaker and educator should know.* National Center for Children in Poverty, Columbia University Mailman School of Public Health.

Kohn, A. (1999). *Punished by rewards: The trouble with gold stars, incentive plans, A's, praise, and other bribes.* Boston: Houghton Mifflin.

Lally, J. R. (2000). Infants have their own curriculum: A responsive approach to curriculum planning for infants and toddlers. *Head Start Bulletin, 67,* 6–7.

Lillard, A. (2005). *Montessori: The science behind the genius.* Cary, NC: Oxford University Press.

Lincoln, A. (1858). House Divided speech. Retrieved November 1, 2007, from http://showcase.netins.net/web/creative/lincoln/speeches/house.htm

Louv, R. (2005). *Last child in the woods: Saving our children from nature deficit disorder.* Chapel Hill, NC: Algonquin.

Maguire-Fong, M. J. (1999). *Investigations: A responsive approach to infant curriculum.* Retrieved October 15, 2007, from http://www.pitc.org/resources/macfonghnd.htm

Marcon, R. A. (1992). Differential effects of three preschool models on inner-city 4-year-olds. *Early Childhood Research Quarterly, 7*(4), 517–530. (ERIC Journal No. EJ458104)

Miller, R. (2006). A brief history of alternative education. *The Education Revolution.* Retrieved January 12, 2007, from http://www.educationrevolution.org/history.html

National Association for the Education of Young Children and National Association of Early Childhood Specialists in State Departments of Education. (2002). *Early learning standards: Creating the conditions for success.* Retrieved July 2, 2007, from http://www.naeyc.org/about/positions/early_learning_standards.asp

National Center for Education Statistics. (2003, September 9). *National Assessment of Educational Progress (NAEP) Questions.* Retrieved January 2, 2008, from http://nces.ed.gov/nationsreportcard/itmrls/

National Head Start Association. (2007). *National Head Start Association 2007 Policy Agenda.* http://www.paheadstart.org/UserFiles/File/2007_policy_agenda.pdf

Nelson, K. (2004). *Busy ants.* Minneapolis, MN: Lerner Books.

New, R. (2000). The Reggio Emilia approach: It's not an approach—it's an attitude (3rd ed.). In J. Roopnarine & J. Johnson (Eds.), *Approaches to early childhood education.* Upper Saddle River, NJ: Merrill/Prentice Hall.

Olfman, S. (2003). *All work and no play: How educational reforms are harming our preschoolers.* Westport CT: Praeger.

Parks, G. (2000). The High/Scope Perry Preschool Project. *Juvenile Justice Bulletin.* Retrieved May 1, 2008, from http://www.ncjrs.gov/pdffiles1/ojjdp/181725.pdf

Pestalozzi, J. (1894). *How Gertrude teaches her children.* London: Swan Sonnenschein.

Rousseau, J-J. (1762). *Émile.* London: Dent. (1911 edition)

Rutsch, H. (2006). *Literacy as freedom: The United Nations launches literacy decade (2003–2012).* United Nations Chronicle Online Edition. Retrieved February 26, 2007, from http://www.un.org/Pubs/chronicle/2003/webArticles/022103_literacy.html

Skinner, B. F. (2002). *Beyond freedom and dignity.* Indianapolis, IN: Hackett Publishing.

Smith, D. (2005). The egg man and the empress. *Montessori Life.* Retrieved January 13, 2007, from http://findarticle.com/p/articles/mi_qa4097/is_200507/ai_n15615284/pg_4

Spodek, B., Saracho, M., & Davis, M. (1987). *Foundations of early childhood education.* Upper Saddle River, NJ: Prentice Hall.

The University of Chicago Lab Schools. (2006). *History of the University of Chicago Lab Schools.* Retrieved February 1, 2007, from http://www.ucls.uchicago.edu/about/history/chapter1.shtml

U.S. Department of Health and Human Services. (2008). *Statutory degree and credentialing requirements for Head Start teaching staff.* Retrieved March 1, 2009, from http://eclkc.ohs.acf.hhs.gov/hslc/Professional%20Development/Staff%20Development/Teaching%20Teams/resour_ime_012_0081908.html

Vygtosky, L. (1986). *Thought and language.* Cambridge, MA: MIT Press.

Watson, J. B. (1930). *Behaviorism* (Rev. ed.). University of Chicago Press.

Chapter 9

Bodrova, E., Leong, D., & Shore, R. (2004). Child outcome standards in preschool programs: What are standards; what is needed to make them work? *Preschool Policy Matters, 5.* Retrieved April 13, 2008, from http://nieer.org/resources/policybriefs/5.pdf

Bredekamp, S., & Rosegrant, T. (1995). Reaching potentials through national standards: Panacea or pipe dream. In S. Bredekamp & T. Rosegrant (Eds.), *Reaching potentials: Transforming early childhood curriculum and assessment* (pp. 5–14). Washington, DC: National Association for the Education of Young Children.

Chicago Public Schools. (2005). *Teacher Resources: Head Start child outcomes framework.* Retrieved April 1, 2009, from http://www.ecechicago.org/teacher/standards/outcomes.html

Council of Chief State School Officers. (2004). *The words we use: A glossary of terms for early childhood education standards and assessment.* Retrieved June 15, 2007, from http://www.ccsso.org/Projects/scass/projects/early_childhood_education_assessment_consortium/publications_and_products/2839.cfm

Early On, Michigan Individualized Family Service Plan (IFSP) Individualized Education Plan (IEP). Retrieved April 1, 2009, from http://www.michigan.gov/documents/8-1-05IFSP-IEPForm_135442_7.pdf

Grace, C. (1992). *The portfolio and its use: Developmentally appropriate assessment of young children.* Clearinghouse on Early Education and Parenting. Retrieved July 2, 2007, from http://ceep.crc.uiuc.edu/eecearchive/digests/1992/grace92.html

Grosvenor, L. (1993). Taking assessment matters into our own hands. In M. Dalheim (Ed.), *Student portfolios* (NEA Professional Library Teacher-to-Teacher Series). Washington, DC: Bookshelf (Editorial Projects in Education).

Hagie, M. U., Gallipo, P. G., & Svien, L. (2003). Traditional culture versus traditional assessment for American Indian students: An investigation of potential test item bias. *Assessment for Effective Intervention, 23*(1), 15–25.

Helm, J., & Gronlund, G. (2000). Linking standards and engaged learning in the early years. *Early Childhood Research and Practice, 2*(1). Retrieved June 4, 2007, from http://ecrp.uiuc.edu/v2n1/helm.html

High/Scope Educational Research Foundation. (2008). *Preschool COR.* Retrieved April 8, 2008, from http://www.highscope.org/Content.asp?ContentId=113

Jablon, J. R., Dombro, A. L., & Dichtelmiller, M. L. (1999). *The power of observation.* Washington, DC: Teaching Strategies.

Jones, E. (1993). *Growing teachers: Partnerships in staff development.* Early Childhood Research Institute. Retrieved July 1, 2007, from http://clas.uiuc.edu/fulltext/cl01141/cl01141.html

Kostelnik, M. (1992). MYTHS associated with developmentally appropriate programs. *Young Children, 47*(4), 17–23.

Meisels, S., Jablon, J., Marsden, D., Dichtelmiller, M., Dorfman, A., & Steele, D. (1995). *The work sampling system: An overview.* Ann Arbor: Rebus Planning Associates.

Mitchell, A., & David, J. (1992). *Explorations with children: A curriculum guide from the Bank Street College of Education.* New York: Bank Street.

National Association for the Education of Young Children. (2003). *Early childhood curriculum, assessment, and program evaluation: Building an effective accountable system in programs for children birth through age eight.* Retrieved July 1, 2007, from http://www.naeyc.org/about/positions/pdf/pscape.pdf

National Association for the Education of Young Children. (2005a). *Code of ethical conduct.* Retrieved January 15, 2007, from http://www.naeyc.org/about/positions/PSETH98.asp

National Association for the Education of Young Children. (2005b). *Screening and assessment of young English-language learners.* Supplement to the NAEYC Position Statement on Early Childhood Curriculum, Assessment, and Program Evaluation. Retrieved June 15, 2007, from http://www.naeyc.org/about/positions/pdf/ELL_Supplement.pdf

National Association for the Education of Young Children and National Association of Early Childhood Specialists in State Departments of Education. (2002). *Early learning standards: Creating the conditions for success.* Retrieved July 2, 2007, from http://www.naeyc.org/about/positions/early_learning_standards.asp

National Conference of State Legislators. (2008). *Newborn hearing screening: State laws.* Retrieved June 8, 2008, from http://www.ncsl.org/programs/health/hear50.htm

National Institute for Early Education Research. (2004). *Preschool assessment: A guide to developing a balanced approach.* Preschool Policy Matters. Retrieved June 30, 2007, from http://nieer.org/resources/policybriefs/7.pdf

National School Boards Association. (2008). *NSBA Issues Brief: Head Start Reauthorization.* Retrieved April 2, 2009, from http://www.nsba.org/MainMenu/Advocacy/FederalLaws/EarlyEducation/NSBAsIssueBriefonHeadStartReauthorization.aspx

Pardini, P. (2002). The history of special education. *Rethinking Schools Online, 16*(3). Retrieved January 30, 2007, from http://www.rethinkingschools.org/archive/16_03/Hist163.shtml

Pett, J. (1990). What is authentic evaluation? Common questions and answers. *Fair Test Examiner, 4,* 8–9.

Scott-Little, C., Lesko, J., Martella, J., & Milburn, P. (2007). Early learning standards: Results from a national survey to document trends in state-level policies and practices. *Early Childhood Research and Practice, 9*(1). Retrieved October 2, 2008, from http://ecrp.uiuc.edu/v9n1/little.html

Segal, M., & Webber, N. T. (1996). Non-structured play observation: Guidelines, benefits and caveats. In S. J. Meisels & E. Fenichel (Eds.), *New visions for the developmental assessment of infants and young children* (pp. 207–30). New York: Zero to Three National Center for Infants, Toddlers and Families.

Vermont Early Childhood Work Group. (2001). *Planning your professional growth: Creating an individualized professional development plan for early care and education.* Retrieved June 29, 2007, from http://humanservices.vermont.gov/publications/early-childhood-work-group/planning-your-professional-growth

Zachary, L. (2000). *The mentor's guide: Facilitating effective learning relationships.* San Francisco: Jossey-Bass.

Chapter 10

Bellini, S. (2003). Making (and keeping) friends: A model for social skills interaction. *The Reporter, 8*(3), 1–10.

Biel, L., & Peske, N. (2005). *Raising a sensory smart child.* New York: Penguin.

Bowlby, J. (1972). *Attachment and loss. Vol. 1: Attachment* (2nd ed.). New York: Basic Books. (New printing, 1999, with a foreword by Allan N. Schore; originally published in 1969)

Bowman, B., & Brownell, C. (2007). Supporting infants and toddlers with challenging behavior. In D. Cicchetti & D. J. Cohen (Eds.), *Developmental psychopathology. Vol. 2: Risk, disorder, and adaptation* (pp. 421–471). New York: Wiley.

Bretherton, I., Fritz, J., Zahn-Waxler, C. & Ridgeway, D. (1986). Learning to talk about emotions: A functionalist perspective. *Child Development, 57,* 529–548.

Cameron, J., Pierce, W. D., Banko, K. M., & Gear, A. (2005). Achievement-based rewards and intrinsic motivation: A test of cognitive mediators. *Journal of Educational Psychology, 97*(4), 641–655.

Catlett, C., Winton, P., & Hemmeter, M. L. (2004). Resources for supporting young children with challenging behaviors and their families. *Young Exceptional Children, 7*(2), 30.

Center on the Social and Emotional Foundations for Early Learning. (2006). *Social emotional teaching strategies PowerPoint presentation.* Retrieved June 14, 2007, from http://www.vanderbilt.edu/csefel/modules/module2/presenters-ppt/presentation.ppt#256,1,Social Emotional Teaching Strategies

Comer, J. (2005). Child and adolescent development: The critical missing focus in school reform. *Phi Delta Kappan, 86,* 757–763.

Cooper, M. (1995). *I got community.* New York: Penguin.

Darling-Hammond, L. (2000). *Solving the dilemmas of teacher supply, demand, and quality.* New York: National Commission on Teaching and America's Future.

Darling-Hammond, L. (2005). New standards and old inequalities: School reform and the education of African American students. In J. E. King (Ed.), *Black education: A transformative research and action agenda for the new century* (pp. 197–223). Mahwah, NJ: Erlbaum.

Dishion, T., French, D., & Patterson, G. (1995). The development and ecology of antisocial behavior. In D. Cicchetti & D. J. Cohen (Eds.), *Manual of developmental psychopathology* (pp. 421–471). New York: Wiley.

Division for Early Childhood of The Council of Exceptional Children. (2006). *Identification of and intervention with challenging behavior*. Retrieved July 1, 2007, from http://www.dec-sped.org/pdf/positionpapers/PositionStatement_ChallBeh.pdf

Erikson, E. (1950). *Childhood and society*. New York: Norton.

Fox, L. (2006). *Supporting infants and toddlers with challenging behavior*. Center on the Social and Emotional Foundations for Early Learning. Retrieved July 8, 2007, from http://www.vanderbilt.edu/csefel/modules/module4/handout6.pdf

Fox, L., Dunlap, G., Hemmeter, M. L., Joseph, G., & Strain, P. (2003). The teaching pyramid: A model for supporting social emotional competence and preventing challenging behavior in young children. *Young Exceptional Children, 58,* 48–52.

Fox, L., & Lentini, R. (2006). "You got it!" Teaching social/emotional skills. *Beyond the Journal*. Retrieved July 17, 2007, from http://www.journal.naeyc.org/btj/200611/

Gartrell, D. (2006). Guidance matters. *Beyond the Journal*. Retrieved August 5, 2007, from http://www.journal.naeyc.org/btj/200603/GuidanceBTJ.asp

Hitz, R., & Driscoll, A. (1989). *Praise in the classroom*. (Eric Digests). Retrieved March 8, 2005, from http//www.ericdigests.org/pre-9213/praise.htm

Honig, A. (2000). *Love and learn: Positive guidance for young children*. Washington, DC: National Association for the Education of Young Children.

Institute of Medicine Committee on Quality of Health Care in America. (2001). *Crossing the quality chasm: A new health system for the 21st century*. Washington, DC: National Academies Press.

Jalongo, M. (2007). Beyond benchmarks and scores: Reasserting the role of motivation and interest in children's academic achievement. *An ACEI Position Paper*. Retrieved February 3, 2009, from http://www.acei.org/motivPosPaper.pdf

Joseph, G., & Strain, P. (2006). *Enhancing emotional vocabulary in young children*. Center on the Social and Emotional Foundations for Early Learning. Retrieved July 17, 2007, from http://www.vanderbilt.edu/csefel/modules/module2/handout6.pdf

Kern, L. (2007). *Addressing persistent challenging behaviors*. Center on the Social and Emotional Foundations for Early Learning. Retrieved July 12, 2007, from http://challengingbehavior.fmhi.usf.edu/Pers_Challenging_Behavior.pdf

Lavigne, J. V., Gibbons, R. D., Christoffel, K. K., Arend, R., Rosenbaum, D., Binns, H., et al. (1996). Prevalence rates and correlates of psychiatric disorders among preschool children. *Journal of the American Academy of Child and Adolescent Psychiatry, 35*(2), 204–214.

Lipsey, M. W., & Derzon, J. H. (1998). Predictors of violent or serious delinquency in adolescence and early adulthood: A synthesis of longitudinal research. In R. Loeber & D. P. Farrington (Eds.), *Serious & violent juvenile offenders: Risk factors and successful interventions* (pp. 86–105). Thousand Oaks, CA: Sage.

Maslow, A. (1998). *Toward a psychology of being*. New York: Wiley.

Michigan Public Policy Initiative. (2002). *Spotlight: Explaining challenging behavior in early childhood*. Retrieved March 1, 2007, from https://www.mnaonline.org/pdf/spotlight3.pdf

Mulligan, S., Morris, S., Green, K., & Harper-Whelan, S. (2003). *Curriculum on inclusion: Practical strategies for early childhood programs*. Missoula, Missouri: Rural Institute on Disabilities.

National Association for the Education of Young Children. (1995). *Teaching children not to be—or be victims of—bullies*. Retrieved August 12, 2007, from http://www.naeyc.org/ece/1996/14.asp

National Association for the Education of Young Children. (1998). Self-esteem and young children: You are the key. *Early Years are Learning Years*. Retrieved November 25, 2008, from http://www.naeyc.org/ece/1998/15.asp

National Scientific Council on the Developing Child. (2005). *Children's emotional development is built in to the architecture of their brains* (Working Paper II). Retrieved March 15, 2008, from http://www.developingchild.net/papers/workingpaperII.pdf

New, R., & Cochran, M. (2007). *Early childhood education: An international encyclopedia*. Westport, CT: Greenwood.

Olson, M., & Hyson, M. (2003). *Early childhood educators and child abuse prevention*. Booklet. Washington, DC: National Association for the Education of Young Children.

Raver, C. C. (2002). Emotions matter: Making the case for the role of young children's emotional development for early school readiness. *Social Policy Report, 16*(3), 3–19.

Ray, A., Bowman, B., & Brownell, J. O'N. (2006). Teacher-child relationships, social-emotional development, and school achievement. In B. Bowman & E. K. Moore (Eds.), *School readiness and social-emotional development: Perspectives on cultural diversity* (pp. 7–22). Washington, DC: National Black Child Development Institute.

Thinkexist. (2008). Mahatma Gandhi quotes. Retrieved April 22, 2008, from http://thinkexist.com/quotation/if_we_wish_to_create_a_lasting_peace_we_must/8067.html

U.S. Department of Education Center for Evidence-Based Practice. (2002). *Young children with challenging behavior*. Retrieved August 1, 2007, from http://challengingbehavior.fmhi.usf.edu/about.html

U.S. Department of Labor, Bureau of Labor Statistics. (2007). *Teachers: Preschool, kindergarten, elementary, and secondary*. Retrieved June 1, 2007, from http://stats.bls.gov/oco/ocos069.htm#emply

Williams, G. A., & Asher, S. R. (1993). Children without friends, Part 4: Improving social skills. In C. M. Todd (Ed.), *School-age connections, 3*(2), pp. 3–5. Urbana-Champaign, IL: University of Illinois Cooperative Extension Service.

Chapter 11

Abbott, A., & Bartlett, D. (2001). Infant motor development and equipment use in the home. *Child: Care, Health & Development, 27*(3), 295–306.

American Academy of Pediatrics. (2004). Keeping your child safe. In S. P. Shevlov & R. E. Hannemann (Eds.), *Caring for your baby and young child: Birth to age 5* (4th ed., pp. 423–470). New York: Bantam.

Anti-Defamation League. (2006). *What is anti-bias education?* Retrieved September 1, 2006, from http://www.adl.org/tools_teachers/tip_antibias_ed.asp

Butin, D. (2000). *Early childhood centers*. Washington, DC: National Clearinghouse for Educational Facilities.

Center for Universal Design North Carolina State University. (1997). *Universal design principles.* Retrieved July 1, 2008, from http://www.design.ncsu.edu/cud/about_ud/udprincipleshtmlformat.html#top

Christensen, K. (2003). *Creating inclusive outdoor play environments; Designing for ability rather than disability.* Retrieved September 26, 2006, from www.adventureislandplayground.org

Consumer Product Safety Commission. (1999). *Safety hazards in child care settings.* Retrieved October 3, 2008, from http://www.cpsc.gov/library/ccstudy.html

Cook, R., Klein, M., & Tessier, A. (2004). *Adapting early childhood curricula for children in inclusive settings* (6th ed.). Upper Saddle River, NJ: Merrill/Prentice Hall.

Cosco, N., & Moore, R. (1999). *Playing in place: Why the physical environment is important in playwork.* Paper presented at the 14th Play Education Annual Play and Human Development Meeting: Theoretical Playwork, Ely, UK.

Council on Rural Services. (2006). *Brain research and its implications for early childhood programs.* Retrieved September 18, 2006, from http://www.corsp.org/kids_family/Parent%20Activities/Brain%20Research%20and%20Its%20Implications%20for%20EC%20Programs.pdf#search=%22early%20childhood%20environments%20senses%22

Egertson, H. (2006). In praise of butterflies: Linking self-esteem and learning. *Beyond the Journal.* Retrieved September 18, 2006, from http://www.journal.naeyc.org/btj/200611/BTJPrimaryinterest.asp

Francis, M. (1995). Childhood's garden: Children's memory & meaning of gardens. *Children's Environments, 11*(1).

Froebel, F. (1974). *The education of man* (W. N. Hailmann, Trans.). Clifton, NJ: A. M. Kelley. (Original work published in 1826)

Herrington, S., & Studtman, K. (1998). Landscape interventions: New directions for the design of children's outdoor play environments. *Landscape and Urban Planning, 42*(2–4), 191–205.

Hohensee, J., & Derman-Sparks, L. (1992). *Implementing an anti-bias curriculum in early childhood classrooms.* Champaign, IL: ERIC Clearinghouse on Early Childhood Education. (ERIC Document Reproduction Service No. ED351146)

Jones, E. (2003). Playing to get smart. *Young Children, 58,* 32–33.

Katz, L. G., & Chard, S. C. (2000). *Engaging children's minds: The project approach* (2nd ed.). Stamford, CT: Ablex.

Kern, P., & Wakeford, L. (2007). Supporting outdoor play for young children: The zone model of playground supervision. *Young Children, 62*(2), 12–16.

Malaguzzi, L. (1994). Your image of the child: Where teaching begins. *Child Care Information Exchange, 96,* pp. 52–61.

Malone, K., & Tranter, P. (2003). Children's environmental learning and the use, design, and management of schoolgrounds. *Children, Youth, and Environments, 13*(2). Retrieved May 3, 2009, from: www.colorado.edu/journals/cye/13_2/Malone_Tranter/ChildrensEnvLearningAbstract.htm

National Lekotek Center. (2006). *Top 10 tips for choosing toys.* Retrieved September 28, 2006, from http://www.lekotek.org/resources/informationontoys/tentips.html

New, R. S., Mardell, B., & Robinson, D. (2005). Early childhood education as risky business: Going beyond what's "safe" to discovering what's possible? *Early Childhood Research and Practice, 7*(2), 1–18.Retrieved October 2, 2008, from: http://ecrp.uiuc.edu/v7n2/new.html

Playing for Keeps. (2005). *Tips for selecting toys.* Retrieved September 20, 2006, from http://www.playingforkeeps.org/site/documents/tip_selecting_toys.pdf

Prescott, E. (1987). The environment as organizer of intent in child-care settings. In C. S. Weinstein & T. G. David (Eds.), *Spaces for children: The built environment and child development* (pp. 159–185). New York: Plenum.

Shonkoff, J., & Phillips, D. (2000). *From neurons to neighborhoods: The science of early childhood development.* Washington, DC: National Academies Press.

Torelli, L., & Durrett, C. (1996). Landscape for learning: The impact of classroom design on infants and toddlers. *Early childhood NEWS, 8*(2), 12–17.

White, R., & Stoeklin, S. (2003). *The great 35 square foot myth.* Retrieved August 31, 2006, from http://www.whitehutchinson.com/children/articles/35footmyth.shtml

Women's History Quotes. (2007). Maria Montessori. Retrieved November 4, 2007, from http://womenshistory.about.com/od/quotes/a/montessori.htm

Chapter 12

American Academy of Pediatrics, Committee on Public Education. Children, adolescents, and television. *Pediatrics, 107,* 423–426.

Cotton, K., & Conklin, N. (2001). *Research on early childhood education.* Retrieved October 8, 2007, from http://www.nwrel.org/scpd/sirs/3/topsyn3.html

Davis, B., & Shade, D. (1994). *Integrate, don't isolate: Computers in the early childhood classroom.* Champaign, IL: ERIC Clearinghouse on Early Childhood Education. (ERIC Document Reproduction Service No. ED376991)

Eisner, E. (2007). *The three R's are essential, but don't forget the A—the arts.* Retrieved October 1, 2007, from http://artsedge.kennedy-center.org/content/3789/

Epstein, A. (2003). How planning and reflection develop young children's thinking skills. *Beyond the Journal: Young Children on the Web.* Retrieved October 11, 2007, from http://www.journal.naeyc.org/btj/200309/Planning&Reflection.pdf

High/Scope. (2007). *Intentional teacher.* High/Scope Press Release. Retrieved October 15, 2007, from http://www.highscope.org/Content.asp?ContentId=279

Hohensee, J., & Derman-Sparks, L. (1992). *Implementing an anti-bias curriculum in early childhood classrooms.* Champaign, IL: ERIC Clearinghouse on Early Childhood Education. (ERIC Document Reproduction Service No. ED351146)

Isenberg, J. P., & Quisenberry, N. (2002). *Play: Essential for all children.* A position paper of the Association for Childhood Education International. Retrieved October 3, 2007, from www.udel.edu/bateman/acei/playpaper.htm

Jablon, J., & Wilkinson, M. (2006). Using engagement strategies to facilitate children's learning and success. *Beyond the Journal: Young Children on the Web.* Retrieved October 13, 2007, from http://www.journal.naeyc.org/btj/200603/JablonBTJ.asp

Katz, L. G. (1992). *Nongraded and mixed-age grouping in early childhood programs.* (ERIC Digest). Retrieved October 13, 2007, from http://www.eric.ed.gov/contentdelivery/servlet/ERICServlet?accno=ED351148

Katz, L. G., & Chard, S. C. (2000). *Engaging children's minds: The project approach* (2nd ed.). Stamford, CT: Ablex.

Knapp-Philo, J., Notari-Syverson, A., & Stice, K. K. (2005). The tools of literacy for infants and toddlers. In E. M. Horn & H. Jones (Eds.), *Supporting early literacy development in young children* (Young Exceptional Children Monograph Series No. 7) (pp. 43–58). Longmont, CO: Sopris West.

Kostelnik, M., & Soderman, A. (1999). *Developmentally appropriate curriculum: Best practices in early childhood education.* (2nd ed.). Upper Saddle River, NJ: Merrill/Prentice Hall.

Mayo Clinic. (2007). *Childhood obesity.* Retrieved October 14, 2007, from http://www.mayoclinic.com/health/childhood-obesity/DS00698

Mindes, G. (2005). Social studies in today's early childhood curriculum. *Beyond the Journal: Young Children on the Web.* Retrieved October 11, 2007, from http://www.journal.naeyc.org/btj/200509/

National Association for the Education of Young Children/International Reading Association. (1998). *Learning to read and write: Developmentally appropriate practices for young children.* A joint position of the International Reading Association (IRA) and the National Association for the Education of Young Children (NAEYC). Retrieved October 3, 2007, from http://www.naeyc.org/about/positions/pdf/psread98.pdf

National Association for the Education of Young Children/National Council of Teachers of Mathematics. (2002). *Early childhood mathematics education: Promoting good beginnings.* A joint position of the NAEYC and the NCTM. Retrieved October 14, 2007, from http://www.nctm.org/about/content.aspx?id=6352

National Council for the Social Studies. (1994). *Curriculum standards for social studies: Expectations for excellence.* Washington, DC: Author.

North Central Regional Education Laboratory. (1999). *Critical issue: Organizing for effective early childhood programs and practices.* Retrieved June 1, 2008, from http://www.ncrel.org/sdrs/areas/issues/students/earlycld/ea100.htm

Northwestern Regional Education Laboratory. (2001). *Technology in early childhood education: Finding the balance.* Retrieved October 5, 2007, from http://www.nwrel.org/request/june01/inequities.html

Nurturing Early Learners. (2007). *A framework for kindergarten curriculum in Singapore.* Retrieved October 1, 2007, from http://www.moe.gov.sg/preschooleducation/docs/framework14-25.pdf

Rudman, M. (1984). *Children's literature: An issues approach* (2nd ed.). New York: Longman.

Sexuality Information and Education Council of the United States. (2004). *Guidelines for comprehensive sexuality education* (3rd ed.). Retrieved April 1, 2008, from http://www.siecus.org/pubs/guidelines/guidelines.pdf

Sietz, H. (2006). The plan: Building on children's interests. *Beyond the Journal.* Retrieved April 1, 2008, from http://www.journal.naeyc.org/btj/200603/SeitzBTJ.pdf#xml=http://naeychq.naeyc.org/texis/search/pdfhi.txt?query=Seitz&pr=naeyc&prox=sentence&rorder=750&rprox=500&rdfreq=1000&rwfreq=1000&rlead=1000&sufs=2&order=r&cq=&id=45225655167

Smith, M. W., Dickinson, D. K., & Sangeorge, A. (2002). *The early language and literacy classroom observation.* Baltimore, MD: Brookes.

Thinkexist. (2007). *Aristotle quotes.* Retrieved June 22, 2008, from http://thinkexist.com/quotation/those_that_know_do_those_that_understand-teach/10325.html

Torelli, L., & Durrett, C. (1996). Landscape for learning: The impact of classroom design on infants and toddlers. *Early Childhood News, 8*(2), 12–17.

U.S. Department of Labor, Bureau of Labor Statistics. (2007). *Teachers: Preschool, kindergarten, elementary, and secondary.* Retrieved June 1, 2007, from http://stats.bls.gov/oco/ocos069.htm#emply

Walling, S. (2003). *A day at the beach.* Yarmouth, ME: Abernathy.

Westminster College. (2007). *Science in the early childhood curriculum.* Retrieved October 11, 2007, from http://www.psych.westminster.edu/preschool/science.htm

Chapter 13

Alliance for Early Childhood Finance. (2006). *Early care and education systems reform: Key elements.* Retrieved October 18, 2007, from http://www.earlychildhoodfinance.org/handouts/Developing%20Systems%20Article.DOC

American Federation of Teachers. (2002). *Early childhood education: Building a strong foundation for the future* (Policy Brief No. 15). Retrieved January 20, 2006, from www.eric.ed.gov/ERICWebPortal/contentdelivery/servlet/ERICServlet?accno=ED478657

Brookings Institution. (2008). *No Child Left Behind and the 2004 campaign.* Retrieved April 13, 2008, from http://www.brookings.edu/opinions/2004/0108education_loveless.aspx

Buysse, V., Wesley, P. W., Bryant, D., & Gardner, D. (1999). Quality of early childhood programs in inclusive and noninclusive settings. *Exceptional Children, 65*(3), 301–314.

Center for Early Childhood Leadership. (2001). Achieving center accreditation: Factors that impact success. *Research Notes,* National Louis University. Retrieved January 25, 2009, from http://cecl.nl.edu/research/issues/rnw01.pdf

Chism, N. V. N. (1998). Developing a philosophy of teaching statement. *Essays on Teaching Excellence 9*(3), 1–2.

Cotton, K., & Conklin, N. (2001). *Research on early childhood education.* Retrieved June 1, 2007, from http://www.nwrel.org/scpd/sirs/3/topsyn3.html

Division for Early Childhood/Council of Exceptional Children. (2007). *Promoting positive outcomes for children with disabilities: Recommendations for curriculum, assessment, and program evaluation.* Missoula, MT: Author. Retrieved October 1, 2007, from http://www.naeyc.org/about/positions/pdf/PrmtgPositiveOutcomes.pdf

Division for Early Childhood and National Association for the Education of Young Children. (2008). Field review draft of draft position statement regarding Early Childhood Inclusion. Retrieved October 19, 2008, from http://community.fpg.unc.edu/resources/articles/Position-Statement-on-EC-Inclusion-draft-10-2008.pdf/view

Harms, T., Clifford, R., & Cryer, D. (1995). *The School-Age Environment Rating Scale (SACERS).* New York: Teachers College Press.

Harms, T., Clifford, R., & Cryer, D. (2003). *The Infant/Toddler Environment Rating Scale, Revised Edition (ITERS-R).* New York: Teachers College Press.

Harms, T., Clifford, R., & Cryer, D. (2005). *The Early Childhood Environment Rating Scale, Revised Edition, Updated (ECERS-R).* New York: Teachers College Press.

Harms, T., Clifford, R., & Cryer, D. (2007). *The Family Child Care Rating Scale, Revised Edition (FCCERS-R)*. New York: Teachers College Press.

Kohn, A. (2007). *Schools matter: Alfie Kohn on NCLB*. Retrieved April 13, 2008, from http://schoolsmatter.blogspot.com/2007/08/alfie-kohn-on-nclb.html

National Association of Child Care Resource and Referral Agencies. (2007). *We can do better: NACCRRA's ranking of state child care center standards and oversight*. Retrieved October 17, 2007, from http://www.naccrra.org/policy/recent_reports/scorecard.php

National Association for the Education of Young Children. (2005). *Code of ethical conduct*. Retrieved June 1, 2008, from http://www.naeyc.org/about/positions/pseth98.asp

National Association for the Education of Young Children. (2007). *Head Start reauthorization*. Retrieved April 13, 2008, from http://www.naeyc.org/policy/federal/pdf/head_start.pdf

National Association for the Education of Young Children and National Association of Early Childhood Specialists in State Departments of Education. (2002). *Early learning standards: Creating conditions for success*. Retrieved October 20, 2007, from http://naecs.crc.uiuc.edu/position/creating_conditions.pdf

National Child Care Information and Technical Assistance Center. (2005). *Tiered-quality strategies: Definitions and state systems*. Retrieved October 4, 2007, from http://www.nccic.org/pubs/tiered-defsystems.html

National Child Care Information and Technical Assistance Center (2006). *Child care center licensing regulations (October 2006): Child: staff ratios and maximum group size requirements*. Retrieved October 19, 2008, from http://www.nccic.org/pubs/cclicensingreq/ratios.html

National Resource Center for Health and Safety in Child Care. (2002). *Caring for our children. National health and safety performance standards: Guidelines for out-of-home care*. A Joint Collaborative Project of the American Academy of Pediatrics, American Public Health Association, and the National Resource Center for Health and Safety in Child Care. Retrieved October 19, 2007, from http://nrc.uchsc.edu/CFOC/HTMLVersion/TOC.html

Onveon. (2008). Educational administrators, preschool, and child care center/program. *Career Profile*. Retrieved May 26, 2008, from http://www.onveon.com/careers/education-administrators-preschool-child-care-center-program/career-profile.htm

Radtke, J. (1998). *Strategic communications for nonprofit organizations: Seven steps to creating a successful plan*. New York: Wiley.

Shonkoff, J. (2004). Evaluating early childhood services: What's really behind the curtain? *The Evaluation Exchange, 10*(2), 3–4.

Spodek, B., & Saracho, O. N. (1990). Preparing early childhood teachers. In B. Spodek & O. N. Saracho (Eds.), *Yearbook in early childhood education, Volume 1: Early childhood teacher preparation* (pp. 23–44). New York: Teachers College Press.

Stipek, D. (2005). Early childhood education at a crossroads. *Harvard Education Letter*. Retrieved October 30, 2007, from http://www.edletter.org/past/issues/2005-ja/crossroads.shtml

Stoney, L., Mitchell, A., & Warner, M. (2006). Smarter reform: Moving beyond single-program solutions to an early care and education system. *Community Development: Journal of the Community Development Society, 37*(2), 101–113.

Thinkexist. (2007). Maria Montessori quotes. Retrieved October 9, 2007, from http://en.thinkexist.com/quotation/one_test_of_the_correctness_of_educational/148632.html

U.S. Department of Health and Human Services. (2007). *Head Start program performance standards and other regulations*. Retrieved October 4, 2007, from http://eclkc.ohs.acf.hhs.gov/hslc/Program%20Design%20and%20Management/Head%20Start%20Requirements/Head%20Start%20Requirements

Whitebook, M. (2003). *Bachelor's degrees are best: Higher qualifications for pre-kindergarten teachers lead to better learning environments for children*. Washington, DC: The Trust for Early Education.

Chapter 14

Brainy Quote. (2007). Marian Wright Edelman quotes. Retrieved June 1, 2008, from http://www.brainyquote.com/quotes/authors/m/marian_wright_edelman.html

Build Strong Foundations for Our Youngest Children. (n.d.). *Building early childhood systems in a multi-ethnic society*. Retrieved April 21, 2009, from http://www.buildinitiative.org/files/Build%20Initiative%20-%20Overview%20of%20Policy.pdf

Calman, L., & Tarr-Whelan, L. (2005). *Early childhood education for all: A wise investment*. Legal Momentum's Family Initiative & MIT Workplace Center. Retrieved May 20, 2006, from http://web.mit.edu/workplacecenter/docs/Full%20Report.pdf

Center for Early Childhood Leadership. (2003). *Financial aid strategies: The key to an early childhood career development system*. Research Notes. Retrieved May 11, 2007, from http://cecl.nl.edu/research/issues/rnw03.pdf

Chang, F., Early, D., & Winton, P. (2005, Winter). Early childhood teacher preparation in special education at 2- and 4-year institutions of higher education. *Journal of Early Intervention 27*(2), 110–124.

Coleman, M., Buysse, V., & Neitzel, J. (2006). *Recognition and response: An early intervening system for young children at-risk for learning disabilities*. Retrieved August 1, 2008, from http://www.fpg.unc.edu/~randr/pdfs/2006FPGSynthesis_RecognitionAndResponse.pdf

Culture of Peace Initiative. (2006). Better world quotes. Retrieved September 1, 2008, from http://www.cultureofpeace.org/quotes/betterworld-quotes.htm

Darling-Hammond, L., & Garcia-Lopez, S. P. (2002). What is diversity? In L. Darling-Hammond, J. French, & S. P. Garcia-Lopez (Eds.), *Learning to teach for social justice* (pp. 9–12). New York: Teachers College Press.

DeLapp, L. (2003). *Supporting early childhood initiatives: Legislative strategies for everyday people*. The Finance Project. Retrieved May 14, 2007, from http://www.financeproject.org/Publications/LegislativeStrategies.pdf

Gallagher, J. J., & Clifford, R. M. (2000). The missing support infrastructure in early childhood. *Early Childhood Research & Practice, 2*(1). Retrieved November 13, 2007, from http://ecrp.uiuc.edu/v2n1/gallagher.html

Gibran, K. (1923). *The prophet.* New York: Alfred A Knopf.

Haflon, N., Uyeda, K., Inkelas, M., & Rice, T. (2004). *Building bridges: A comprehensive system for healthy development and school readiness*. National Center for Infant and Early Childhood Health Policy (1). Retrieved November 4, 2007, from http://www.healthychild.ucla.edu/NationalCenter/bb.brief.no1.final.pdf

Harwood, P. (2006). *To Anne Frank, On her 75th birthday*. Retrieved January 1, 2008, from http://www.libranpoet.com/anne_frank.htm

Kirp, D. (2007). *The sandbox investment: The preschool movement and kids first politics*. Cambridge: Harvard University Press.

Kovaleski, J. F. (2007). Potential pitfalls of response to intervention. In S. R. Jimerson, M. K. Burns, & A. M. VanDerHeyden (Eds.), *The handbook of response to intervention: The science and practice of assessment and intervention* (pp. 80–92). New York: Springer.

McDonald, D. (2005). *Raising your voice for children: Advocacy training.* National Association for the Education of Young Children. Retrieved June 4, 2007, from http://www.naeyc.org/policy/presentation.ppt#396,5

Mitchell, A. (2007). Defining our field. *Young Children, 62*(5), pp. 6–7.

National Association for the Education of Young Children. (2000). *A call for excellence in early childhood education.* Retrieved April 12, 2007, from http://www.naeyc.org/policy/excellence.asp

National Association for the Education of Young Children. (2002). *Compensation for the early childhood workforce.* Retrieved June 1, 2007, from http://www.naeyc.org/ece/critical/compensation.asp

National Association for the Education of Young Children. (2004). *Advocacy toolkit.* Retrieved April 19, 2009, from http://www.naeyc.org/policy/toolbox/pdf/toolkit.pdf

National Black Child Development Institute. (2007). *Parent empowerment project.* Retrieved April 20, 2009, from http://www.nbcdi.org/programs/pep/default.asp

National Black Child Development Institute. (2009). *Public policy recommendations.* Retrieved April 20, 2009, from www.nbcdi.org/media/policyrecommendations.doc

National Center for Family Literacy. (n.d.). *Current initiatives.* Retrieved April 20, 2009, from http://www.famlit.org/site/c.gtJWJdMQIsE/b.1423167/k.33D/Current_Initiatives.htm

National Child Care Information Center. (2006). *State professional development systems and early childhood workforce initiatives.* Retrieved December 2, 2007, from http://nccic.acf.hhs.gov/pubs/goodstart/state-ece.html

National Early Childhood Accountability Task Force. (2007). *Taking stock: Assessing and improving early childhood learning and program quality. Final report.* Retrieved December 1, 2007, from http://www.fcd-us.org/resources/resources_show.htm?doc_id=579564

National Governors Association. (2009). *State opportunities under the American Recovery and Reinvestment Act: Early childhood programs.* Retrieved April 19, 2009, from http://www.nga.org/Files/pdf/arraearlychildhood.pdf

National Institute for Early Education Research. (2007). *The state of preschool 2007.* Retrieved December 1, 2008, from http://nieer.org/yearbook/pdf/yearbook.pdf

National Institute for Early Childhood Research. (2008). *The state of preschool, 2008.* Retrieved April 21, 2009, from http://nieer.org/yearbook/pdf/yearbook.pdf

Obama, B. (2008). South Carolina presidential primary speech, January 27, 2008.

Pianta, R. (2007). Opportunity in early education: Improving the quality of teacher-child interactions through classroom observation and professional development. NAEYC Annual Conference, Chicago, Illinois, November 7–10, 2007.

Rolnick, A., & Grunewald, R. (2003). Early childhood development: Economic development with a high public return. *Fedgazette.* Retrieved May 17, 2006, from http://minneapolisfed.org/pubs/fedgaz/03-03/earlychild.cfm

Shonkoff, J., & Phillips, D. (Eds.). (2000). *From neurons to neighborhoods: The science of early childhood development.* Committee on Integrating the Science of Early Childhood Development, Board on Children, Youth, and Families. Washington, DC: National Academies Press.

T.E.A.C.H. Early Childhood. (2006). *Early childhood workforce investments: A national strategy.* 2005–2006 Annual Report. Retrieved June 1, 2007, from http://www.childcareservices.org/_downloads/TEACH_annual_report_06.pdf

Thinkexist. (2008). Nelson Mandela quotes. Retrieved October 1, 2007, from http://thinkexist.com/quotation/education_is_the_most_powerful_weapon_which_you/144638.html

U.S. Department of Labor, Bureau of Labor Statistics. (2007). *Teachers: Preschool, kindergarten, elementary, and secondary.* Retrieved June 1, 2007, from http://stats.bls.gov/oco/ocos069.htm#emply

Whitebook, M. (1997). *Who's missing at the table? Leadership opportunities and barriers for teachers and providers.* Center for the Child Care Workforce. Retrieved April 19, 2009, from http://www.ccw.org/pubs/whosmissing.pdf

Whitebook, M., & Eichberg, A. (2002). Finding a better way: Defining policies to improve child care workforce compensation. *Young Children, 7*(3), pp. 66–72.

Wilkins D. (2000). *It's a human thing.* Retrieved September 1, 2008, from http://www.ncsd.org/thoughts/human.htm

Women's History. (2000). Marian Wright Edelman quotes. Retrieved June 1, 2008, from http://womenshistory.about.com/od/quotes/a/marian_edelman.htm

Zero to Three Policy Center. (2008). *Early learning guidelines for infants and toddlers: Recommendations for states.* Retrieved April 13, 2008, from http://www.zerotothree.org/site/DocServer/Early_Learning_Guidelines_for_Infants_and_Toddlers.pdf

Name Index

McBride, R., 29
McCartney, K., 82
McCormick Tribune Center
   for Early Childhood
   Leadership, 186
McDonald, D., 432
McKeown, M., 131
McLaughlin, M. W., 23, 29
McMillan, R., 196
McNeil, J., 27
McVicker, J., 27
McWilliams, R., 36
Meisels, S., 62, 255
Meredith, L., 161
Meyer, L., 29
Michigan Public Policy
   Initiative, 278
Milburn, P., 237
Miller, M., 163
Miller, R., 207
Mindes, G., 381
Minnes, P., 169
Mitchell, A., 249, 255, 399, 426
Moll, L., 166
Moore, E., 49
Moore, R., 329
Morris, J., 152
Morris, S., 32, 289
Moss, L., 184
Mueller, M., 49
Mulligan, S., 32, 289
Myers, M., 138, 143
Myers-Walls, J. A., 136

Nachen, J., 169
NASBE Task Force on Early
   Childhood Education, 50
National Association for Child
   Care Resource and Referral
   Agencies (NACCRRA), 8,
   156, 397, 404, 419
National Association for Music
   Education, 84
National Association for the
   Education of Young Children
   (NAEYC), 6, 9, 13, 14, 61,
   67, 77, 78, 81, 82, 87, 88,
   89, 90, 91, 93, 96, 97, 129,
   130, 131, 136, 155, 156,
   161, 178, 180, 181, 186,
   188, 212, 236, 238, 239,
   240, 246, 276, 304, 376,
   379, 397, 402, 406, 425,
   428, 429, 430, 433
National Association of Early
   Childhood Specialists in
   State Departments of
   Education (NAECS/SDE),
   212, 236, 238, 406

National Association of
   Elementary School
   Principals, 158
National Association of Nursery
   School Educators, 24
National Black Child
   Development Institute,
   442, 443
National Campaign to Prevent
   Teen Pregnancy, 151
National Center for Children in
   Poverty, 50
National Center for Early
   Development and Learning,
   56, 60, 61, 184, 185, 186
National Center for Education
   Statistics, 60, 65, 158, 219
National Center for Family
   Literacy, 441
National Center on Family
   Homelessness, 137, 138
National Child Care
   Information and Technical
   Assistance Center, 400, 401,
   402, 445
National Clearinghouse for
   English Language
   Acquisition, 85
National Coalition on Health
   Care, 7
National Conference of State
   Legislators, 85, 130, 259
National Council for the Social
   Studies, 380
National Council of Teachers of
   Mathematics (NCTM), 379
National Dissemination Center
   for Children with
   Disabilities, 114
National Early Childhood
   Accountability Task
   Force, 426
National Early Childhood
   Technical Assistance Center
   (NECTAC), 33
National Education Goals
   Panel, 156
National Governors
   Association, 427
National Head Start
   Association, 221
National Information Center
   for Children and Youth with
   Disabilities, 30
National Institute for Early
   Education Research, 10, 66,
   244, 446
National Institute on Out-of-
   School Time, 65

National Lekotek Center, 335
National Mental Health
   Information Center, 126
National Resource Center for
   Health and Safety in Child
   Care, 400
National School Boards
   Association, 247
National Scientific Council on
   the Developing Child, 132,
   143, 144, 277
Neitzel, J., 443
Nelson, B., 190
Nelson, K., 229
New, R., 222, 280, 350
Nichols, A., 157
Noddings, N., 143
Noppe, I., 94
Noppe, L., 94
North Carolina Institute for
   Early Childhood, 186
North Central Regional
   Laboratory, 163
Northwestern Regional
   Education Laboratory,
   365, 380
Notari-Syverson, A., 376
Nunez, R. D., 139, 143
Nurturing Early Learners, 357

Office for Civil Rights, 32
Olfman, S., 202
Olson, M., 89, 276
Onveon, 403
Organisation for Economic
   Cooperation and
   Development (OECD), 156
Osgood, R. L., 35
Osofsky, J., 151
Ounce of Prevention Fund, 51
Owen, M., 95, 96

Palmaffy, T., 27, 30
Pang, V. O., 66
Pardini, P., 21, 31, 260
Parks, G., 217
Patterson, C., 190, 192
Patterson, G., 276
Patterson, K., 196
Pavan, B. N., 63
Peebles, C., 151
Perkins, D., 169
Perry, B. D., 51, 139
Peske, N., 292
Pestalozzi, J., 233
Peth-Pierce, R., 89
Pett, J., 254
Phillips, D., 51, 186, 347, 437
Piaget, J., 78

Pianta, R., 426
Pierce, W. D., 282
Piesner-Feinberg, E., 35, 186
Playing for Keeps, 335
Pollard, R., 139
Popp, P., 138, 143
Porter, T., 57
Pre-Elementary Educational
   Longitudinal Study, 59
Pre-K Now, 158
Prescott, E., 344
President's Panel on Mental
   Retardation, 30
Proper, E., 29

Quisenberry, N., 94, 362

Radtke, J., 413
Raines, S., 10
Randall, W., 100
Raudenbush, S. W., 61
Rauscher, F., 84
Raver, C., 89–90
Ray, A., 66, 276
Reed-Victor, E., 143
Rennert-Ariev, P., 66
Rice, P. F., 134
Rice, T., 437
Richards, J. C., 131
Richmond, J., 134
Riddle, E. M., 92
Ridgeway, D., 287
Risley, T., 50
Robbins, J., 66
Robertson, A., 57, 58
Robinson, D., 350
Rodgers, W., 49
Rolnick, A., 435
Rose, E., 21, 22, 23, 24, 25, 34
Rosegrant, T., 201, 235
Rosenbaum, J., 50
Ros-Voseles, D., 285
Rothstein, R., 163
Rous, B., 36
Rousseau, J-J., 206
Rudman, M., 383
Runyan, D., 139
Rutsch, H., 203

Sablan, V. A., 66
St. Pierre, R., 29
Sakai, L., 8
Salembrier, G., 33
Sánchez, S. Y., 131
Sangeorge, A., 376
Saracho, O., 7, 208, 419
Saunders, W., 131
Scarborough, A., 34, 58, 186
Scarr, S., 82

Subject Index